QUEEN & COUNTRY™

GREG RUCKA

oni
PRESS

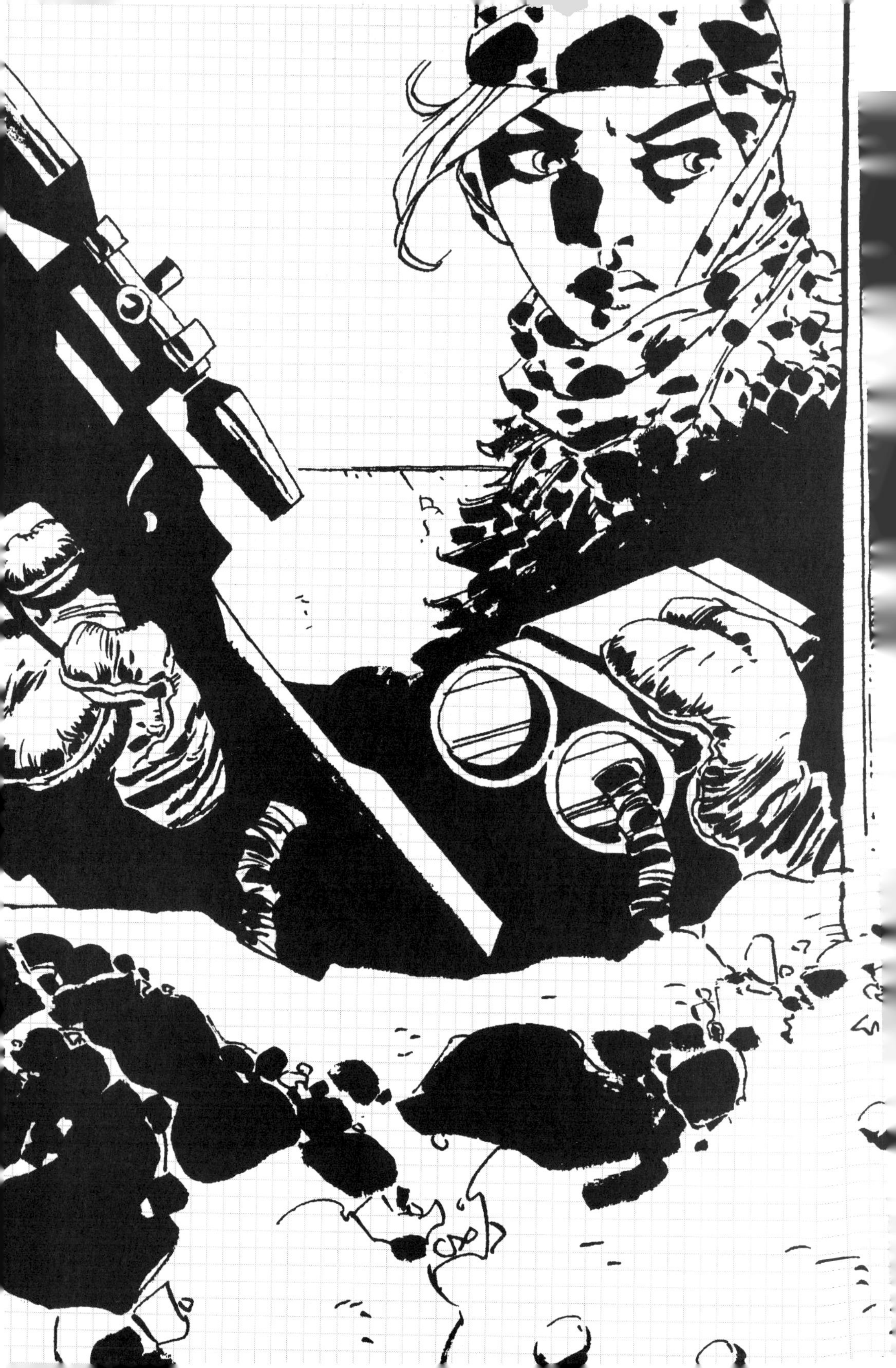

QUEEN & COUNTRY ™

WRITTEN BY
GREG RUCKA

ILLUSTRATED BY
**JASON SHAWN ALEXANDER, CARLA SPEED McNEIL,
& MIKE HAWTHORNE**

LETTERING BY
JOHN DRANSKI & CARLA SPEED McNEIL

COVER BY
TIM SALE

BOOK DESIGN BY
KEITH WOOD

COLLECTION EDITED BY
JAMES LUCAS JONES & JILL BEATON

ORIGINAL SERIES EDITED BY
JAMIE S. RICH & JAMES LUCAS JONES

Published by Oni Press, Inc.
Joe Nozemack, publisher
James Lucas Jones, editor in chief
Randal C. Jarrell, managing editor
Cory Casoni, marketing director
Jill Beaton, assistant editor
Douglas E. Sherwood, editorial assistant

This collects issues 13-24 of the Oni Press comics
series *Queen & Country*.

ONI PRESS, INC.
1305 SE Martin Luther King Jr. Blvd.
Suite A
Portland, OR 97214
USA

www.onipress.com

First edition: April 2008
ISBN-13: 978-1-932664-89-8
ISBN-10: 1-929998-89-0

1 3 5 7 9 10 8 6 4 2

PRINTED IN CANADA.

TABLE OF CONTENTS

OPERATION: BLACKWALL

WRITTEN BY
GREG RUCKA

ILLUSTRATED BY
JASON SHAWN ALEXANDER

LETTERED BY
JOHN DRANSKI

ORIGINALLY EDITED BY
JAMIE S. RICH & JAMES LUCAS JONES

ROSTER

C—Ubiquitous code-name for the current head of SIS. Real name is Sir Wilson Stanton Davies.

DONALD WELDON—Deputy Chief of Service, has oversight of all aspects of Intelligence gathering and operations. Immediate superior to Crocker.

PAUL CROCKER—Director of Operations, encompassing all field work in all theaters of operations. In addition to commanding individual stations, has direct command of the Special Section—sometimes referred to as Minders —used for special operations.

TOM WALLACE—Head of the Special Section, a Special Operations Officer with the designation Minder One. Responsible for the training and continued well-being of his unit, both at home and in the field. Six year veteran of the Minders.

TARA CHACE—Special Operations Officer, designated Minder Two. Entering her third year as Minder.

EDWARD KITTERING—Special Operations Officer, designated Minder Three. Has been with the Special Section for less than a year.

OPS ROOM STAFF   OTHERS

ALEXIS—Mission Control Officer (also called Main Communications Officer)– responsible for maintaining communications between the Operations Room and the agents in the field.

RON—Duty Operations Officer, responsible for monitoring the status and importance of all incoming intelligence, both from foreign stations and other sources.

KATE—Personal Assistant to Paul Crocker, termed PA to D.Ops. Possibly the hardest and most important job in the Service.

COLIN BECK—Mid-fifties, self-made billionaire known for his aggressive business tactics, savvy, and willpower. Owns or has interests in technology, mass media, entertainment, and communication industries.

RACHEL BECK—Mid-twenties dilettante, currently living in Paris on a substantial allowance from her father. Aspiring fashion designer.

RENE DUPUIS—Also mid-fifties, head of IID, a company with almost three hundred years of history in France. Under Rene, IID has moved its focus from its traditional shipping and transport lines to the communications and tech industries.

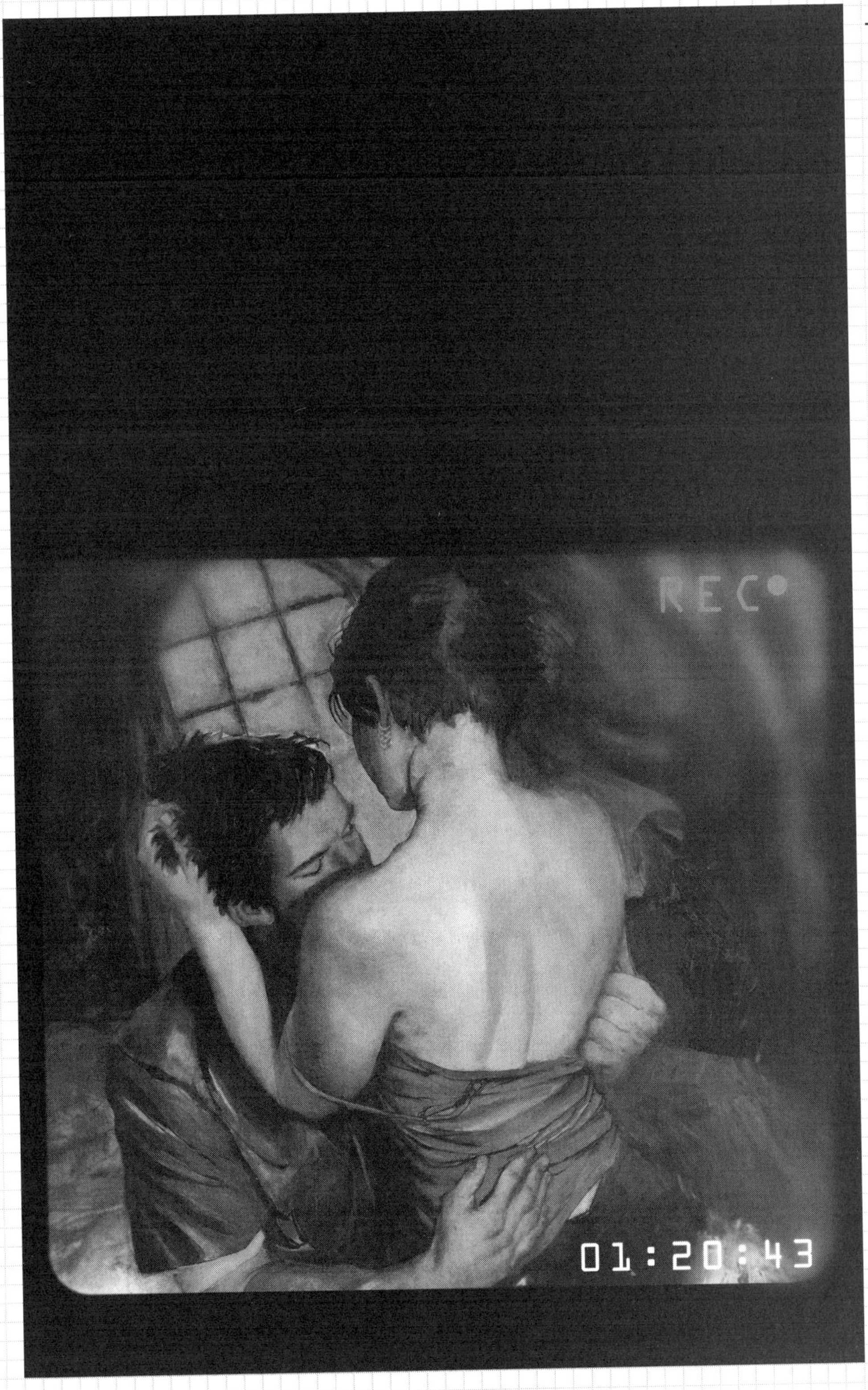
REC
01:20:43

CHAPTER 1

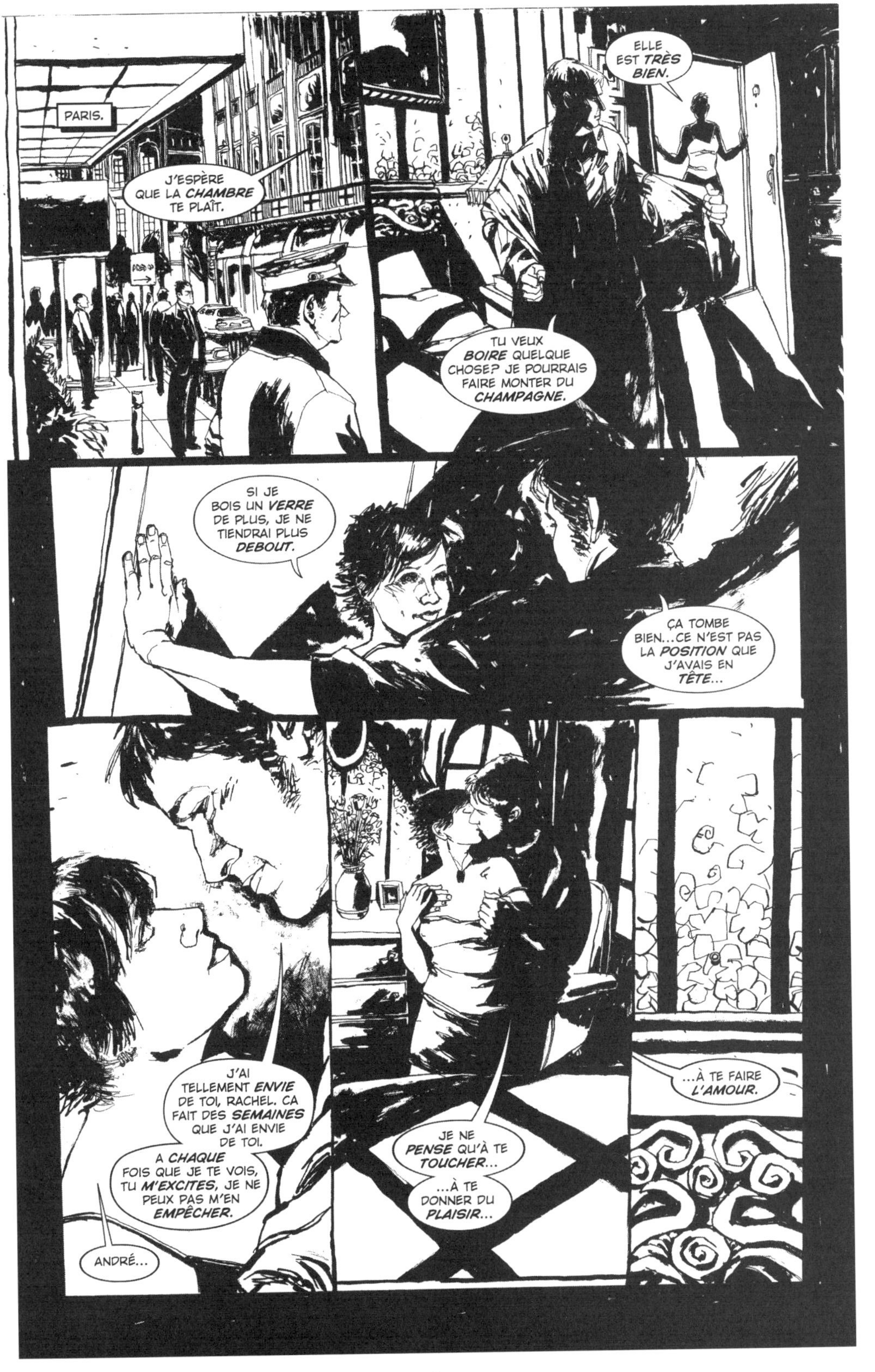
PARIS.
J'ESPÈRE QUE LA CHAMBRE TE PLAÎT.
ELLE EST TRÈS BIEN.
TU VEUX BOIRE QUELQUE CHOSE? JE POURRAIS FAIRE MONTER DU CHAMPAGNE.
SI JE BOIS UN VERRE DE PLUS, JE NE TIENDRAI PLUS DEBOUT.
ÇA TOMBE BIEN...CE N'EST PAS LA POSITION QUE J'AVAIS EN TÊTE...
J'AI TELLEMENT ENVIE DE TOI, RACHEL. CA FAIT DES SEMAINES QUE J'AI ENVIE DE TOI.
A CHAQUE FOIS QUE JE TE VOIS, TU M'EXCITES, JE NE PEUX PAS M'EN EMPÊCHER.
ANDRÉ...
JE NE PENSE QU'À TE TOUCHER...
...À TE DONNER DU PLAISIR...
...À TE FAIRE L'AMOUR.

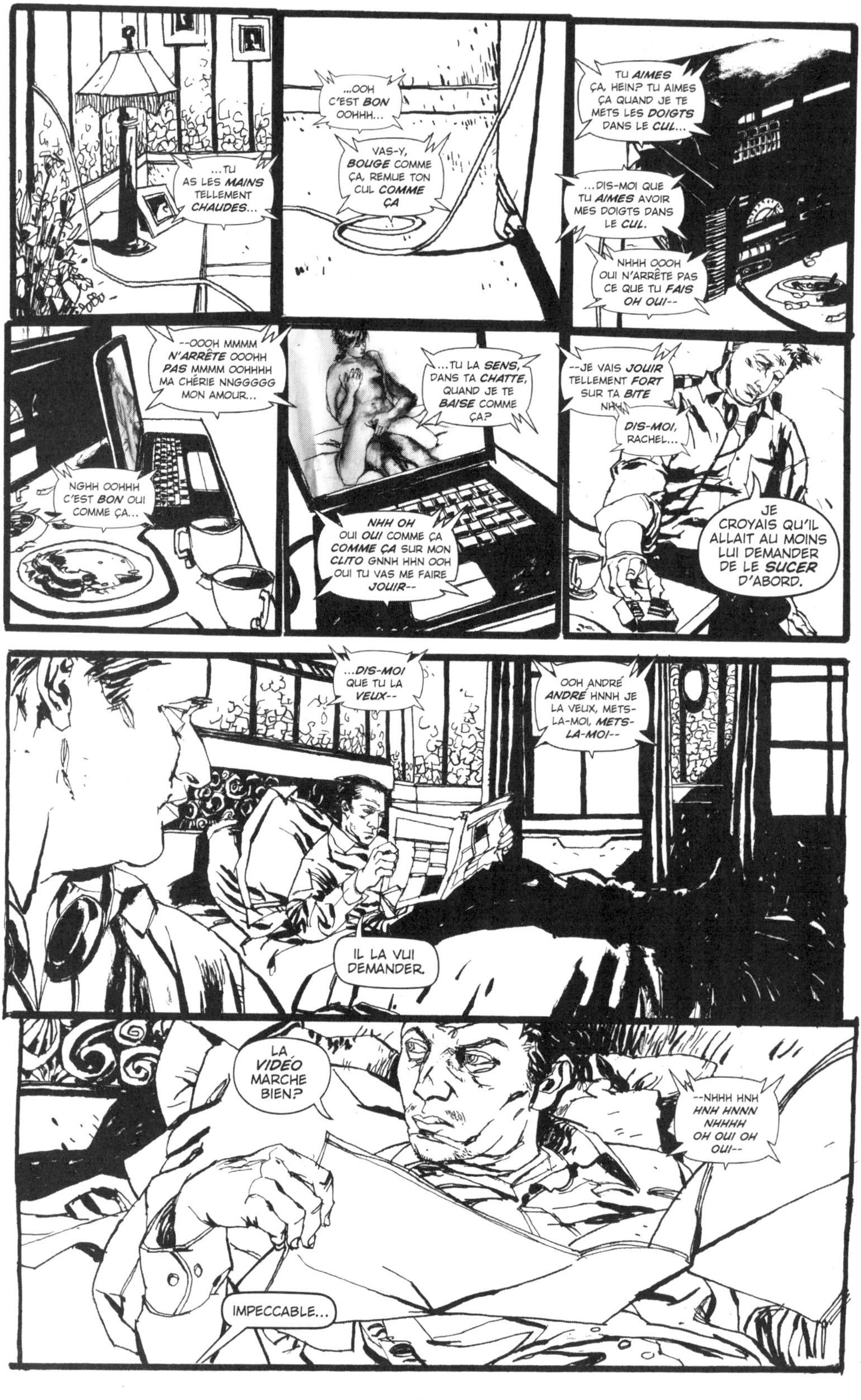
...TU AS LES MAINS TELLEMENT CHAUDES...
...OOH C'EST BON OOHHH...
VAS-Y, BOUGE COMME ÇA, REMUE TON CUL COMME ÇA
TU AIMES ÇA, HEIN? TU AIMES ÇA QUAND JE TE METS LES DOIGTS DANS LE CUL...
...DIS-MOI QUE TU AIMES AVOIR MES DOIGTS DANS LE CUL.
NHHH OOOH OUI N'ARRÊTE PAS CE QUE TU FAIS OH OUI--
--OOOH MMMM N'ARRÊTE OOOHH PAS MMMM OOHHHH MA CHÉRIE NNGGGGG MON AMOUR...
NGHH OOHHH C'EST BON OUI COMME ÇA...
...TU LA SENS, DANS TA CHATTE, QUAND JE TE BAISE COMME ÇA?
NHH OH OUI OUI COMME ÇA COMME ÇA SUR MON CLITO GNNH HHN OOH OUI TU VAS ME FAIRE JOUIR--
--JE VAIS JOUIR TELLEMENT FORT SUR TA BITE NHH
DIS-MOI, RACHEL...
JE CROYAIS QU'IL ALLAIT AU MOINS LUI DEMANDER DE LE SUCER D'ABORD.
...DIS-MOI QUE TU LA VEUX--
OOH ANDRÉ ANDRÉ HNNH JE LA VEUX, METS-LA-MOI, METS-LA-MOI--
IL LA VUI DEMANDER.
LA VIDÉO MARCHE BIEN?
--NHHH HNH HNH HNNN NHHHH OH OUI OH OUI--
IMPECCABLE...

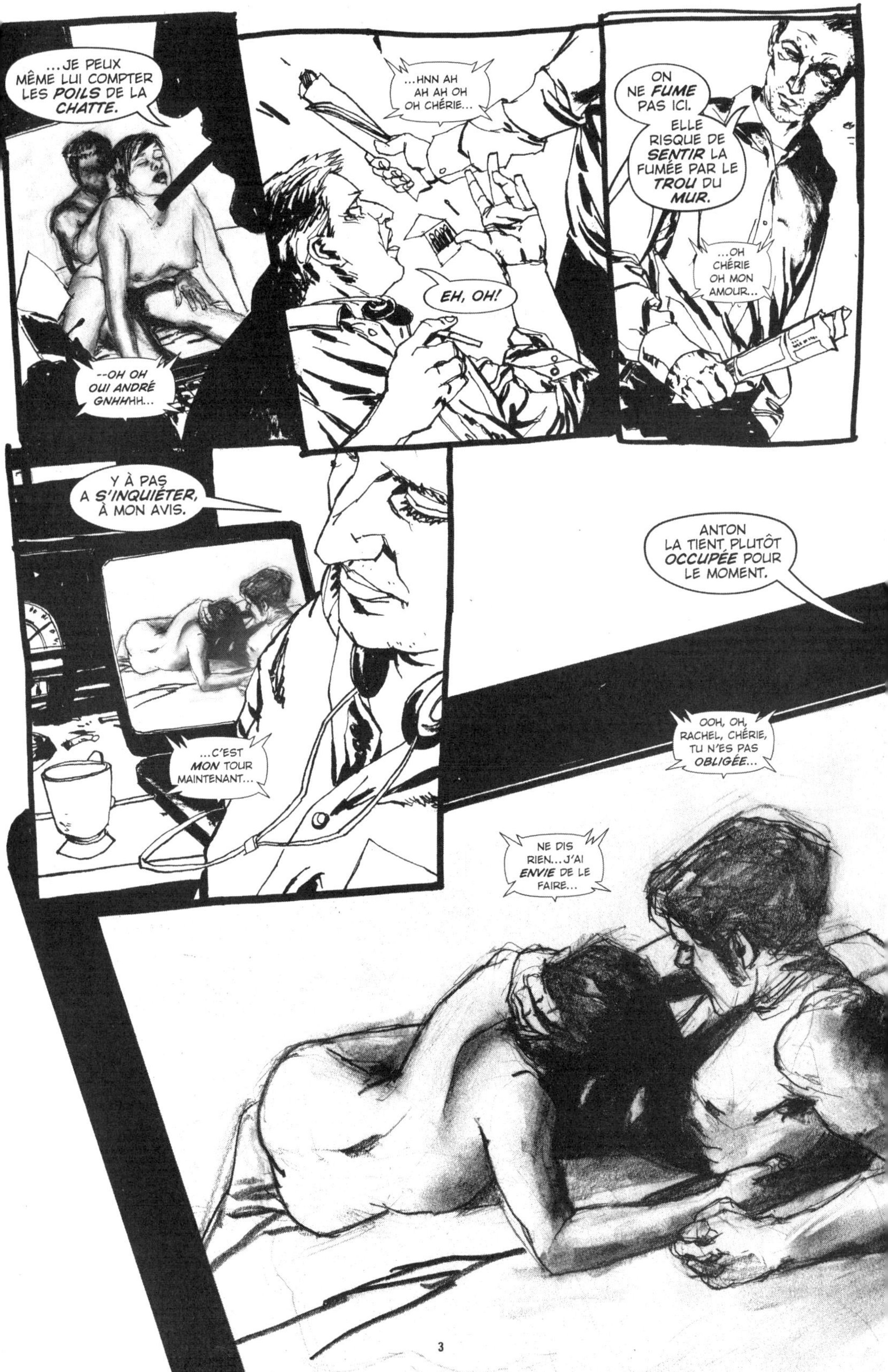
...JE PEUX MÊME LUI COMPTER LES POILS DE LA CHATTE.
--OH OH OUI ANDRÉ GNHHHHH...
...HNN AH AH AH OH OH CHÉRIE...
EH, OH!
ON NE FUME PAS ICI.
ELLE RISQUE DE SENTIR LA FUMÉE PAR LE TROU DU MUR.
...OH CHÉRIE OH MON AMOUR...
Y À PAS A S'INQUIÉTER, À MON AVIS.
...C'EST MON TOUR MAINTENANT...
ANTON LA TIENT PLUTÔT OCCUPÉE POUR LE MOMENT.
OOH, OH, RACHEL, CHÉRIE, TU N'ES PAS OBLIGÉE...
NE DIS RIEN... J'AI ENVIE DE LE FAIRE...

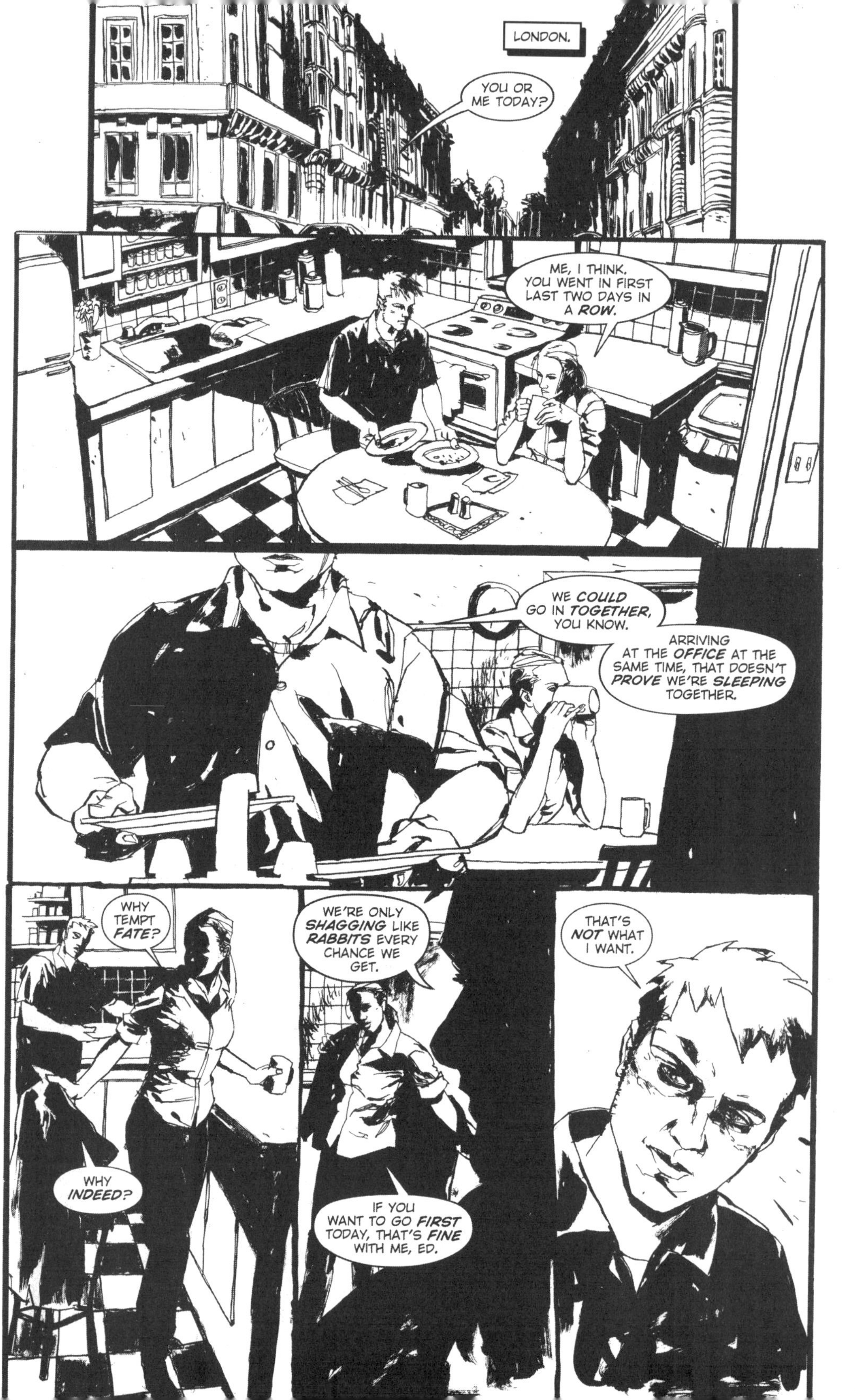
LONDON.
YOU OR ME TODAY?
ME, I THINK. YOU WENT IN FIRST LAST TWO DAYS IN A ROW.
WE COULD GO IN TOGETHER, YOU KNOW.
ARRIVING AT THE OFFICE AT THE SAME TIME, THAT DOESN'T PROVE WE'RE SLEEPING TOGETHER.
WHY TEMPT FATE?
WHY INDEED?
WE'RE ONLY SHAGGING LIKE RABBITS EVERY CHANCE WE GET.
IF YOU WANT TO GO FIRST TODAY, THAT'S FINE WITH ME, ED.
THAT'S NOT WHAT I WANT.

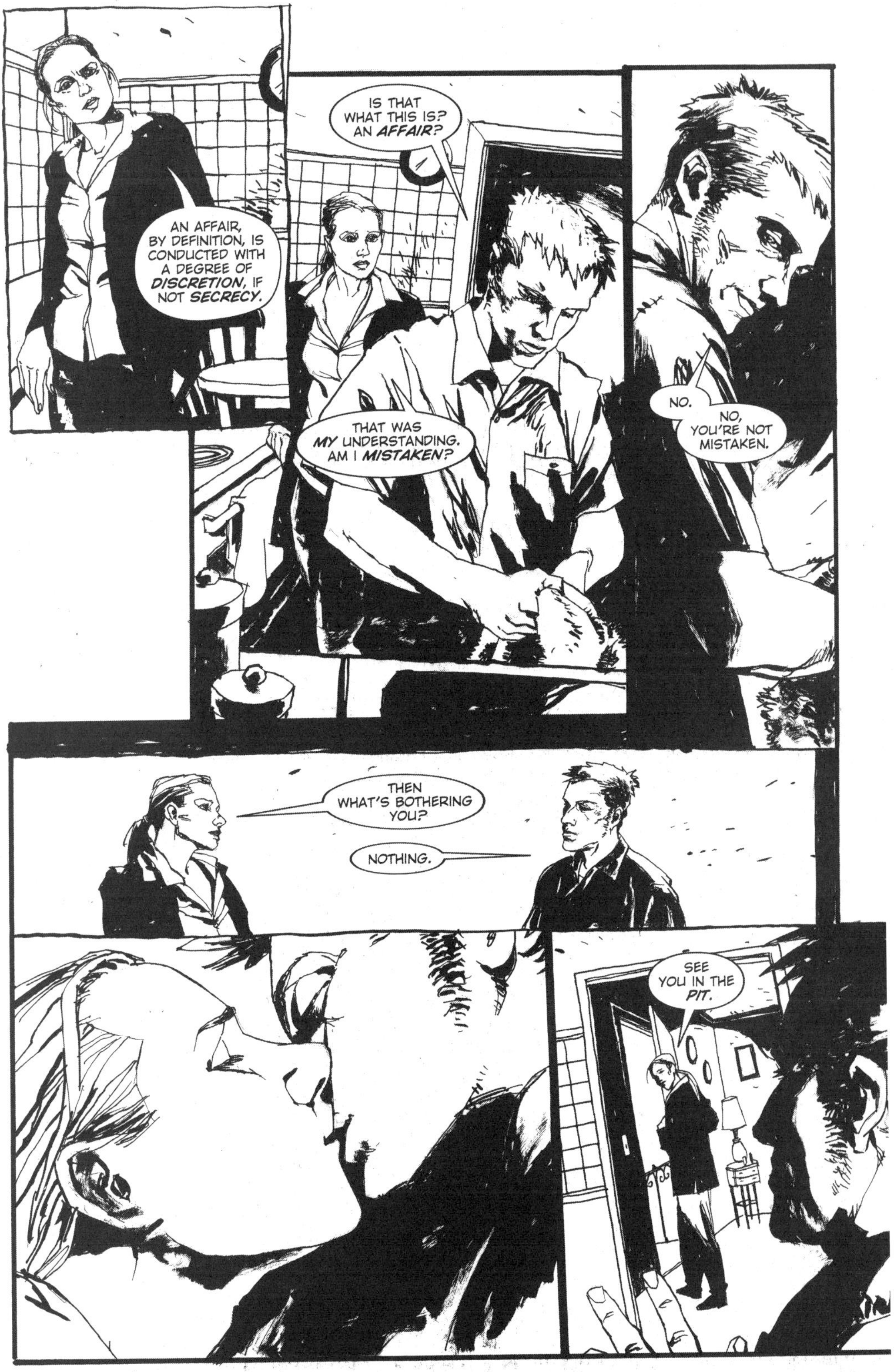

AN AFFAIR, BY DEFINITION, IS CONDUCTED WITH A DEGREE OF *DISCRETION*, IF NOT *SECRECY*.
IS THAT WHAT THIS IS? AN *AFFAIR*?
THAT WAS *MY* UNDERSTANDING. AM I *MISTAKEN*?
NO.
NO, YOU'RE NOT MISTAKEN.
THEN WHAT'S BOTHERING YOU?
NOTHING.
SEE YOU IN THE *PIT*.

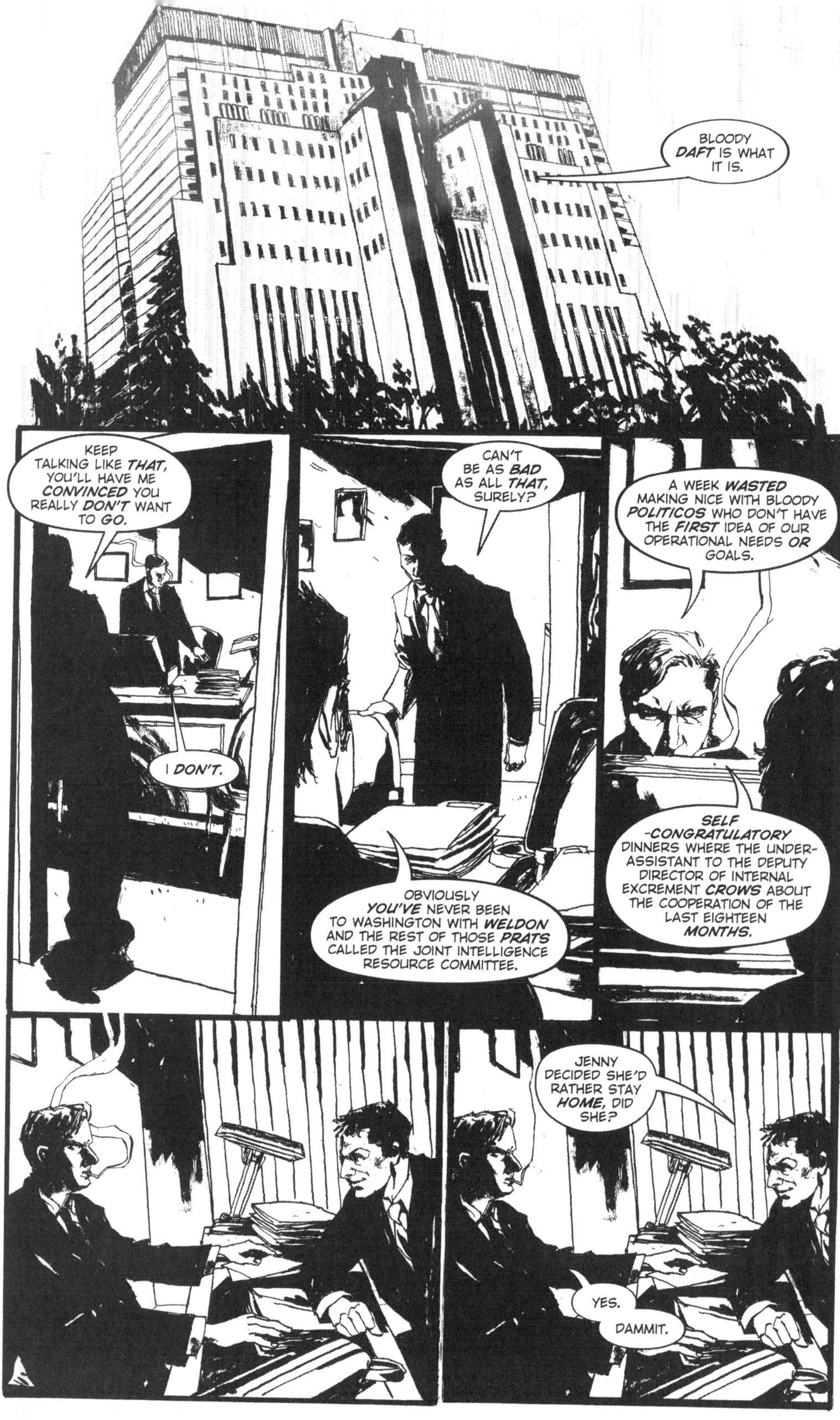
BLOODY DAFT IS WHAT IT IS.
KEEP TALKING LIKE THAT, YOU'LL HAVE ME CONVINCED YOU REALLY DON'T WANT TO GO.
I DON'T.
CAN'T BE AS BAD AS ALL THAT, SURELY?
OBVIOUSLY YOU'VE NEVER BEEN TO WASHINGTON WITH WELDON AND THE REST OF THOSE PRATS CALLED THE JOINT INTELLIGENCE RESOURCE COMMITTEE.
A WEEK WASTED MAKING NICE WITH BLOODY POLITICOS WHO DON'T HAVE THE FIRST IDEA OF OUR OPERATIONAL NEEDS OR GOALS.
SELF -CONGRATULATORY DINNERS WHERE THE UNDER-ASSISTANT TO THE DEPUTY DIRECTOR OF INTERNAL EXCREMENT CROWS ABOUT THE COOPERATION OF THE LAST EIGHTEEN MONTHS.
JENNY DECIDED SHE'D RATHER STAY HOME, DID SHE?
YES.
DAMMIT.

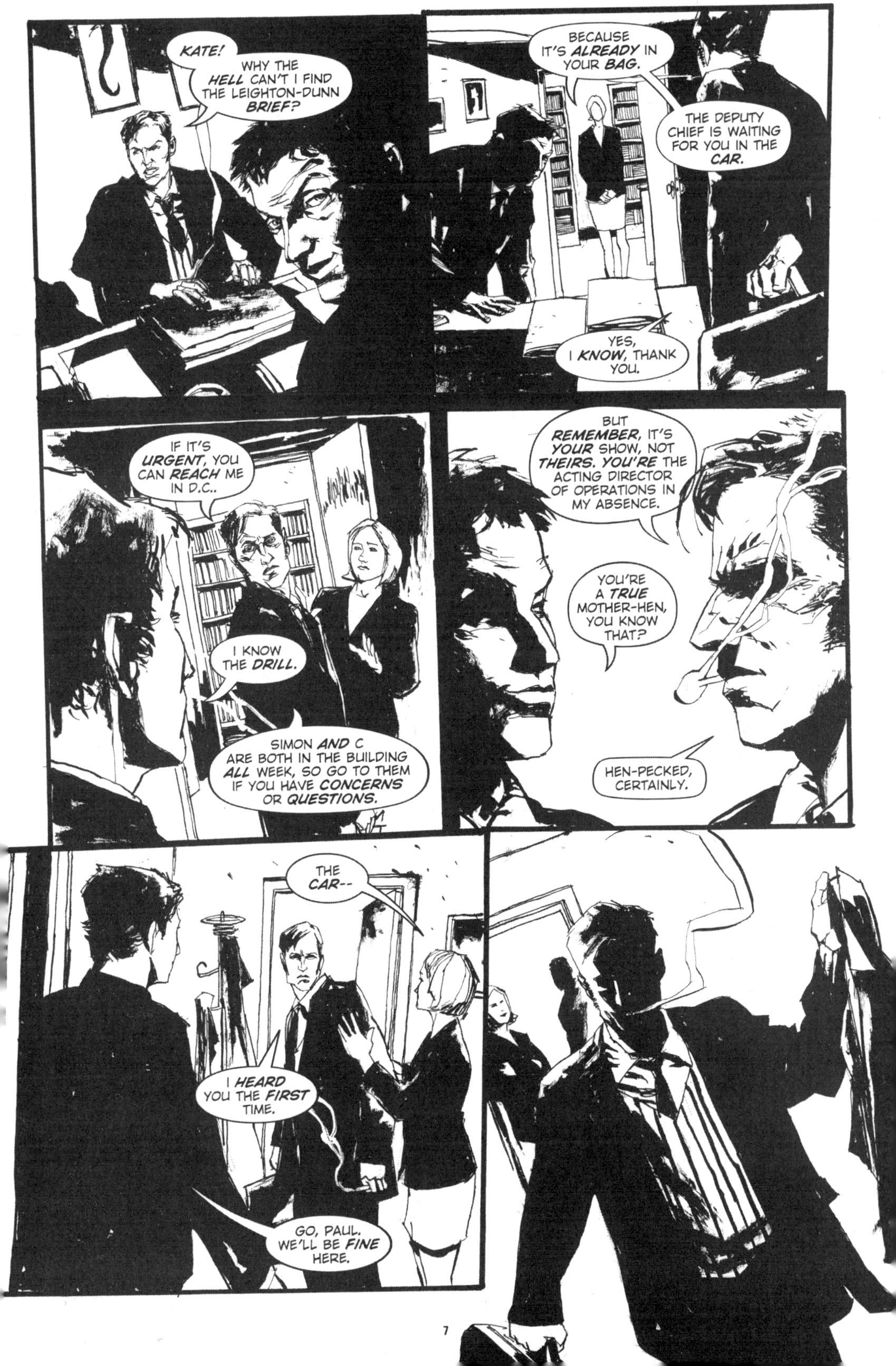
KATE! WHY THE HELL CAN'T I FIND THE LEIGHTON-DUNN BRIEF?
BECAUSE IT'S ALREADY IN YOUR BAG.
THE DEPUTY CHIEF IS WAITING FOR YOU IN THE CAR.
YES, I KNOW, THANK YOU.
IF IT'S URGENT, YOU CAN REACH ME IN D.C..
I KNOW THE DRILL.
SIMON AND C ARE BOTH IN THE BUILDING ALL WEEK, SO GO TO THEM IF YOU HAVE CONCERNS OR QUESTIONS.
BUT REMEMBER, IT'S YOUR SHOW, NOT THEIRS. YOU'RE THE ACTING DIRECTOR OF OPERATIONS IN MY ABSENCE.
YOU'RE A TRUE MOTHER-HEN, YOU KNOW THAT?
HEN-PECKED, CERTAINLY.
THE CAR--
I HEARD YOU THE FIRST TIME.
GO, PAUL. WE'LL BE FINE HERE.

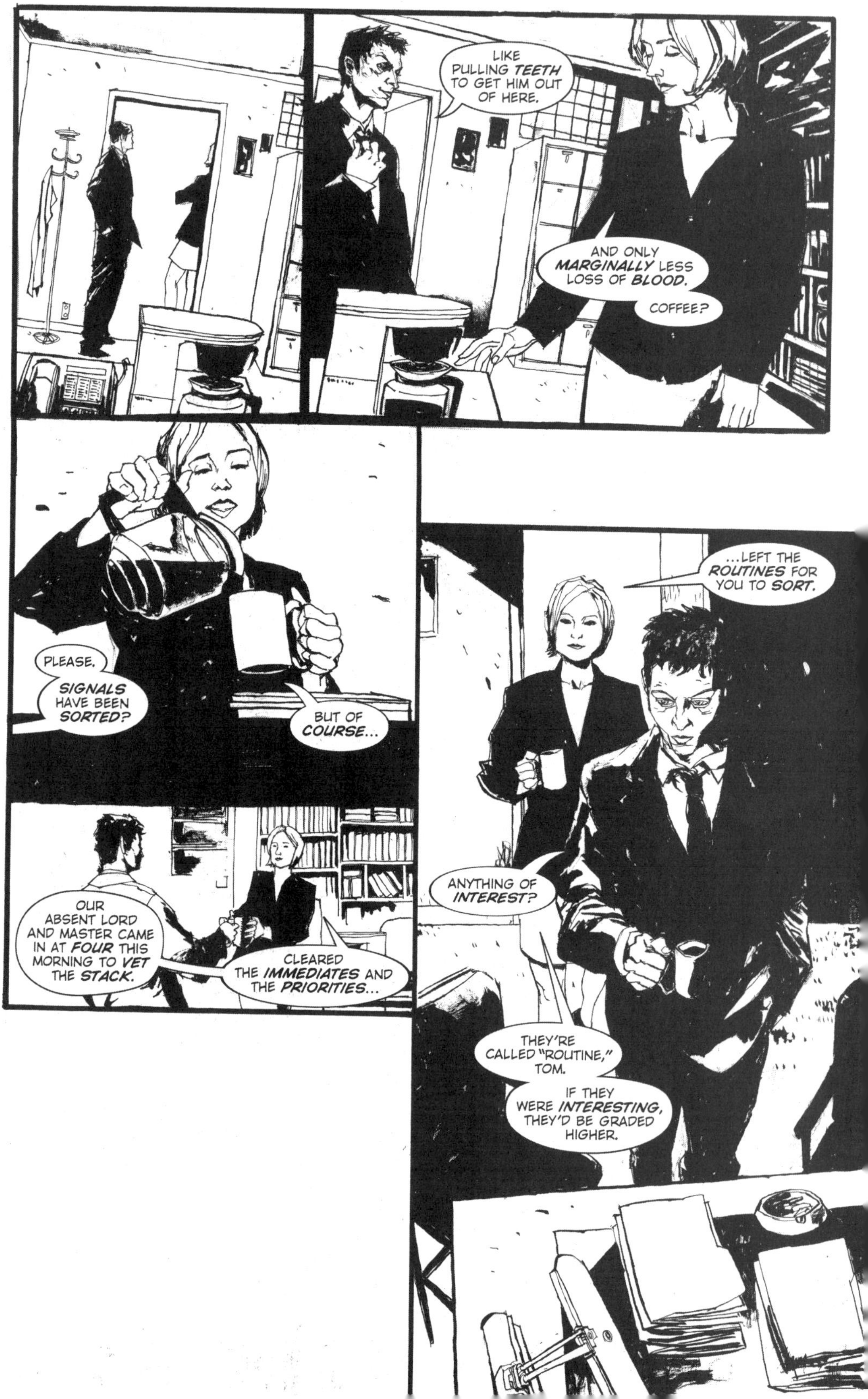
LIKE PULLING TEETH TO GET HIM OUT OF HERE.
AND ONLY MARGINALLY LESS LOSS OF BLOOD.
COFFEE?
PLEASE.
SIGNALS HAVE BEEN SORTED?
BUT OF COURSE...
OUR ABSENT LORD AND MASTER CAME IN AT FOUR THIS MORNING TO VET THE STACK.
CLEARED THE IMMEDIATES AND THE PRIORITIES...
...LEFT THE ROUTINES FOR YOU TO SORT.
ANYTHING OF INTEREST?
THEY'RE CALLED "ROUTINE," TOM.
IF THEY WERE INTERESTING, THEY'D BE GRADED HIGHER.

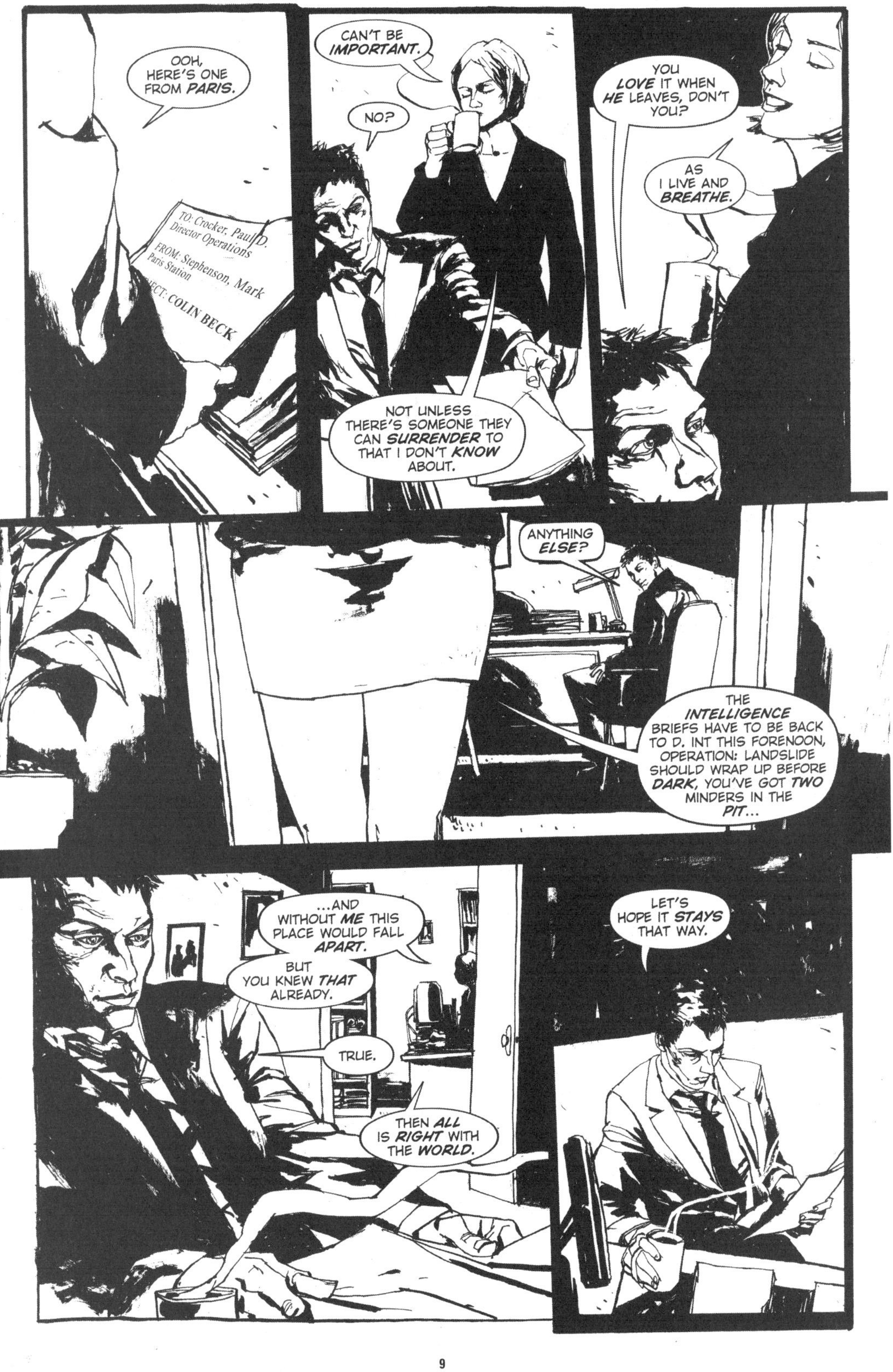
OOH, HERE'S ONE FROM PARIS.
TO: Crocker, Paul D. Director Operations
FROM: Stephenson, Mark Paris Station
COLIN BECK
CAN'T BE IMPORTANT.
NO?
NOT UNLESS THERE'S SOMEONE THEY CAN SURRENDER TO THAT I DON'T KNOW ABOUT.
YOU LOVE IT WHEN HE LEAVES, DON'T YOU?
AS I LIVE AND BREATHE.
ANYTHING ELSE?
THE INTELLIGENCE BRIEFS HAVE TO BE BACK TO D. INT THIS FORENOON, OPERATION: LANDSLIDE SHOULD WRAP UP BEFORE DARK, YOU'VE GOT TWO MINDERS IN THE PIT...
...AND WITHOUT ME THIS PLACE WOULD FALL APART.
BUT YOU KNEW THAT ALREADY.
TRUE.
THEN ALL IS RIGHT WITH THE WORLD.
LET'S HOPE IT STAYS THAT WAY.

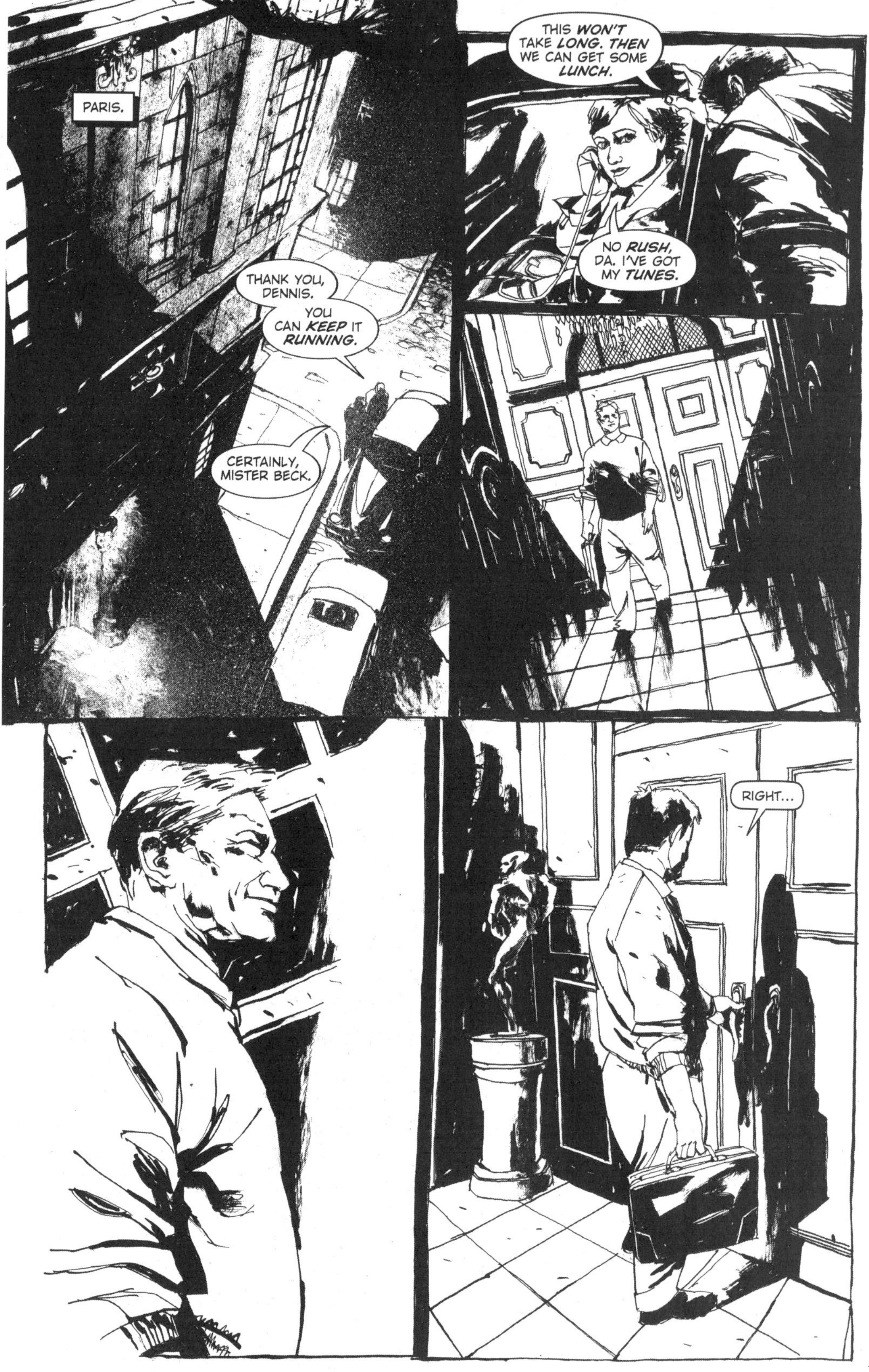
PARIS.
THANK YOU, DENNIS.
YOU CAN KEEP IT RUNNING.
CERTAINLY, MISTER BECK.
THIS WON'T TAKE LONG. THEN WE CAN GET SOME LUNCH.
NO RUSH, DA. I'VE GOT MY TUNES.
RIGHT...

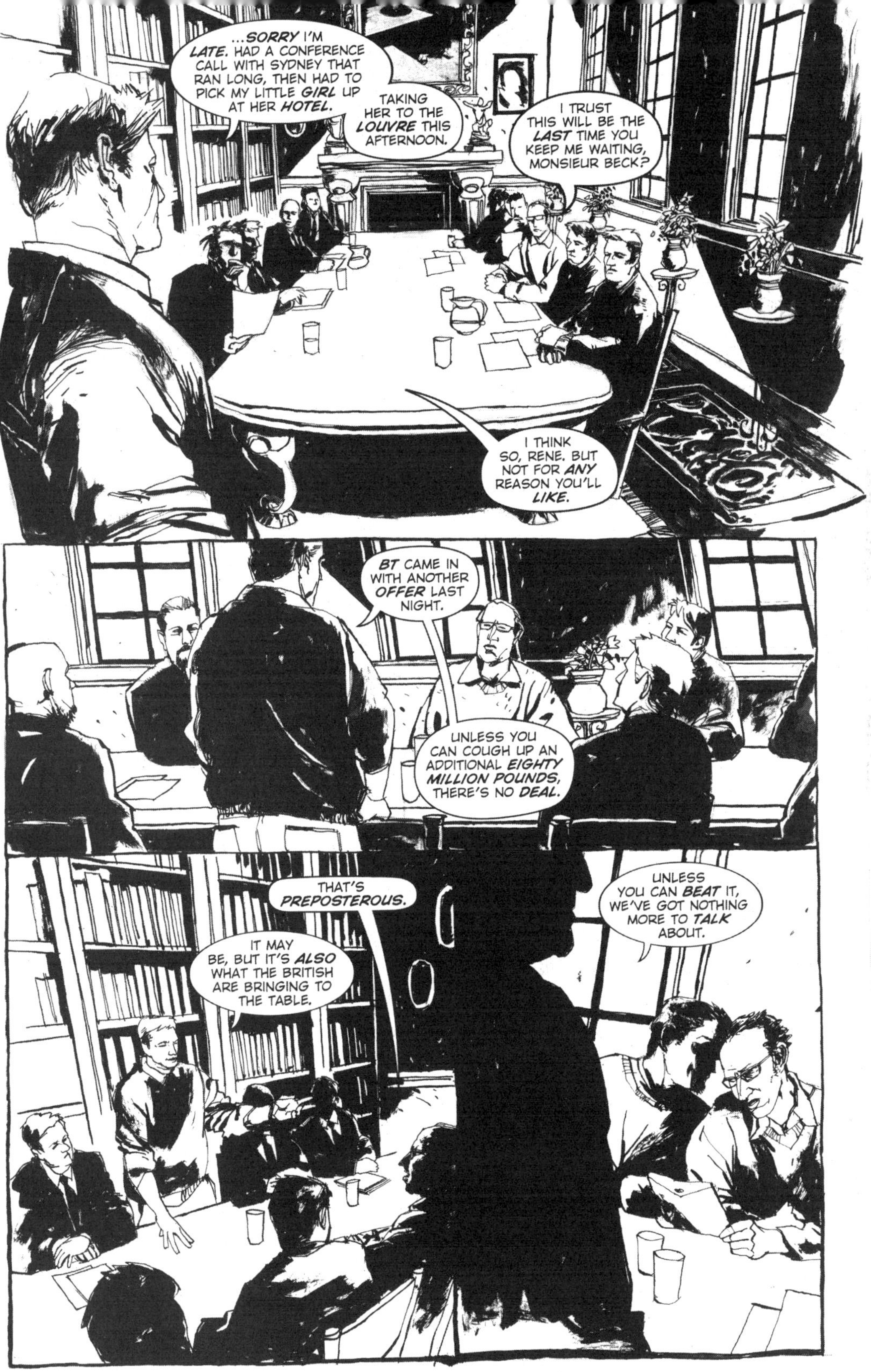
...SORRY I'M LATE. HAD A CONFERENCE CALL WITH SYDNEY THAT RAN LONG, THEN HAD TO PICK MY LITTLE GIRL UP AT HER HOTEL.
TAKING HER TO THE LOUVRE THIS AFTERNOON.
I TRUST THIS WILL BE THE LAST TIME YOU KEEP ME WAITING, MONSIEUR BECK?
I THINK SO, RENE. BUT NOT FOR ANY REASON YOU'LL LIKE.
BT CAME IN WITH ANOTHER OFFER LAST NIGHT.
UNLESS YOU CAN COUGH UP AN ADDITIONAL EIGHTY MILLION POUNDS, THERE'S NO DEAL.
THAT'S PREPOSTEROUS.
IT MAY BE, BUT IT'S ALSO WHAT THE BRITISH ARE BRINGING TO THE TABLE.
UNLESS YOU CAN BEAT IT, WE'VE GOT NOTHING MORE TO TALK ABOUT.

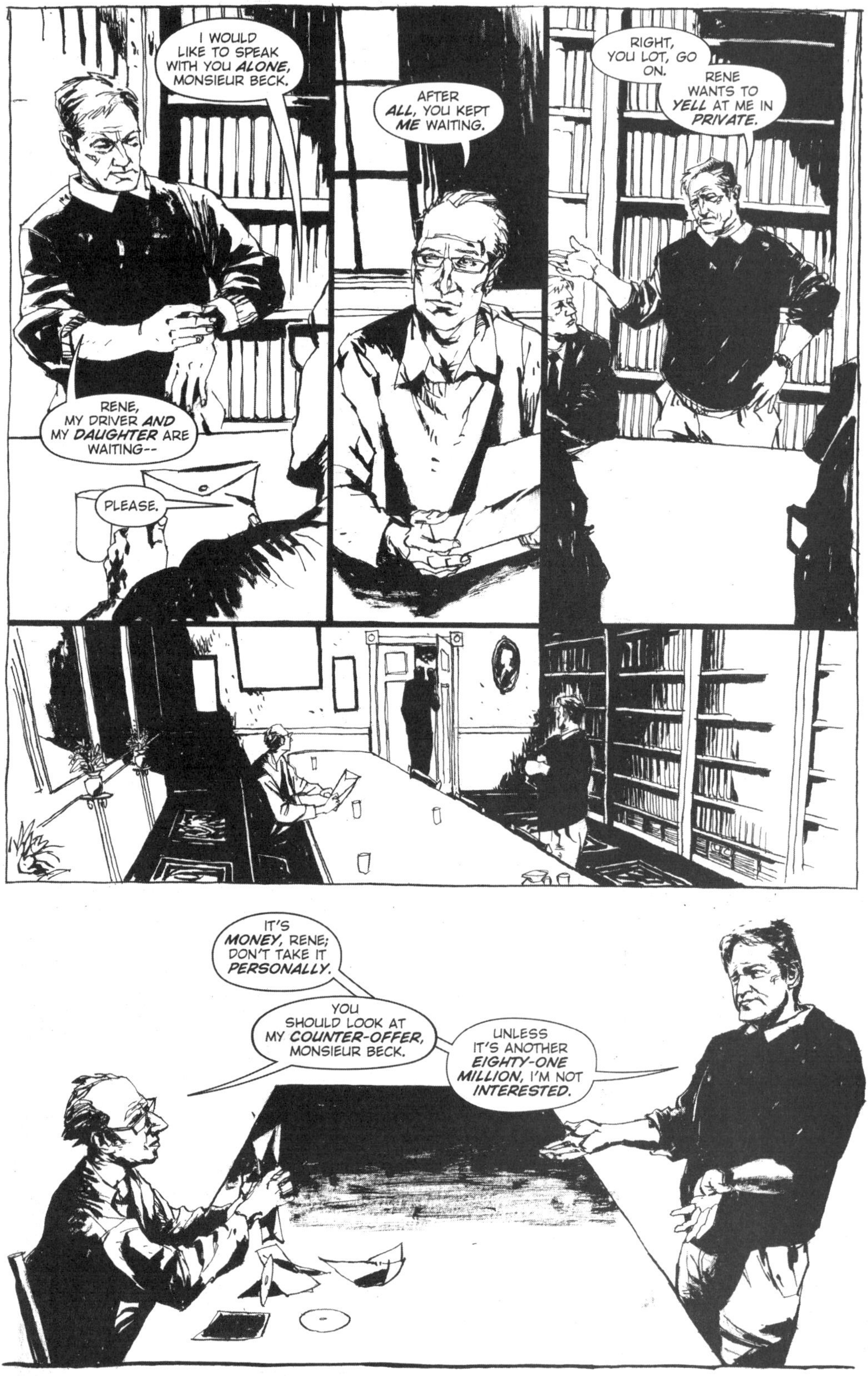
I WOULD LIKE TO SPEAK WITH YOU ALONE, MONSIEUR BECK.
RENE, MY DRIVER AND MY DAUGHTER ARE WAITING--
PLEASE.
AFTER ALL, YOU KEPT ME WAITING.
RIGHT, YOU LOT, GO ON.
RENE WANTS TO YELL AT ME IN PRIVATE.
IT'S MONEY, RENE; DON'T TAKE IT PERSONALLY.
YOU SHOULD LOOK AT MY COUNTER-OFFER, MONSIEUR BECK.
UNLESS IT'S ANOTHER EIGHTY-ONE MILLION, I'M NOT INTERESTED.

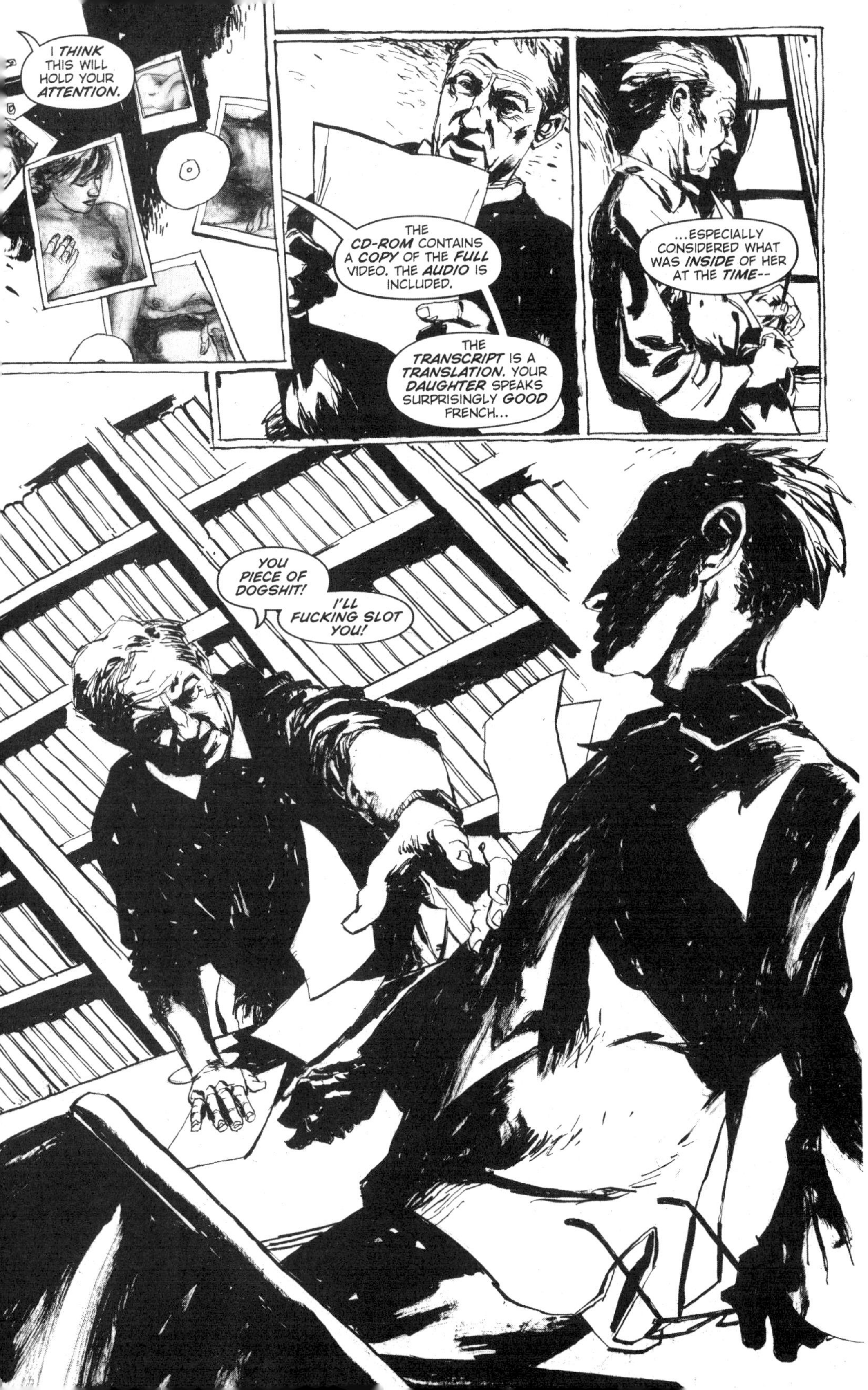
I THINK THIS WILL HOLD YOUR ATTENTION.
THE CD-ROM CONTAINS A COPY OF THE FULL VIDEO. THE AUDIO IS INCLUDED.
THE TRANSCRIPT IS A TRANSLATION. YOUR DAUGHTER SPEAKS SURPRISINGLY GOOD FRENCH...
...ESPECIALLY CONSIDERED WHAT WAS INSIDE OF HER AT THE TIME--
YOU PIECE OF DOGSHIT!
I'LL FUCKING SLOT YOU!

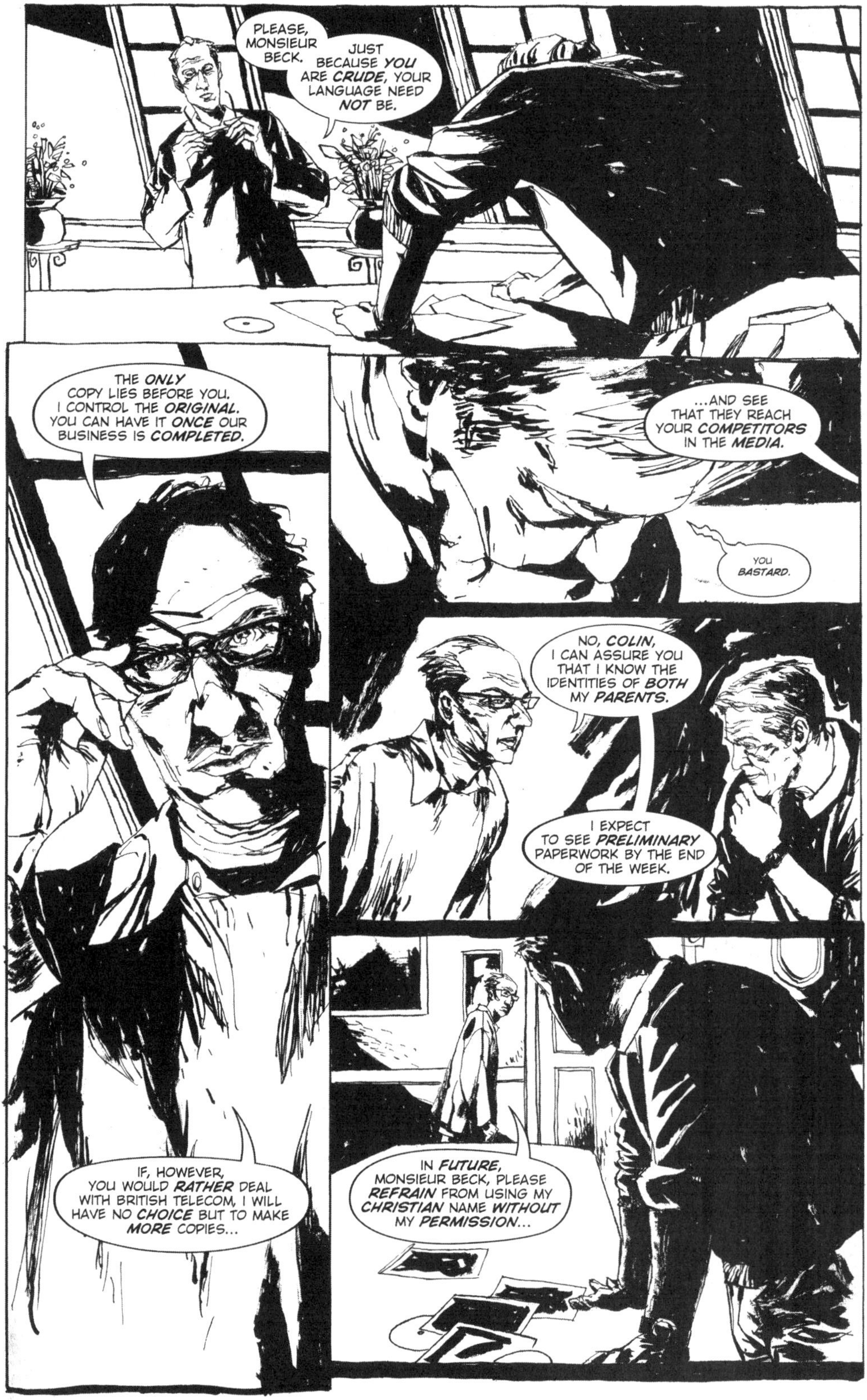
PLEASE, MONSIEUR BECK.
JUST BECAUSE YOU ARE CRUDE, YOUR LANGUAGE NEED NOT BE.
THE ONLY COPY LIES BEFORE YOU. I CONTROL THE ORIGINAL. YOU CAN HAVE IT ONCE OUR BUSINESS IS COMPLETED.
IF, HOWEVER, YOU WOULD RATHER DEAL WITH BRITISH TELECOM, I WILL HAVE NO CHOICE BUT TO MAKE MORE COPIES...
...AND SEE THAT THEY REACH YOUR COMPETITORS IN THE MEDIA.
YOU BASTARD.
NO, COLIN, I CAN ASSURE YOU THAT I KNOW THE IDENTITIES OF BOTH MY PARENTS.
I EXPECT TO SEE PRELIMINARY PAPERWORK BY THE END OF THE WEEK.
IN FUTURE, MONSIEUR BECK, PLEASE REFRAIN FROM USING MY CHRISTIAN NAME WITHOUT MY PERMISSION...

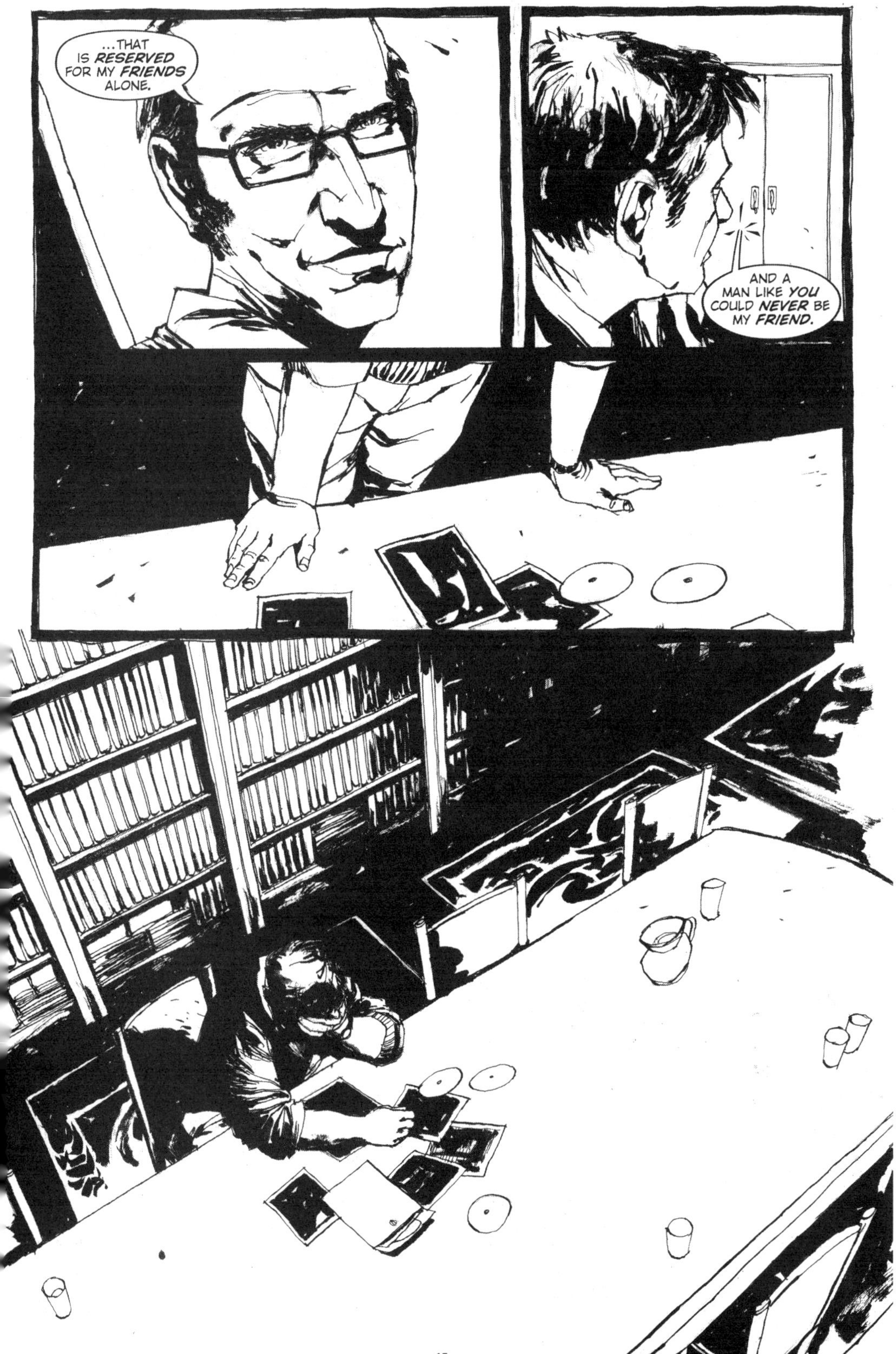
...THAT IS RESERVED FOR MY FRIENDS ALONE.
AND A MAN LIKE YOU COULD NEVER BE MY FRIEND.

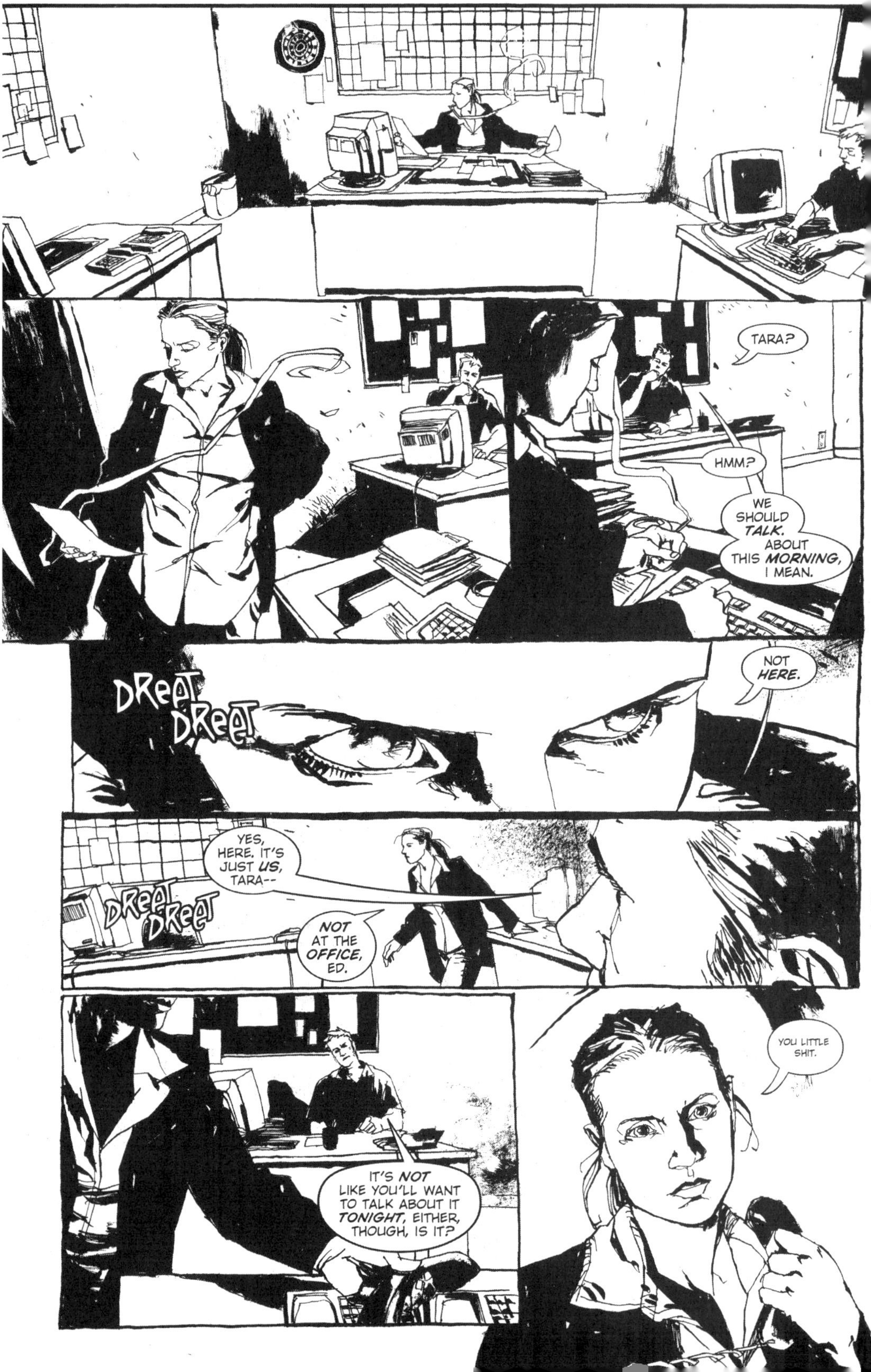
TARA?
HMM?
WE SHOULD TALK. ABOUT THIS MORNING, I MEAN.
DREET DREET
NOT HERE.
YES, HERE. IT'S JUST US, TARA--
DREET DREET
NOT AT THE OFFICE, ED.
IT'S NOT LIKE YOU'LL WANT TO TALK ABOUT IT TONIGHT, EITHER, THOUGH, IS IT?
YOU LITTLE SHIT.

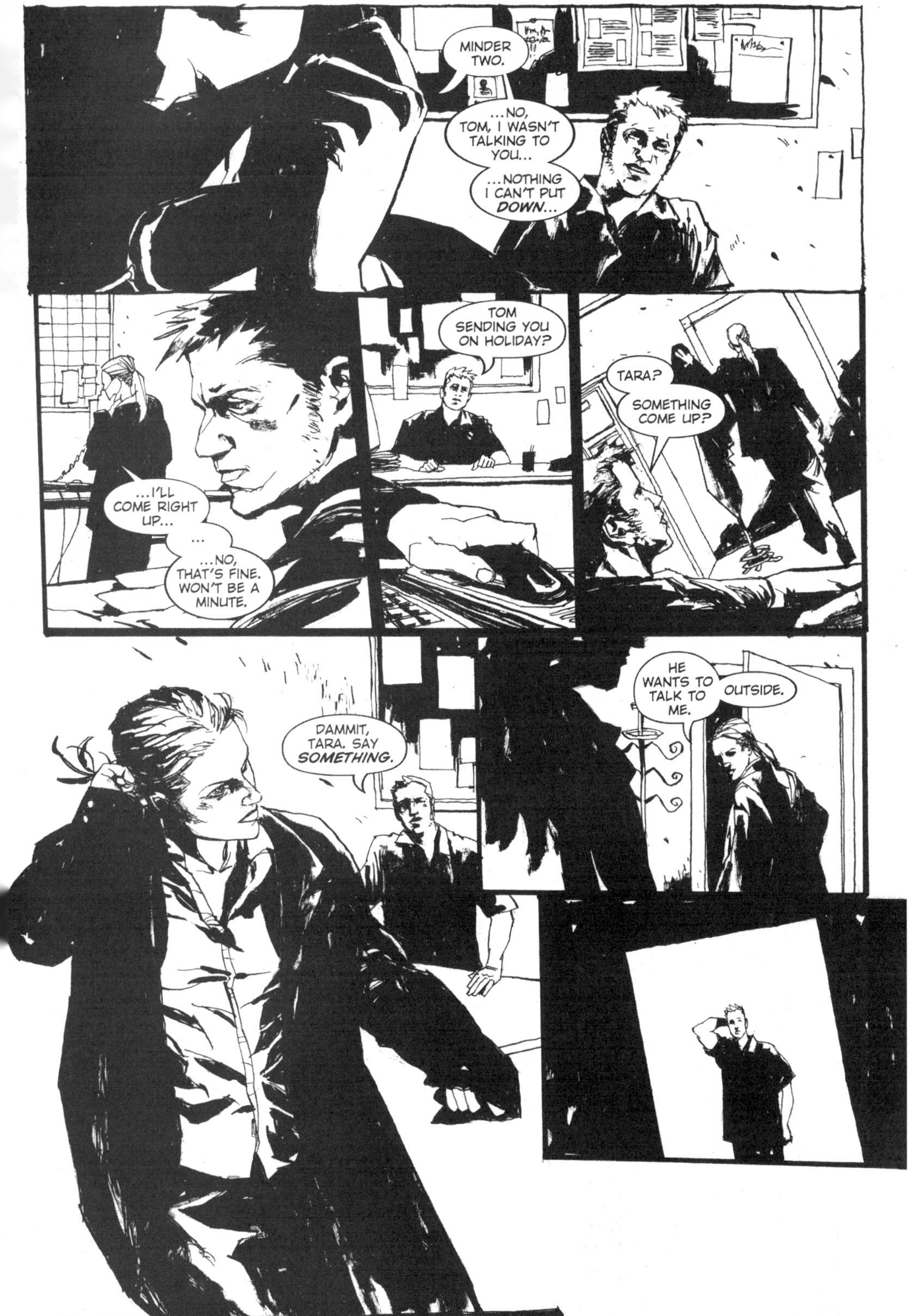
MINDER TWO.
...NO, TOM, I WASN'T TALKING TO YOU...
...NOTHING I CAN'T PUT DOWN...
...I'LL COME RIGHT UP...
...
...NO, THAT'S FINE. WON'T BE A MINUTE.
TOM SENDING YOU ON HOLIDAY?
TARA?
SOMETHING COME UP?
DAMMIT, TARA. SAY SOMETHING.
HE WANTS TO TALK TO ME.
OUTSIDE.

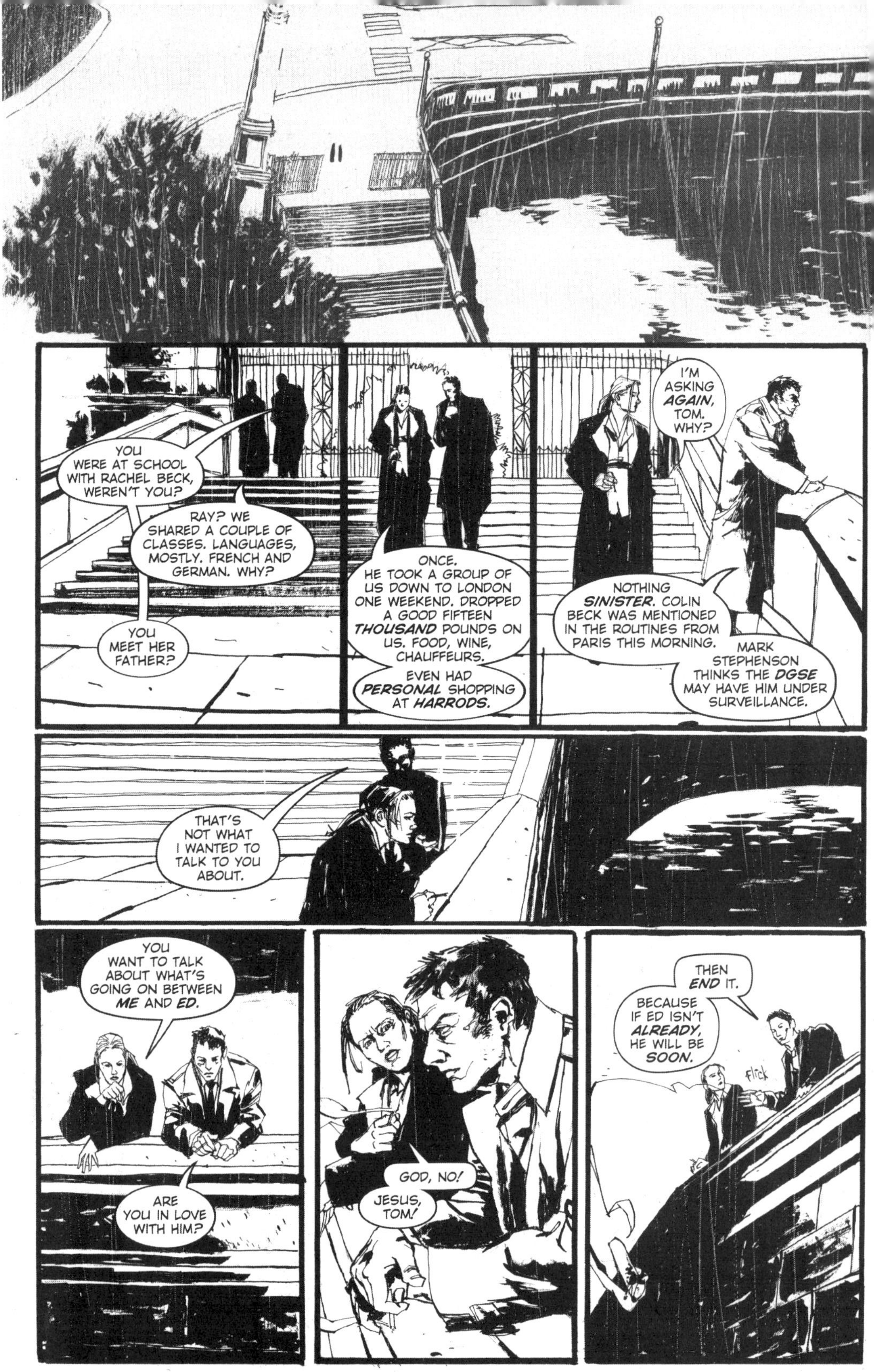

YOU WERE AT SCHOOL WITH RACHEL BECK, WEREN'T YOU?
RAY? WE SHARED A COUPLE OF CLASSES. LANGUAGES, MOSTLY. FRENCH AND GERMAN. WHY?
YOU MEET HER FATHER?
ONCE. HE TOOK A GROUP OF US DOWN TO LONDON ONE WEEKEND. DROPPED A GOOD FIFTEEN THOUSAND POUNDS ON US. FOOD, WINE, CHAUFFEURS.
EVEN HAD PERSONAL SHOPPING AT HARRODS.
I'M ASKING AGAIN, TOM. WHY?
NOTHING SINISTER. COLIN BECK WAS MENTIONED IN THE ROUTINES FROM PARIS THIS MORNING.
MARK STEPHENSON THINKS THE DGSE MAY HAVE HIM UNDER SURVEILLANCE.
THAT'S NOT WHAT I WANTED TO TALK TO YOU ABOUT.
YOU WANT TO TALK ABOUT WHAT'S GOING ON BETWEEN ME AND ED.
ARE YOU IN LOVE WITH HIM?
GOD, NO!
JESUS, TOM!
THEN END IT.
BECAUSE IF ED ISN'T ALREADY, HE WILL BE SOON.
FLICK

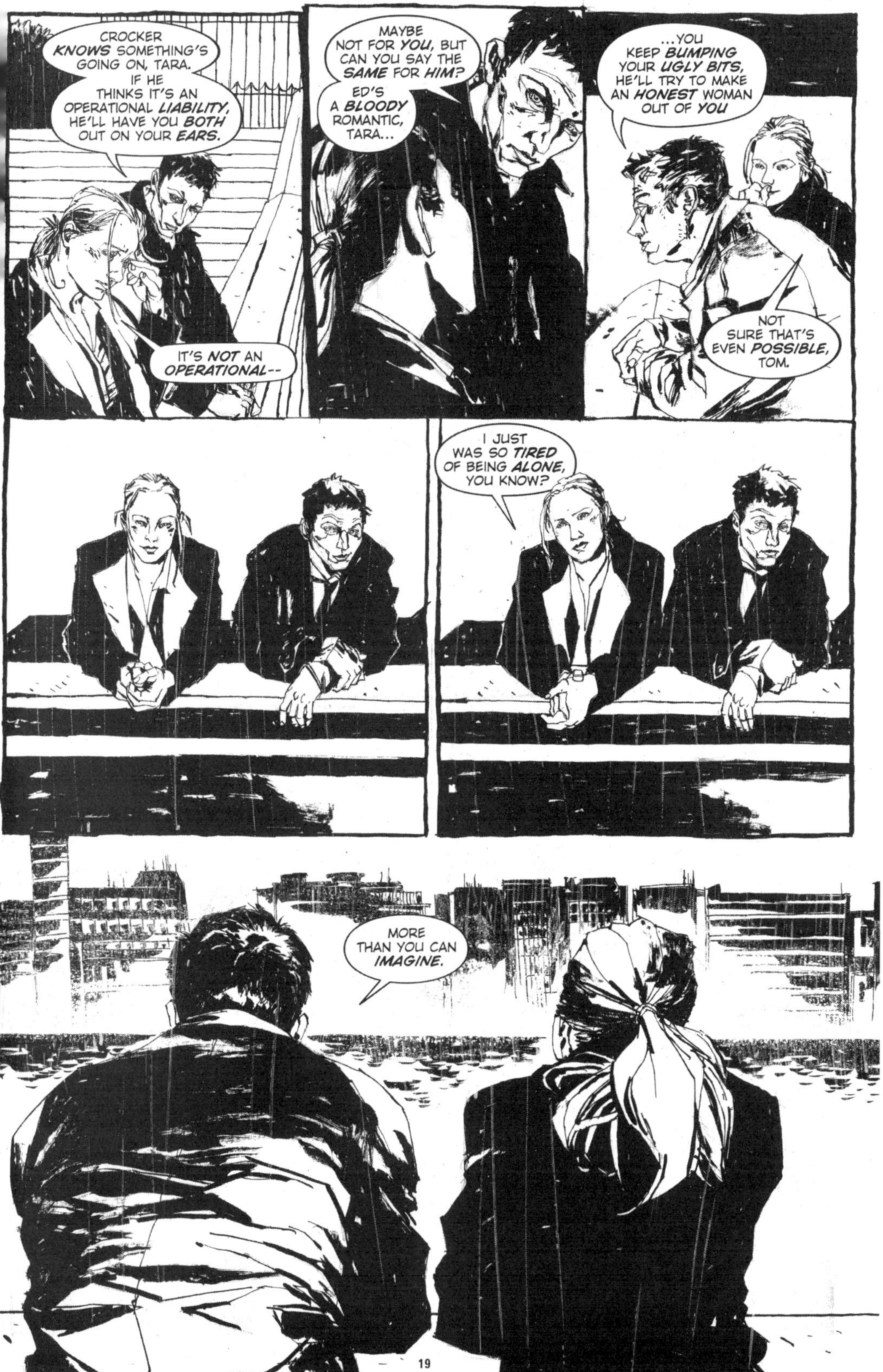
CROCKER KNOWS SOMETHING'S GOING ON, TARA.
IF HE THINKS IT'S AN OPERATIONAL LIABILITY, HE'LL HAVE YOU BOTH OUT ON YOUR EARS.
IT'S NOT AN OPERATIONAL--
MAYBE NOT FOR YOU, BUT CAN YOU SAY THE SAME FOR HIM?
ED'S A BLOODY ROMANTIC, TARA...
...YOU KEEP BUMPING YOUR UGLY BITS, HE'LL TRY TO MAKE AN HONEST WOMAN OUT OF YOU
NOT SURE THAT'S EVEN POSSIBLE, TOM.
I JUST WAS SO TIRED OF BEING ALONE, YOU KNOW?
MORE THAN YOU CAN IMAGINE.

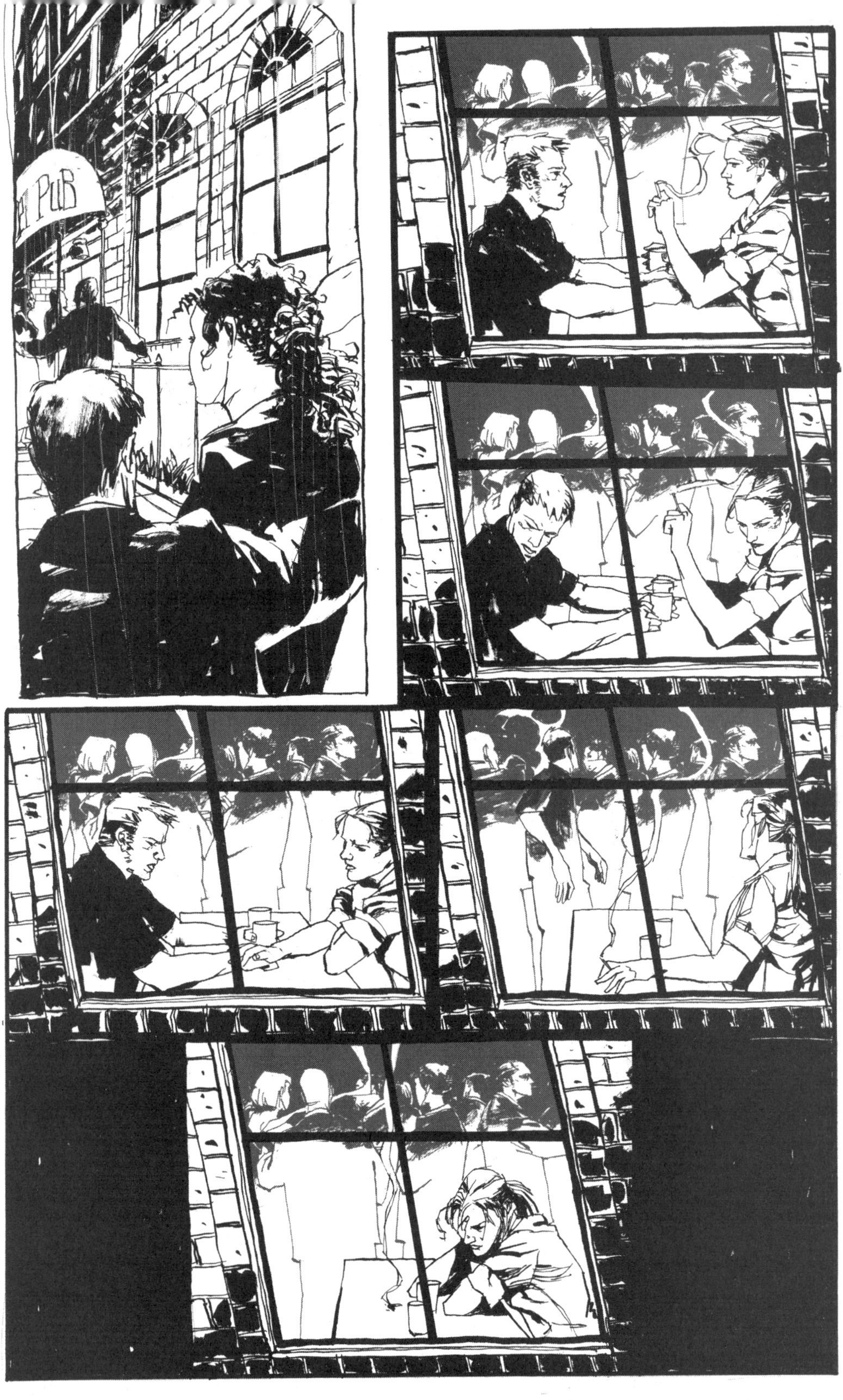
PUB

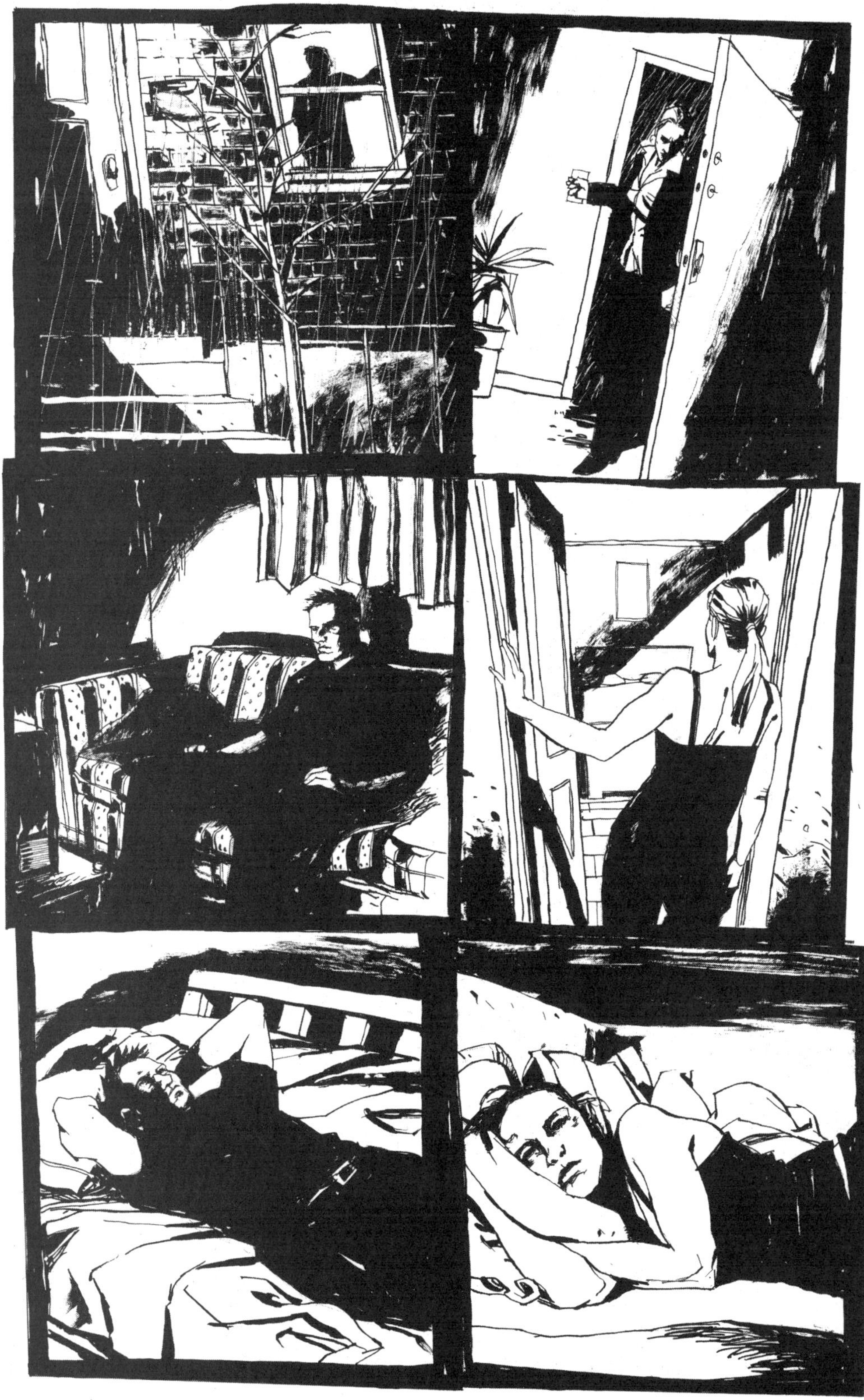

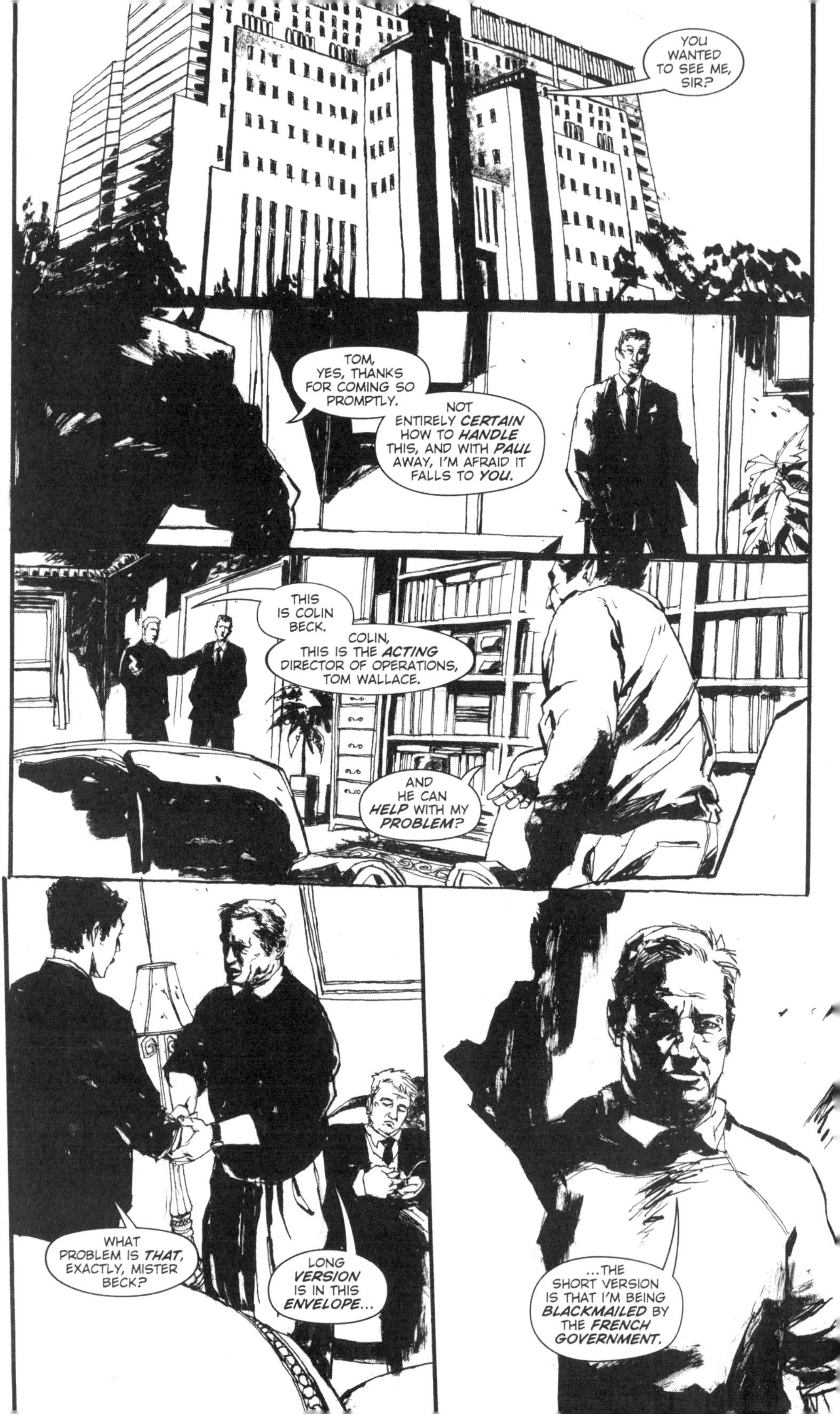
YOU WANTED TO SEE ME, SIR?
TOM, YES, THANKS FOR COMING SO PROMPTLY.
NOT ENTIRELY CERTAIN HOW TO HANDLE THIS, AND WITH PAUL AWAY, I'M AFRAID IT FALLS TO YOU.
THIS IS COLIN BECK.
COLIN, THIS IS THE ACTING DIRECTOR OF OPERATIONS, TOM WALLACE.
AND HE CAN HELP WITH MY PROBLEM?
WHAT PROBLEM IS THAT, EXACTLY, MISTER BECK?
LONG VERSION IS IN THIS ENVELOPE...
...THE SHORT VERSION IS THAT I'M BEING BLACKMAILED BY THE FRENCH GOVERNMENT.

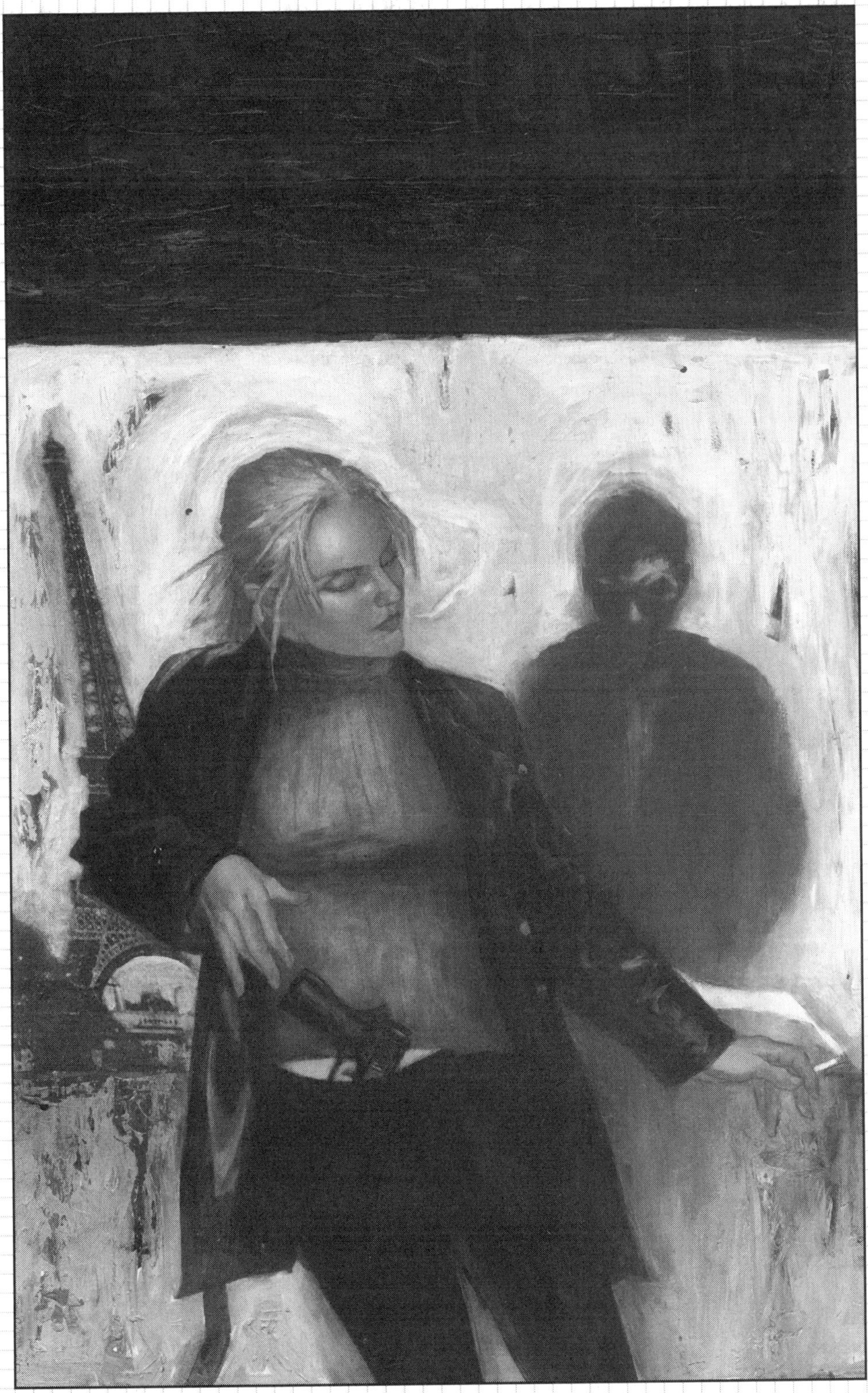

CHAPTER 2

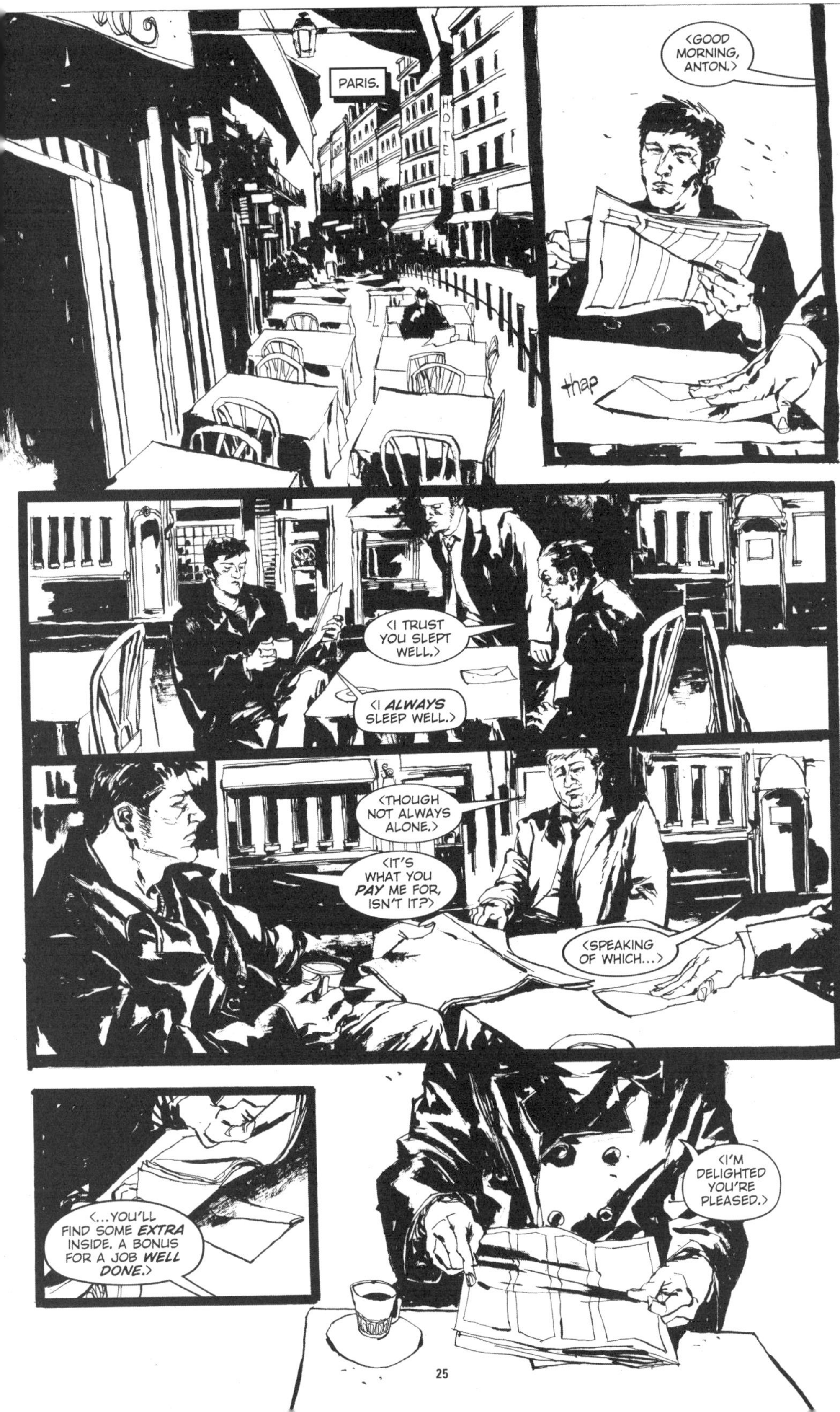
PARIS.
<GOOD MORNING, ANTON.>
thap
<I TRUST YOU SLEPT WELL.>
<I ALWAYS SLEEP WELL.>
<THOUGH NOT ALWAYS ALONE.>
<IT'S WHAT YOU PAY ME FOR, ISN'T IT?>
<SPEAKING OF WHICH...>
<...YOU'LL FIND SOME EXTRA INSIDE. A BONUS FOR A JOB WELL DONE.>
<I'M DELIGHTED YOU'RE PLEASED.>

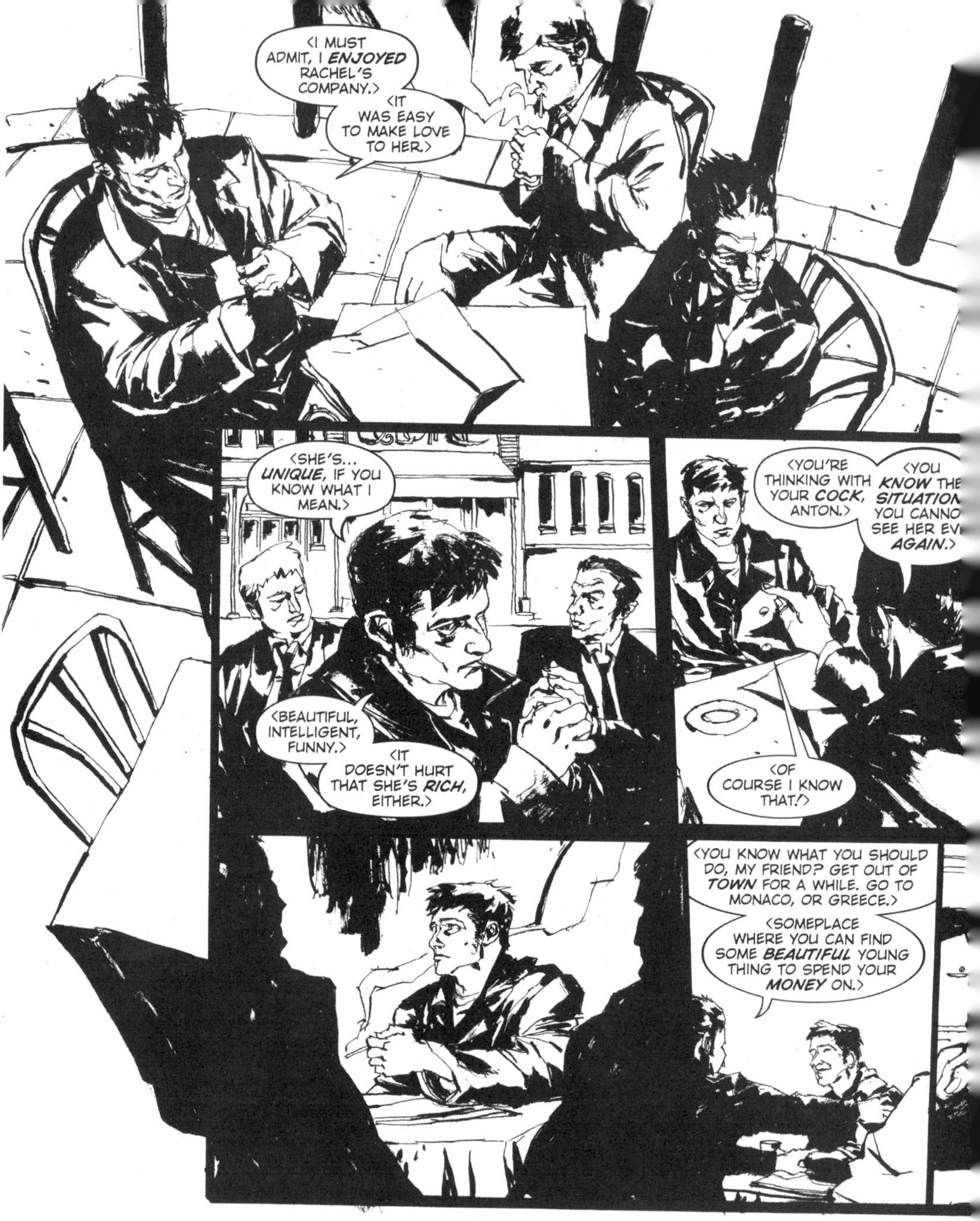

<I MUST ADMIT, I **ENJOYED** RACHEL'S COMPANY.>
<IT WAS EASY TO MAKE LOVE TO HER.>
<SHE'S... **UNIQUE**, IF YOU KNOW WHAT I MEAN.>
<BEAUTIFUL, INTELLIGENT, FUNNY.>
<IT DOESN'T HURT THAT SHE'S **RICH**, EITHER.>
<YOU'RE THINKING WITH YOUR **COCK**, ANTON.>
<YOU **KNOW** THE **SITUATION** YOU CANNO SEE HER EV **AGAIN**.>
<OF COURSE I KNOW THAT!>
<YOU KNOW WHAT YOU SHOULD DO, MY FRIEND? GET OUT OF **TOWN** FOR A WHILE. GO TO MONACO, OR GREECE.>
<SOMEPLACE WHERE YOU CAN FIND SOME **BEAUTIFUL** YOUNG THING TO SPEND YOUR **MONEY** ON.>

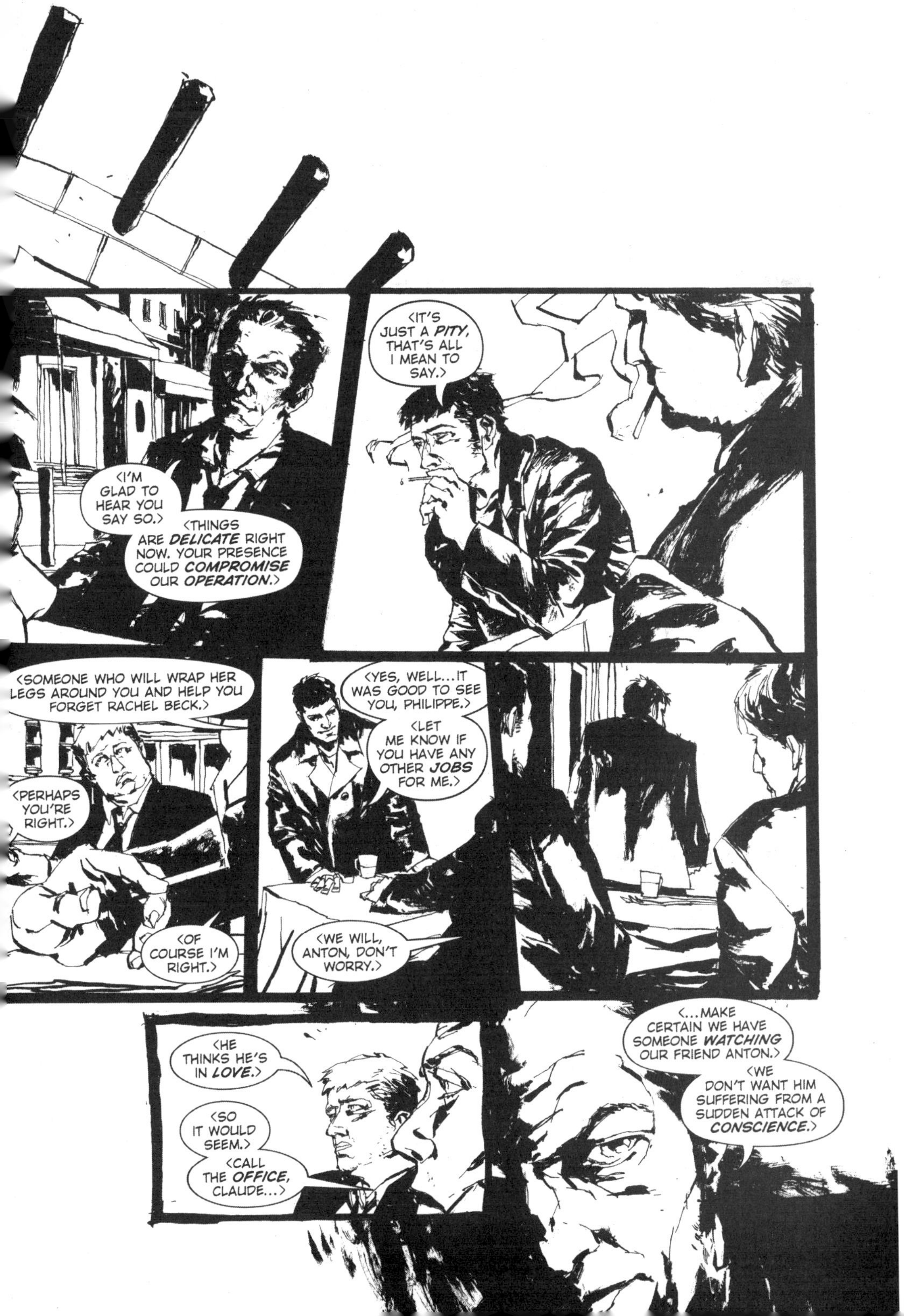

<I'M GLAD TO HEAR YOU SAY SO.>
<THINGS ARE DELICATE RIGHT NOW. YOUR PRESENCE COULD COMPROMISE OUR OPERATION.>
<IT'S JUST A PITY, THAT'S ALL I MEAN TO SAY.>
<SOMEONE WHO WILL WRAP HER LEGS AROUND YOU AND HELP YOU FORGET RACHEL BECK.>
<PERHAPS YOU'RE RIGHT.>
<OF COURSE I'M RIGHT.>
<YES, WELL...IT WAS GOOD TO SEE YOU, PHILIPPE.>
<LET ME KNOW IF YOU HAVE ANY OTHER JOBS FOR ME.>
<WE WILL, ANTON, DON'T WORRY.>
<HE THINKS HE'S IN LOVE.>
<SO IT WOULD SEEM.>
<CALL THE OFFICE, CLAUDE...>
<...MAKE CERTAIN WE HAVE SOMEONE WATCHING OUR FRIEND ANTON.>
<WE DON'T WANT HIM SUFFERING FROM A SUDDEN ATTACK OF CONSCIENCE.>

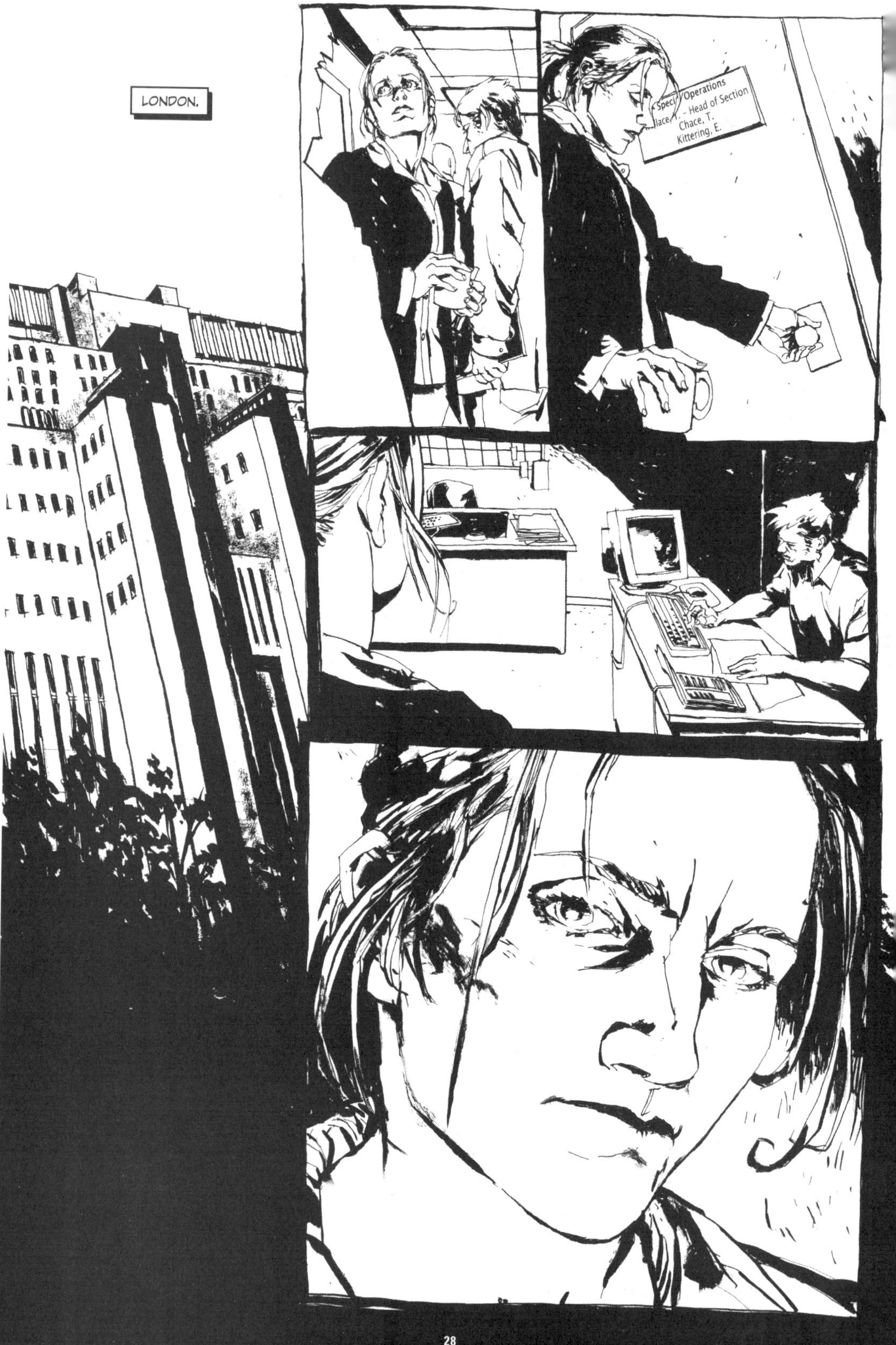
LONDON.
Operations
Head of Section
Chace, T.
Kittering, E.

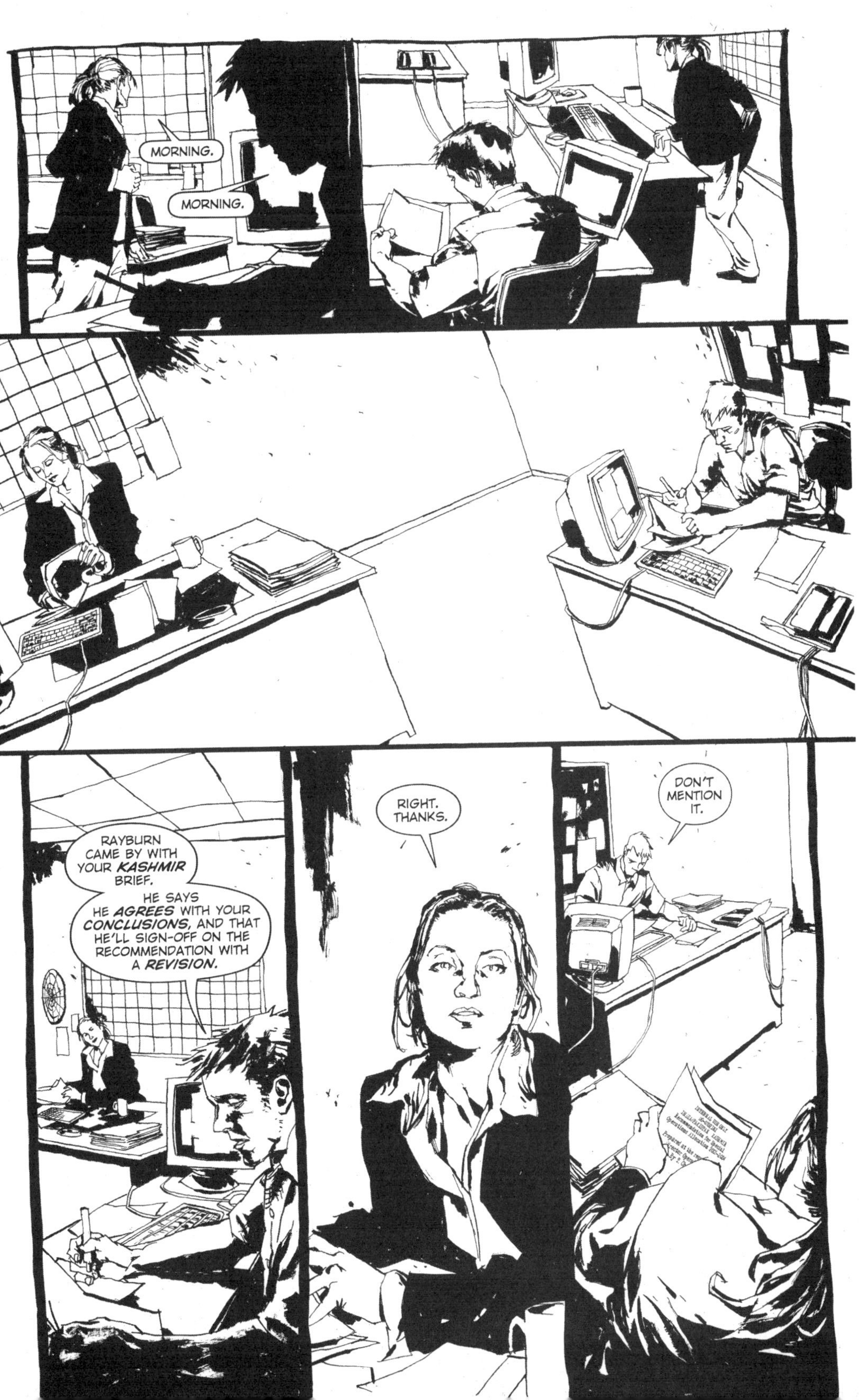
MORNING.
MORNING.
RAYBURN CAME BY WITH YOUR *KASHMIR* BRIEF.
HE SAYS HE *AGREES* WITH YOUR *CONCLUSIONS,* AND THAT HE'LL SIGN-OFF ON THE RECOMMENDATION WITH A *REVISION.*
RIGHT. THANKS.
DON'T MENTION IT.

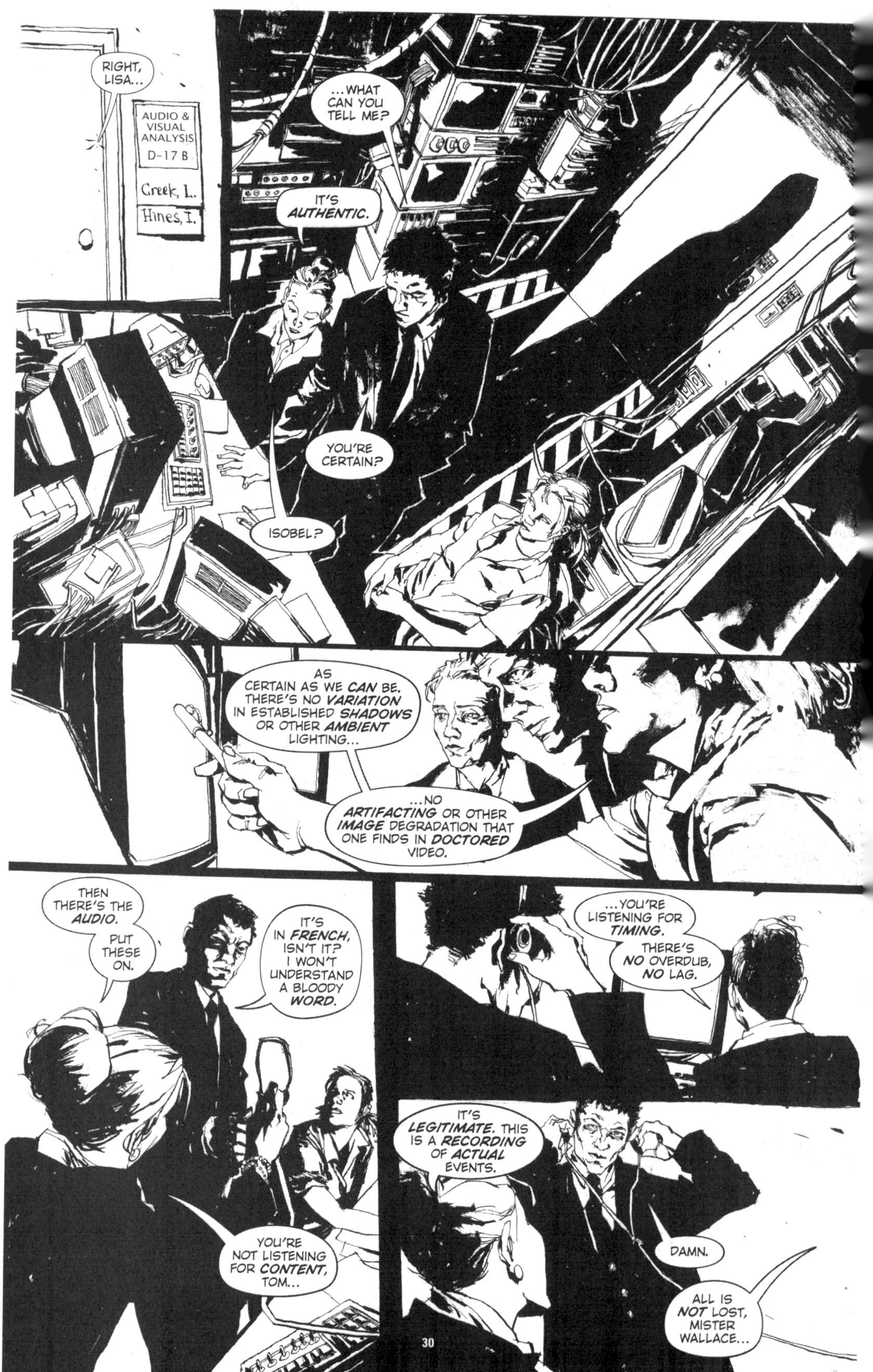
RIGHT, LISA...
AUDIO & VISUAL ANALYSIS D-17 B
Creek, L.
Hines, I.
...WHAT CAN YOU TELL ME?
IT'S *AUTHENTIC*.
YOU'RE CERTAIN?
ISOBEL?
AS CERTAIN AS WE *CAN* BE. THERE'S NO *VARIATION* IN ESTABLISHED *SHADOWS* OR OTHER *AMBIENT* LIGHTING...
...NO *ARTIFACTING* OR OTHER *IMAGE* DEGRADATION THAT ONE FINDS IN *DOCTORED* VIDEO.
THEN THERE'S THE *AUDIO*.
PUT THESE ON.
IT'S IN *FRENCH*, ISN'T IT? I WON'T UNDERSTAND A BLOODY *WORD*.
YOU'RE NOT LISTENING FOR *CONTENT*, TOM...
...YOU'RE LISTENING FOR *TIMING*.
THERE'S *NO* OVERDUB, *NO* LAG.
IT'S *LEGITIMATE*. THIS IS A *RECORDING* OF *ACTUAL* EVENTS.
DAMN.
ALL IS *NOT* LOST, MISTER WALLACE...

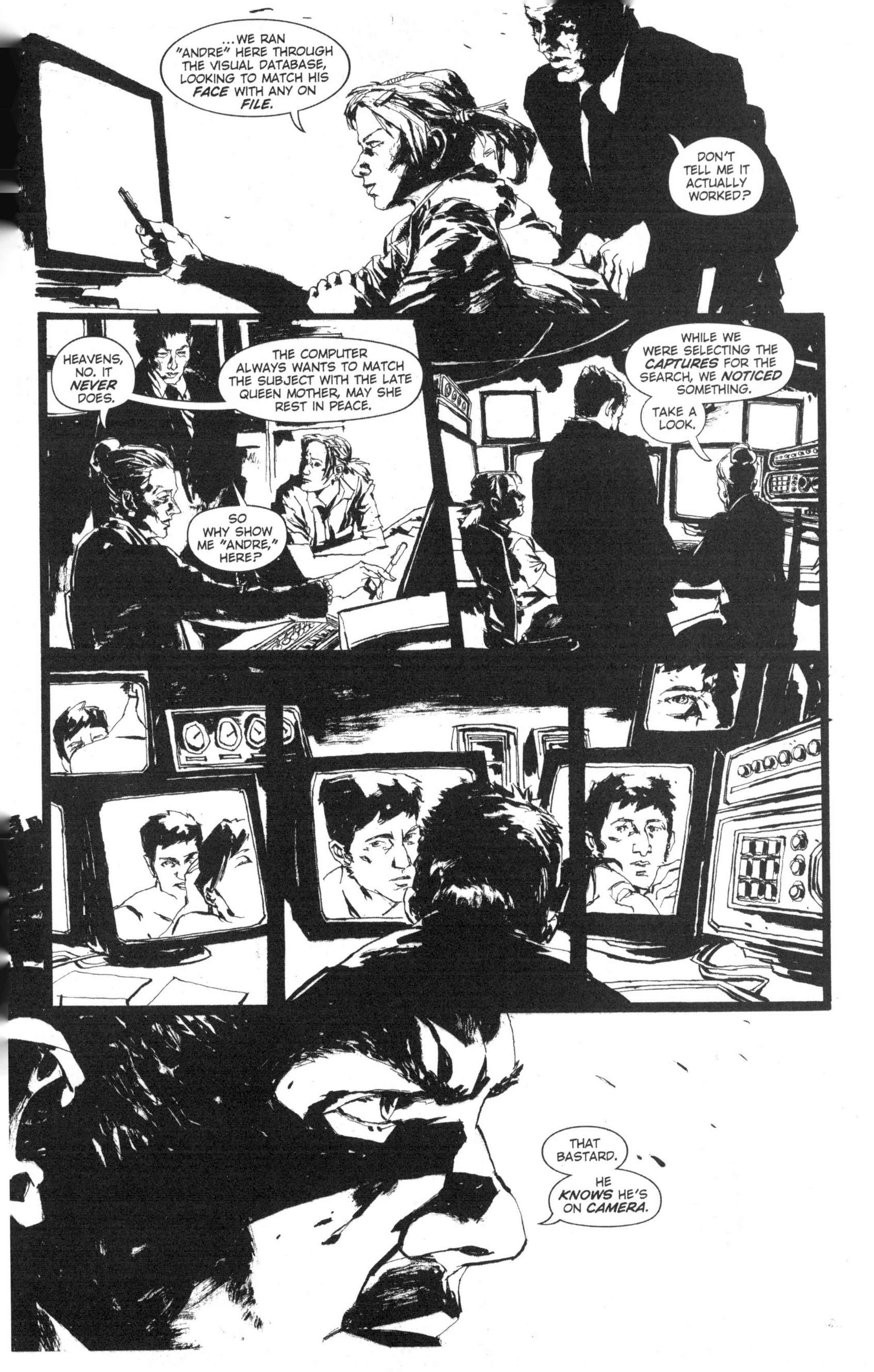
...WE RAN "ANDRE" HERE THROUGH THE VISUAL DATABASE, LOOKING TO MATCH HIS FACE WITH ANY ON FILE.
DON'T TELL ME IT ACTUALLY WORKED?
HEAVENS, NO. IT NEVER DOES.
THE COMPUTER ALWAYS WANTS TO MATCH THE SUBJECT WITH THE LATE QUEEN MOTHER, MAY SHE REST IN PEACE.
SO WHY SHOW ME "ANDRE," HERE?
WHILE WE WERE SELECTING THE CAPTURES FOR THE SEARCH, WE NOTICED SOMETHING.
TAKE A LOOK.
THAT BASTARD.
HE KNOWS HE'S ON CAMERA.

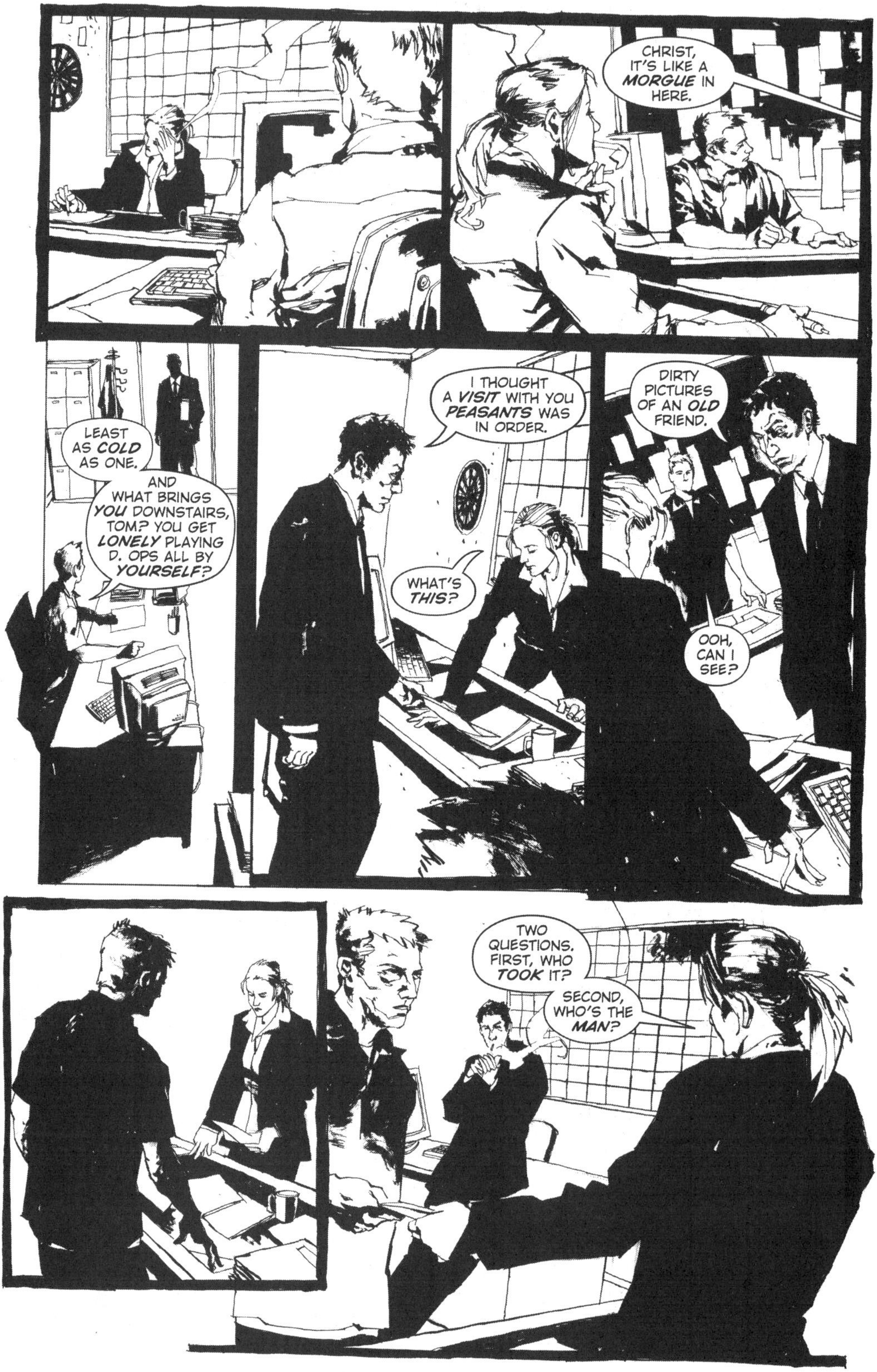
CHRIST, IT'S LIKE A MORGUE IN HERE.
LEAST AS COLD AS ONE.
AND WHAT BRINGS YOU DOWNSTAIRS, TOM? YOU GET LONELY PLAYING D. OPS ALL BY YOURSELF?
I THOUGHT A VISIT WITH YOU PEASANTS WAS IN ORDER.
WHAT'S THIS?
DIRTY PICTURES OF AN OLD FRIEND.
OOH, CAN I SEE?
TWO QUESTIONS. FIRST, WHO TOOK IT?
SECOND, WHO'S THE MAN?

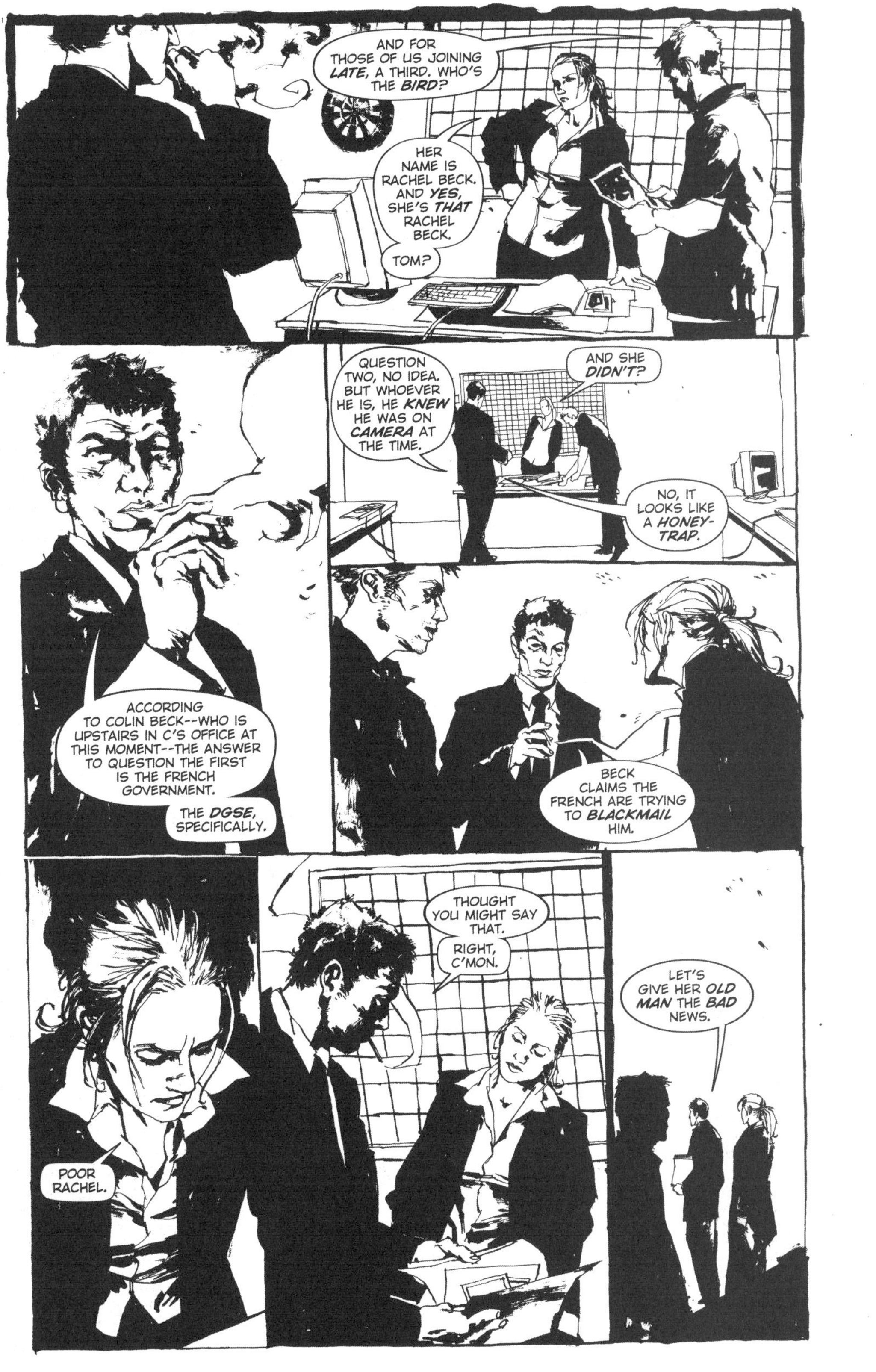
AND FOR THOSE OF US JOINING LATE, A THIRD. WHO'S THE BIRD?
HER NAME IS RACHEL BECK. AND YES, SHE'S THAT RACHEL BECK.
TOM?
ACCORDING TO COLIN BECK--WHO IS UPSTAIRS IN C'S OFFICE AT THIS MOMENT--THE ANSWER TO QUESTION THE FIRST IS THE FRENCH GOVERNMENT.
THE DGSE, SPECIFICALLY.
QUESTION TWO, NO IDEA. BUT WHOEVER HE IS, HE KNEW HE WAS ON CAMERA AT THE TIME.
AND SHE DIDN'T?
NO, IT LOOKS LIKE A HONEY-TRAP.
BECK CLAIMS THE FRENCH ARE TRYING TO BLACKMAIL HIM.
POOR RACHEL.
THOUGHT YOU MIGHT SAY THAT.
RIGHT, C'MON.
LET'S GIVE HER OLD MAN THE BAD NEWS.

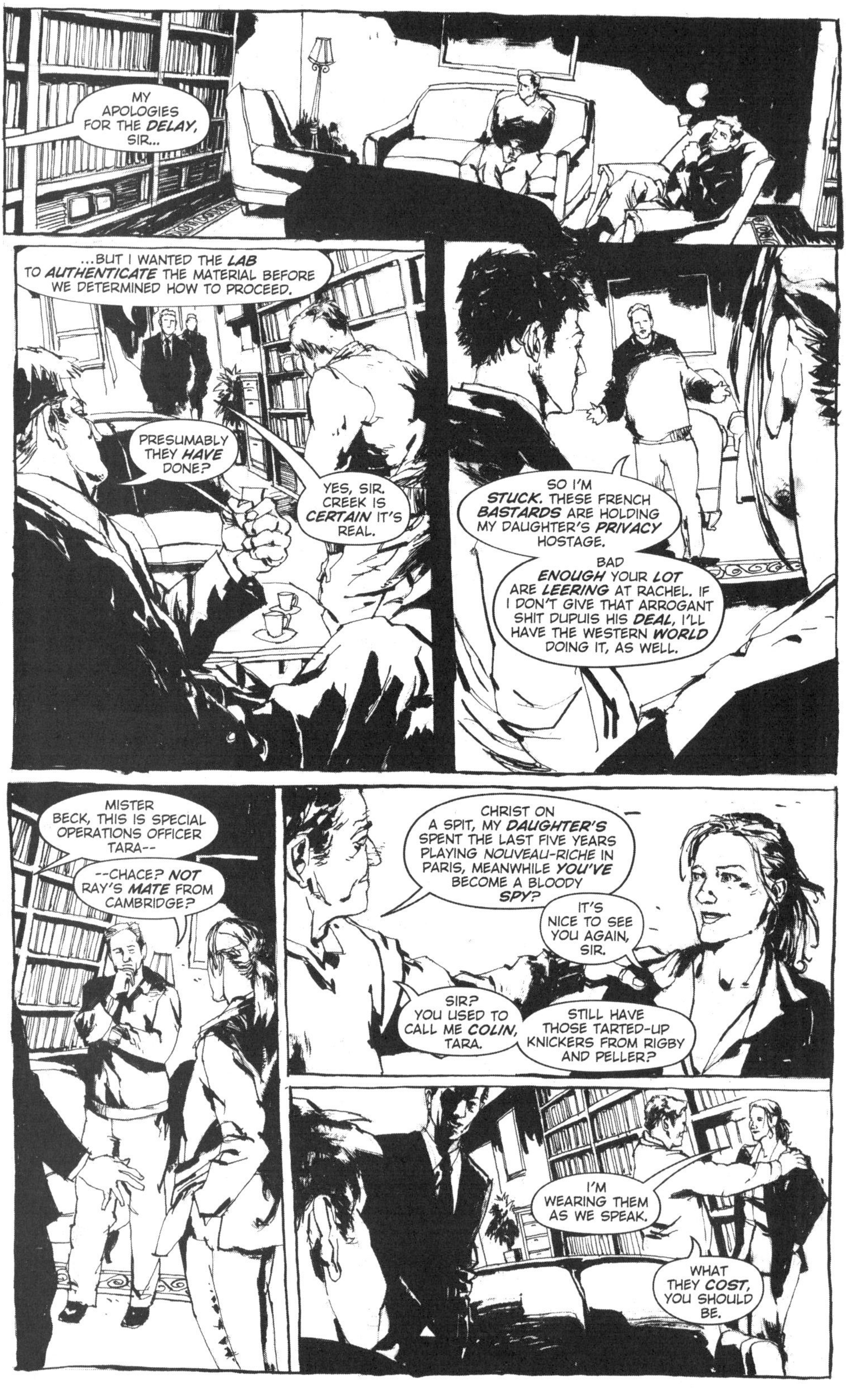
MY APOLOGIES FOR THE *DELAY,* SIR...
...BUT I WANTED THE *LAB* TO *AUTHENTICATE* THE MATERIAL BEFORE WE DETERMINED HOW TO PROCEED.
PRESUMABLY THEY *HAVE* DONE?
YES, SIR. CREEK IS *CERTAIN* IT'S REAL.
SO I'M *STUCK.* THESE FRENCH *BASTARDS* ARE HOLDING MY DAUGHTER'S *PRIVACY* HOSTAGE.
BAD *ENOUGH* YOUR *LOT* ARE *LEERING* AT RACHEL. IF I DON'T GIVE THAT ARROGANT SHIT DUPUIS HIS *DEAL,* I'LL HAVE THE WESTERN *WORLD* DOING IT, AS WELL.
MISTER BECK, THIS IS SPECIAL OPERATIONS OFFICER TARA--
--CHACE? *NOT* RAY'S *MATE* FROM CAMBRIDGE?
CHRIST ON A SPIT, MY *DAUGHTER'S* SPENT THE LAST FIVE YEARS PLAYING *NOUVEAU-RICHE* IN PARIS, MEANWHILE *YOU'VE* BECOME A BLOODY *SPY?*
IT'S NICE TO SEE YOU AGAIN, SIR.
SIR? YOU USED TO CALL ME *COLIN,* TARA.
STILL HAVE THOSE TARTED-UP KNICKERS FROM RIGBY AND PELLER?
I'M WEARING THEM AS WE SPEAK.
WHAT THEY *COST,* YOU SHOULD BE.

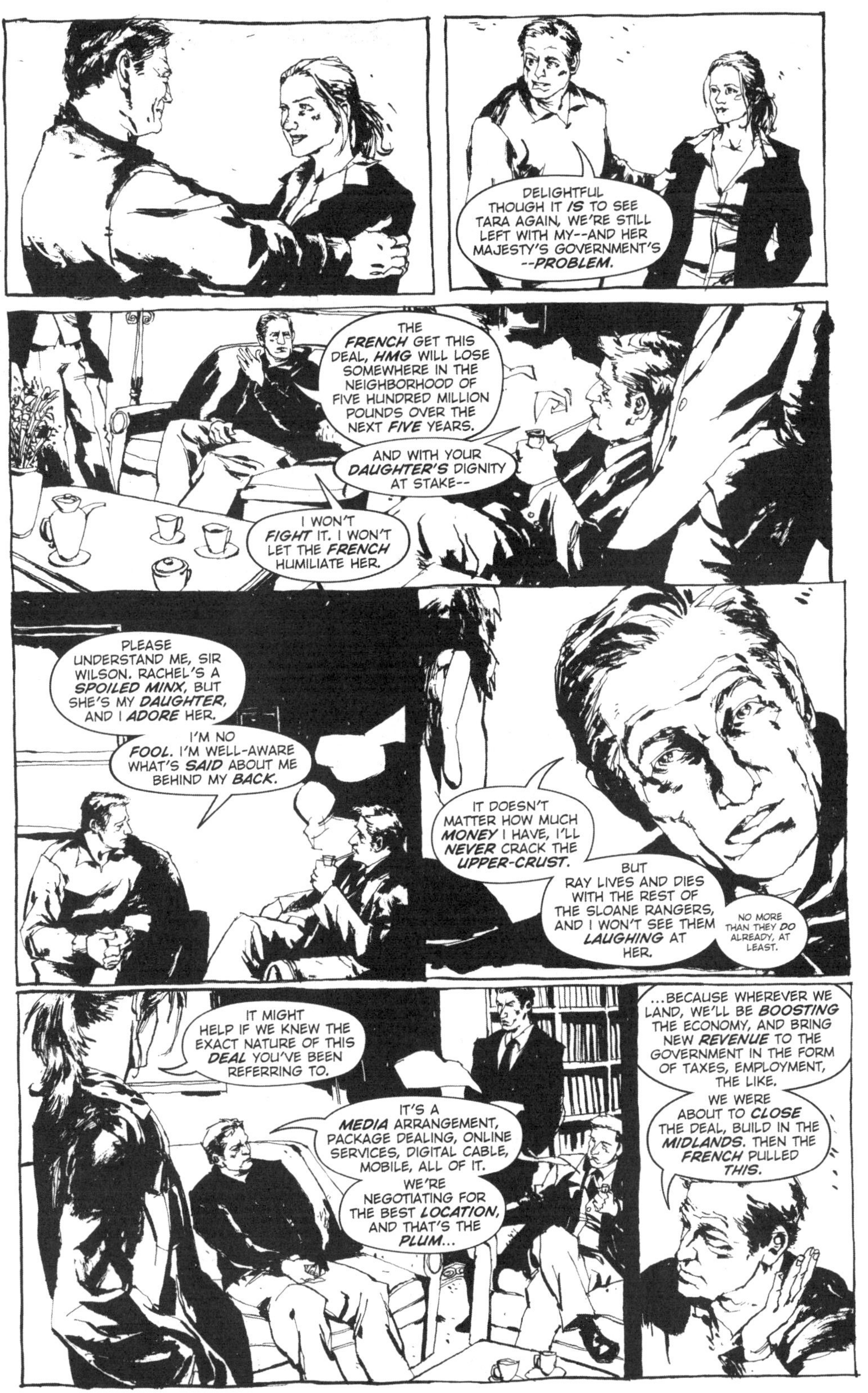
DELIGHTFUL THOUGH IT IS TO SEE TARA AGAIN, WE'RE STILL LEFT WITH MY--AND HER MAJESTY'S GOVERNMENT'S --PROBLEM.
THE FRENCH GET THIS DEAL, HMG WILL LOSE SOMEWHERE IN THE NEIGHBORHOOD OF FIVE HUNDRED MILLION POUNDS OVER THE NEXT FIVE YEARS.
AND WITH YOUR DAUGHTER'S DIGNITY AT STAKE--
I WON'T FIGHT IT. I WON'T LET THE FRENCH HUMILIATE HER.
PLEASE UNDERSTAND ME, SIR WILSON. RACHEL'S A SPOILED MINX, BUT SHE'S MY DAUGHTER, AND I ADORE HER.
I'M NO FOOL. I'M WELL-AWARE WHAT'S SAID ABOUT ME BEHIND MY BACK.
IT DOESN'T MATTER HOW MUCH MONEY I HAVE, I'LL NEVER CRACK THE UPPER-CRUST.
BUT RAY LIVES AND DIES WITH THE REST OF THE SLOANE RANGERS, AND I WON'T SEE THEM LAUGHING AT HER.
NO MORE THAN THEY DO ALREADY, AT LEAST.
IT MIGHT HELP IF WE KNEW THE EXACT NATURE OF THIS DEAL YOU'VE BEEN REFERRING TO.
IT'S A MEDIA ARRANGEMENT, PACKAGE DEALING, ONLINE SERVICES, DIGITAL CABLE, MOBILE, ALL OF IT.
WE'RE NEGOTIATING FOR THE BEST LOCATION, AND THAT'S THE PLUM...
...BECAUSE WHEREVER WE LAND, WE'LL BE BOOSTING THE ECONOMY, AND BRING NEW REVENUE TO THE GOVERNMENT IN THE FORM OF TAXES, EMPLOYMENT, THE LIKE.
WE WERE ABOUT TO CLOSE THE DEAL, BUILD IN THE MIDLANDS. THEN THE FRENCH PULLED THIS.

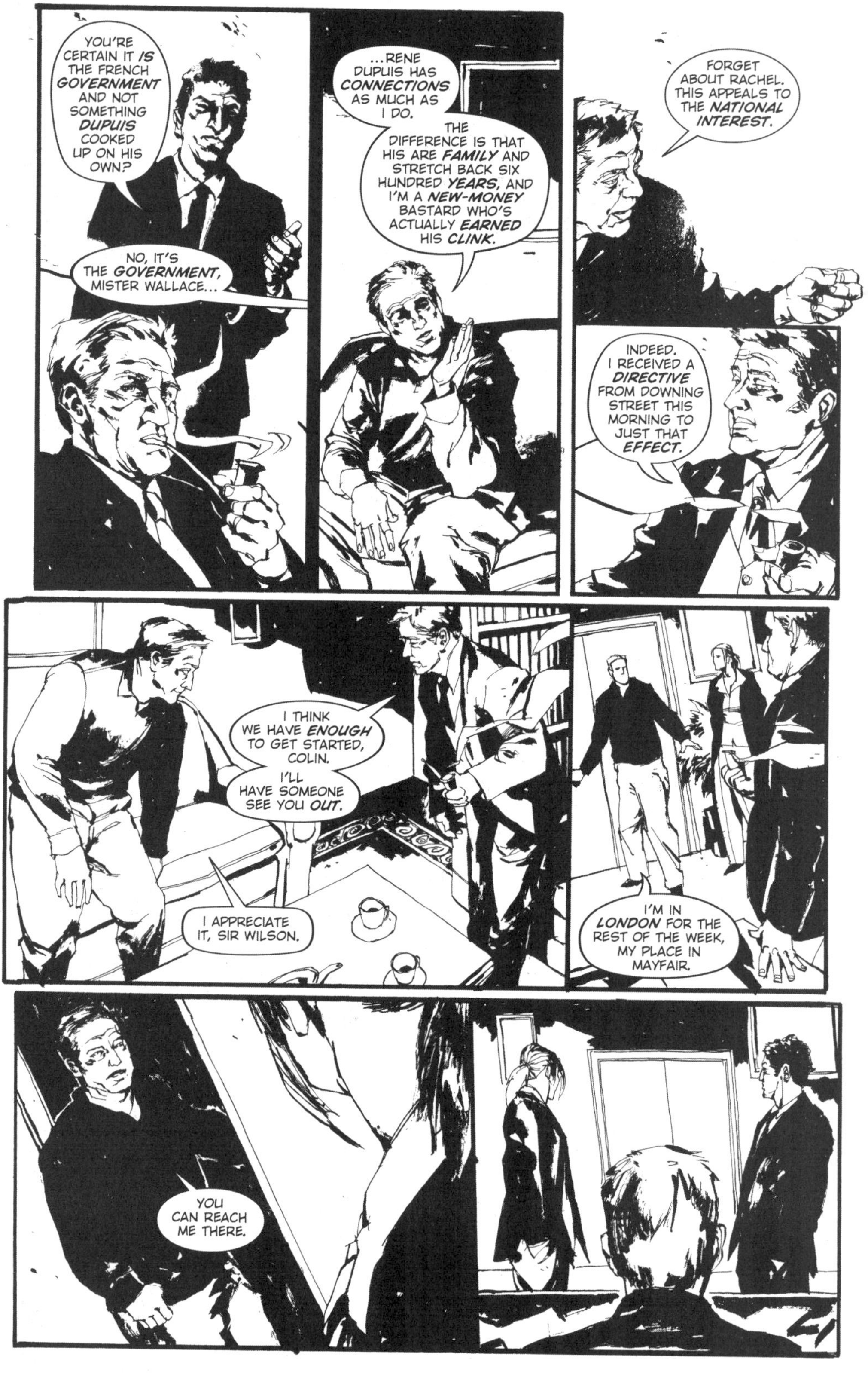
YOU'RE CERTAIN IT IS THE FRENCH GOVERNMENT AND NOT SOMETHING DUPUIS COOKED UP ON HIS OWN?
NO, IT'S THE GOVERNMENT, MISTER WALLACE...
...RENE DUPUIS HAS CONNECTIONS AS MUCH AS I DO.
THE DIFFERENCE IS THAT HIS ARE FAMILY AND STRETCH BACK SIX HUNDRED YEARS, AND I'M A NEW-MONEY BASTARD WHO'S ACTUALLY EARNED HIS CLINK.
FORGET ABOUT RACHEL. THIS APPEALS TO THE NATIONAL INTEREST.
INDEED. I RECEIVED A DIRECTIVE FROM DOWNING STREET THIS MORNING TO JUST THAT EFFECT.
I THINK WE HAVE ENOUGH TO GET STARTED, COLIN.
I'LL HAVE SOMEONE SEE YOU OUT.
I APPRECIATE IT, SIR WILSON.
I'M IN LONDON FOR THE REST OF THE WEEK, MY PLACE IN MAYFAIR.
YOU CAN REACH ME THERE.

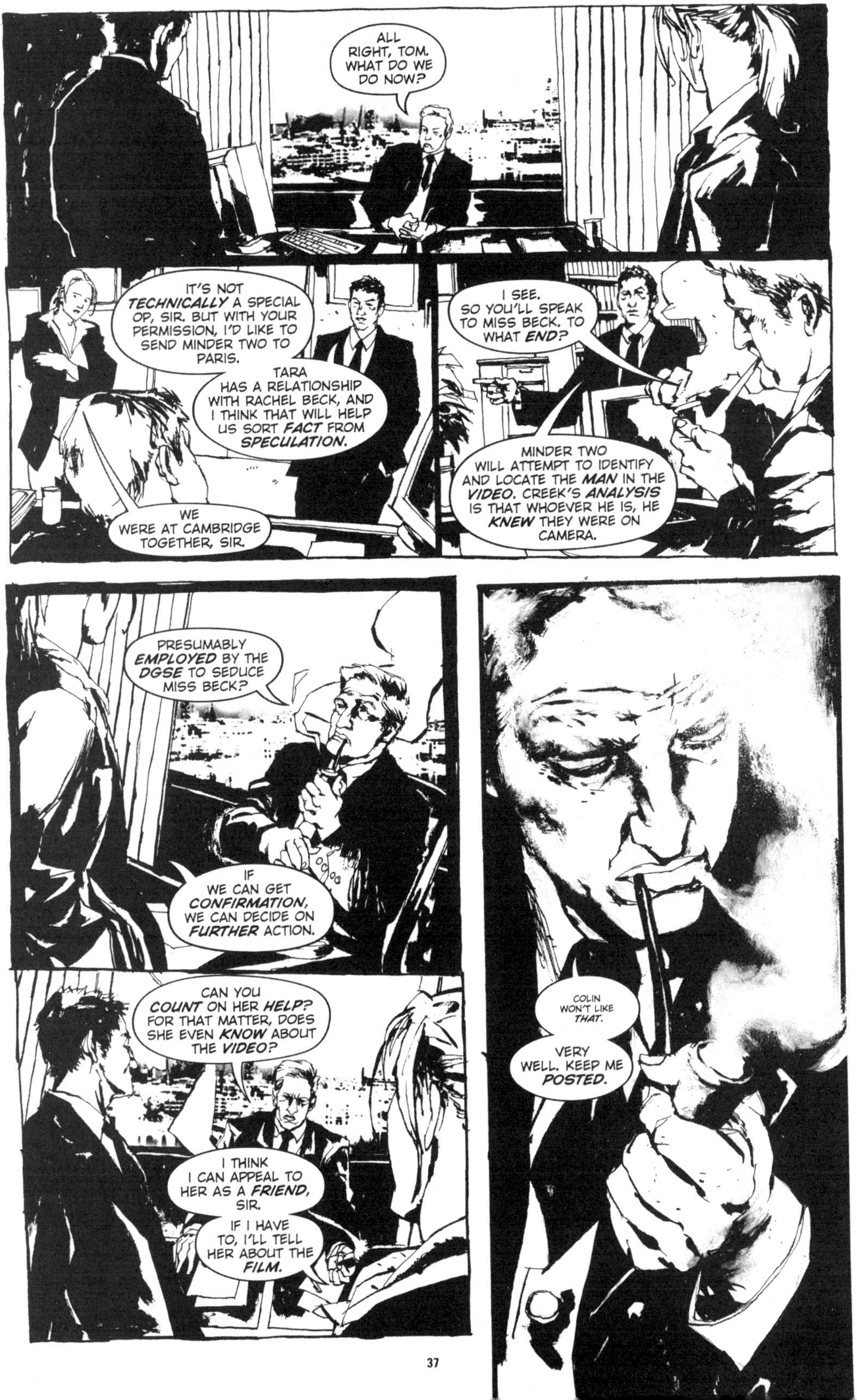
ALL RIGHT, TOM. WHAT DO WE DO NOW?
IT'S NOT *TECHNICALLY* A SPECIAL OP, SIR. BUT WITH YOUR PERMISSION, I'D LIKE TO SEND MINDER TWO TO PARIS.
TARA HAS A RELATIONSHIP WITH RACHEL BECK, AND I THINK THAT WILL HELP US SORT *FACT* FROM *SPECULATION*.
WE WERE AT CAMBRIDGE TOGETHER, SIR.
I SEE. SO YOU'LL SPEAK TO MISS BECK. TO WHAT *END*?
MINDER TWO WILL ATTEMPT TO IDENTIFY AND LOCATE THE *MAN* IN THE *VIDEO*. CREEK'S *ANALYSIS* IS THAT WHOEVER HE IS, HE *KNEW* THEY WERE ON CAMERA.
PRESUMABLY *EMPLOYED* BY THE *DGSE* TO SEDUCE MISS BECK?
IF WE CAN GET *CONFIRMATION*, WE CAN DECIDE ON *FURTHER* ACTION.
CAN YOU *COUNT* ON HER *HELP*? FOR THAT MATTER, DOES SHE EVEN *KNOW* ABOUT THE *VIDEO*?
I THINK I CAN APPEAL TO HER AS A *FRIEND*, SIR.
IF I HAVE TO, I'LL TELL HER ABOUT THE *FILM*.
COLIN WON'T LIKE *THAT*.
VERY WELL. KEEP ME *POSTED*.

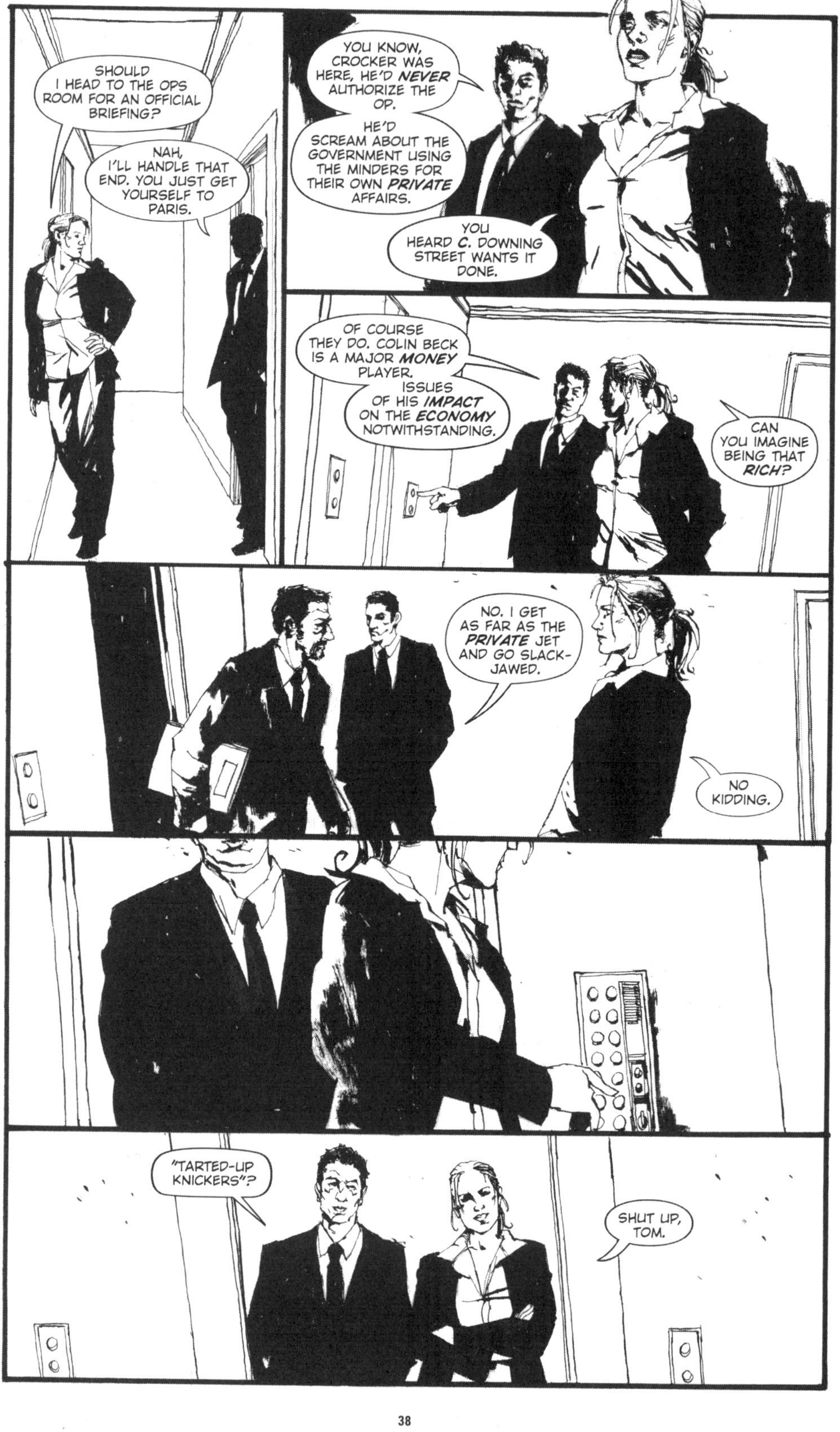
SHOULD I HEAD TO THE OPS ROOM FOR AN OFFICIAL BRIEFING?
NAH, I'LL HANDLE THAT END. YOU JUST GET YOURSELF TO PARIS.
YOU KNOW, CROCKER WAS HERE, HE'D NEVER AUTHORIZE THE OP.
HE'D SCREAM ABOUT THE GOVERNMENT USING THE MINDERS FOR THEIR OWN PRIVATE AFFAIRS.
YOU HEARD C. DOWNING STREET WANTS IT DONE.
OF COURSE THEY DO. COLIN BECK IS A MAJOR MONEY PLAYER.
ISSUES OF HIS IMPACT ON THE ECONOMY NOTWITHSTANDING.
CAN YOU IMAGINE BEING THAT RICH?
NO. I GET AS FAR AS THE PRIVATE JET AND GO SLACK-JAWED.
NO KIDDING.
"TARTED-UP KNICKERS"?
SHUT UP, TOM.

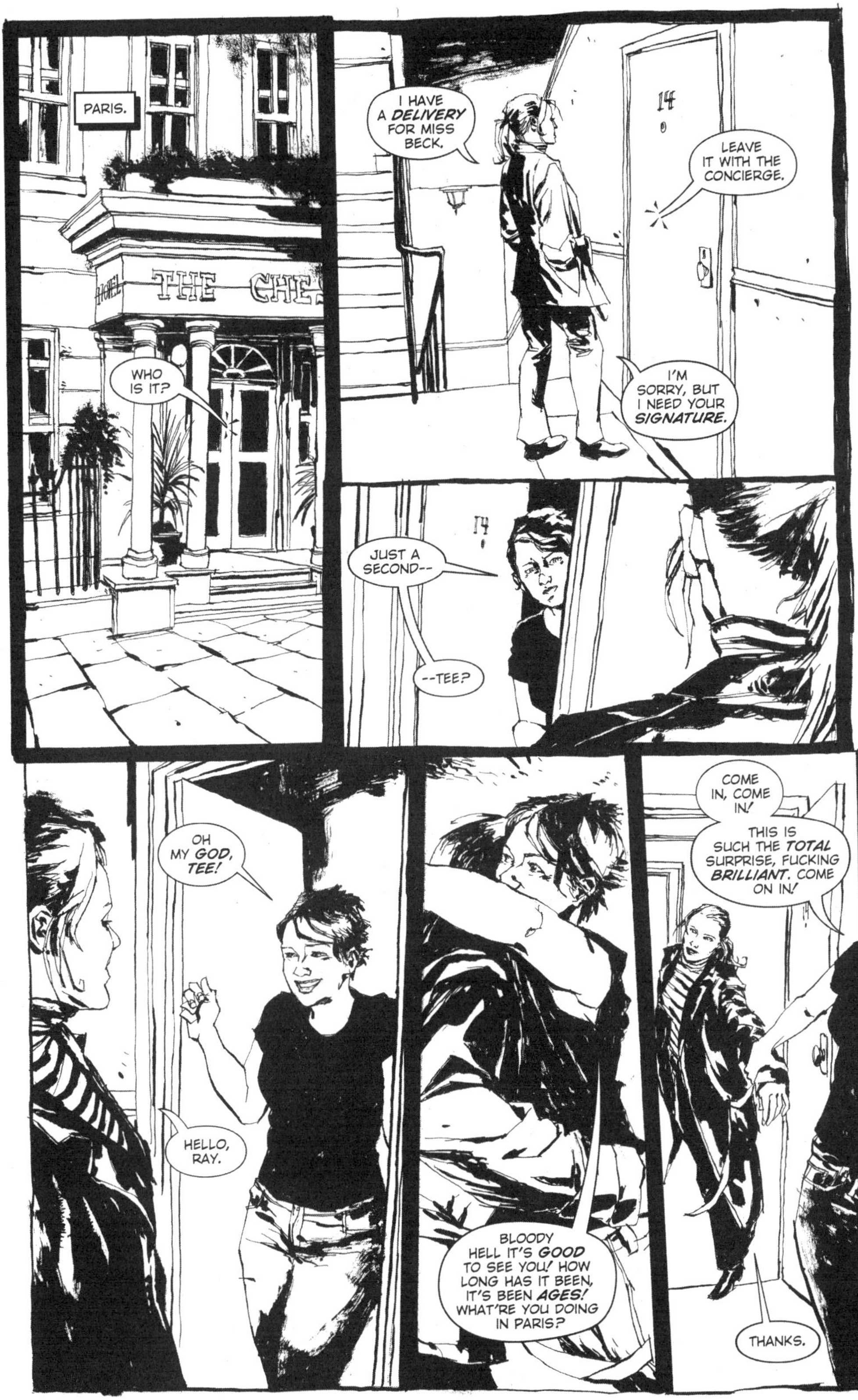
PARIS.
WHO IS IT?
I HAVE A DELIVERY FOR MISS BECK.
LEAVE IT WITH THE CONCIERGE.
I'M SORRY, BUT I NEED YOUR SIGNATURE.
JUST A SECOND--
--TEE?
OH MY GOD, TEE!
HELLO, RAY.
BLOODY HELL IT'S GOOD TO SEE YOU! HOW LONG HAS IT BEEN, IT'S BEEN AGES! WHAT'RE YOU DOING IN PARIS?
COME IN, COME IN!
THIS IS SUCH THE TOTAL SURPRISE, FUCKING BRILLIANT. COME ON IN!
THANKS.

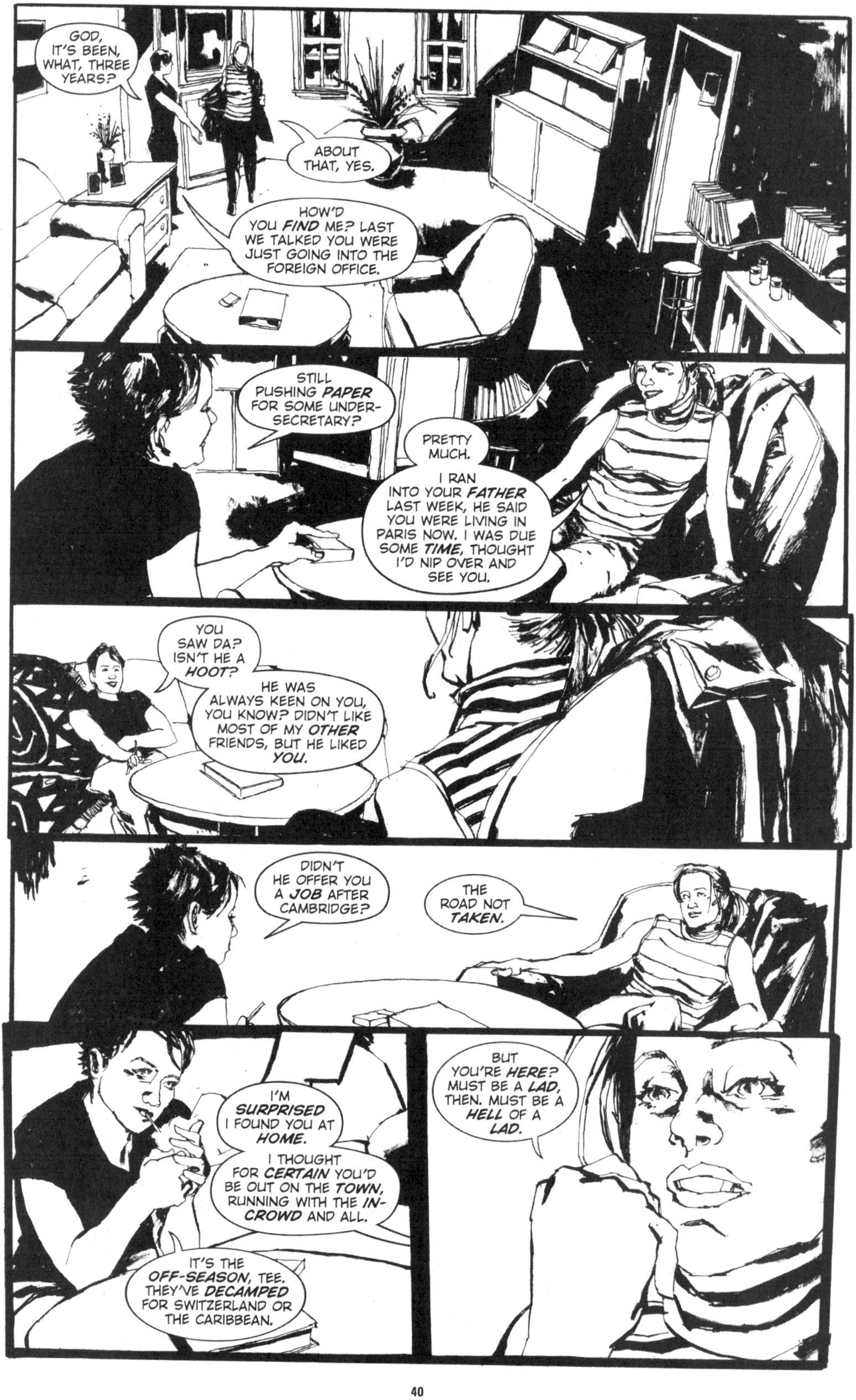

GOD, IT'S BEEN, WHAT, THREE YEARS?
ABOUT THAT, YES.
HOW'D YOU FIND ME? LAST WE TALKED YOU WERE JUST GOING INTO THE FOREIGN OFFICE.
STILL PUSHING PAPER FOR SOME UNDER-SECRETARY?
PRETTY MUCH.
I RAN INTO YOUR FATHER LAST WEEK, HE SAID YOU WERE LIVING IN PARIS NOW. I WAS DUE SOME TIME, THOUGHT I'D NIP OVER AND SEE YOU.
YOU SAW DA? ISN'T HE A HOOT?
HE WAS ALWAYS KEEN ON YOU, YOU KNOW? DIDN'T LIKE MOST OF MY OTHER FRIENDS, BUT HE LIKED YOU.
DIDN'T HE OFFER YOU A JOB AFTER CAMBRIDGE?
THE ROAD NOT TAKEN.
I'M SURPRISED I FOUND YOU AT HOME.
I THOUGHT FOR CERTAIN YOU'D BE OUT ON THE TOWN, RUNNING WITH THE IN-CROWD AND ALL.
IT'S THE OFF-SEASON, TEE. THEY'VE DECAMPED FOR SWITZERLAND OR THE CARIBBEAN.
BUT YOU'RE HERE? MUST BE A LAD, THEN. MUST BE A HELL OF A LAD.

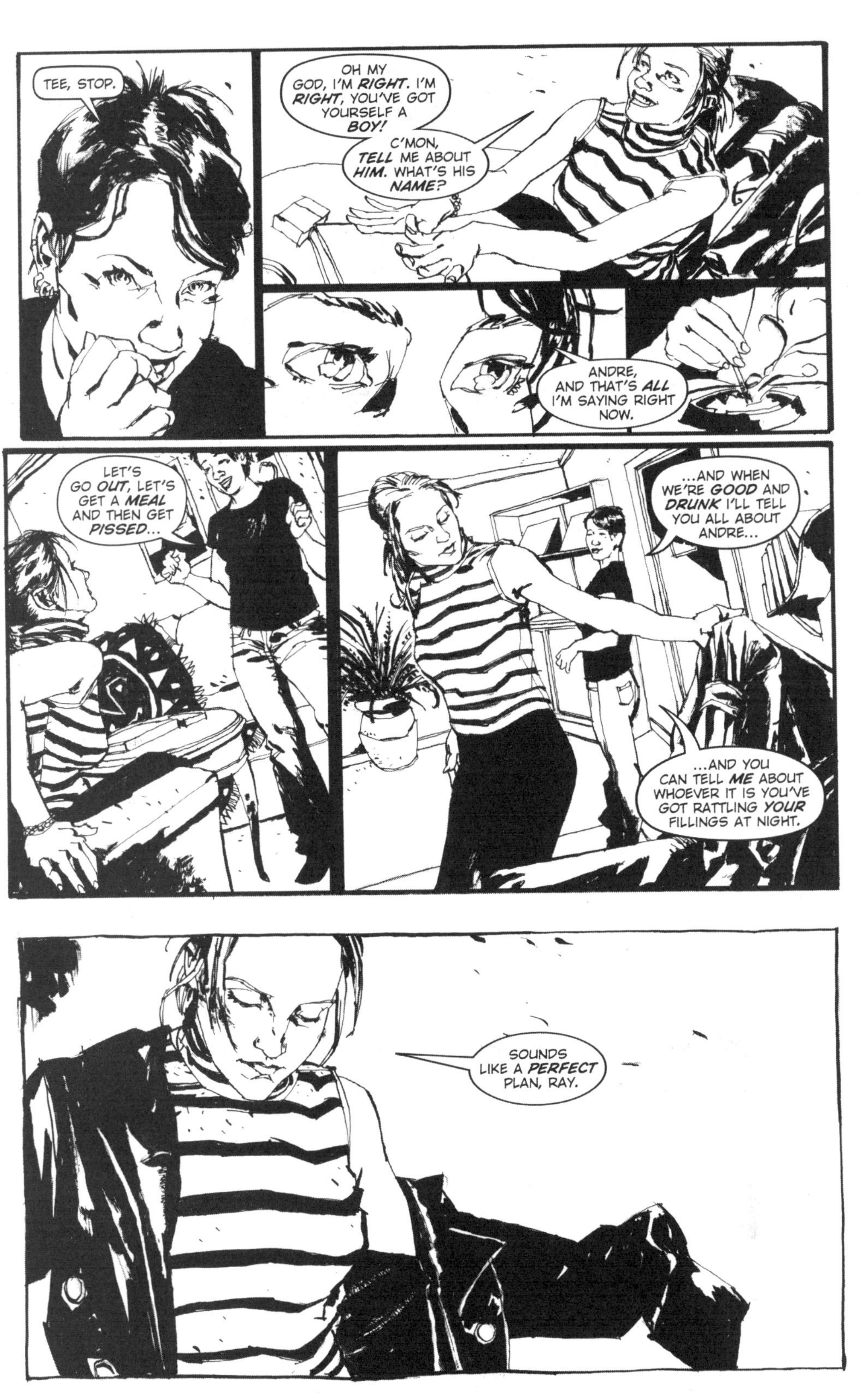
TEE, STOP.
OH MY GOD, I'M RIGHT. I'M RIGHT, YOU'VE GOT YOURSELF A BOY!
C'MON, TELL ME ABOUT HIM. WHAT'S HIS NAME?
ANDRE, AND THAT'S ALL I'M SAYING RIGHT NOW.
LET'S GO OUT, LET'S GET A MEAL AND THEN GET PISSED...
...AND WHEN WE'RE GOOD AND DRUNK I'LL TELL YOU ALL ABOUT ANDRE...
...AND YOU CAN TELL ME ABOUT WHOEVER IT IS YOU'VE GOT RATTLING YOUR FILLINGS AT NIGHT.
SOUNDS LIKE A PERFECT PLAN, RAY.

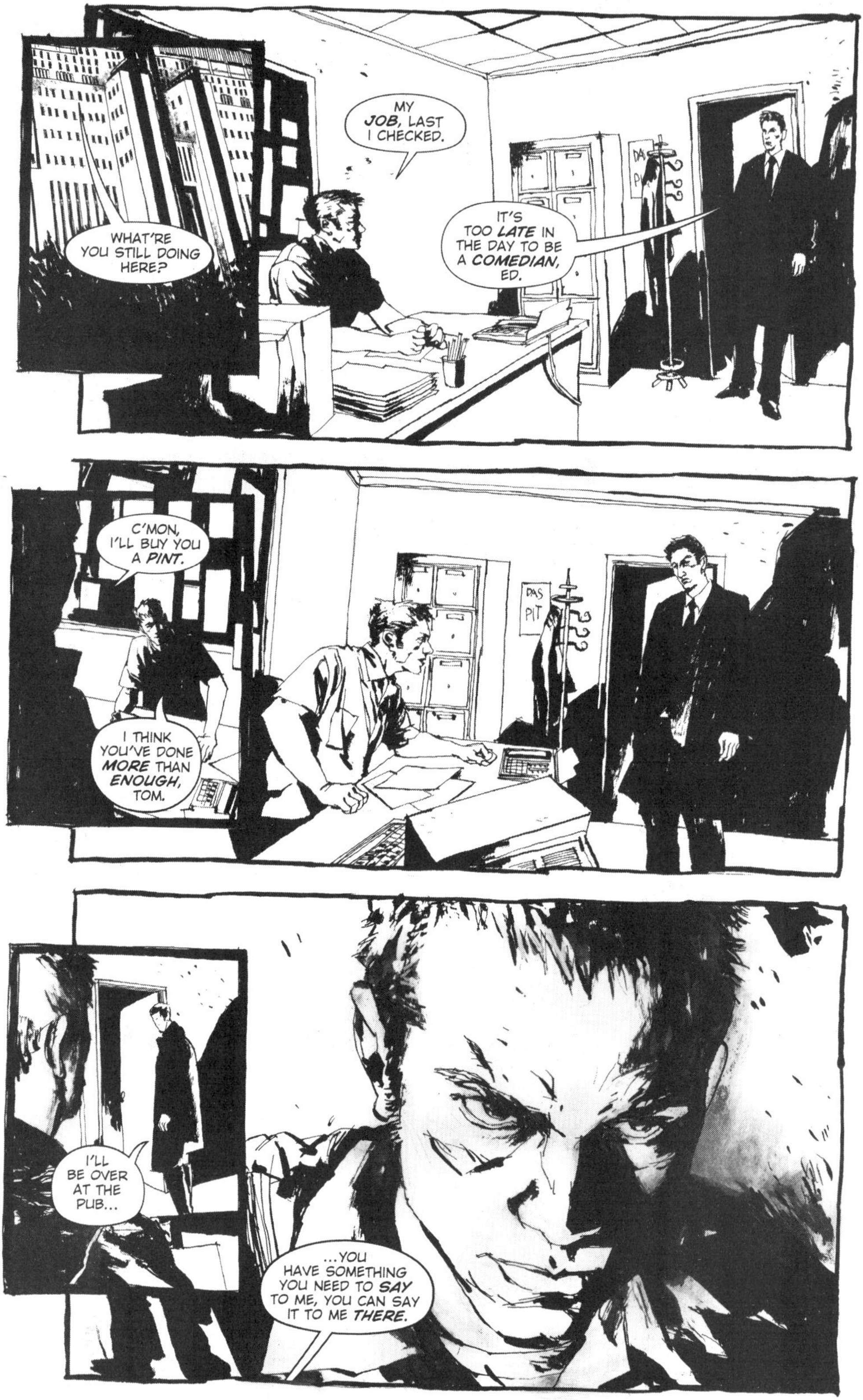
WHAT'RE YOU STILL DOING HERE?
MY JOB, LAST I CHECKED.
IT'S TOO LATE IN THE DAY TO BE A COMEDIAN, ED.
C'MON, I'LL BUY YOU A PINT.
DAS PIT
I THINK YOU'VE DONE MORE THAN ENOUGH, TOM.
I'LL BE OVER AT THE PUB...
...YOU HAVE SOMETHING YOU NEED TO SAY TO ME, YOU CAN SAY IT TO ME THERE.

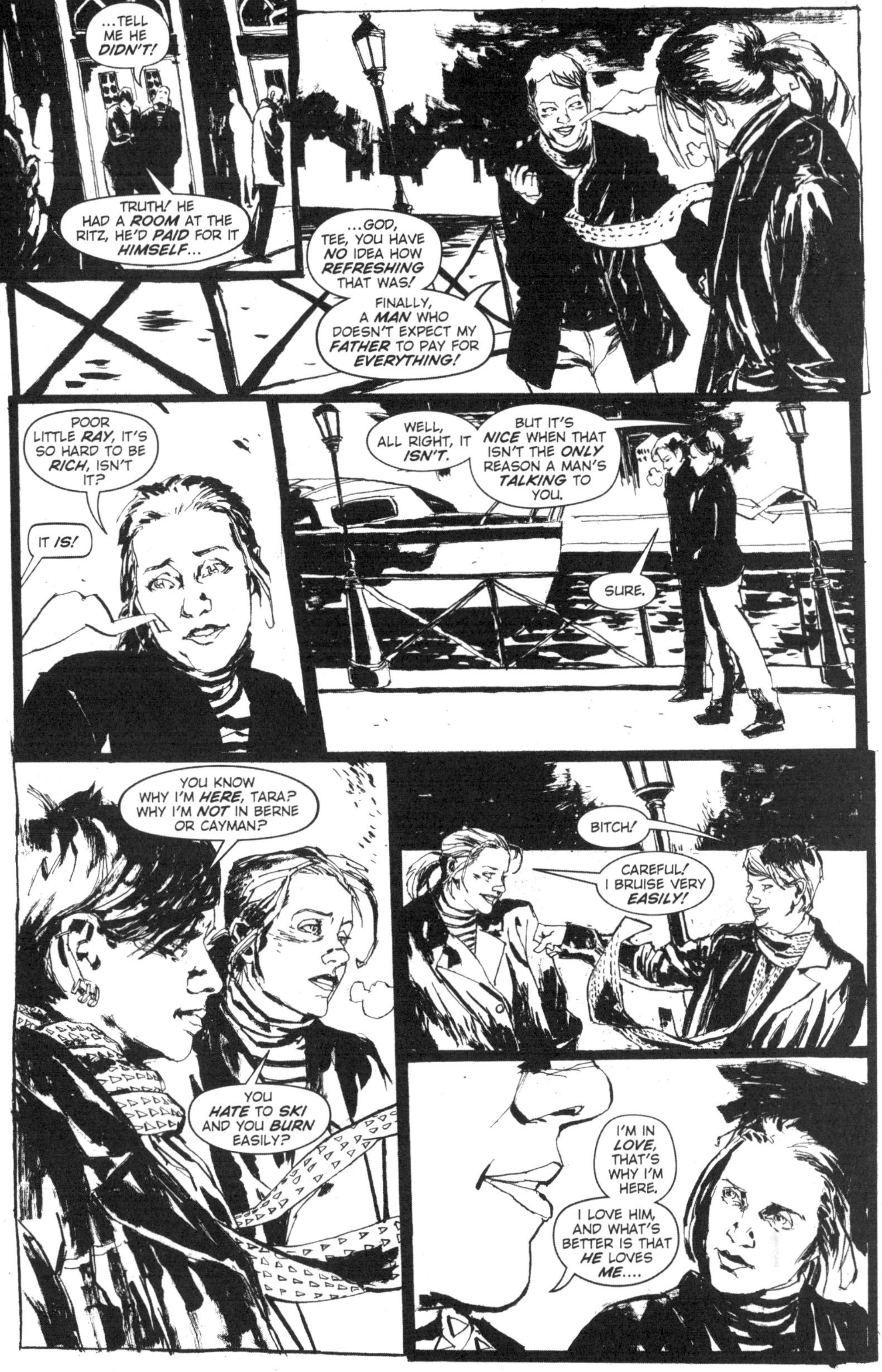
...TELL ME HE DIDN'T!
TRUTH! HE HAD A ROOM AT THE RITZ, HE'D PAID FOR IT HIMSELF...
...GOD, TEE, YOU HAVE NO IDEA HOW REFRESHING THAT WAS!
FINALLY, A MAN WHO DOESN'T EXPECT MY FATHER TO PAY FOR EVERYTHING!
POOR LITTLE RAY, IT'S SO HARD TO BE RICH, ISN'T IT?
IT IS!
WELL, ALL RIGHT, IT ISN'T.
BUT IT'S NICE WHEN THAT ISN'T THE ONLY REASON A MAN'S TALKING TO YOU.
SURE.
YOU KNOW WHY I'M HERE, TARA? WHY I'M NOT IN BERNE OR CAYMAN?
YOU HATE TO SKI AND YOU BURN EASILY?
BITCH!
CAREFUL! I BRUISE VERY EASILY!
I'M IN LOVE, THAT'S WHY I'M HERE.
I LOVE HIM, AND WHAT'S BETTER IS THAT HE LOVES ME....

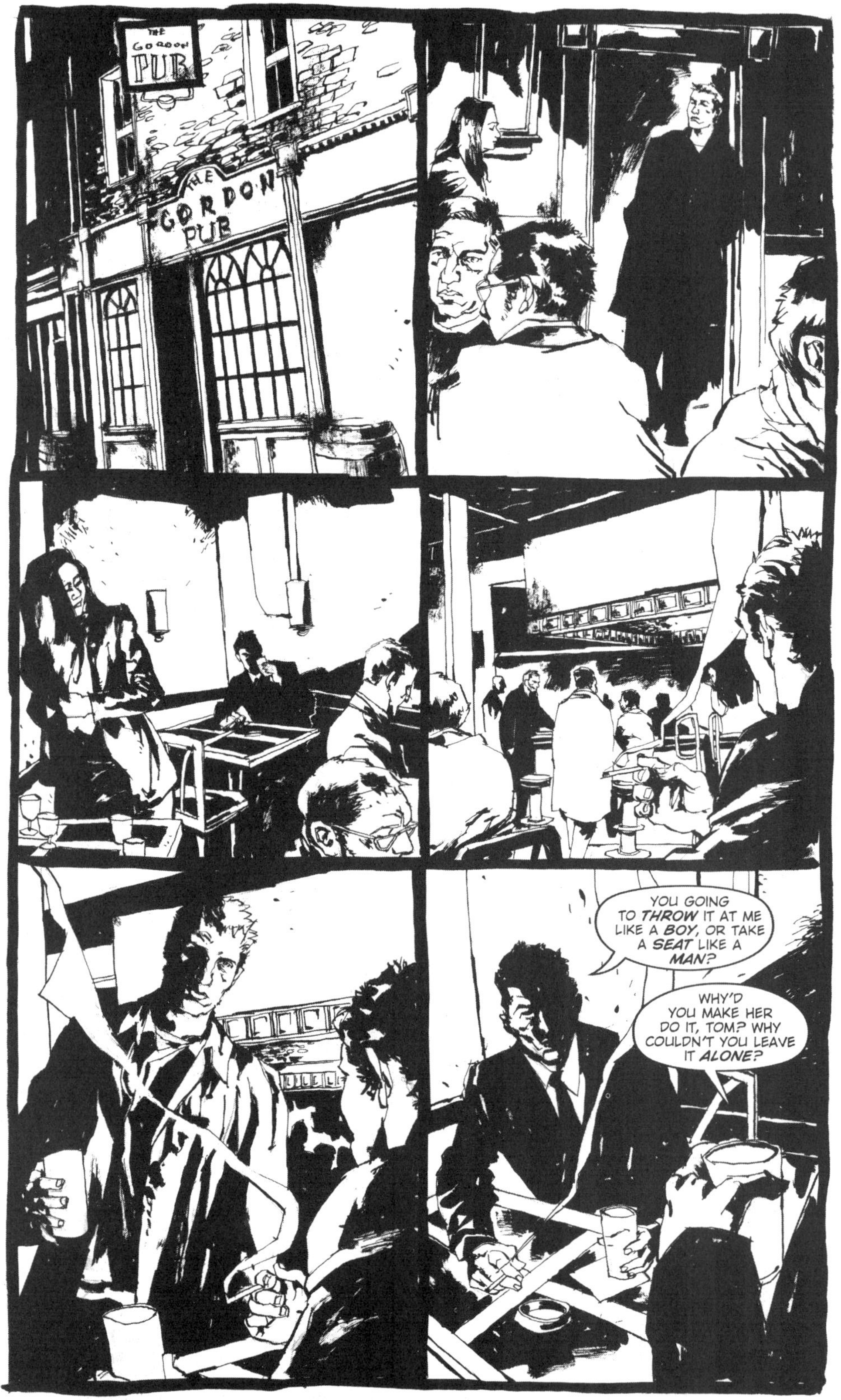
THE GORDON PUB
THE GORDON PUB
YOU GOING TO THROW IT AT ME LIKE A BOY, OR TAKE A SEAT LIKE A MAN?
WHY'D YOU MAKE HER DO IT, TOM? WHY COULDN'T YOU LEAVE IT ALONE?

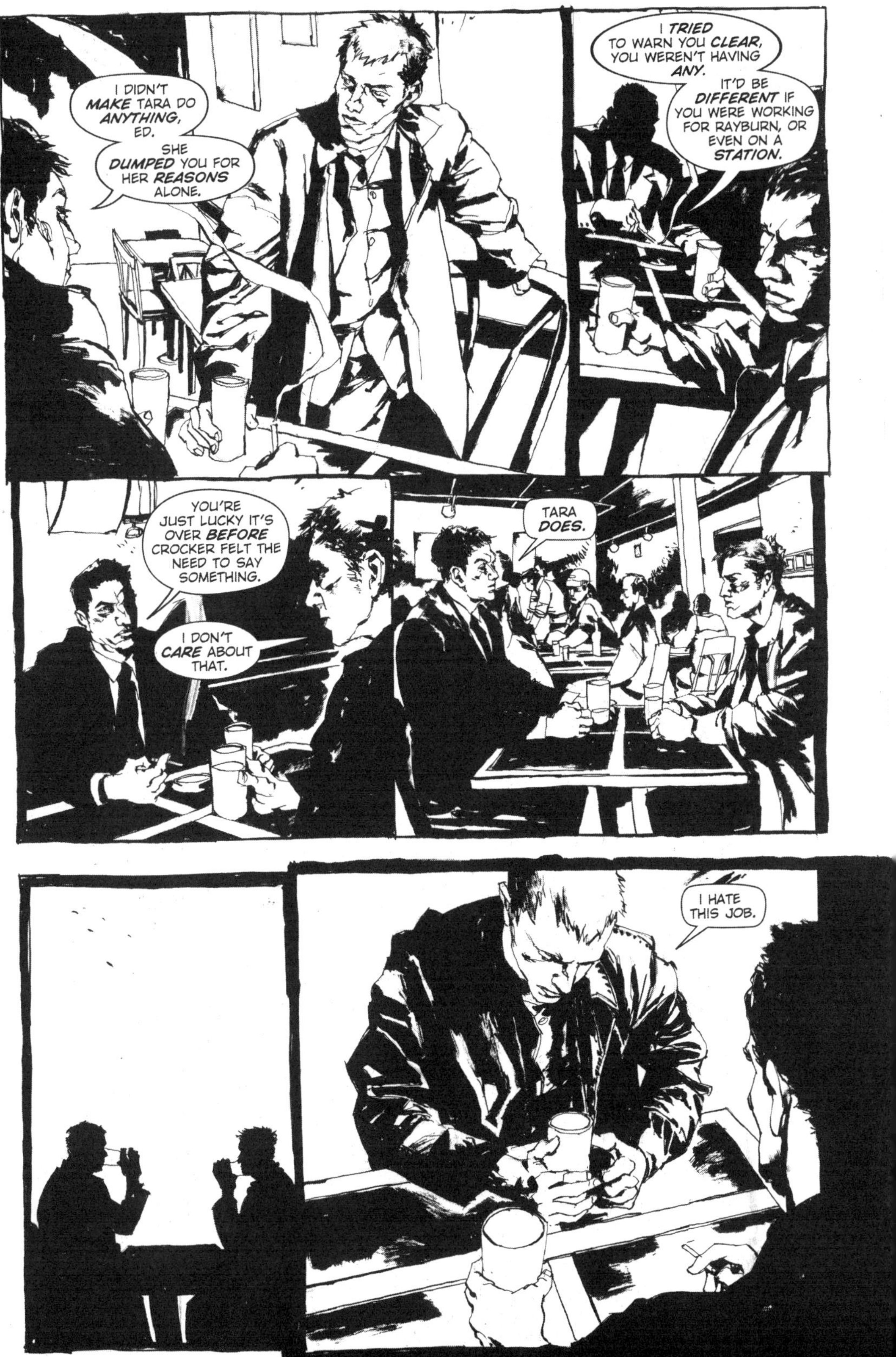
I DIDN'T MAKE TARA DO ANYTHING, ED.
SHE DUMPED YOU FOR HER REASONS ALONE.
I TRIED TO WARN YOU CLEAR, YOU WEREN'T HAVING ANY.
IT'D BE DIFFERENT IF YOU WERE WORKING FOR RAYBURN, OR EVEN ON A STATION.
YOU'RE JUST LUCKY IT'S OVER BEFORE CROCKER FELT THE NEED TO SAY SOMETHING.
I DON'T CARE ABOUT THAT.
TARA DOES.
I HATE THIS JOB.

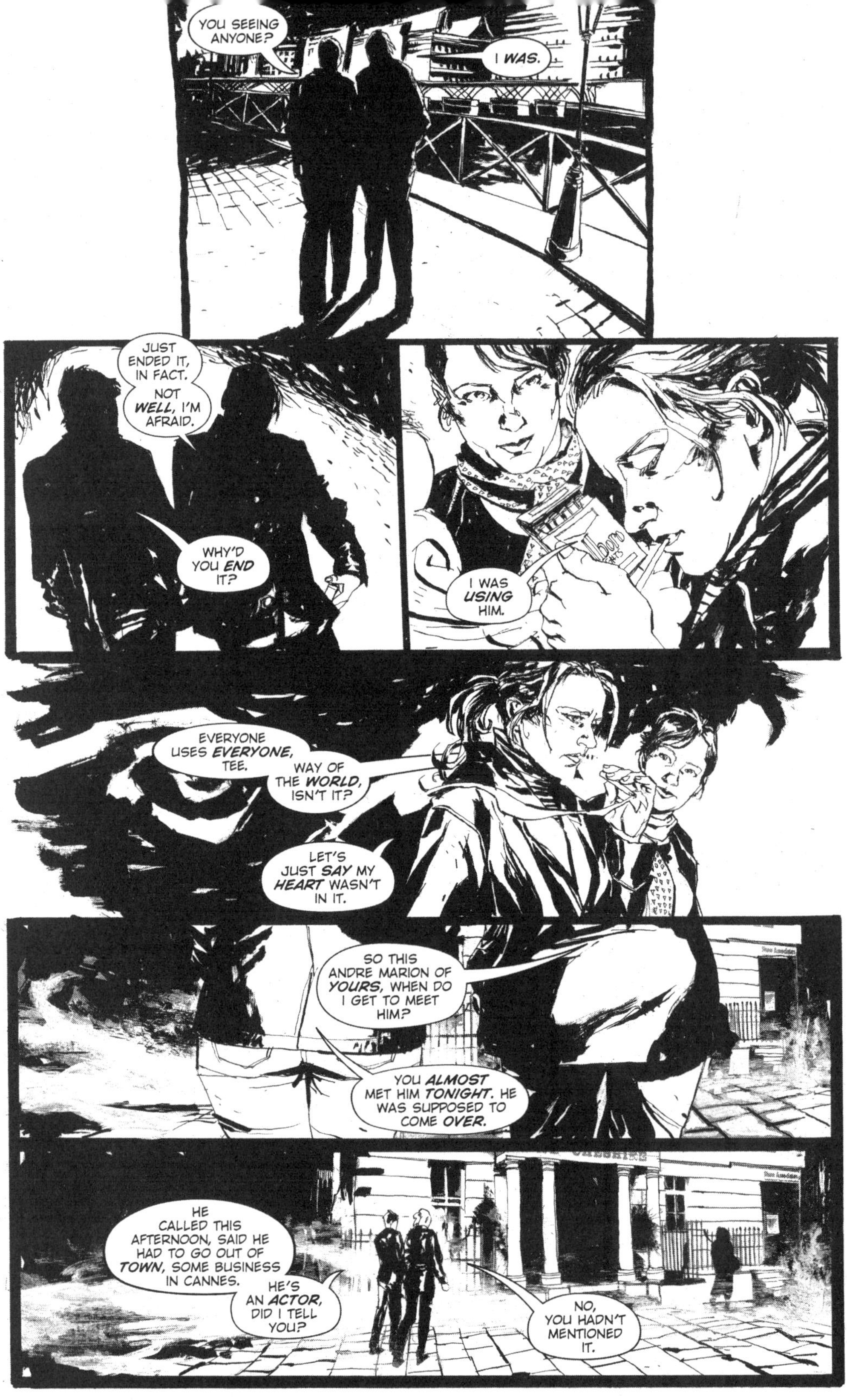
YOU SEEING ANYONE?
I WAS.
JUST ENDED IT, IN FACT.
NOT WELL, I'M AFRAID.
WHY'D YOU END IT?
I WAS USING HIM.
EVERYONE USES EVERYONE, TEE.
WAY OF THE WORLD, ISN'T IT?
LET'S JUST SAY MY HEART WASN'T IN IT.
SO THIS ANDRE MARION OF YOURS, WHEN DO I GET TO MEET HIM?
YOU ALMOST MET HIM TONIGHT. HE WAS SUPPOSED TO COME OVER.
HE CALLED THIS AFTERNOON, SAID HE HAD TO GO OUT OF TOWN, SOME BUSINESS IN CANNES.
HE'S AN ACTOR, DID I TELL YOU?
NO, YOU HADN'T MENTIONED IT.

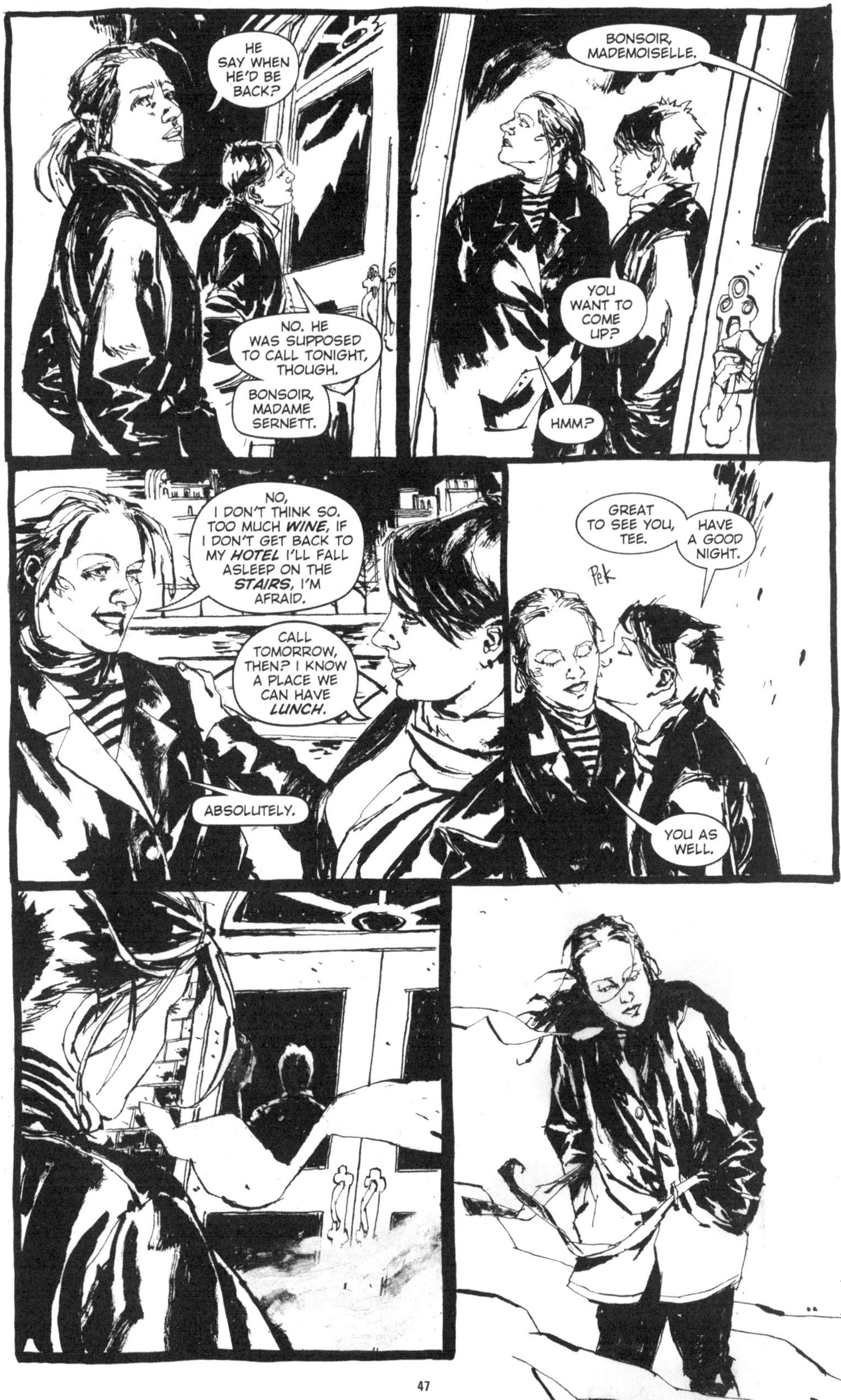
HE SAY WHEN HE'D BE BACK?
NO. HE WAS SUPPOSED TO CALL TONIGHT, THOUGH.
BONSOIR, MADAME SERNETT.
BONSOIR, MADEMOISELLE.
YOU WANT TO COME UP?
HMM?
NO, I DON'T THINK SO. TOO MUCH WINE, IF I DON'T GET BACK TO MY HOTEL I'LL FALL ASLEEP ON THE STAIRS, I'M AFRAID.
CALL TOMORROW, THEN? I KNOW A PLACE WE CAN HAVE LUNCH.
ABSOLUTELY.
GREAT TO SEE YOU, TEE.
HAVE A GOOD NIGHT.
PEK
YOU AS WELL.

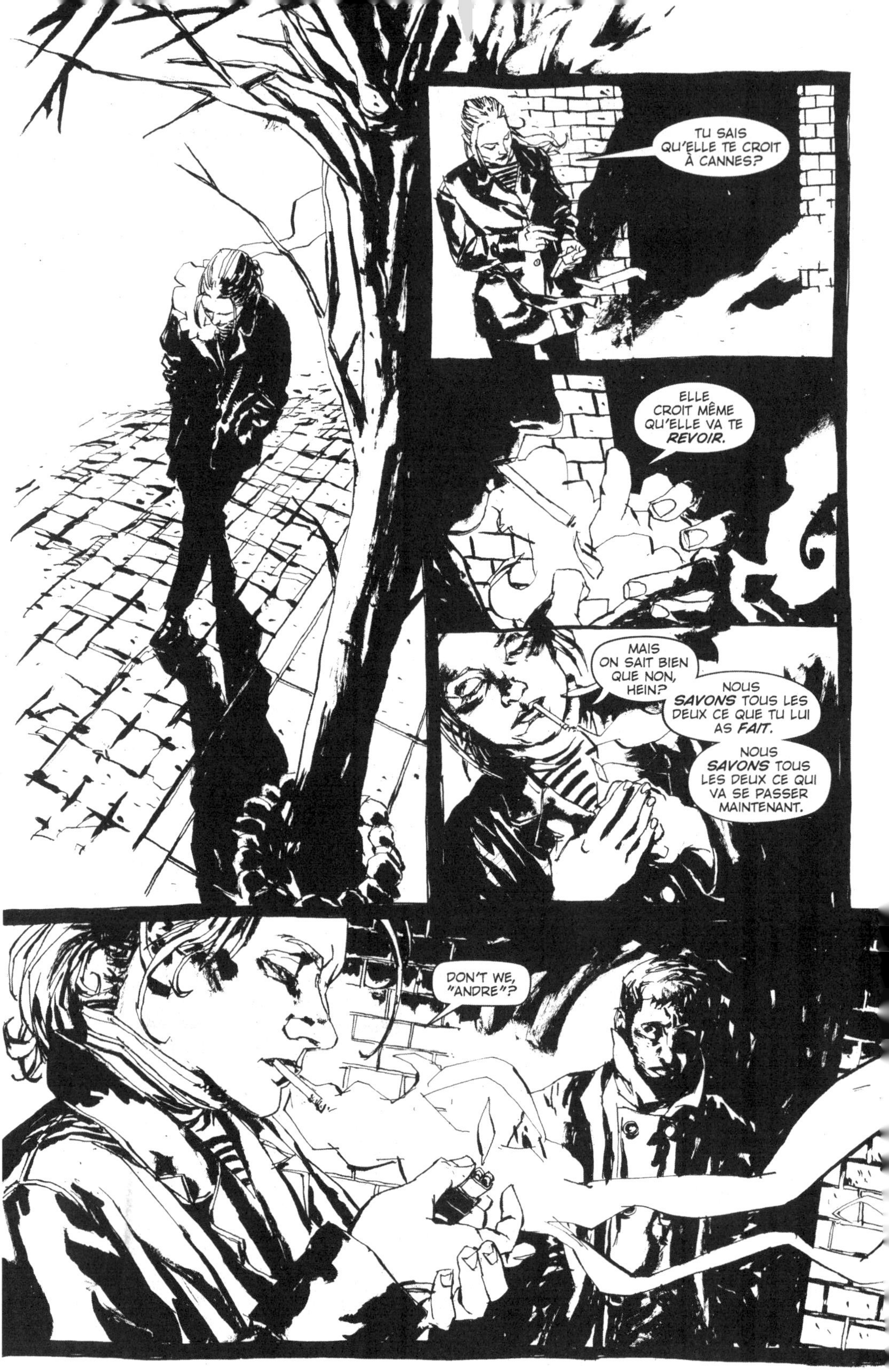
TU SAIS QU'ELLE TE CROIT À CANNES?
ELLE CROIT MÊME QU'ELLE VA TE **REVOIR**.
MAIS ON SAIT BIEN QUE NON, HEIN?
NOUS **SAVONS** TOUS LES DEUX CE QUE TU LUI AS **FAIT**.
NOUS **SAVONS** TOUS LES DEUX CE QUI VA SE PASSER MAINTENANT.
DON'T WE, "ANDRE"?

CHAPTER 3

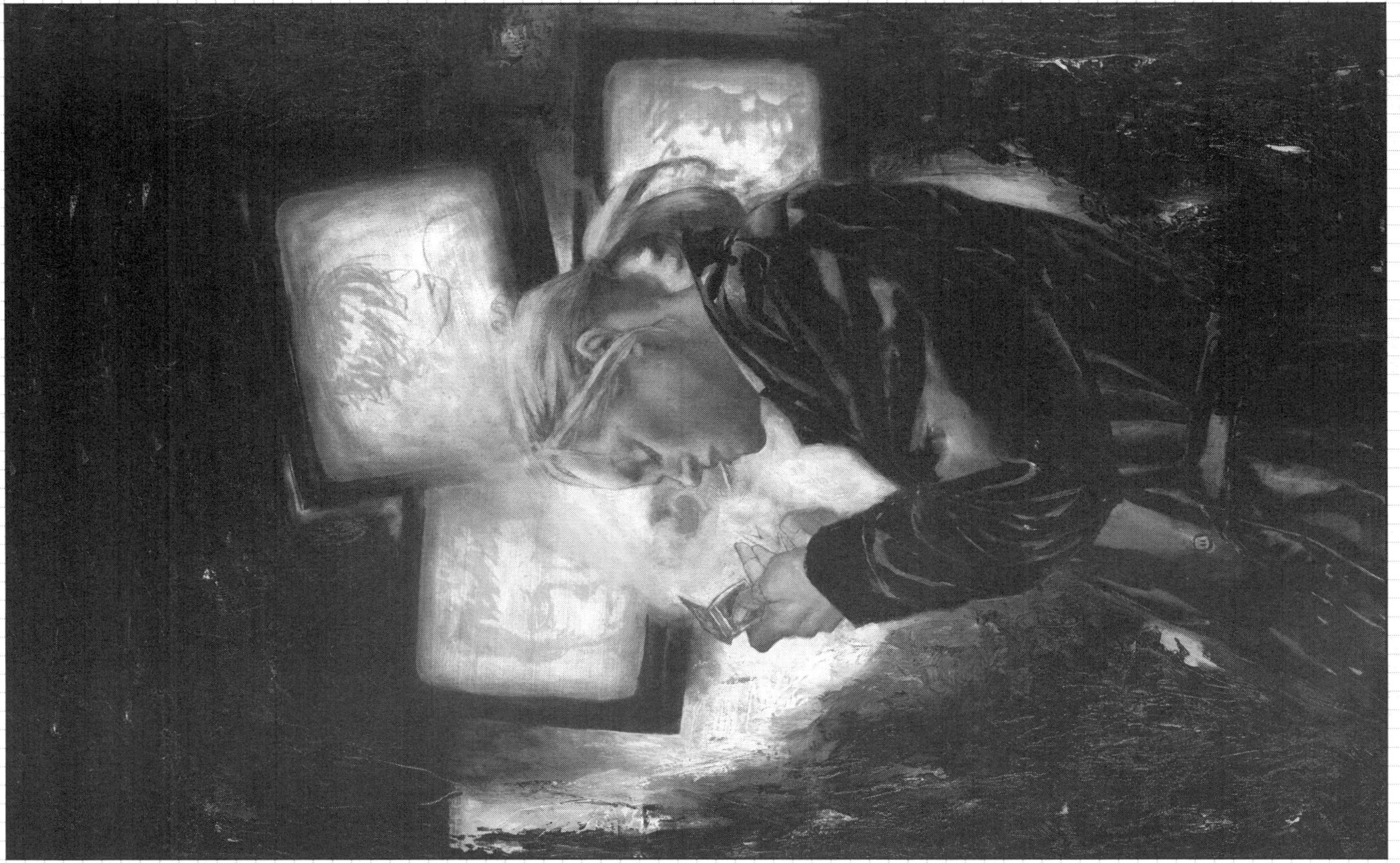

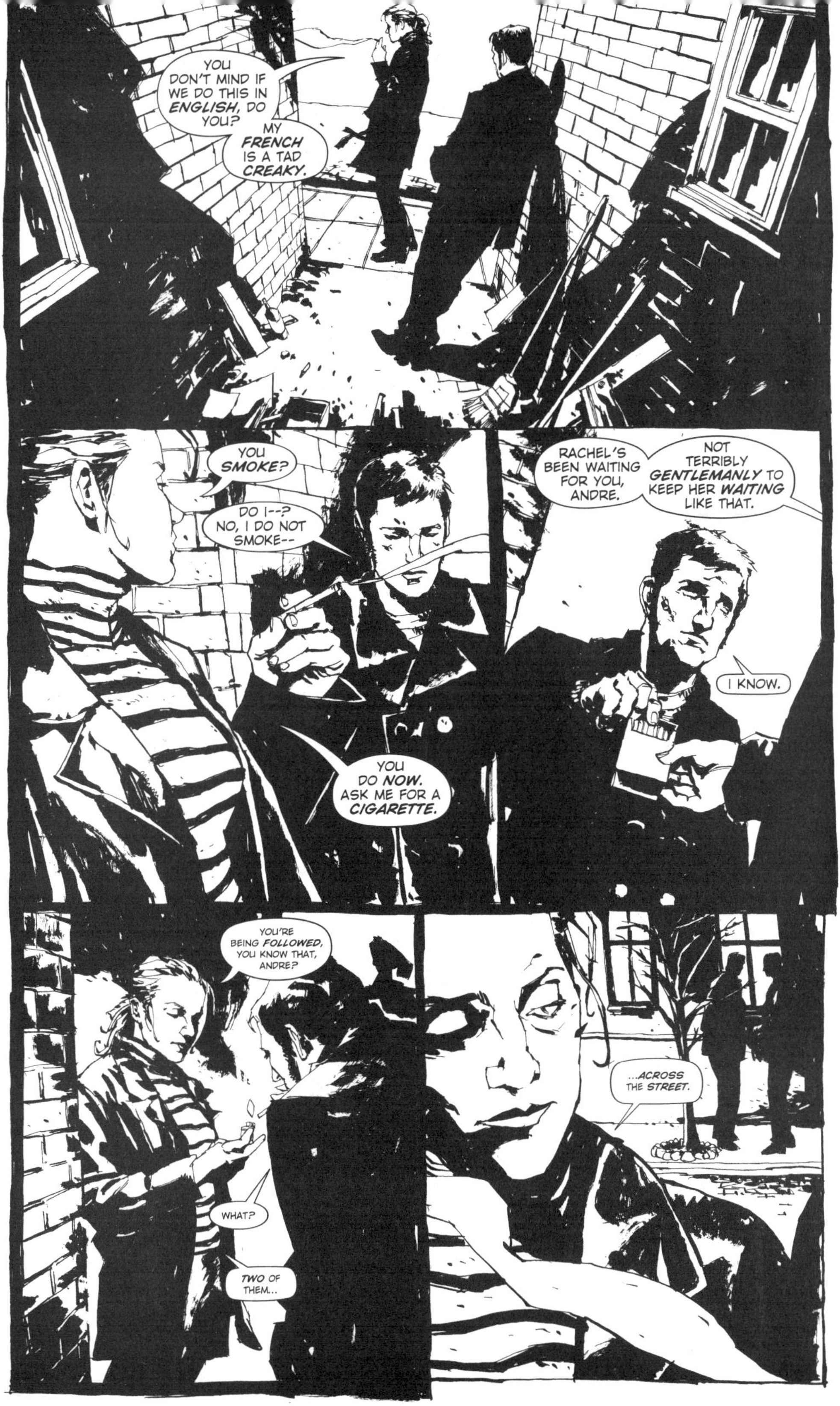
YOU DON'T MIND IF WE DO THIS IN ENGLISH, DO YOU?
MY FRENCH IS A TAD CREAKY.
YOU SMOKE?
DO I--? NO, I DO NOT SMOKE--
YOU DO NOW. ASK ME FOR A CIGARETTE.
RACHEL'S BEEN WAITING FOR YOU, ANDRE.
NOT TERRIBLY GENTLEMANLY TO KEEP HER WAITING LIKE THAT.
I KNOW.
YOU'RE BEING FOLLOWED, YOU KNOW THAT, ANDRE?
WHAT?
TWO OF THEM...
...ACROSS THE STREET.

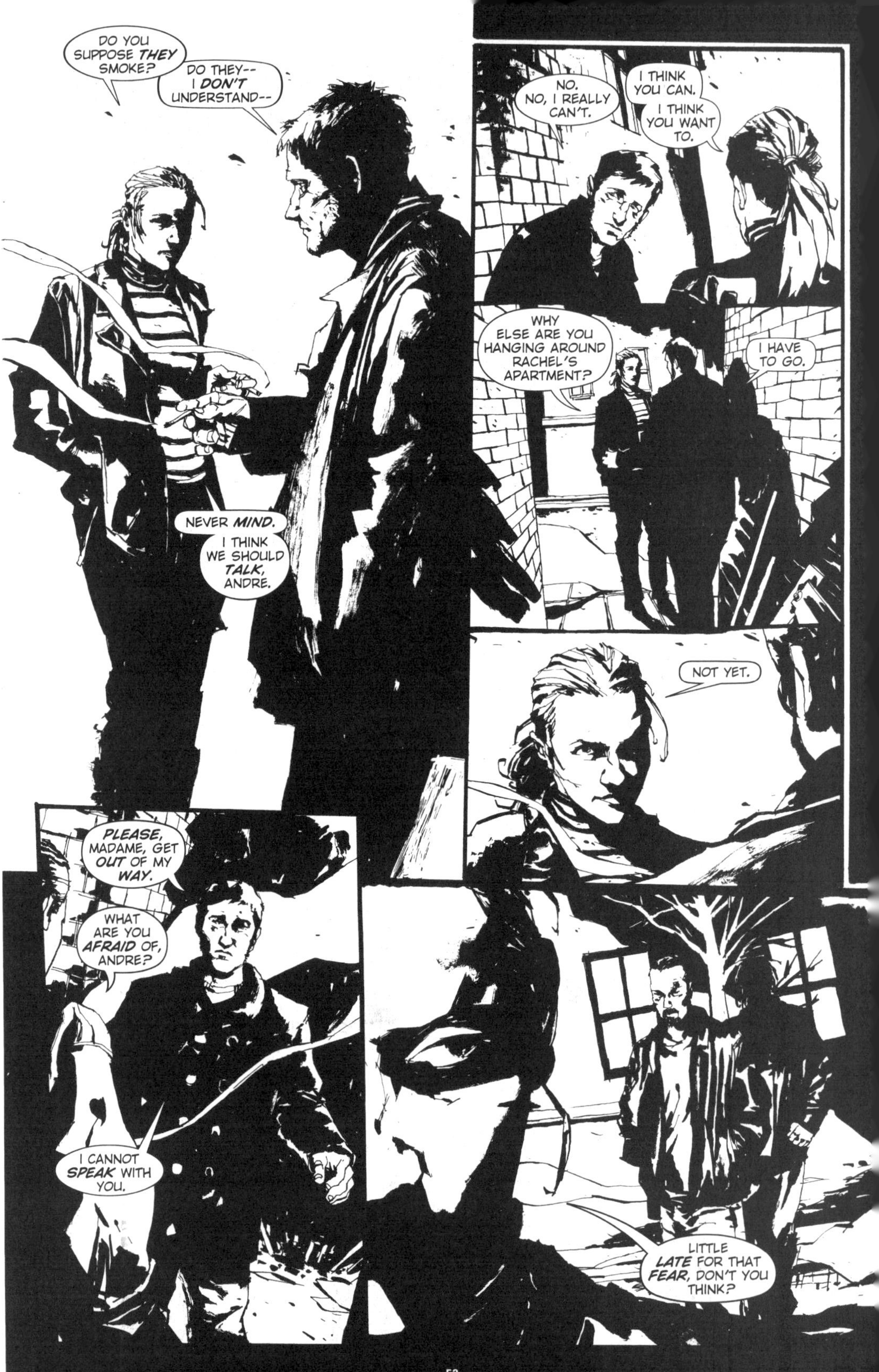
DO YOU SUPPOSE THEY SMOKE?
DO THEY-- I DON'T UNDERSTAND--
NEVER MIND.
I THINK WE SHOULD TALK, ANDRE.
NO. NO, I REALLY CAN'T.
I THINK YOU CAN.
I THINK YOU WANT TO.
WHY ELSE ARE YOU HANGING AROUND RACHEL'S APARTMENT?
I HAVE TO GO.
NOT YET.
PLEASE, MADAME, GET OUT OF MY WAY.
WHAT ARE YOU AFRAID OF, ANDRE?
I CANNOT SPEAK WITH YOU.
LITTLE LATE FOR THAT FEAR, DON'T YOU THINK?

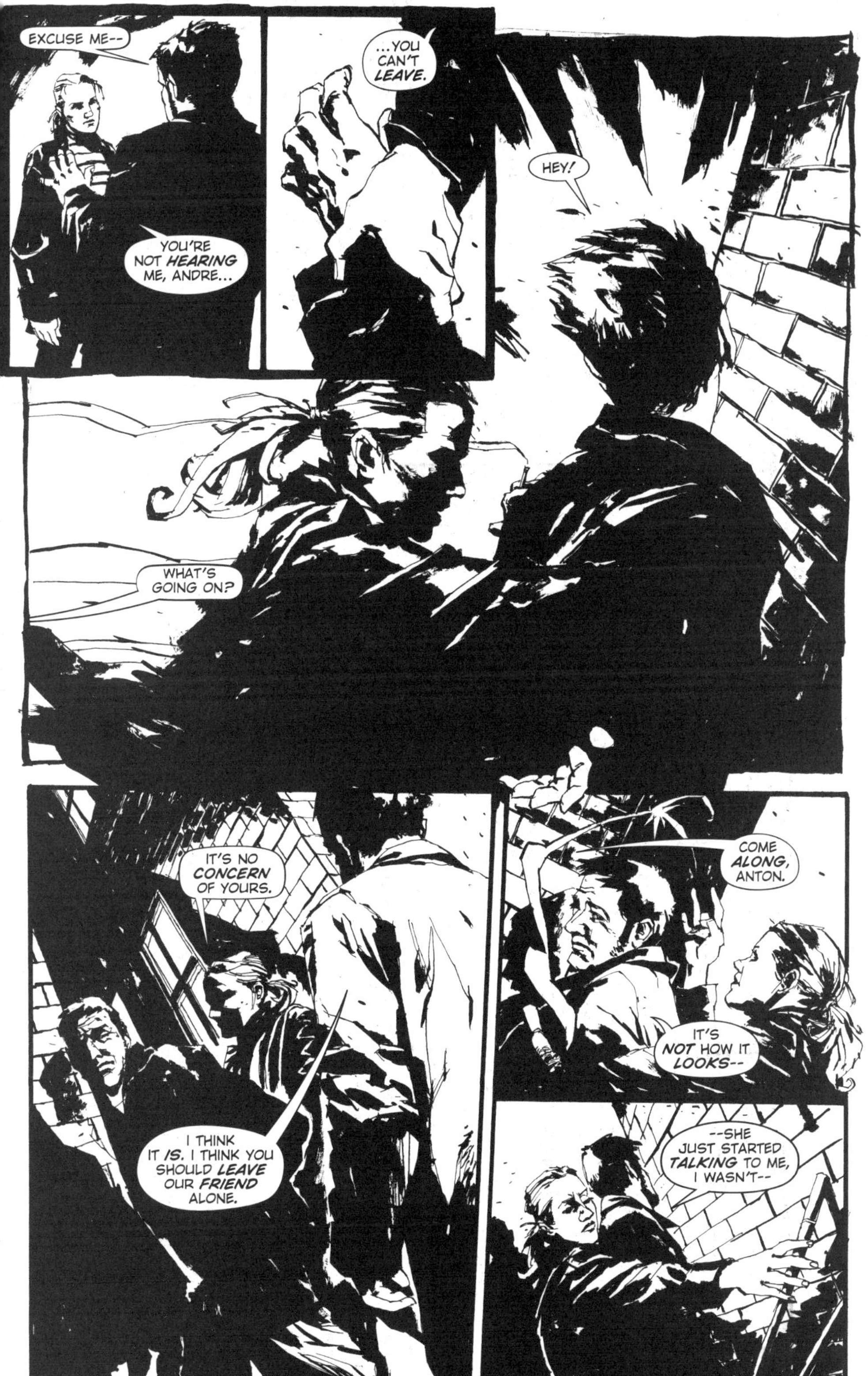
EXCUSE ME--
YOU'RE NOT HEARING ME, ANDRE...
...YOU CAN'T LEAVE.
HEY!
WHAT'S GOING ON?
IT'S NO CONCERN OF YOURS.
I THINK IT IS. I THINK YOU SHOULD LEAVE OUR FRIEND ALONE.
COME ALONG, ANTON.
IT'S NOT HOW IT LOOKS--
--SHE JUST STARTED TALKING TO ME, I WASN'T--

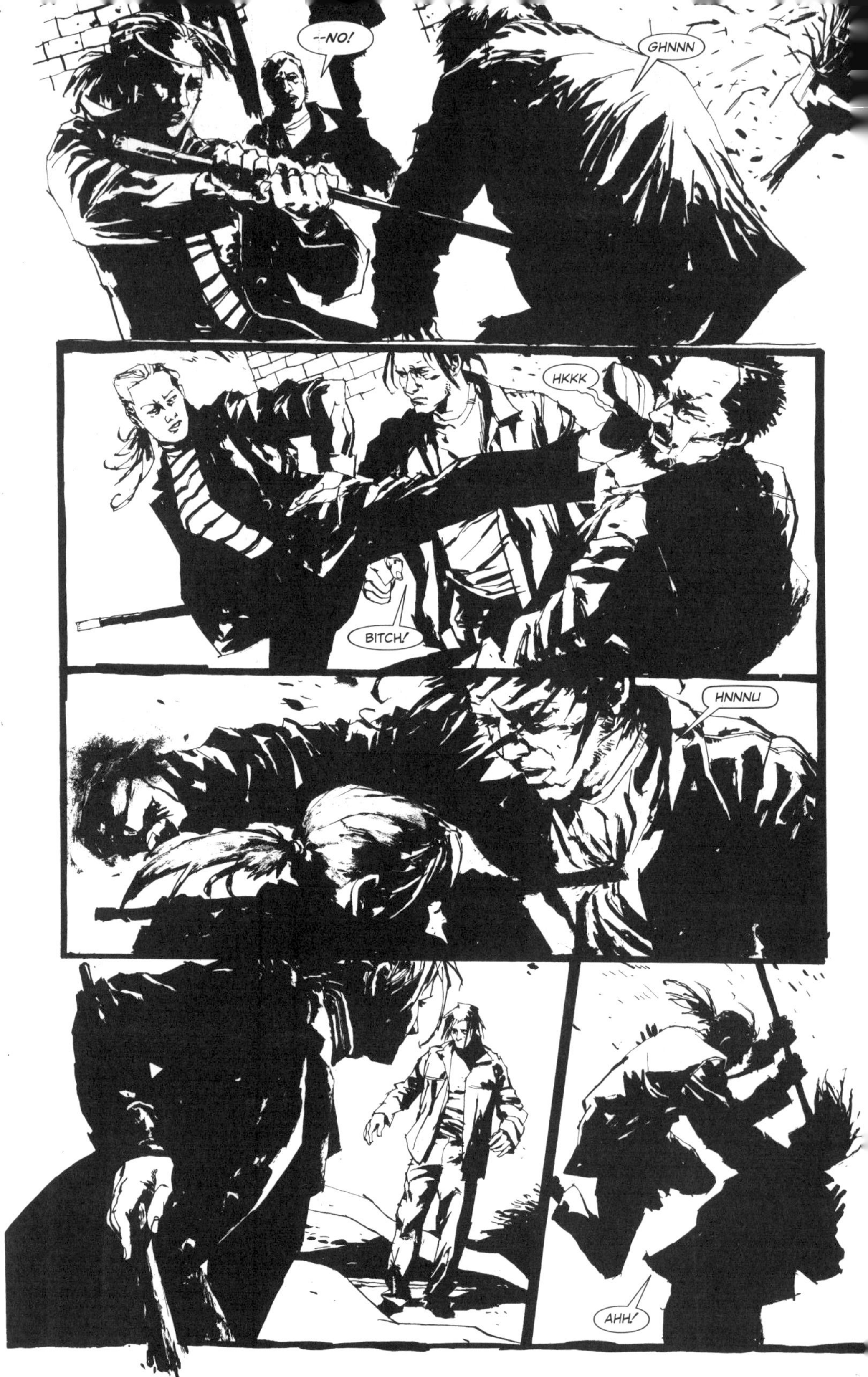
--NO!
GHNNN
HKKK
BITCH!
HNNNU
AHH!

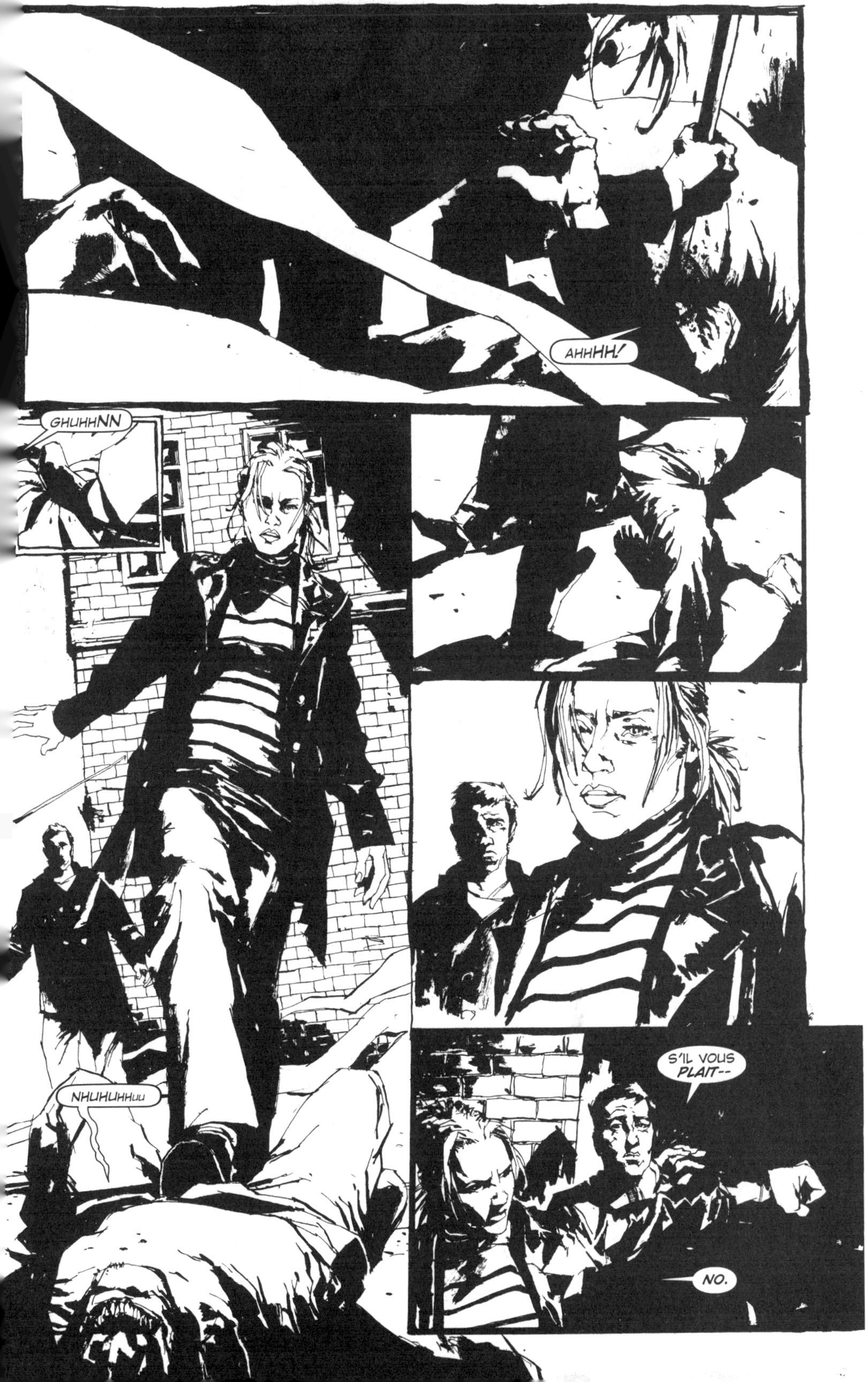
AHHHH!
GHUHHNN
NHUHUHHuu
S'IL VOUS PLAIT--
NO.

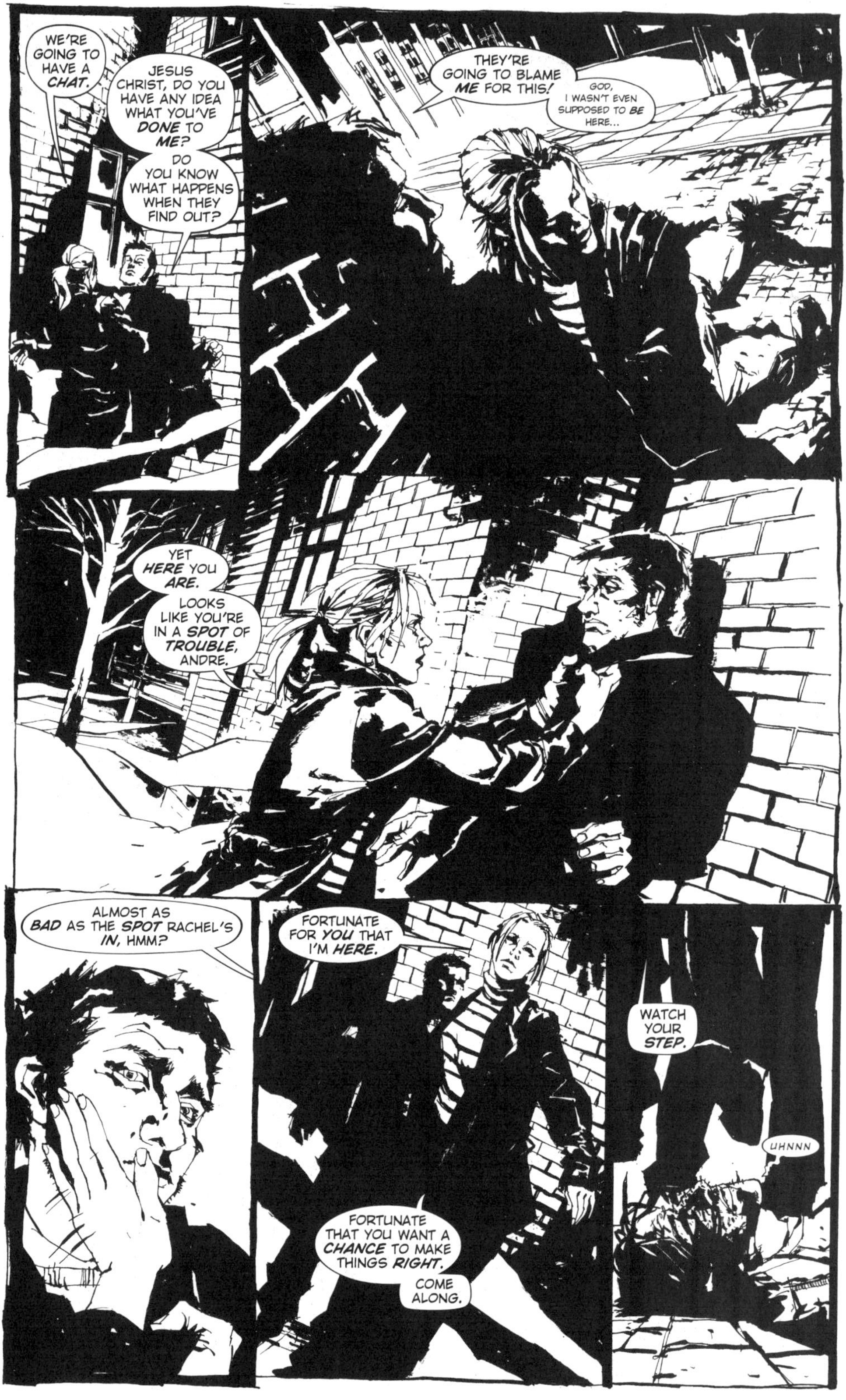
WE'RE GOING TO HAVE A CHAT.
JESUS CHRIST, DO YOU HAVE ANY IDEA WHAT YOU'VE DONE TO ME?
DO YOU KNOW WHAT HAPPENS WHEN THEY FIND OUT?
THEY'RE GOING TO BLAME ME FOR THIS!
GOD, I WASN'T EVEN SUPPOSED TO BE HERE...
YET HERE YOU ARE.
LOOKS LIKE YOU'RE IN A SPOT OF TROUBLE, ANDRE.
ALMOST AS BAD AS THE SPOT RACHEL'S IN, HMM?
FORTUNATE FOR YOU THAT I'M HERE.
FORTUNATE THAT YOU WANT A CHANCE TO MAKE THINGS RIGHT.
COME ALONG.
WATCH YOUR STEP.
UHNNN

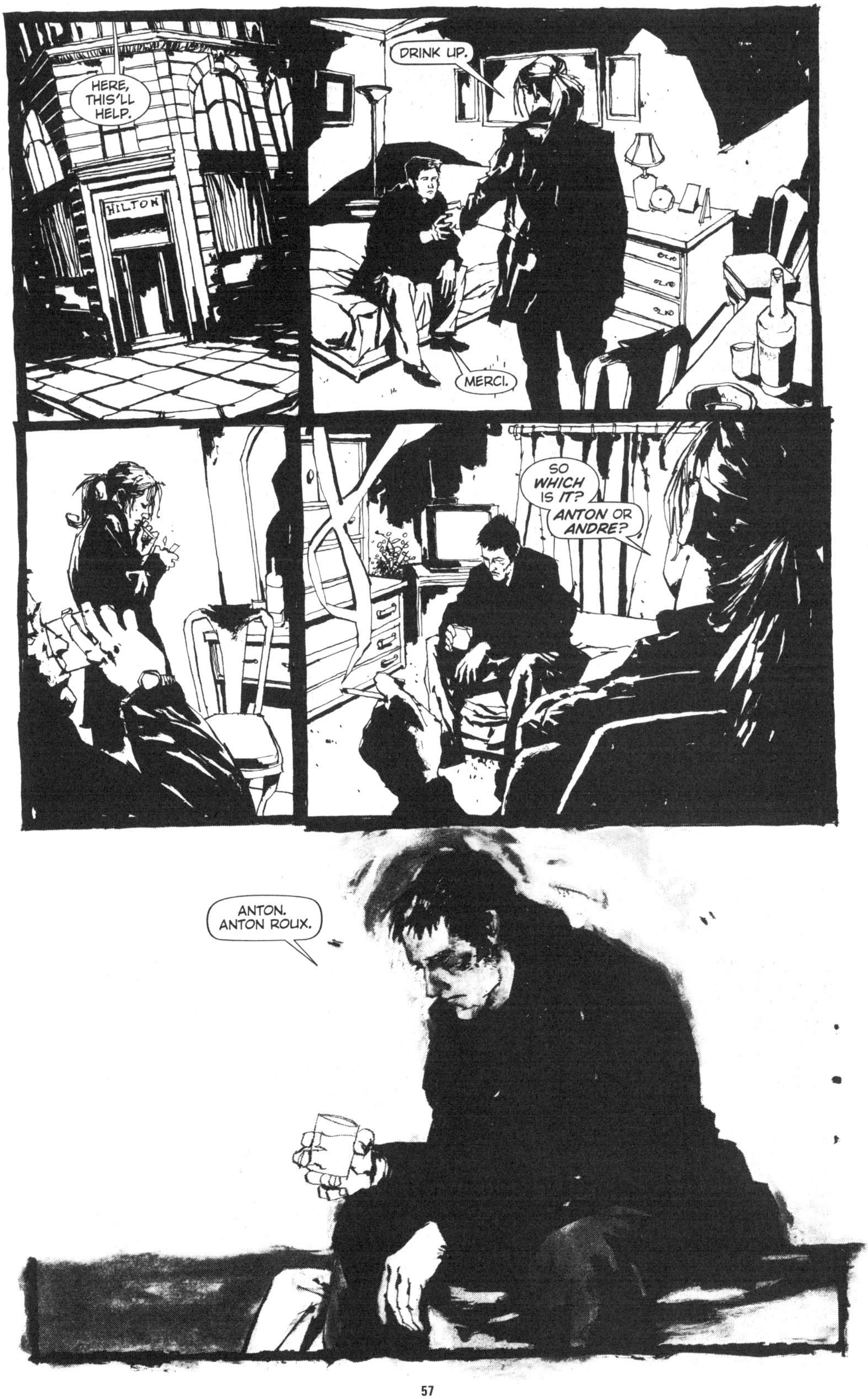

HERE, THIS'LL HELP.
HILTON
DRINK UP.
MERCI.
SO WHICH IS IT?
ANTON OR ANDRE?
ANTON. ANTON ROUX.

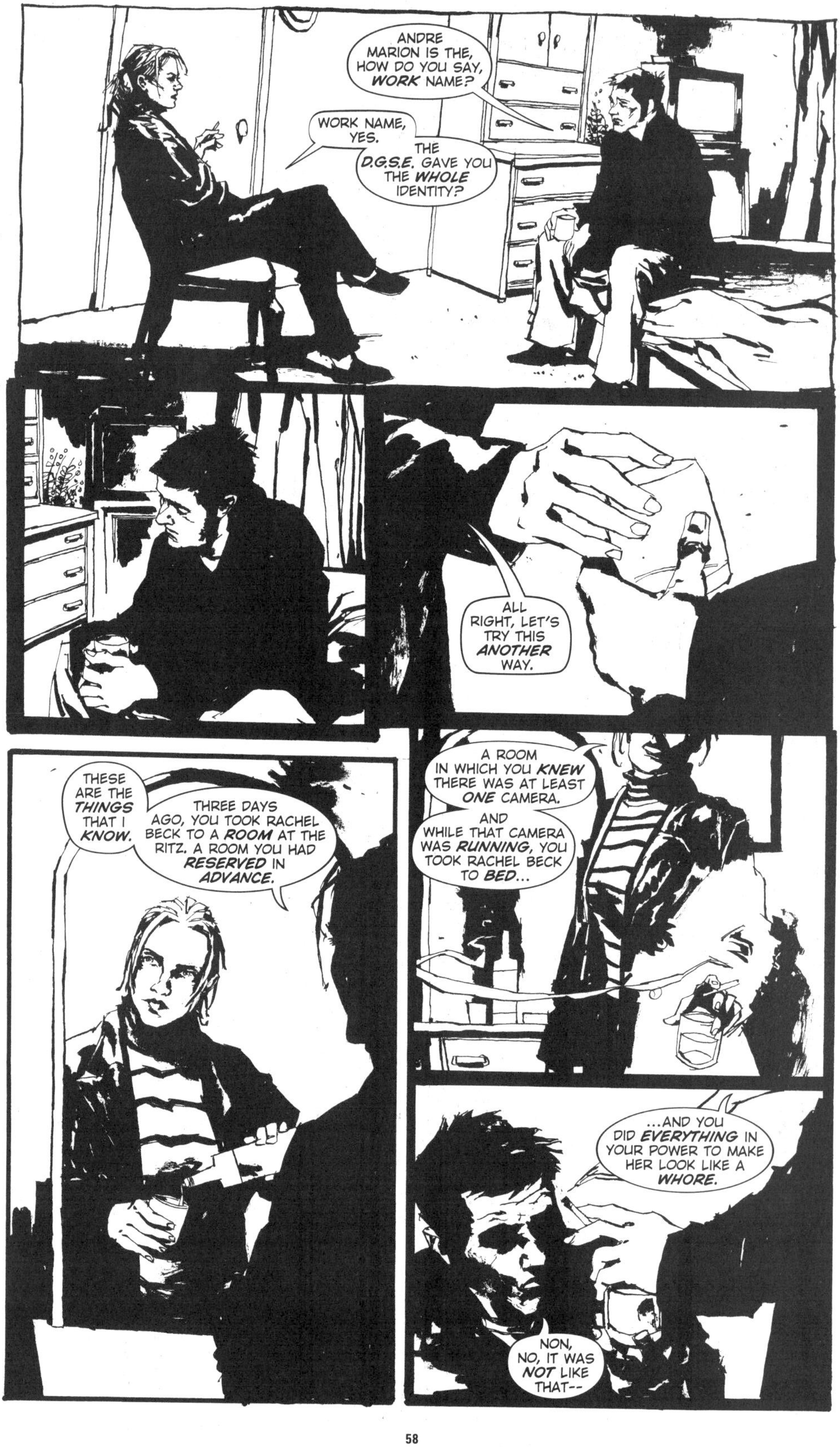

ANDRE MARION IS THE, HOW DO YOU SAY, *WORK* NAME?
WORK NAME, YES.
THE *D.G.S.E.* GAVE YOU THE *WHOLE* IDENTITY?
ALL RIGHT, LET'S TRY THIS *ANOTHER* WAY.
THESE ARE THE *THINGS* THAT I *KNOW.*
THREE DAYS AGO, YOU TOOK RACHEL BECK TO A *ROOM* AT THE RITZ. A ROOM YOU HAD *RESERVED* IN *ADVANCE.*
A ROOM IN WHICH YOU *KNEW* THERE WAS AT LEAST *ONE* CAMERA.
AND WHILE THAT CAMERA WAS *RUNNING,* YOU TOOK RACHEL BECK TO *BED*...
...AND YOU DID *EVERYTHING* IN YOUR POWER TO MAKE HER LOOK LIKE A *WHORE.*
NON, NO, IT WAS *NOT* LIKE THAT--

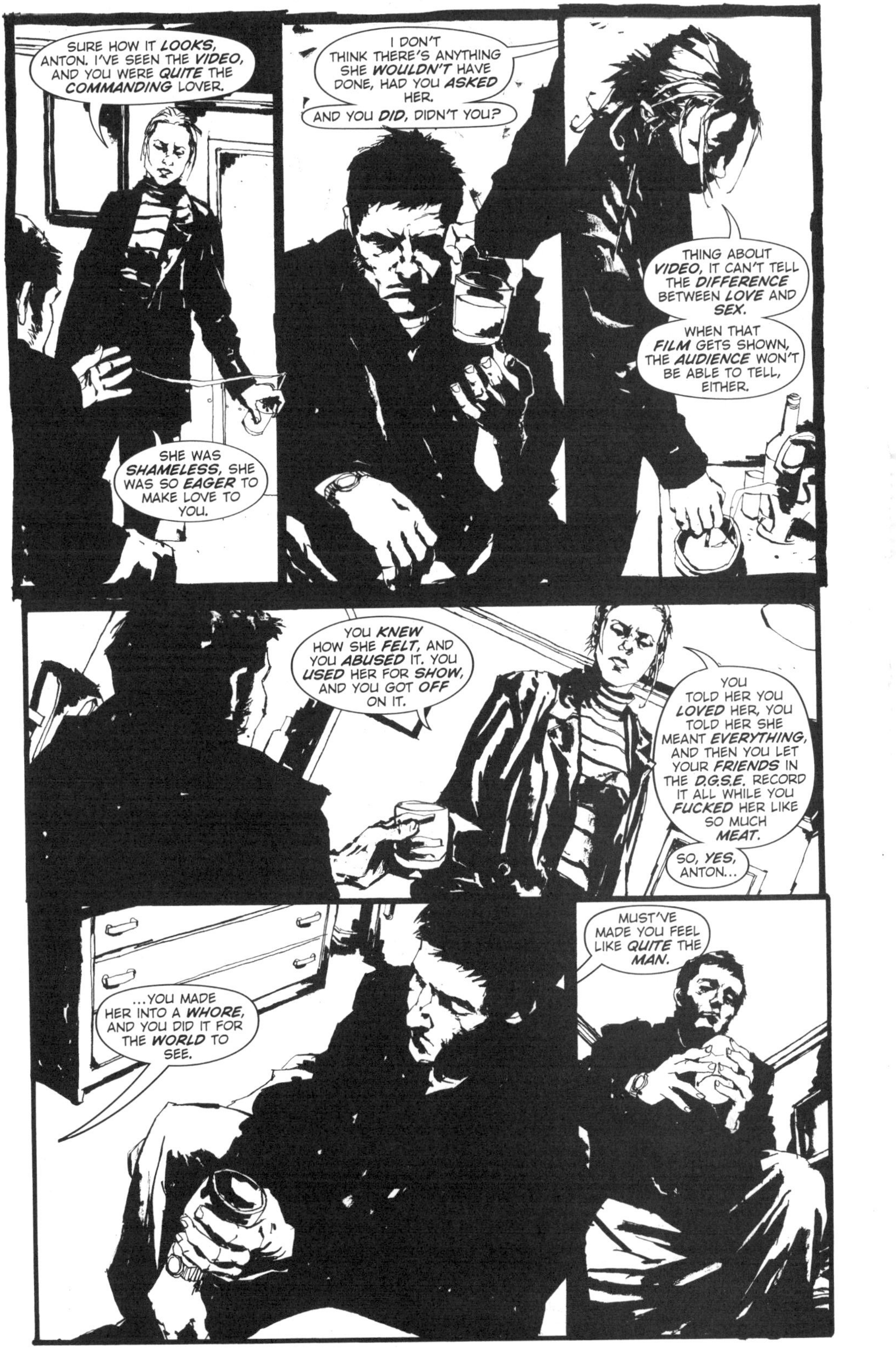
SURE HOW IT LOOKS, ANTON. I'VE SEEN THE VIDEO, AND YOU WERE QUITE THE COMMANDING LOVER.
SHE WAS SHAMELESS, SHE WAS SO EAGER TO MAKE LOVE TO YOU.
I DON'T THINK THERE'S ANYTHING SHE WOULDN'T HAVE DONE, HAD YOU ASKED HER.
AND YOU DID, DIDN'T YOU?
THING ABOUT VIDEO, IT CAN'T TELL THE DIFFERENCE BETWEEN LOVE AND SEX.
WHEN THAT FILM GETS SHOWN, THE AUDIENCE WON'T BE ABLE TO TELL, EITHER.
YOU KNEW HOW SHE FELT, AND YOU ABUSED IT. YOU USED HER FOR SHOW, AND YOU GOT OFF ON IT.
YOU TOLD HER YOU LOVED HER, YOU TOLD HER SHE MEANT EVERYTHING, AND THEN YOU LET YOUR FRIENDS IN THE D.G.S.E. RECORD IT ALL WHILE YOU FUCKED HER LIKE SO MUCH MEAT.
SO, YES, ANTON...
...YOU MADE HER INTO A WHORE, AND YOU DID IT FOR THE WORLD TO SEE.
MUST'VE MADE YOU FEEL LIKE QUITE THE MAN.

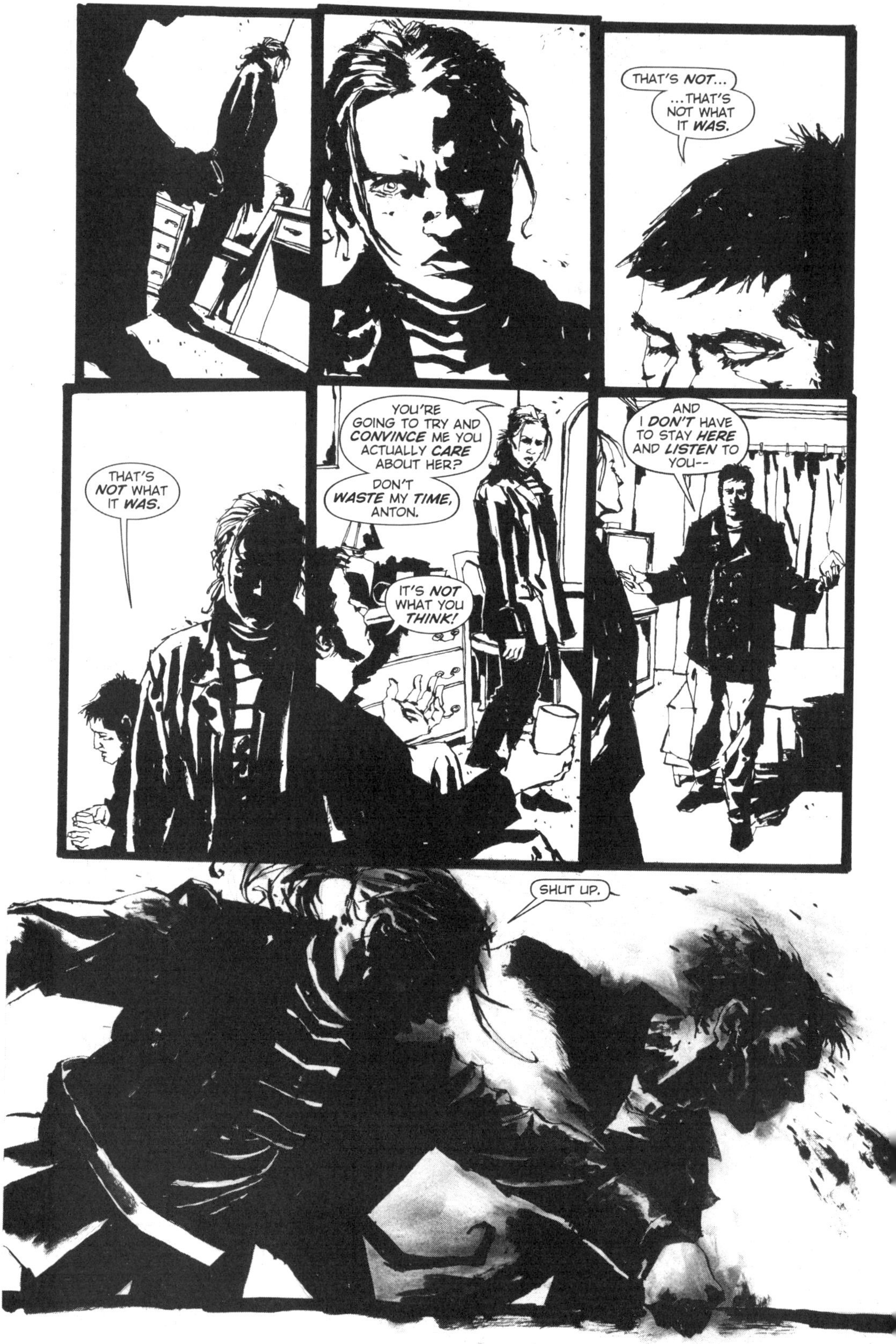
THAT'S NOT...
...THAT'S NOT WHAT IT WAS.
THAT'S NOT WHAT IT WAS.
YOU'RE GOING TO TRY AND CONVINCE ME YOU ACTUALLY CARE ABOUT HER?
DON'T WASTE MY TIME, ANTON.
IT'S NOT WHAT YOU THINK!
AND I DON'T HAVE TO STAY HERE AND LISTEN TO YOU--
SHUT UP.

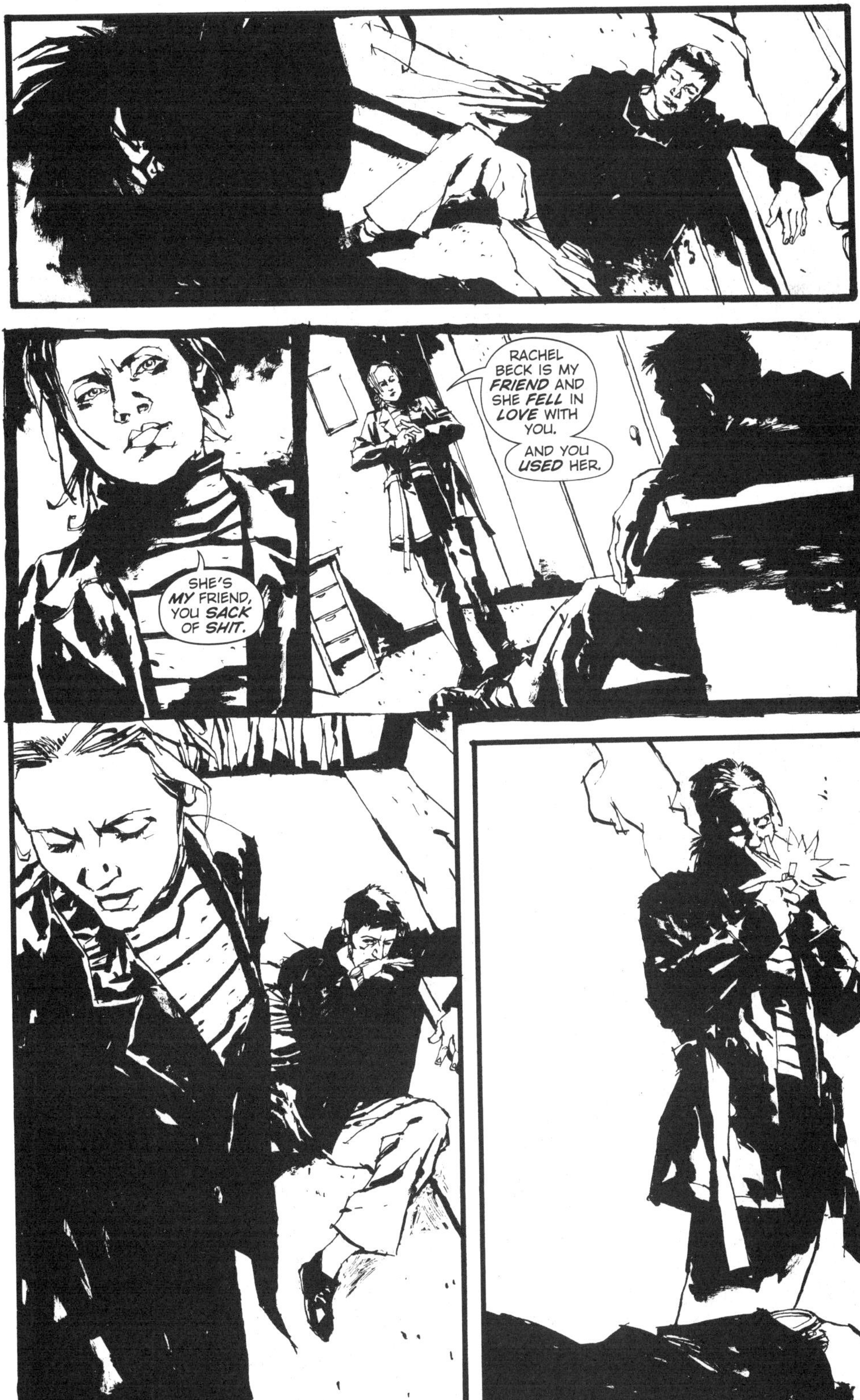
SHE'S MY FRIEND, YOU SACK OF SHIT.
RACHEL BECK IS MY FRIEND AND SHE FELL IN LOVE WITH YOU.
AND YOU USED HER.

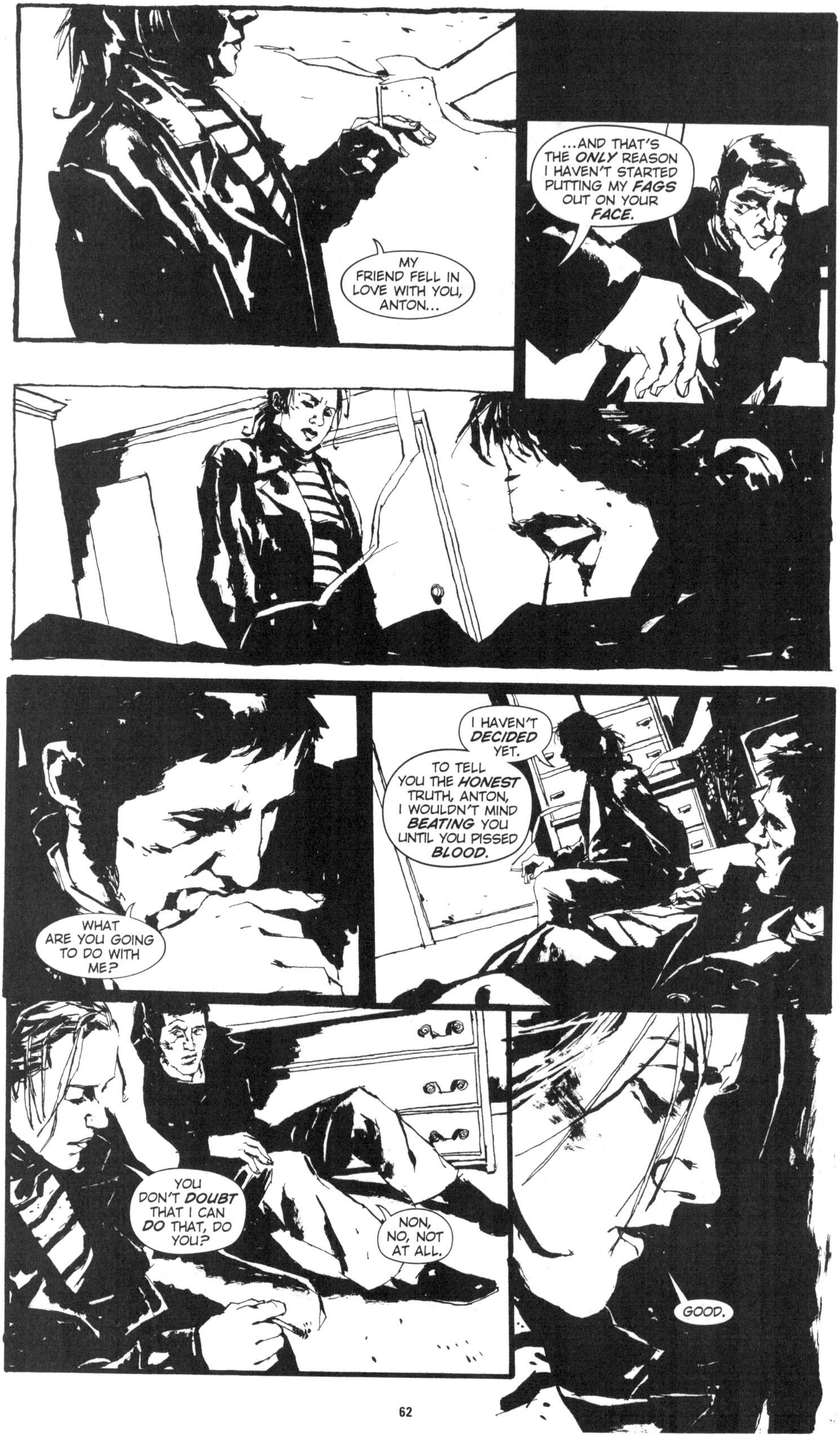
MY FRIEND FELL IN LOVE WITH YOU, ANTON...
...AND THAT'S THE ONLY REASON I HAVEN'T STARTED PUTTING MY FAGS OUT ON YOUR FACE.
WHAT ARE YOU GOING TO DO WITH ME?
I HAVEN'T DECIDED YET.
TO TELL YOU THE HONEST TRUTH, ANTON, I WOULDN'T MIND BEATING YOU UNTIL YOU PISSED BLOOD.
YOU DON'T DOUBT THAT I CAN DO THAT, DO YOU?
NON, NO, NOT AT ALL.
GOOD.

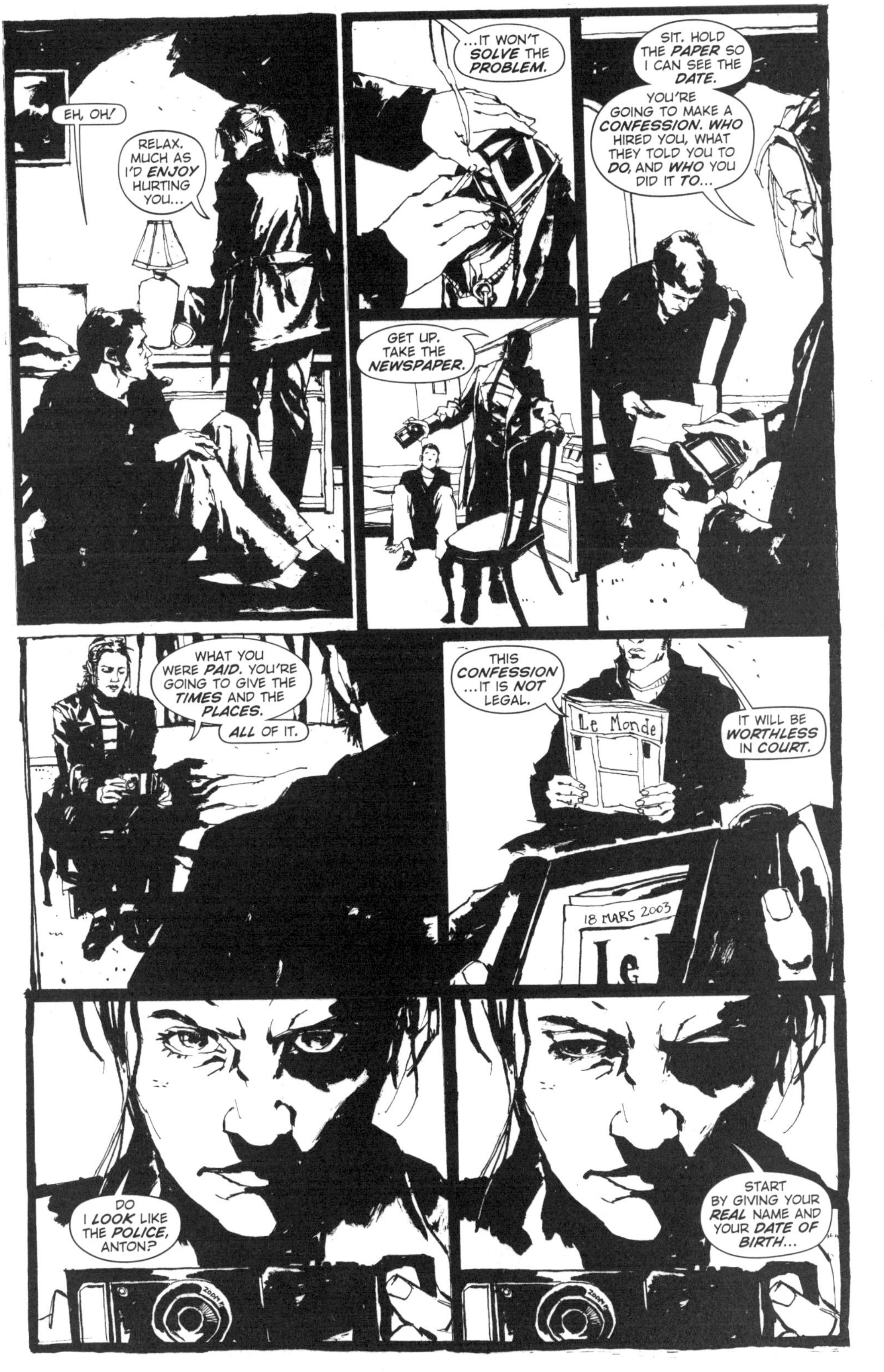
EH, OH!
RELAX. MUCH AS I'D ENJOY HURTING YOU...
...IT WON'T SOLVE THE PROBLEM.
GET UP. TAKE THE NEWSPAPER.
SIT. HOLD THE PAPER SO I CAN SEE THE DATE.
YOU'RE GOING TO MAKE A CONFESSION. WHO HIRED YOU, WHAT THEY TOLD YOU TO DO, AND WHO YOU DID IT TO...
WHAT YOU WERE PAID. YOU'RE GOING TO GIVE THE TIMES AND THE PLACES.
ALL OF IT.
THIS CONFESSION ...IT IS NOT LEGAL.
Le Monde
IT WILL BE WORTHLESS IN COURT.
18 MARS 2003
DO I LOOK LIKE THE POLICE, ANTON?
START BY GIVING YOUR REAL NAME AND YOUR DATE OF BIRTH...

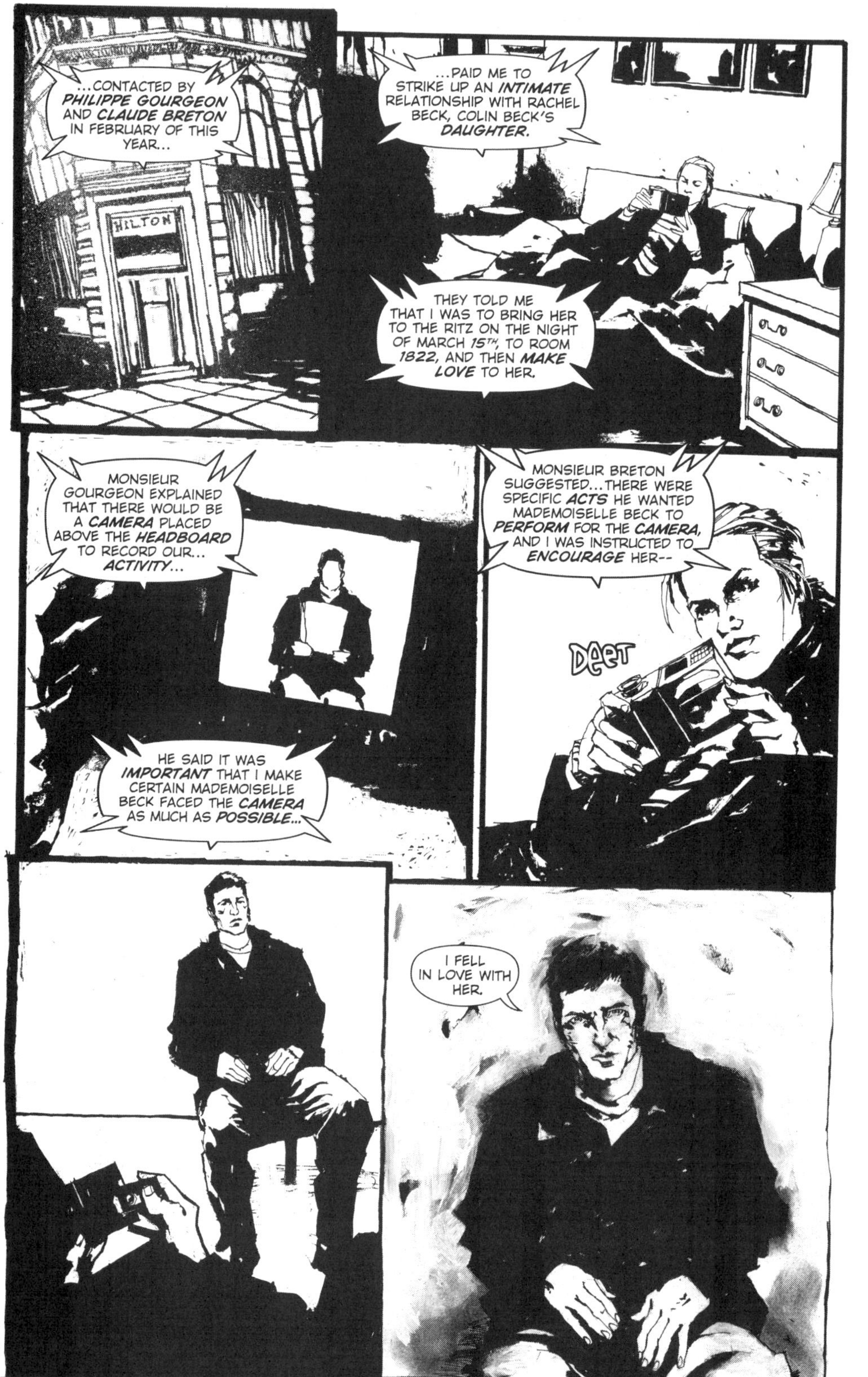
...CONTACTED BY PHILIPPE GOURGEON AND CLAUDE BRETON IN FEBRUARY OF THIS YEAR...
HILTON
...PAID ME TO STRIKE UP AN INTIMATE RELATIONSHIP WITH RACHEL BECK, COLIN BECK'S DAUGHTER.
THEY TOLD ME THAT I WAS TO BRING HER TO THE RITZ ON THE NIGHT OF MARCH 15TH, TO ROOM 1822, AND THEN MAKE LOVE TO HER.
MONSIEUR GOURGEON EXPLAINED THAT THERE WOULD BE A CAMERA PLACED ABOVE THE HEADBOARD TO RECORD OUR... ACTIVITY...
HE SAID IT WAS IMPORTANT THAT I MAKE CERTAIN MADEMOISELLE BECK FACED THE CAMERA AS MUCH AS POSSIBLE...
MONSIEUR BRETON SUGGESTED...THERE WERE SPECIFIC ACTS HE WANTED MADEMOISELLE BECK TO PERFORM FOR THE CAMERA, AND I WAS INSTRUCTED TO ENCOURAGE HER--
DEET
I FELL IN LOVE WITH HER.

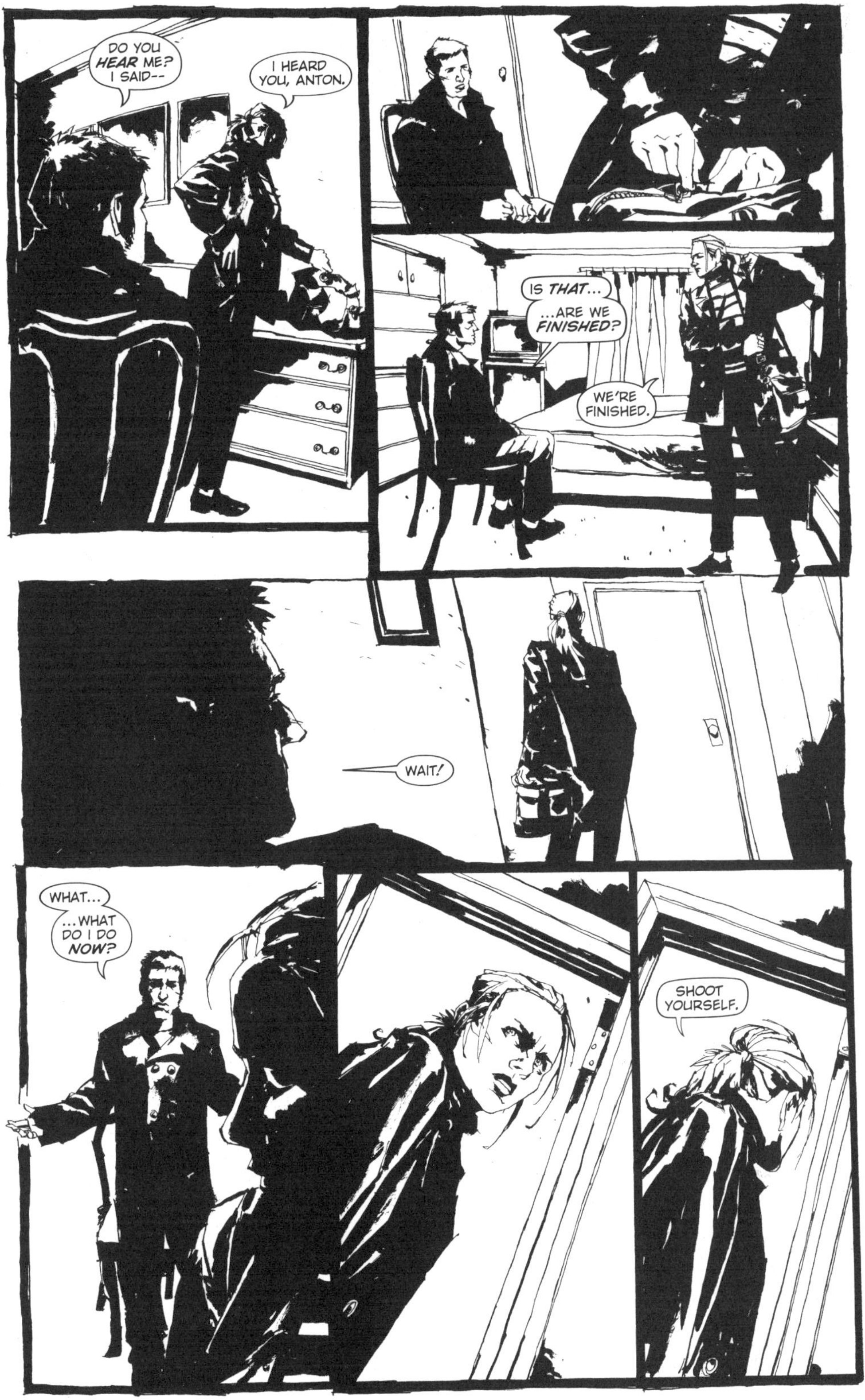
DO YOU HEAR ME? I SAID--
I HEARD YOU, ANTON.
IS THAT...
...ARE WE FINISHED?
WE'RE FINISHED.
WAIT!
WHAT...
...WHAT DO I DO NOW?
SHOOT YOURSELF.

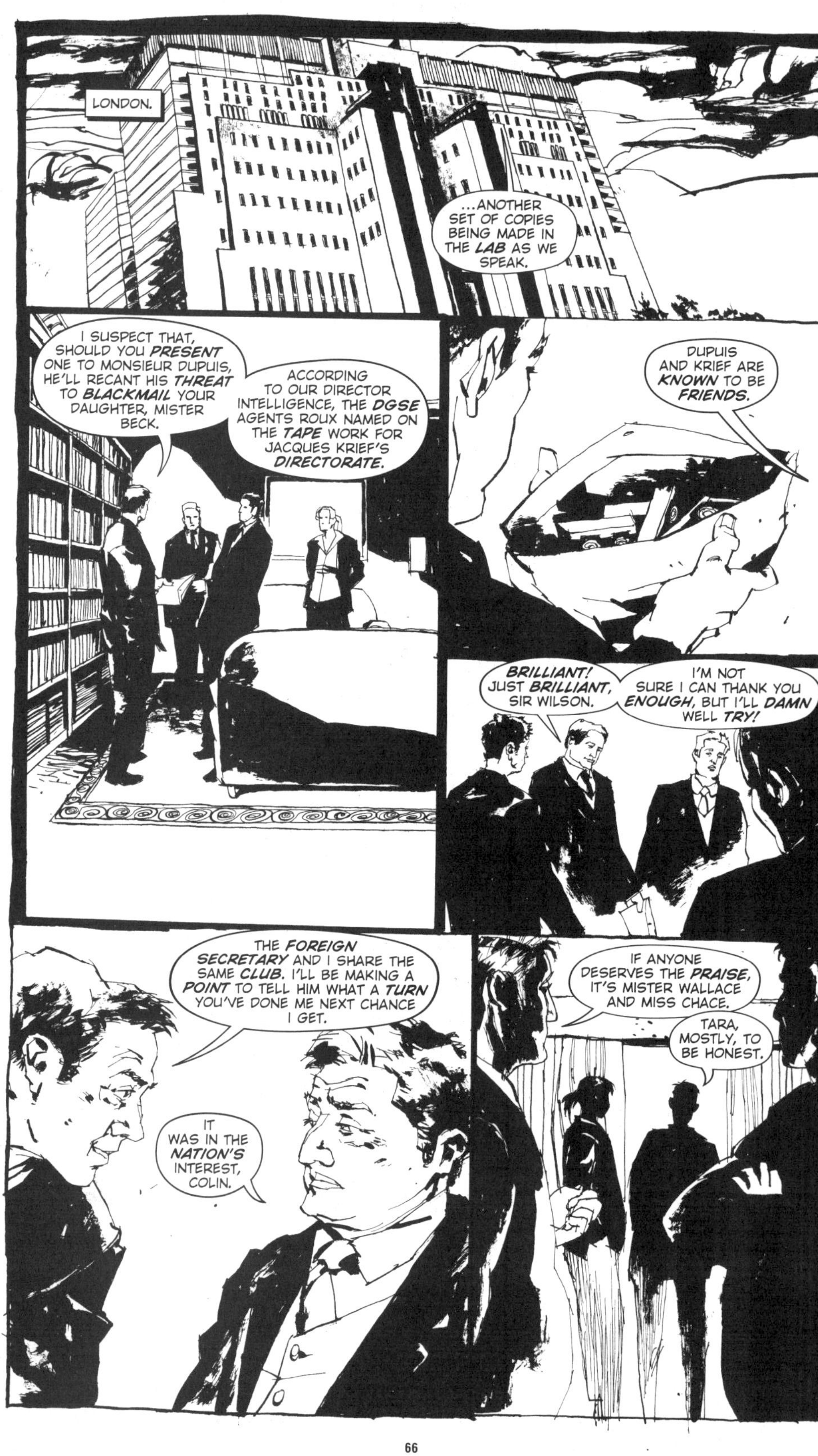

LONDON.
...ANOTHER SET OF COPIES BEING MADE IN THE LAB AS WE SPEAK.
I SUSPECT THAT, SHOULD YOU PRESENT ONE TO MONSIEUR DUPUIS, HE'LL RECANT HIS THREAT TO BLACKMAIL YOUR DAUGHTER, MISTER BECK.
ACCORDING TO OUR DIRECTOR INTELLIGENCE, THE DGSE AGENTS ROUX NAMED ON THE TAPE WORK FOR JACQUES KRIEF'S DIRECTORATE.
DUPUIS AND KRIEF ARE KNOWN TO BE FRIENDS.
BRILLIANT! JUST BRILLIANT, SIR WILSON.
I'M NOT SURE I CAN THANK YOU ENOUGH, BUT I'LL DAMN WELL TRY!
THE FOREIGN SECRETARY AND I SHARE THE SAME CLUB. I'LL BE MAKING A POINT TO TELL HIM WHAT A TURN YOU'VE DONE ME NEXT CHANCE I GET.
IT WAS IN THE NATION'S INTEREST, COLIN.
IF ANYONE DESERVES THE PRAISE, IT'S MISTER WALLACE AND MISS CHACE.
TARA, MOSTLY, TO BE HONEST.

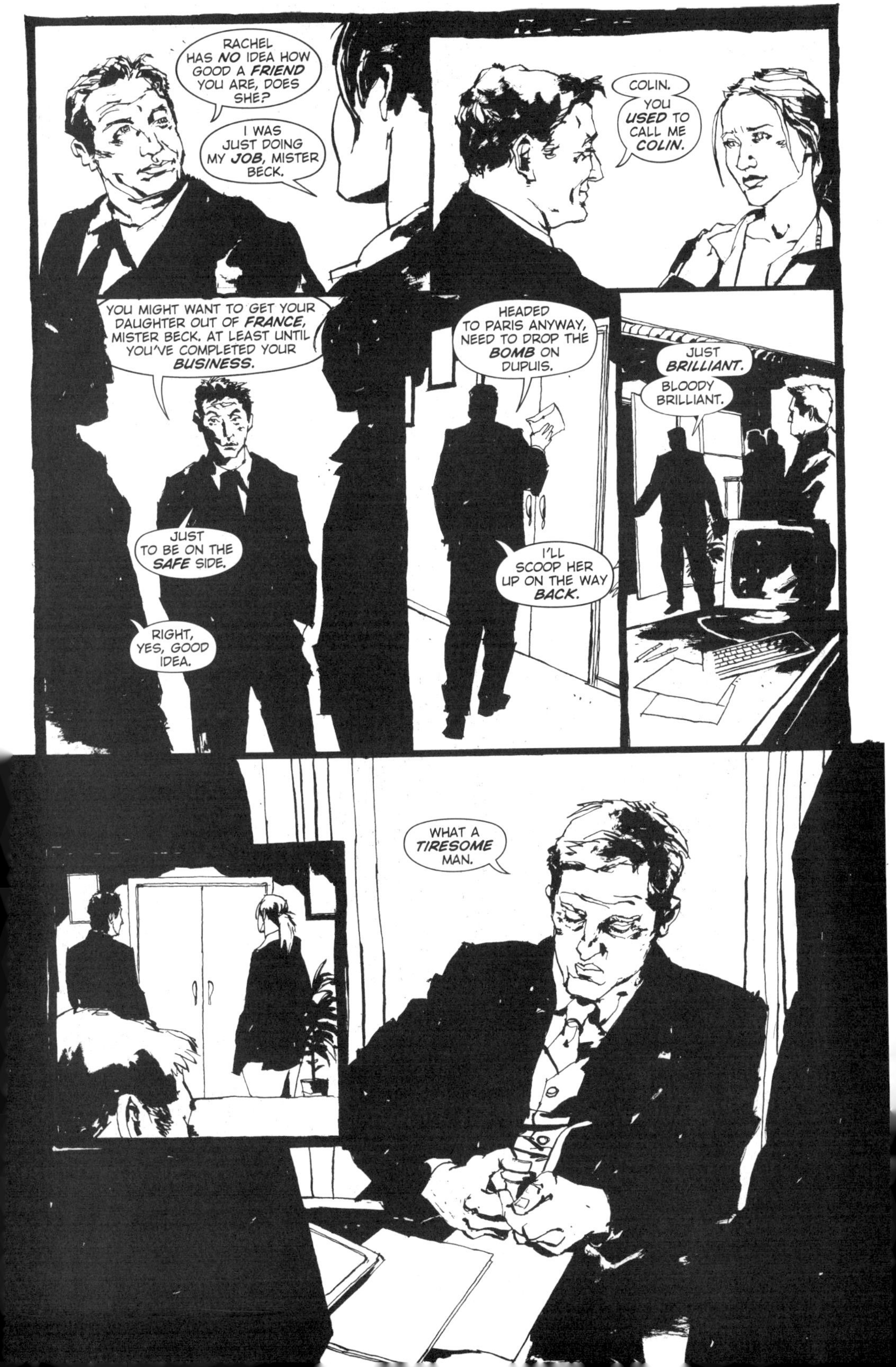
RACHEL HAS NO IDEA HOW GOOD A FRIEND YOU ARE, DOES SHE?
I WAS JUST DOING MY JOB, MISTER BECK.
COLIN.
YOU USED TO CALL ME COLIN.
YOU MIGHT WANT TO GET YOUR DAUGHTER OUT OF FRANCE, MISTER BECK. AT LEAST UNTIL YOU'VE COMPLETED YOUR BUSINESS.
JUST TO BE ON THE SAFE SIDE.
RIGHT, YES, GOOD IDEA.
HEADED TO PARIS ANYWAY, NEED TO DROP THE BOMB ON DUPUIS.
I'LL SCOOP HER UP ON THE WAY BACK.
JUST BRILLIANT.
BLOODY BRILLIANT.
WHAT A TIRESOME MAN.

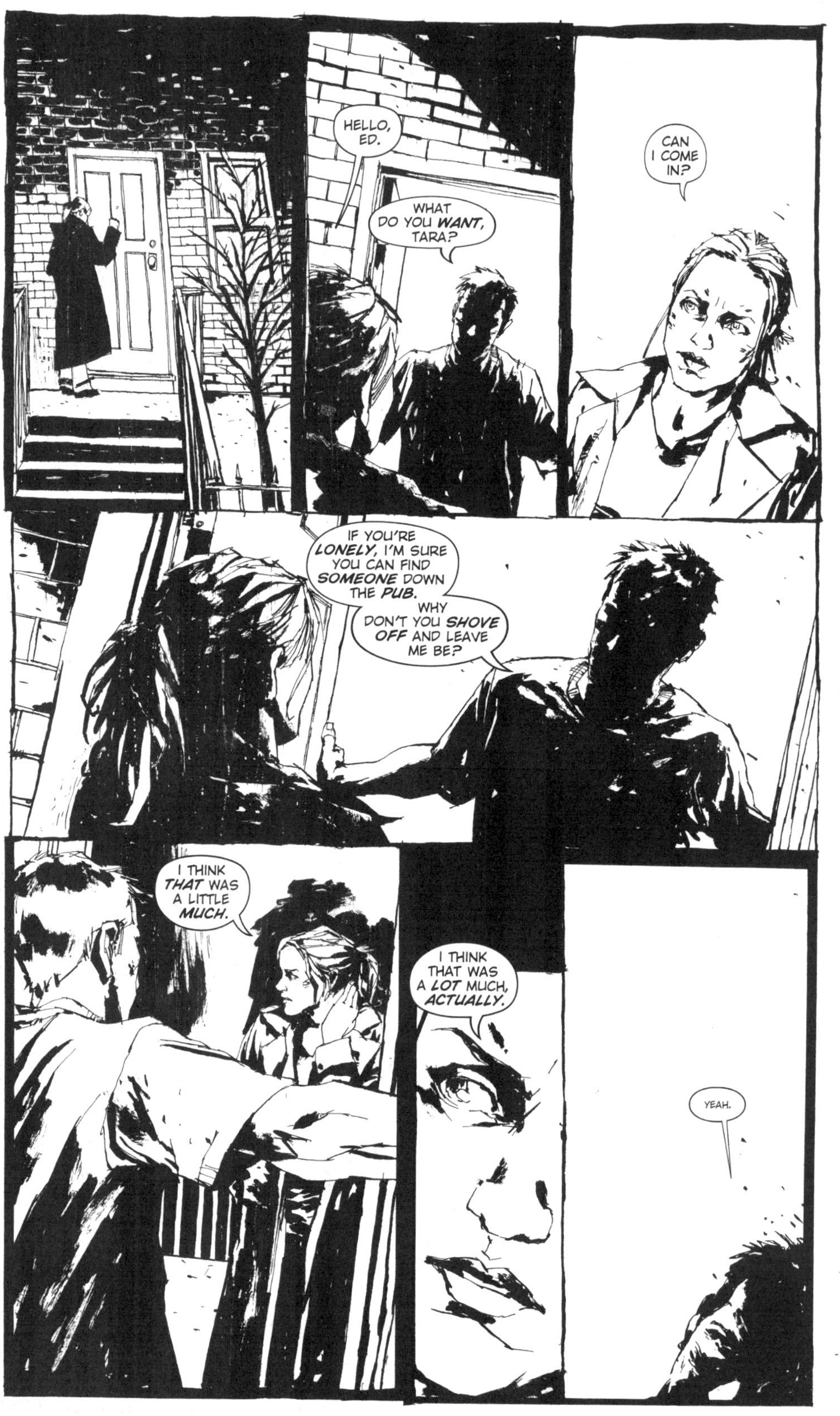
HELLO, ED.
WHAT DO YOU WANT, TARA?
CAN I COME IN?
IF YOU'RE LONELY, I'M SURE YOU CAN FIND SOMEONE DOWN THE PUB.
WHY DON'T YOU SHOVE OFF AND LEAVE ME BE?
I THINK THAT WAS A LITTLE MUCH.
I THINK THAT WAS A LOT MUCH, ACTUALLY.
YEAH.

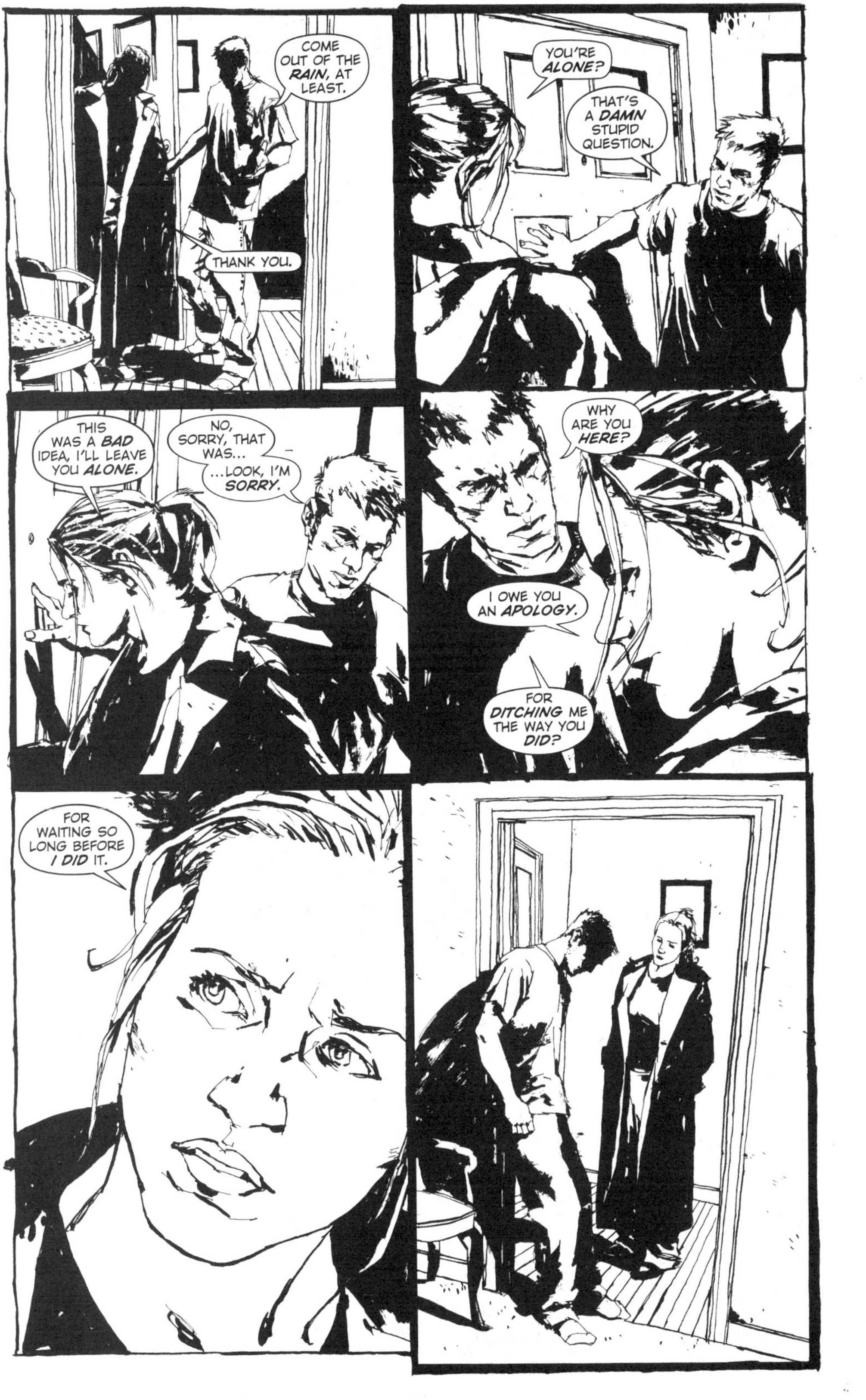
COME OUT OF THE RAIN, AT LEAST.
THANK YOU.
YOU'RE ALONE?
THAT'S A DAMN STUPID QUESTION.
THIS WAS A BAD IDEA, I'LL LEAVE YOU ALONE.
NO, SORRY, THAT WAS... ...LOOK, I'M SORRY.
WHY ARE YOU HERE?
I OWE YOU AN APOLOGY.
FOR DITCHING ME THE WAY YOU DID?
FOR WAITING SO LONG BEFORE I DID IT.

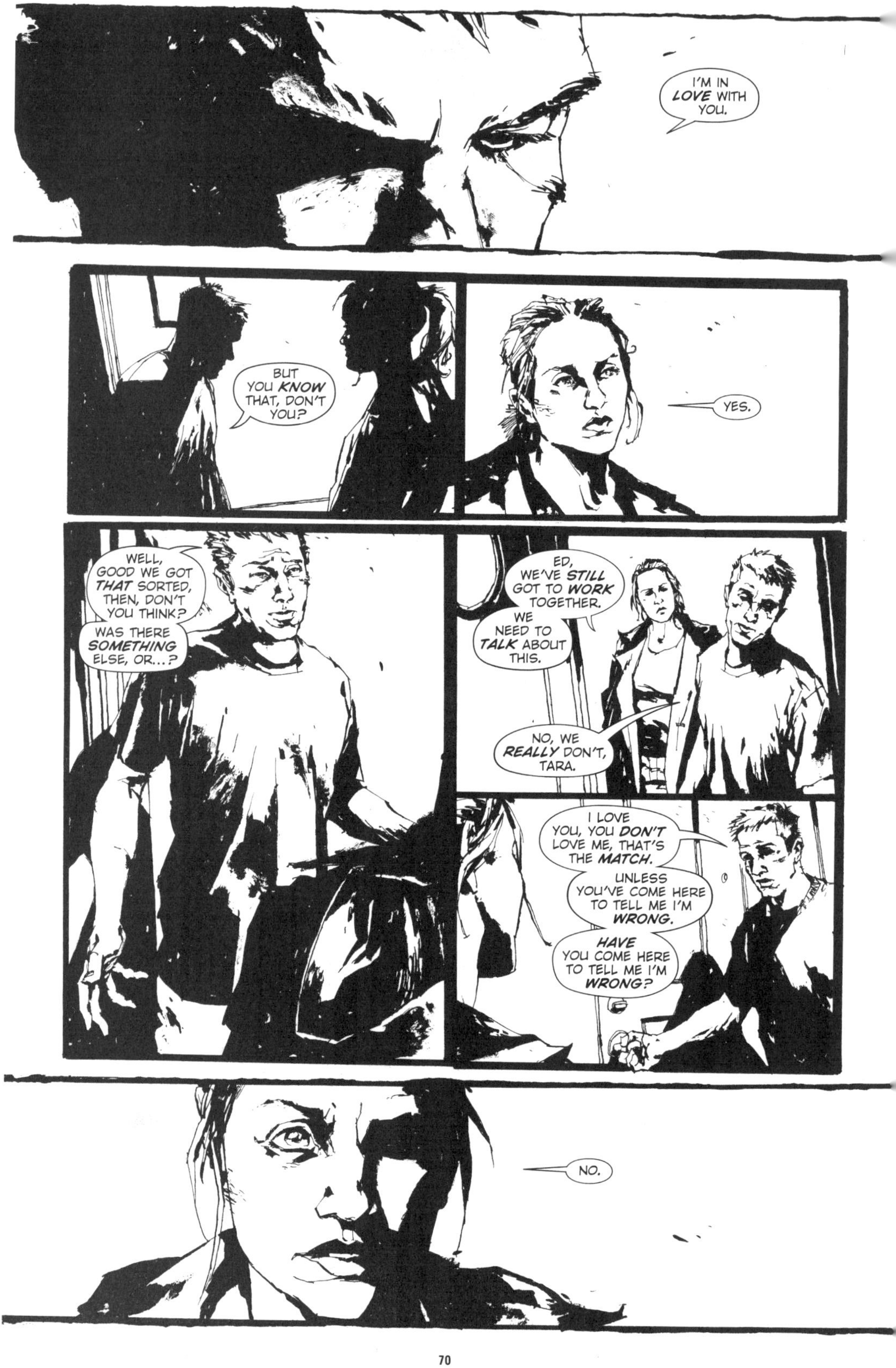
I'M IN LOVE WITH YOU.
BUT YOU KNOW THAT, DON'T YOU?
YES.
WELL, GOOD WE GOT THAT SORTED, THEN, DON'T YOU THINK?
WAS THERE SOMETHING ELSE, OR...?
ED, WE'VE STILL GOT TO WORK TOGETHER.
WE NEED TO TALK ABOUT THIS.
NO, WE REALLY DON'T, TARA.
I LOVE YOU, YOU DON'T LOVE ME, THAT'S THE MATCH.
UNLESS YOU'VE COME HERE TO TELL ME I'M WRONG.
HAVE YOU COME HERE TO TELL ME I'M WRONG?
NO.

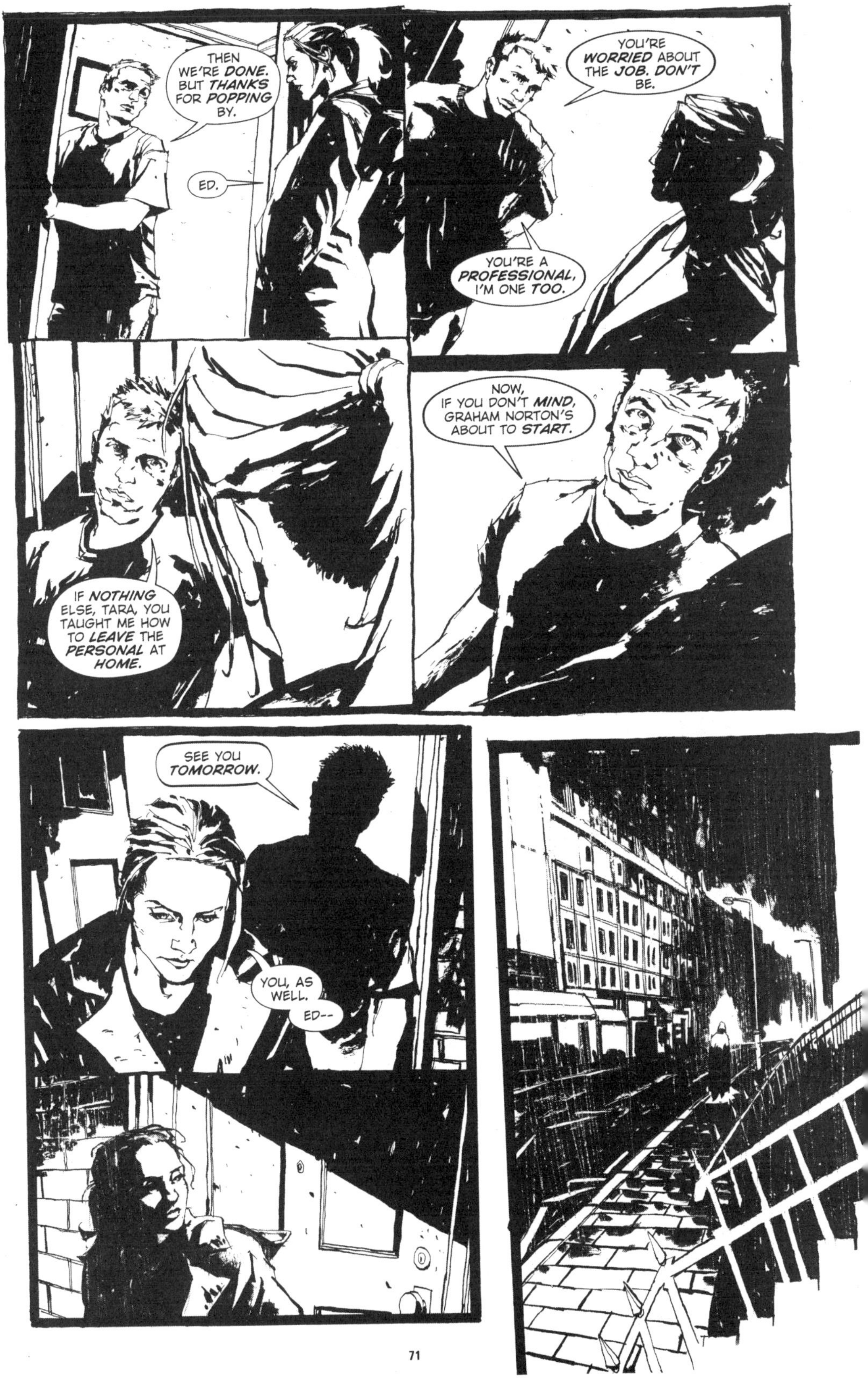

THEN WE'RE DONE. BUT THANKS FOR POPPING BY.
ED.
YOU'RE WORRIED ABOUT THE JOB. DON'T BE.
YOU'RE A PROFESSIONAL, I'M ONE TOO.
IF NOTHING ELSE, TARA, YOU TAUGHT ME HOW TO LEAVE THE PERSONAL AT HOME.
NOW, IF YOU DON'T MIND, GRAHAM NORTON'S ABOUT TO START.
SEE YOU TOMORROW.
YOU, AS WELL.
ED--

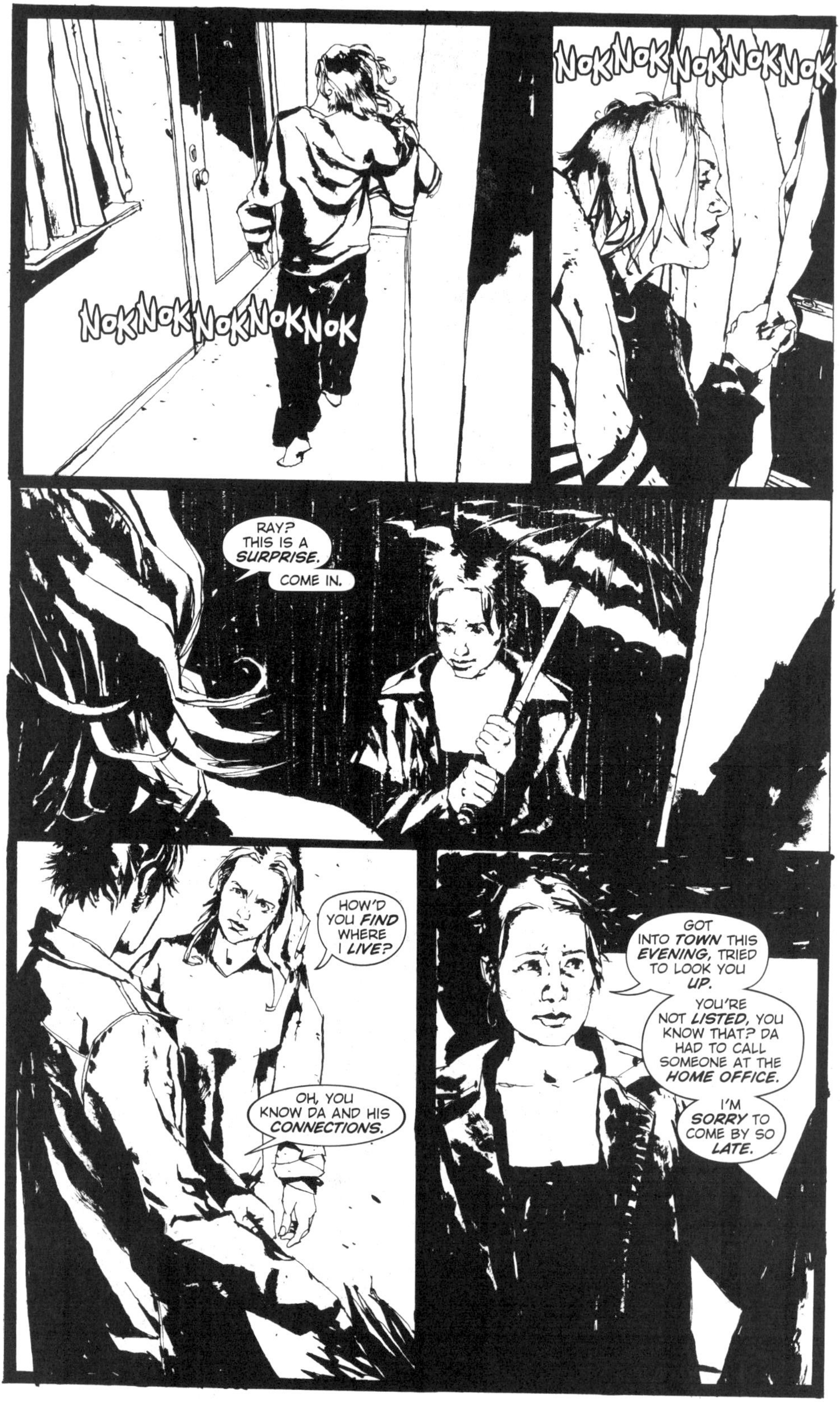
NOKNOKNOKNOKNOK
NOKNOKNOKNOKNOK
RAY? THIS IS A SURPRISE.
COME IN.
HOW'D YOU FIND WHERE I LIVE?
OH, YOU KNOW DA AND HIS CONNECTIONS.
GOT INTO TOWN THIS EVENING, TRIED TO LOOK YOU UP.
YOU'RE NOT LISTED, YOU KNOW THAT? DA HAD TO CALL SOMEONE AT THE HOME OFFICE.
I'M SORRY TO COME BY SO LATE.

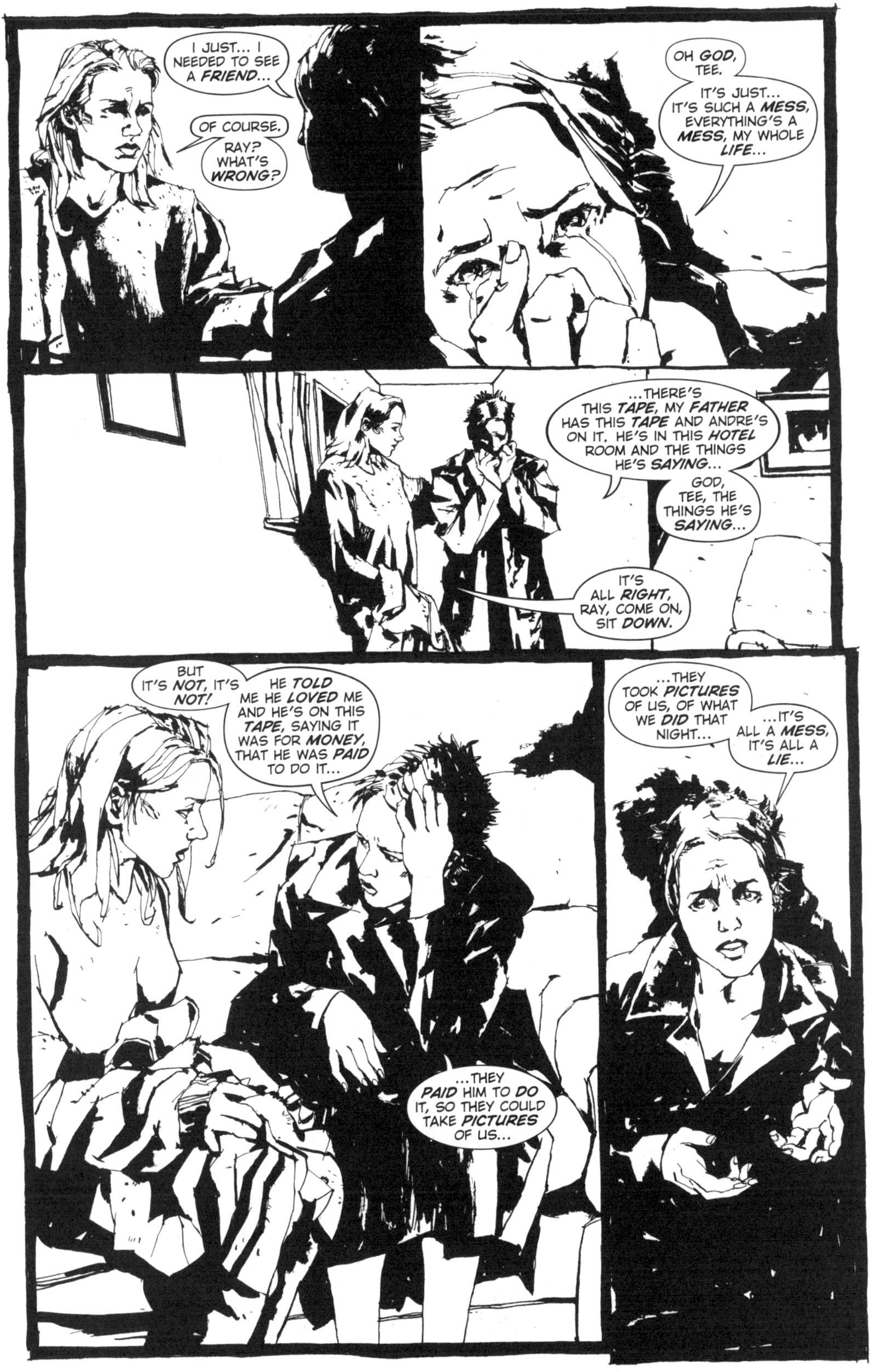
I JUST... I NEEDED TO SEE A *FRIEND*...
OF COURSE. RAY? WHAT'S *WRONG*?
OH *GOD*, TEE.
IT'S JUST... IT'S SUCH A *MESS*, EVERYTHING'S A *MESS*, MY WHOLE *LIFE*...
...THERE'S THIS *TAPE*, MY *FATHER* HAS THIS *TAPE* AND ANDRE'S ON IT. HE'S IN THIS *HOTEL* ROOM AND THE THINGS HE'S *SAYING*...
GOD, TEE, THE THINGS HE'S *SAYING*...
IT'S ALL *RIGHT*, RAY, COME ON, SIT *DOWN*.
BUT IT'S *NOT*, IT'S *NOT!*
HE *TOLD* ME HE *LOVED* ME AND HE'S ON THIS *TAPE*, SAYING IT WAS FOR *MONEY*, THAT HE WAS *PAID* TO DO IT...
...THEY *PAID* HIM TO *DO* IT, SO THEY COULD TAKE *PICTURES* OF US...
...THEY TOOK *PICTURES* OF US, OF WHAT WE *DID* THAT NIGHT...
...IT'S ALL A *MESS*, IT'S ALL A *LIE*...

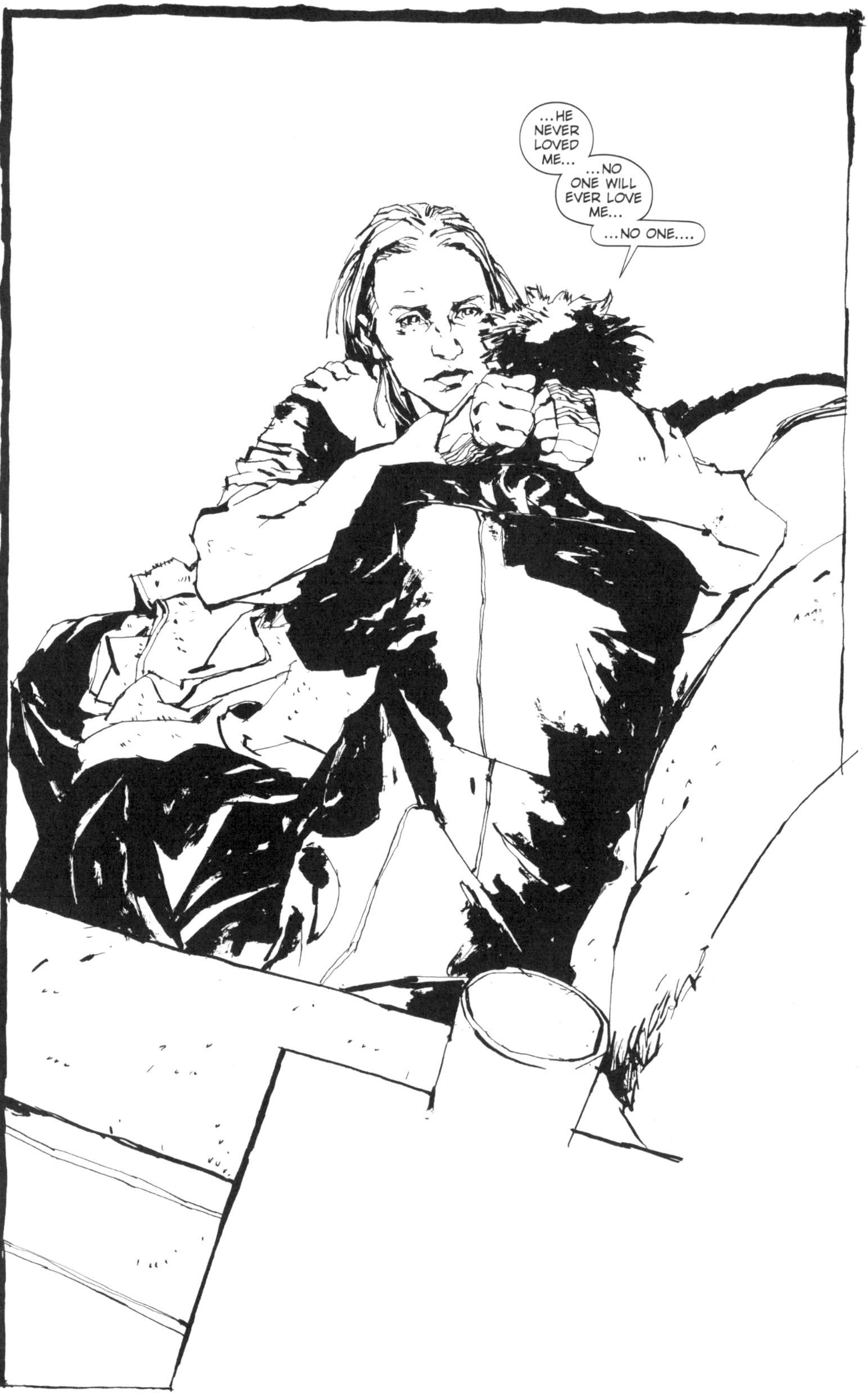
...HE NEVER LOVED ME...
...NO ONE WILL EVER LOVE ME...
...NO ONE....

OPERATION: STORM FRONT

WRITTEN BY
GREG RUCKA

ILLUSTRATED & LETTERED BY
CARLA SPEED McNEIL

ORIGINAL SERIES EDITED BY
JAMIE S. RICH & JAMES LUCAS JONES

ROSTER

C—Ubiquitous code-name for the current head of SIS. Real name is Sir Wilson Stanton Davies.

DONALD WELDON—Deputy Chief of Service, has oversight of all aspects of Intelligence gathering and operations. Immediate superior to Crocker.

PAUL CROCKER—Director of Operations, encompassing all field work in all theaters of operations. In addition to commanding individual stations, has direct command of the Special Section—sometimes referred to as Minders—used for special operations.

TOM WALLACE—Head of the Special Section, a Special Operations Officer with the designation Minder One. Responsible for the training and continued well-being of his unit, both at home and in the field. Six year veteran of the Minders.

TARA CHACE—Special Operations Officer, designated Minder Two. Entering her third year as Minder.

EDWARD KITTERING—Special Operations Officer, designated Minder Three. Has been with the Special Section for less than a year.

OPS ROOM STAFF   OTHERS

ALEXIS—Mission Control Officer (also called Main Communications Officer)– responsible for maintaining communications between the Operations Room and the agents in the field.

RON—Duty Operations Officer, responsible for monitoring the status and importance of all incoming intelligence, both from foreign stations and other sources.

KATE—Personal Assistant to Paul Crocker, termed PA to D.Ops. Possibly the hardest and most important job in the Service.

SIMON RAYBURN—Director of Intelligence for SIS (D. Int), essentially Crocker's opposite number. Responsible for the evaluation, interpretation, and dissemination of all acquired intelligence.

BRIAN BUTLER—A former sergeant in one of the British Army's oldest and most respected regiments. An unique individual who actually requested assignment with special section.

LASHA KARPIN—Son of would-be Soviet defector Valery Karpin. A savvy businessman with a shrewd mind for politics, Karpin is a vice-president of Varita Technologies.

CHAPTER 1

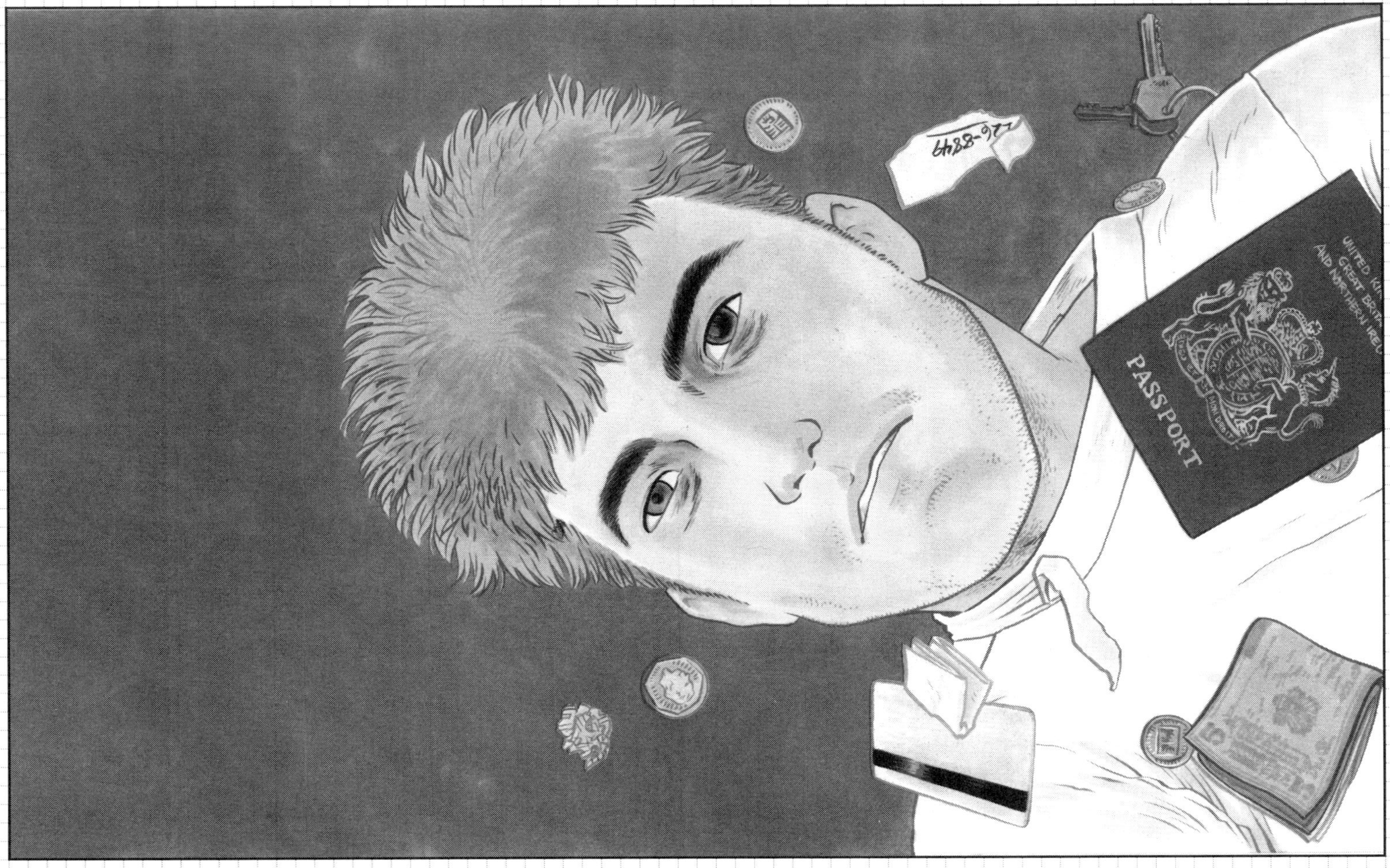

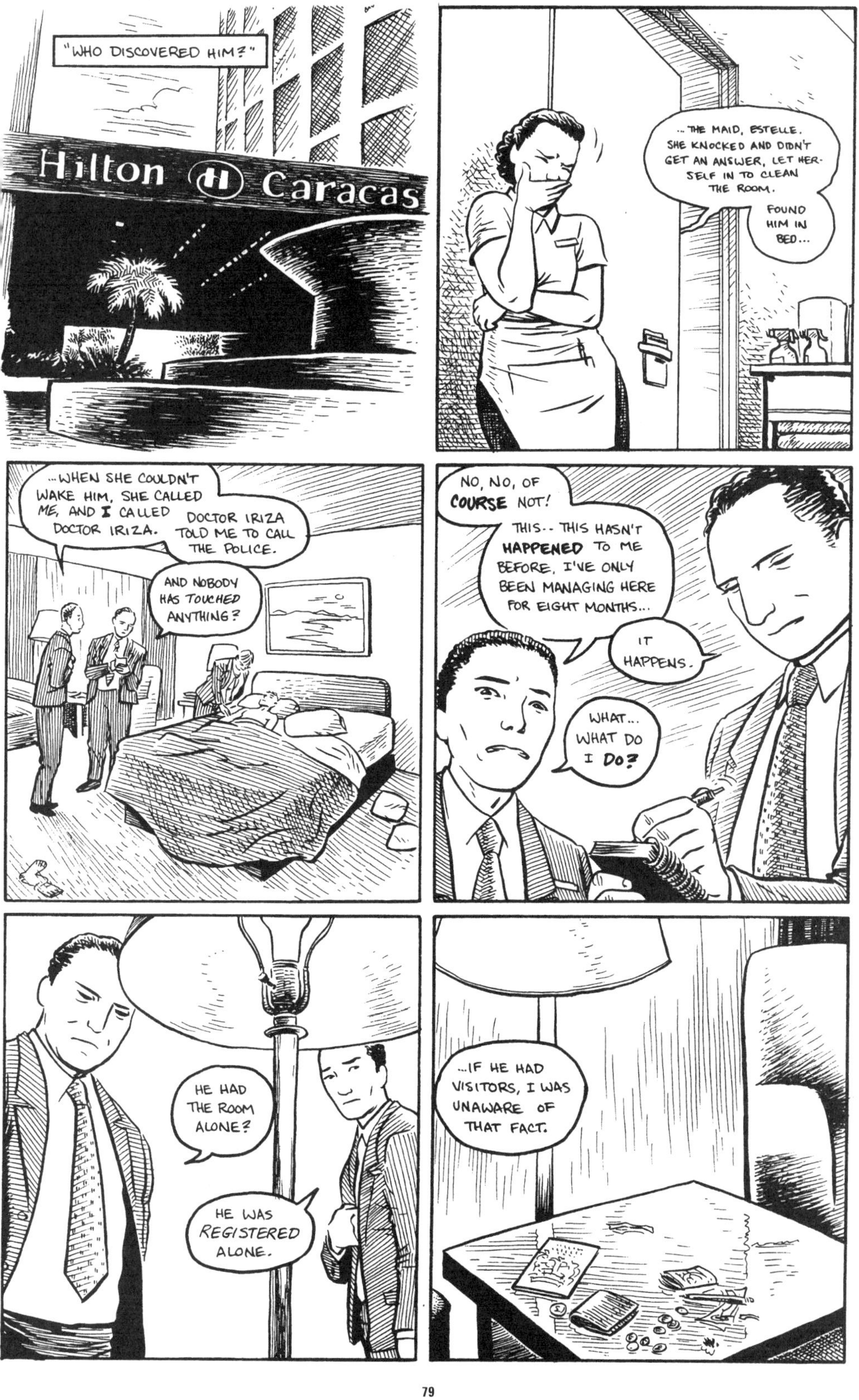
"WHO DISCOVERED HIM?"
Hilton Caracas
...THE MAID, ESTELLE. SHE KNOCKED AND DIDN'T GET AN ANSWER, LET HER-SELF IN TO CLEAN THE ROOM.
FOUND HIM IN BED...
...WHEN SHE COULDN'T WAKE HIM, SHE CALLED ME, AND I CALLED DOCTOR IRIZA.
DOCTOR IRIZA TOLD ME TO CALL THE POLICE.
AND NOBODY HAS TOUCHED ANYTHING?
NO, NO, OF COURSE NOT!
THIS.. THIS HASN'T HAPPENED TO ME BEFORE. I'VE ONLY BEEN MANAGING HERE FOR EIGHT MONTHS...
IT HAPPENS.
WHAT... WHAT DO I DO?
HE HAD THE ROOM ALONE?
HE WAS REGISTERED ALONE.
...IF HE HAD VISITORS, I WAS UNAWARE OF THAT FACT.

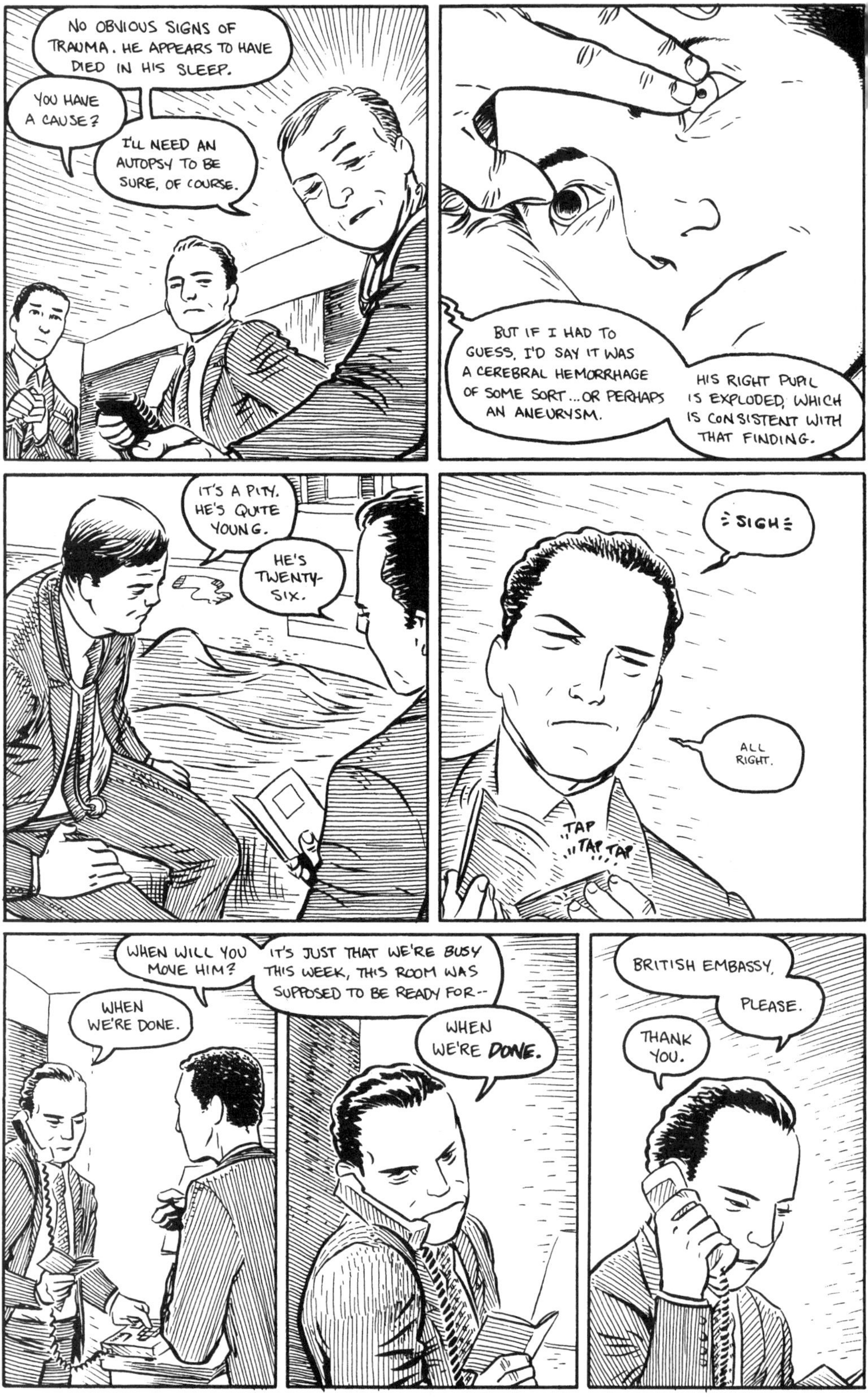
NO OBVIOUS SIGNS OF TRAUMA. HE APPEARS TO HAVE DIED IN HIS SLEEP.
YOU HAVE A CAUSE?
I'LL NEED AN AUTOPSY TO BE SURE, OF COURSE.
BUT IF I HAD TO GUESS, I'D SAY IT WAS A CEREBRAL HEMORRHAGE OF SOME SORT...OR PERHAPS AN ANEURYSM.
HIS RIGHT PUPIL IS EXPLODED, WHICH IS CONSISTENT WITH THAT FINDING.
IT'S A PITY. HE'S QUITE YOUNG.
HE'S TWENTY-SIX.
SIGH
ALL RIGHT.
TAP TAP TAP
WHEN WILL YOU MOVE HIM?
WHEN WE'RE DONE.
IT'S JUST THAT WE'RE BUSY THIS WEEK, THIS ROOM WAS SUPPOSED TO BE READY FOR--
WHEN WE'RE DONE.
BRITISH EMBASSY,
PLEASE.
THANK YOU.

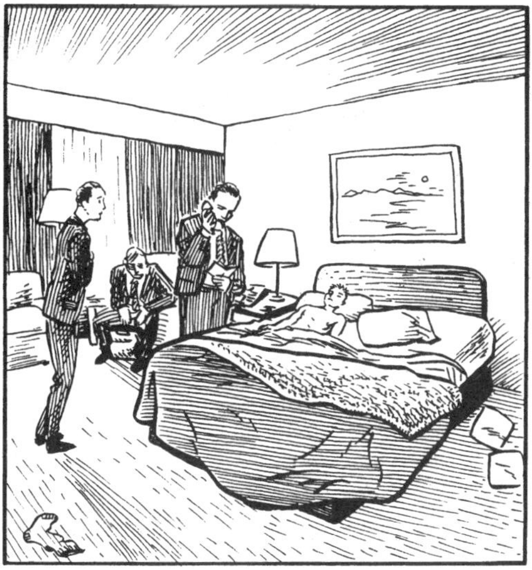

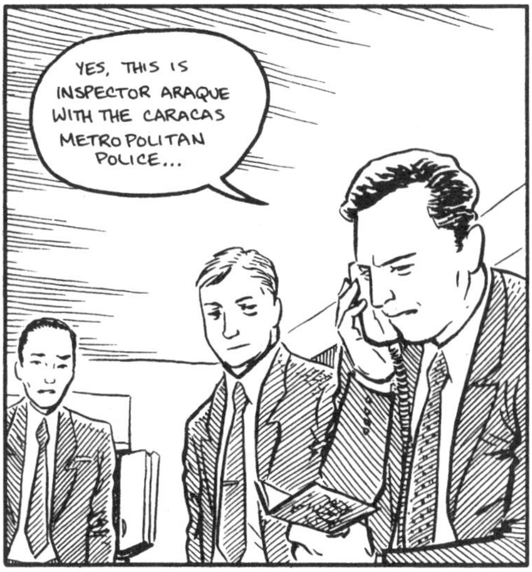
YES, THIS IS INSPECTOR ARAQUE WITH THE CARACAS METROPOLITAN POLICE...

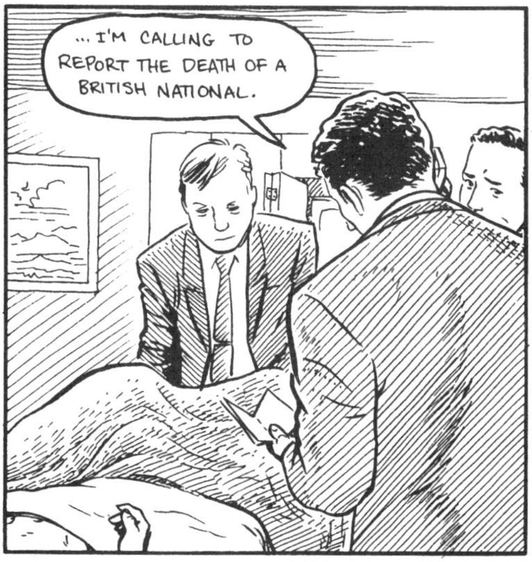
...I'M CALLING TO REPORT THE DEATH OF A BRITISH NATIONAL.

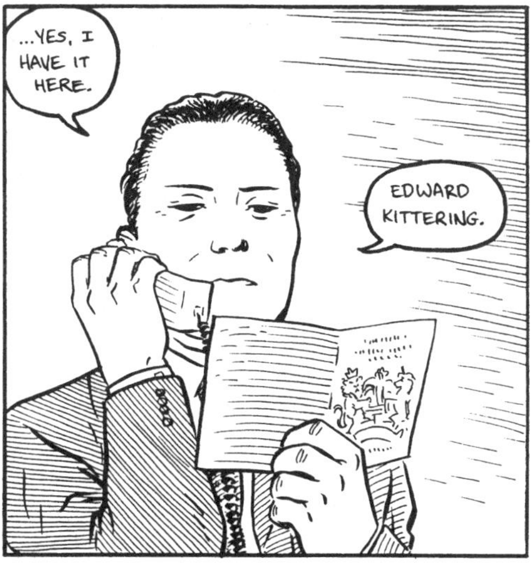
...YES, I HAVE IT HERE.
EDWARD KITTERING.

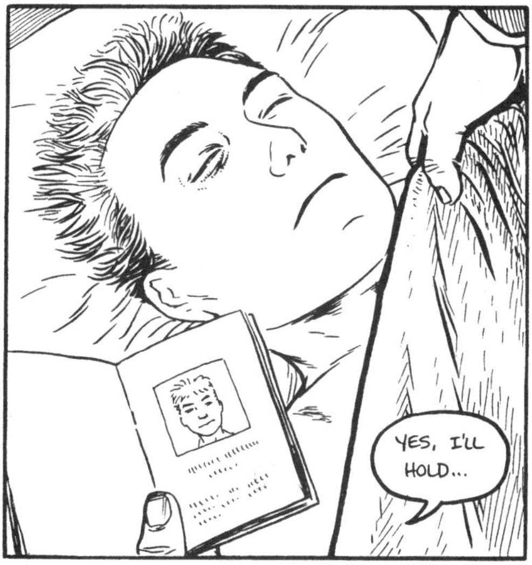
YES, I'LL HOLD...

LONDON

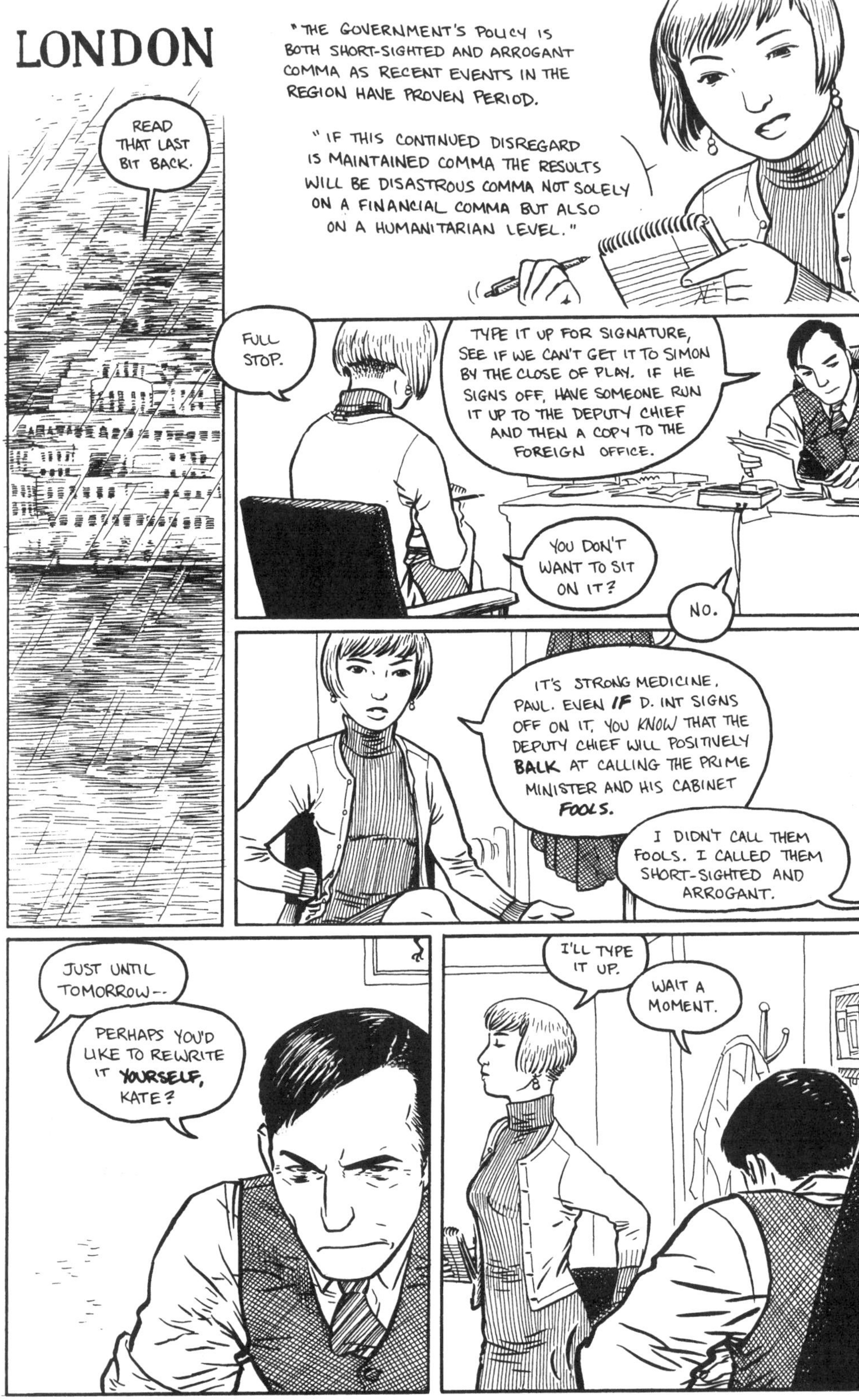

"THE GOVERNMENT'S POLICY IS BOTH SHORT-SIGHTED AND ARROGANT COMMA AS RECENT EVENTS IN THE REGION HAVE PROVEN PERIOD.
"IF THIS CONTINUED DISREGARD IS MAINTAINED COMMA THE RESULTS WILL BE DISASTROUS COMMA NOT SOLELY ON A FINANCIAL COMMA BUT ALSO ON A HUMANITARIAN LEVEL."
READ THAT LAST BIT BACK.
FULL STOP.
TYPE IT UP FOR SIGNATURE, SEE IF WE CAN'T GET IT TO SIMON BY THE CLOSE OF PLAY. IF HE SIGNS OFF, HAVE SOMEONE RUN IT UP TO THE DEPUTY CHIEF AND THEN A COPY TO THE FOREIGN OFFICE.
YOU DON'T WANT TO SIT ON IT?
NO.
IT'S STRONG MEDICINE, PAUL. EVEN IF D. INT SIGNS OFF ON IT, YOU KNOW THAT THE DEPUTY CHIEF WILL POSITIVELY BALK AT CALLING THE PRIME MINISTER AND HIS CABINET FOOLS.
I DIDN'T CALL THEM FOOLS. I CALLED THEM SHORT-SIGHTED AND ARROGANT.
JUST UNTIL TOMORROW--
PERHAPS YOU'D LIKE TO REWRITE IT YOURSELF, KATE?
I'LL TYPE IT UP.
WAIT A MOMENT.

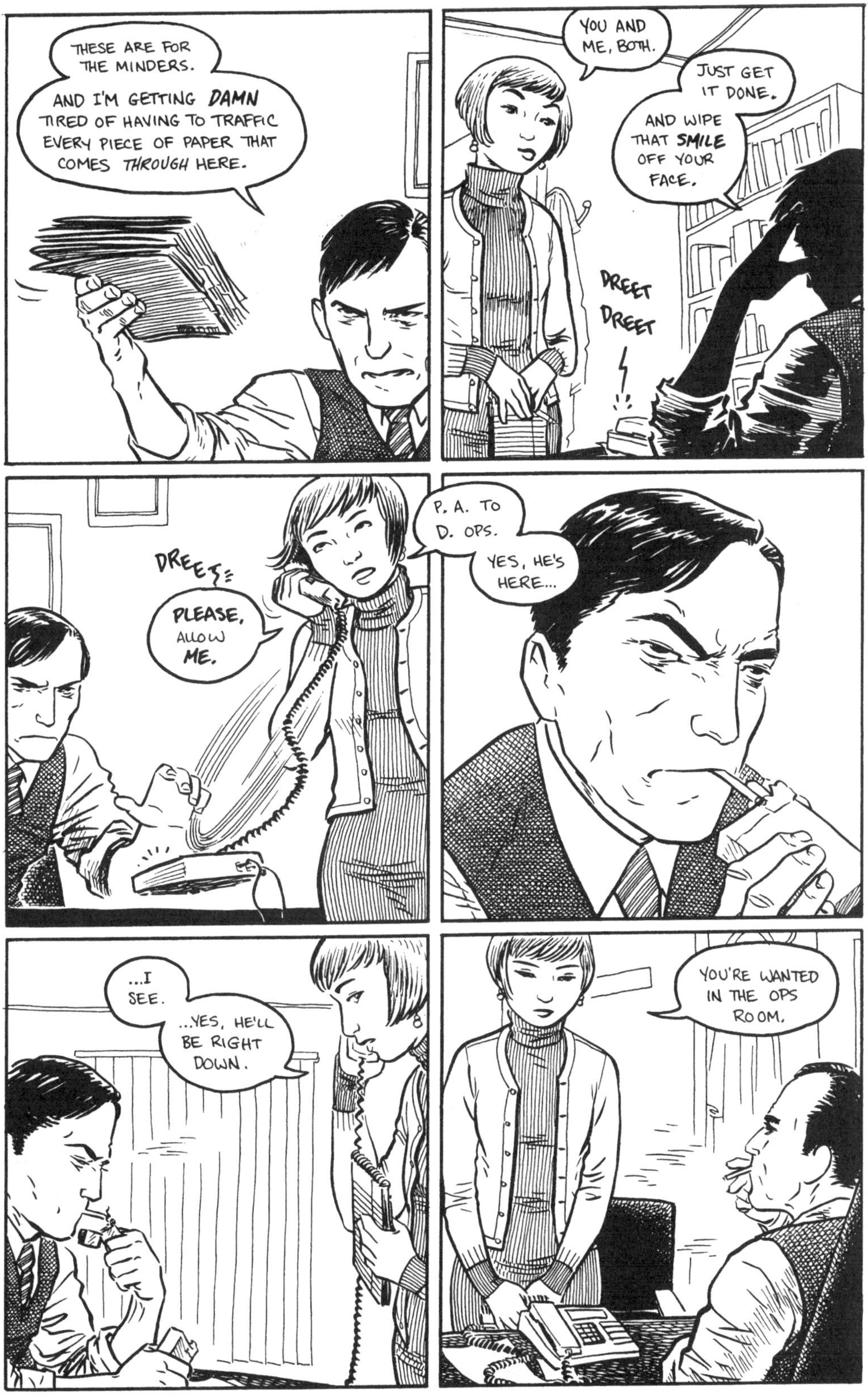
THESE ARE FOR THE MINDERS.
AND I'M GETTING DAMN TIRED OF HAVING TO TRAFFIC EVERY PIECE OF PAPER THAT COMES THROUGH HERE.
YOU AND ME, BOTH.
JUST GET IT DONE.
AND WIPE THAT SMILE OFF YOUR FACE.
DREET DREET
DREET
PLEASE, ALLOW ME.
P. A. TO D. OPS.
YES, HE'S HERE...
...I SEE.
...YES, HE'LL BE RIGHT DOWN.
YOU'RE WANTED IN THE OPS ROOM.

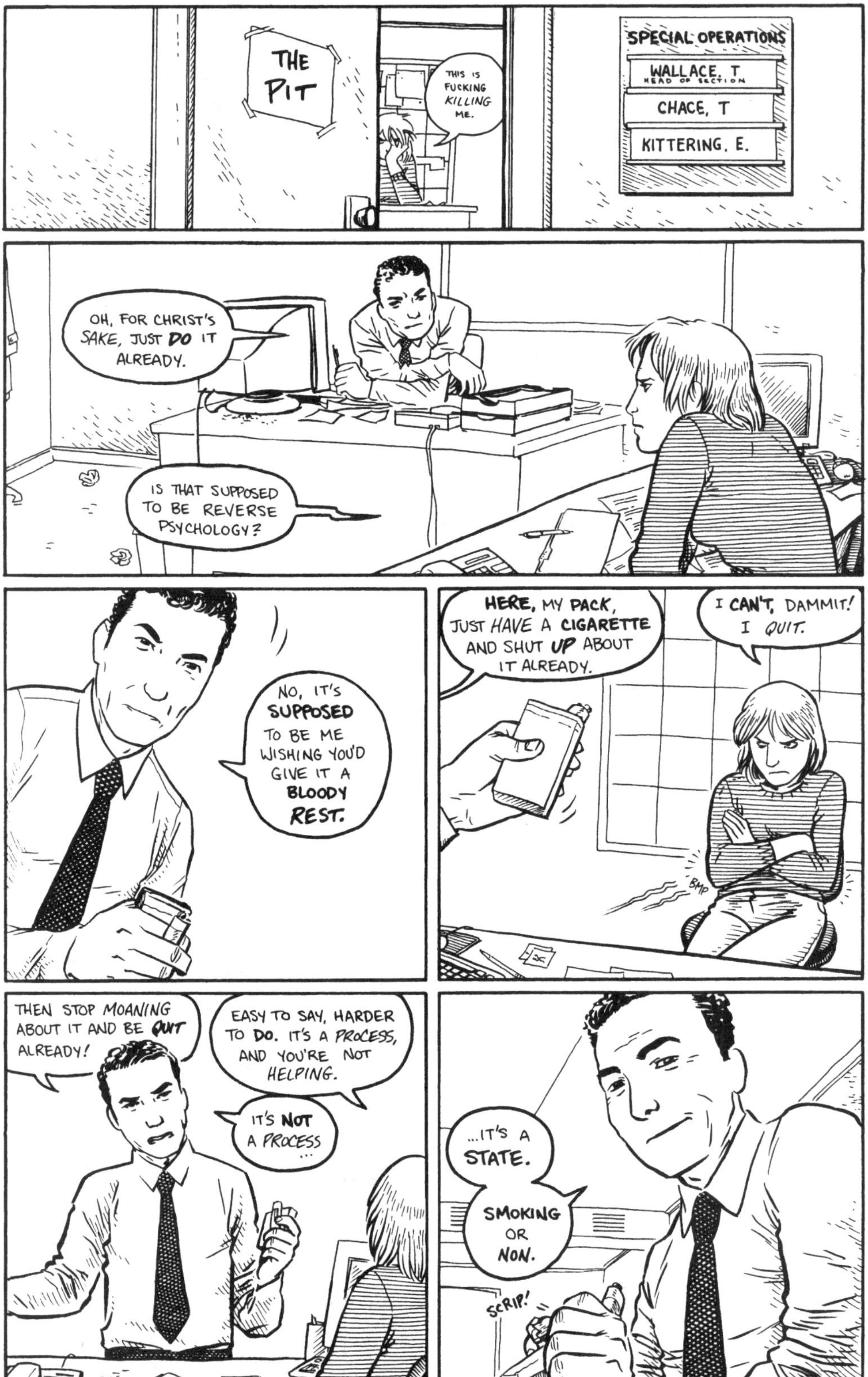
THE PIT
THIS IS FUCKING KILLING ME.
SPECIAL OPERATIONS
WALLACE, T
HEAD OF SECTION
CHACE, T
KITTERING, E.
OH, FOR CHRIST'S SAKE, JUST DO IT ALREADY.
IS THAT SUPPOSED TO BE REVERSE PSYCHOLOGY?
NO, IT'S SUPPOSED TO BE ME WISHING YOU'D GIVE IT A BLOODY REST.
HERE, MY PACK, JUST HAVE A CIGARETTE AND SHUT UP ABOUT IT ALREADY.
I CAN'T, DAMMIT! I QUIT.
BMP
THEN STOP MOANING ABOUT IT AND BE QUIT ALREADY!
EASY TO SAY, HARDER TO DO. IT'S A PROCESS, AND YOU'RE NOT HELPING.
IT'S NOT A PROCESS ...
...IT'S A STATE.
SMOKING OR NON.
SCRIP!

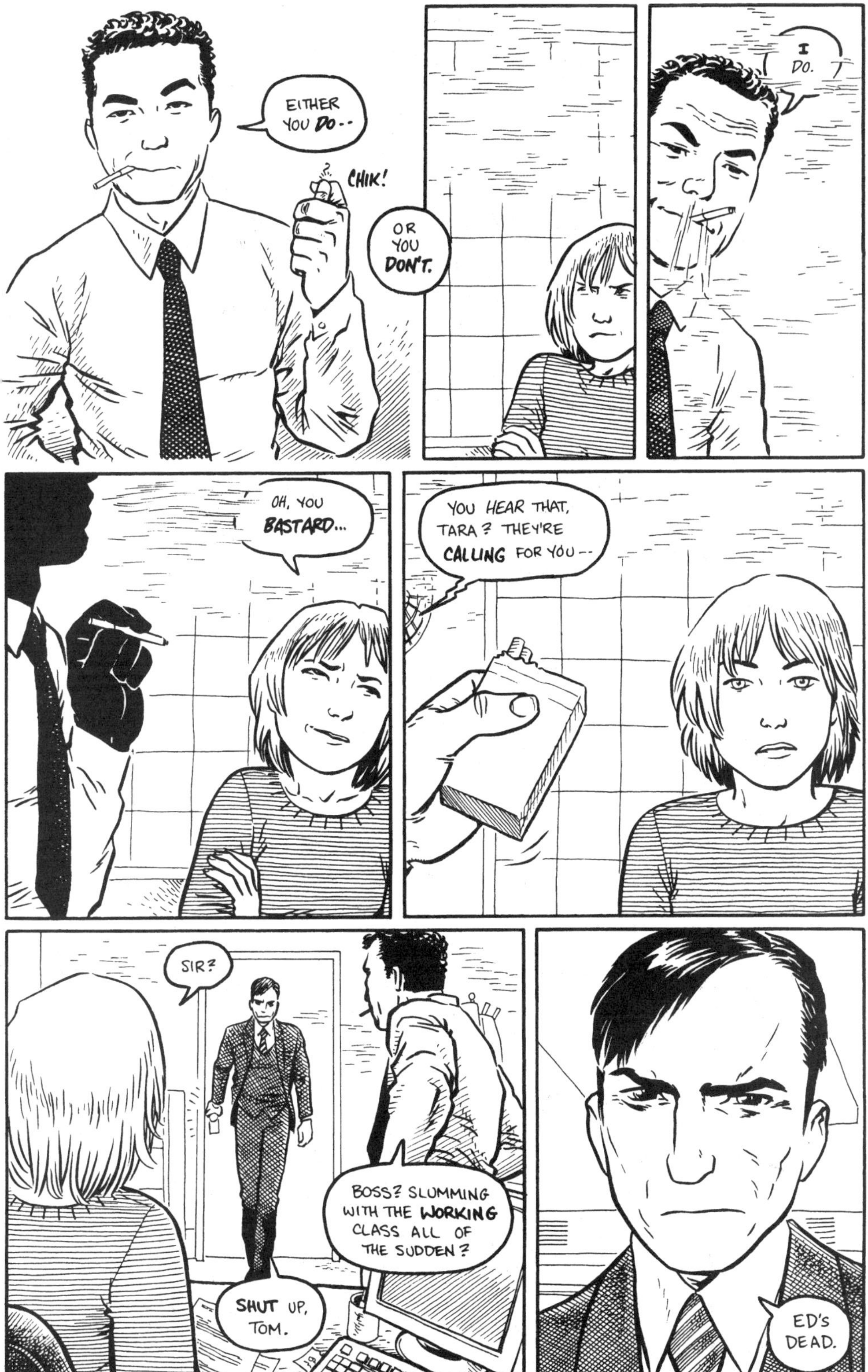
EITHER YOU DO--
CHIK!
OR YOU DON'T.
I DO.
OH, YOU BASTARD...
YOU HEAR THAT, TARA? THEY'RE CALLING FOR YOU--
SIR?
BOSS? SLUMMING WITH THE WORKING CLASS ALL OF THE SUDDEN?
SHUT UP, TOM.
ED'S DEAD.

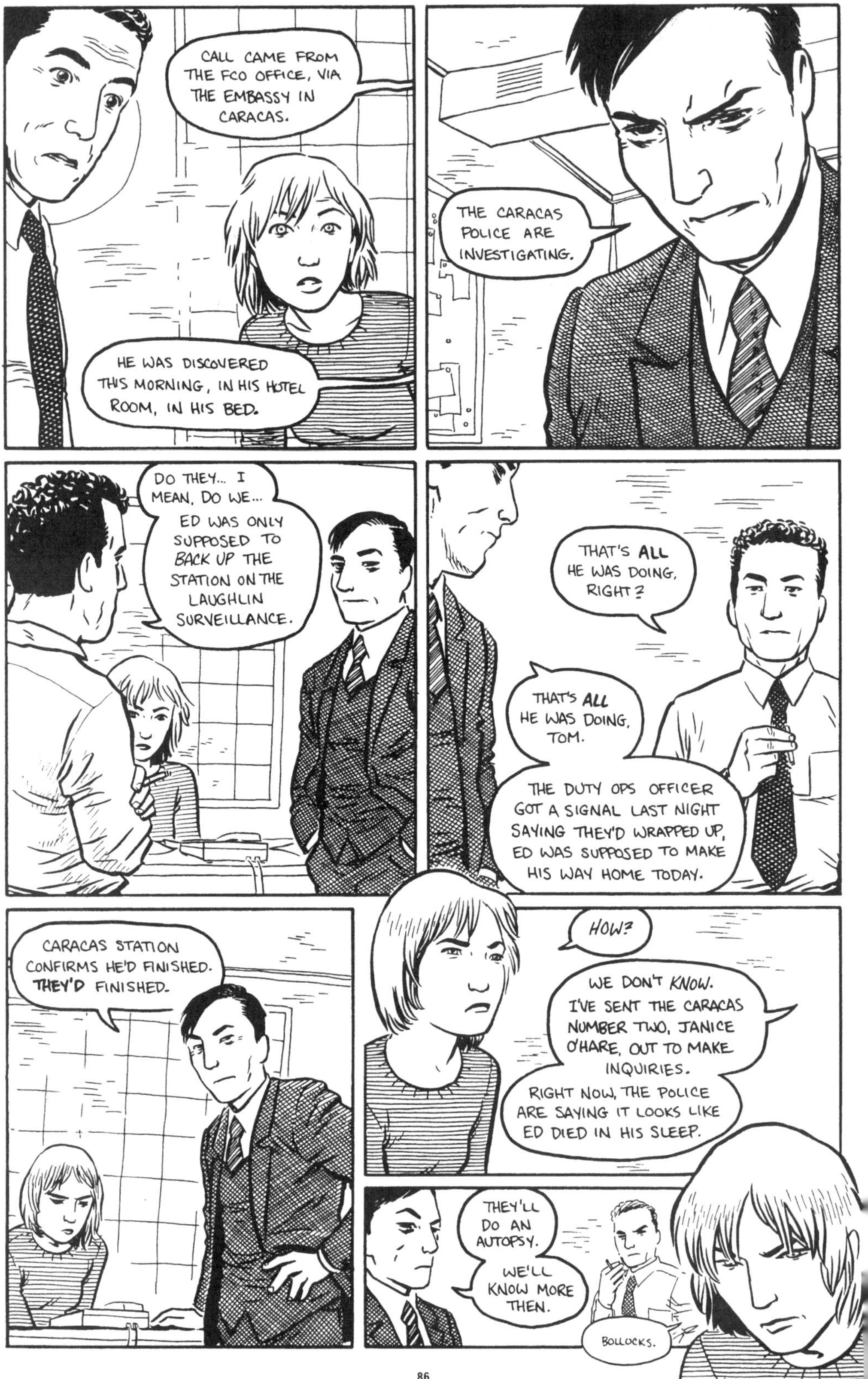
CALL CAME FROM THE FCO OFFICE, VIA THE EMBASSY IN CARACAS.
HE WAS DISCOVERED THIS MORNING, IN HIS HOTEL ROOM, IN HIS BED.
THE CARACAS POLICE ARE INVESTIGATING.
DO THEY... I MEAN, DO WE...
ED WAS ONLY SUPPOSED TO BACK UP THE STATION ON THE LAUGHLIN SURVEILLANCE.
THAT'S ALL HE WAS DOING, RIGHT?
THAT'S ALL HE WAS DOING, TOM.
THE DUTY OPS OFFICER GOT A SIGNAL LAST NIGHT SAYING THEY'D WRAPPED UP, ED WAS SUPPOSED TO MAKE HIS WAY HOME TODAY.
CARACAS STATION CONFIRMS HE'D FINISHED. THEY'D FINISHED.
HOW?
WE DON'T KNOW. I'VE SENT THE CARACAS NUMBER TWO, JANICE O'HARE, OUT TO MAKE INQUIRIES.
RIGHT NOW, THE POLICE ARE SAYING IT LOOKS LIKE ED DIED IN HIS SLEEP.
THEY'LL DO AN AUTOPSY.
WE'LL KNOW MORE THEN.
BOLLOCKS.

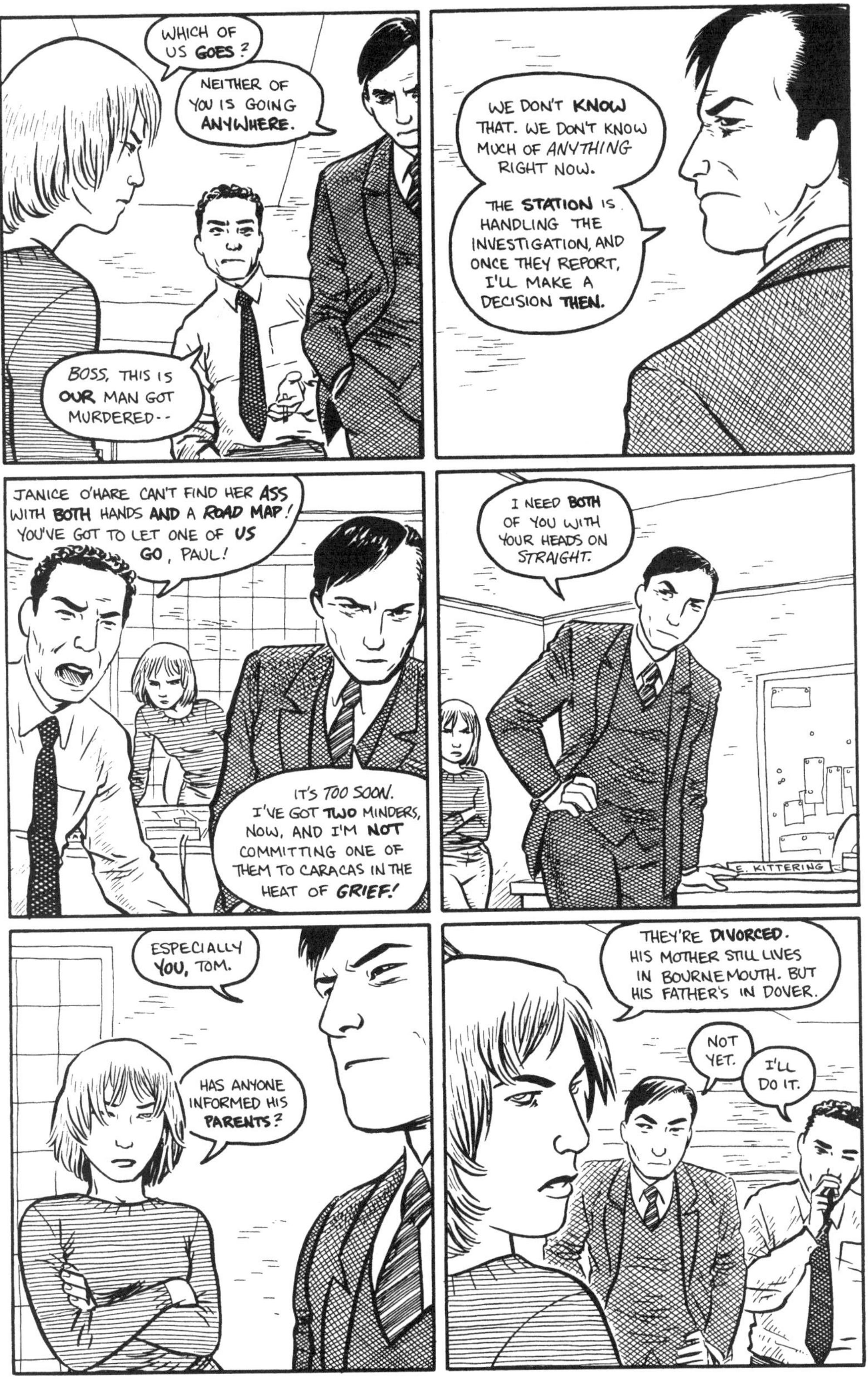
WHICH OF US GOES?
NEITHER OF YOU IS GOING ANYWHERE.
BOSS, THIS IS OUR MAN GOT MURDERED--
WE DON'T KNOW THAT. WE DON'T KNOW MUCH OF ANYTHING RIGHT NOW.
THE STATION IS HANDLING THE INVESTIGATION, AND ONCE THEY REPORT, I'LL MAKE A DECISION THEN.
JANICE O'HARE CAN'T FIND HER ASS WITH BOTH HANDS AND A ROAD MAP! YOU'VE GOT TO LET ONE OF US GO, PAUL!
IT'S TOO SOON. I'VE GOT TWO MINDERS, NOW, AND I'M NOT COMMITTING ONE OF THEM TO CARACAS IN THE HEAT OF GRIEF!
I NEED BOTH OF YOU WITH YOUR HEADS ON STRAIGHT.
E. KITTERING
ESPECIALLY YOU, TOM.
HAS ANYONE INFORMED HIS PARENTS?
THEY'RE DIVORCED. HIS MOTHER STILL LIVES IN BOURNEMOUTH. BUT HIS FATHER'S IN DOVER.
NOT YET.
I'LL DO IT.

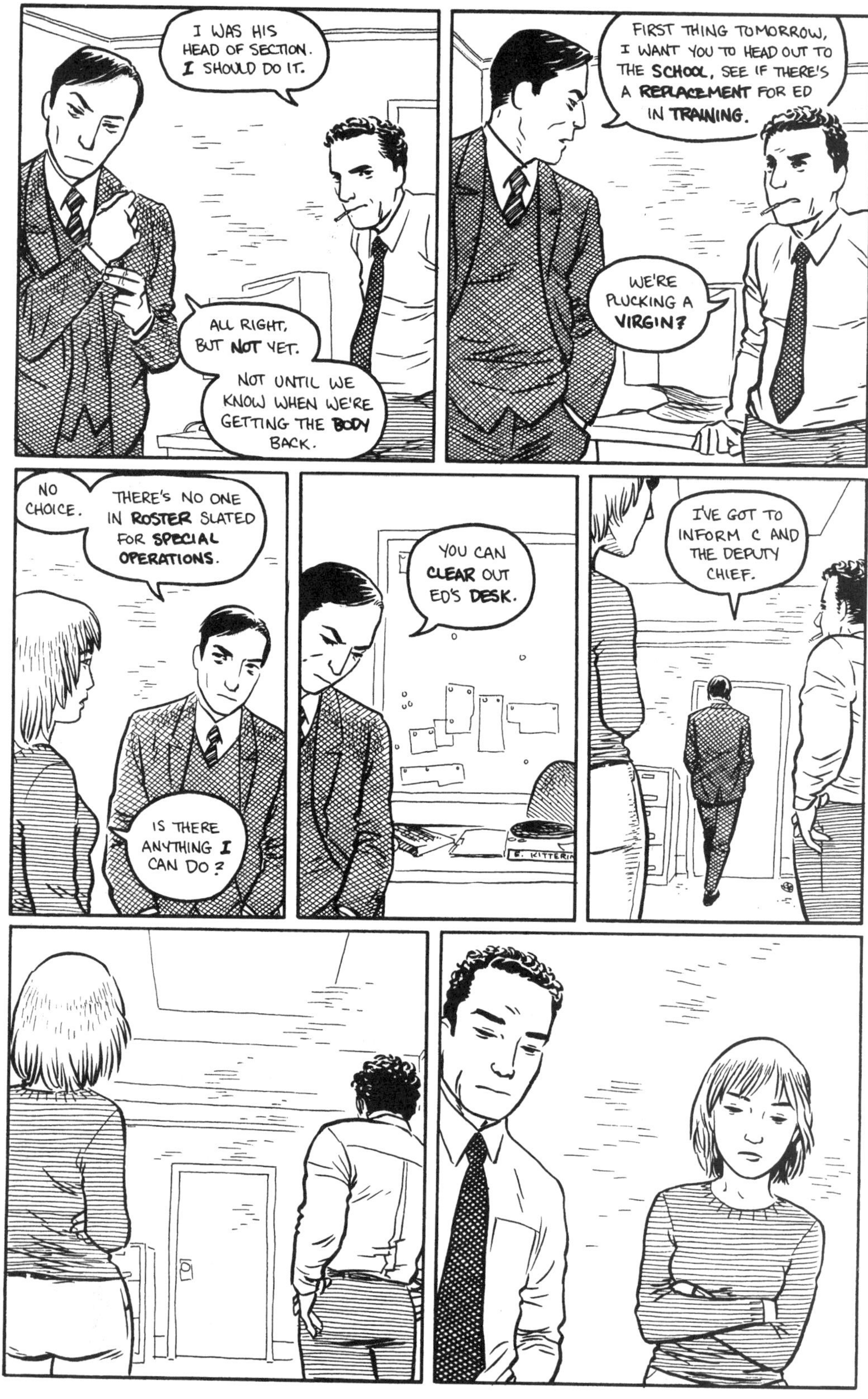
I WAS HIS HEAD OF SECTION. I SHOULD DO IT.
ALL RIGHT, BUT NOT YET.
NOT UNTIL WE KNOW WHEN WE'RE GETTING THE BODY BACK.
FIRST THING TOMORROW, I WANT YOU TO HEAD OUT TO THE SCHOOL, SEE IF THERE'S A REPLACEMENT FOR ED IN TRAINING.
WE'RE PLUCKING A VIRGIN?
NO CHOICE.
THERE'S NO ONE IN ROSTER SLATED FOR SPECIAL OPERATIONS.
IS THERE ANYTHING I CAN DO?
YOU CAN CLEAR OUT ED'S DESK.
E. KITTERIN
I'VE GOT TO INFORM C AND THE DEPUTY CHIEF.

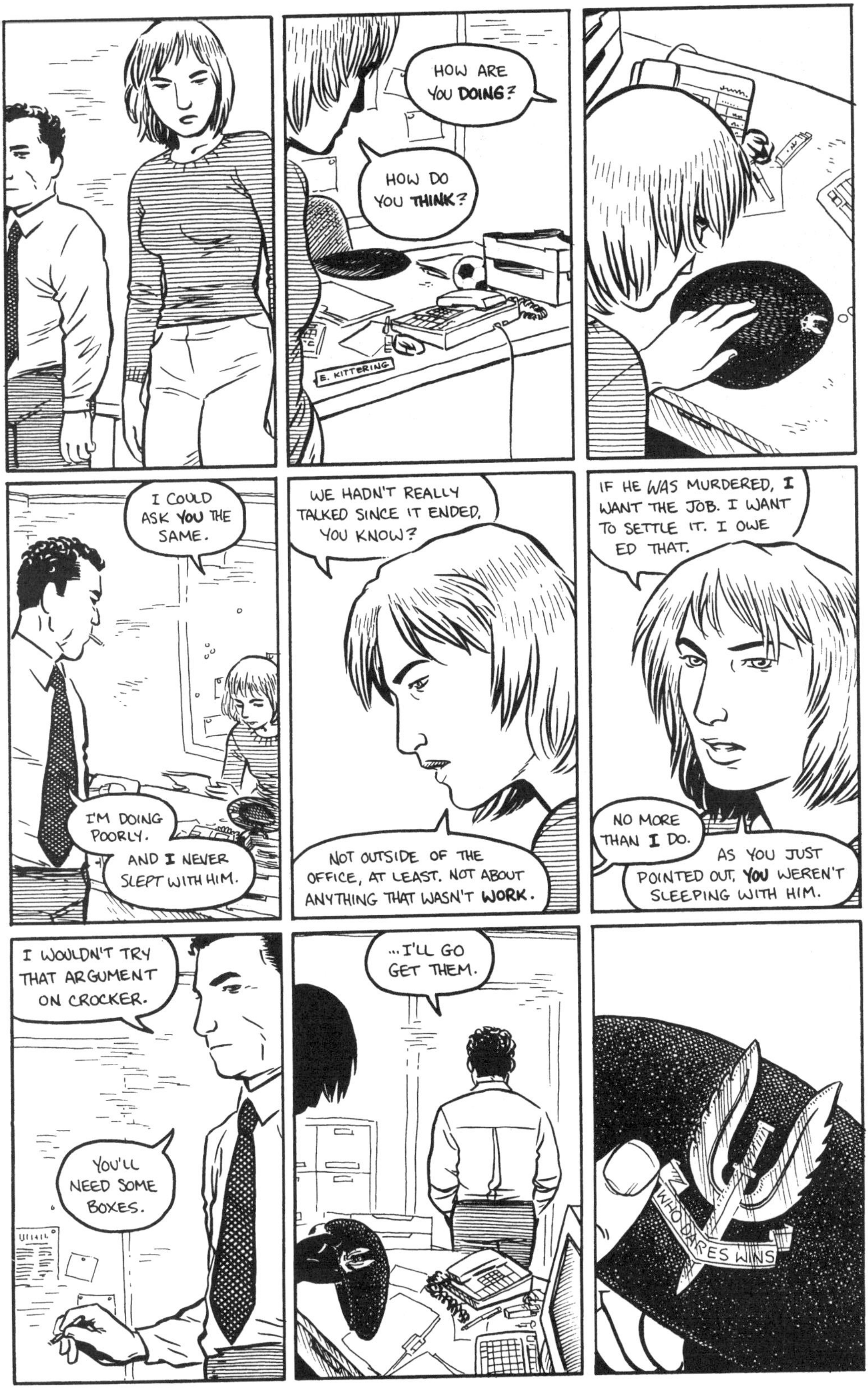
HOW ARE YOU DOING?
HOW DO YOU THINK?
E. KITTERING
I COULD ASK YOU THE SAME.
I'M DOING POORLY.
AND I NEVER SLEPT WITH HIM.
WE HADN'T REALLY TALKED SINCE IT ENDED, YOU KNOW?
NOT OUTSIDE OF THE OFFICE, AT LEAST. NOT ABOUT ANYTHING THAT WASN'T WORK.
IF HE WAS MURDERED, I WANT THE JOB. I WANT TO SETTLE IT. I OWE ED THAT.
NO MORE THAN I DO.
AS YOU JUST POINTED OUT, YOU WEREN'T SLEEPING WITH HIM.
I WOULDN'T TRY THAT ARGUMENT ON CROCKER.
YOU'LL NEED SOME BOXES.
...I'LL GO GET THEM.
WHO DARES WINS

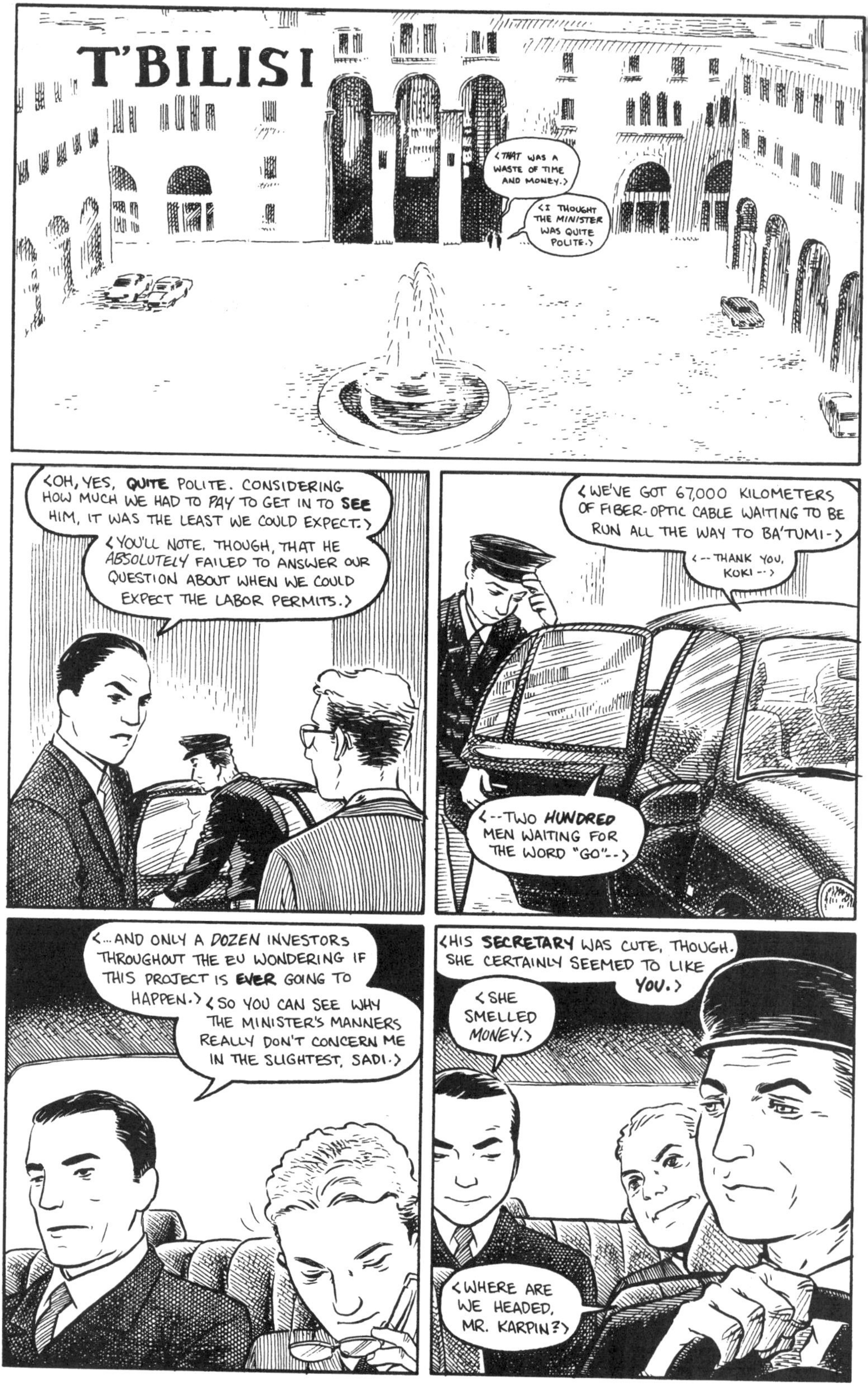
T'BILISI
<THAT WAS A WASTE OF TIME AND MONEY.>
<I THOUGHT THE MINISTER WAS QUITE POLITE.>
<OH, YES, QUITE POLITE. CONSIDERING HOW MUCH WE HAD TO PAY TO GET IN TO SEE HIM, IT WAS THE LEAST WE COULD EXPECT.>
<YOU'LL NOTE, THOUGH, THAT HE ABSOLUTELY FAILED TO ANSWER OUR QUESTION ABOUT WHEN WE COULD EXPECT THE LABOR PERMITS.>
<WE'VE GOT 67,000 KILOMETERS OF FIBER-OPTIC CABLE WAITING TO BE RUN ALL THE WAY TO BA'TUMI->
<--THANK YOU, KOKI-->
<--TWO HUNDRED MEN WAITING FOR THE WORD "GO"-->
<...AND ONLY A DOZEN INVESTORS THROUGHOUT THE EU WONDERING IF THIS PROJECT IS EVER GOING TO HAPPEN.>
<SO YOU CAN SEE WHY THE MINISTER'S MANNERS REALLY DON'T CONCERN ME IN THE SLIGHTEST, SADI.>
<HIS SECRETARY WAS CUTE, THOUGH. SHE CERTAINLY SEEMED TO LIKE YOU.>
<SHE SMELLED MONEY.>
<WHERE ARE WE HEADED, MR. KARPIN?>

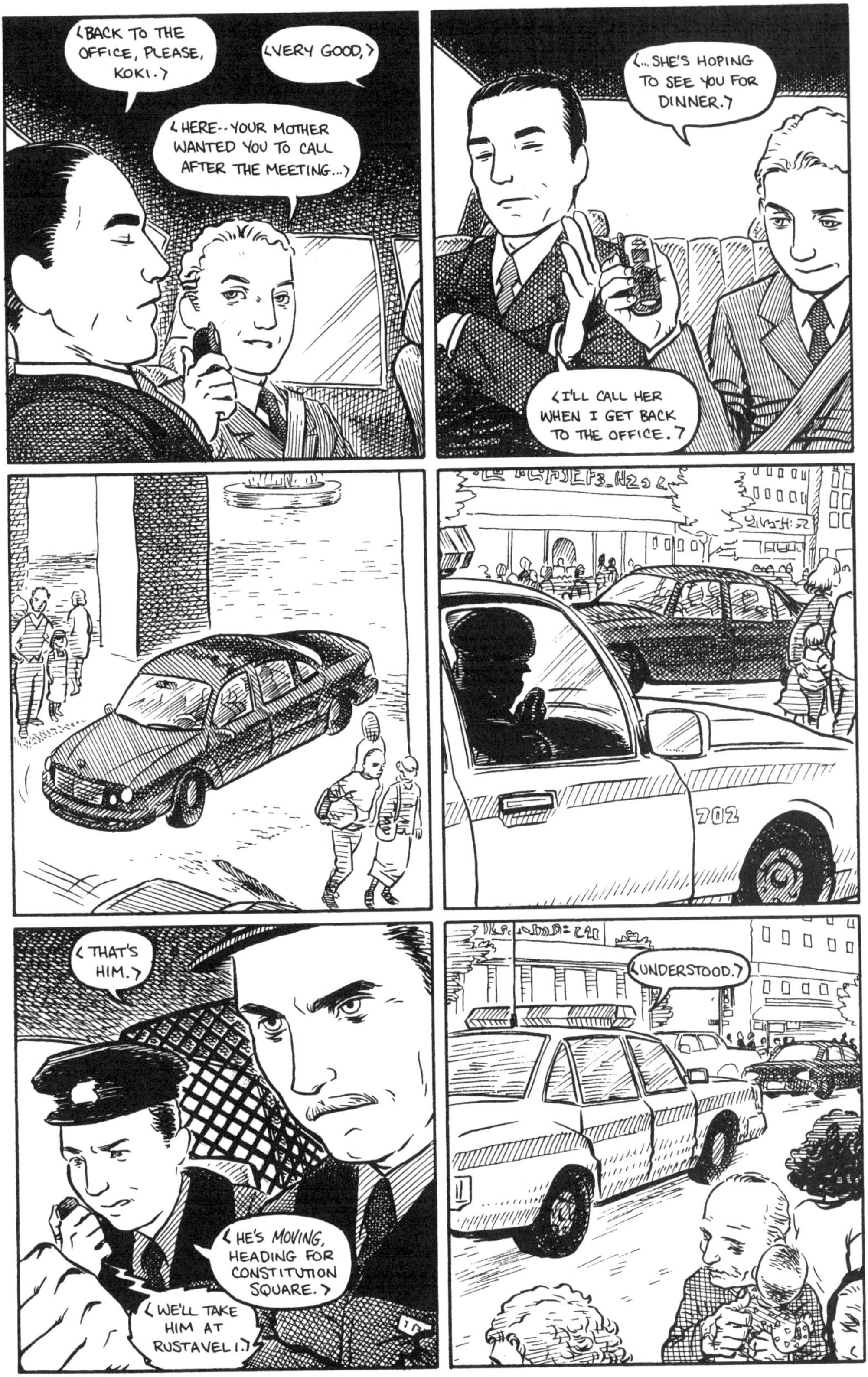
‹BACK TO THE OFFICE, PLEASE, KOKI.›
‹VERY GOOD.›
‹HERE--YOUR MOTHER WANTED YOU TO CALL AFTER THE MEETING...›
‹...SHE'S HOPING TO SEE YOU FOR DINNER.›
‹I'LL CALL HER WHEN I GET BACK TO THE OFFICE.›
702
‹THAT'S HIM.›
‹HE'S *MOVING*, HEADING FOR CONSTITUTION SQUARE.›
‹WE'LL TAKE HIM AT RUSTAVELI.›
‹UNDERSTOOD.›

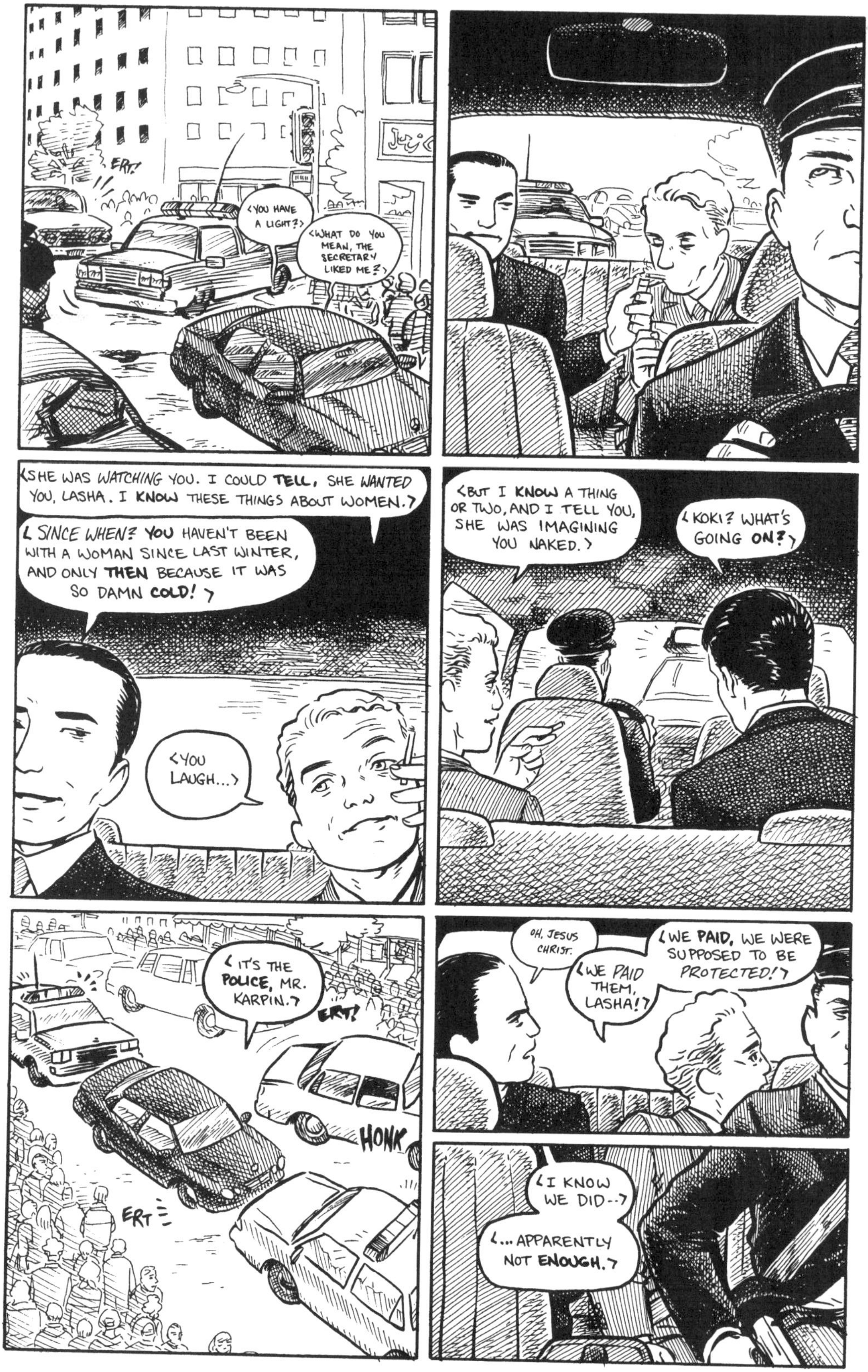
ERT!
<YOU HAVE A LIGHT?>
<WHAT DO YOU MEAN, THE SECRETARY LIKED ME?>
<SHE WAS WATCHING YOU. I COULD TELL, SHE WANTED YOU, LASHA. I KNOW THESE THINGS ABOUT WOMEN.>
<SINCE WHEN? YOU HAVEN'T BEEN WITH A WOMAN SINCE LAST WINTER, AND ONLY THEN BECAUSE IT WAS SO DAMN COLD!>
<YOU LAUGH...>
<BUT I KNOW A THING OR TWO, AND I TELL YOU, SHE WAS IMAGINING YOU NAKED.>
<KOKI? WHAT'S GOING ON?>
<IT'S THE POLICE, MR. KARPIN.>
ERT!
HONK
ERT
OH, JESUS CHRIST.
<WE PAID THEM, LASHA!>
<WE PAID, WE WERE SUPPOSED TO BE PROTECTED!>
<I KNOW WE DID-->
<...APPARENTLY NOT ENOUGH.>

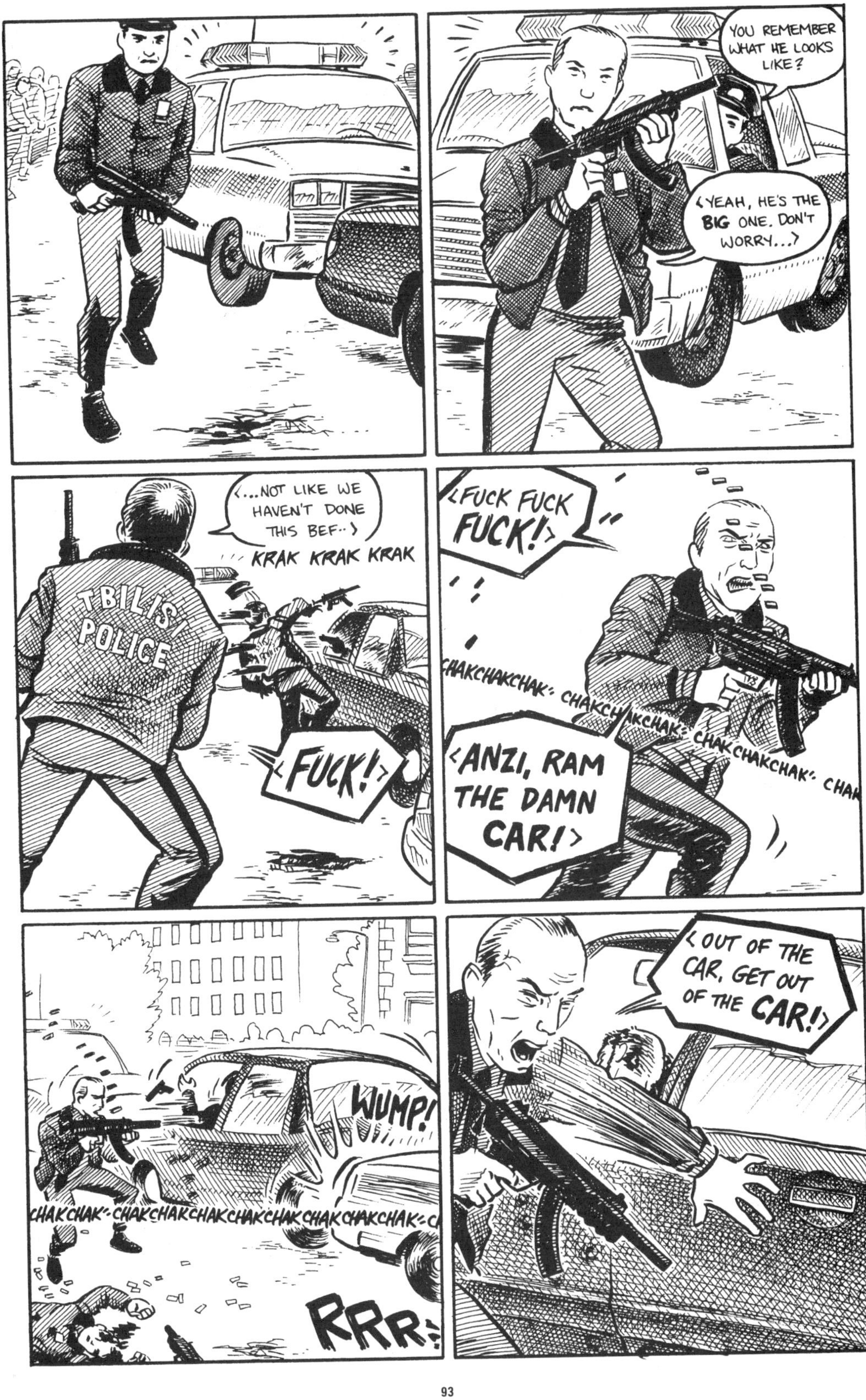

YOU REMEMBER WHAT HE LOOKS LIKE?
‹YEAH, HE'S THE **BIG** ONE. DON'T WORRY...›
‹...NOT LIKE WE HAVEN'T DONE THIS BEF..›
KRAK KRAK KRAK
‹FUCK!›
‹FUCK FUCK FUCK!›
CHAKCHAKCHAK- CHAKCHAKCHAK- CHAKCHAKCHAK- CHAK
‹ANZI, RAM THE DAMN CAR!›
WUMP!
CHAKCHAK- CHAKCHAKCHAKCHAKCHAKCHAKCHAKCHAK- C
RRR
‹OUT OF THE CAR, GET OUT OF THE CAR!›

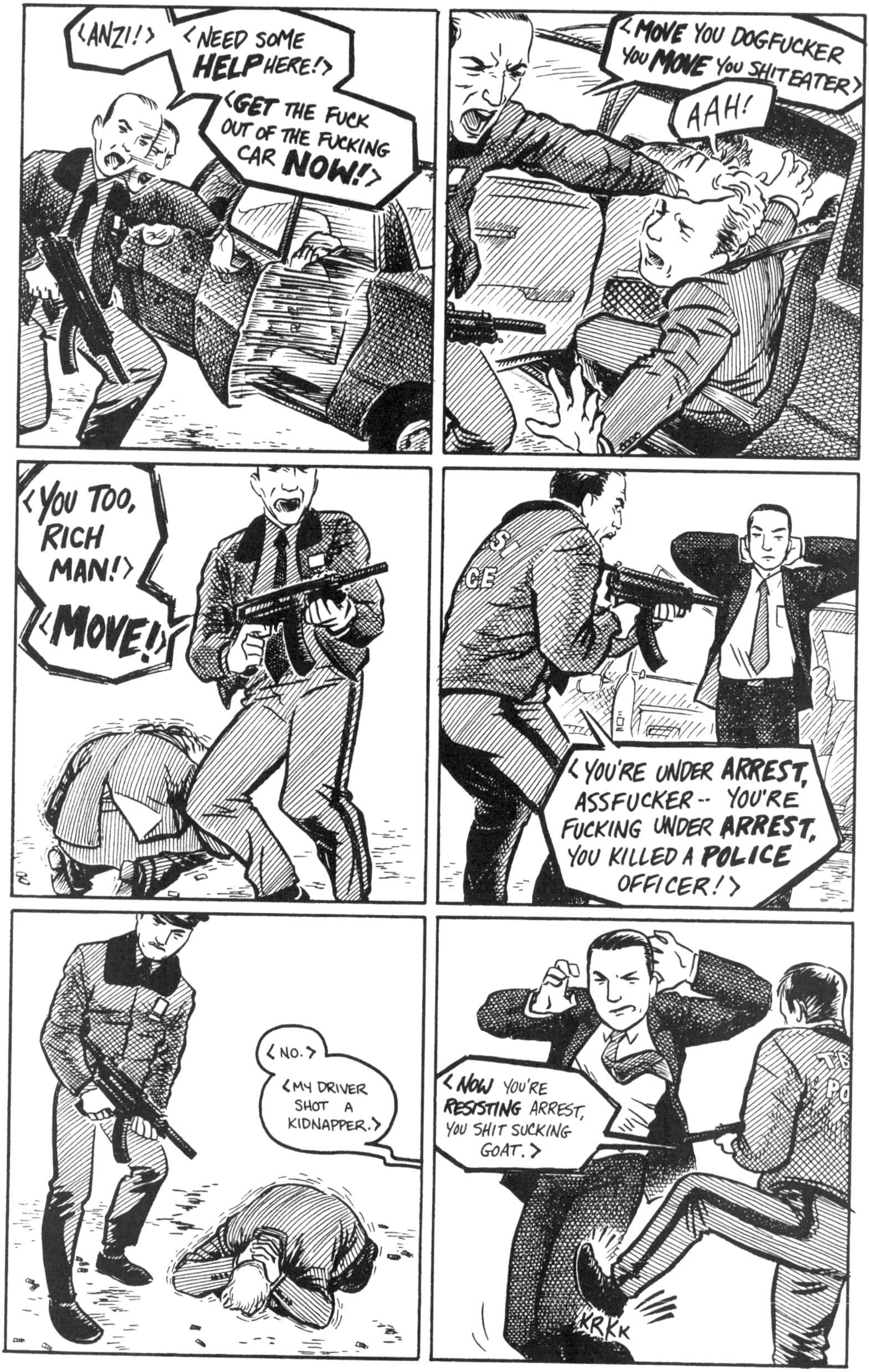
<ANZI!>
<NEED SOME HELP HERE!>
<GET THE FUCK OUT OF THE FUCKING CAR NOW!>
<MOVE YOU DOGFUCKER YOU MOVE YOU SHITEATER>
AAH!
<YOU TOO, RICH MAN!>
<MOVE!>
<YOU'RE UNDER ARREST, ASSFUCKER-- YOU'RE FUCKING UNDER ARREST, YOU KILLED A POLICE OFFICER!>
<NO.>
<MY DRIVER SHOT A KIDNAPPER.>
<NOW YOU'RE RESISTING ARREST, YOU SHIT SUCKING GOAT.>
KRKK

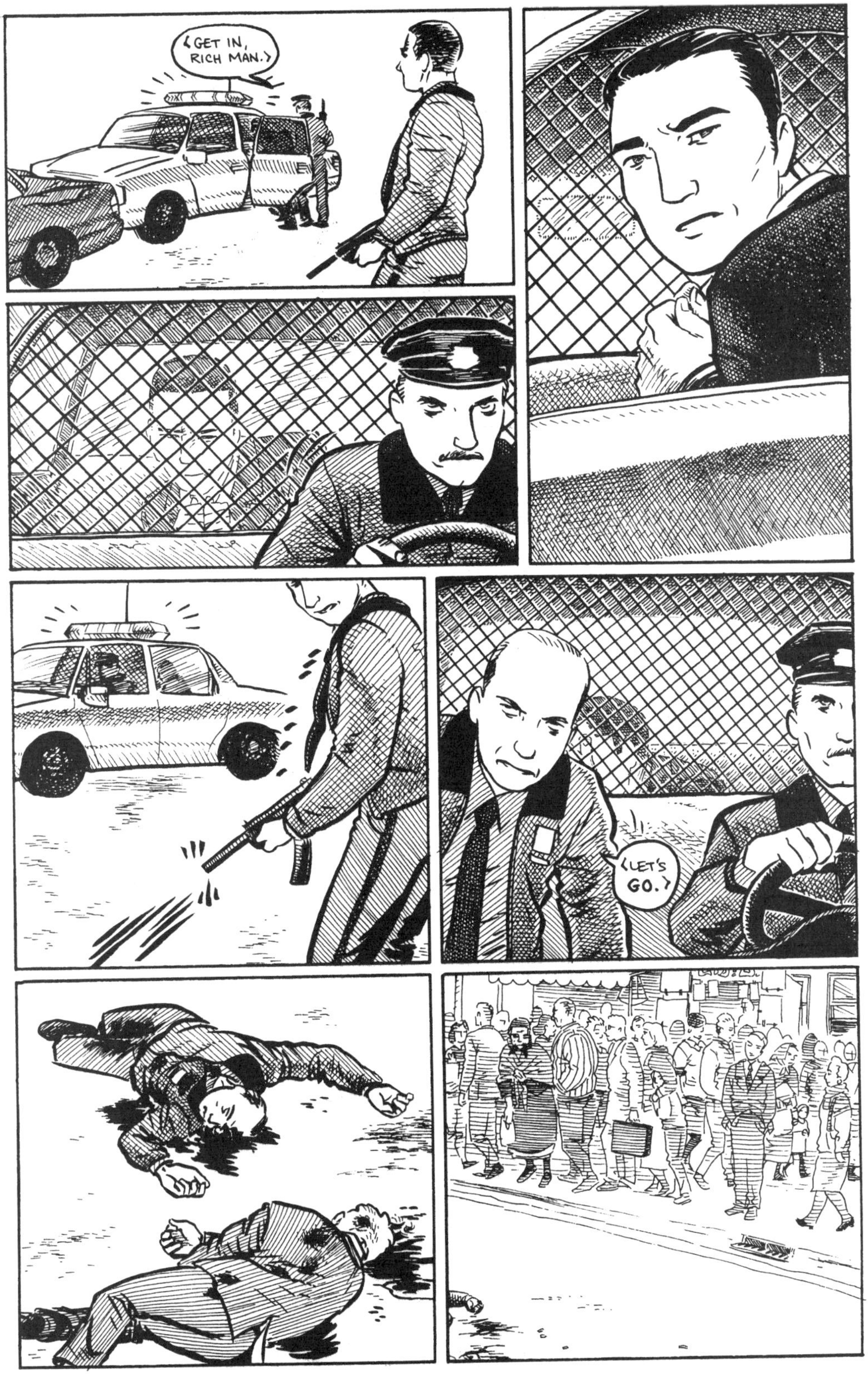
‹GET IN, RICH MAN.›
‹LET'S GO.›

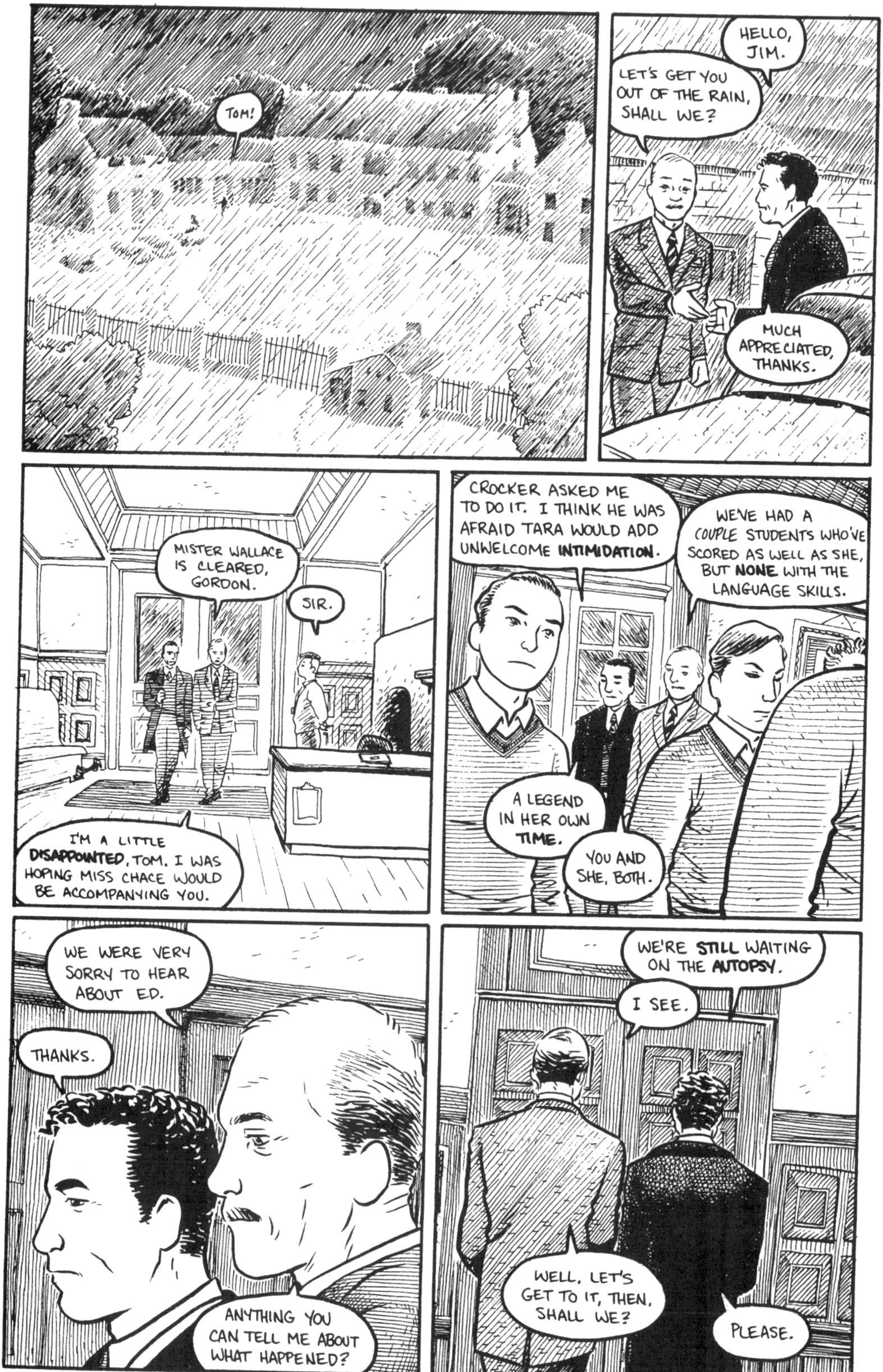

TOM!
HELLO, JIM.
LET'S GET YOU OUT OF THE RAIN, SHALL WE?
MUCH APPRECIATED, THANKS.
MISTER WALLACE IS CLEARED, GORDON.
SIR.
I'M A LITTLE DISAPPOINTED, TOM. I WAS HOPING MISS CHACE WOULD BE ACCOMPANYING YOU.
CROCKER ASKED ME TO DO IT. I THINK HE WAS AFRAID TARA WOULD ADD UNWELCOME INTIMIDATION.
WE'VE HAD A COUPLE STUDENTS WHO'VE SCORED AS WELL AS SHE, BUT NONE WITH THE LANGUAGE SKILLS.
A LEGEND IN HER OWN TIME.
YOU AND SHE, BOTH.
WE WERE VERY SORRY TO HEAR ABOUT ED.
THANKS.
ANYTHING YOU CAN TELL ME ABOUT WHAT HAPPENED?
WE'RE STILL WAITING ON THE AUTOPSY.
I SEE.
WELL, LET'S GET TO IT, THEN, SHALL WE?
PLEASE.

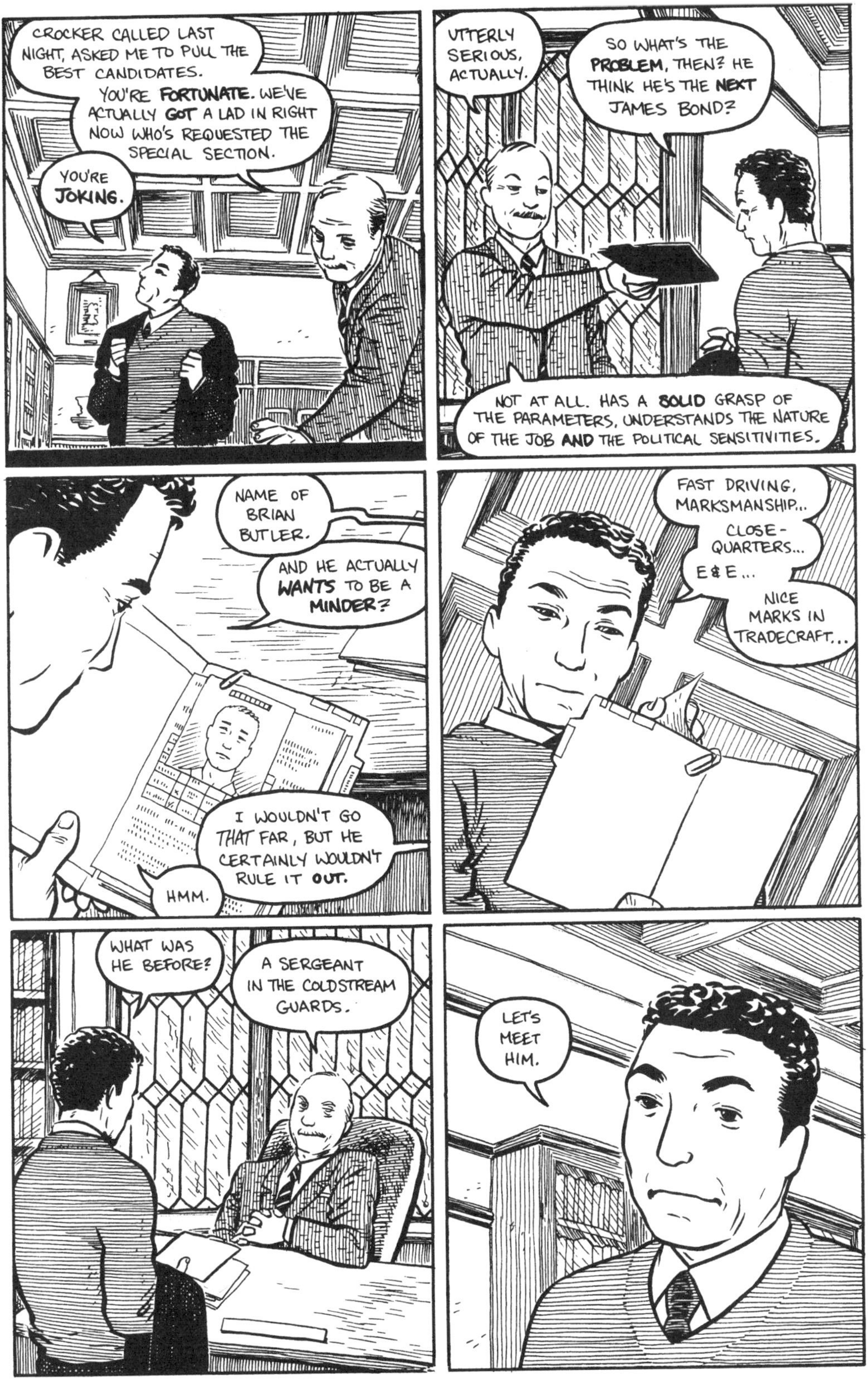
CROCKER CALLED LAST NIGHT, ASKED ME TO PULL THE BEST CANDIDATES.
YOU'RE **FORTUNATE**. WE'VE ACTUALLY **GOT** A LAD IN RIGHT NOW WHO'S REQUESTED THE SPECIAL SECTION.
YOU'RE **JOKING**.
UTTERLY SERIOUS, ACTUALLY.
SO WHAT'S THE **PROBLEM**, THEN? HE THINK HE'S THE **NEXT** JAMES BOND?
NOT AT ALL. HAS A **SOLID** GRASP OF THE PARAMETERS, UNDERSTANDS THE NATURE OF THE JOB **AND** THE POLITICAL SENSITIVITIES.
NAME OF BRIAN BUTLER.
AND HE ACTUALLY **WANTS** TO BE A **MINDER**?
I WOULDN'T GO *THAT* FAR, BUT HE CERTAINLY WOULDN'T RULE IT **OUT**.
HMM.
FAST DRIVING, MARKSMANSHIP...
CLOSE-QUARTERS...
E&E...
NICE MARKS IN TRADECRAFT...
WHAT WAS HE BEFORE?
A SERGEANT IN THE COLDSTREAM GUARDS.
LET'S MEET HIM.

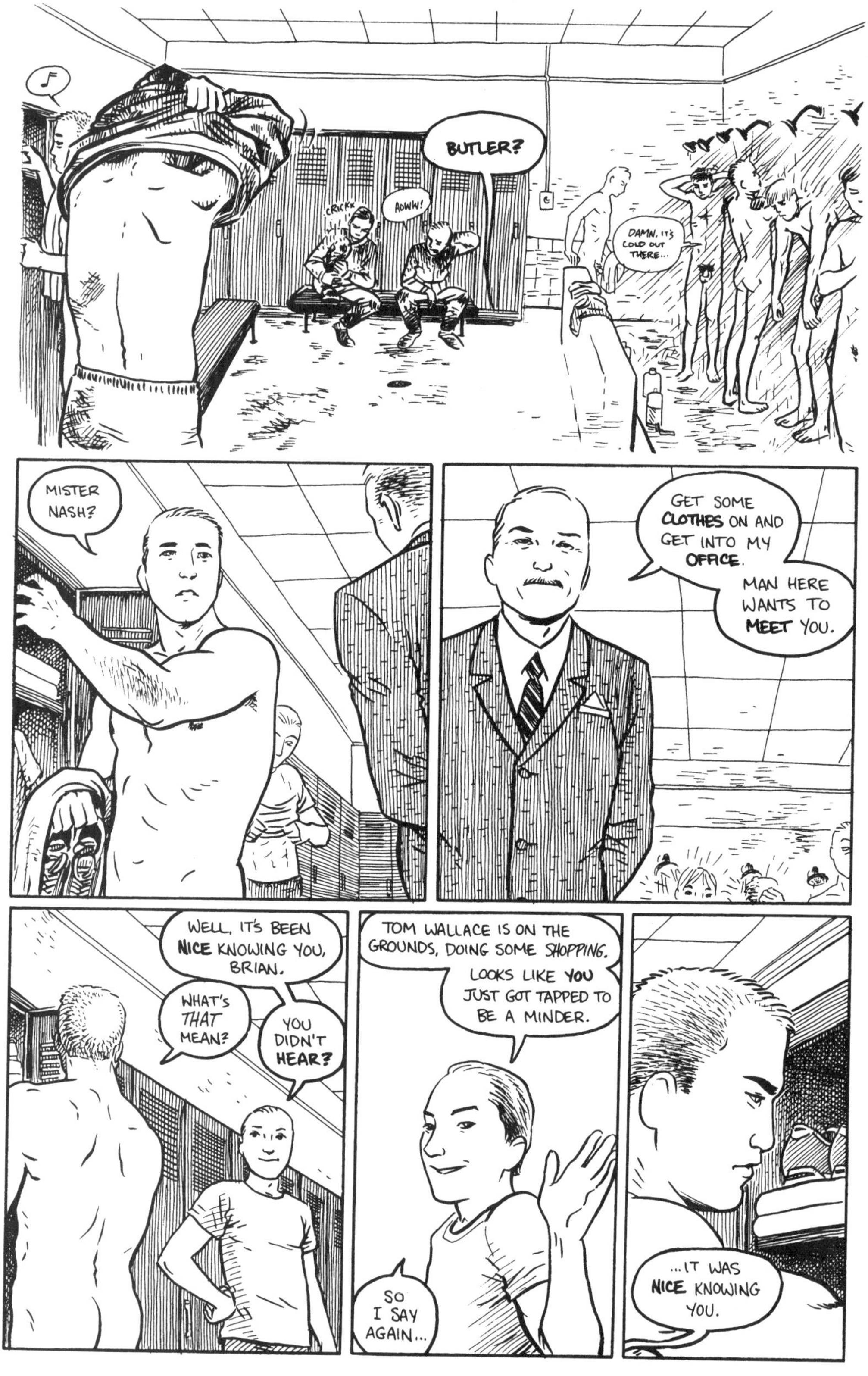
♪
BUTLER?
CRICKK
AOWW!
DAMN, IT'S COLD OUT THERE...
MISTER NASH?
GET SOME CLOTHES ON AND GET INTO MY OFFICE.
MAN HERE WANTS TO MEET YOU.
WELL, IT'S BEEN NICE KNOWING YOU, BRIAN.
WHAT'S THAT MEAN?
YOU DIDN'T HEAR?
TOM WALLACE IS ON THE GROUNDS, DOING SOME SHOPPING.
LOOKS LIKE YOU JUST GOT TAPPED TO BE A MINDER.
SO I SAY AGAIN...
...IT WAS NICE KNOWING YOU.

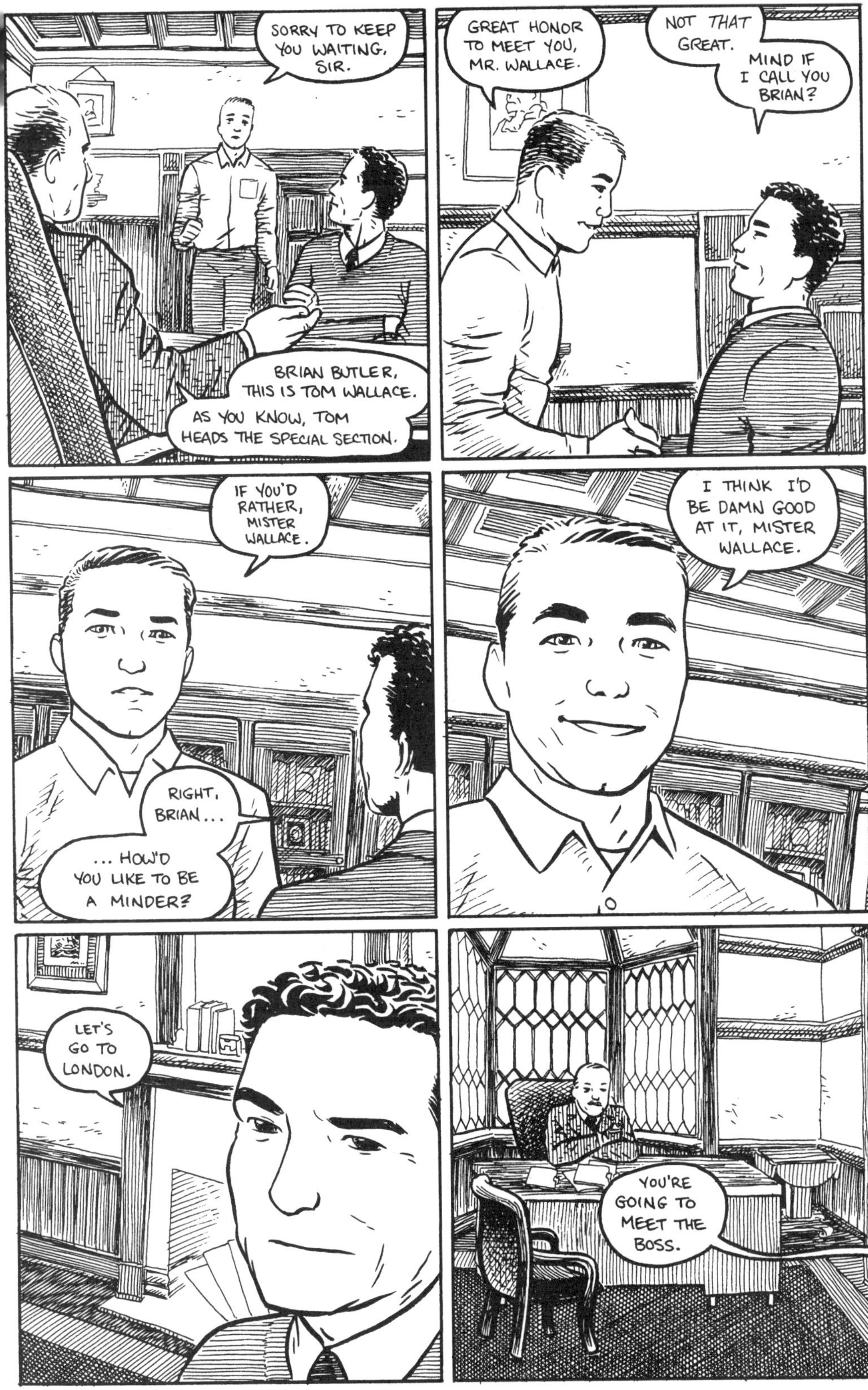
SORRY TO KEEP YOU WAITING, SIR.
BRIAN BUTLER, THIS IS TOM WALLACE.
AS YOU KNOW, TOM HEADS THE SPECIAL SECTION.
GREAT HONOR TO MEET YOU, MR. WALLACE.
NOT THAT GREAT.
MIND IF I CALL YOU BRIAN?
IF YOU'D RATHER, MISTER WALLACE.
RIGHT, BRIAN...
... HOW'D YOU LIKE TO BE A MINDER?
I THINK I'D BE DAMN GOOD AT IT, MISTER WALLACE.
LET'S GO TO LONDON.
YOU'RE GOING TO MEET THE BOSS.

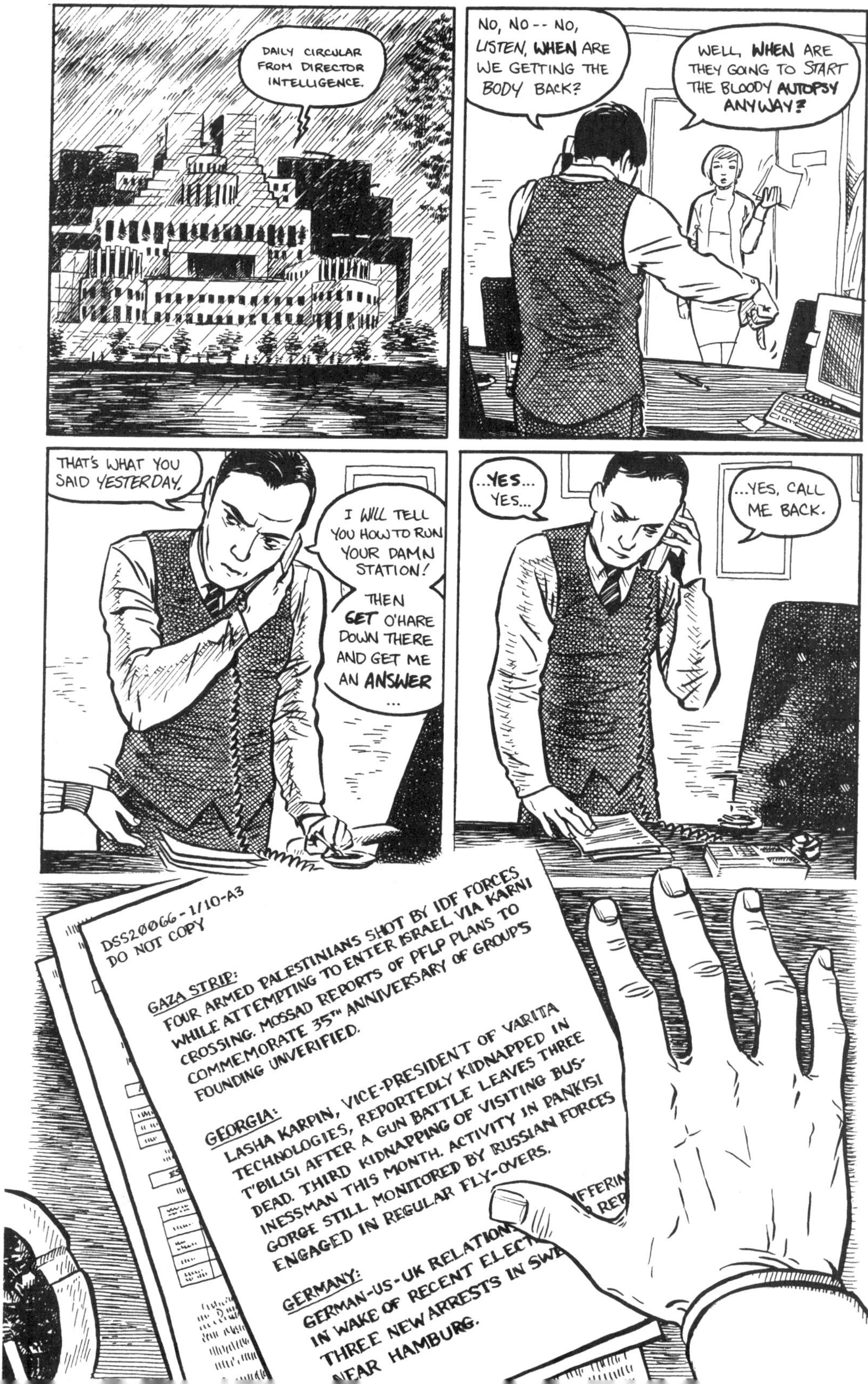

DAILY CIRCULAR FROM DIRECTOR INTELLIGENCE.
NO, NO -- NO, LISTEN, WHEN ARE WE GETTING THE BODY BACK?
WELL, WHEN ARE THEY GOING TO START THE BLOODY AUTOPSY ANYWAY?
THAT'S WHAT YOU SAID YESTERDAY.
I WILL TELL YOU HOW TO RUN YOUR DAMN STATION!
THEN GET O'HARE DOWN THERE AND GET ME AN ANSWER ...
...YES... YES...
...YES, CALL ME BACK.
DSS20066-1/10-A3
DO NOT COPY
GAZA STRIP:
FOUR ARMED PALESTINIANS SHOT BY IDF FORCES WHILE ATTEMPTING TO ENTER ISRAEL VIA KARNI CROSSING. MOSSAD REPORTS OF PFLP PLANS TO COMMEMORATE 35TH ANNIVERSARY OF GROUP'S FOUNDING UNVERIFIED.
GEORGIA:
LASHA KARPIN, VICE-PRESIDENT OF VARITA TECHNOLOGIES, REPORTEDLY KIDNAPPED IN T'BILISI AFTER A GUN BATTLE LEAVES THREE DEAD. THIRD KIDNAPPING OF VISITING BUSINESSMAN THIS MONTH. ACTIVITY IN PANKISI GORGE STILL MONITORED BY RUSSIAN FORCES ENGAGED IN REGULAR FLY-OVERS.
GERMANY:
GERMAN-US-UK RELATION
IN WAKE OF RECENT ELECT
THREE NEW ARRESTS IN SW
NEAR HAMBURG.

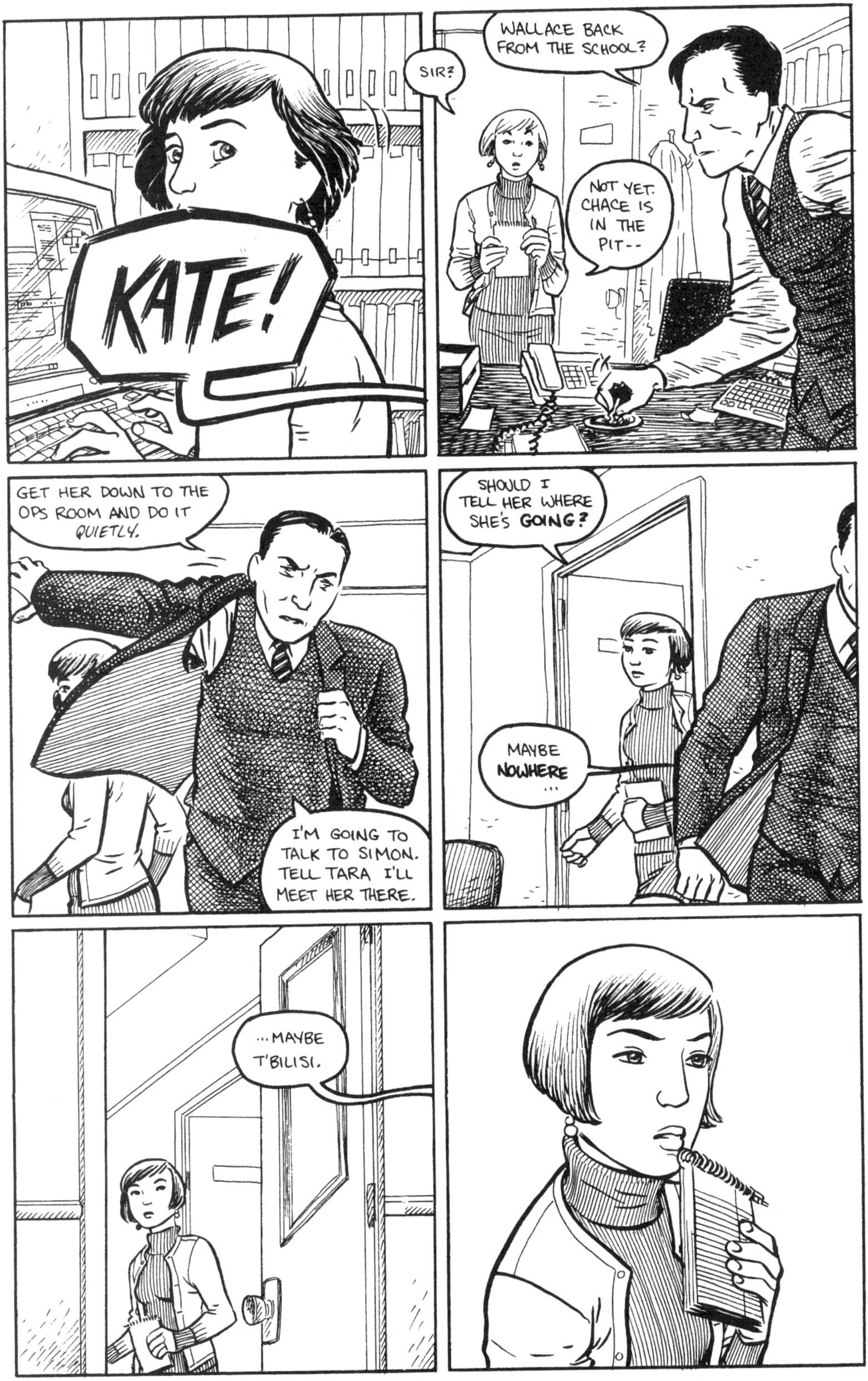
KATE!
SIR?
WALLACE BACK FROM THE SCHOOL?
NOT YET. CHACE IS IN THE PIT--
GET HER DOWN TO THE OPS ROOM AND DO IT QUIETLY.
I'M GOING TO TALK TO SIMON. TELL TARA I'LL MEET HER THERE.
SHOULD I TELL HER WHERE SHE'S GOING?
MAYBE NOWHERE ...
...MAYBE T'BILISI.

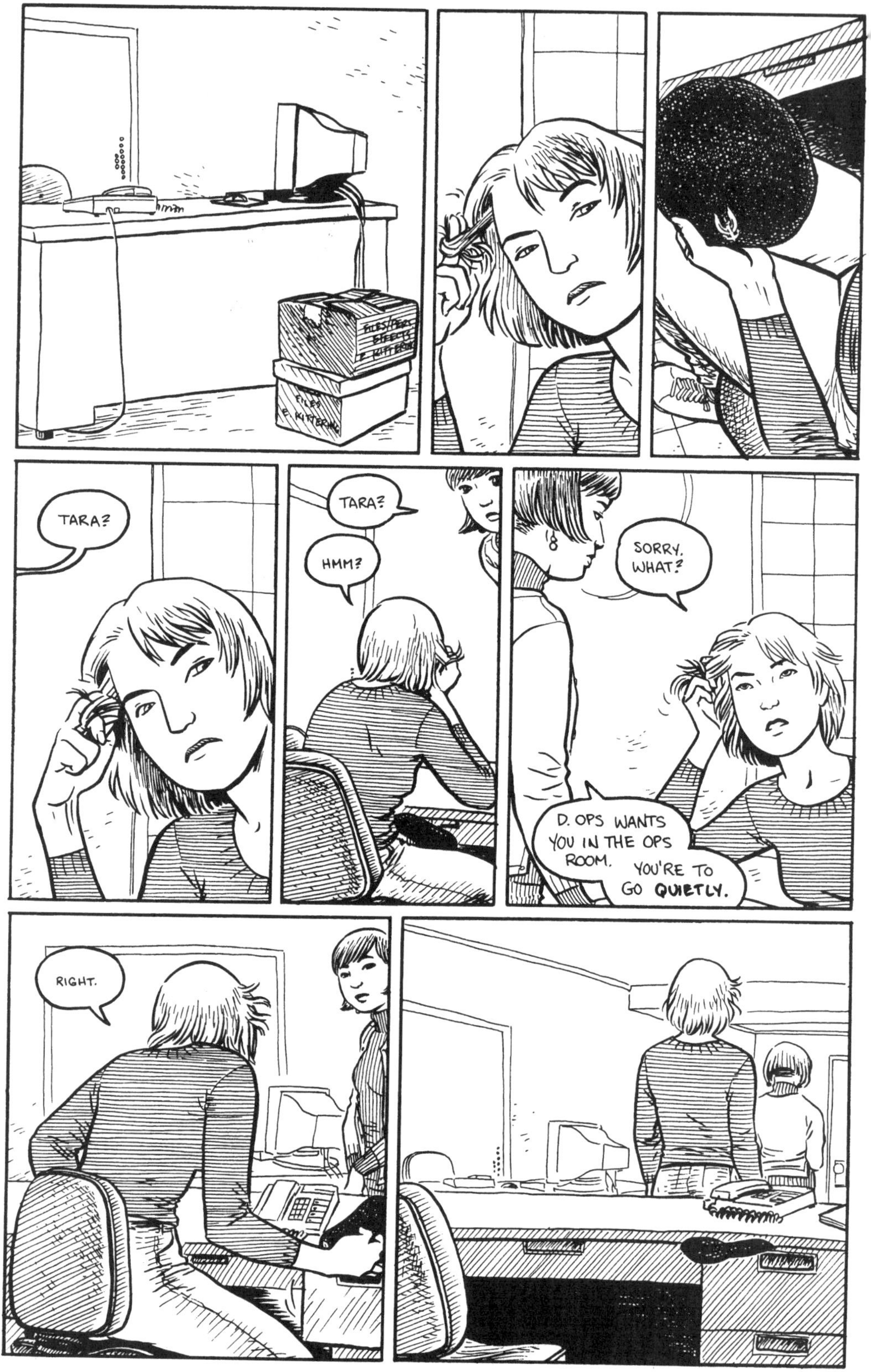
TARA?
TARA?
HMM?
SORRY. WHAT?
D. OPS WANTS YOU IN THE OPS ROOM.
YOU'RE TO GO **QUIETLY.**
RIGHT.

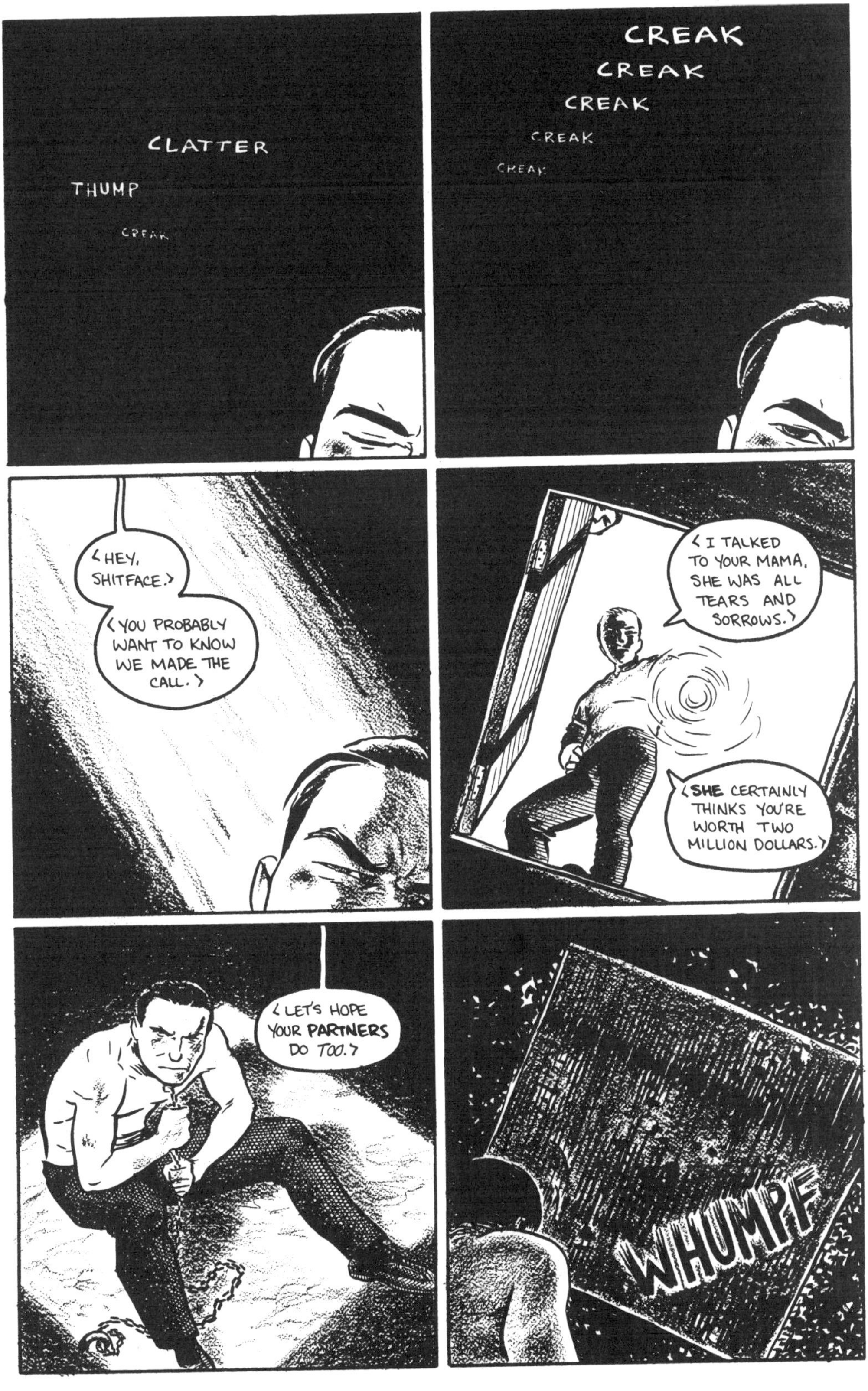
CLATTER
THUMP
CREAK
CREAK
CREAK
CREAK
CREAK
CREAK
‹HEY, SHITFACE.›
‹YOU PROBABLY WANT TO KNOW WE MADE THE CALL.›
‹I TALKED TO YOUR MAMA, SHE WAS ALL TEARS AND SORROWS.›
‹**SHE** CERTAINLY THINKS YOU'RE WORTH TWO MILLION DOLLARS.›
‹LET'S HOPE YOUR **PARTNERS** DO *TOO*.›
WHUMPF

CHAPTER 2

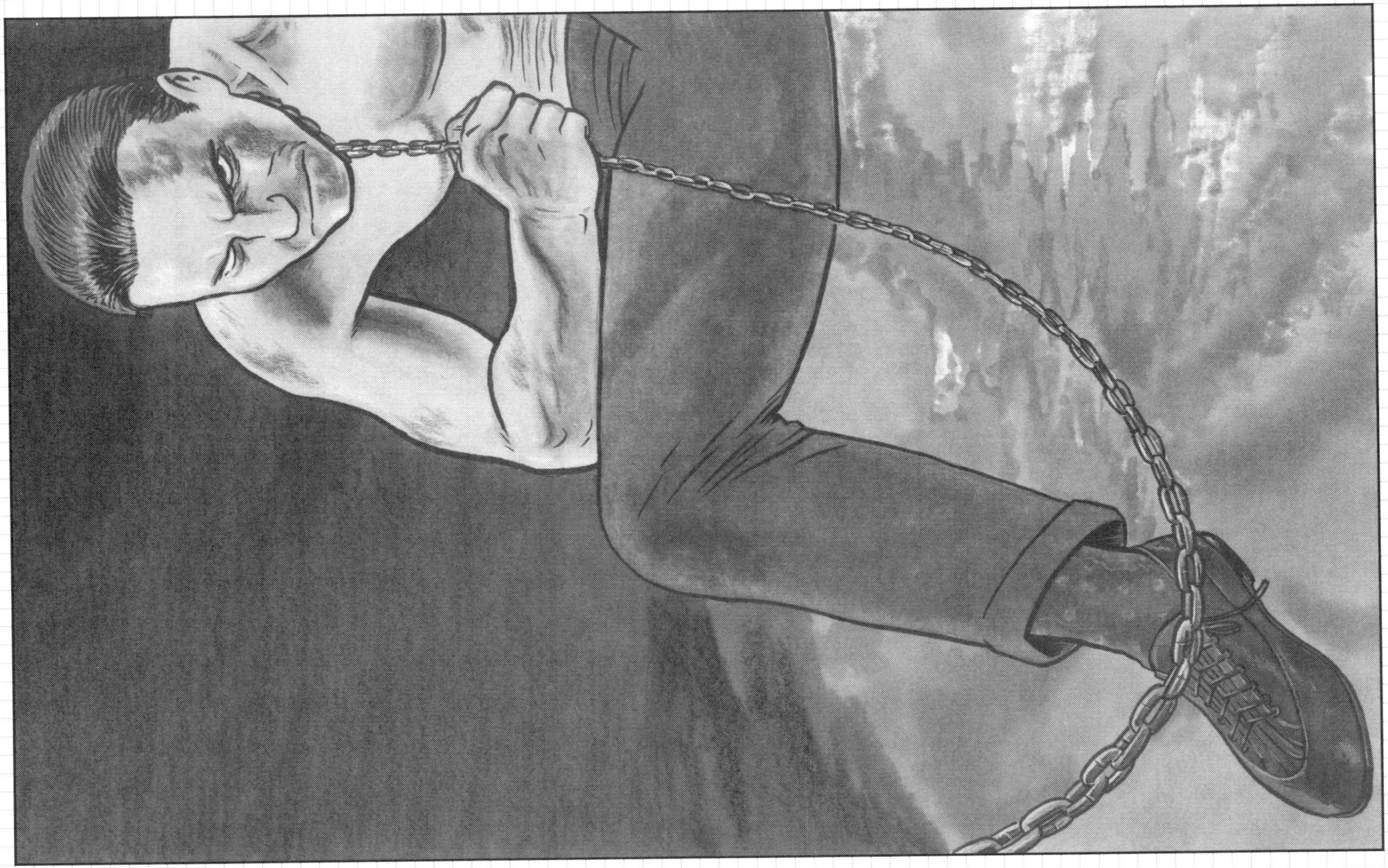

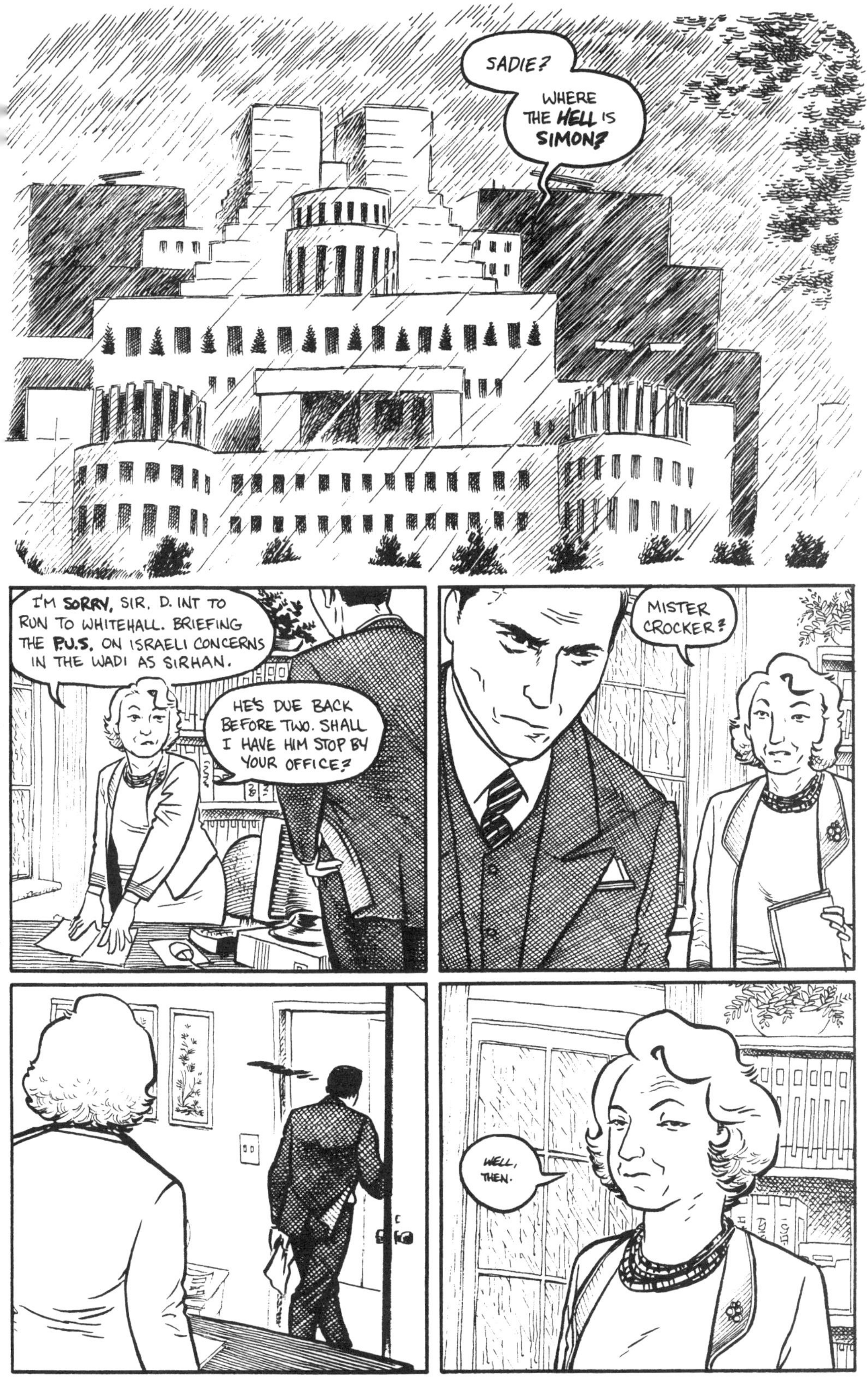
SADIE?
WHERE THE HELL IS SIMON?
I'M SORRY, SIR. D. INT TO RUN TO WHITEHALL. BRIEFING THE P.U.S. ON ISRAELI CONCERNS IN THE WADI AS SIRHAN.
HE'S DUE BACK BEFORE TWO. SHALL I HAVE HIM STOP BY YOUR OFFICE?
MISTER CROCKER?
WELL, THEN.

TARA.

TARA, LASS, YOU'VE **GOT** TO STOP **DOING** THAT. I'M AFRAID YOU'LL TRY TO SMOKE **ME**.

I **MIGHT.** HOW MUCH NICOTINE DO YOU CONTAIN?

TWENTY YEARS, PACK A DAY... FAIR **AMOUNT**, AT A **GUESS.**

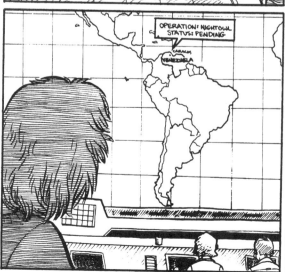

OPERATION: NIGHTOWL
STATUS: PENDING

CARACAS
VENEZUELA

FUCKING HELL.

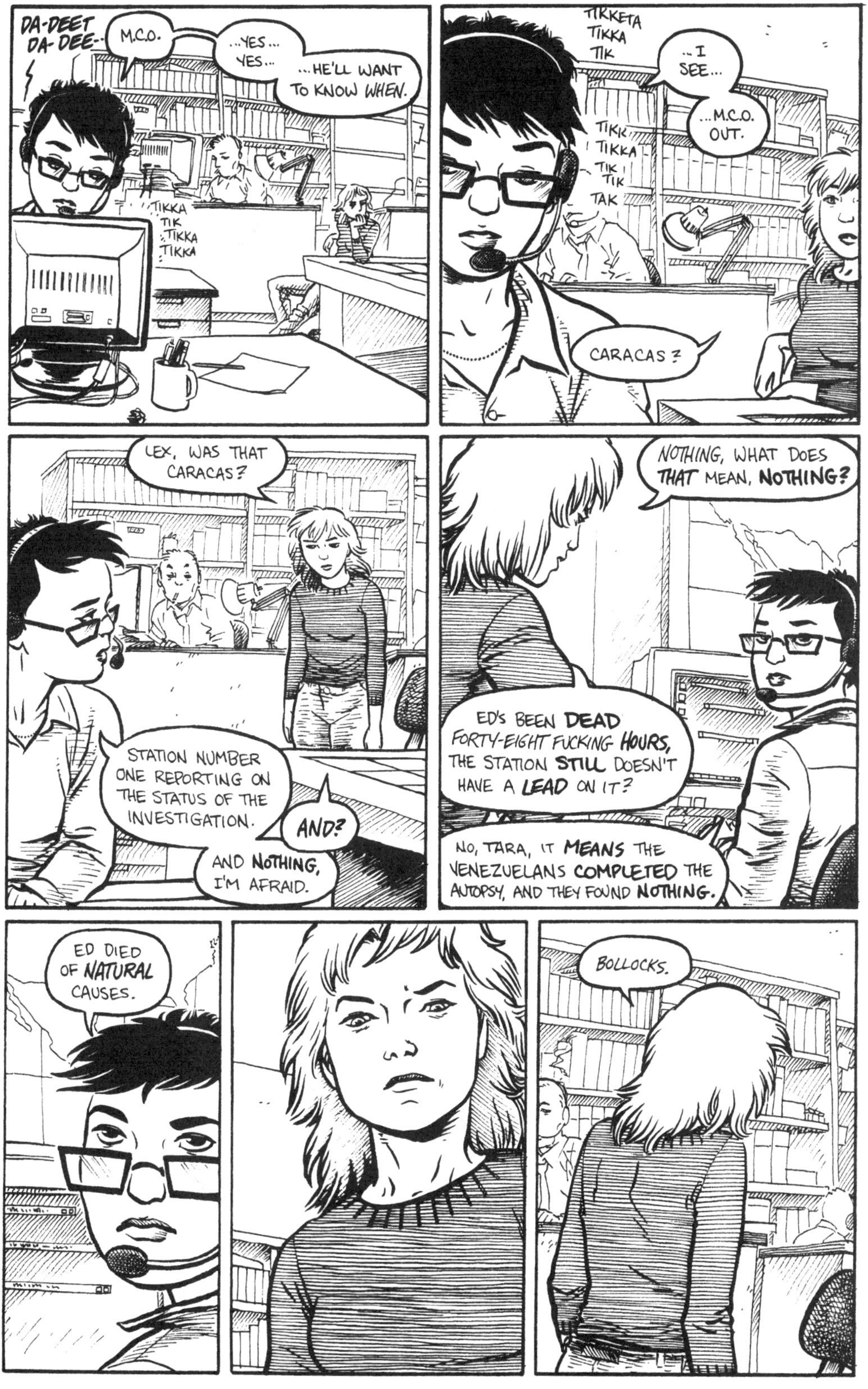
DA-DEET DA-DEE
M.C.O.
...YES... YES...
...HE'LL WANT TO KNOW WHEN.
TIKKA TIK TIKKA TIKKA
TIKKETA TIKKA TIK
..I SEE...
TIKK TIKKA TIK TIK TAK
...M.C.O. OUT.
CARACAS?
LEX, WAS THAT CARACAS?
STATION NUMBER ONE REPORTING ON THE STATUS OF THE INVESTIGATION.
AND?
AND NOTHING, I'M AFRAID.
NOTHING, WHAT DOES THAT MEAN, NOTHING?
ED'S BEEN DEAD FORTY-EIGHT FUCKING HOURS, THE STATION STILL DOESN'T HAVE A LEAD ON IT?
NO, TARA, IT MEANS THE VENEZUELANS COMPLETED THE AUTOPSY, AND THEY FOUND NOTHING.
ED DIED OF NATURAL CAUSES.
BOLLOCKS.

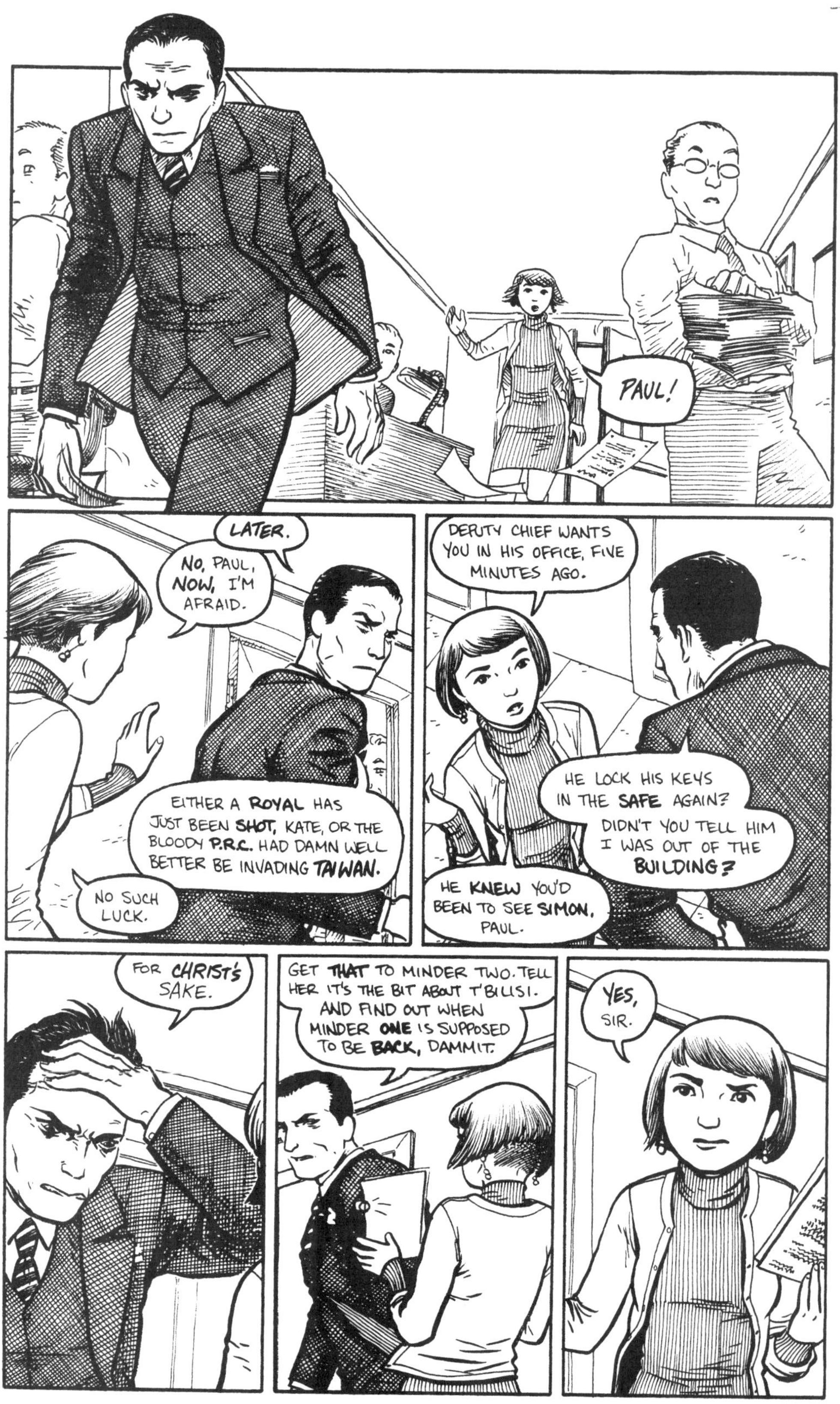
PAUL!
LATER.
NO, PAUL, NOW, I'M AFRAID.
EITHER A ROYAL HAS JUST BEEN SHOT, KATE, OR THE BLOODY P.R.C. HAD DAMN WELL BETTER BE INVADING TAIWAN.
NO SUCH LUCK.
DEPUTY CHIEF WANTS YOU IN HIS OFFICE, FIVE MINUTES AGO.
HE LOCK HIS KEYS IN THE SAFE AGAIN?
DIDN'T YOU TELL HIM I WAS OUT OF THE BUILDING?
HE KNEW YOU'D BEEN TO SEE SIMON, PAUL.
FOR CHRIST'S SAKE.
GET THAT TO MINDER TWO. TELL HER IT'S THE BIT ABOUT T'BILISI.
AND FIND OUT WHEN MINDER ONE IS SUPPOSED TO BE BACK, DAMMIT.
YES, SIR.

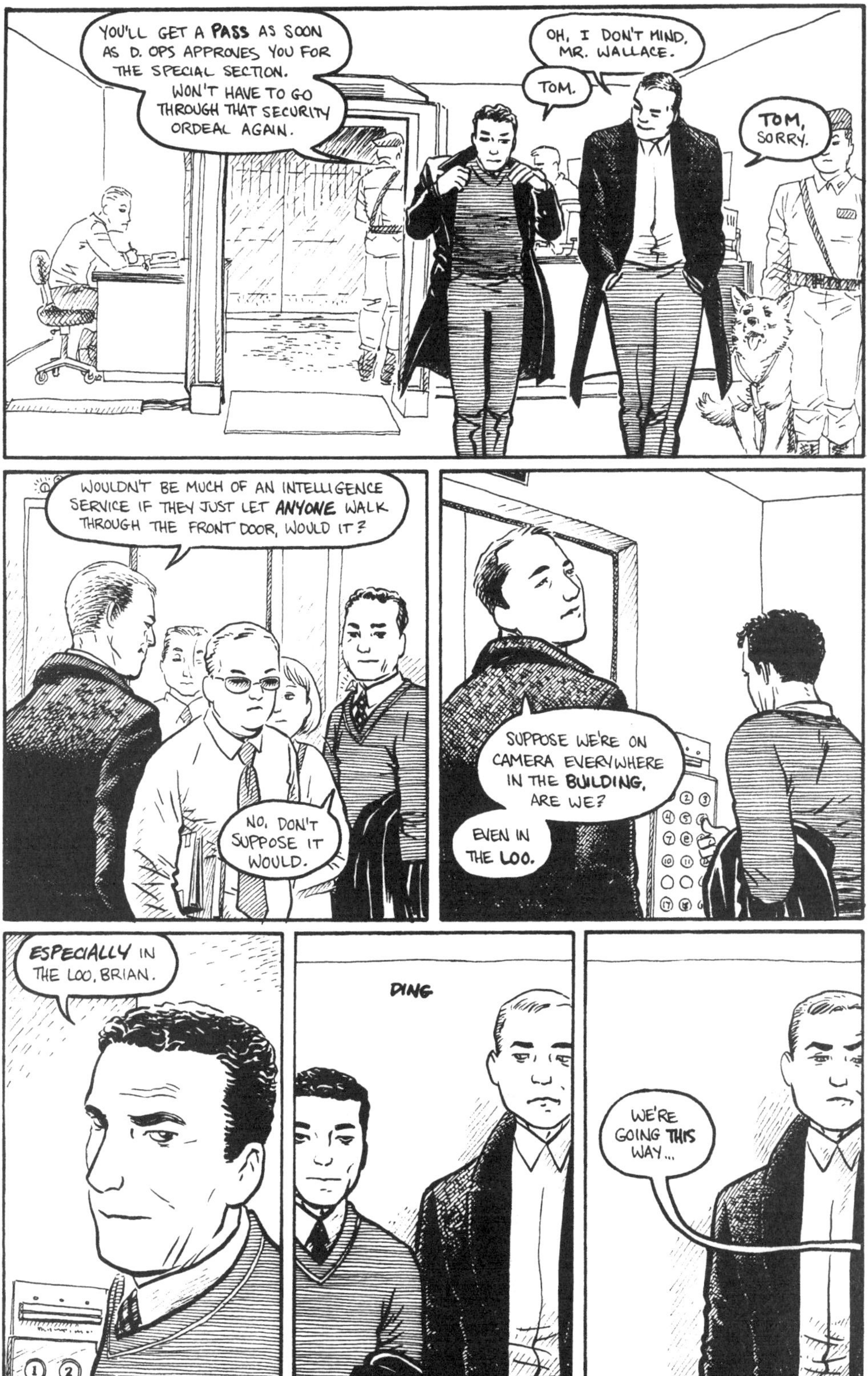
YOU'LL GET A PASS AS SOON AS D. OPS APPROVES YOU FOR THE SPECIAL SECTION.
WON'T HAVE TO GO THROUGH THAT SECURITY ORDEAL AGAIN.
OH, I DON'T MIND, MR. WALLACE.
TOM.
TOM, SORRY.
WOULDN'T BE MUCH OF AN INTELLIGENCE SERVICE IF THEY JUST LET ANYONE WALK THROUGH THE FRONT DOOR, WOULD IT?
NO, DON'T SUPPOSE IT WOULD.
SUPPOSE WE'RE ON CAMERA EVERYWHERE IN THE BUILDING, ARE WE?
EVEN IN THE LOO.
ESPECIALLY IN THE LOO, BRIAN.
DING
WE'RE GOING THIS WAY...

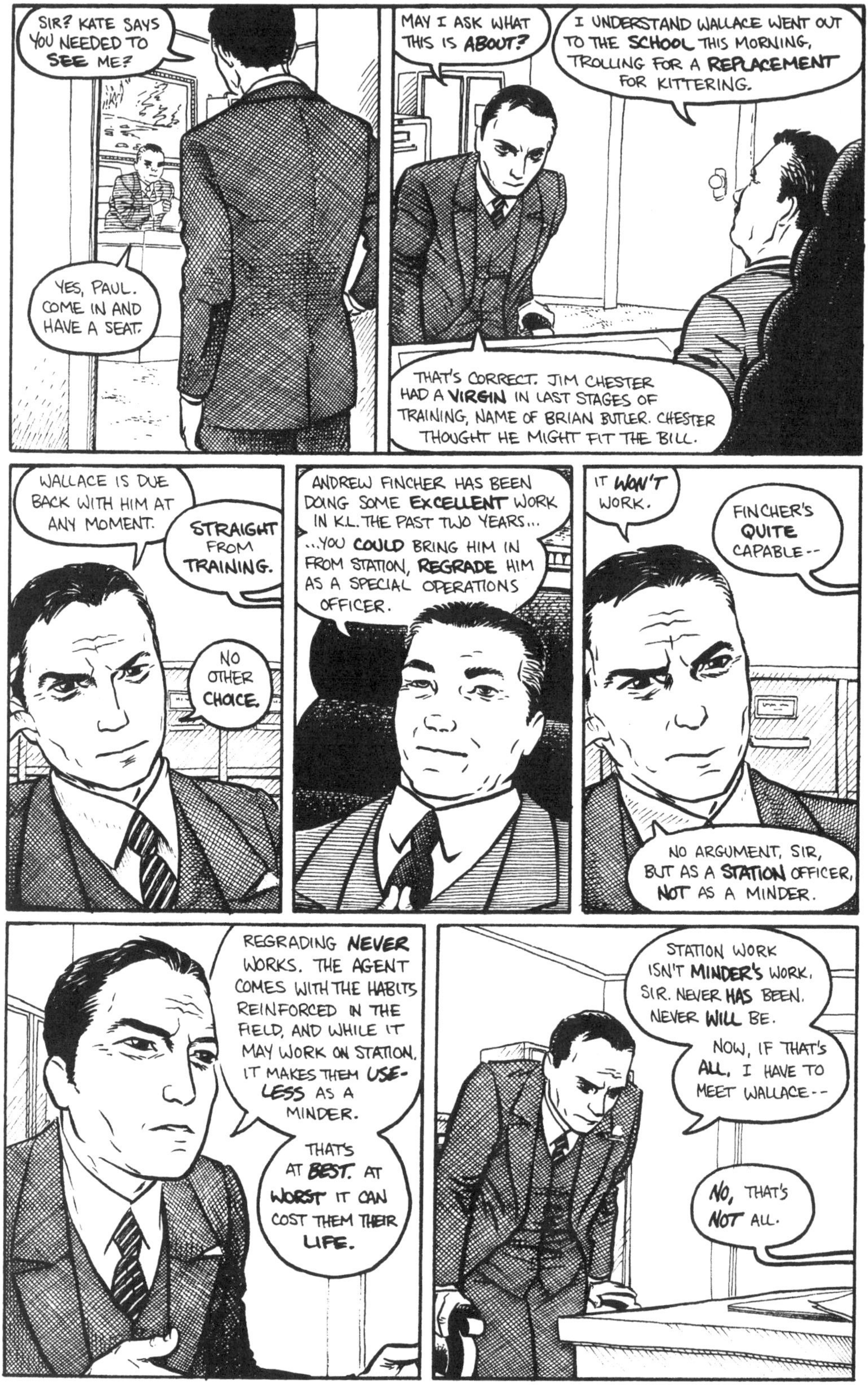
SIR? KATE SAYS YOU NEEDED TO SEE ME?
YES, PAUL. COME IN AND HAVE A SEAT.
MAY I ASK WHAT THIS IS ABOUT?
I UNDERSTAND WALLACE WENT OUT TO THE SCHOOL THIS MORNING, TROLLING FOR A REPLACEMENT FOR KITTERING.
THAT'S CORRECT. JIM CHESTER HAD A VIRGIN IN LAST STAGES OF TRAINING, NAME OF BRIAN BUTLER. CHESTER THOUGHT HE MIGHT FIT THE BILL.
WALLACE IS DUE BACK WITH HIM AT ANY MOMENT.
STRAIGHT FROM TRAINING.
NO OTHER CHOICE.
ANDREW FINCHER HAS BEEN DOING SOME EXCELLENT WORK IN K.L. THE PAST TWO YEARS... ...YOU COULD BRING HIM IN FROM STATION, REGRADE HIM AS A SPECIAL OPERATIONS OFFICER.
IT WON'T WORK.
FINCHER'S QUITE CAPABLE--
NO ARGUMENT, SIR, BUT AS A STATION OFFICER, NOT AS A MINDER.
REGRADING NEVER WORKS. THE AGENT COMES WITH THE HABITS REINFORCED IN THE FIELD, AND WHILE IT MAY WORK ON STATION, IT MAKES THEM USE-LESS AS A MINDER.
THAT'S AT BEST. AT WORST IT CAN COST THEM THEIR LIFE.
STATION WORK ISN'T MINDER'S WORK, SIR. NEVER HAS BEEN. NEVER WILL BE.
NOW, IF THAT'S ALL, I HAVE TO MEET WALLACE--
NO, THAT'S NOT ALL.

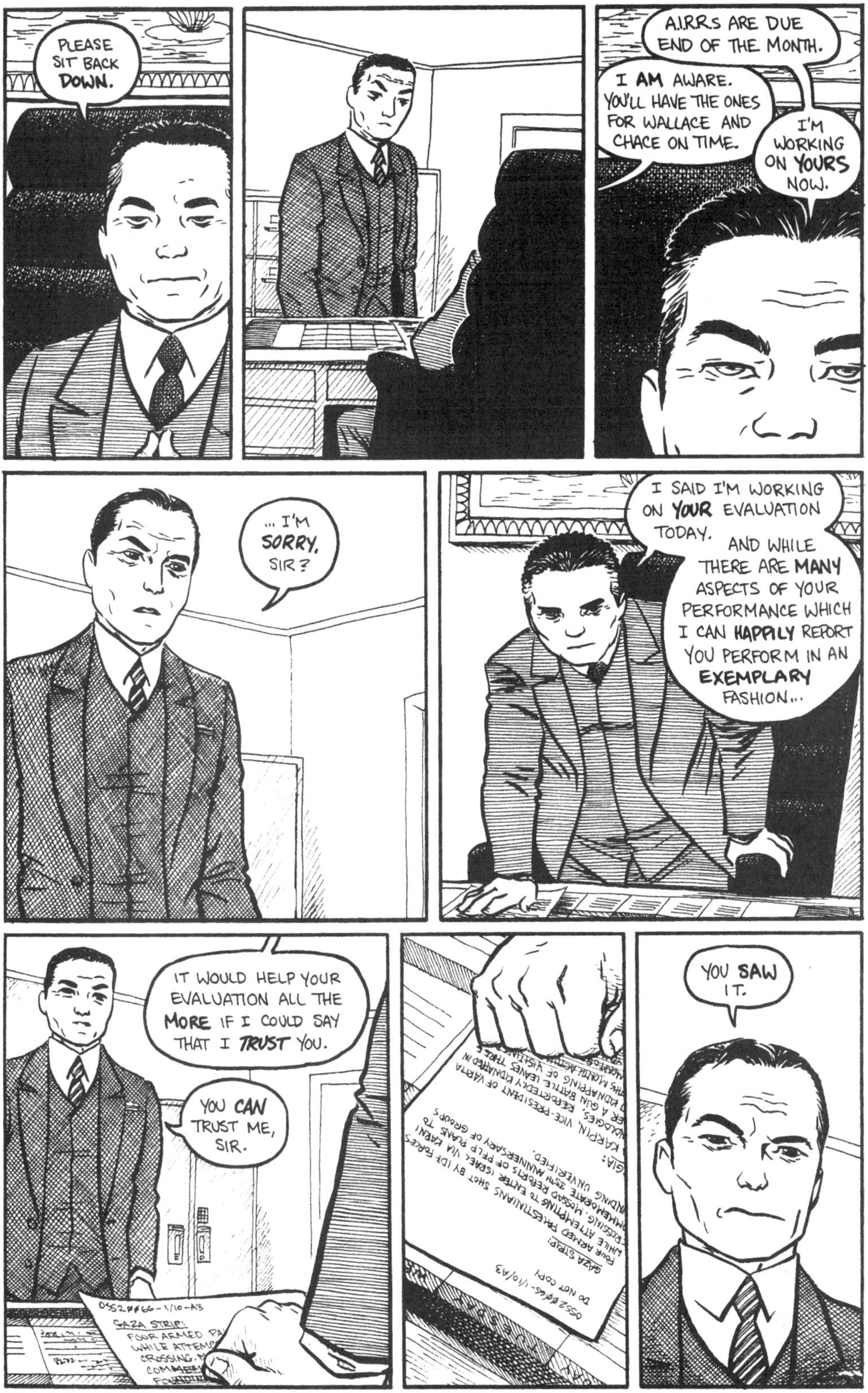
PLEASE SIT BACK DOWN.
A.I.R.R.S ARE DUE END OF THE MONTH.
I AM AWARE. YOU'LL HAVE THE ONES FOR WALLACE AND CHACE ON TIME.
I'M WORKING ON YOURS NOW.
... I'M SORRY, SIR?
I SAID I'M WORKING ON YOUR EVALUATION TODAY.
AND WHILE THERE ARE MANY ASPECTS OF YOUR PERFORMANCE WHICH I CAN HAPPILY REPORT YOU PERFORM IN AN EXEMPLARY FASHION...
IT WOULD HELP YOUR EVALUATION ALL THE MORE IF I COULD SAY THAT I TRUST YOU.
YOU CAN TRUST ME, SIR.
GAZA STRIP:
YOU SAW IT.

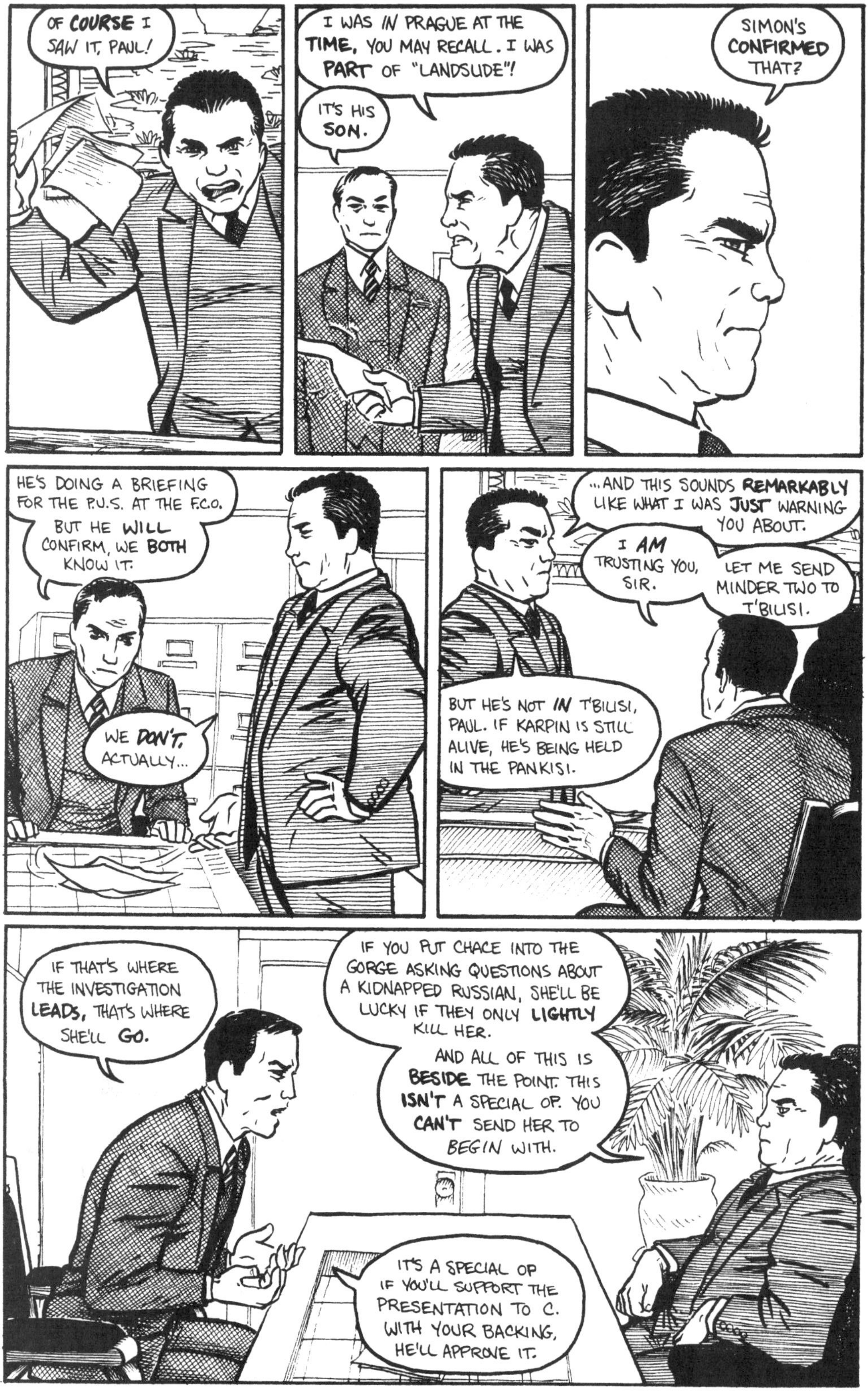
OF COURSE I SAW IT, PAUL!
I WAS IN PRAGUE AT THE TIME, YOU MAY RECALL. I WAS PART OF "LANDSLIDE"!
IT'S HIS SON.
SIMON'S CONFIRMED THAT?
HE'S DOING A BRIEFING FOR THE P.U.S. AT THE F.C.O.
BUT HE WILL CONFIRM, WE BOTH KNOW IT.
WE DON'T, ACTUALLY...
...AND THIS SOUNDS REMARKABLY LIKE WHAT I WAS JUST WARNING YOU ABOUT.
I AM TRUSTING YOU, SIR.
LET ME SEND MINDER TWO TO T'BILISI.
BUT HE'S NOT IN T'BILISI, PAUL. IF KARPIN IS STILL ALIVE, HE'S BEING HELD IN THE PANKISI.
IF THAT'S WHERE THE INVESTIGATION LEADS, THAT'S WHERE SHE'LL GO.
IF YOU PUT CHACE INTO THE GORGE ASKING QUESTIONS ABOUT A KIDNAPPED RUSSIAN, SHE'LL BE LUCKY IF THEY ONLY LIGHTLY KILL HER.
AND ALL OF THIS IS BESIDE THE POINT. THIS ISN'T A SPECIAL OP. YOU CAN'T SEND HER TO BEGIN WITH.
IT'S A SPECIAL OP IF YOU'LL SUPPORT THE PRESENTATION TO C. WITH YOUR BACKING, HE'LL APPROVE IT.

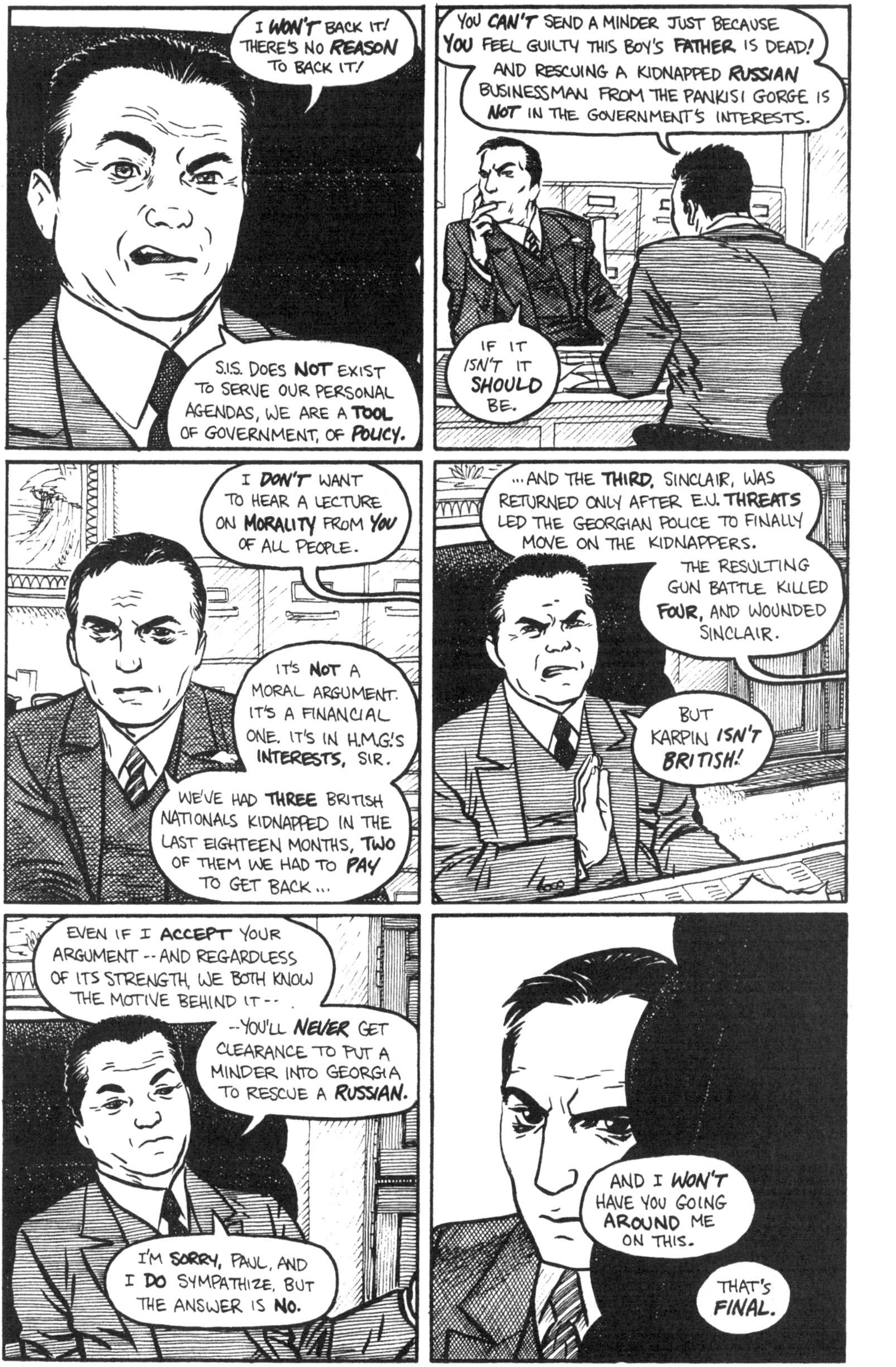
I WON'T BACK IT! THERE'S NO REASON TO BACK IT!
S.I.S. DOES NOT EXIST TO SERVE OUR PERSONAL AGENDAS, WE ARE A TOOL OF GOVERNMENT, OF POLICY.
YOU CAN'T SEND A MINDER JUST BECAUSE YOU FEEL GUILTY THIS BOY'S FATHER IS DEAD! AND RESCUING A KIDNAPPED RUSSIAN BUSINESSMAN FROM THE PANKISI GORGE IS NOT IN THE GOVERNMENT'S INTERESTS.
IF IT ISN'T IT SHOULD BE.
I DON'T WANT TO HEAR A LECTURE ON MORALITY FROM YOU OF ALL PEOPLE.
IT'S NOT A MORAL ARGUMENT. IT'S A FINANCIAL ONE. IT'S IN H.M.G.'S INTERESTS, SIR.
WE'VE HAD THREE BRITISH NATIONALS KIDNAPPED IN THE LAST EIGHTEEN MONTHS, TWO OF THEM WE HAD TO PAY TO GET BACK...
...AND THE THIRD, SINCLAIR, WAS RETURNED ONLY AFTER E.U. THREATS LED THE GEORGIAN POLICE TO FINALLY MOVE ON THE KIDNAPPERS.
THE RESULTING GUN BATTLE KILLED FOUR, AND WOUNDED SINCLAIR.
BUT KARPIN ISN'T BRITISH!
EVEN IF I ACCEPT YOUR ARGUMENT -- AND REGARDLESS OF ITS STRENGTH, WE BOTH KNOW THE MOTIVE BEHIND IT --
--YOU'LL NEVER GET CLEARANCE TO PUT A MINDER INTO GEORGIA TO RESCUE A RUSSIAN.
I'M SORRY, PAUL, AND I DO SYMPATHIZE, BUT THE ANSWER IS NO.
AND I WON'T HAVE YOU GOING AROUND ME ON THIS.
THAT'S FINAL.

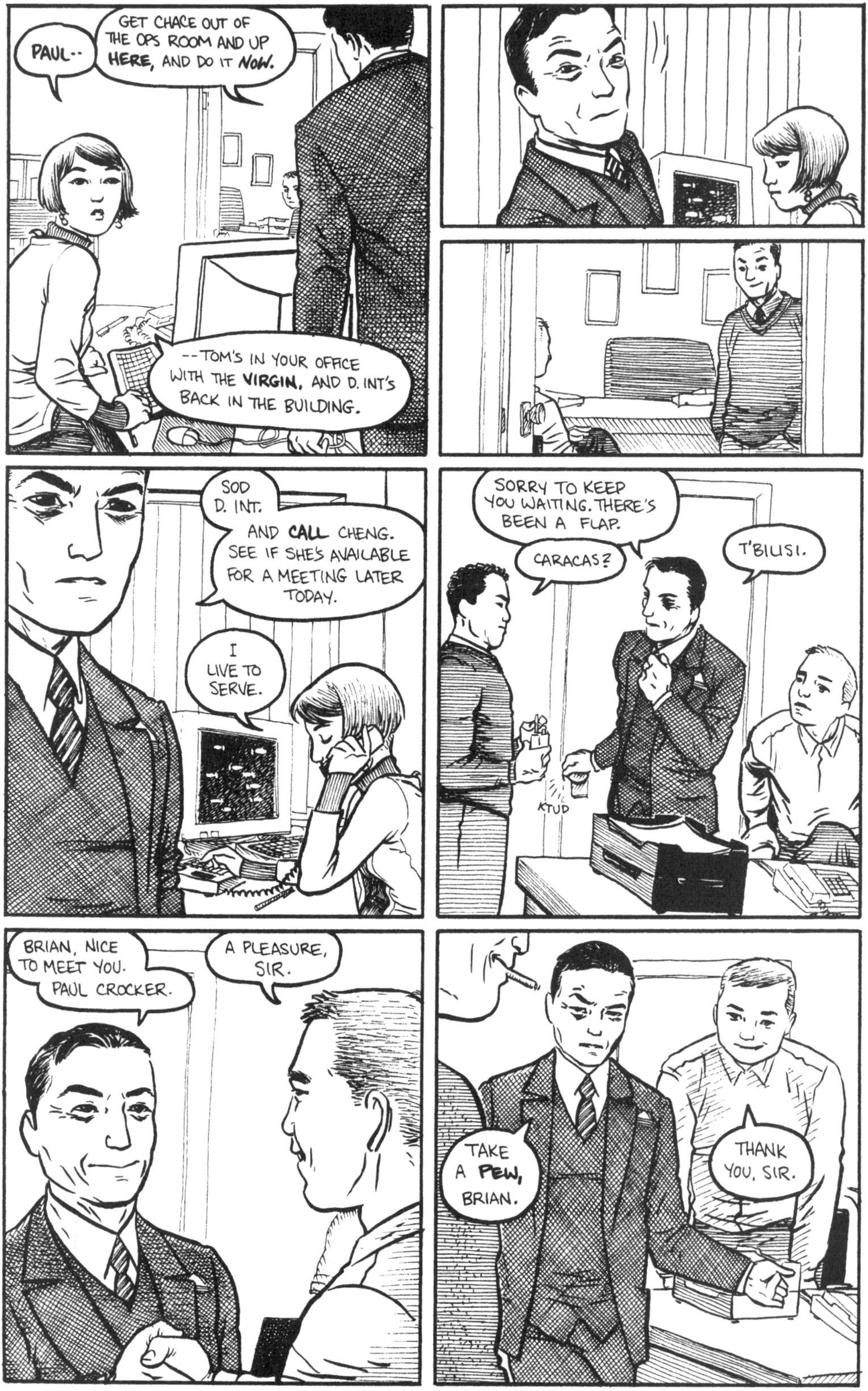
PAUL..
GET CHACE OUT OF THE OPS ROOM AND UP **HERE**, AND DO IT ***NOW***.
--TOM'S IN YOUR OFFICE WITH THE **VIRGIN**, AND D. INT'S BACK IN THE BUILDING.
SOD D. INT.
AND **CALL** CHENG. SEE IF SHE'S AVAILABLE FOR A MEETING LATER TODAY.
I LIVE TO SERVE.
SORRY TO KEEP YOU WAITING. THERE'S BEEN A FLAP.
CARACAS?
T'BILISI.
KTUD
BRIAN, NICE TO MEET YOU. PAUL CROCKER.
A PLEASURE, SIR.
TAKE A **PEW**, BRIAN.
THANK YOU, SIR.

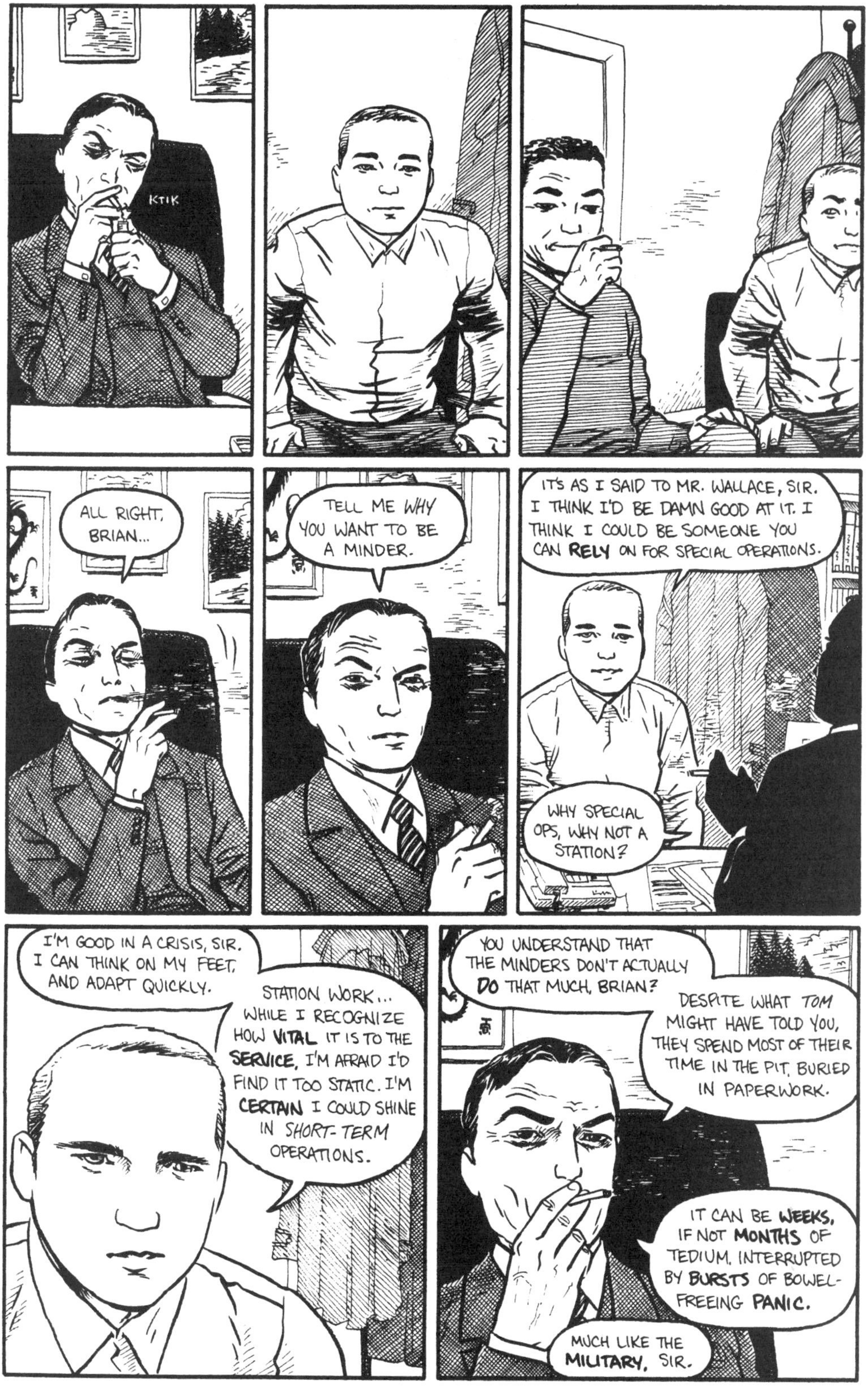
KTIK
ALL RIGHT, BRIAN...
TELL ME WHY YOU WANT TO BE A MINDER.
IT'S AS I SAID TO MR. WALLACE, SIR. I THINK I'D BE DAMN GOOD AT IT. I THINK I COULD BE SOMEONE YOU CAN RELY ON FOR SPECIAL OPERATIONS.
WHY SPECIAL OPS, WHY NOT A STATION?
I'M GOOD IN A CRISIS, SIR. I CAN THINK ON MY FEET, AND ADAPT QUICKLY.
STATION WORK... WHILE I RECOGNIZE HOW VITAL IT IS TO THE SERVICE, I'M AFRAID I'D FIND IT TOO STATIC. I'M CERTAIN I COULD SHINE IN SHORT-TERM OPERATIONS.
YOU UNDERSTAND THAT THE MINDERS DON'T ACTUALLY DO THAT MUCH, BRIAN?
DESPITE WHAT TOM MIGHT HAVE TOLD YOU, THEY SPEND MOST OF THEIR TIME IN THE PIT, BURIED IN PAPERWORK.
IT CAN BE WEEKS, IF NOT MONTHS OF TEDIUM, INTERRUPTED BY BURSTS OF BOWEL-FREEING PANIC.
MUCH LIKE THE MILITARY, SIR.

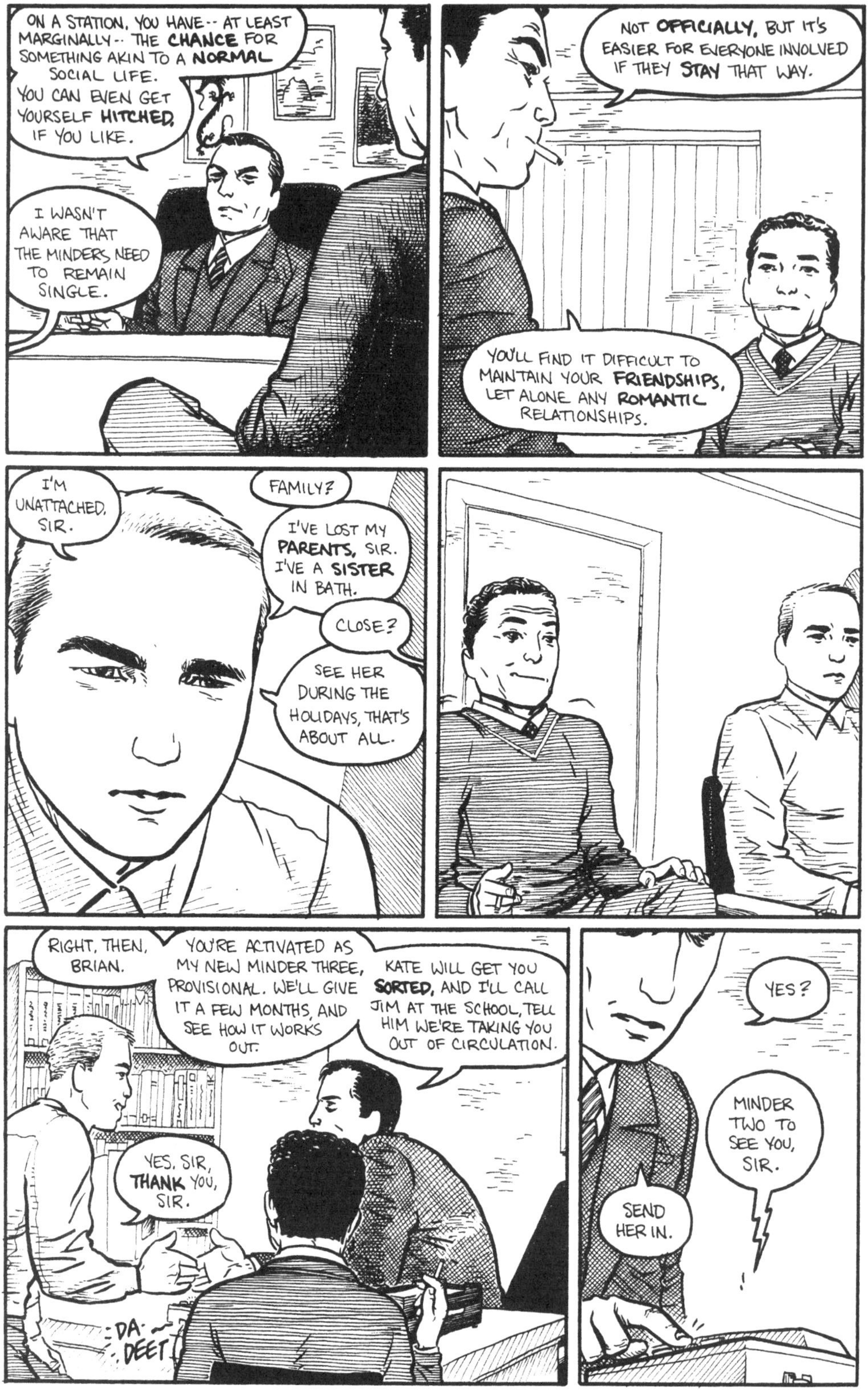
ON A STATION, YOU HAVE-- AT LEAST MARGINALLY-- THE **CHANCE** FOR SOMETHING AKIN TO A **NORMAL** SOCIAL LIFE.
YOU CAN EVEN GET YOURSELF **HITCHED**, IF YOU LIKE.
I WASN'T AWARE THAT THE MINDERS NEED TO REMAIN SINGLE.
NOT **OFFICIALLY**, BUT IT'S EASIER FOR EVERYONE INVOLVED IF THEY **STAY** THAT WAY.
YOU'LL FIND IT DIFFICULT TO MAINTAIN YOUR **FRIENDSHIPS**, LET ALONE ANY **ROMANTIC** RELATIONSHIPS.
I'M UNATTACHED, SIR.
FAMILY?
I'VE LOST MY **PARENTS**, SIR. I'VE A **SISTER** IN BATH.
CLOSE?
SEE HER DURING THE HOLIDAYS, THAT'S ABOUT ALL.
RIGHT, THEN, BRIAN.
YOU'RE ACTIVATED AS MY NEW MINDER THREE, PROVISIONAL. WE'LL GIVE IT A FEW MONTHS, AND SEE HOW IT WORKS OUT.
KATE WILL GET YOU **SORTED**, AND I'LL CALL JIM AT THE SCHOOL, TELL HIM WE'RE TAKING YOU OUT OF CIRCULATION.
YES, SIR, **THANK** YOU, SIR.
DA-DEET
YES?
MINDER TWO TO SEE YOU, SIR.
SEND HER IN.

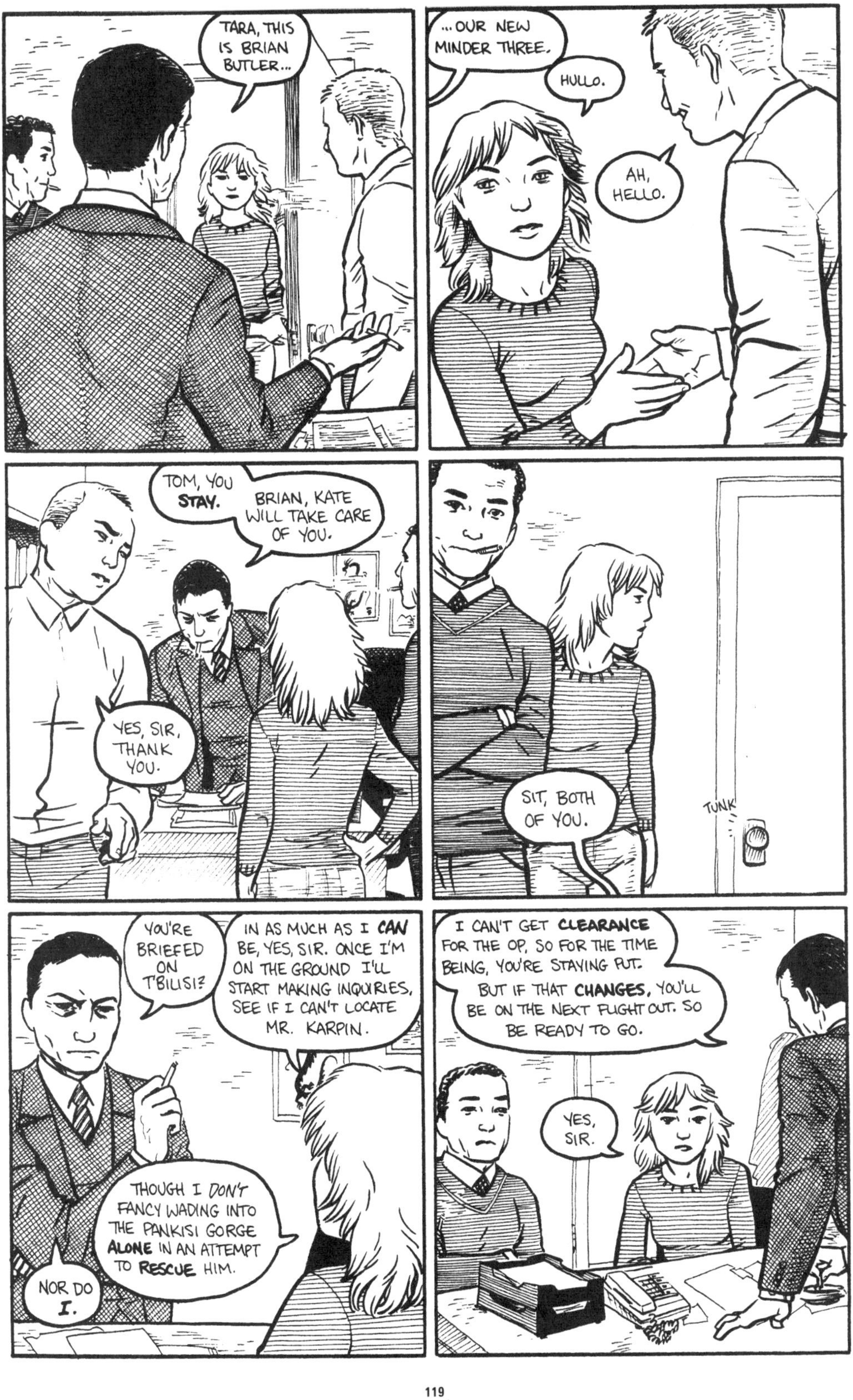
TARA, THIS IS BRIAN BUTLER...
...OUR NEW MINDER THREE.
HULLO.
AH, HELLO.
TOM, YOU **STAY.**
BRIAN, KATE WILL TAKE CARE OF YOU.
YES, SIR, THANK YOU.
SIT, BOTH OF YOU.
TUNK
YOU'RE BRIEFED ON T'BILISI?
IN AS MUCH AS I **CAN** BE, YES, SIR. ONCE I'M ON THE GROUND I'LL START MAKING INQUIRIES, SEE IF I CAN'T LOCATE MR. KARPIN.
THOUGH I *DON'T* FANCY WADING INTO THE PANKISI GORGE **ALONE** IN AN ATTEMPT TO **RESCUE** HIM.
NOR DO **I.**
I CAN'T GET **CLEARANCE** FOR THE OP, SO FOR THE TIME BEING, YOU'RE STAYING PUT.
BUT IF THAT **CHANGES,** YOU'LL BE ON THE NEXT FLIGHT OUT. SO BE READY TO GO.
YES, SIR.

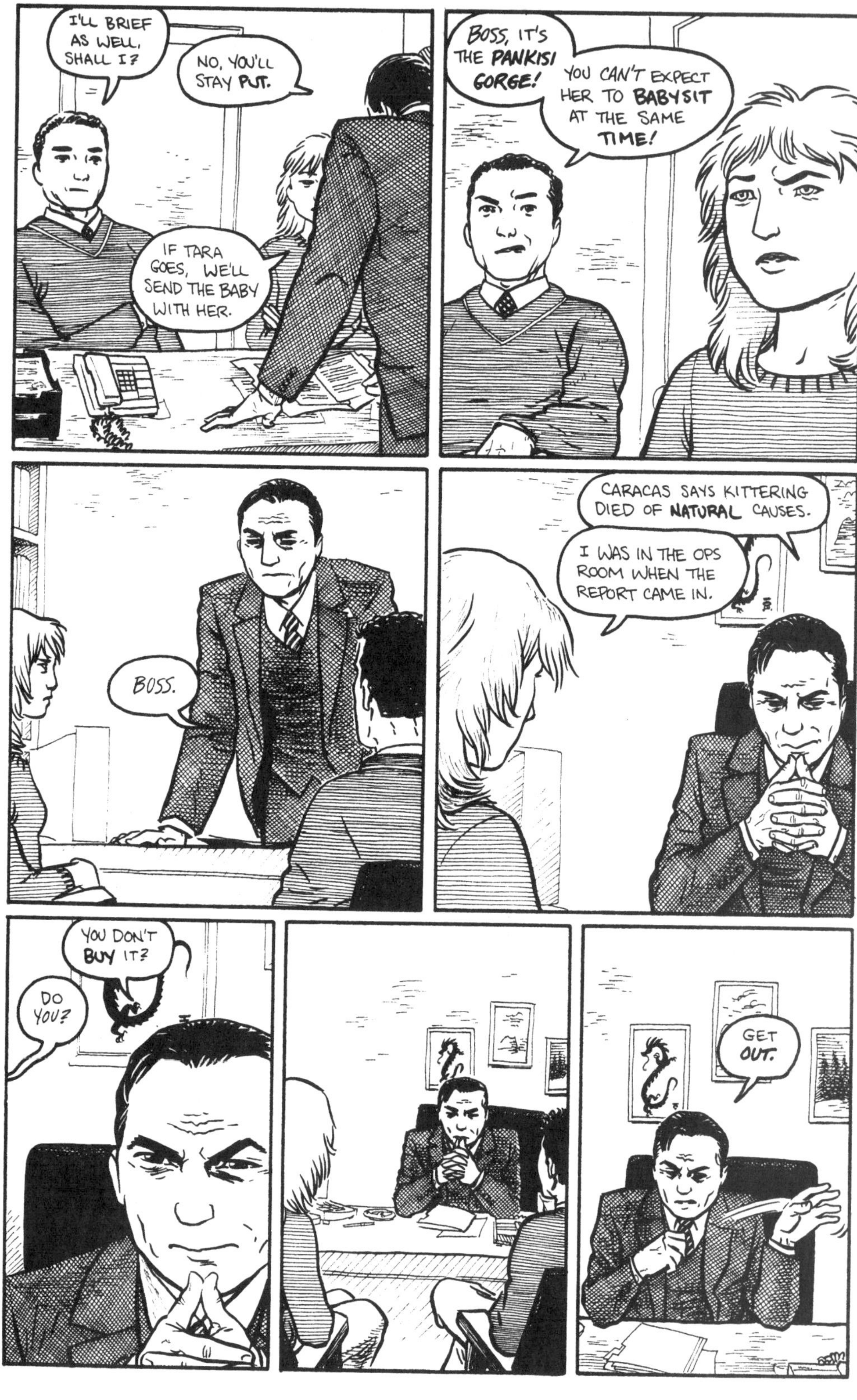
I'LL BRIEF AS WELL, SHALL I?
NO, YOU'LL STAY PUT.
IF TARA GOES, WE'LL SEND THE BABY WITH HER.
BOSS, IT'S THE PANKISI GORGE!
YOU CAN'T EXPECT HER TO BABYSIT AT THE SAME TIME!
BOSS.
CARACAS SAYS KITTERING DIED OF NATURAL CAUSES.
I WAS IN THE OPS ROOM WHEN THE REPORT CAME IN.
YOU DON'T BUY IT?
DO YOU?
GET OUT.

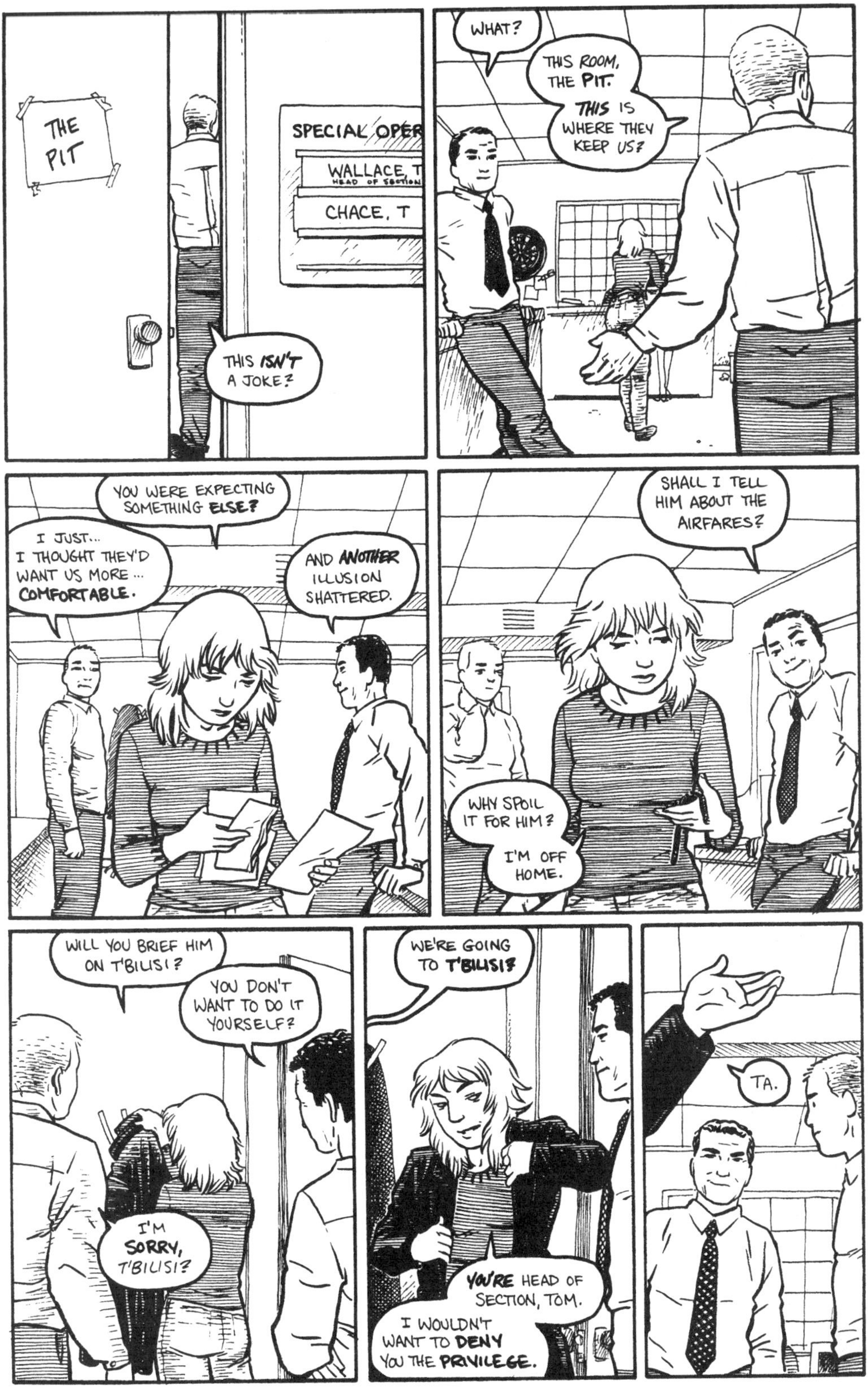
THE PIT
SPECIAL OPER
WALLACE, T
HEAD OF SECTION
CHACE, T
THIS ISN'T A JOKE?
WHAT?
THIS ROOM, THE PIT. THIS IS WHERE THEY KEEP US?
YOU WERE EXPECTING SOMETHING ELSE?
I JUST... I THOUGHT THEY'D WANT US MORE... COMFORTABLE.
AND ANOTHER ILLUSION SHATTERED.
SHALL I TELL HIM ABOUT THE AIRFARES?
WHY SPOIL IT FOR HIM?
I'M OFF HOME.
WILL YOU BRIEF HIM ON T'BILISI?
YOU DON'T WANT TO DO IT YOURSELF?
I'M SORRY, T'BILISI?
WE'RE GOING TO T'BILISI?
YOU'RE HEAD OF SECTION, TOM.
I WOULDN'T WANT TO DENY YOU THE PRIVILEGE.
TA.

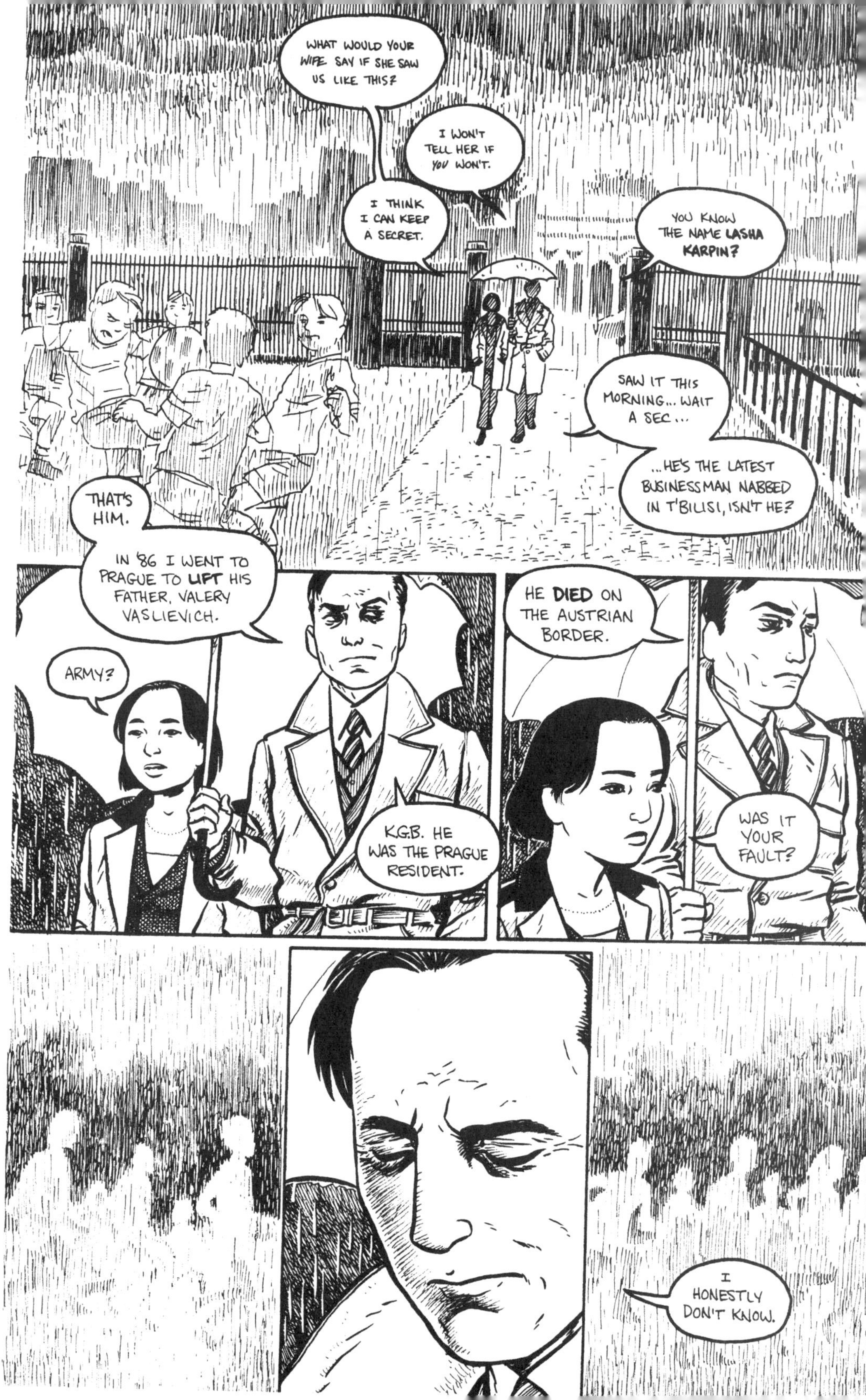

WHAT WOULD YOUR WIFE SAY IF SHE SAW US LIKE THIS?
I WON'T TELL HER IF YOU WON'T.
I THINK I CAN KEEP A SECRET.
YOU KNOW THE NAME **LASHA KARPIN?**
SAW IT THIS MORNING... WAIT A SEC...
...HE'S THE LATEST BUSINESSMAN NABBED IN T'BILISI, ISN'T HE?
THAT'S HIM.
IN '86 I WENT TO PRAGUE TO **LIFT** HIS FATHER, VALERY VASLIEVICH.
ARMY?
K.G.B. HE WAS THE PRAGUE RESIDENT.
HE **DIED** ON THE AUSTRIAN BORDER.
WAS IT YOUR FAULT?
I HONESTLY DON'T KNOW.

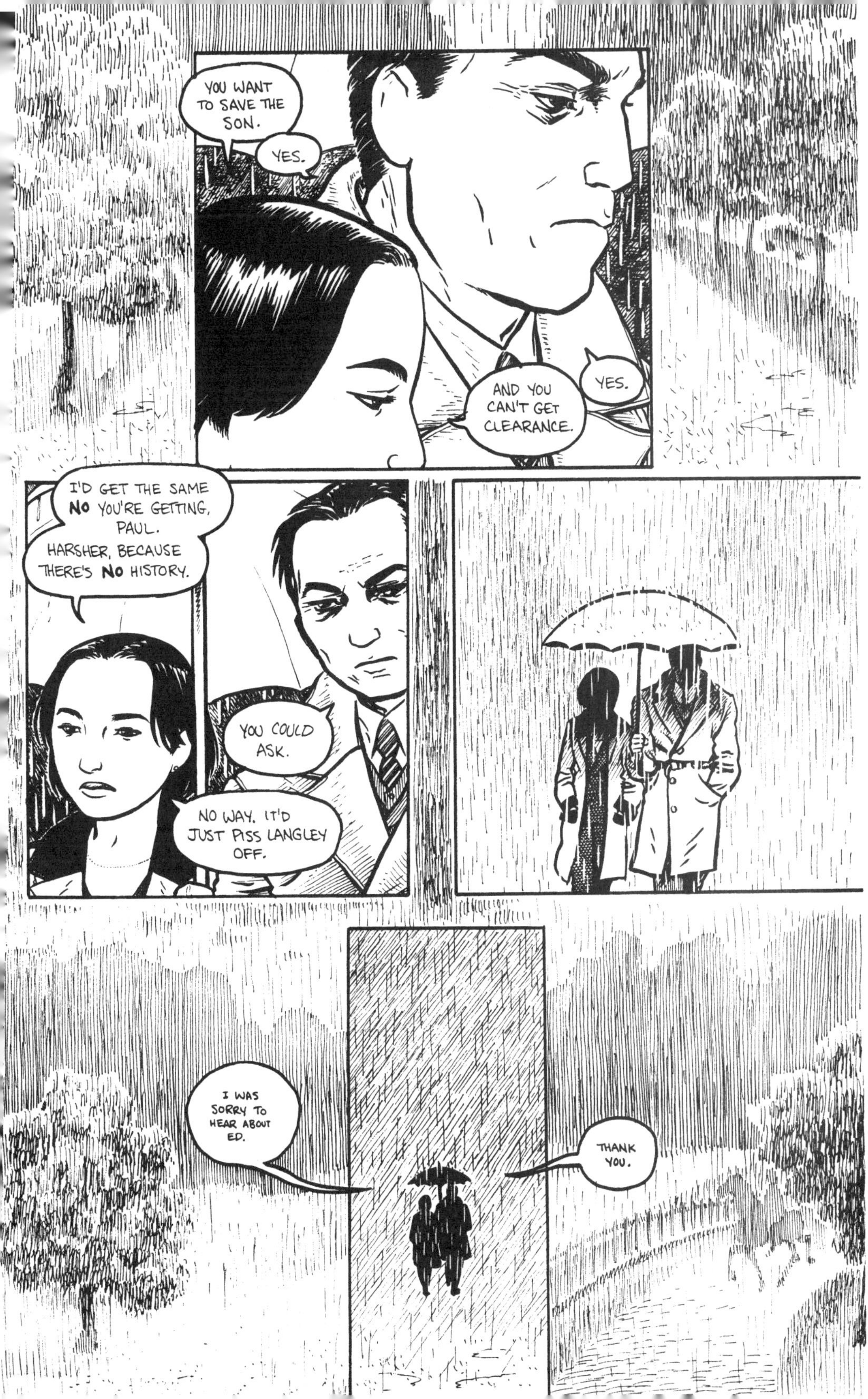
YOU WANT TO SAVE THE SON.
YES.
AND YOU CAN'T GET CLEARANCE.
YES.
I'D GET THE SAME NO YOU'RE GETTING, PAUL.
HARSHER, BECAUSE THERE'S NO HISTORY.
YOU COULD ASK.
NO WAY. IT'D JUST PISS LANGLEY OFF.
I WAS SORRY TO HEAR ABOUT ED.
THANK YOU.

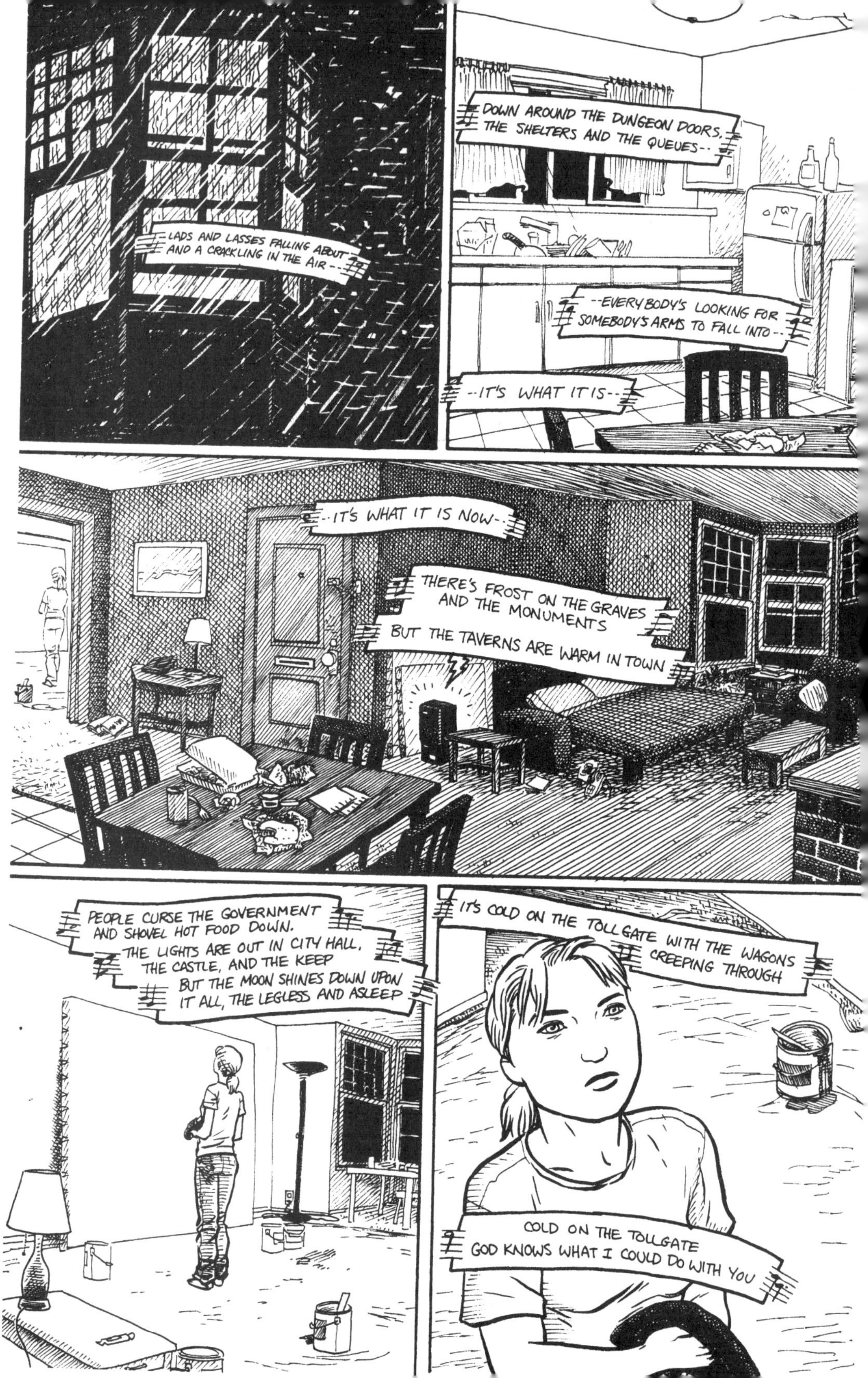
LADS AND LASSES FALLING ABOUT AND A CRACKLING IN THE AIR--
DOWN AROUND THE DUNGEON DOORS, THE SHELTERS AND THE QUEUES--
--EVERYBODY'S LOOKING FOR SOMEBODY'S ARMS TO FALL INTO--
--IT'S WHAT IT IS--
--IT'S WHAT IT IS NOW--
THERE'S FROST ON THE GRAVES AND THE MONUMENTS
BUT THE TAVERNS ARE WARM IN TOWN
PEOPLE CURSE THE GOVERNMENT AND SHOVEL HOT FOOD DOWN.
THE LIGHTS ARE OUT IN CITY HALL, THE CASTLE, AND THE KEEP
BUT THE MOON SHINES DOWN UPON IT ALL, THE LEGLESS AND ASLEEP
IT'S COLD ON THE TOLLGATE WITH THE WAGONS CREEPING THROUGH
COLD ON THE TOLLGATE
GOD KNOWS WHAT I COULD DO WITH YOU

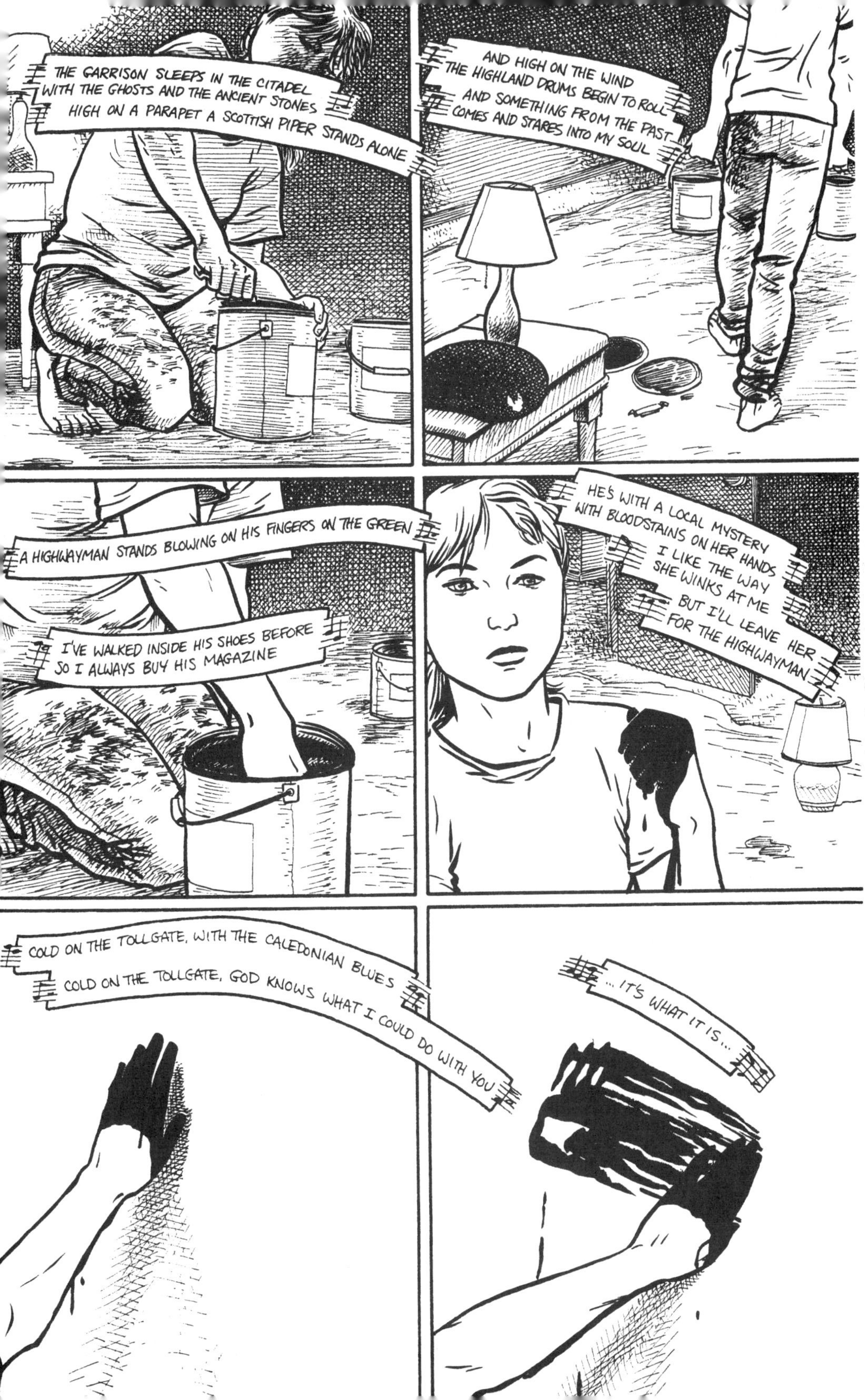
THE GARRISON SLEEPS IN THE CITADEL
WITH THE GHOSTS AND THE ANCIENT STONES
HIGH ON A PARAPET A SCOTTISH PIPER STANDS ALONE
AND HIGH ON THE WIND
THE HIGHLAND DRUMS BEGIN TO ROLL
AND SOMETHING FROM THE PAST
COMES AND STARES INTO MY SOUL
A HIGHWAYMAN STANDS BLOWING ON HIS FINGERS ON THE GREEN
I'VE WALKED INSIDE HIS SHOES BEFORE
SO I ALWAYS BUY HIS MAGAZINE
HE'S WITH A LOCAL MYSTERY
WITH BLOODSTAINS ON HER HANDS
I LIKE THE WAY
SHE WINKS AT ME
BUT I'LL LEAVE HER
FOR THE HIGHWAYMAN
COLD ON THE TOLLGATE, WITH THE CALEDONIAN BLUES
COLD ON THE TOLLGATE, GOD KNOWS WHAT I COULD DO WITH YOU
... IT'S WHAT IT IS...

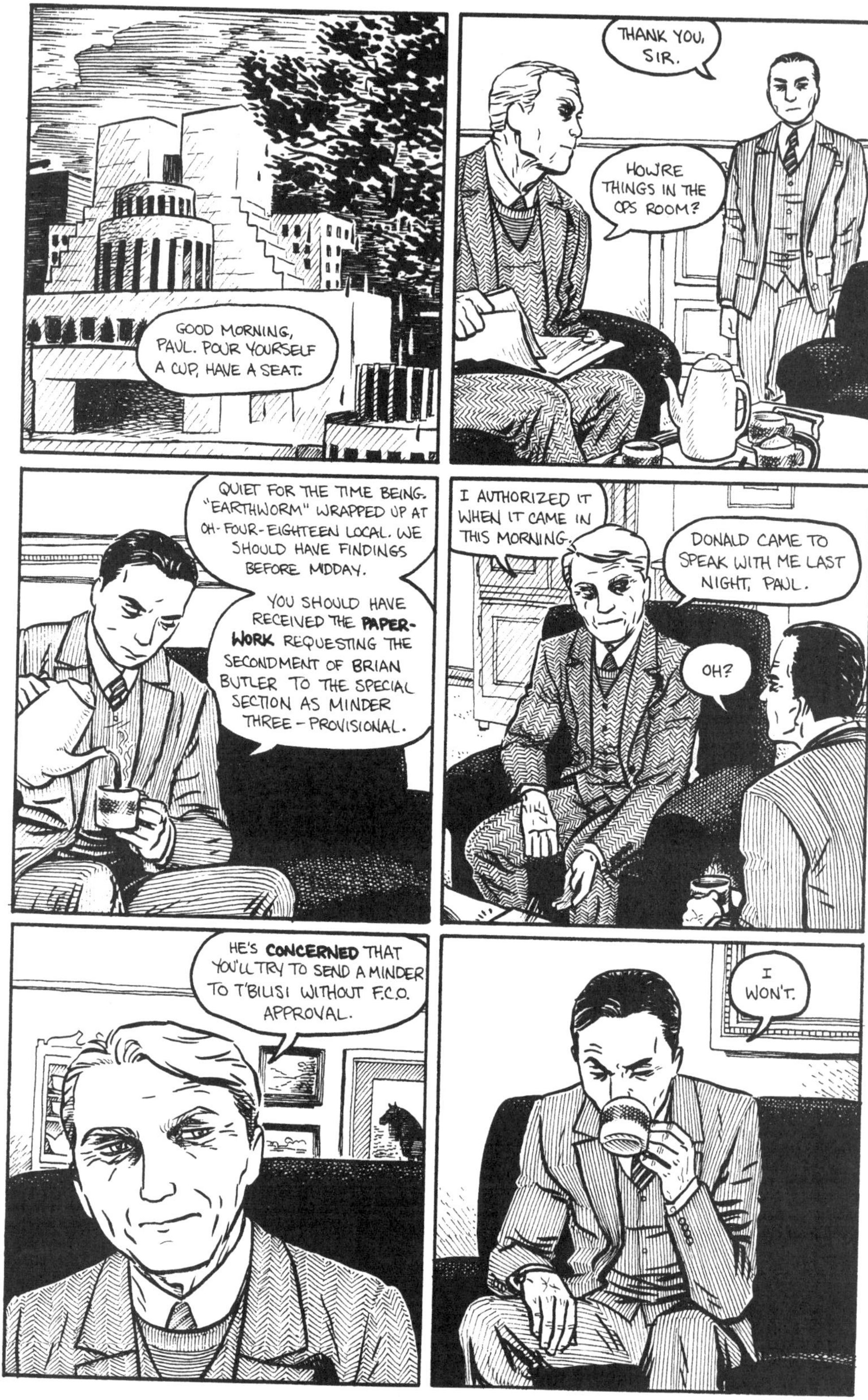
GOOD MORNING, PAUL. POUR YOURSELF A CUP, HAVE A SEAT.
THANK YOU, SIR.
HOW'RE THINGS IN THE OPS ROOM?
QUIET FOR THE TIME BEING. "EARTHWORM" WRAPPED UP AT OH-FOUR-EIGHTEEN LOCAL. WE SHOULD HAVE FINDINGS BEFORE MIDDAY.
YOU SHOULD HAVE RECEIVED THE **PAPERWORK** REQUESTING THE SECONDMENT OF BRIAN BUTLER TO THE SPECIAL SECTION AS MINDER THREE-PROVISIONAL.
I AUTHORIZED IT WHEN IT CAME IN THIS MORNING.
DONALD CAME TO SPEAK WITH ME LAST NIGHT, PAUL.
OH?
HE'S **CONCERNED** THAT YOU'LL TRY TO SEND A MINDER TO T'BILISI WITHOUT F.C.O. APPROVAL.
I WON'T.

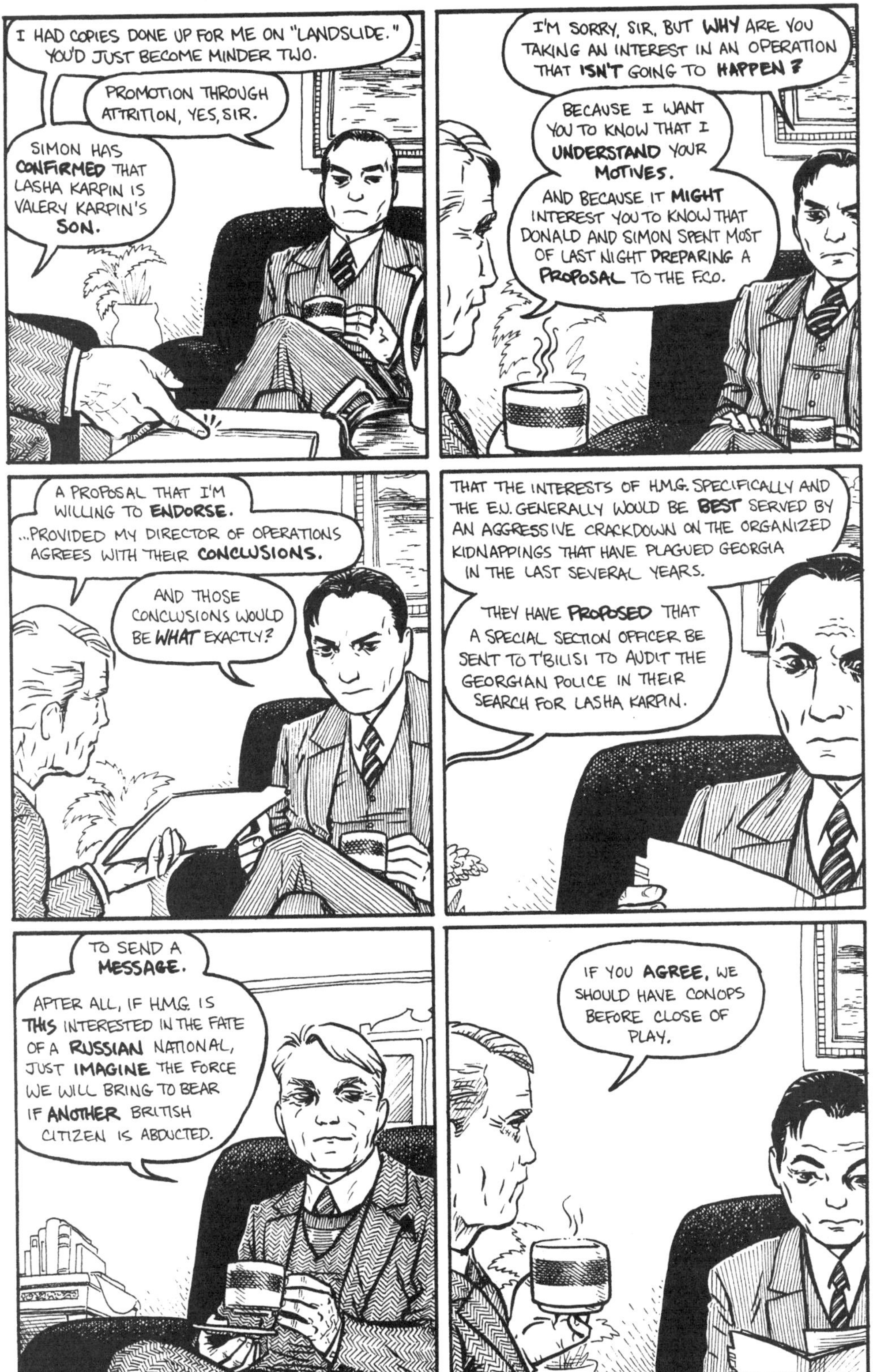

I HAD COPIES DONE UP FOR ME ON "LANDSLIDE." YOU'D JUST BECOME MINDER TWO.
PROMOTION THROUGH ATTRITION, YES, SIR.
SIMON HAS CONFIRMED THAT LASHA KARPIN IS VALERY KARPIN'S SON.
I'M SORRY, SIR, BUT WHY ARE YOU TAKING AN INTEREST IN AN OPERATION THAT ISN'T GOING TO HAPPEN?
BECAUSE I WANT YOU TO KNOW THAT I UNDERSTAND YOUR MOTIVES.
AND BECAUSE IT MIGHT INTEREST YOU TO KNOW THAT DONALD AND SIMON SPENT MOST OF LAST NIGHT PREPARING A PROPOSAL TO THE F.C.O.
A PROPOSAL THAT I'M WILLING TO ENDORSE. ...PROVIDED MY DIRECTOR OF OPERATIONS AGREES WITH THEIR CONCLUSIONS.
AND THOSE CONCLUSIONS WOULD BE WHAT EXACTLY?
THAT THE INTERESTS OF H.M.G. SPECIFICALLY AND THE E.U. GENERALLY WOULD BE BEST SERVED BY AN AGGRESSIVE CRACKDOWN ON THE ORGANIZED KIDNAPPINGS THAT HAVE PLAGUED GEORGIA IN THE LAST SEVERAL YEARS.
THEY HAVE PROPOSED THAT A SPECIAL SECTION OFFICER BE SENT TO T'BILISI TO AUDIT THE GEORGIAN POLICE IN THEIR SEARCH FOR LASHA KARPIN.
TO SEND A MESSAGE.
AFTER ALL, IF H.M.G. IS THIS INTERESTED IN THE FATE OF A RUSSIAN NATIONAL, JUST IMAGINE THE FORCE WE WILL BRING TO BEAR IF ANOTHER BRITISH CITIZEN IS ABDUCTED.
IF YOU AGREE, WE SHOULD HAVE CONOPS BEFORE CLOSE OF PLAY.

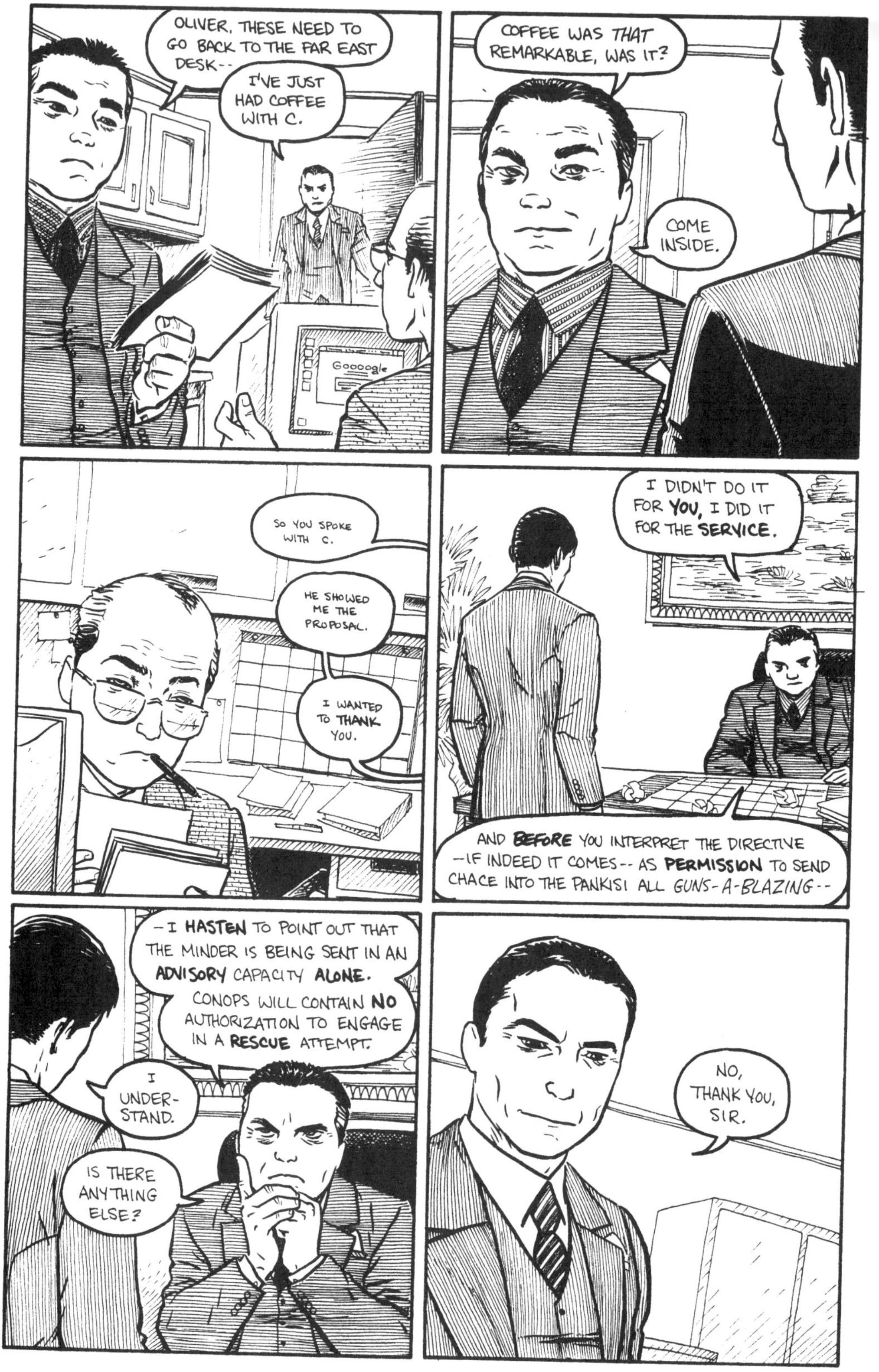
OLIVER, THESE NEED TO GO BACK TO THE FAR EAST DESK--
I'VE JUST HAD COFFEE WITH C.
Goooogle
COFFEE WAS THAT REMARKABLE, WAS IT?
COME INSIDE.
SO YOU SPOKE WITH C.
HE SHOWED ME THE PROPOSAL.
I WANTED TO THANK YOU.
I DIDN'T DO IT FOR YOU, I DID IT FOR THE SERVICE.
AND BEFORE YOU INTERPRET THE DIRECTIVE --IF INDEED IT COMES-- AS PERMISSION TO SEND CHACE INTO THE PANKISI ALL GUNS-A-BLAZING--
--I HASTEN TO POINT OUT THAT THE MINDER IS BEING SENT IN AN ADVISORY CAPACITY ALONE.
CONOPS WILL CONTAIN NO AUTHORIZATION TO ENGAGE IN A RESCUE ATTEMPT.
I UNDERSTAND.
IS THERE ANYTHING ELSE?
NO, THANK YOU, SIR.

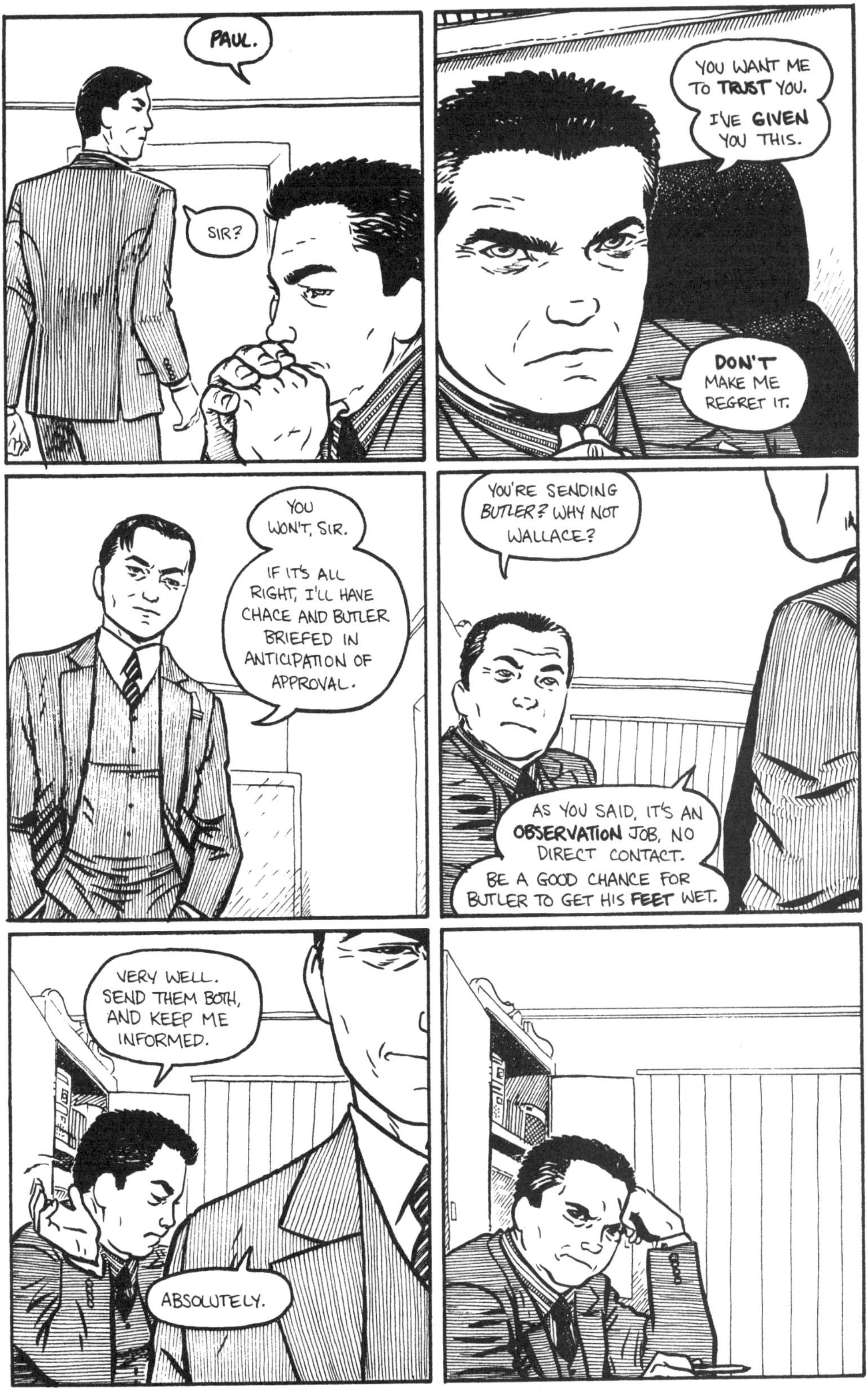

PAUL.
SIR?
YOU WANT ME TO TRUST YOU.
I'VE GIVEN YOU THIS.
DON'T MAKE ME REGRET IT.
YOU WON'T, SIR.
IF IT'S ALL RIGHT, I'LL HAVE CHACE AND BUTLER BRIEFED IN ANTICIPATION OF APPROVAL.
YOU'RE SENDING BUTLER? WHY NOT WALLACE?
AS YOU SAID, IT'S AN OBSERVATION JOB, NO DIRECT CONTACT.
BE A GOOD CHANCE FOR BUTLER TO GET HIS FEET WET.
VERY WELL. SEND THEM BOTH, AND KEEP ME INFORMED.
ABSOLUTELY.

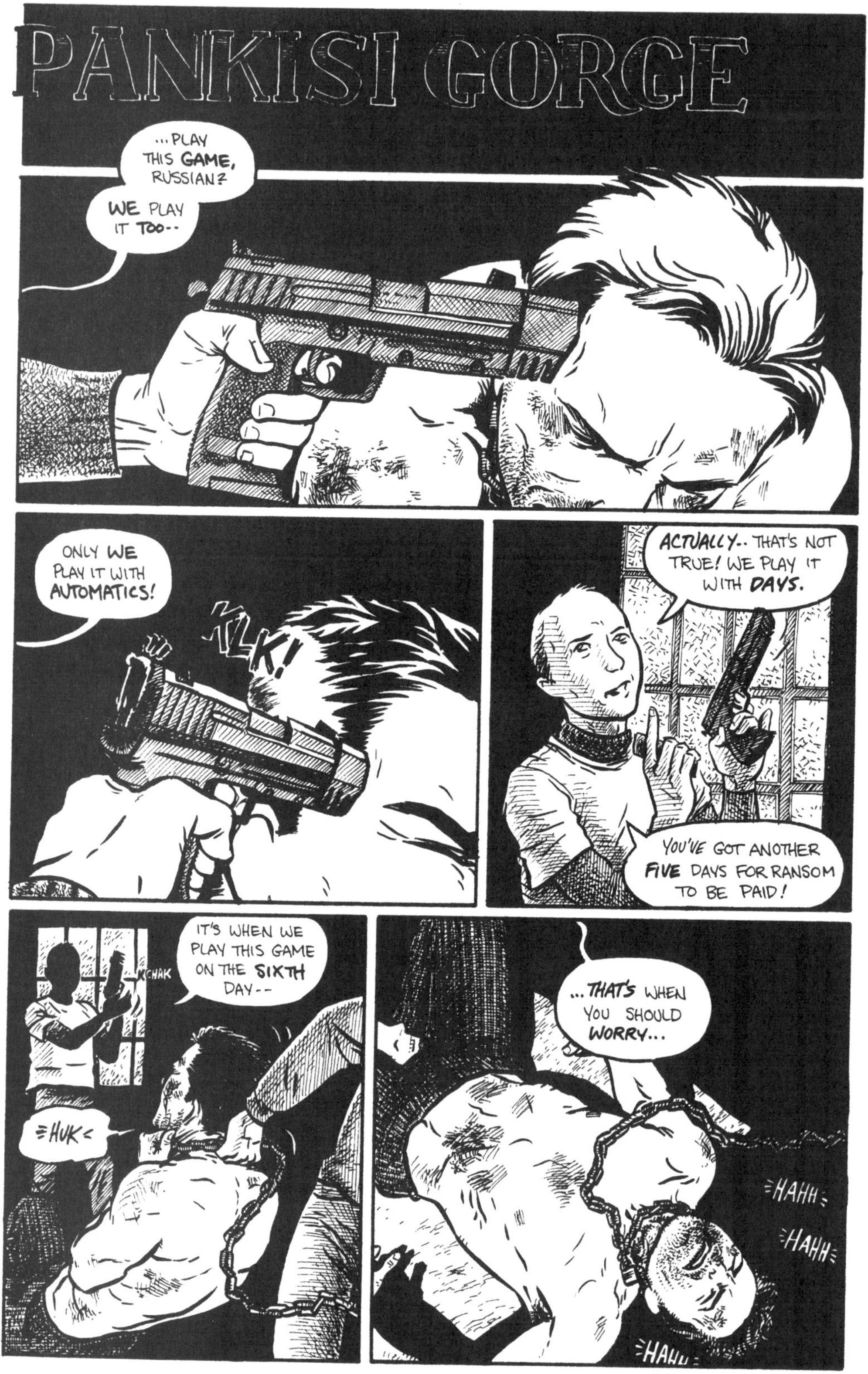
PANKISI GORGE
...PLAY THIS GAME, RUSSIAN?
WE PLAY IT TOO--
ONLY WE PLAY IT WITH AUTOMATICS!
KLIK!
ACTUALLY.. THAT'S NOT TRUE! WE PLAY IT WITH DAYS.
YOU'VE GOT ANOTHER FIVE DAYS FOR RANSOM TO BE PAID!
KCHAK
IT'S WHEN WE PLAY THIS GAME ON THE SIXTH DAY--
HUK
...THAT'S WHEN YOU SHOULD WORRY...
HAHH
HAHH

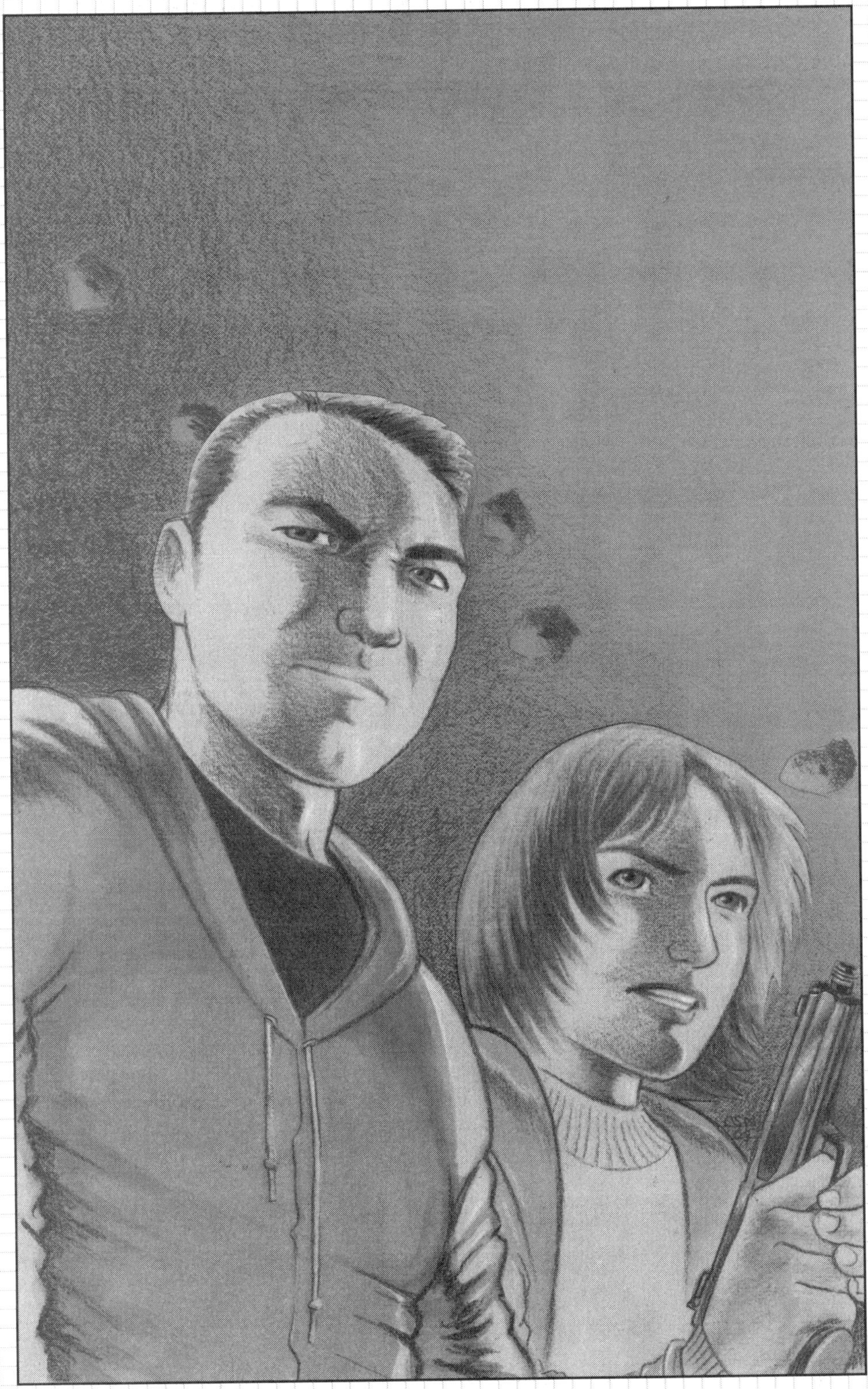

CHAPTER 3

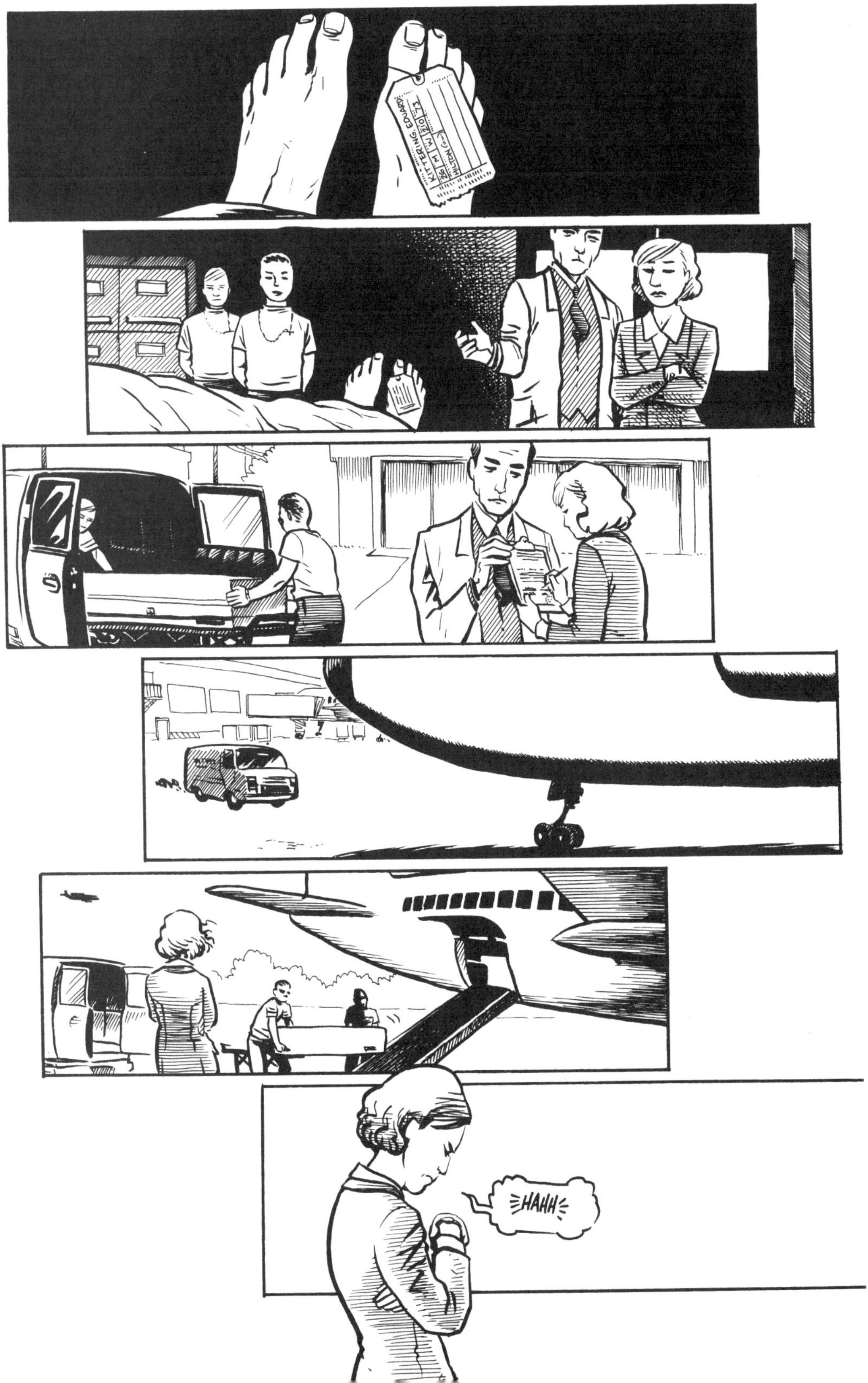
KITTERING, EDUARD
26 M W 2/10 73
HILTON
HAHH

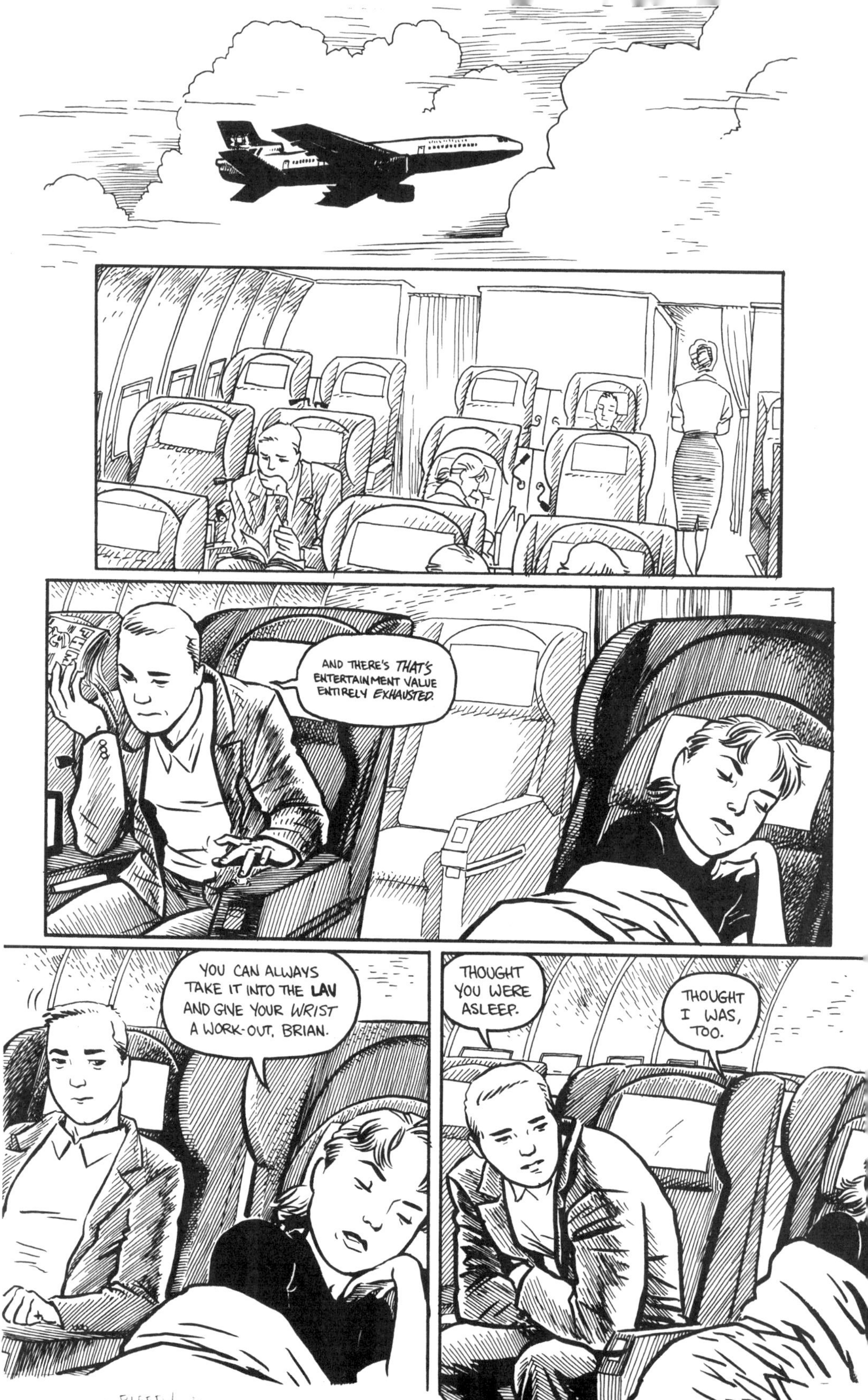
AND THERE'S THAT'S ENTERTAINMENT VALUE ENTIRELY EXHAUSTED.
YOU CAN ALWAYS TAKE IT INTO THE LAV AND GIVE YOUR WRIST A WORK-OUT, BRIAN.
THOUGHT YOU WERE ASLEEP.
THOUGHT I WAS, TOO.

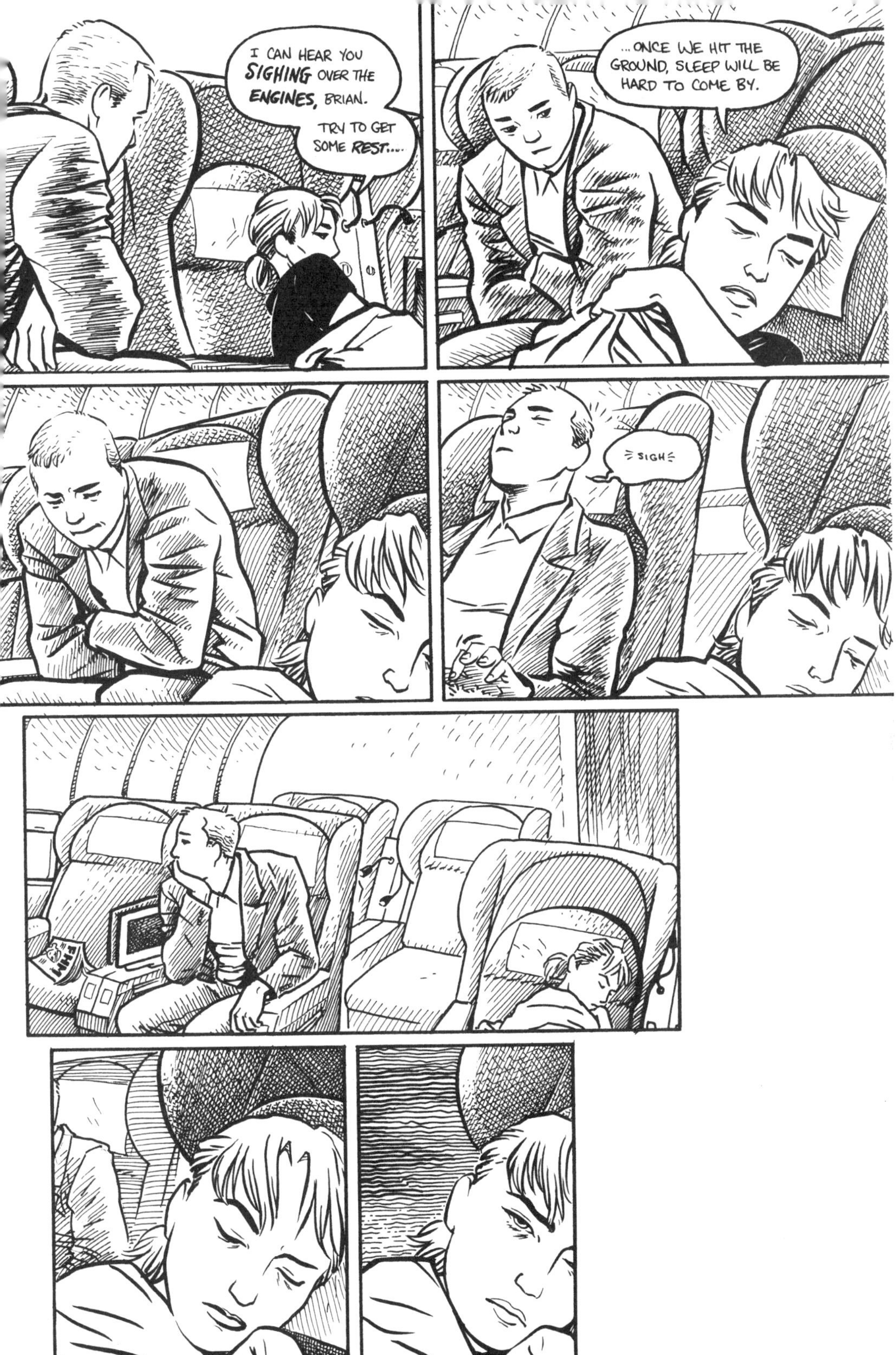
I CAN HEAR YOU SIGHING OVER THE ENGINES, BRIAN.
TRY TO GET SOME REST....
...ONCE WE HIT THE GROUND, SLEEP WILL BE HARD TO COME BY.
SIGH

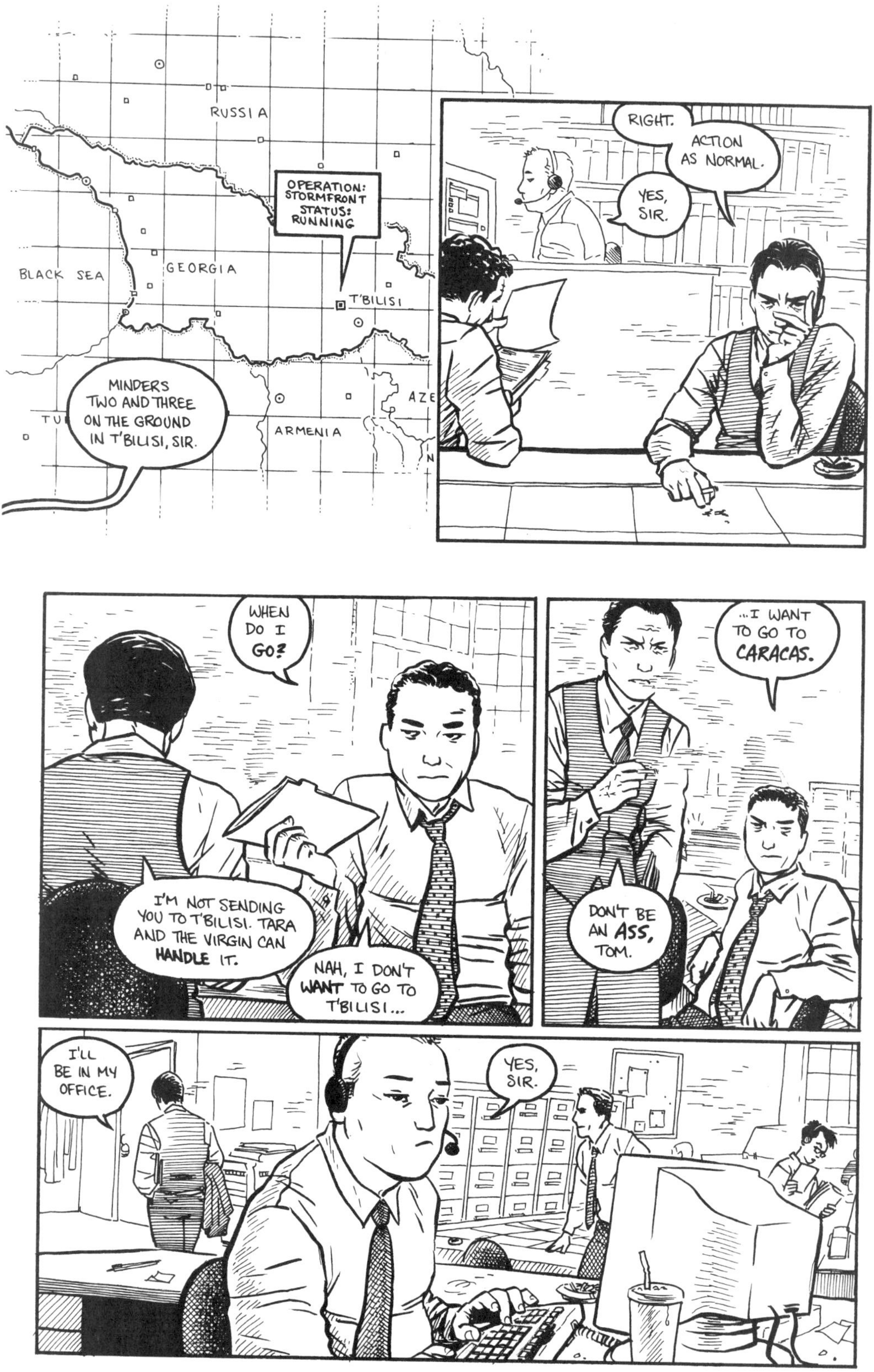
RUSSIA
OPERATION: STORMFRONT STATUS: RUNNING
BLACK SEA
GEORGIA
T'BILISI
ARMENIA
MINDERS TWO AND THREE ON THE GROUND IN T'BILISI, SIR.
RIGHT.
ACTION AS NORMAL.
YES, SIR.
WHEN DO I GO?
I'M NOT SENDING YOU TO T'BILISI. TARA AND THE VIRGIN CAN HANDLE IT.
NAH, I DON'T WANT TO GO TO T'BILISI...
...I WANT TO GO TO CARACAS.
DON'T BE AN ASS, TOM.
I'LL BE IN MY OFFICE.
YES, SIR.

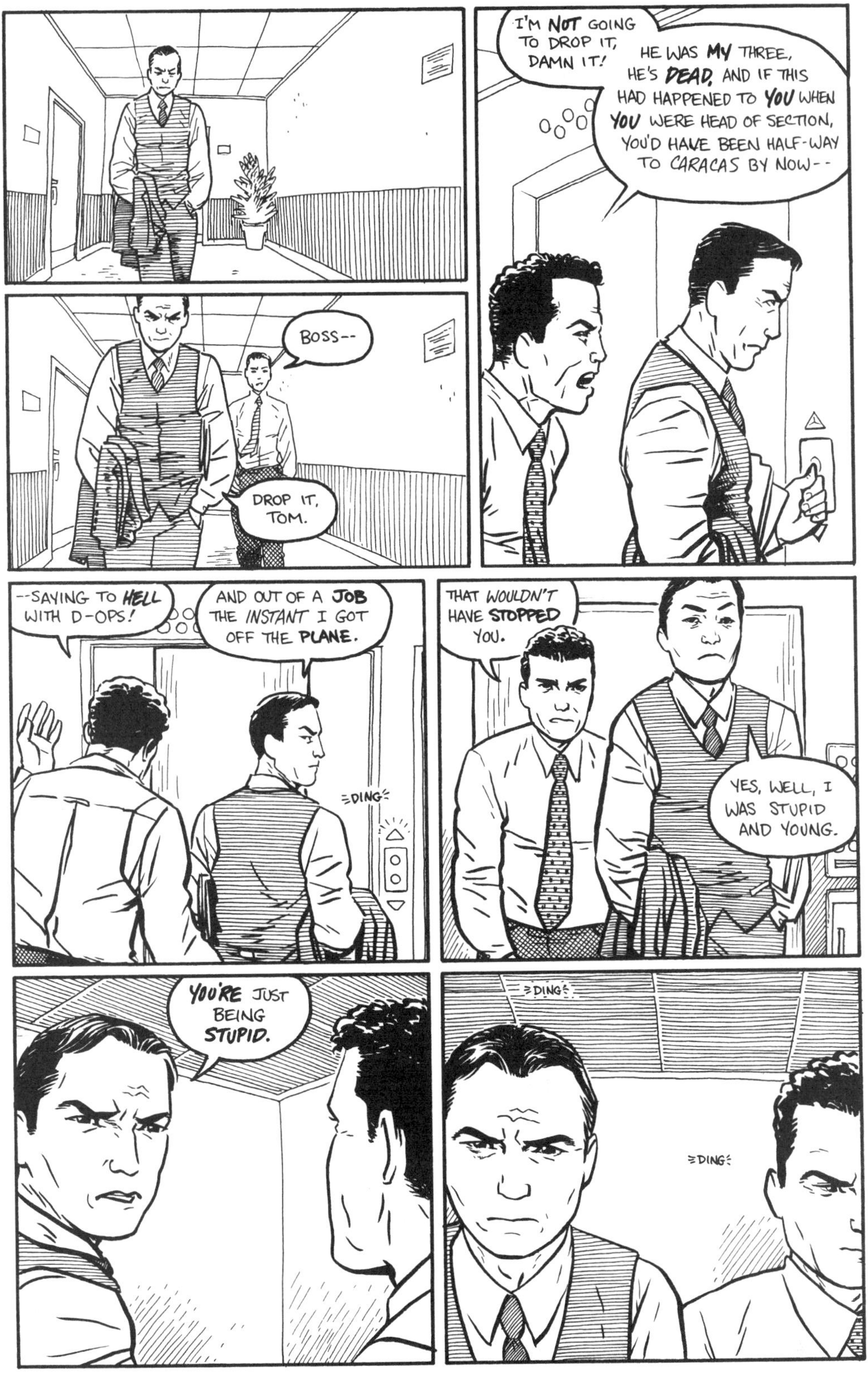
BOSS--
DROP IT, TOM.
I'M NOT GOING TO DROP IT, DAMN IT!
HE WAS MY THREE, HE'S DEAD, AND IF THIS HAD HAPPENED TO YOU WHEN YOU WERE HEAD OF SECTION, YOU'D HAVE BEEN HALF-WAY TO CARACAS BY NOW--
--SAYING TO HELL WITH D-OPS!
AND OUT OF A JOB THE INSTANT I GOT OFF THE PLANE.
DING
THAT WOULDN'T HAVE STOPPED YOU.
YES, WELL, I WAS STUPID AND YOUNG.
YOU'RE JUST BEING STUPID.
DING
DING

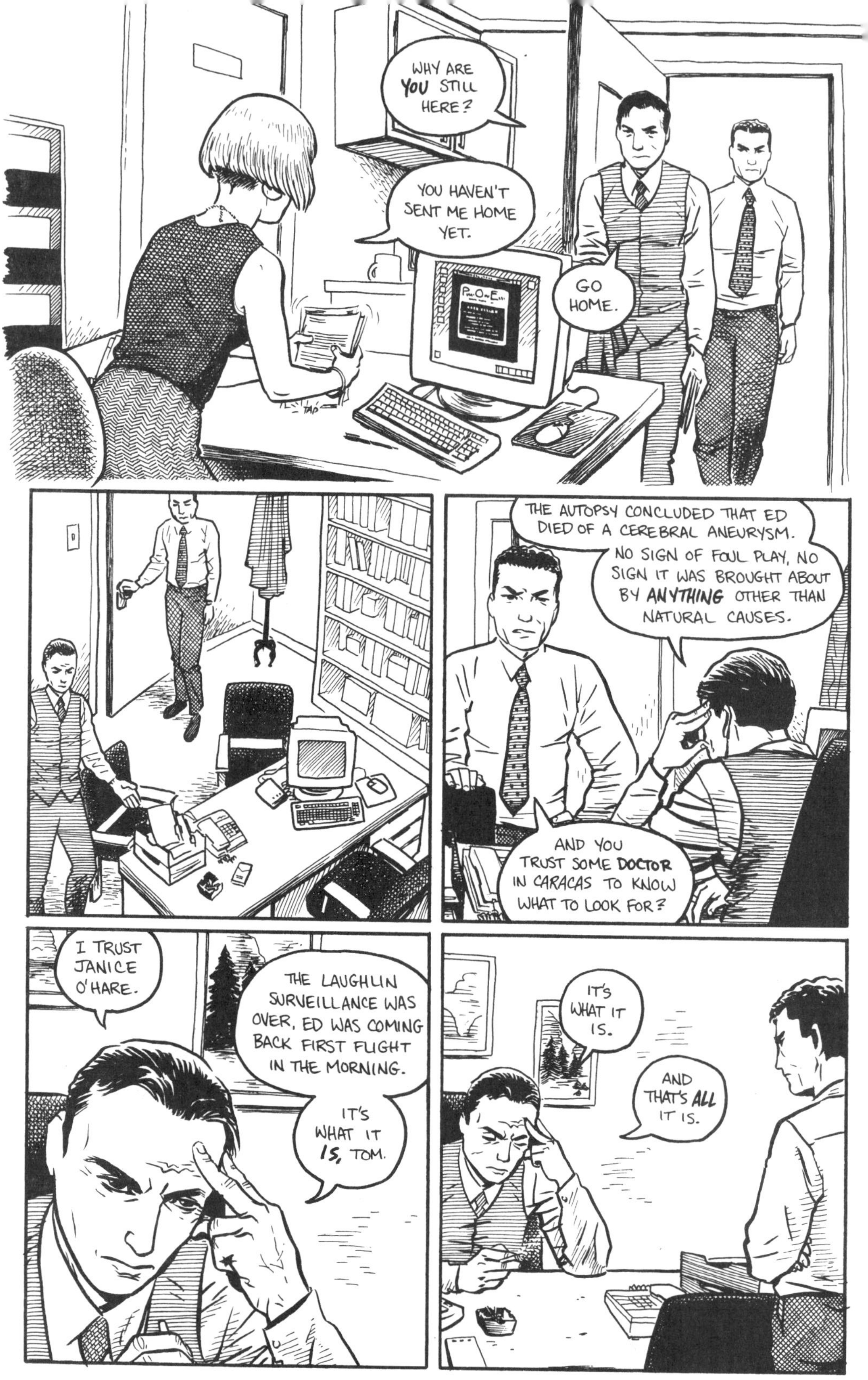
WHY ARE YOU STILL HERE?
YOU HAVEN'T SENT ME HOME YET.
GO HOME.
TAP
THE AUTOPSY CONCLUDED THAT ED DIED OF A CEREBRAL ANEURYSM.
NO SIGN OF FOUL PLAY, NO SIGN IT WAS BROUGHT ABOUT BY ANYTHING OTHER THAN NATURAL CAUSES.
AND YOU TRUST SOME DOCTOR IN CARACAS TO KNOW WHAT TO LOOK FOR?
I TRUST JANICE O'HARE.
THE LAUGHLIN SURVEILLANCE WAS OVER. ED WAS COMING BACK FIRST FLIGHT IN THE MORNING.
IT'S WHAT IT IS, TOM.
IT'S WHAT IT IS.
AND THAT'S ALL IT IS.

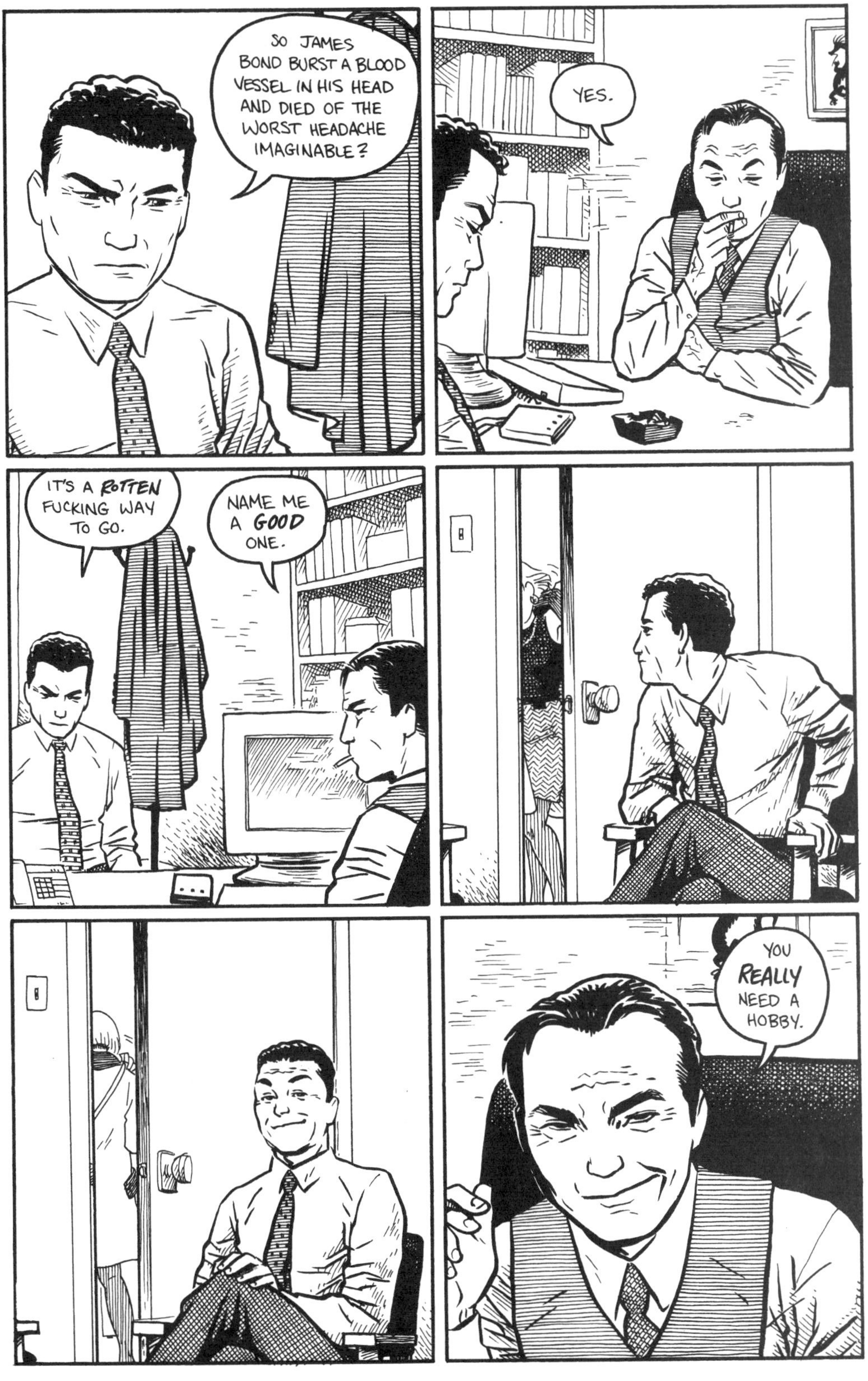
SO JAMES BOND BURST A BLOOD VESSEL IN HIS HEAD AND DIED OF THE WORST HEADACHE IMAGINABLE?
YES.
IT'S A ROTTEN FUCKING WAY TO GO.
NAME ME A GOOD ONE.
YOU REALLY NEED A HOBBY.

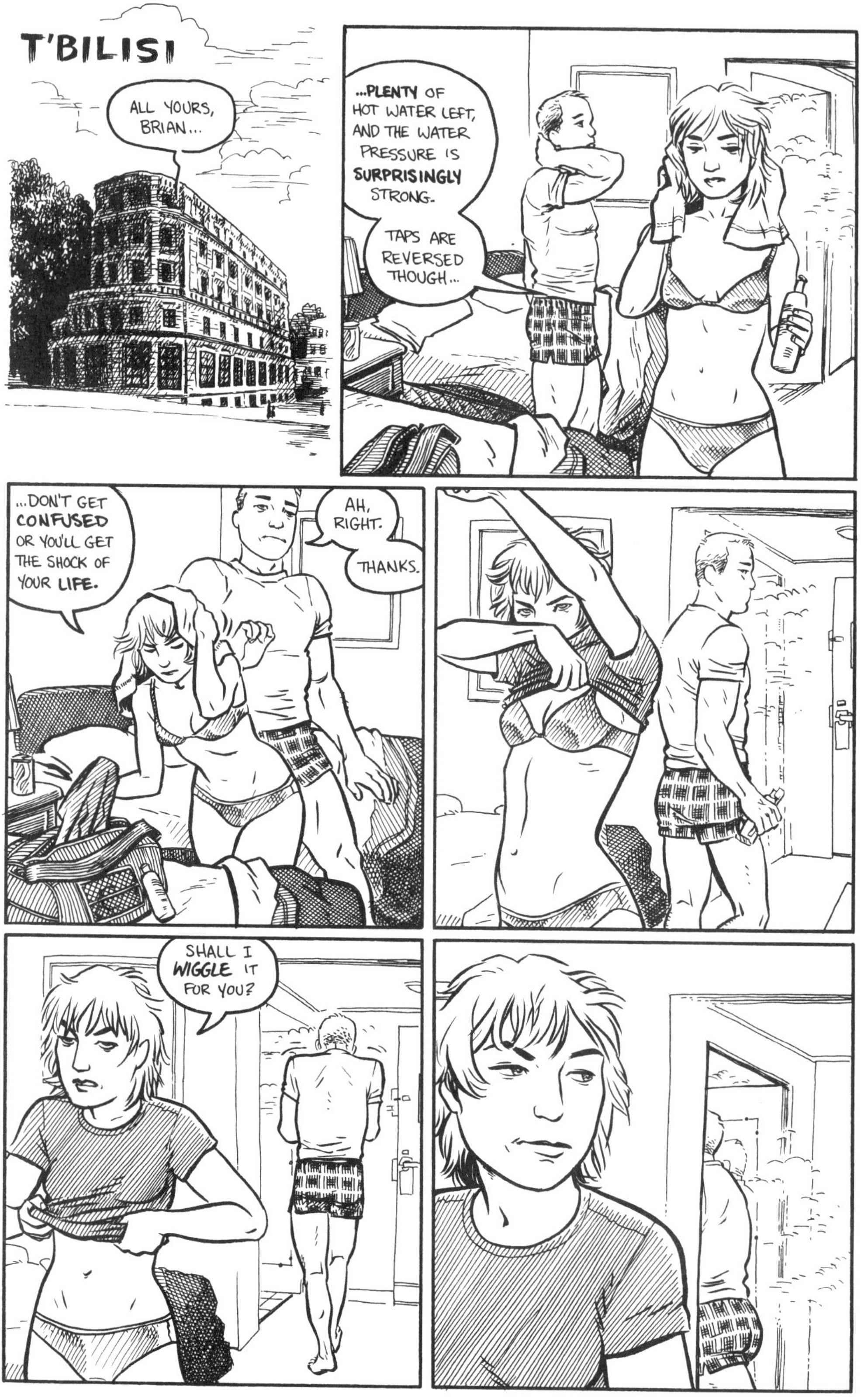
T'BILISI
ALL YOURS, BRIAN...
...PLENTY OF HOT WATER LEFT, AND THE WATER PRESSURE IS SURPRISINGLY STRONG.
TAPS ARE REVERSED THOUGH...
...DON'T GET CONFUSED OR YOU'LL GET THE SHOCK OF YOUR LIFE.
AH, RIGHT.
THANKS.
SHALL I WIGGLE IT FOR YOU?

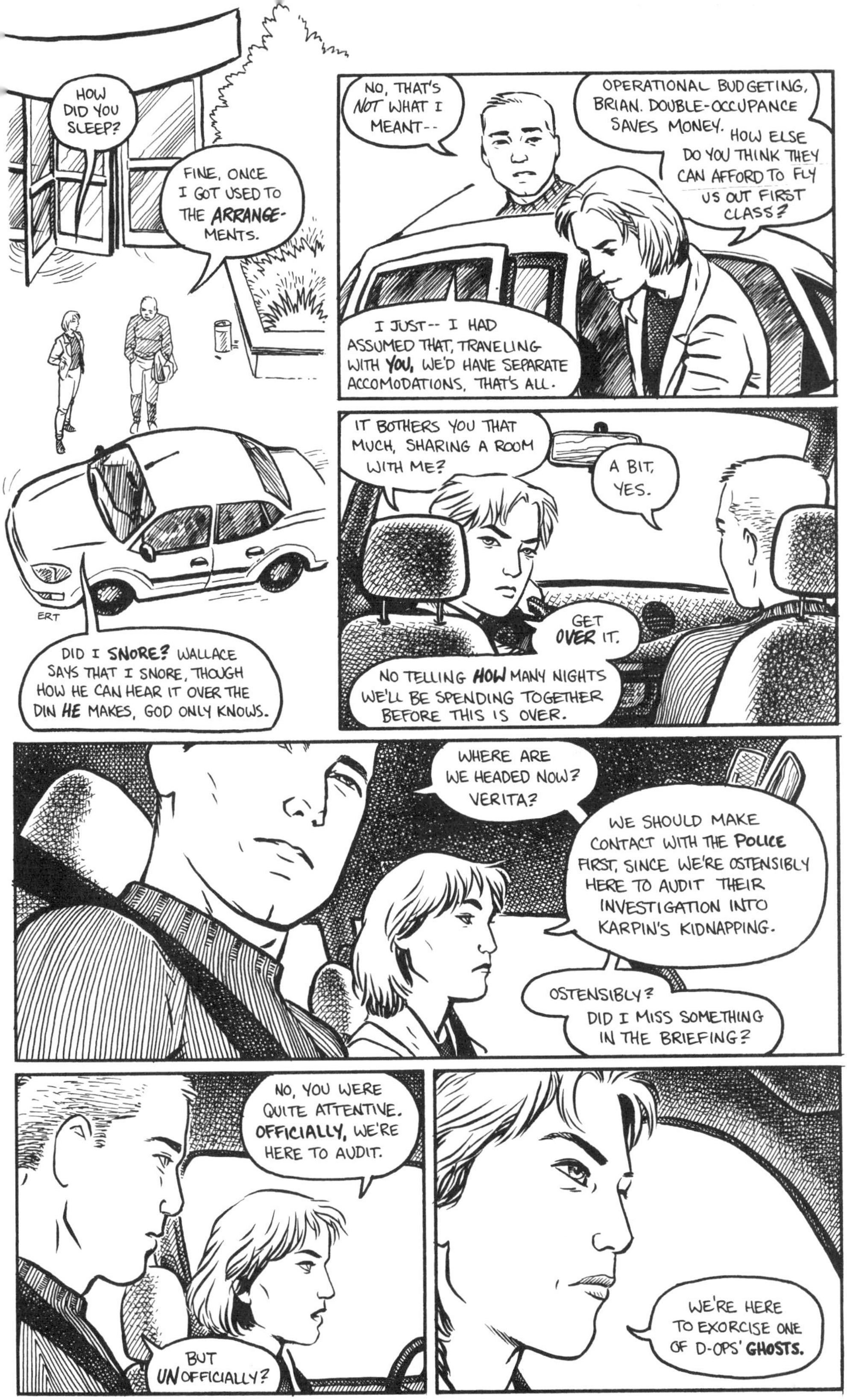
HOW DID YOU SLEEP?
FINE, ONCE I GOT USED TO THE ARRANGE-MENTS.
NO, THAT'S NOT WHAT I MEANT--
OPERATIONAL BUDGETING, BRIAN. DOUBLE-OCCUPANCE SAVES MONEY.
HOW ELSE DO YOU THINK THEY CAN AFFORD TO FLY US OUT FIRST CLASS?
I JUST-- I HAD ASSUMED THAT, TRAVELING WITH YOU, WE'D HAVE SEPARATE ACCOMODATIONS, THAT'S ALL.
ERT
DID I SNORE? WALLACE SAYS THAT I SNORE, THOUGH HOW HE CAN HEAR IT OVER THE DIN HE MAKES, GOD ONLY KNOWS.
IT BOTHERS YOU THAT MUCH, SHARING A ROOM WITH ME?
A BIT, YES.
GET OVER IT.
NO TELLING HOW MANY NIGHTS WE'LL BE SPENDING TOGETHER BEFORE THIS IS OVER.
WHERE ARE WE HEADED NOW? VERITA?
WE SHOULD MAKE CONTACT WITH THE POLICE FIRST, SINCE WE'RE OSTENSIBLY HERE TO AUDIT THEIR INVESTIGATION INTO KARPIN'S KIDNAPPING.
OSTENSIBLY?
DID I MISS SOMETHING IN THE BRIEFING?
NO, YOU WERE QUITE ATTENTIVE. OFFICIALLY, WE'RE HERE TO AUDIT.
BUT UNOFFICIALLY?
WE'RE HERE TO EXORCISE ONE OF D-OPS' GHOSTS.

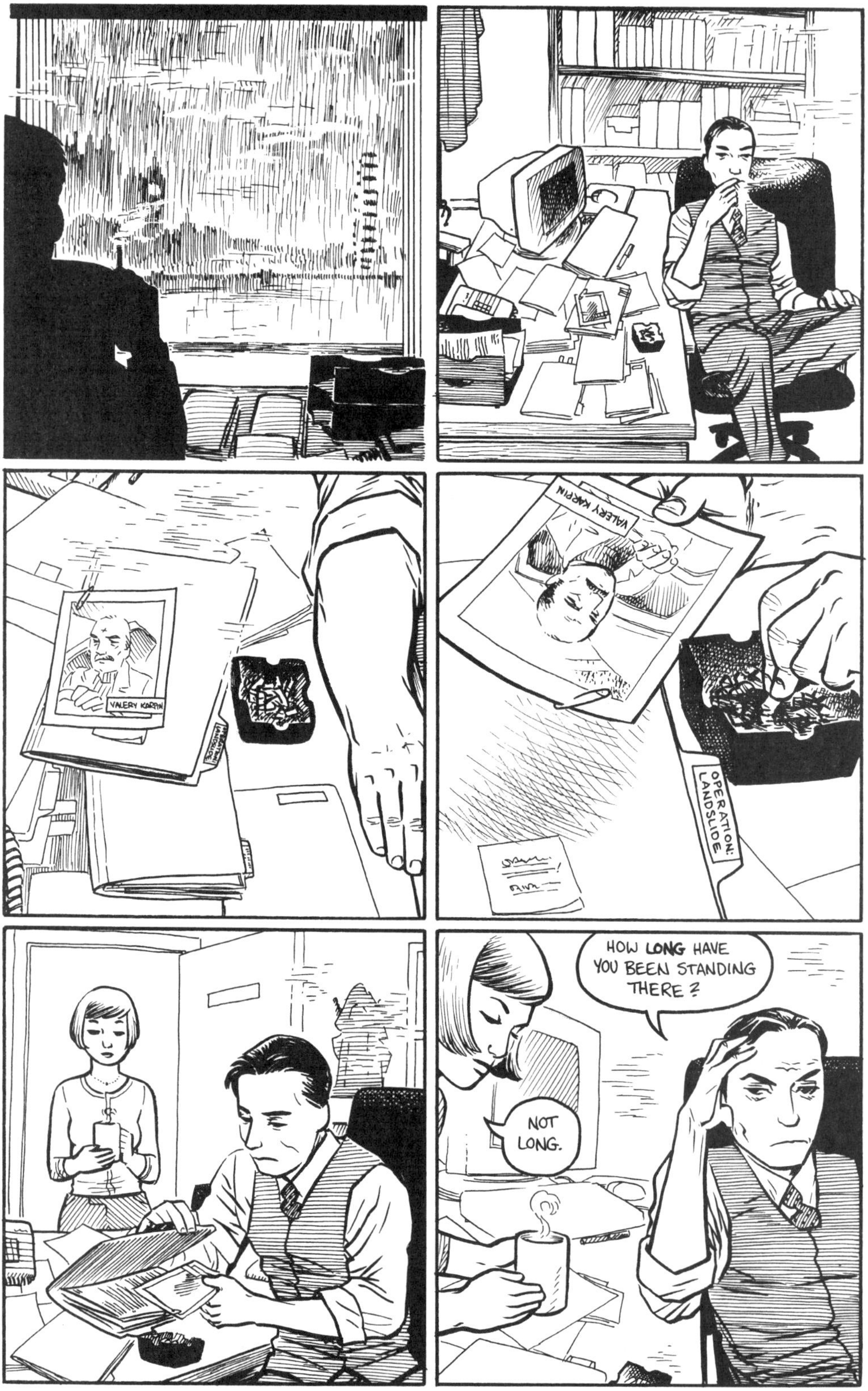
VALERY KARPIN
VALERY KARPIN
OPERATION: LANDSLIDE
HOW **LONG** HAVE YOU BEEN STANDING THERE?
NOT LONG.

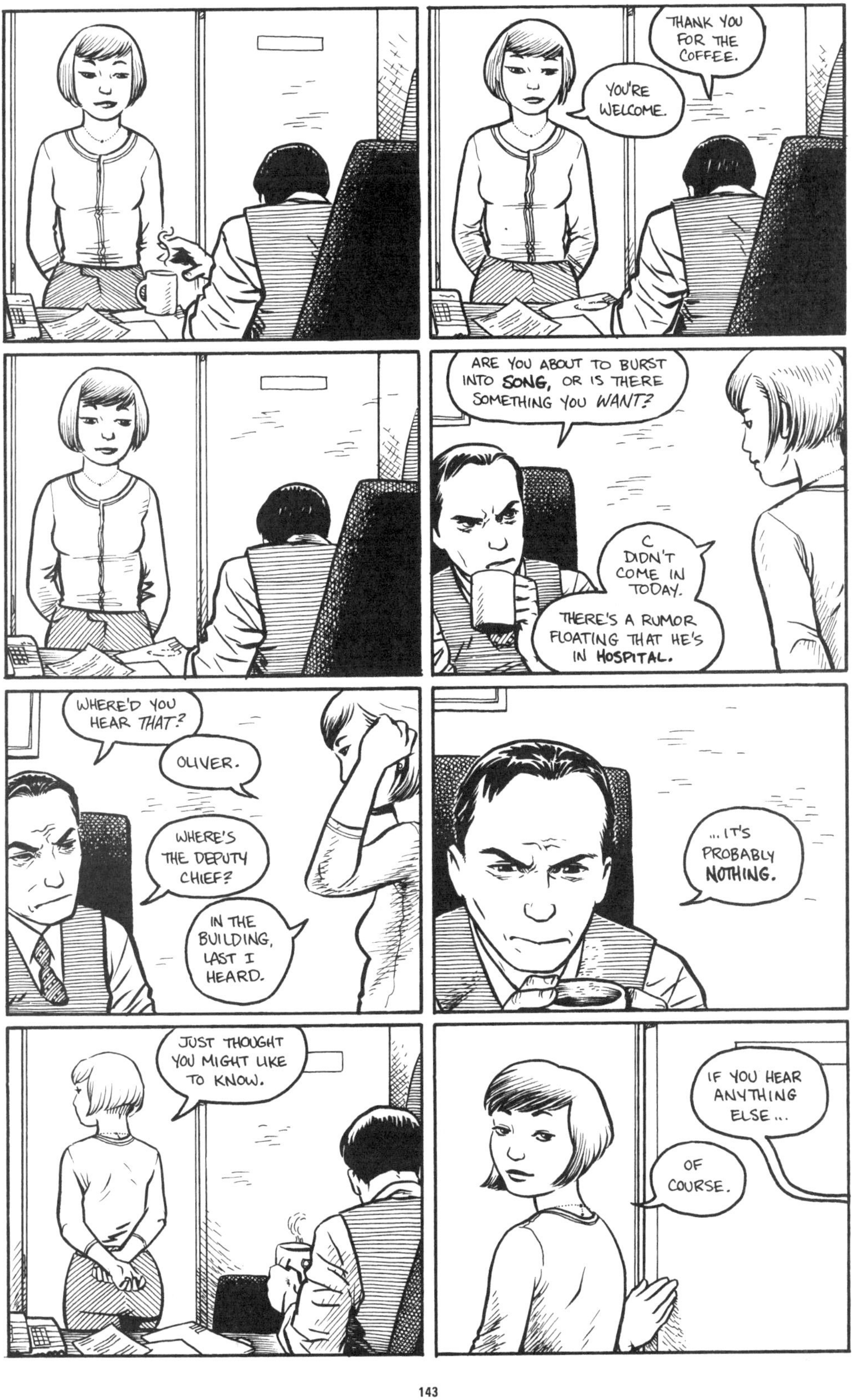
THANK YOU FOR THE COFFEE.
YOU'RE WELCOME.
ARE YOU ABOUT TO BURST INTO SONG, OR IS THERE SOMETHING YOU WANT?
C DIDN'T COME IN TODAY.
THERE'S A RUMOR FLOATING THAT HE'S IN HOSPITAL.
WHERE'D YOU HEAR THAT?
OLIVER.
WHERE'S THE DEPUTY CHIEF?
IN THE BUILDING, LAST I HEARD.
...IT'S PROBABLY NOTHING.
JUST THOUGHT YOU MIGHT LIKE TO KNOW.
IF YOU HEAR ANYTHING ELSE...
OF COURSE.

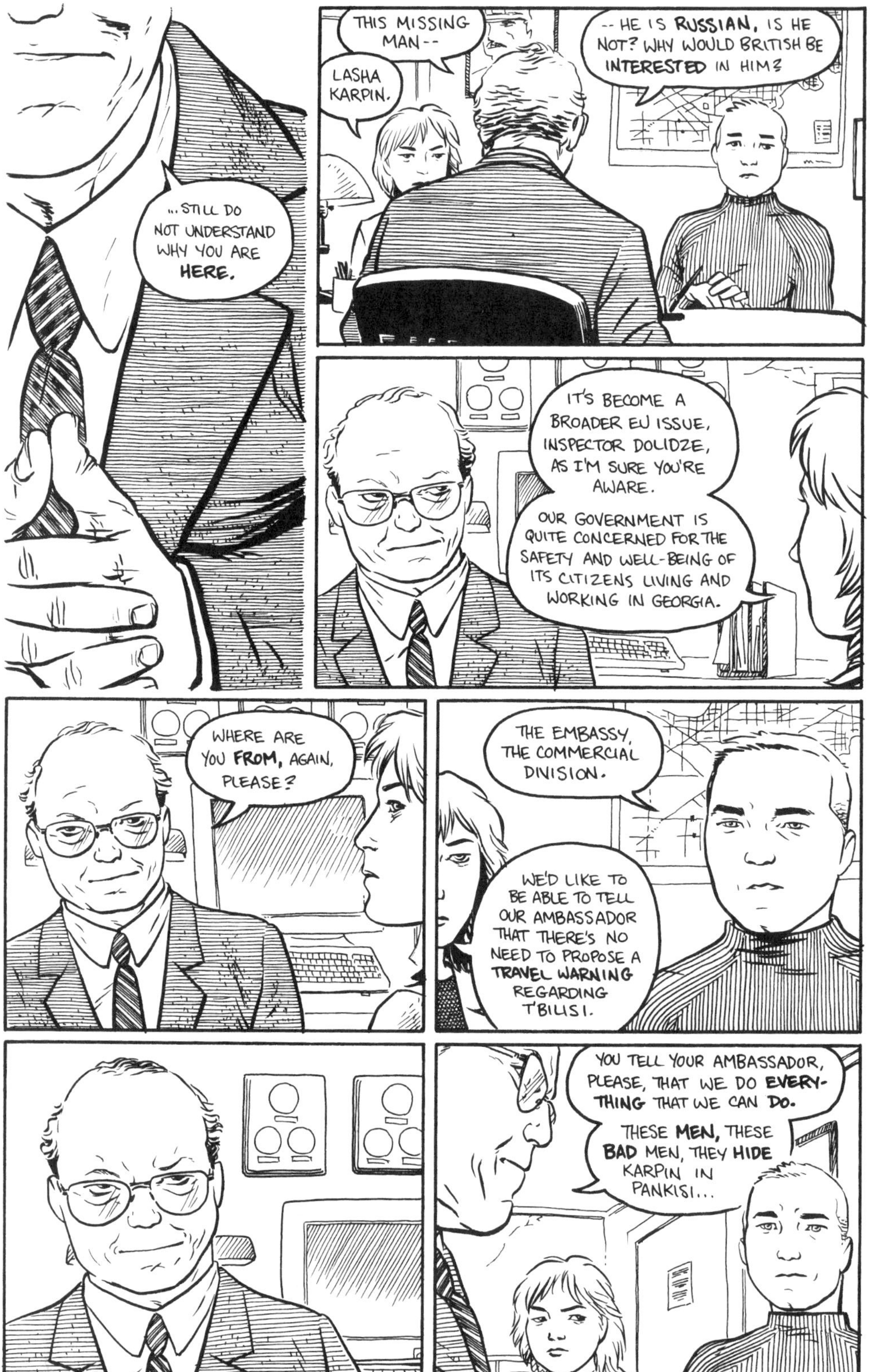
...STILL DO NOT UNDERSTAND WHY YOU ARE HERE.
THIS MISSING MAN--
LASHA KARPIN.
--HE IS RUSSIAN, IS HE NOT? WHY WOULD BRITISH BE INTERESTED IN HIM?
IT'S BECOME A BROADER EU ISSUE, INSPECTOR DOLIDZE, AS I'M SURE YOU'RE AWARE.
OUR GOVERNMENT IS QUITE CONCERNED FOR THE SAFETY AND WELL-BEING OF ITS CITIZENS LIVING AND WORKING IN GEORGIA.
WHERE ARE YOU FROM, AGAIN, PLEASE?
THE EMBASSY, THE COMMERCIAL DIVISION.
WE'D LIKE TO BE ABLE TO TELL OUR AMBASSADOR THAT THERE'S NO NEED TO PROPOSE A TRAVEL WARNING REGARDING T'BILISI.
YOU TELL YOUR AMBASSADOR, PLEASE, THAT WE DO EVERYTHING THAT WE CAN DO.
THESE MEN, THESE BAD MEN, THEY HIDE KARPIN IN PANKISI...

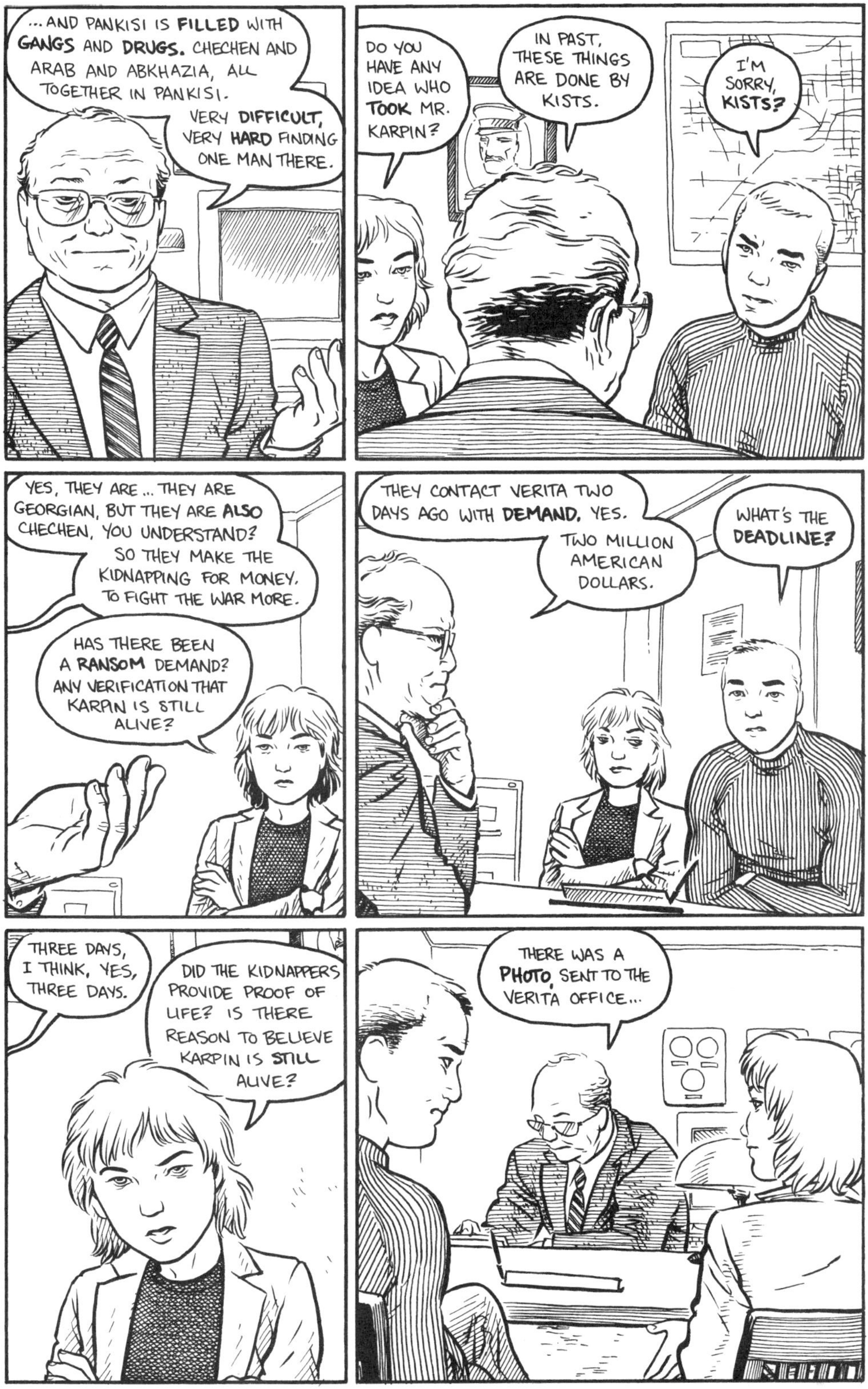
...AND PANKISI IS FILLED WITH GANGS AND DRUGS. CHECHEN AND ARAB AND ABKHAZIA, ALL TOGETHER IN PANKISI.
VERY DIFFICULT, VERY HARD FINDING ONE MAN THERE.
DO YOU HAVE ANY IDEA WHO TOOK MR. KARPIN?
IN PAST, THESE THINGS ARE DONE BY KISTS.
I'M SORRY, KISTS?
YES, THEY ARE... THEY ARE GEORGIAN, BUT THEY ARE ALSO CHECHEN, YOU UNDERSTAND?
SO THEY MAKE THE KIDNAPPING FOR MONEY. TO FIGHT THE WAR MORE.
HAS THERE BEEN A RANSOM DEMAND? ANY VERIFICATION THAT KARPIN IS STILL ALIVE?
THEY CONTACT VERITA TWO DAYS AGO WITH DEMAND. YES.
TWO MILLION AMERICAN DOLLARS.
WHAT'S THE DEADLINE?
THREE DAYS, I THINK, YES, THREE DAYS.
DID THE KIDNAPPERS PROVIDE PROOF OF LIFE? IS THERE REASON TO BELIEVE KARPIN IS STILL ALIVE?
THERE WAS A PHOTO, SENT TO THE VERITA OFFICE...

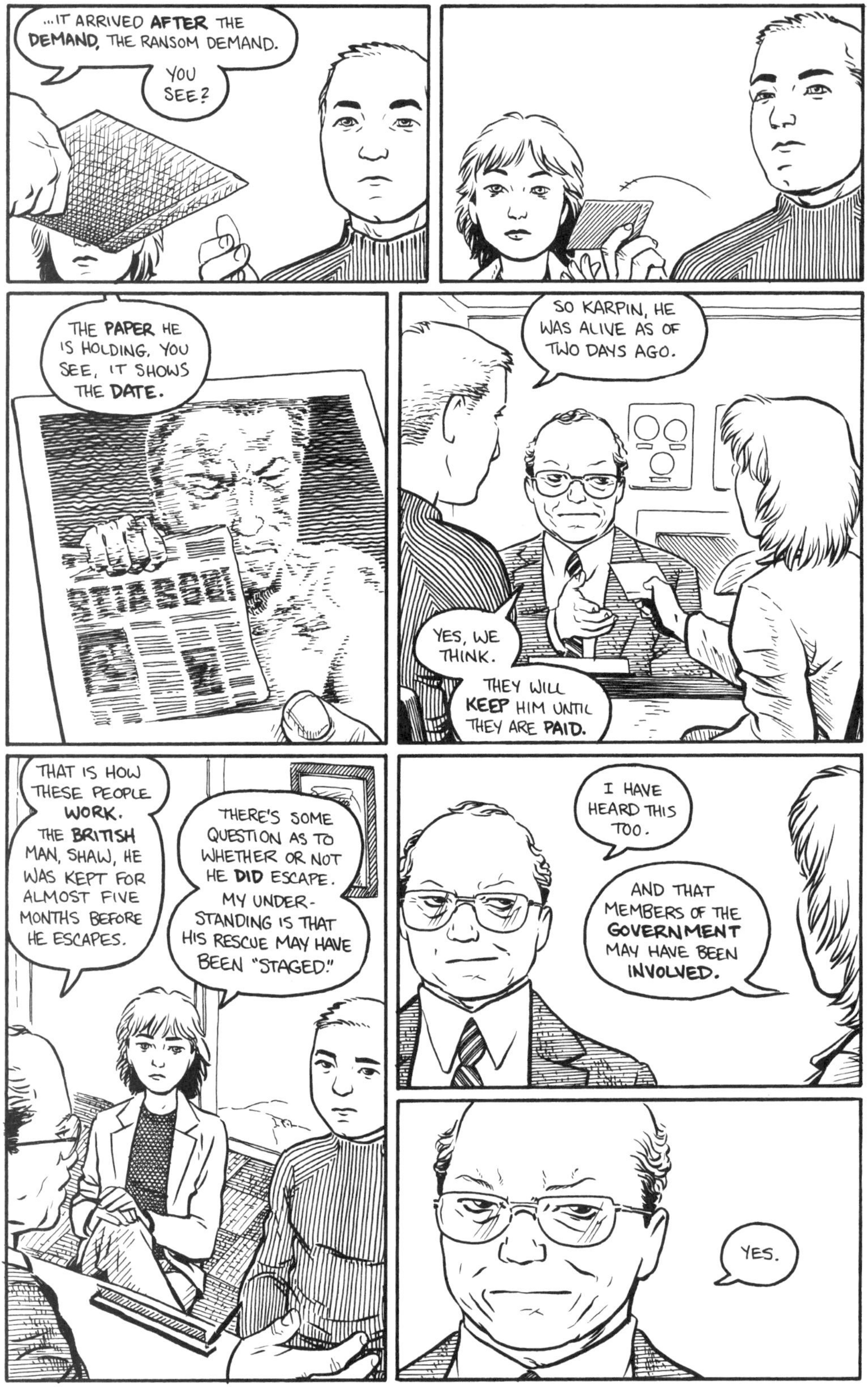

...IT ARRIVED AFTER THE DEMAND, THE RANSOM DEMAND.
YOU SEE?
THE PAPER HE IS HOLDING. YOU SEE, IT SHOWS THE DATE.
SO KARPIN, HE WAS ALIVE AS OF TWO DAYS AGO.
YES, WE THINK.
THEY WILL KEEP HIM UNTIL THEY ARE PAID.
THAT IS HOW THESE PEOPLE WORK. THE BRITISH MAN, SHAW, HE WAS KEPT FOR ALMOST FIVE MONTHS BEFORE HE ESCAPES.
THERE'S SOME QUESTION AS TO WHETHER OR NOT HE DID ESCAPE. MY UNDER-STANDING IS THAT HIS RESCUE MAY HAVE BEEN "STAGED."
I HAVE HEARD THIS TOO.
AND THAT MEMBERS OF THE GOVERNMENT MAY HAVE BEEN INVOLVED.
YES.

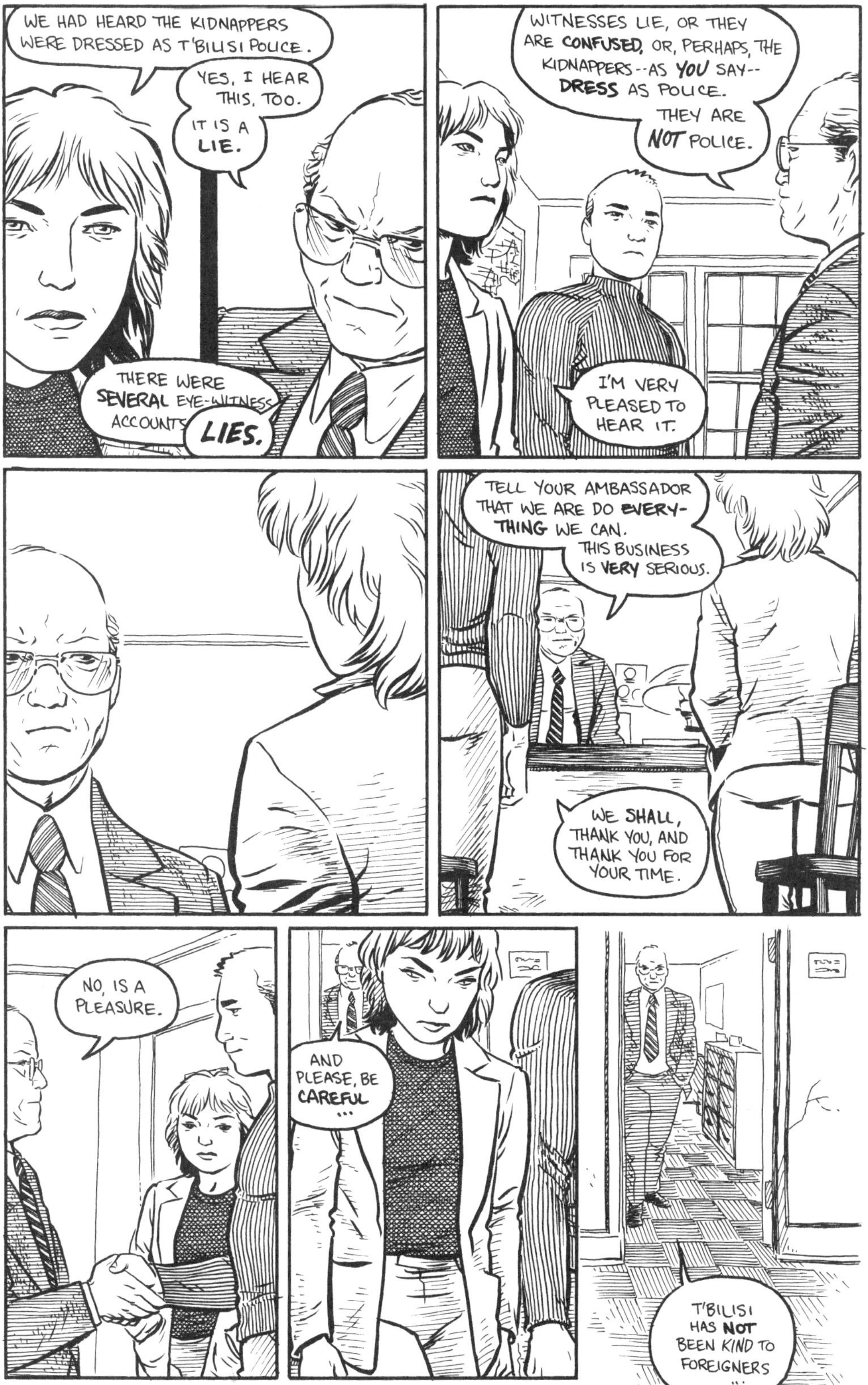
WE HAD HEARD THE KIDNAPPERS WERE DRESSED AS T'BILISI POLICE.
YES, I HEAR THIS, TOO.
IT IS A **LIE.**
THERE WERE **SEVERAL** EYE-WITNESS ACCOUNTS
LIES.
WITNESSES LIE, OR THEY ARE **CONFUSED,** OR, PERHAPS, THE KIDNAPPERS--AS **YOU** SAY-- **DRESS** AS POLICE.
THEY ARE **NOT** POLICE.
I'M VERY PLEASED TO HEAR IT.
TELL YOUR AMBASSADOR THAT WE ARE DO **EVERY-THING** WE CAN.
THIS BUSINESS IS **VERY** SERIOUS.
WE **SHALL,** THANK YOU, AND THANK YOU FOR YOUR TIME.
NO, IS A PLEASURE.
AND PLEASE, BE **CAREFUL** ...
T'BILISI HAS **NOT** BEEN KIND TO FOREIGNERS ...

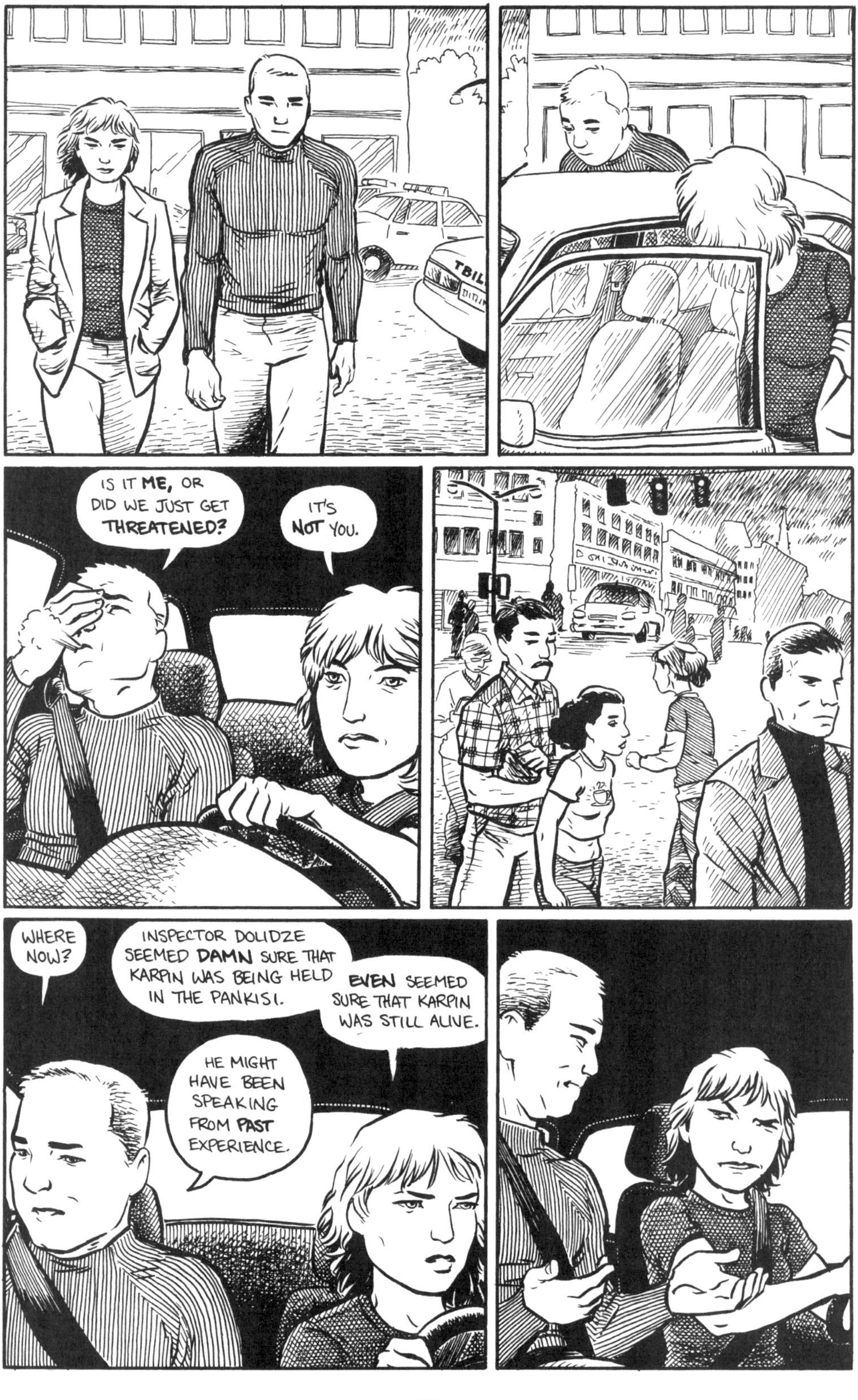
IS IT **ME,** OR DID WE JUST GET **THREATENED?**
IT'S **NOT** YOU.
WHERE NOW?
INSPECTOR DOLIDZE SEEMED **DAMN** SURE THAT KARPIN WAS BEING HELD IN THE PANKISI.
EVEN SEEMED SURE THAT KARPIN WAS STILL ALIVE.
HE MIGHT HAVE BEEN SPEAKING FROM **PAST** EXPERIENCE.

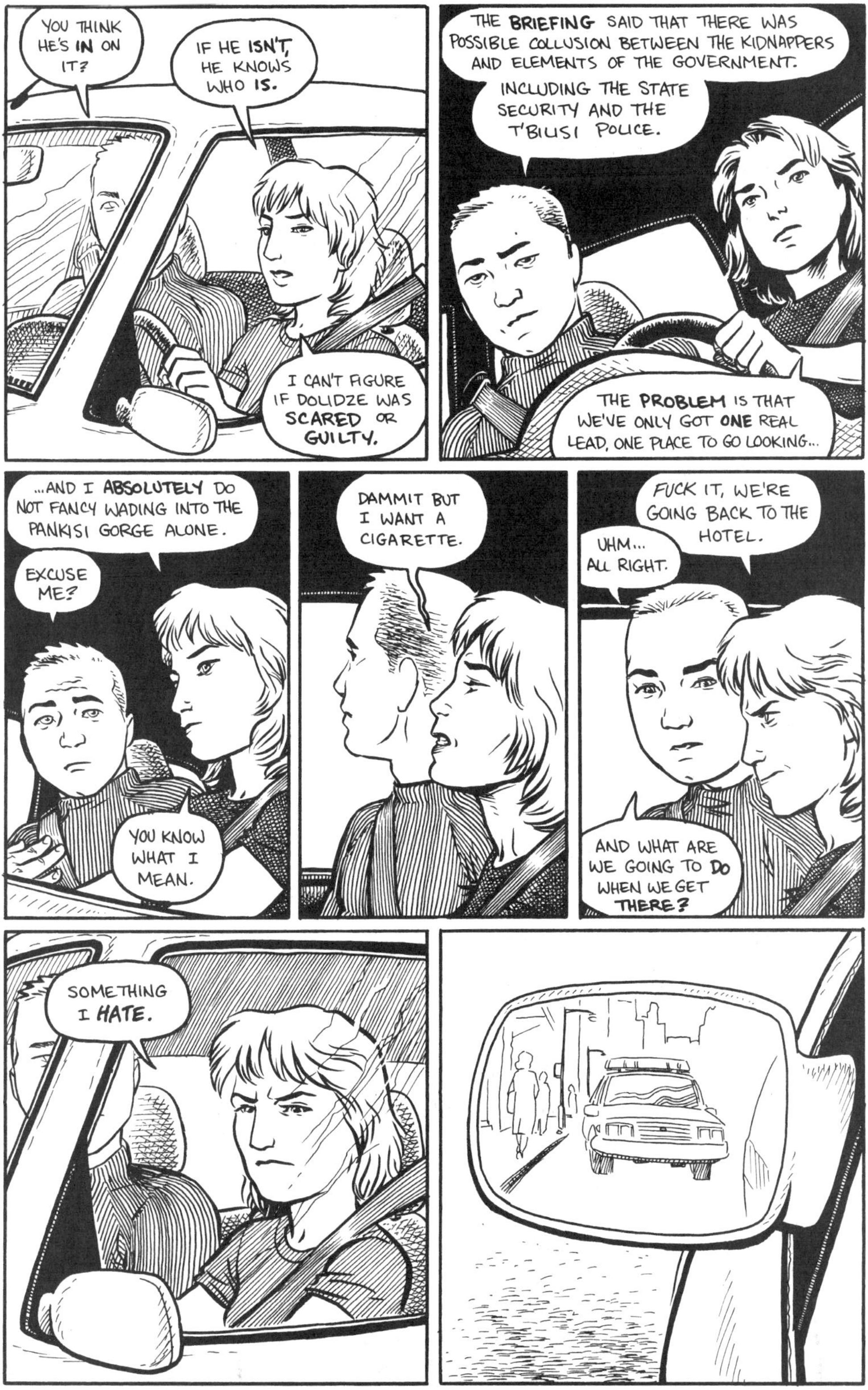
YOU THINK HE'S IN ON IT?
IF HE ISN'T, HE KNOWS WHO IS.
I CAN'T FIGURE IF DOLIDZE WAS SCARED OR GUILTY.
THE BRIEFING SAID THAT THERE WAS POSSIBLE COLLUSION BETWEEN THE KIDNAPPERS AND ELEMENTS OF THE GOVERNMENT.
INCLUDING THE STATE SECURITY AND THE T'BILISI POLICE.
THE PROBLEM IS THAT WE'VE ONLY GOT ONE REAL LEAD, ONE PLACE TO GO LOOKING...
...AND I ABSOLUTELY DO NOT FANCY WADING INTO THE PANKISI GORGE ALONE.
EXCUSE ME?
YOU KNOW WHAT I MEAN.
DAMMIT BUT I WANT A CIGARETTE.
FUCK IT, WE'RE GOING BACK TO THE HOTEL.
UHM... ALL RIGHT.
AND WHAT ARE WE GOING TO DO WHEN WE GET THERE?
SOMETHING I HATE.

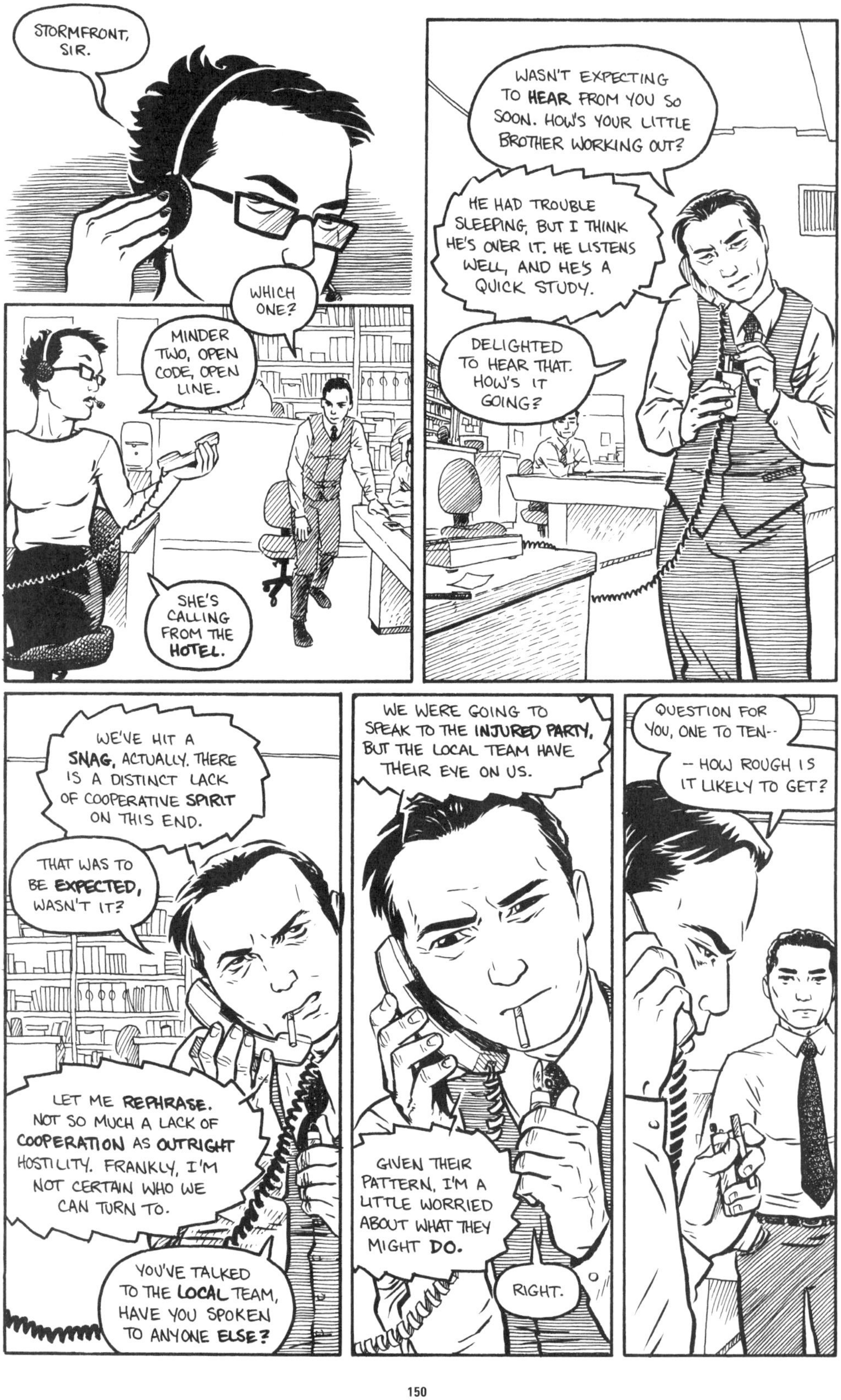
STORMFRONT, SIR.
WASN'T EXPECTING TO HEAR FROM YOU SO SOON. HOW'S YOUR LITTLE BROTHER WORKING OUT?
HE HAD TROUBLE SLEEPING, BUT I THINK HE'S OVER IT. HE LISTENS WELL, AND HE'S A QUICK STUDY.
WHICH ONE?
MINDER TWO, OPEN CODE, OPEN LINE.
SHE'S CALLING FROM THE HOTEL.
DELIGHTED TO HEAR THAT. HOW'S IT GOING?
WE'VE HIT A SNAG, ACTUALLY. THERE IS A DISTINCT LACK OF COOPERATIVE SPIRIT ON THIS END.
THAT WAS TO BE EXPECTED, WASN'T IT?
LET ME REPHRASE. NOT SO MUCH A LACK OF COOPERATION AS OUTRIGHT HOSTILITY. FRANKLY, I'M NOT CERTAIN WHO WE CAN TURN TO.
YOU'VE TALKED TO THE LOCAL TEAM, HAVE YOU SPOKEN TO ANYONE ELSE?
WE WERE GOING TO SPEAK TO THE INJURED PARTY, BUT THE LOCAL TEAM HAVE THEIR EYE ON US.
GIVEN THEIR PATTERN, I'M A LITTLE WORRIED ABOUT WHAT THEY MIGHT DO.
RIGHT.
QUESTION FOR YOU, ONE TO TEN--
-- HOW ROUGH IS IT LIKELY TO GET?

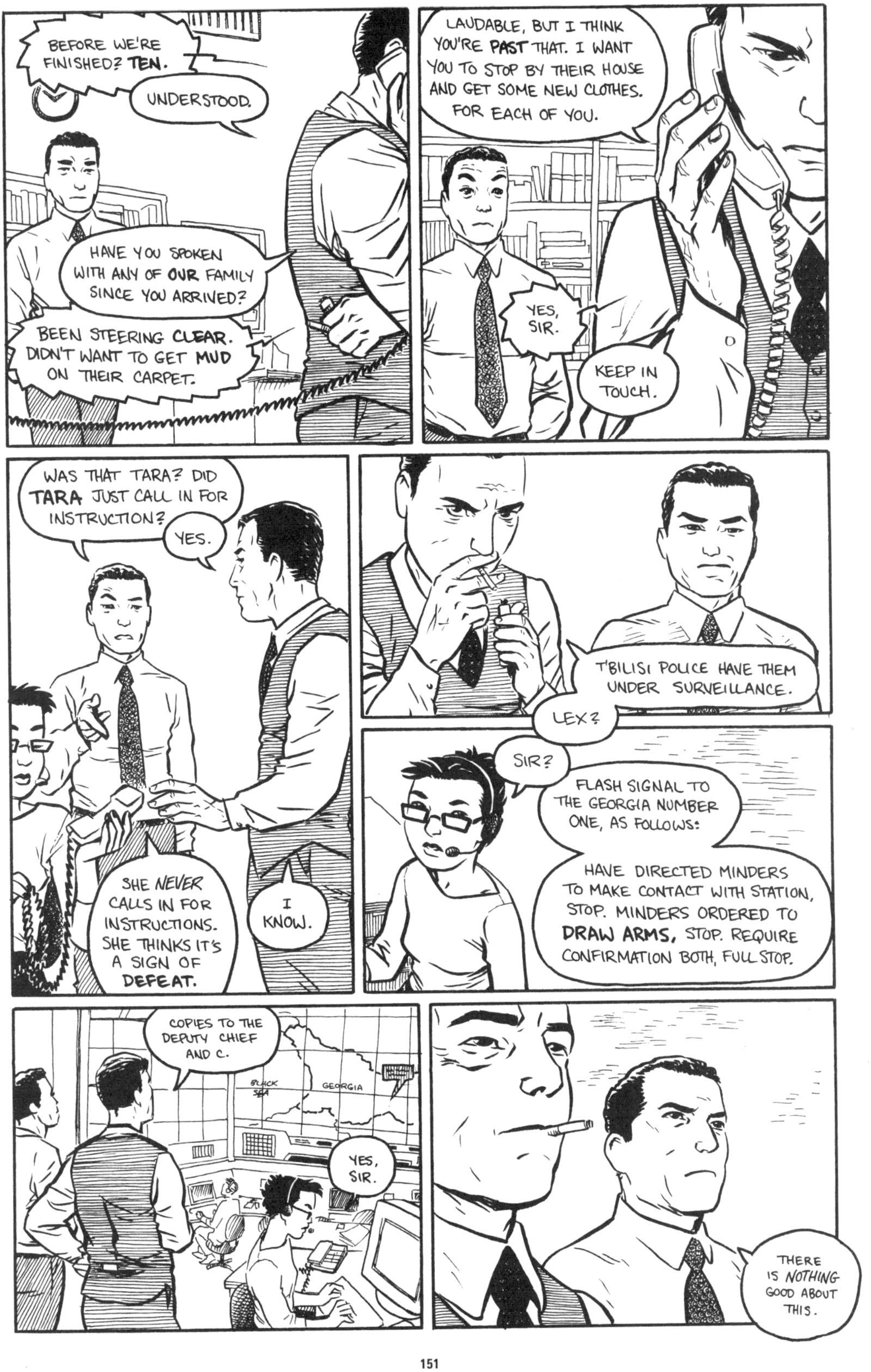
BEFORE WE'RE FINISHED? TEN.
UNDERSTOOD.
HAVE YOU SPOKEN WITH ANY OF OUR FAMILY SINCE YOU ARRIVED?
BEEN STEERING CLEAR. DIDN'T WANT TO GET MUD ON THEIR CARPET.
LAUDABLE, BUT I THINK YOU'RE PAST THAT. I WANT YOU TO STOP BY THEIR HOUSE AND GET SOME NEW CLOTHES. FOR EACH OF YOU.
YES, SIR.
KEEP IN TOUCH.
WAS THAT TARA? DID TARA JUST CALL IN FOR INSTRUCTION?
YES.
SHE NEVER CALLS IN FOR INSTRUCTIONS. SHE THINKS IT'S A SIGN OF DEFEAT.
I KNOW.
T'BILISI POLICE HAVE THEM UNDER SURVEILLANCE.
LEX?
SIR?
FLASH SIGNAL TO THE GEORGIA NUMBER ONE, AS FOLLOWS:
HAVE DIRECTED MINDERS TO MAKE CONTACT WITH STATION, STOP. MINDERS ORDERED TO DRAW ARMS, STOP. REQUIRE CONFIRMATION BOTH, FULL STOP.
COPIES TO THE DEPUTY CHIEF AND C.
BLACK SEA
GEORGIA
YES, SIR.
THERE IS NOTHING GOOD ABOUT THIS.

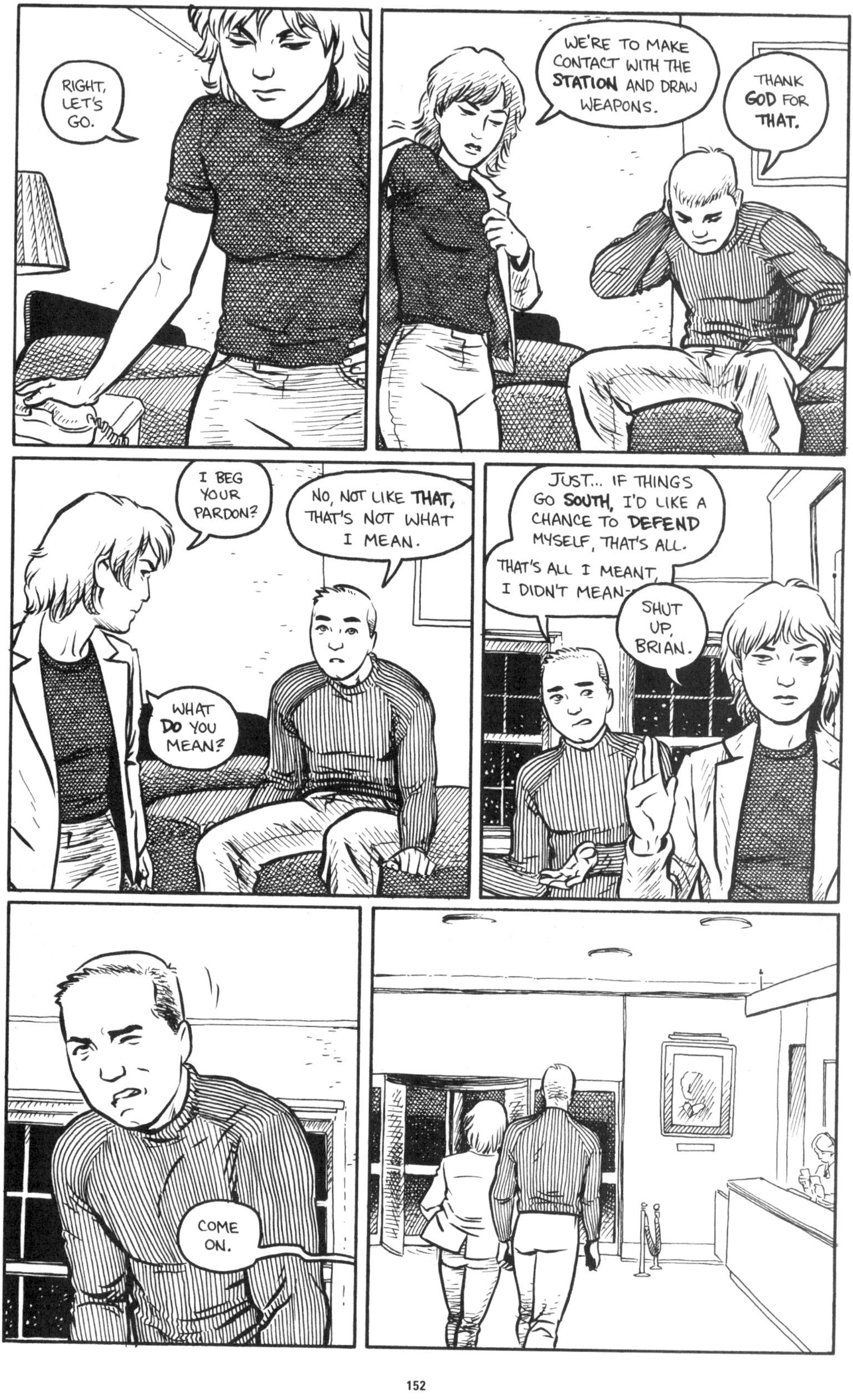
RIGHT, LET'S GO.
WE'RE TO MAKE CONTACT WITH THE STATION AND DRAW WEAPONS.
THANK GOD FOR THAT.
I BEG YOUR PARDON?
NO, NOT LIKE THAT, THAT'S NOT WHAT I MEAN.
WHAT DO YOU MEAN?
JUST... IF THINGS GO SOUTH, I'D LIKE A CHANCE TO DEFEND MYSELF, THAT'S ALL.
THAT'S ALL I MEANT, I DIDN'T MEAN--
SHUT UP, BRIAN.
COME ON.

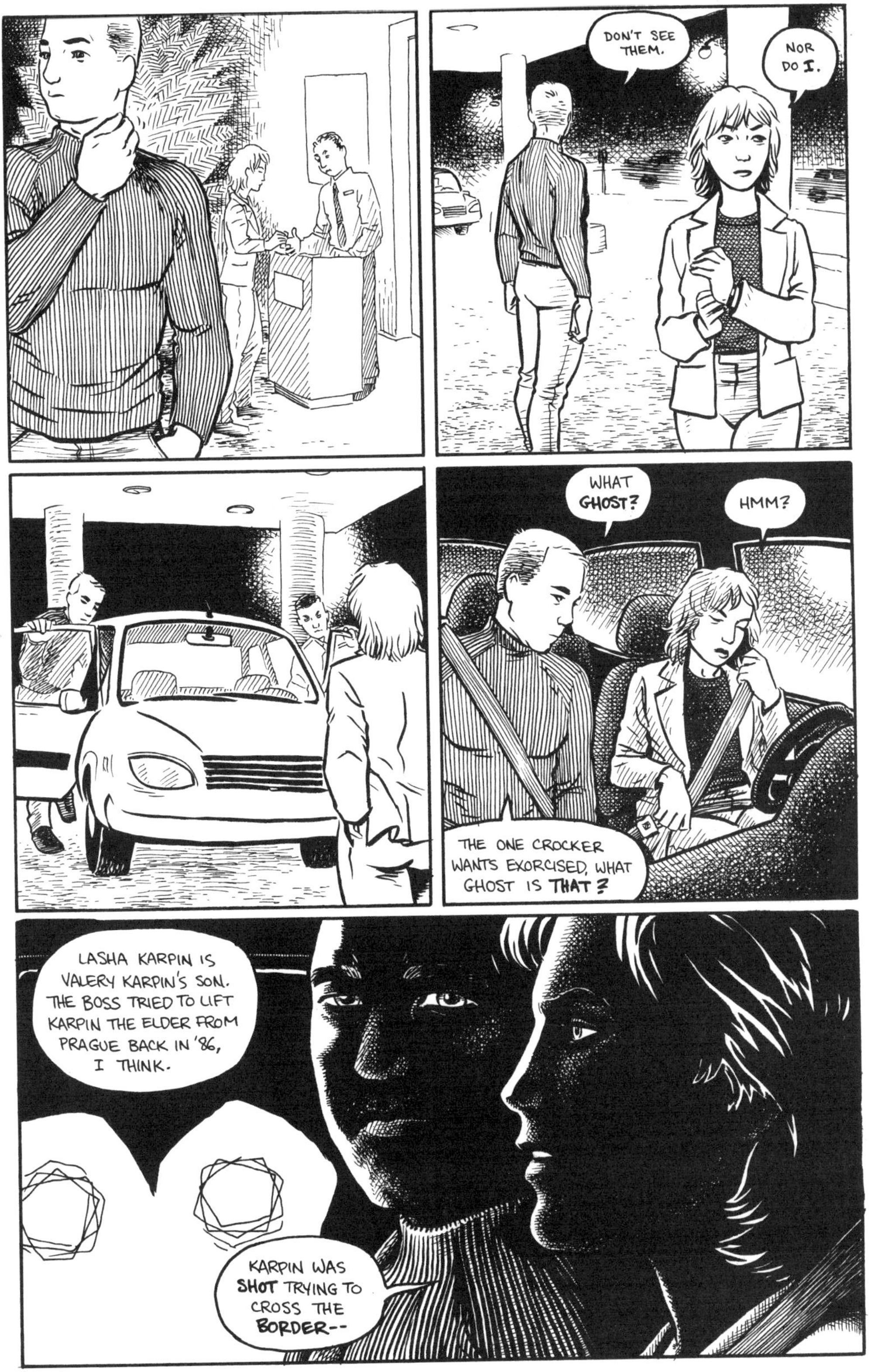
DON'T SEE THEM.
NOR DO I.
WHAT GHOST?
HMM?
THE ONE CROCKER WANTS EXORCISED, WHAT GHOST IS THAT?
LASHA KARPIN IS VALERY KARPIN'S SON. THE BOSS TRIED TO LIFT KARPIN THE ELDER FROM PRAGUE BACK IN '86, I THINK.
KARPIN WAS SHOT TRYING TO CROSS THE BORDER--

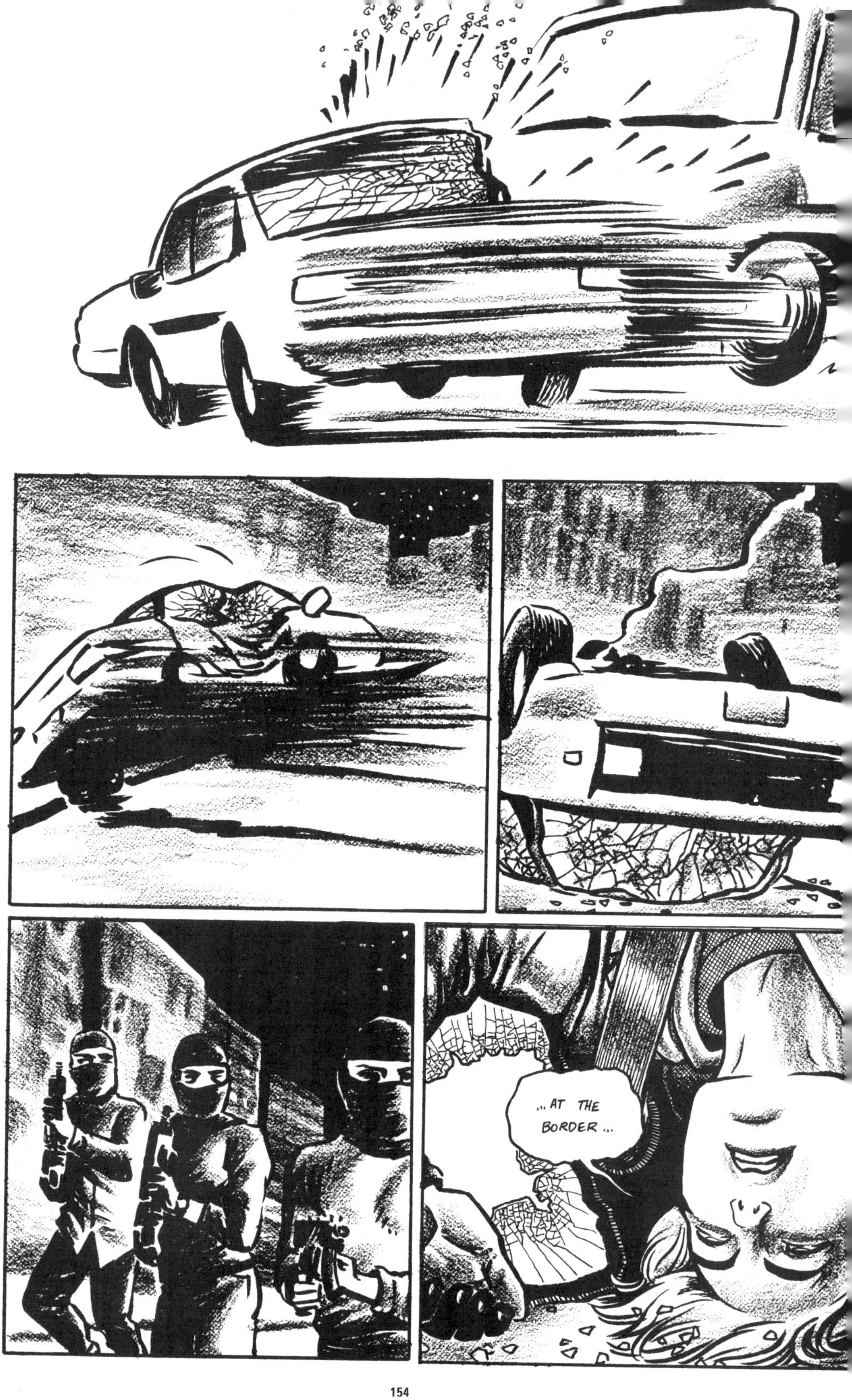
... AT THE BORDER ...

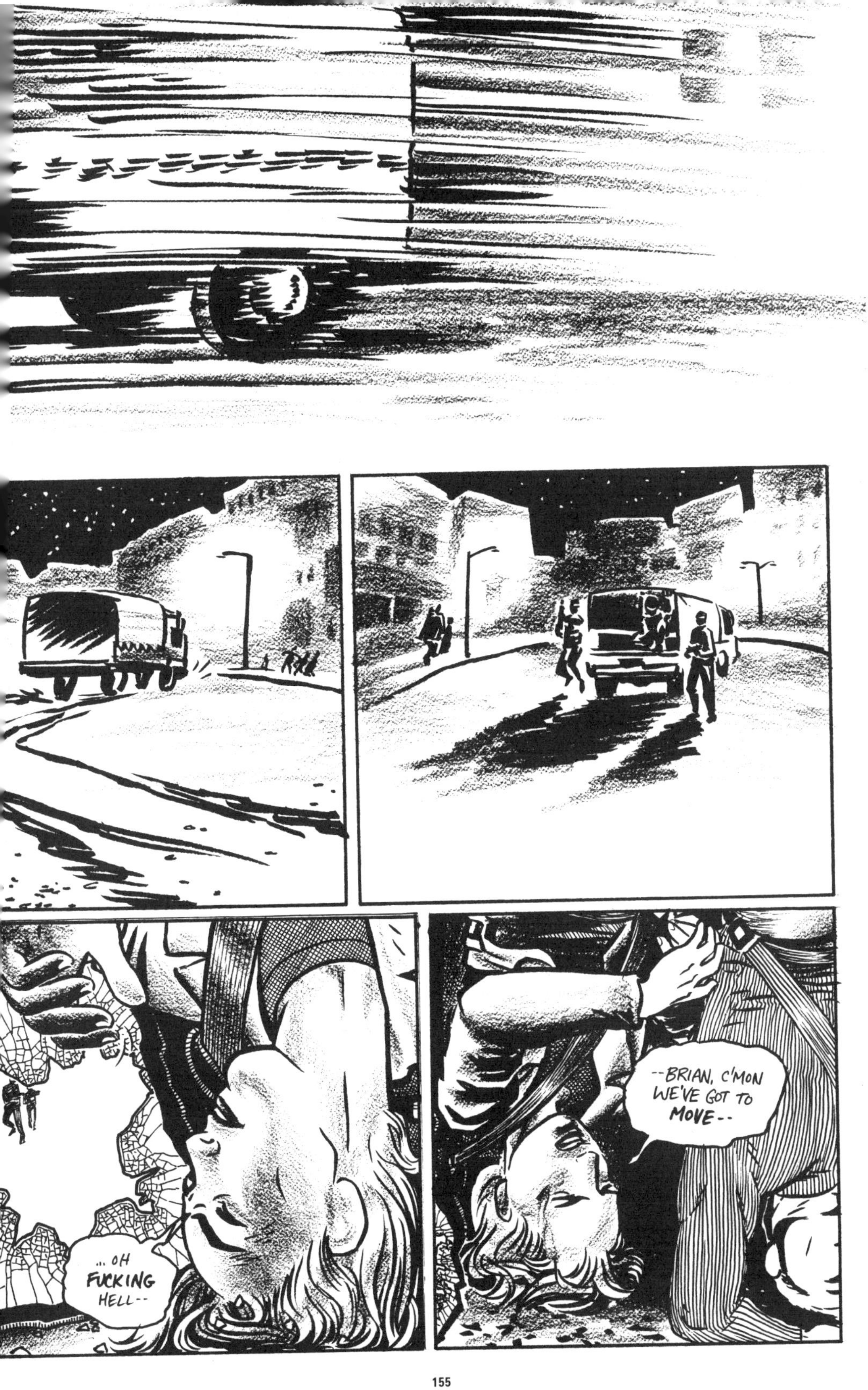
...OH FUCKING HELL--
--BRIAN, C'MON WE'VE GOT TO MOVE--

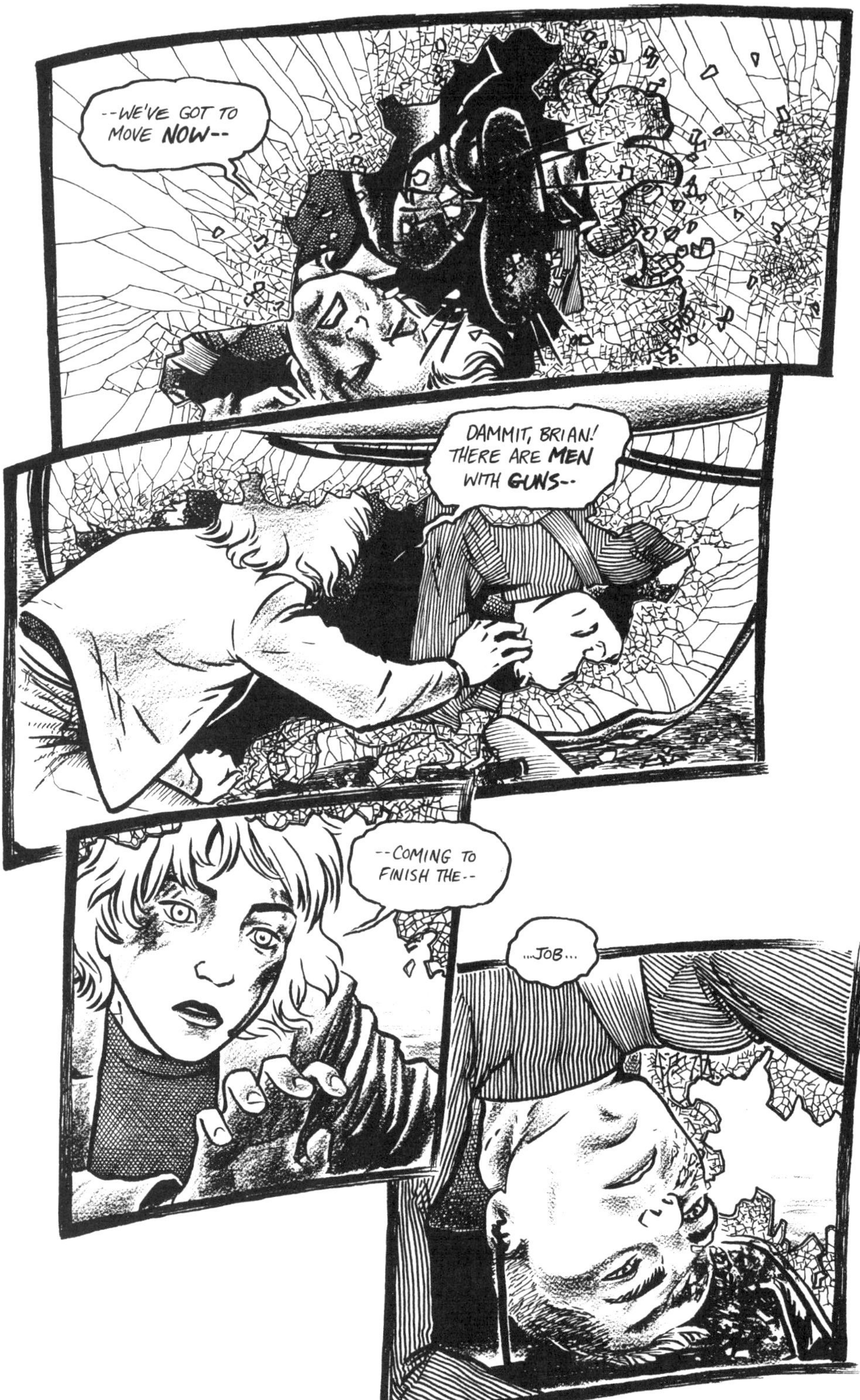
--WE'VE GOT TO MOVE NOW--
DAMMIT, BRIAN! THERE ARE MEN WITH GUNS--
--COMING TO FINISH THE--
...JOB...

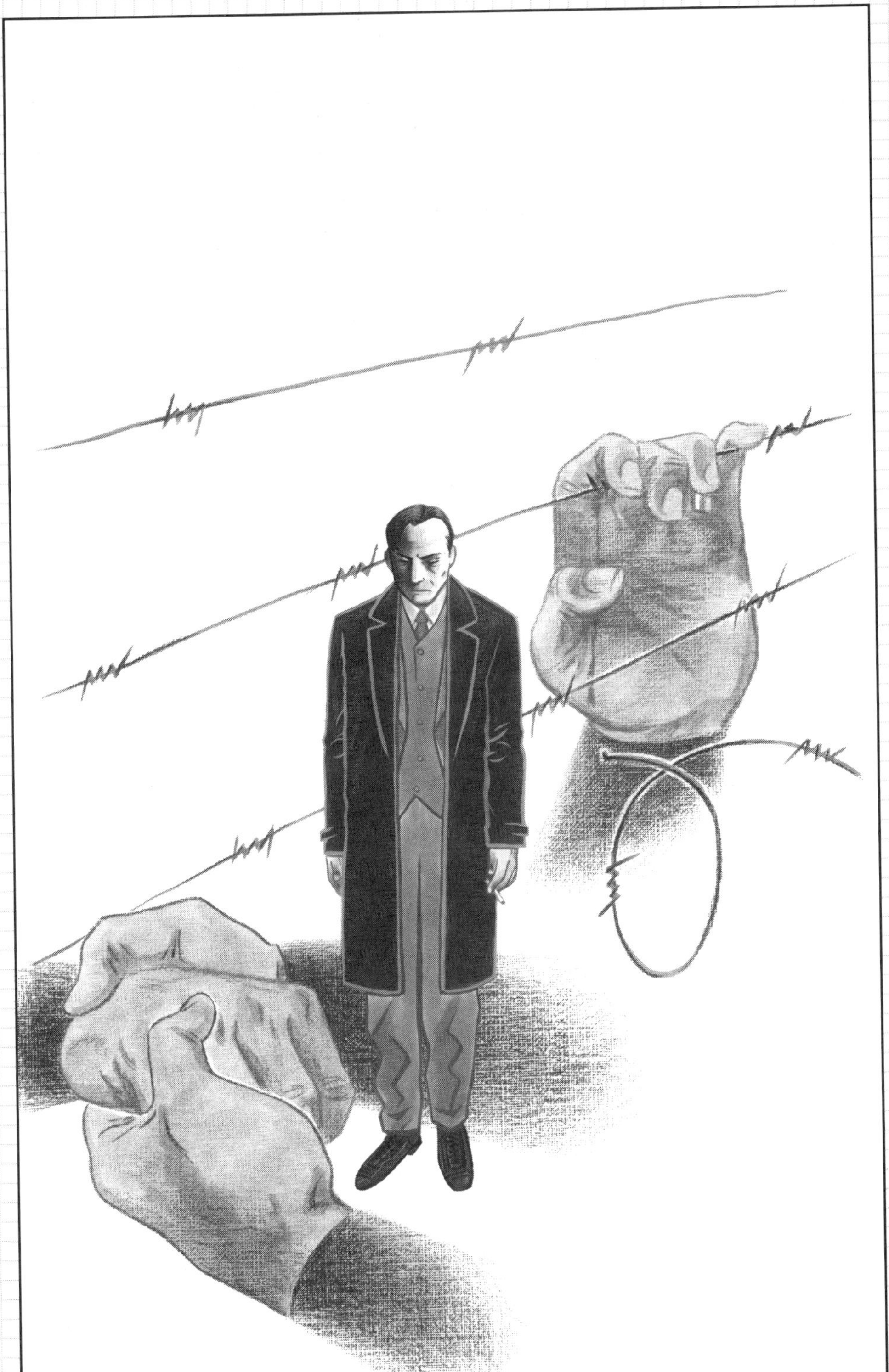

CHAPTER 4

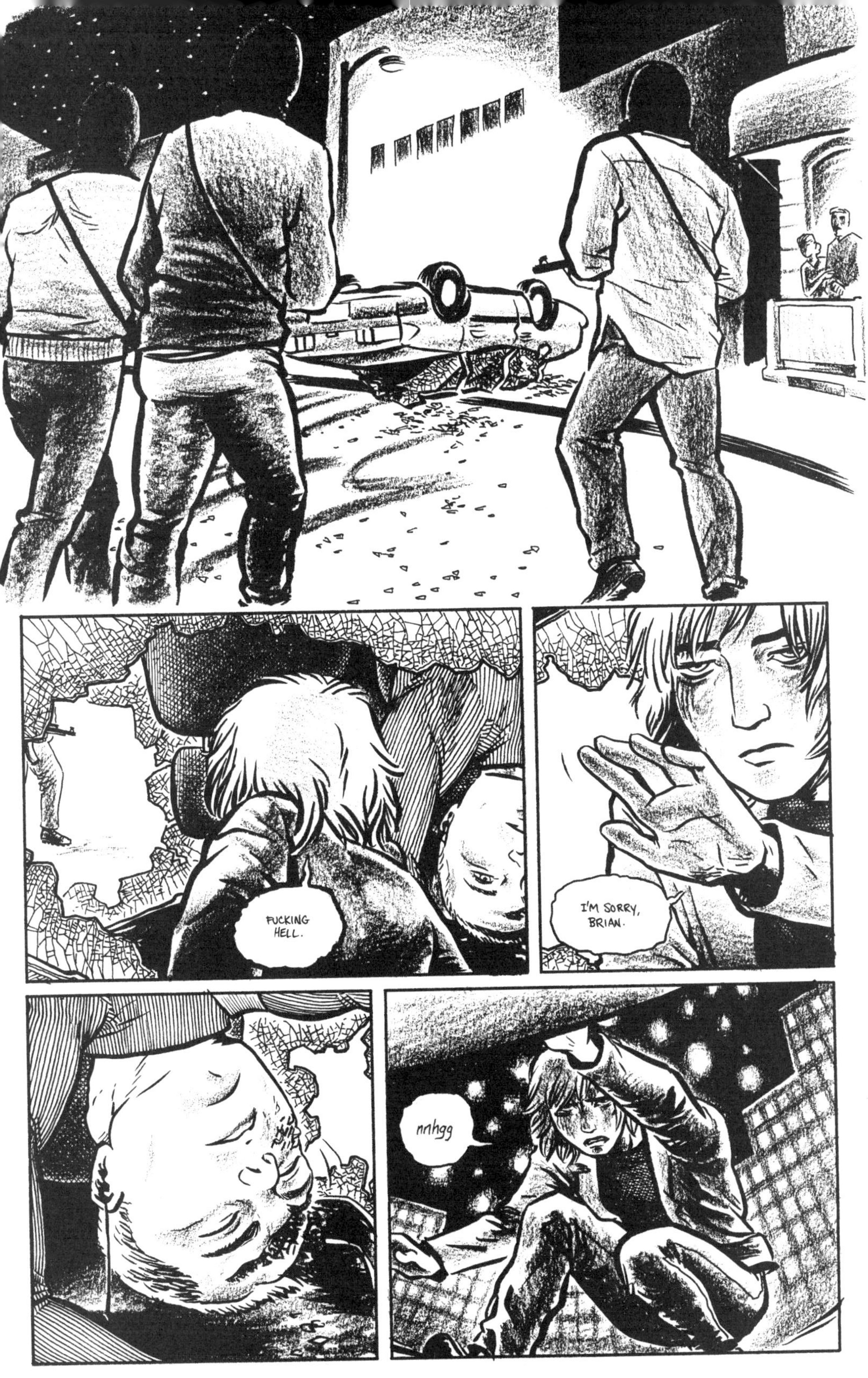
FUCKING HELL.
I'M SORRY, BRIAN.
nnhgg

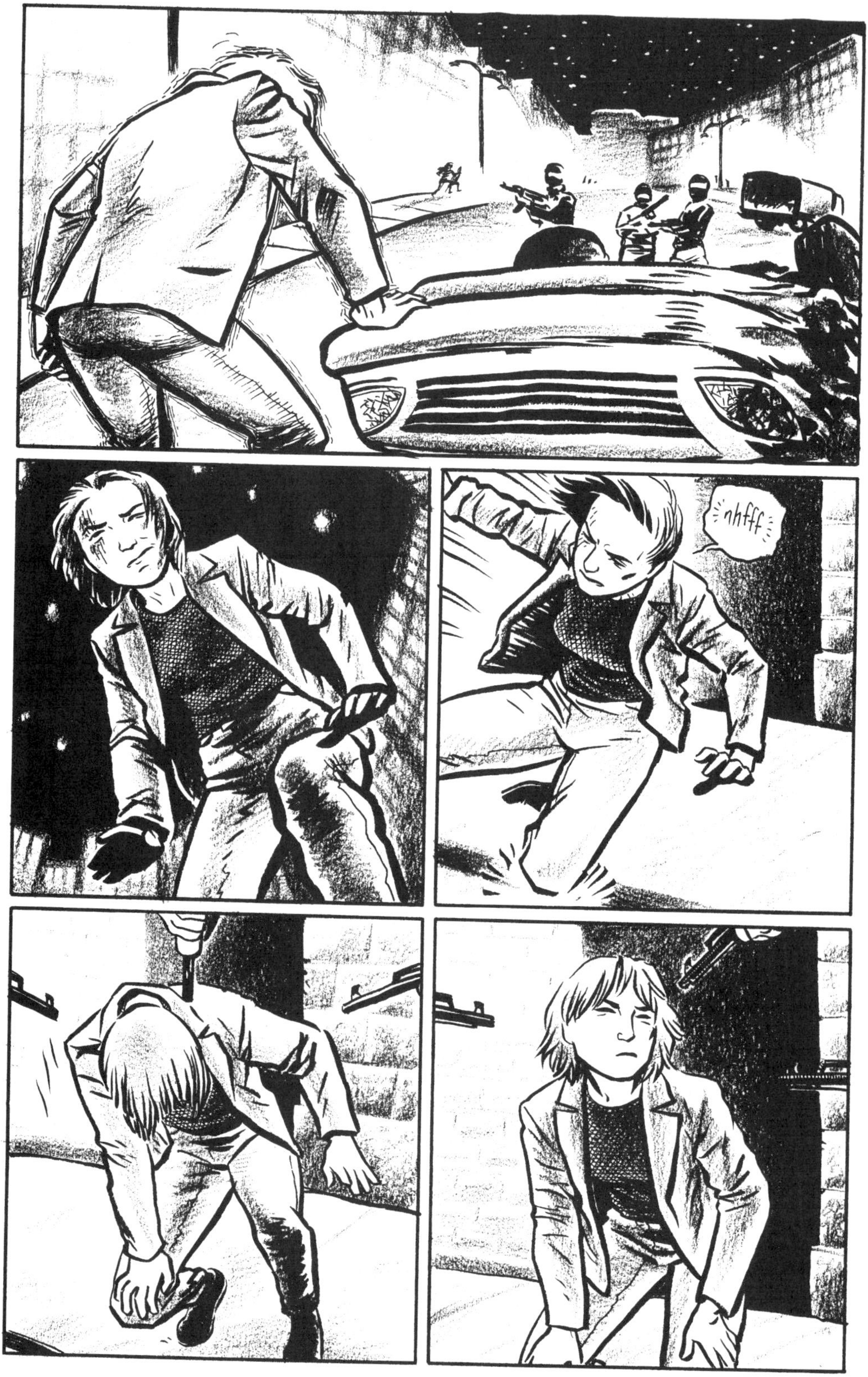
nhfff

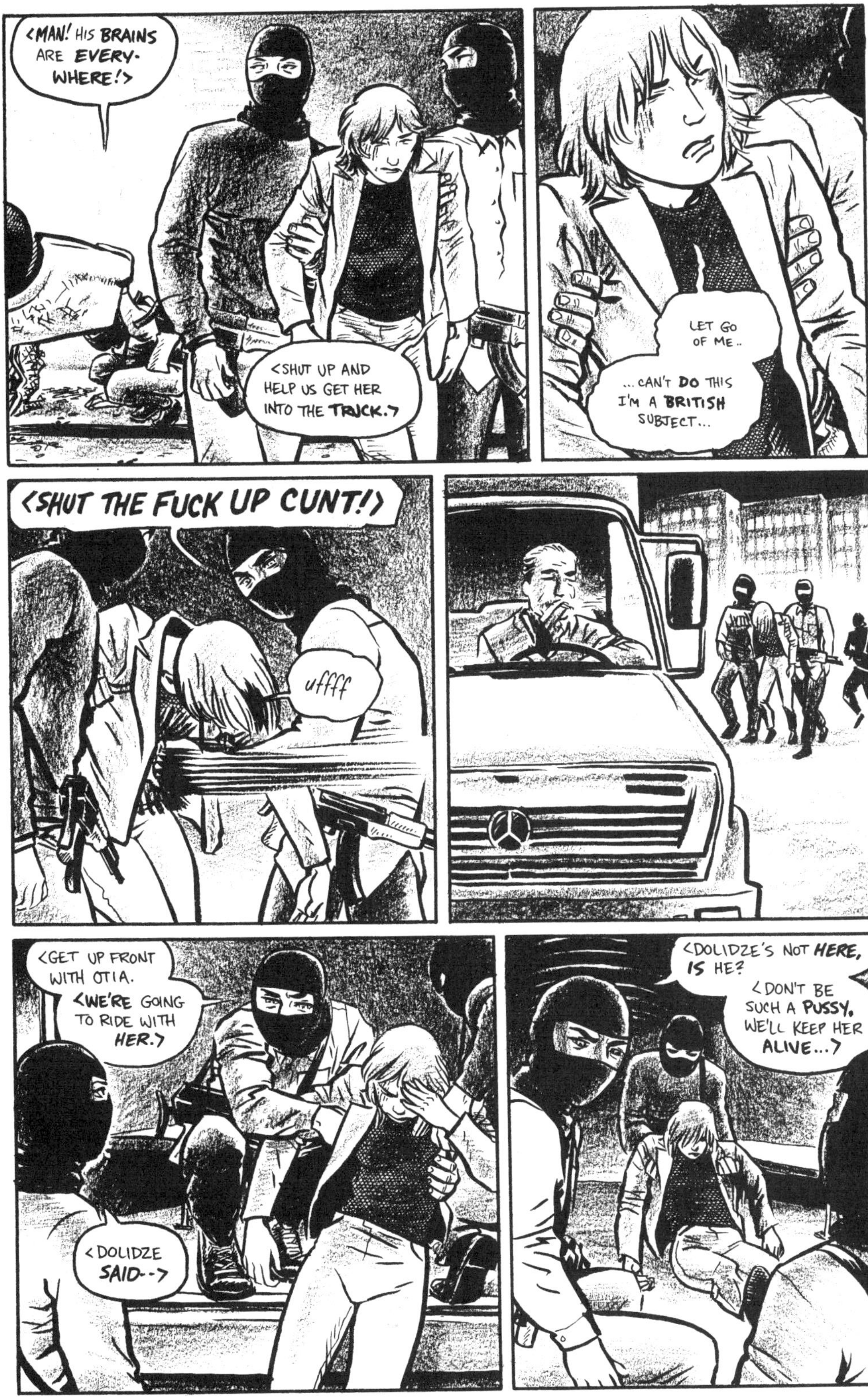
<MAN! HIS BRAINS ARE EVERY-WHERE!>
<SHUT UP AND HELP US GET HER INTO THE TRUCK.>
LET GO OF ME..
...CAN'T DO THIS I'M A BRITISH SUBJECT...
<SHUT THE FUCK UP CUNT!>
uffff
<GET UP FRONT WITH OTIA.
<WE'RE GOING TO RIDE WITH HER.>
<DOLIDZE SAID-->
<DOLIDZE'S NOT HERE, IS HE?
<DON'T BE SUCH A PUSSY. WE'LL KEEP HER ALIVE...>

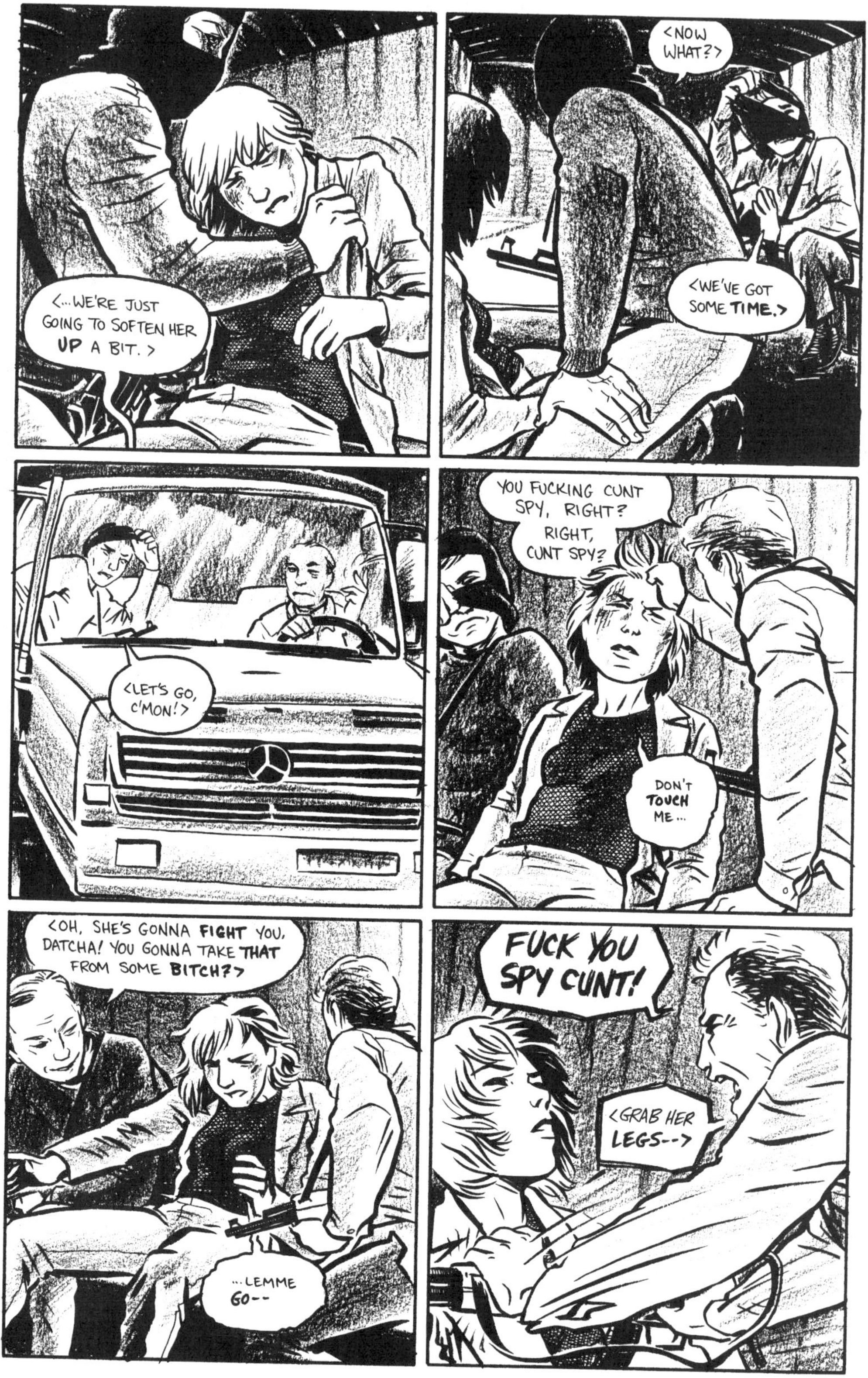
<...WE'RE JUST GOING TO SOFTEN HER UP A BIT.>
<NOW WHAT?>
<WE'VE GOT SOME TIME.>
<LET'S GO, C'MON!>
YOU FUCKING CUNT SPY, RIGHT? RIGHT, CUNT SPY?
DON'T TOUCH ME...
<OH, SHE'S GONNA FIGHT YOU, DATCHA! YOU GONNA TAKE THAT FROM SOME BITCH?>
...LEMME GO--
FUCK YOU SPY CUNT!
<GRAB HER LEGS-->

<-- GET HER PANTS OFF HER -->

YOUR MUZZLE CONTROL SUCKS, MATE.

CHAK
CHAK
CHAK

(HOLY FUCKING SHIT!)

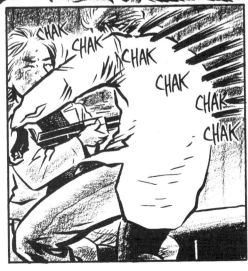

CHAK
CHAK
CHAK
CHAK
CHAK
CHAK

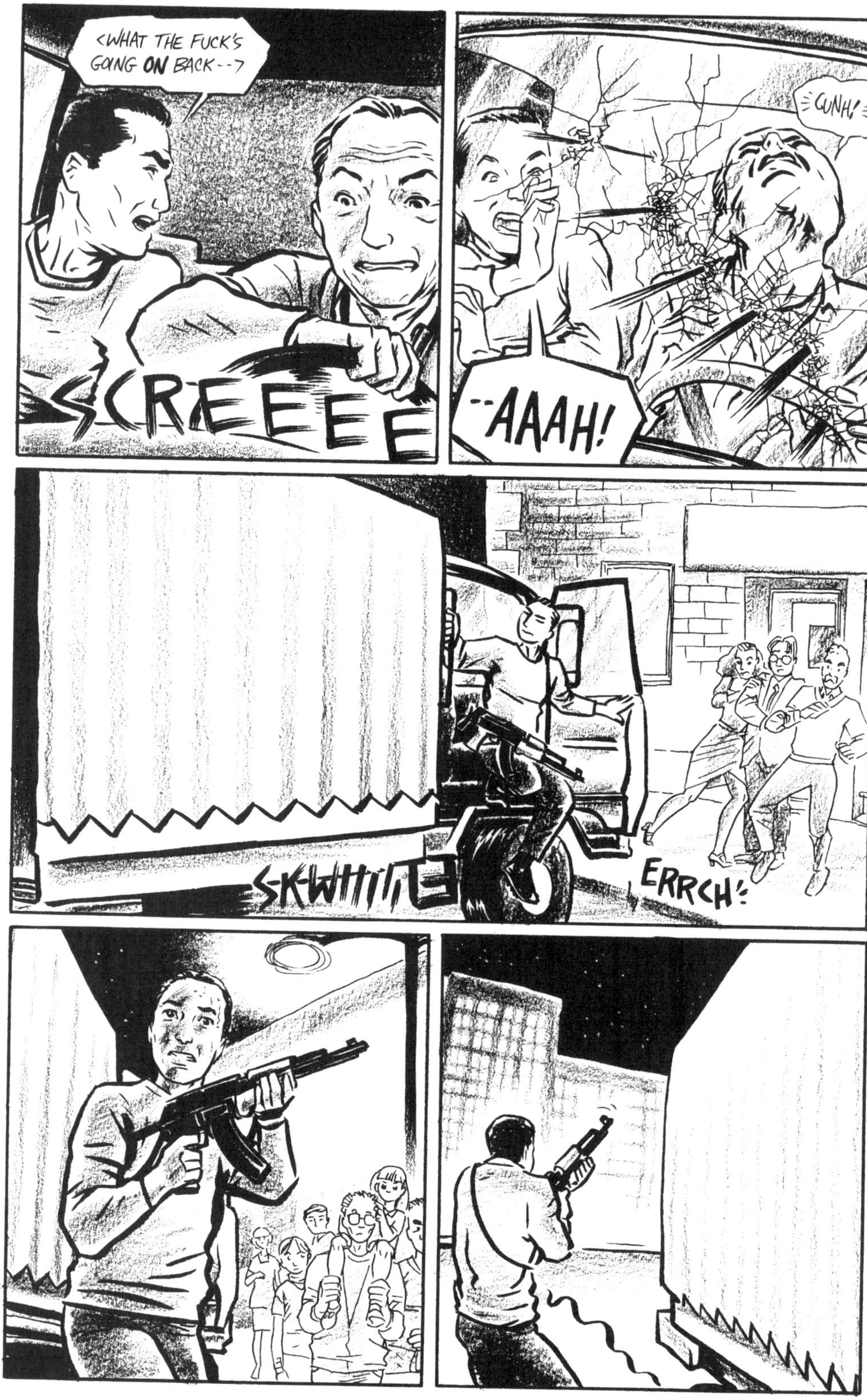
<WHAT THE FUCK'S GOING **ON** BACK-->
SCREEEEE
GUNH!
--AAAH!
SKWHIIIEEERRRCH!

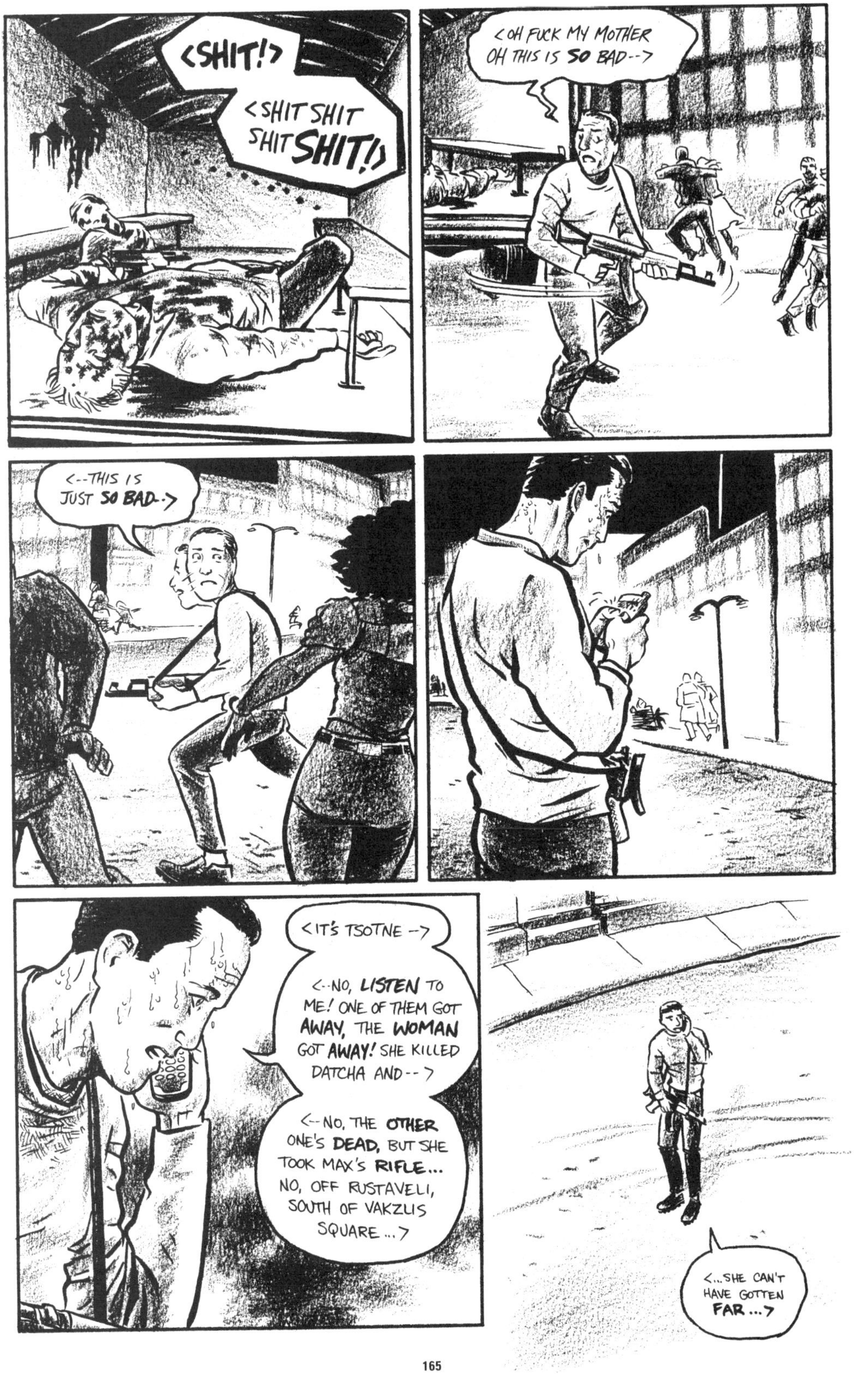

<SHIT!>
<SHIT SHIT SHIT SHIT!>
<OH FUCK MY MOTHER OH THIS IS SO BAD-->
<--THIS IS JUST SO BAD-->
<IT'S TSOTNE -->
<--NO, LISTEN TO ME! ONE OF THEM GOT AWAY, THE WOMAN GOT AWAY! SHE KILLED DATCHA AND-->
<--NO, THE OTHER ONE'S DEAD, BUT SHE TOOK MAX'S RIFLE... NO, OFF RUSTAVELI, SOUTH OF VAKZLIS SQUARE...>
<...SHE CAN'T HAVE GOTTEN FAR...>

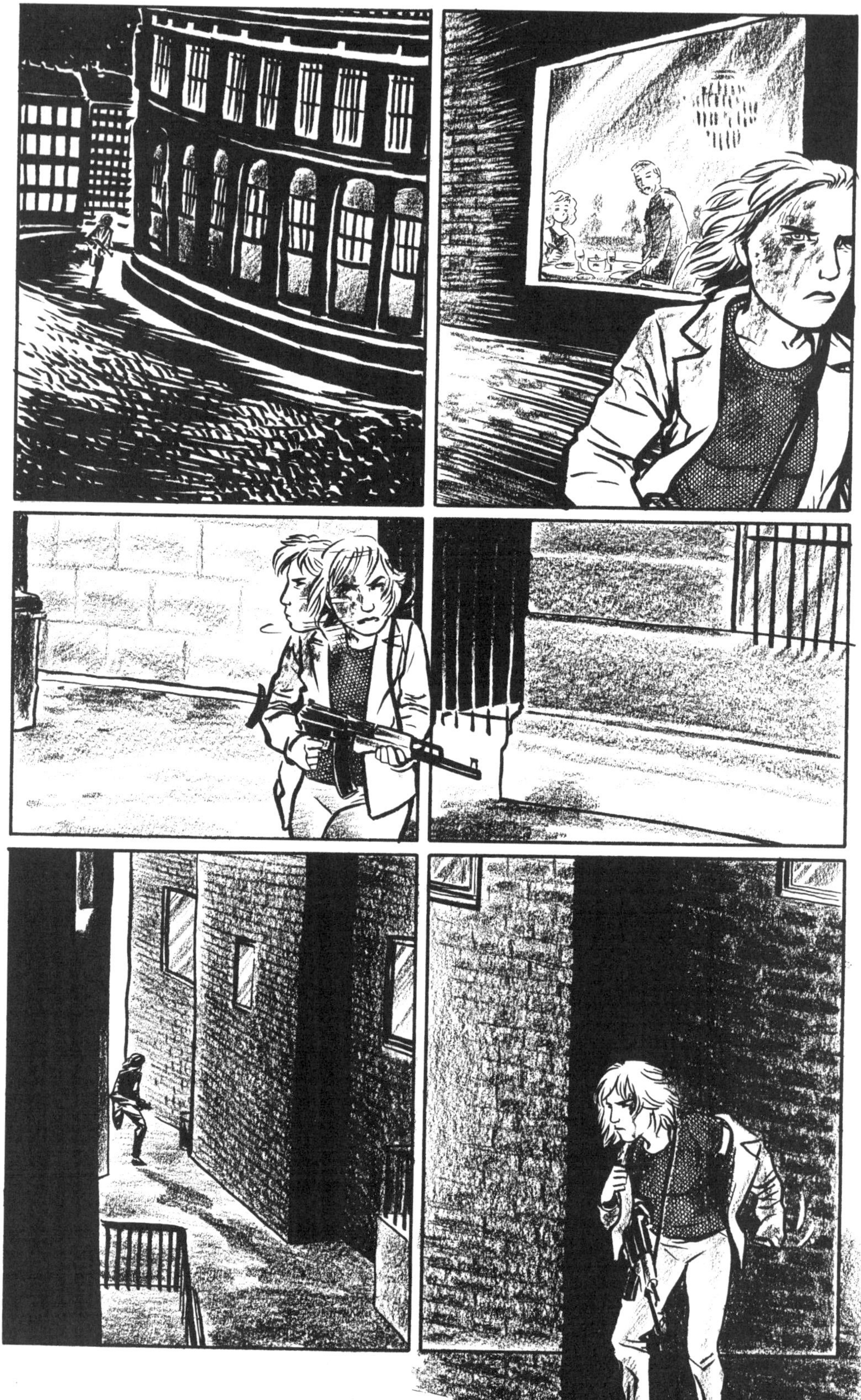

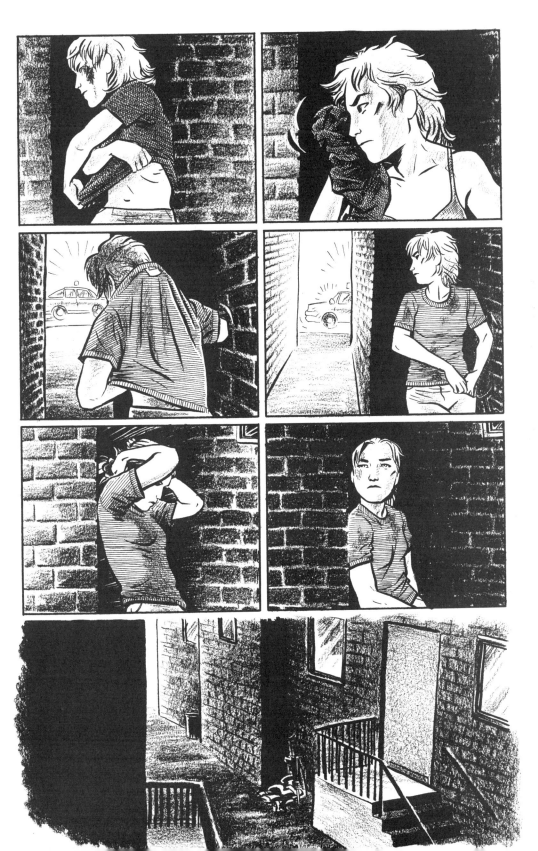

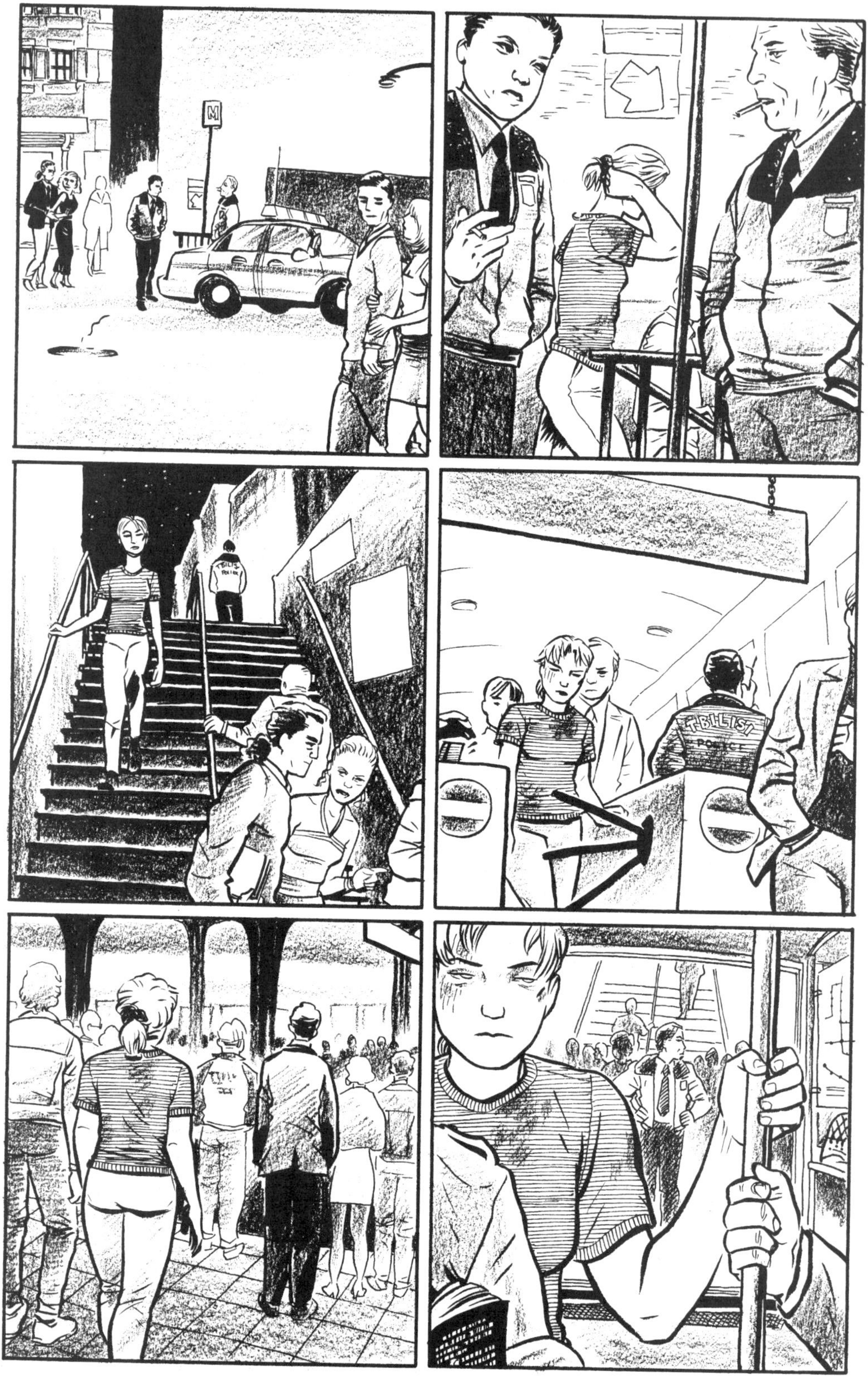
M
TBILISI
POLICE

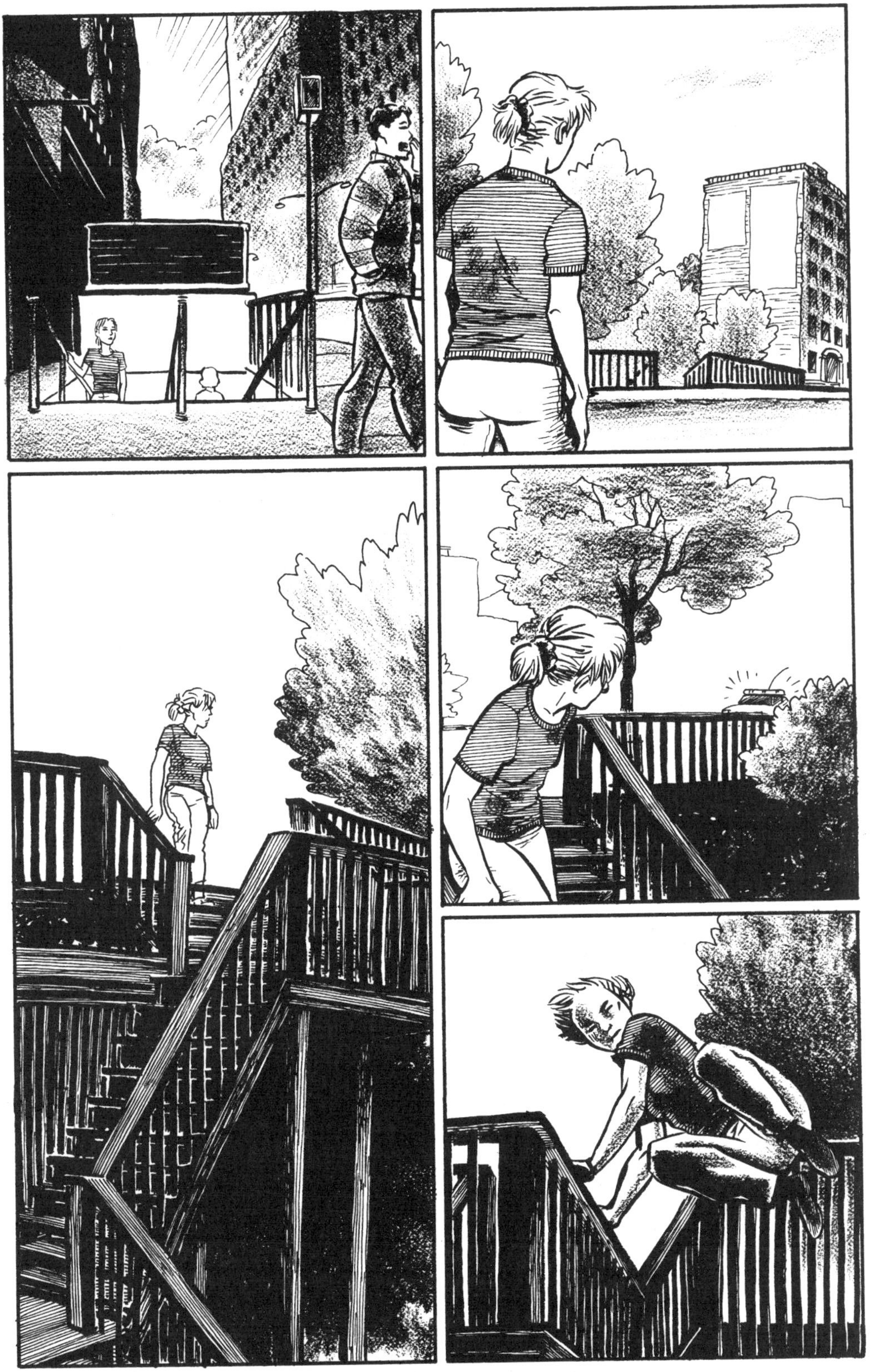

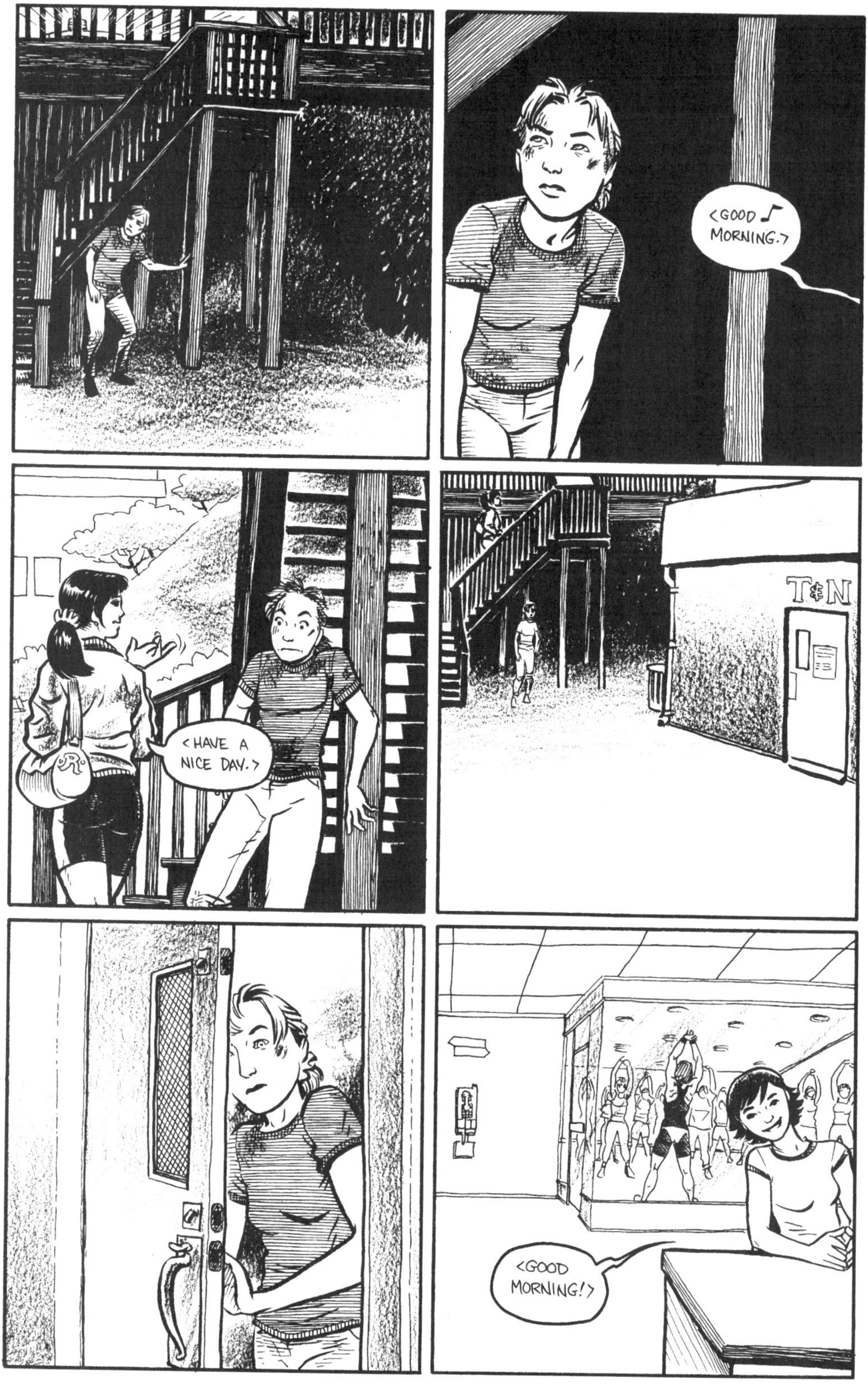
<GOOD ♪ MORNING.>
<HAVE A NICE DAY.>
T&N
<GOOD MORNING!>

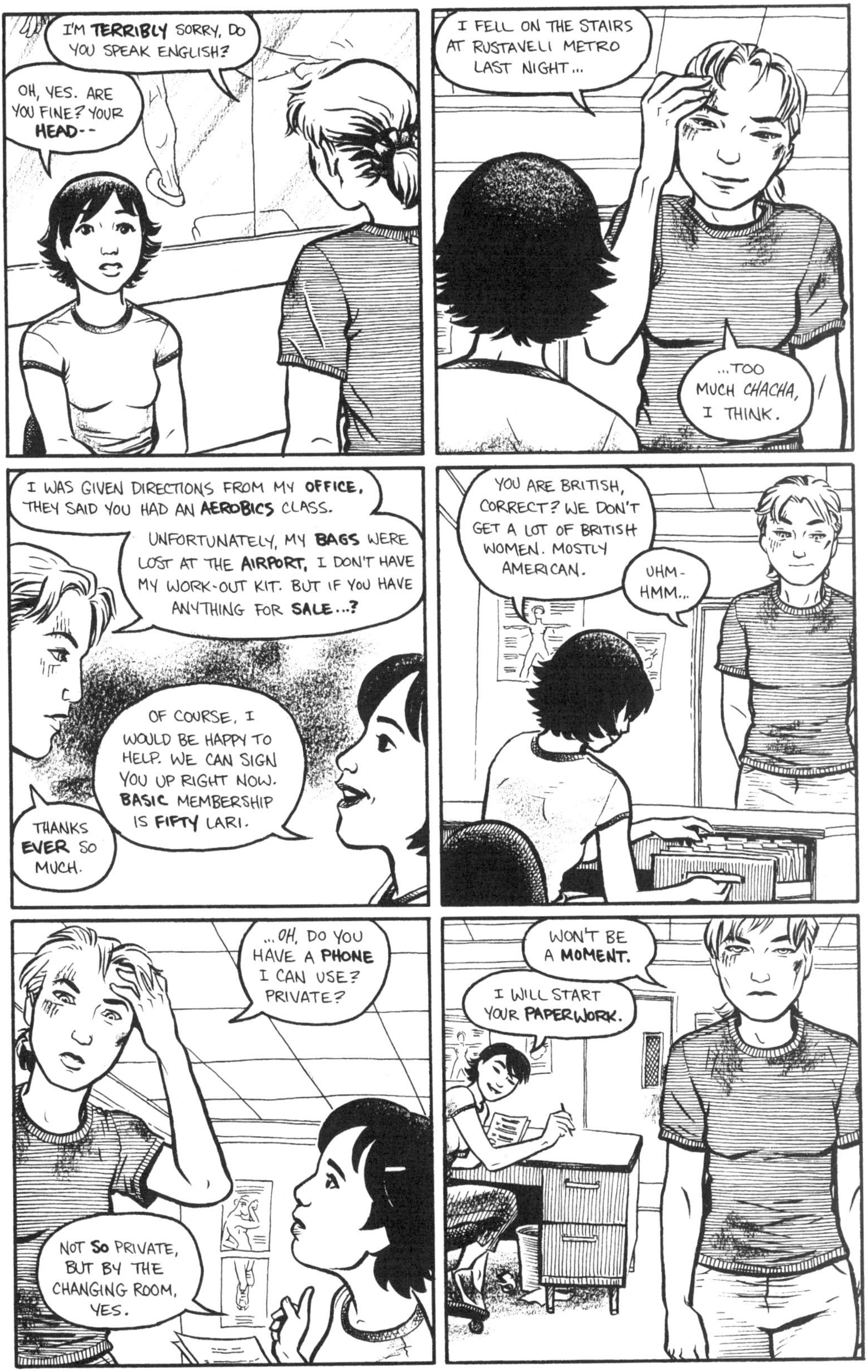
I'M TERRIBLY SORRY, DO YOU SPEAK ENGLISH?
OH, YES. ARE YOU FINE? YOUR HEAD--
I FELL ON THE STAIRS AT RUSTAVELI METRO LAST NIGHT...
...TOO MUCH CHACHA, I THINK.
I WAS GIVEN DIRECTIONS FROM MY OFFICE. THEY SAID YOU HAD AN AEROBICS CLASS.
UNFORTUNATELY, MY BAGS WERE LOST AT THE AIRPORT, I DON'T HAVE MY WORK-OUT KIT. BUT IF YOU HAVE ANYTHING FOR SALE...?
OF COURSE, I WOULD BE HAPPY TO HELP. WE CAN SIGN YOU UP RIGHT NOW. BASIC MEMBERSHIP IS FIFTY LARI.
THANKS EVER SO MUCH.
YOU ARE BRITISH, CORRECT? WE DON'T GET A LOT OF BRITISH WOMEN. MOSTLY AMERICAN.
UHM-HMM...
...OH, DO YOU HAVE A PHONE I CAN USE? PRIVATE?
NOT SO PRIVATE, BUT BY THE CHANGING ROOM, YES.
WON'T BE A MOMENT.
I WILL START YOUR PAPERWORK.

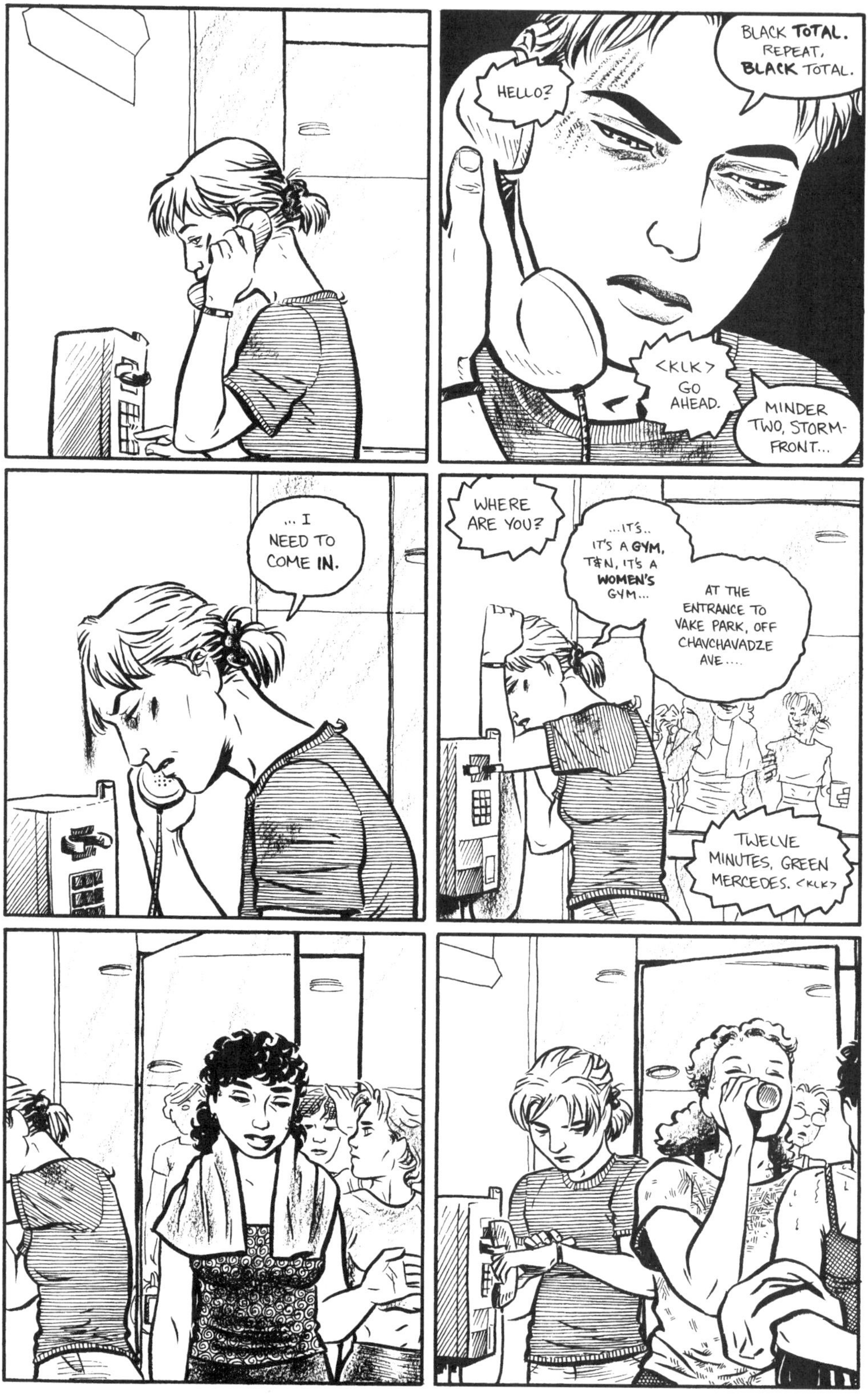
HELLO?
BLACK TOTAL. REPEAT, BLACK TOTAL.
<KLK> GO AHEAD.
MINDER TWO, STORM-FRONT...
... I NEED TO COME IN.
WHERE ARE YOU?
...IT'S.. IT'S A GYM, T&N, IT'S A WOMEN'S GYM...
AT THE ENTRANCE TO VAKE PARK, OFF CHAVCHAVADZE AVE....
TWELVE MINUTES, GREEN MERCEDES. <KLK>

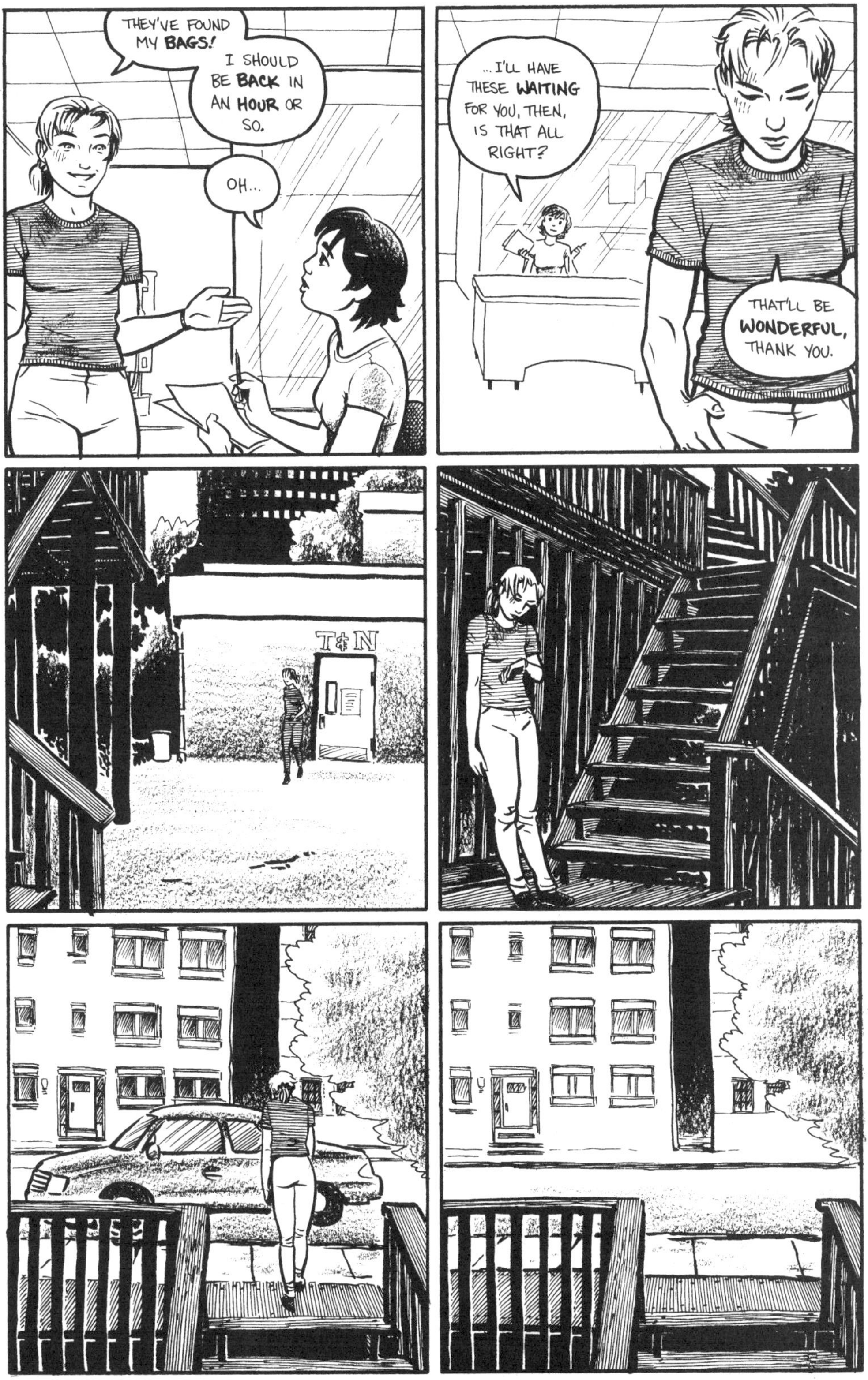
THEY'VE FOUND MY BAGS!
I SHOULD BE BACK IN AN HOUR OR SO.
OH...
...I'LL HAVE THESE WAITING FOR YOU, THEN, IS THAT ALL RIGHT?
THAT'LL BE WONDERFUL, THANK YOU.
T&N

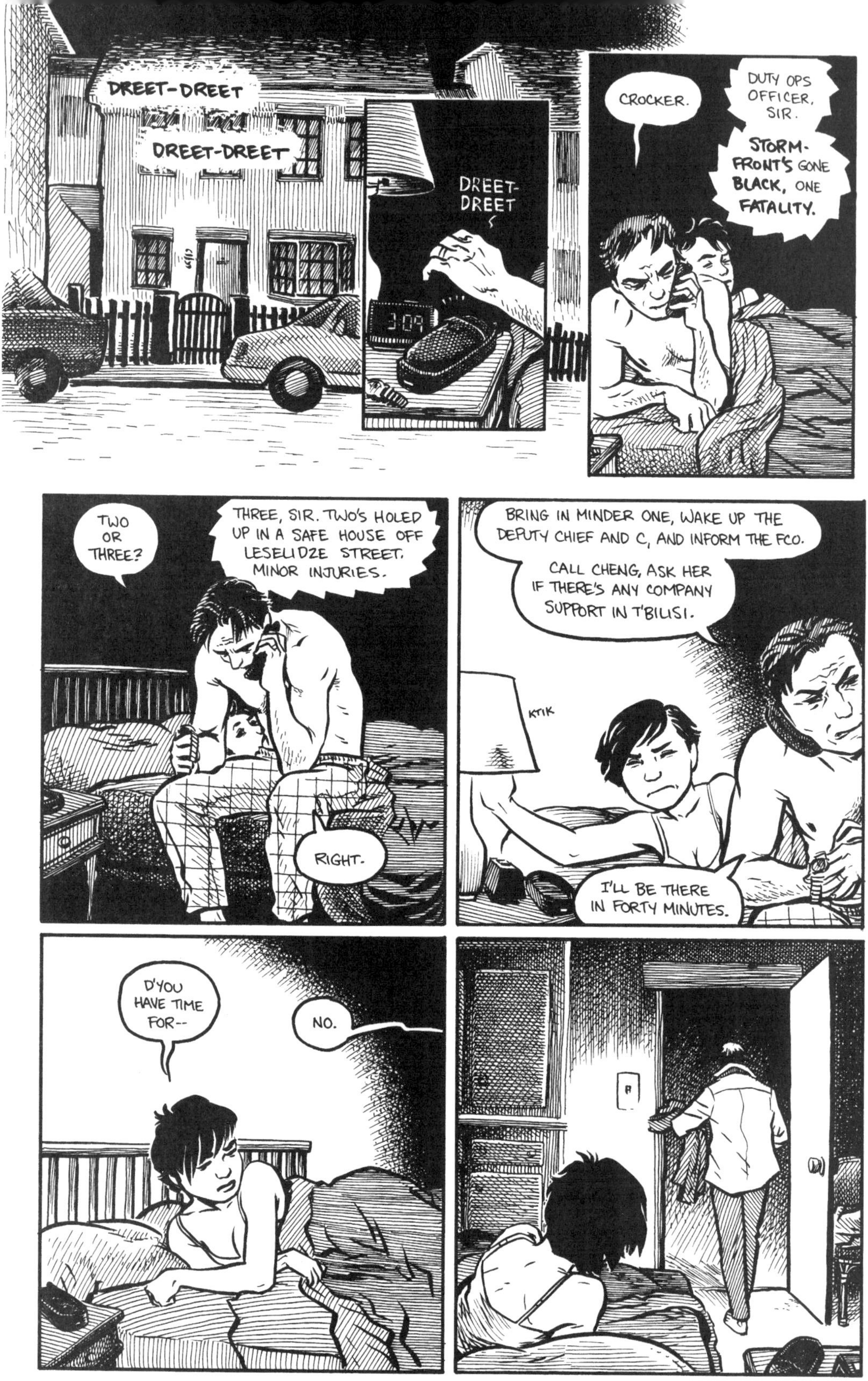
DREET-DREET
DREET-DREET
DREET-DREET
3:09
CROCKER.
DUTY OPS OFFICER, SIR.
STORM-FRONT'S GONE BLACK, ONE FATALITY.
TWO OR THREE?
THREE, SIR. TWO'S HOLED UP IN A SAFE HOUSE OFF LESELIDZE STREET. MINOR INJURIES.
RIGHT.
BRING IN MINDER ONE, WAKE UP THE DEPUTY CHIEF AND C, AND INFORM THE FCO.
CALL CHENG, ASK HER IF THERE'S ANY COMPANY SUPPORT IN T'BILISI.
KTIK
I'LL BE THERE IN FORTY MINUTES.
D'YOU HAVE TIME FOR--
NO.

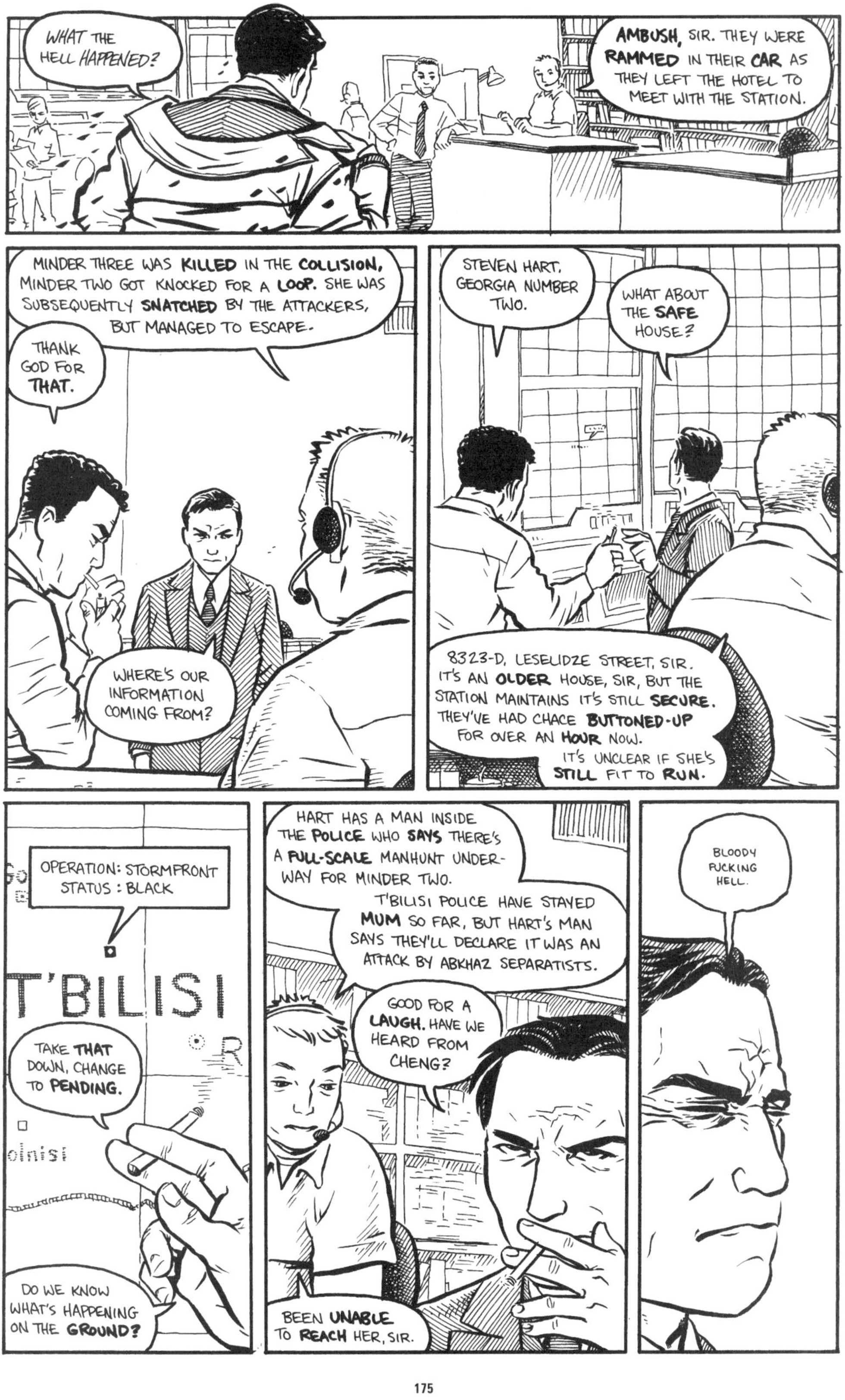
WHAT THE HELL HAPPENED?
AMBUSH, SIR. THEY WERE RAMMED IN THEIR CAR AS THEY LEFT THE HOTEL TO MEET WITH THE STATION.
MINDER THREE WAS KILLED IN THE COLLISION, MINDER TWO GOT KNOCKED FOR A LOOP. SHE WAS SUBSEQUENTLY SNATCHED BY THE ATTACKERS, BUT MANAGED TO ESCAPE.
THANK GOD FOR THAT.
WHERE'S OUR INFORMATION COMING FROM?
STEVEN HART, GEORGIA NUMBER TWO.
WHAT ABOUT THE SAFE HOUSE?
8323-D, LESELIDZE STREET, SIR. IT'S AN OLDER HOUSE, SIR, BUT THE STATION MAINTAINS IT'S STILL SECURE. THEY'VE HAD CHACE BUTTONED-UP FOR OVER AN HOUR NOW.
IT'S UNCLEAR IF SHE'S STILL FIT TO RUN.
OPERATION: STORMFRONT STATUS : BLACK
T'BILISI
TAKE THAT DOWN, CHANGE TO PENDING.
DO WE KNOW WHAT'S HAPPENING ON THE GROUND?
HART HAS A MAN INSIDE THE POLICE WHO SAYS THERE'S A FULL-SCALE MANHUNT UNDER-WAY FOR MINDER TWO.
T'BILISI POLICE HAVE STAYED MUM SO FAR, BUT HART'S MAN SAYS THEY'LL DECLARE IT WAS AN ATTACK BY ABKHAZ SEPARATISTS.
GOOD FOR A LAUGH. HAVE WE HEARD FROM CHENG?
BEEN UNABLE TO REACH HER, SIR.
BLOODY FUCKING HELL.

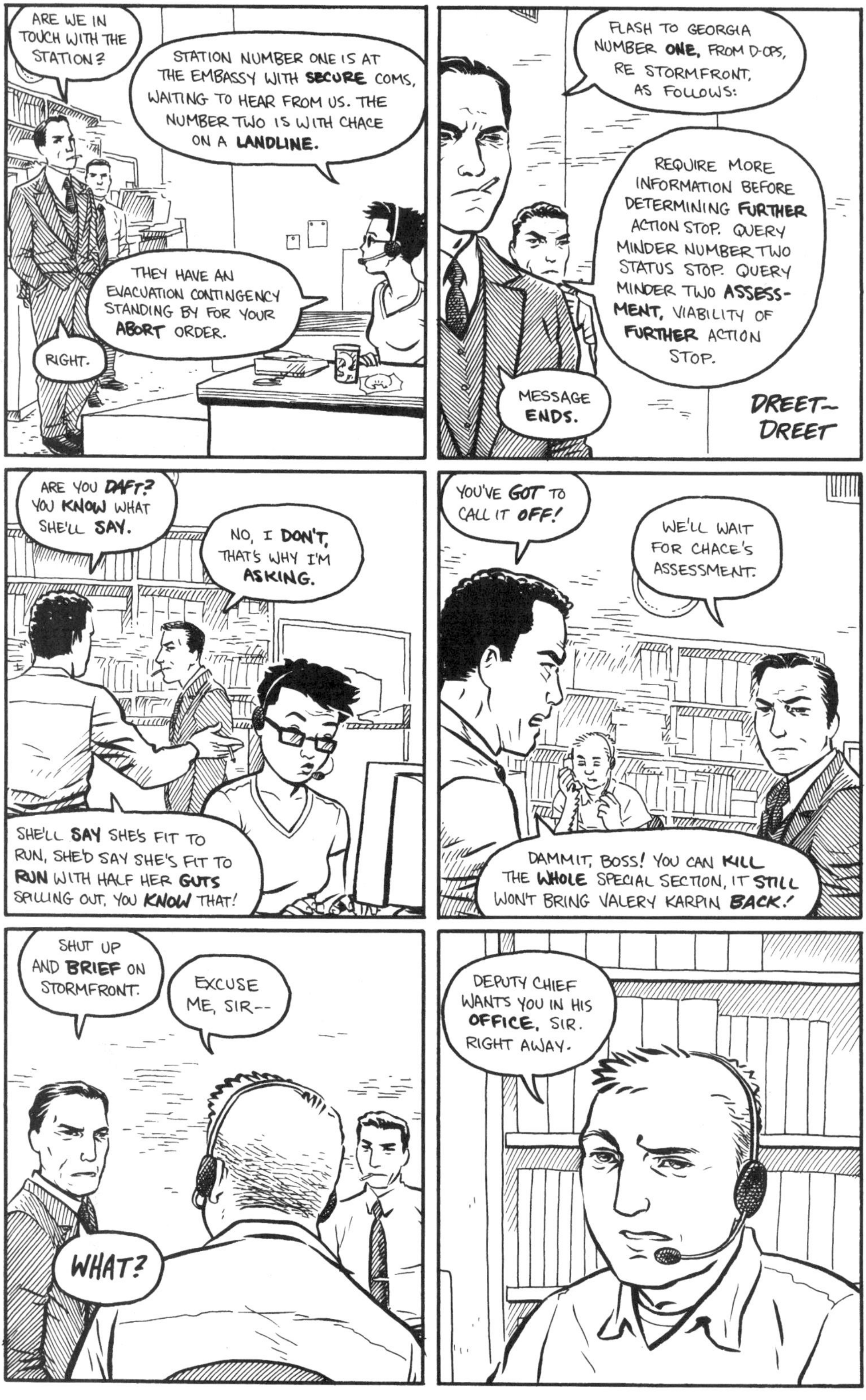
ARE WE IN TOUCH WITH THE STATION?
STATION NUMBER ONE IS AT THE EMBASSY WITH SECURE COMS, WAITING TO HEAR FROM US. THE NUMBER TWO IS WITH CHACE ON A LANDLINE.
THEY HAVE AN EVACUATION CONTINGENCY STANDING BY FOR YOUR ABORT ORDER.
RIGHT.
FLASH TO GEORGIA NUMBER ONE, FROM D-OPS, RE STORMFRONT, AS FOLLOWS:
REQUIRE MORE INFORMATION BEFORE DETERMINING FURTHER ACTION STOP. QUERY MINDER NUMBER TWO STATUS STOP. QUERY MINDER TWO ASSESS-MENT, VIABILITY OF FURTHER ACTION STOP.
MESSAGE ENDS.
DREET-DREET
ARE YOU DAFT? YOU KNOW WHAT SHE'LL SAY.
NO, I DON'T, THAT'S WHY I'M ASKING.
SHE'LL SAY SHE'S FIT TO RUN, SHE'D SAY SHE'S FIT TO RUN WITH HALF HER GUTS SPILLING OUT. YOU KNOW THAT!
YOU'VE GOT TO CALL IT OFF!
WE'LL WAIT FOR CHACE'S ASSESSMENT.
DAMMIT, BOSS! YOU CAN KILL THE WHOLE SPECIAL SECTION, IT STILL WON'T BRING VALERY KARPIN BACK!
SHUT UP AND BRIEF ON STORMFRONT.
EXCUSE ME, SIR--
WHAT?
DEPUTY CHIEF WANTS YOU IN HIS OFFICE, SIR. RIGHT AWAY.

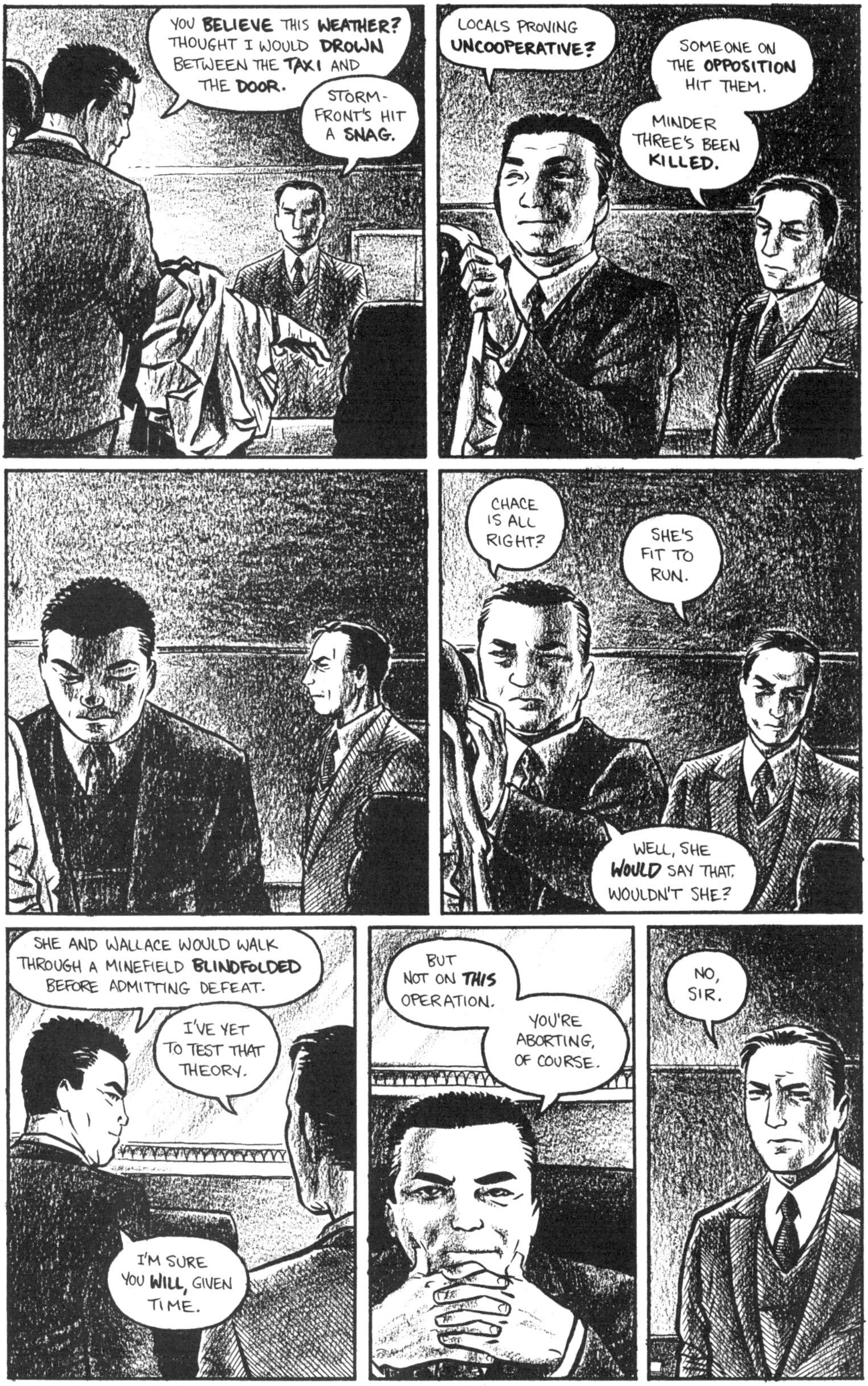
YOU BELIEVE THIS WEATHER? THOUGHT I WOULD DROWN BETWEEN THE TAXI AND THE DOOR.
STORM-FRONT'S HIT A SNAG.
LOCALS PROVING UNCOOPERATIVE?
SOMEONE ON THE OPPOSITION HIT THEM.
MINDER THREE'S BEEN KILLED.
CHACE IS ALL RIGHT?
SHE'S FIT TO RUN.
WELL, SHE WOULD SAY THAT, WOULDN'T SHE?
SHE AND WALLACE WOULD WALK THROUGH A MINEFIELD BLINDFOLDED BEFORE ADMITTING DEFEAT.
I'VE YET TO TEST THAT THEORY.
I'M SURE YOU WILL, GIVEN TIME.
BUT NOT ON THIS OPERATION.
YOU'RE ABORTING, OF COURSE.
NO, SIR.

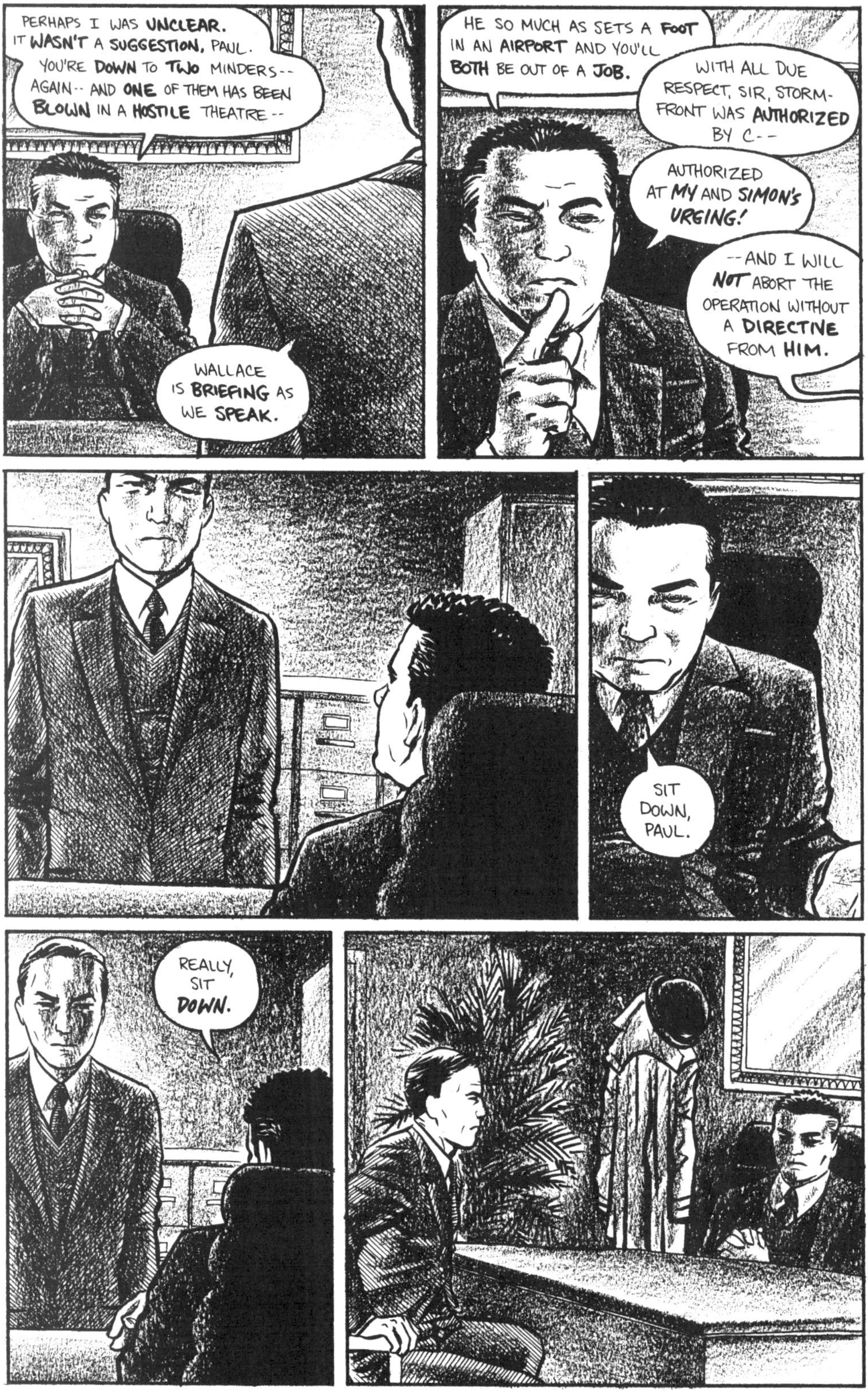
PERHAPS I WAS UNCLEAR. IT WASN'T A SUGGESTION, PAUL. YOU'RE DOWN TO TWO MINDERS-- AGAIN-- AND ONE OF THEM HAS BEEN BLOWN IN A HOSTILE THEATRE--
WALLACE IS BRIEFING AS WE SPEAK.
HE SO MUCH AS SETS A FOOT IN AN AIRPORT AND YOU'LL BOTH BE OUT OF A JOB.
WITH ALL DUE RESPECT, SIR, STORM-FRONT WAS AUTHORIZED BY C--
AUTHORIZED AT MY AND SIMON'S URGING!
--AND I WILL NOT ABORT THE OPERATION WITHOUT A DIRECTIVE FROM HIM.
SIT DOWN, PAUL.
REALLY, SIT DOWN.

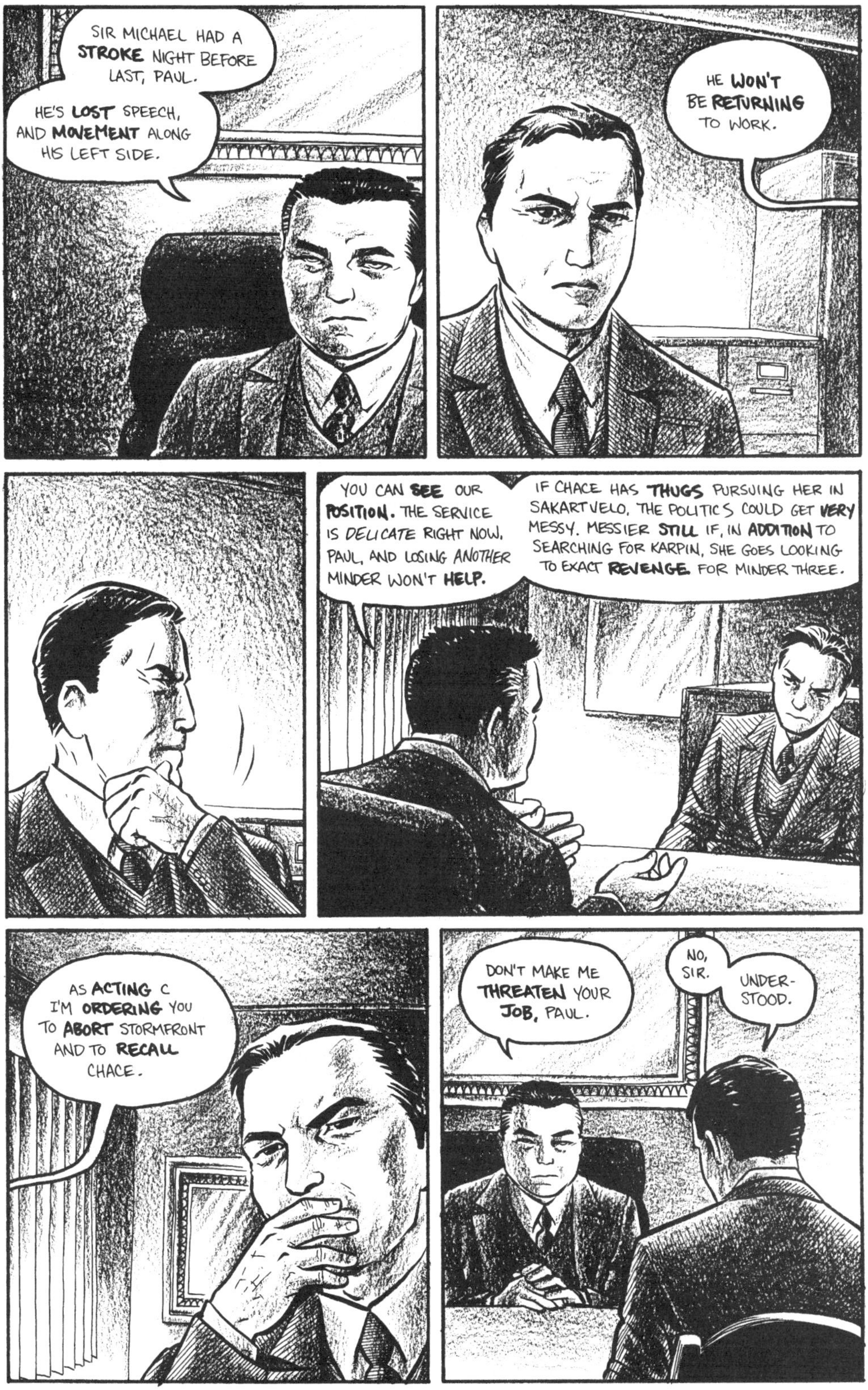
SIR MICHAEL HAD A STROKE NIGHT BEFORE LAST, PAUL.
HE'S LOST SPEECH, AND MOVEMENT ALONG HIS LEFT SIDE.
HE WON'T BE RETURNING TO WORK.
YOU CAN SEE OUR POSITION. THE SERVICE IS DELICATE RIGHT NOW, PAUL, AND LOSING ANOTHER MINDER WON'T HELP.
IF CHACE HAS THUGS PURSUING HER IN SAKARTVELO, THE POLITICS COULD GET VERY MESSY. MESSIER STILL IF, IN ADDITION TO SEARCHING FOR KARPIN, SHE GOES LOOKING TO EXACT REVENGE FOR MINDER THREE.
AS ACTING C I'M ORDERING YOU TO ABORT STORMFRONT AND TO RECALL CHACE.
DON'T MAKE ME THREATEN YOUR JOB, PAUL.
NO, SIR.
UNDER-STOOD.

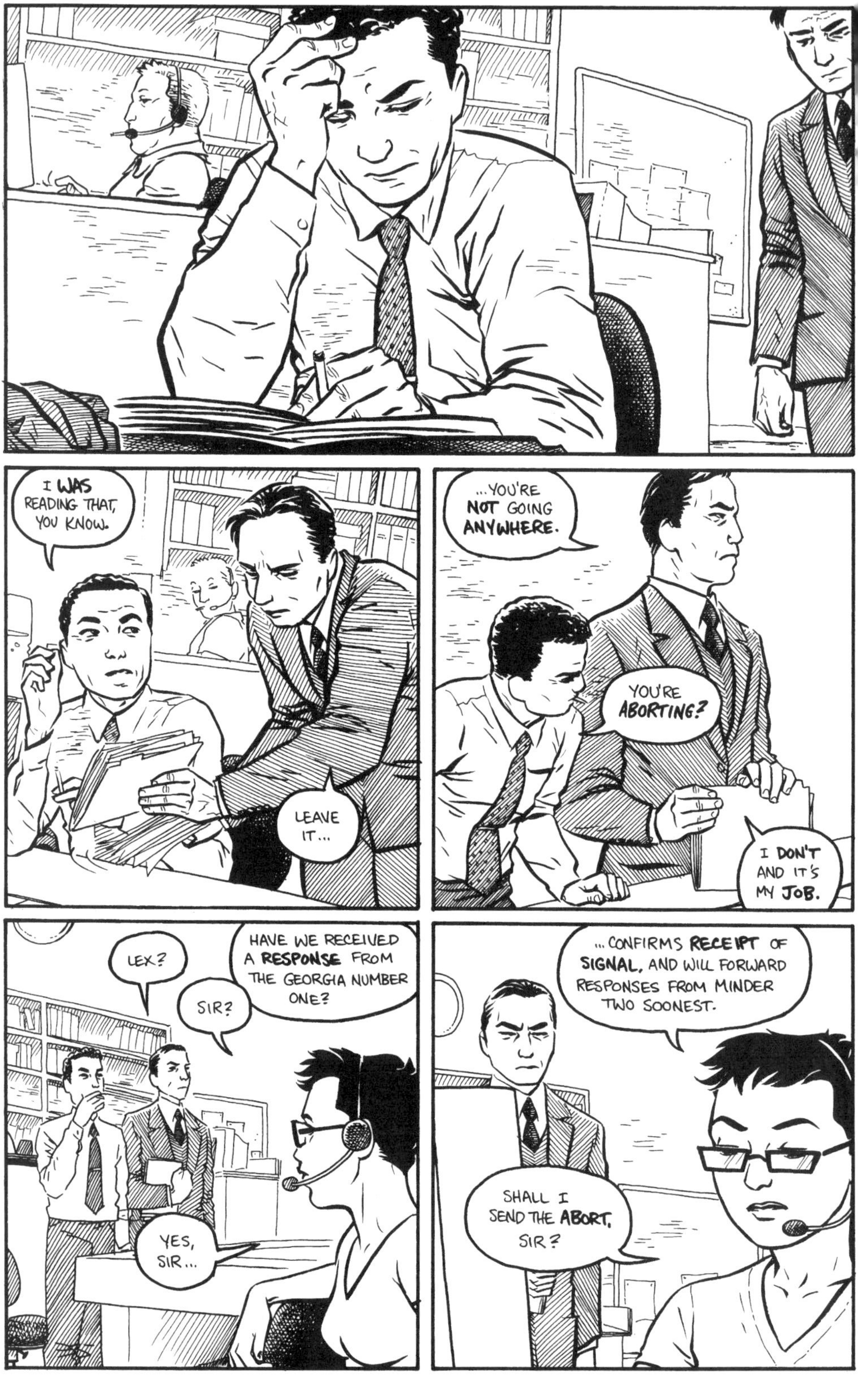
I WAS READING THAT, YOU KNOW.
LEAVE IT...
...YOU'RE NOT GOING ANYWHERE.
YOU'RE ABORTING?
I DON'T AND IT'S MY JOB.
LEX?
SIR?
HAVE WE RECEIVED A RESPONSE FROM THE GEORGIA NUMBER ONE?
YES, SIR...
...CONFIRMS RECEIPT OF SIGNAL, AND WILL FORWARD RESPONSES FROM MINDER TWO SOONEST.
SHALL I SEND THE ABORT, SIR?

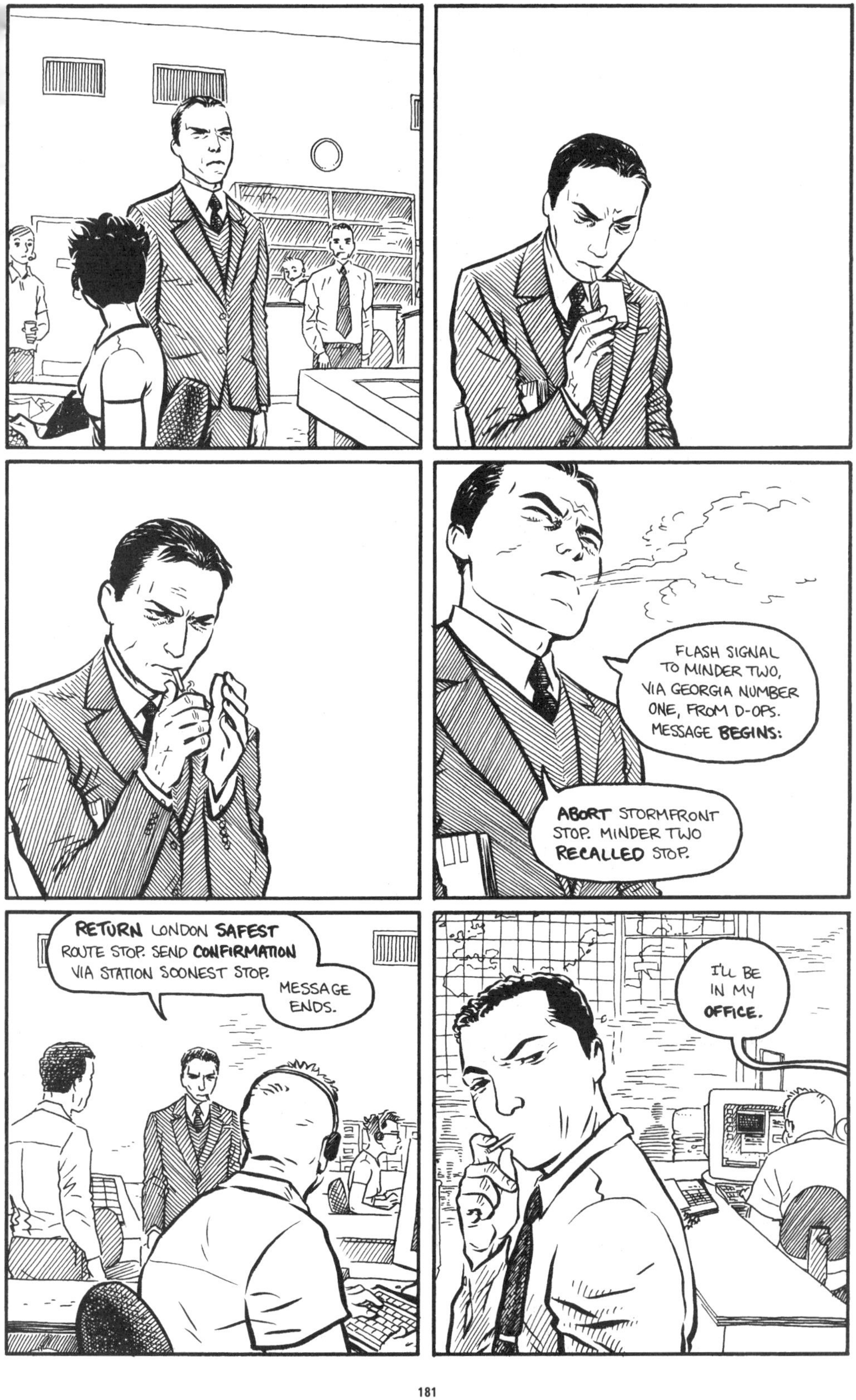
FLASH SIGNAL TO MINDER TWO, VIA GEORGIA NUMBER ONE, FROM D-OPS. MESSAGE BEGINS:
ABORT STORMFRONT STOP. MINDER TWO RECALLED STOP.
RETURN LONDON SAFEST ROUTE STOP. SEND CONFIRMATION VIA STATION SOONEST STOP.
MESSAGE ENDS.
I'LL BE IN MY OFFICE.

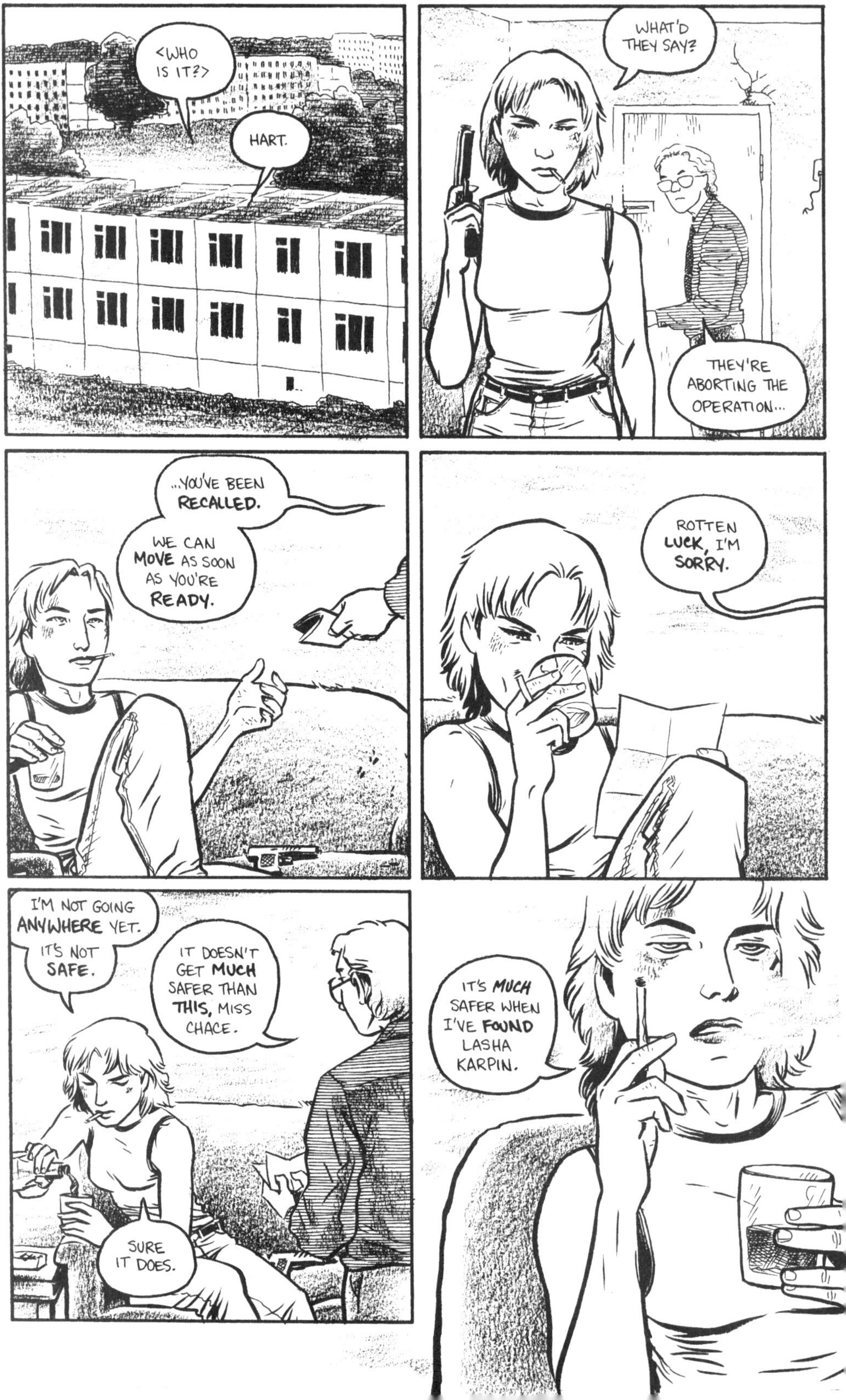
<WHO IS IT?>
HART.
WHAT'D THEY SAY?
THEY'RE ABORTING THE OPERATION...
...YOU'VE BEEN **RECALLED.**
WE CAN **MOVE** AS SOON AS YOU'RE **READY.**
ROTTEN **LUCK**, I'M **SORRY.**
I'M NOT GOING **ANYWHERE** YET.
IT'S NOT **SAFE.**
IT DOESN'T GET **MUCH** SAFER THAN **THIS,** MISS CHACE.
SURE IT DOES.
IT'S **MUCH** SAFER WHEN I'VE **FOUND** LASHA KARPIN.

CHAPTER 5

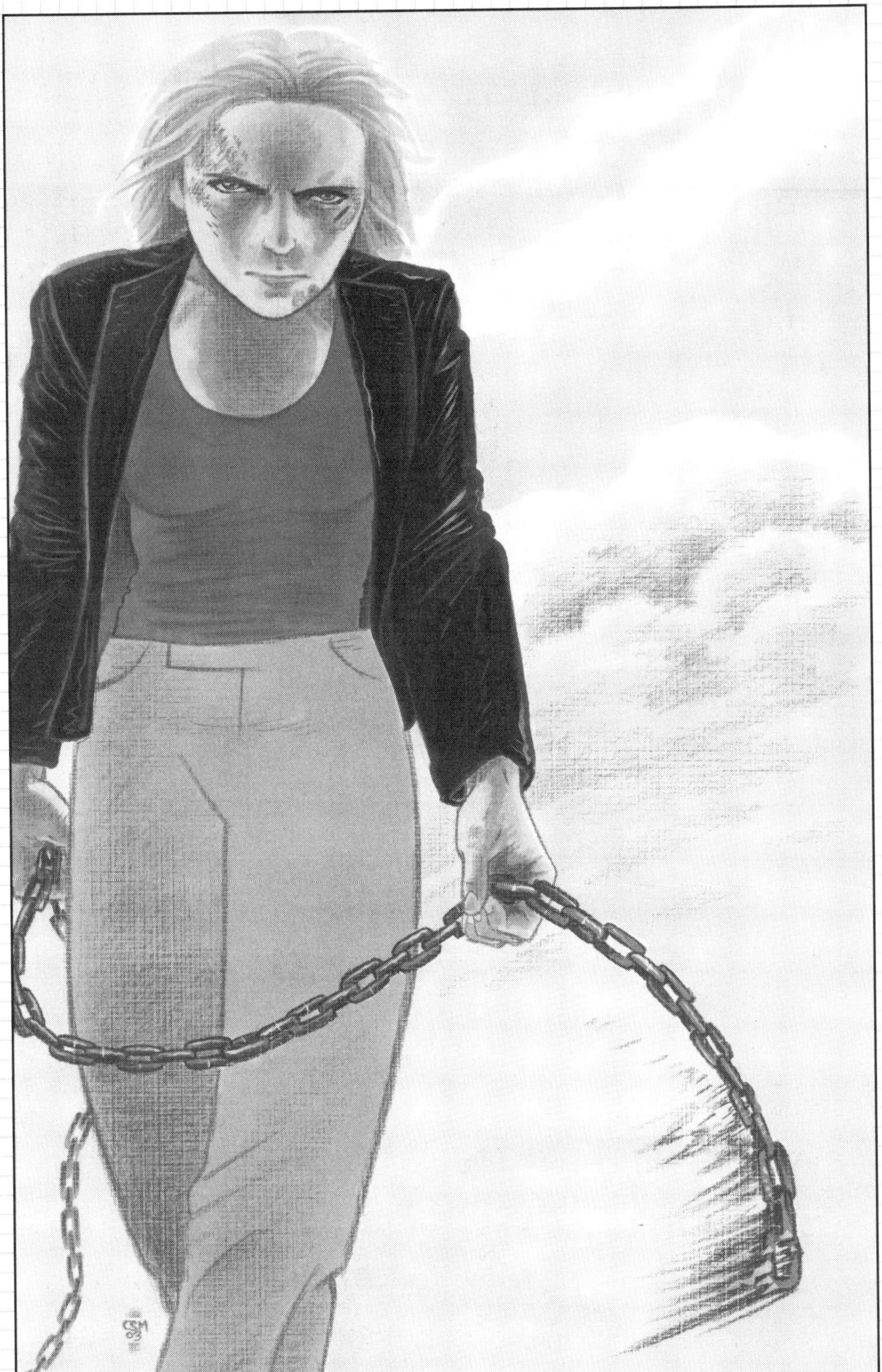

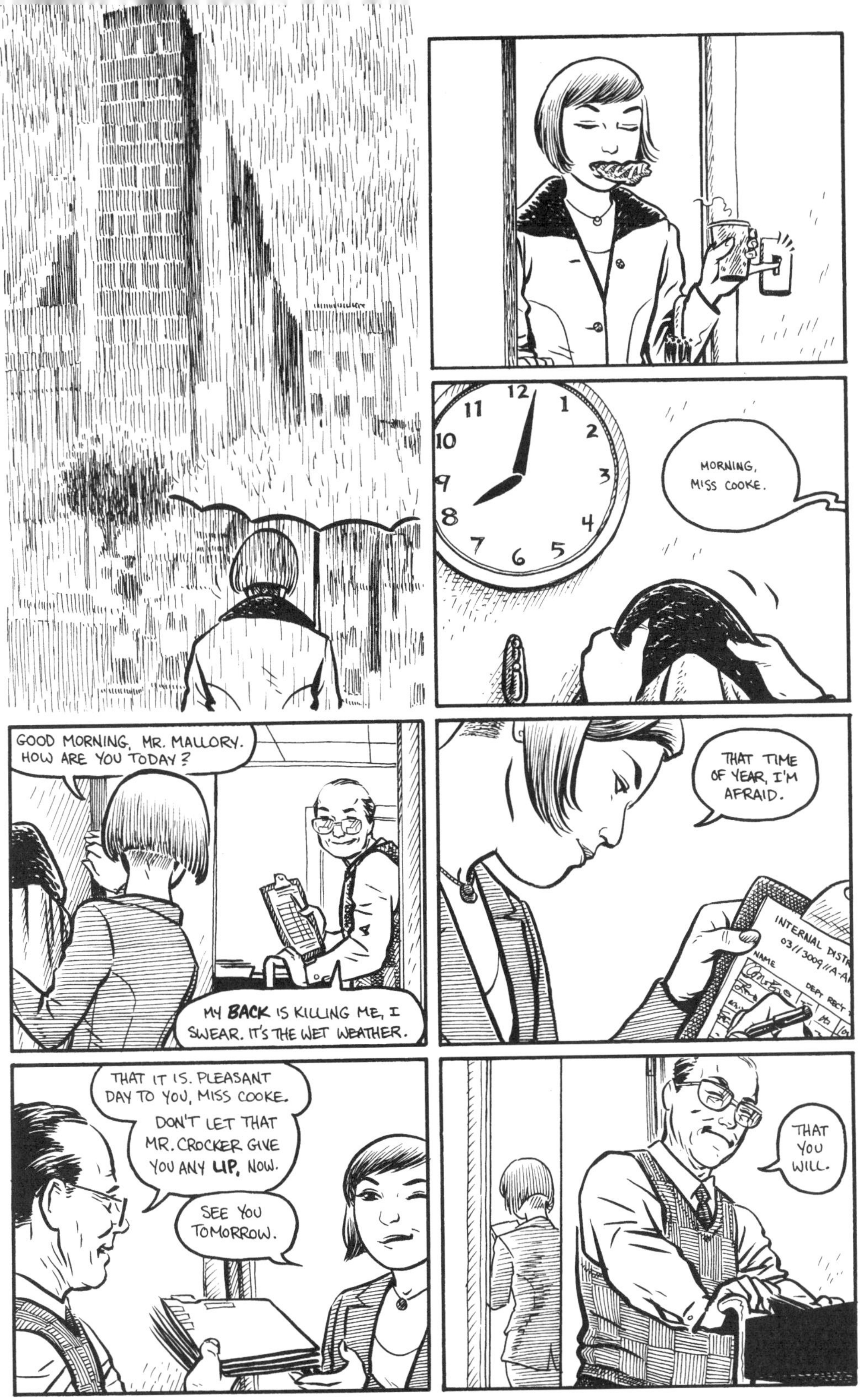
MORNING, MISS COOKE.
GOOD MORNING, MR. MALLORY. HOW ARE YOU TODAY?
MY BACK IS KILLING ME, I SWEAR. IT'S THE WET WEATHER.
THAT TIME OF YEAR, I'M AFRAID.
THAT IT IS. PLEASANT DAY TO YOU, MISS COOKE.
DON'T LET THAT MR. CROCKER GIVE YOU ANY LIP, NOW.
SEE YOU TOMORROW.
THAT YOU WILL.

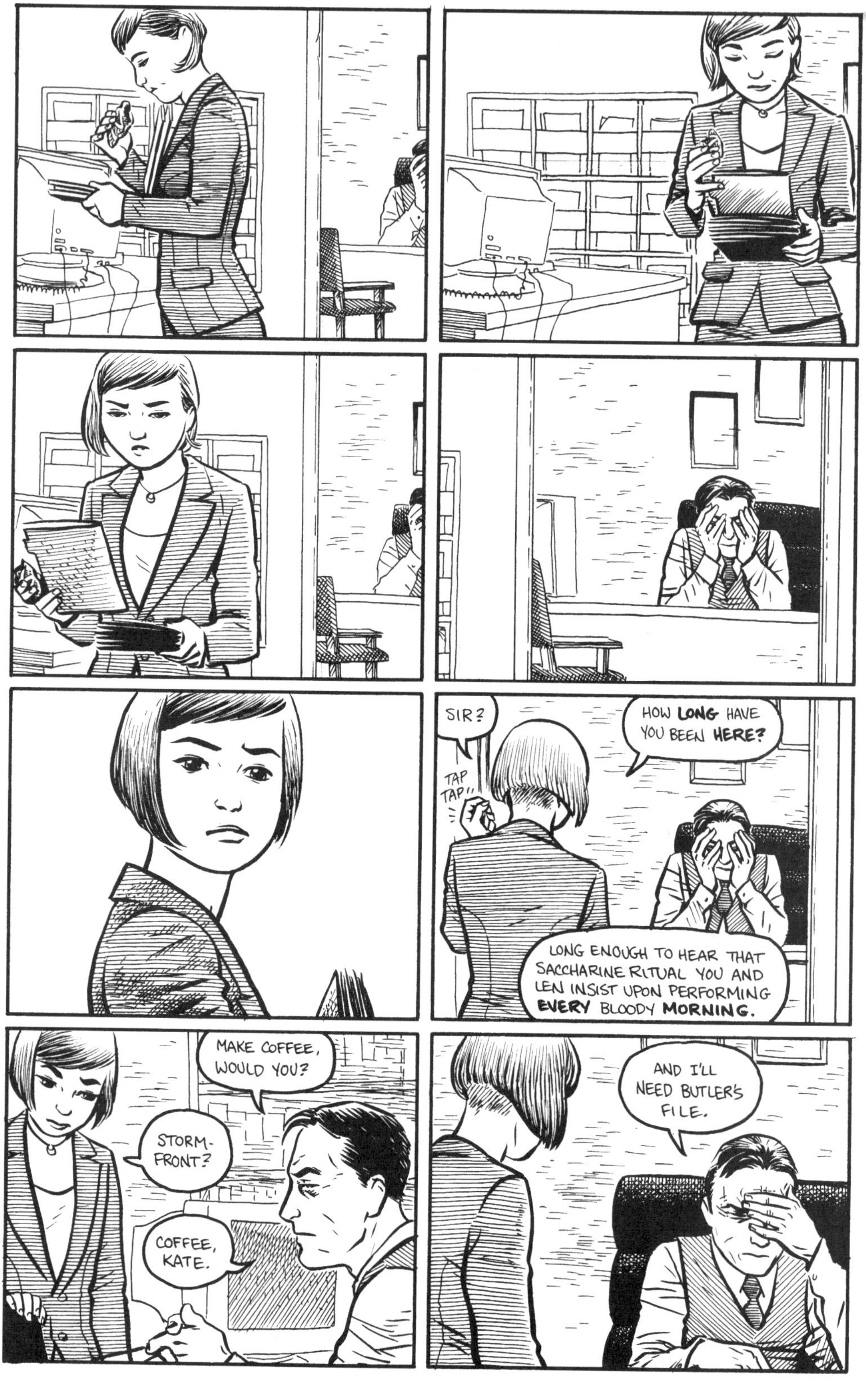
SIR?
TAP TAP
HOW LONG HAVE YOU BEEN HERE?
LONG ENOUGH TO HEAR THAT SACCHARINE RITUAL YOU AND LEN INSIST UPON PERFORMING EVERY BLOODY MORNING.
MAKE COFFEE, WOULD YOU?
STORM-FRONT?
COFFEE, KATE.
AND I'LL NEED BUTLER'S FILE.

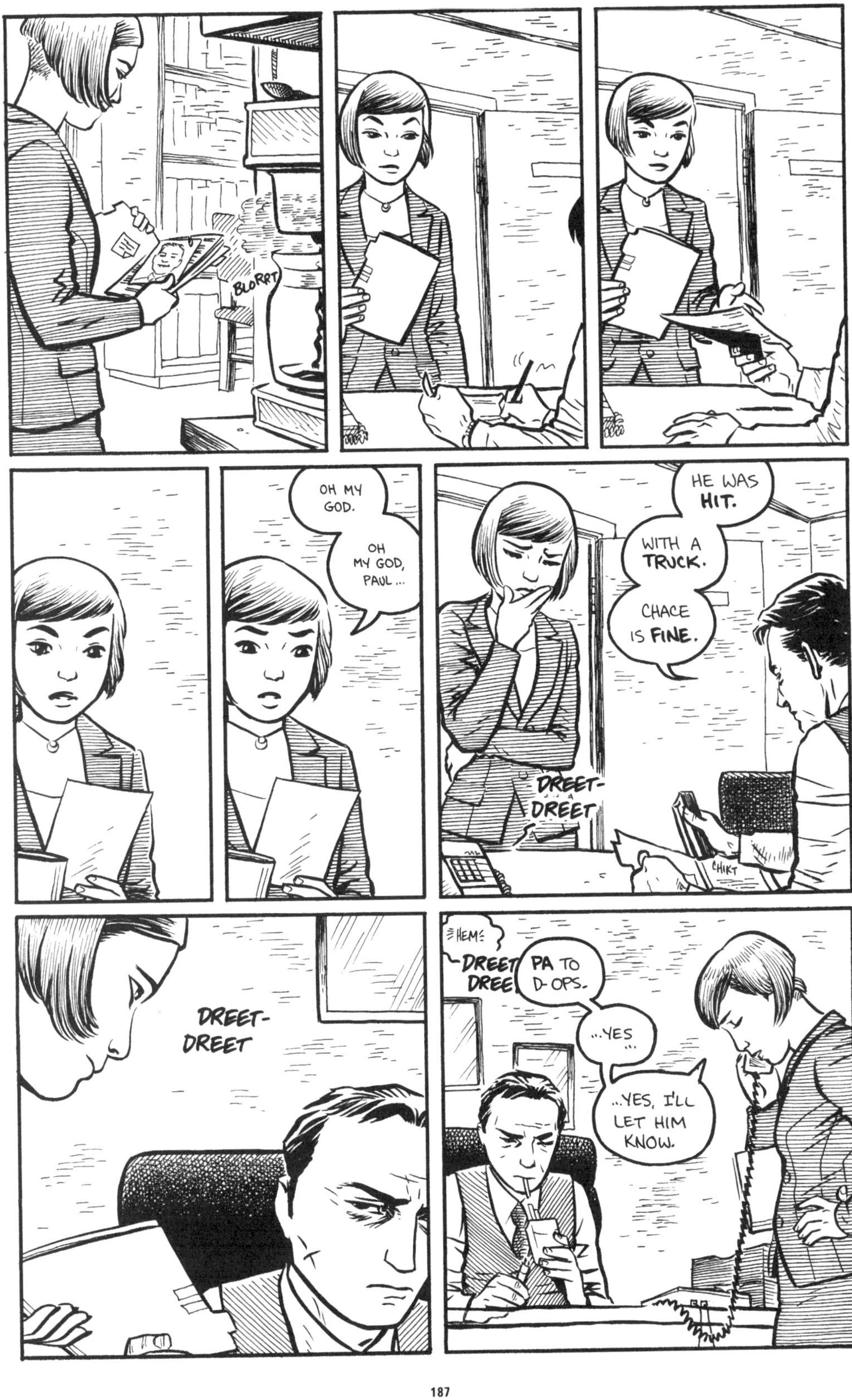
BLORRT
OH MY GOD.
OH MY GOD, PAUL...
HE WAS HIT.
WITH A TRUCK.
CHACE IS FINE.
DREET-DREET
CHIKT
DREET-DREET
HEM
DREET DREE
PA TO D-OPS.
...YES...
...YES, I'LL LET HIM KNOW.

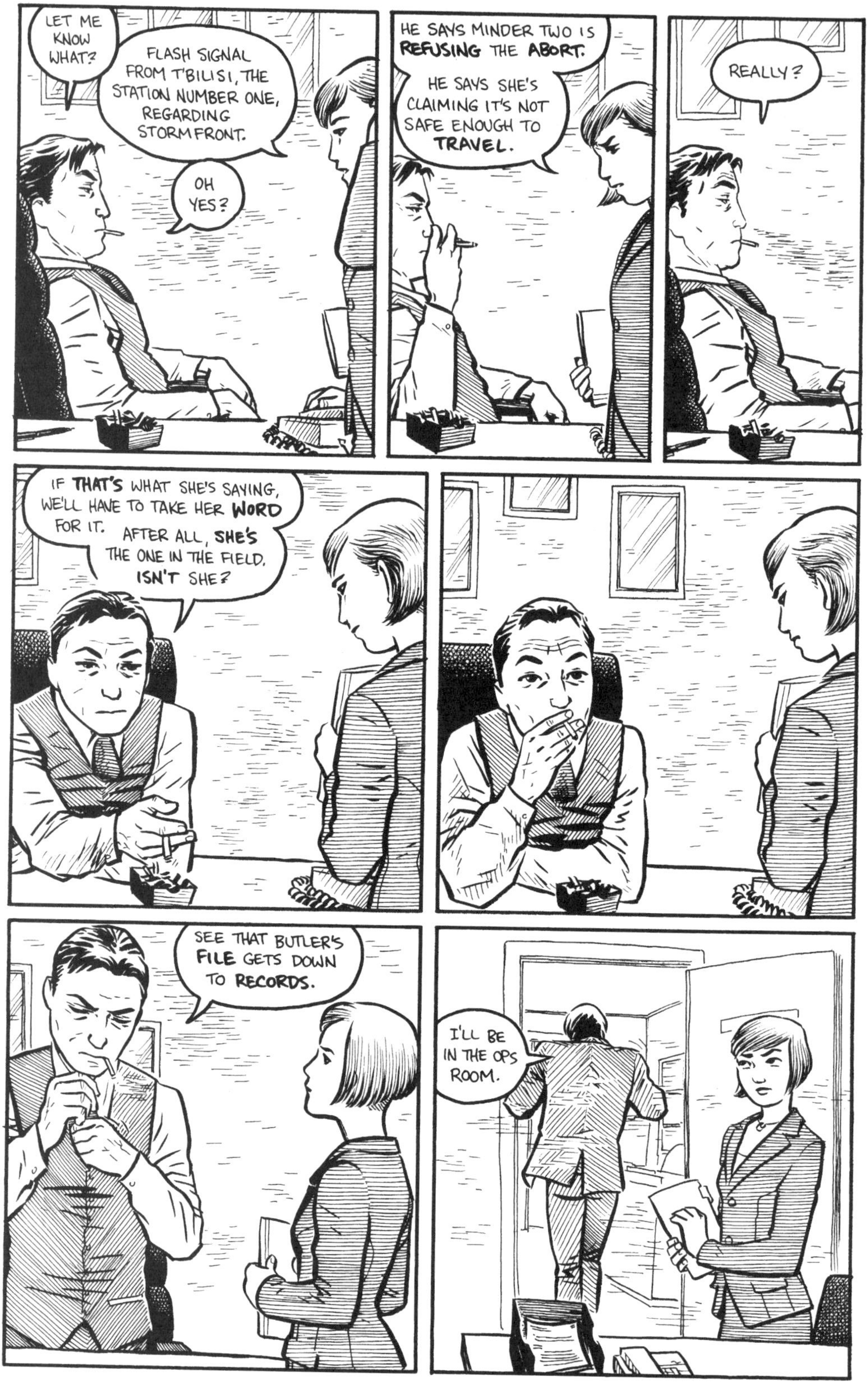

LET ME KNOW WHAT?
FLASH SIGNAL FROM T'BILISI, THE STATION NUMBER ONE, REGARDING STORMFRONT.
OH YES?
HE SAYS MINDER TWO IS REFUSING THE ABORT.
HE SAYS SHE'S CLAIMING IT'S NOT SAFE ENOUGH TO TRAVEL.
REALLY?
IF THAT'S WHAT SHE'S SAYING, WE'LL HAVE TO TAKE HER WORD FOR IT.
AFTER ALL, SHE'S THE ONE IN THE FIELD, ISN'T SHE?
SEE THAT BUTLER'S FILE GETS DOWN TO RECORDS.
I'LL BE IN THE OPS ROOM.

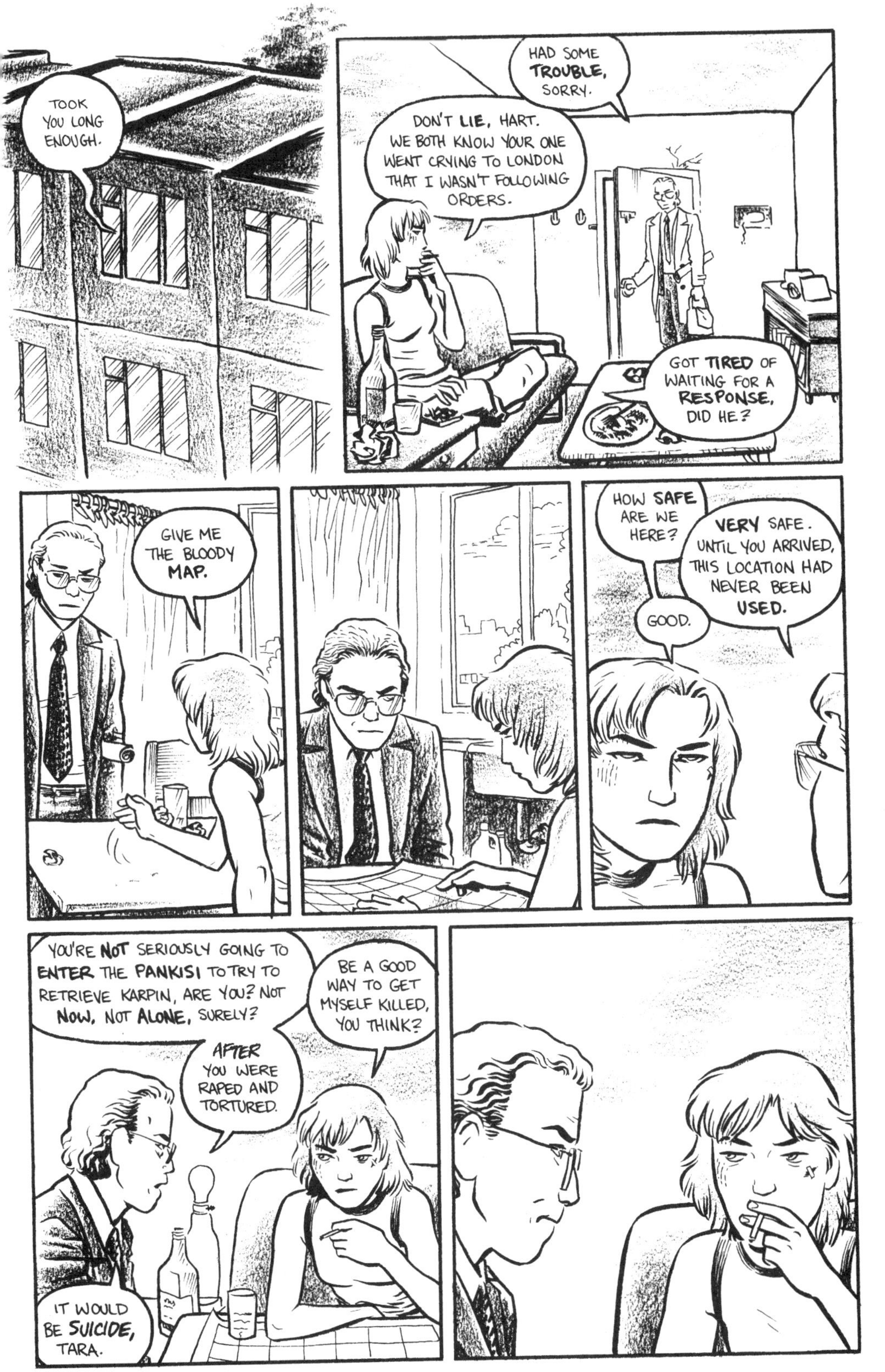
TOOK YOU LONG ENOUGH.
HAD SOME TROUBLE, SORRY.
DON'T LIE, HART. WE BOTH KNOW YOUR ONE WENT CRYING TO LONDON THAT I WASN'T FOLLOWING ORDERS.
GOT TIRED OF WAITING FOR A RESPONSE, DID HE?
GIVE ME THE BLOODY MAP.
HOW SAFE ARE WE HERE?
VERY SAFE. UNTIL YOU ARRIVED, THIS LOCATION HAD NEVER BEEN USED.
GOOD.
YOU'RE NOT SERIOUSLY GOING TO ENTER THE PANKISI TO TRY TO RETRIEVE KARPIN, ARE YOU? NOT NOW, NOT ALONE, SURELY?
AFTER YOU WERE RAPED AND TORTURED.
BE A GOOD WAY TO GET MYSELF KILLED, YOU THINK?
IT WOULD BE SUICIDE, TARA.

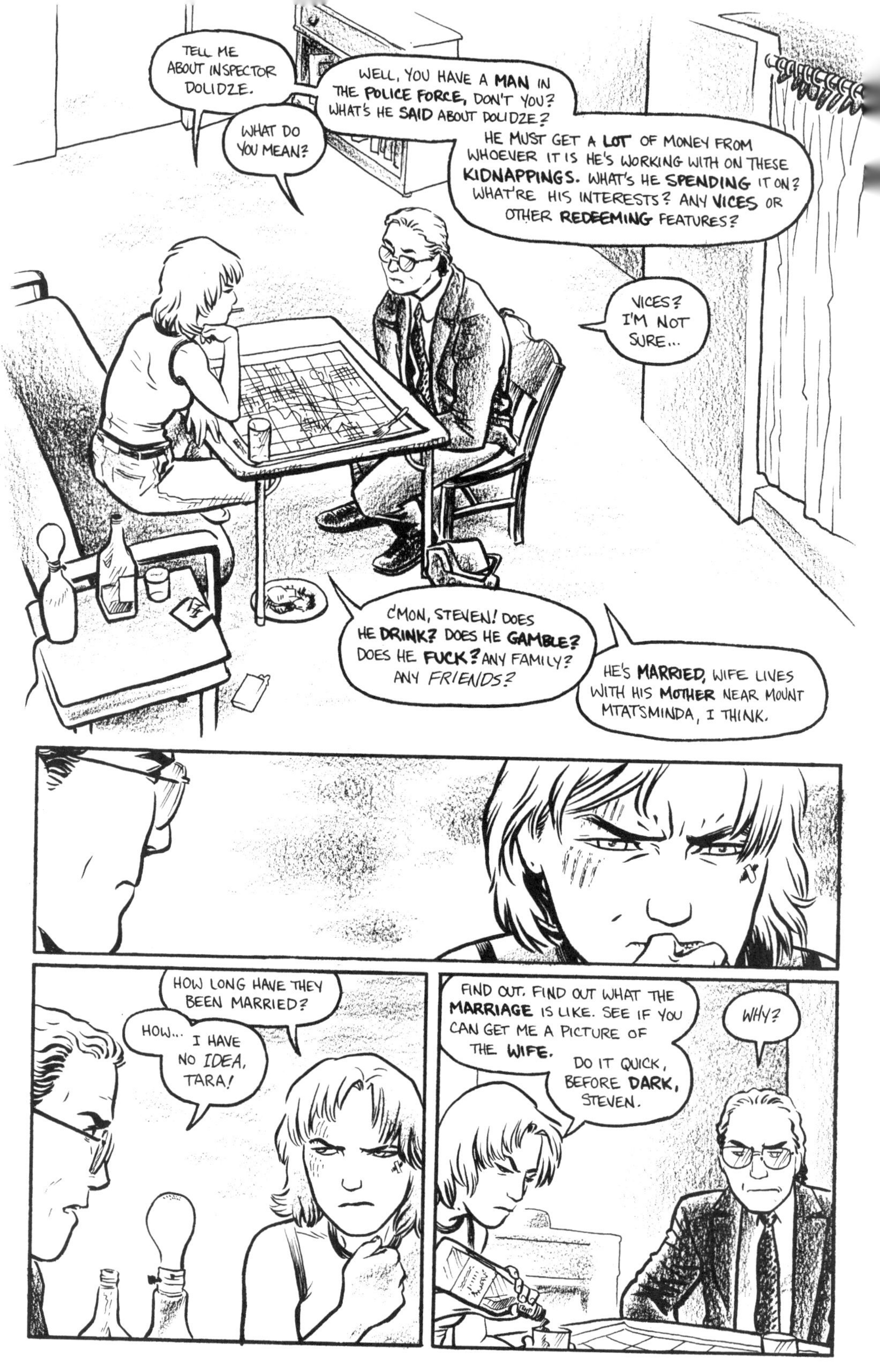
TELL ME ABOUT INSPECTOR DOLIDZE.
WHAT DO YOU MEAN?
WELL, YOU HAVE A MAN IN THE POLICE FORCE, DON'T YOU? WHAT'S HE SAID ABOUT DOLIDZE?
HE MUST GET A LOT OF MONEY FROM WHOEVER IT IS HE'S WORKING WITH ON THESE KIDNAPPINGS. WHAT'S HE SPENDING IT ON? WHAT'RE HIS INTERESTS? ANY VICES OR OTHER REDEEMING FEATURES?
VICES? I'M NOT SURE...
C'MON, STEVEN! DOES HE DRINK? DOES HE GAMBLE? DOES HE FUCK? ANY FAMILY? ANY FRIENDS?
HE'S MARRIED, WIFE LIVES WITH HIS MOTHER NEAR MOUNT MTATSMINDA, I THINK.
HOW LONG HAVE THEY BEEN MARRIED?
HOW... I HAVE NO IDEA, TARA!
FIND OUT. FIND OUT WHAT THE MARRIAGE IS LIKE. SEE IF YOU CAN GET ME A PICTURE OF THE WIFE.
WHY?
DO IT QUICK, BEFORE DARK, STEVEN.

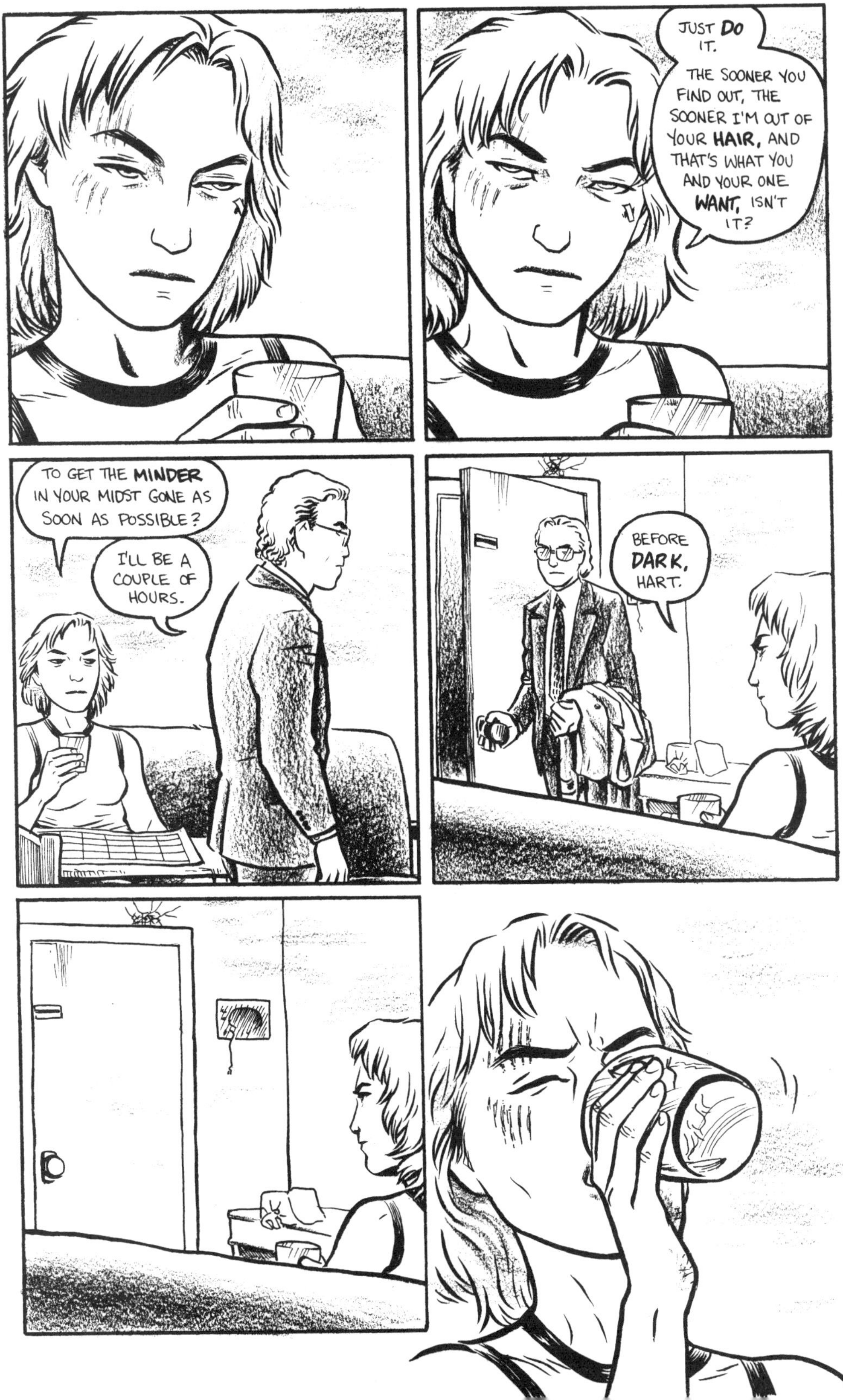
JUST DO IT.
THE SOONER YOU FIND OUT, THE SOONER I'M OUT OF YOUR HAIR, AND THAT'S WHAT YOU AND YOUR ONE WANT, ISN'T IT?
TO GET THE MINDER IN YOUR MIDST GONE AS SOON AS POSSIBLE?
I'LL BE A COUPLE OF HOURS.
BEFORE DARK, HART.

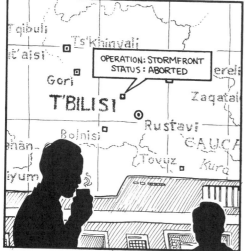

OPERATION: STORMFRONT
STATUS: ABORTED

Gori

T'BILISI

Rustavi

Bolnisi

CAUCA

Tovuz

Kura

NO WORD?

UNLESS YOU COUNT THE **HOURLY** WHINING FROM THE STATION NUMBER ONE ABOUT THE FACT THAT HE'S GOT A MINDER WHO **WON'T** LEAVE, NO.

THAT'S FULLER?

THANKS.

JAMES FULLER, YES. HE'S **COMPLAINING** THAT CHACE HAS HART RUNNING AROUND ON **ERRANDS** FOR HER.

HE'S **DEMANDING** I DO SOMETHING.

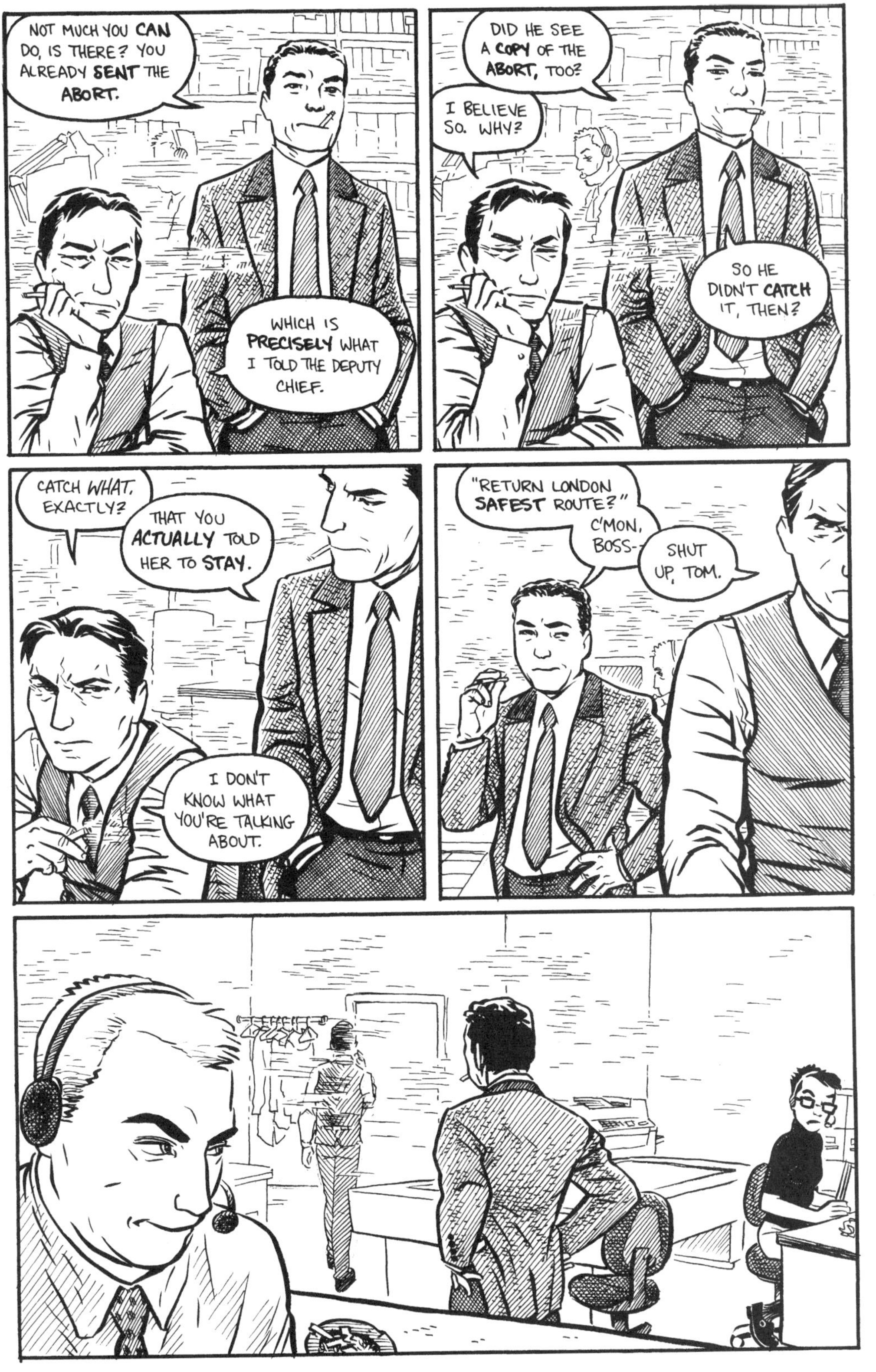
NOT MUCH YOU CAN DO, IS THERE? YOU ALREADY SENT THE ABORT.
WHICH IS PRECISELY WHAT I TOLD THE DEPUTY CHIEF.
DID HE SEE A COPY OF THE ABORT, TOO?
I BELIEVE SO. WHY?
SO HE DIDN'T CATCH IT, THEN?
CATCH WHAT, EXACTLY?
THAT YOU ACTUALLY TOLD HER TO STAY.
I DON'T KNOW WHAT YOU'RE TALKING ABOUT.
"RETURN LONDON SAFEST ROUTE?"
C'MON, BOSS-
SHUT UP, TOM.

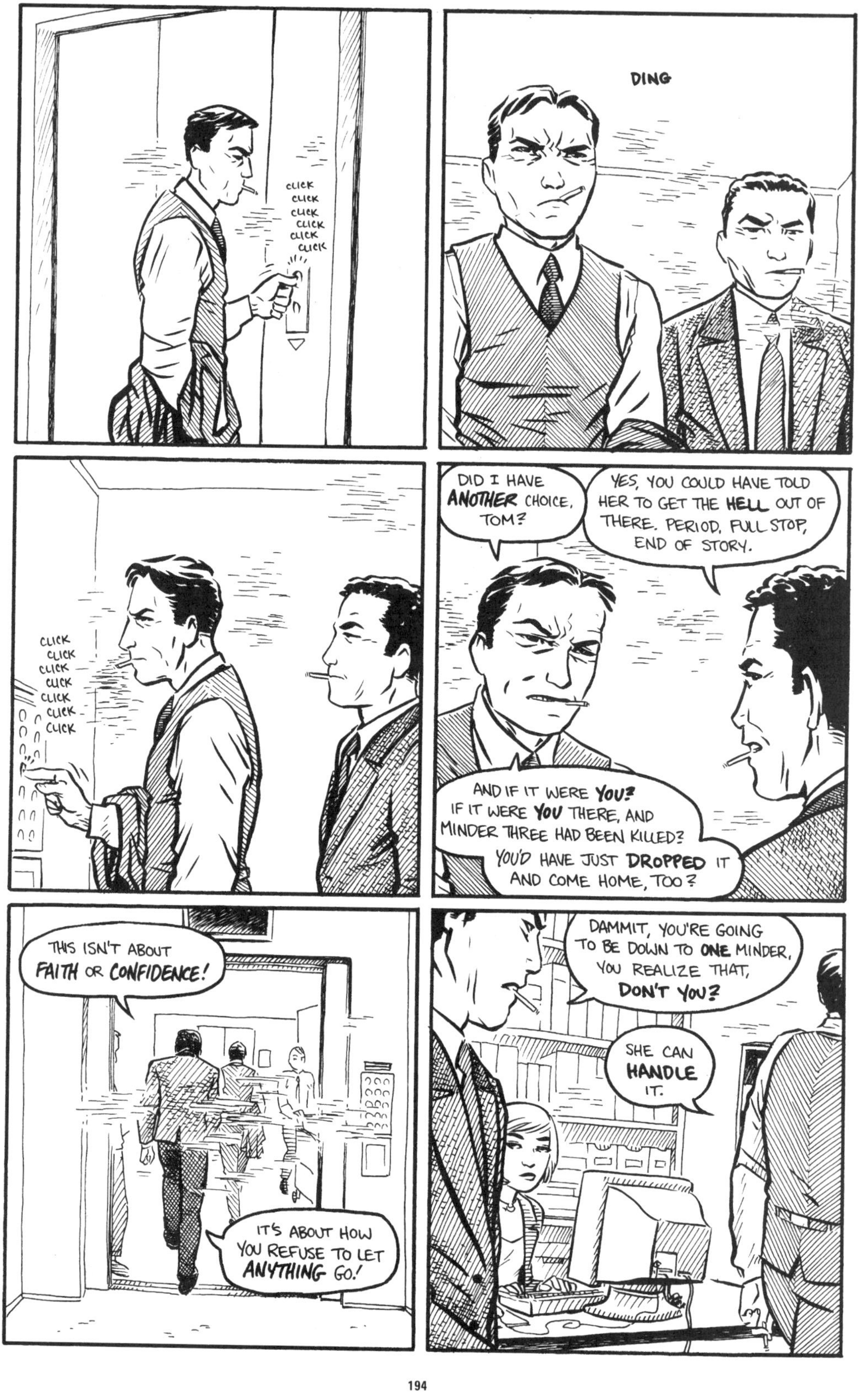
CLICK
CLICK
CLICK
CLICK
CLICK
CLICK
DING
CLICK
CLICK
CLICK
CLICK
CLICK
CLICK
CLICK
DID I HAVE ANOTHER CHOICE, TOM?
YES, YOU COULD HAVE TOLD HER TO GET THE HELL OUT OF THERE. PERIOD, FULL STOP, END OF STORY.
AND IF IT WERE YOU? IF IT WERE YOU THERE, AND MINDER THREE HAD BEEN KILLED?
YOU'D HAVE JUST DROPPED IT AND COME HOME, TOO?
THIS ISN'T ABOUT FAITH OR CONFIDENCE!
IT'S ABOUT HOW YOU REFUSE TO LET ANYTHING GO!
DAMMIT, YOU'RE GOING TO BE DOWN TO ONE MINDER, YOU REALIZE THAT, DON'T YOU?
SHE CAN HANDLE IT.

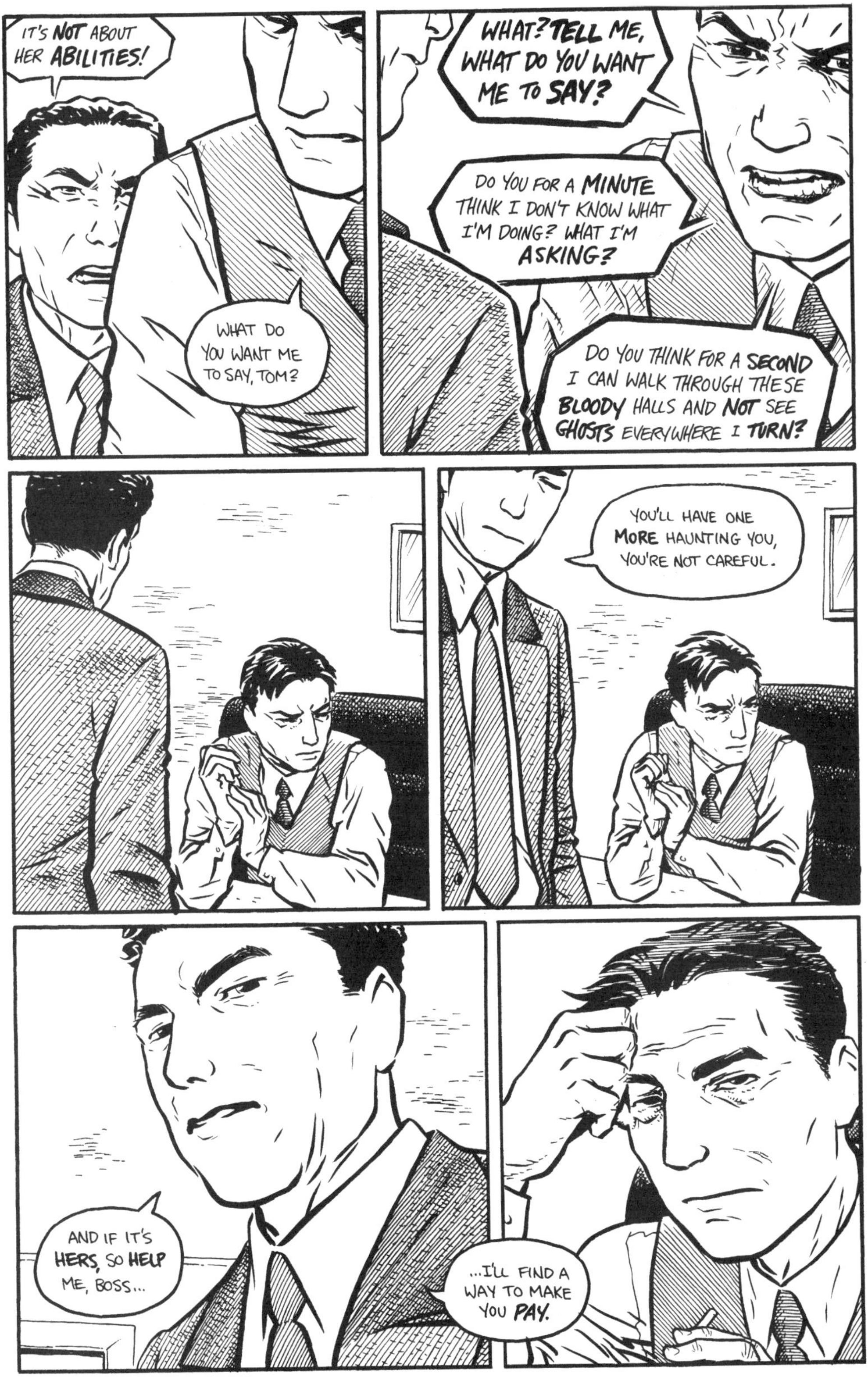
IT'S NOT ABOUT HER ABILITIES!
WHAT DO YOU WANT ME TO SAY, TOM?
WHAT? TELL ME, WHAT DO YOU WANT ME TO SAY?
DO YOU FOR A MINUTE THINK I DON'T KNOW WHAT I'M DOING? WHAT I'M ASKING?
DO YOU THINK FOR A SECOND I CAN WALK THROUGH THESE BLOODY HALLS AND NOT SEE GHOSTS EVERYWHERE I TURN?
YOU'LL HAVE ONE MORE HAUNTING YOU, YOU'RE NOT CAREFUL.
AND IF IT'S HERS, SO HELP ME, BOSS...
...I'LL FIND A WAY TO MAKE YOU PAY.

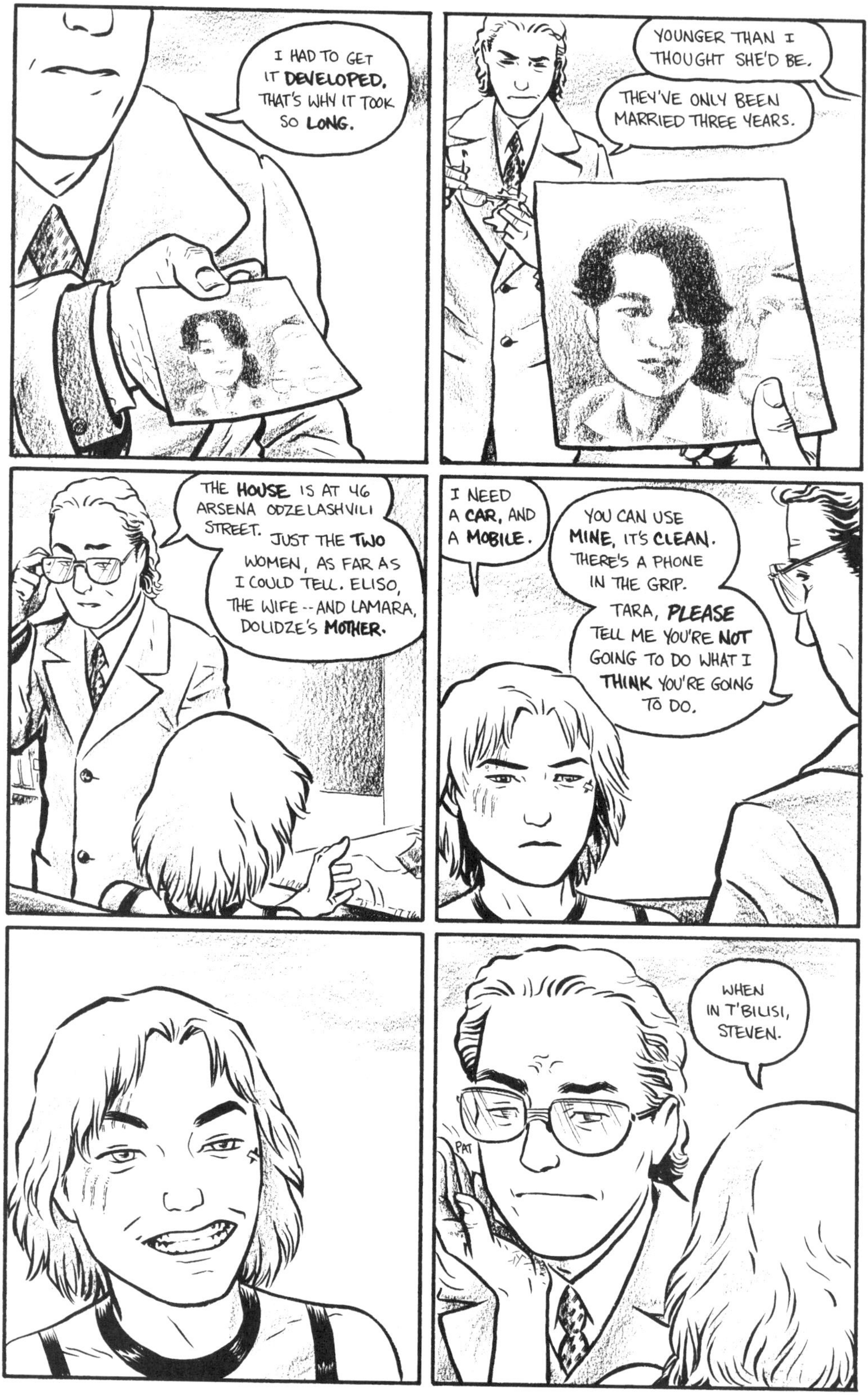
I HAD TO GET IT DEVELOPED. THAT'S WHY IT TOOK SO LONG.
YOUNGER THAN I THOUGHT SHE'D BE.
THEY'VE ONLY BEEN MARRIED THREE YEARS.
THE HOUSE IS AT 46 ARSENA ODZELASHVILI STREET.
JUST THE TWO WOMEN, AS FAR AS I COULD TELL. ELISO, THE WIFE--AND LAMARA, DOLIDZE'S MOTHER.
I NEED A CAR, AND A MOBILE.
YOU CAN USE MINE, IT'S CLEAN. THERE'S A PHONE IN THE GRIP.
TARA, PLEASE TELL ME YOU'RE NOT GOING TO DO WHAT I THINK YOU'RE GOING TO DO.
PAT
WHEN IN T'BILISI, STEVEN.

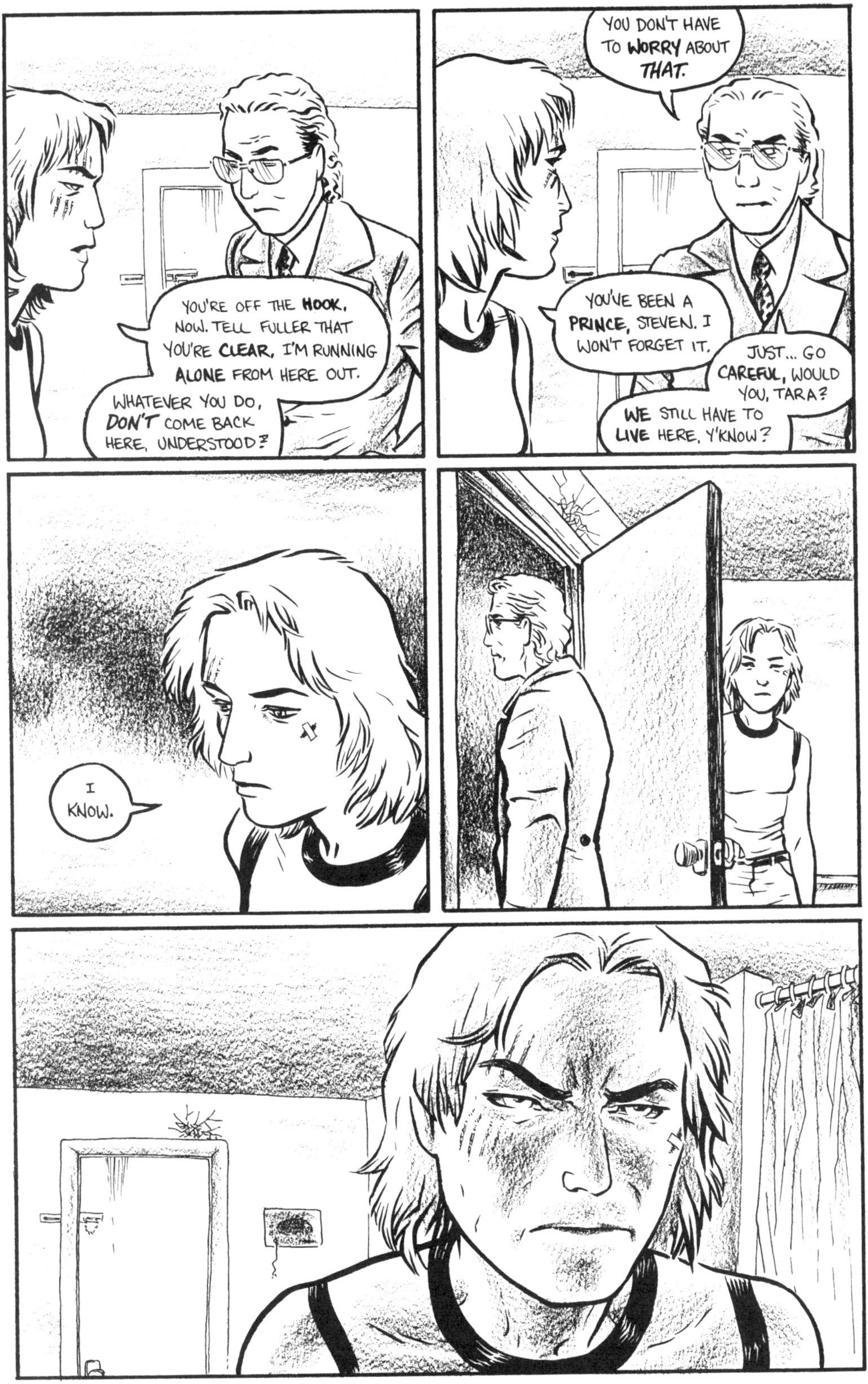
YOU'RE OFF THE HOOK, NOW. TELL FULLER THAT YOU'RE CLEAR, I'M RUNNING ALONE FROM HERE OUT.
WHATEVER YOU DO, DON'T COME BACK HERE, UNDERSTOOD?
YOU DON'T HAVE TO WORRY ABOUT THAT.
YOU'VE BEEN A PRINCE, STEVEN. I WON'T FORGET IT.
JUST... GO CAREFUL, WOULD YOU, TARA?
WE STILL HAVE TO LIVE HERE, Y'KNOW?
I KNOW.

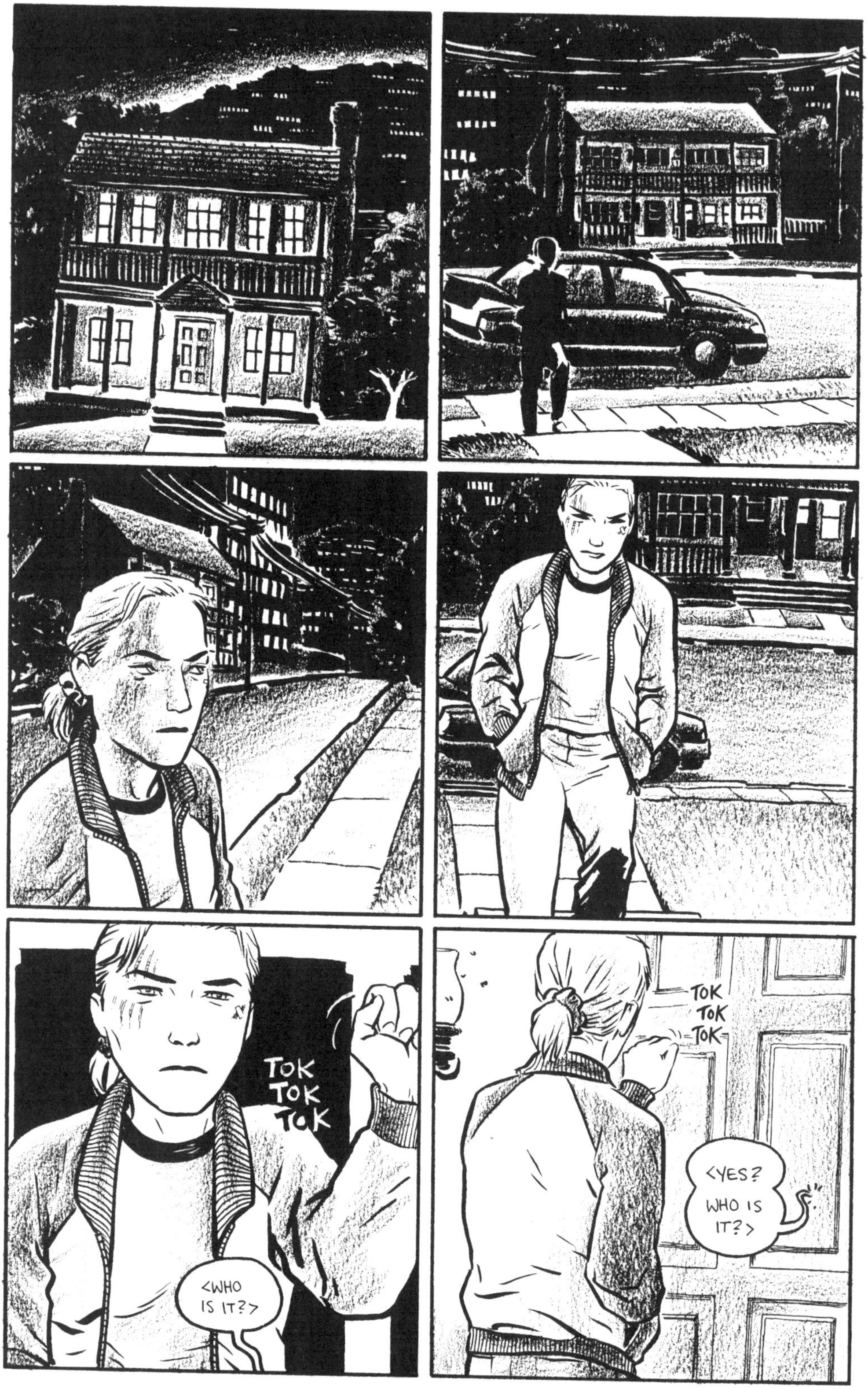
TOK
TOK
TOK
<WHO IS IT?>
TOK
TOK
TOK
<YES? WHO IS IT?>

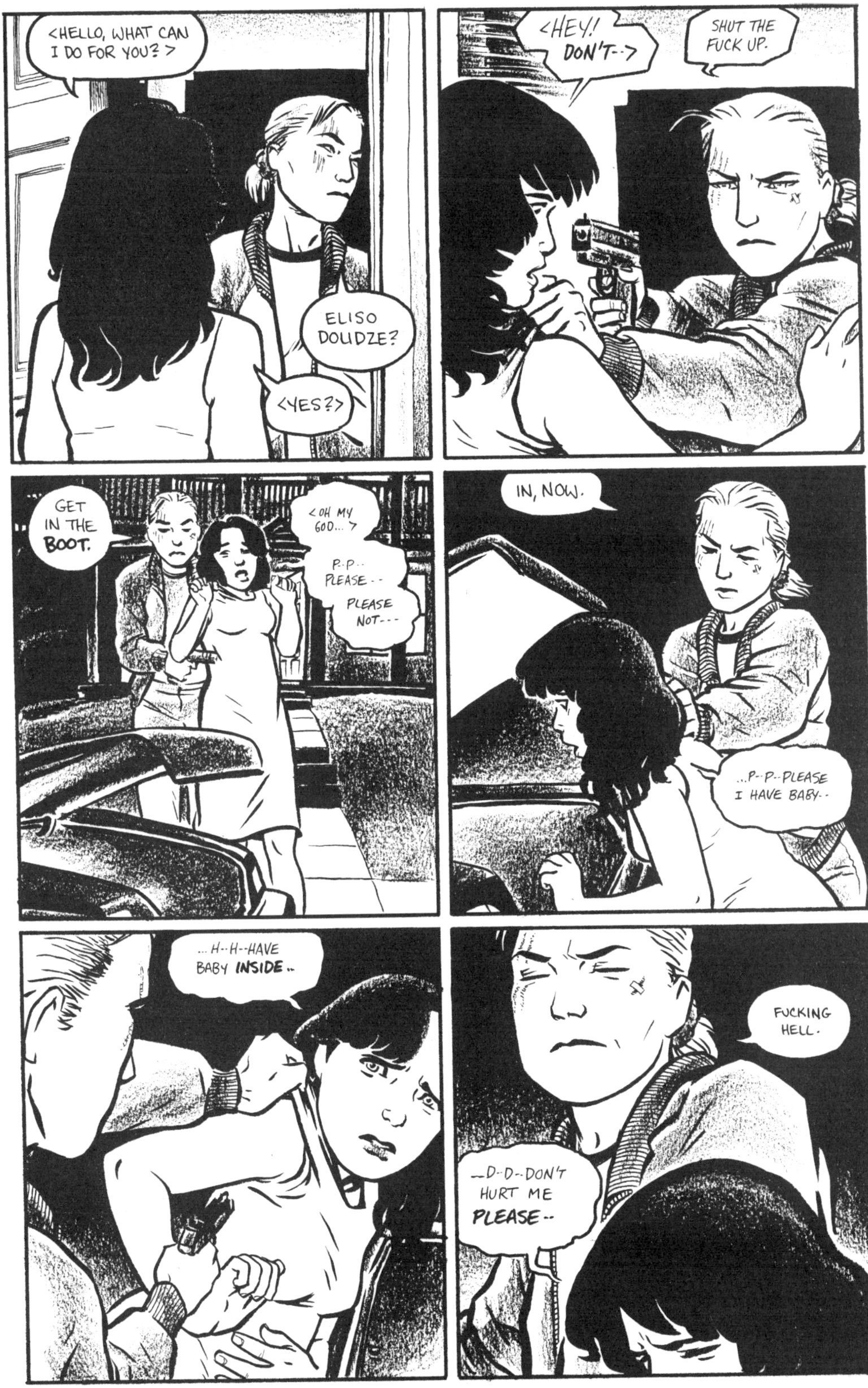
<HELLO, WHAT CAN I DO FOR YOU?>
ELISO DOUDZE?
<YES?>
<HEY! DON'T-->
SHUT THE FUCK UP.
GET IN THE BOOT.
<OH MY GOD...>
P-P-- PLEASE--
PLEASE NOT---
IN, NOW.
...P--P--PLEASE I HAVE BABY--
...H--H--HAVE BABY INSIDE..
FUCKING HELL.
--D-D--DON'T HURT ME PLEASE--

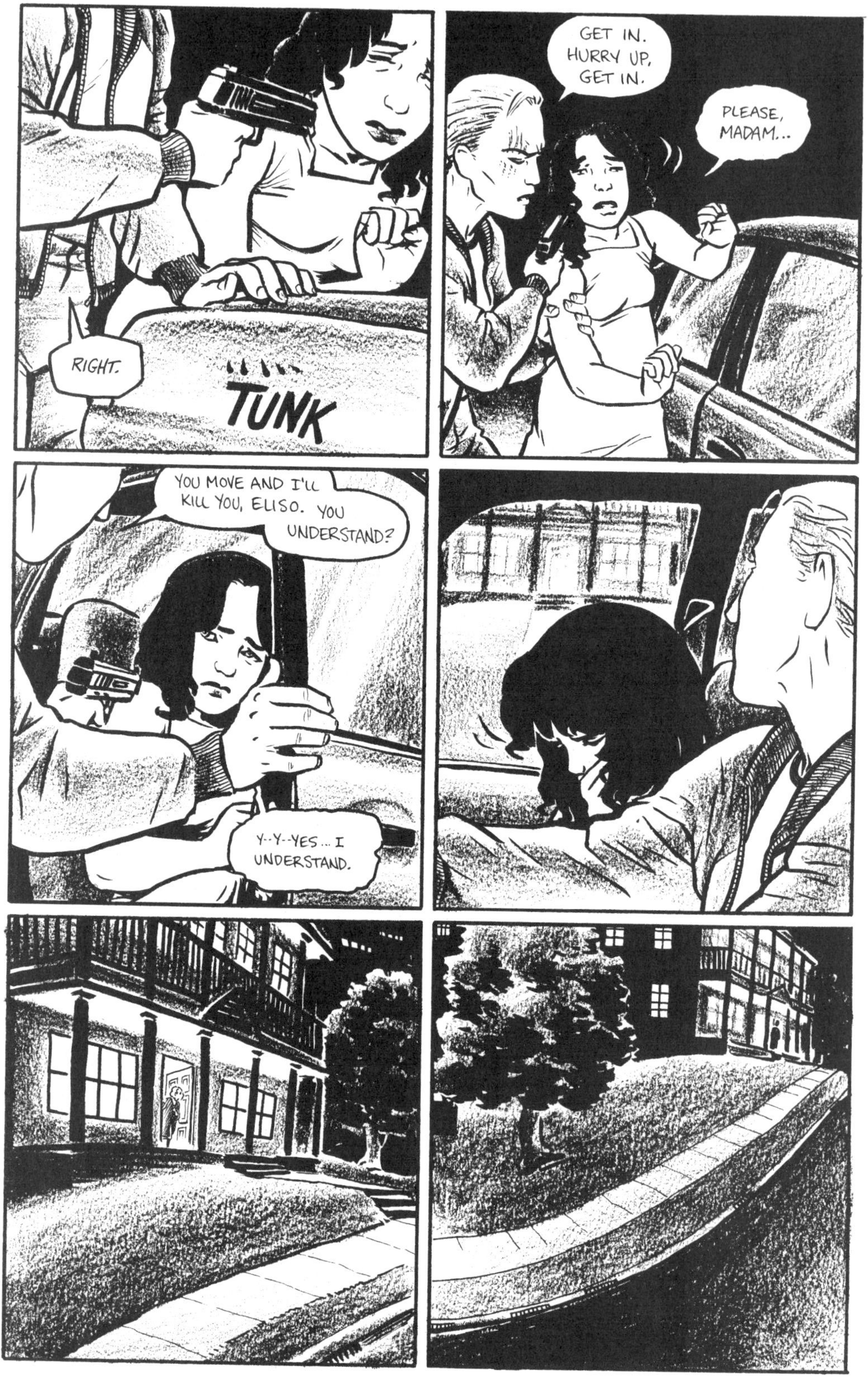
RIGHT.
TUNK
GET IN. HURRY UP, GET IN.
PLEASE, MADAM...
YOU MOVE AND I'LL KILL YOU, ELISO. YOU UNDERSTAND?
Y--Y--YES... I UNDERSTAND.

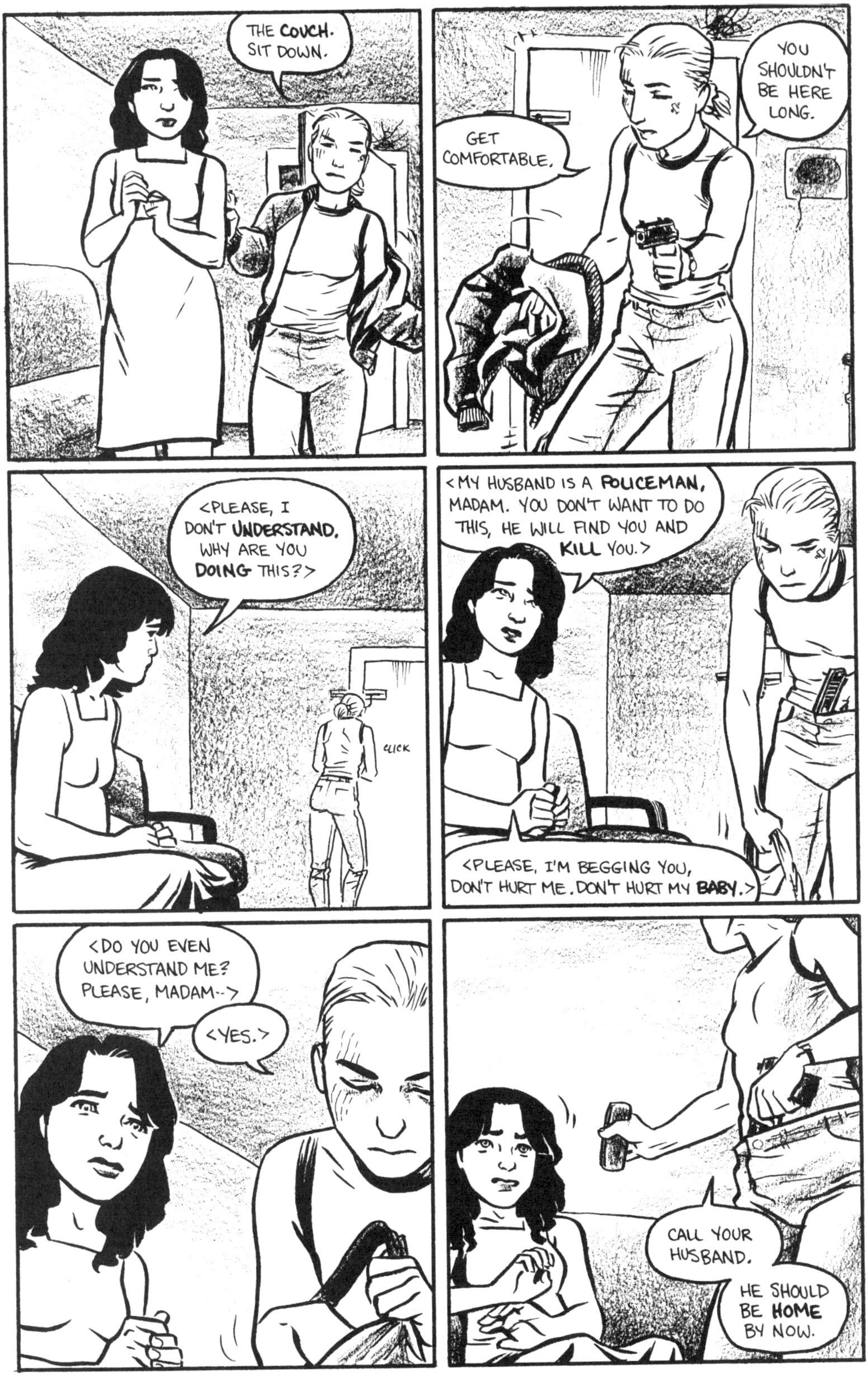
THE COUCH. SIT DOWN.
GET COMFORTABLE.
YOU SHOULDN'T BE HERE LONG.
<PLEASE, I DON'T UNDERSTAND. WHY ARE YOU DOING THIS?>
CLICK
<MY HUSBAND IS A POLICEMAN, MADAM. YOU DON'T WANT TO DO THIS, HE WILL FIND YOU AND KILL YOU.>
<PLEASE, I'M BEGGING YOU, DON'T HURT ME. DON'T HURT MY BABY.>
<DO YOU EVEN UNDERSTAND ME? PLEASE, MADAM-->
<YES.>
CALL YOUR HUSBAND.
HE SHOULD BE HOME BY NOW.

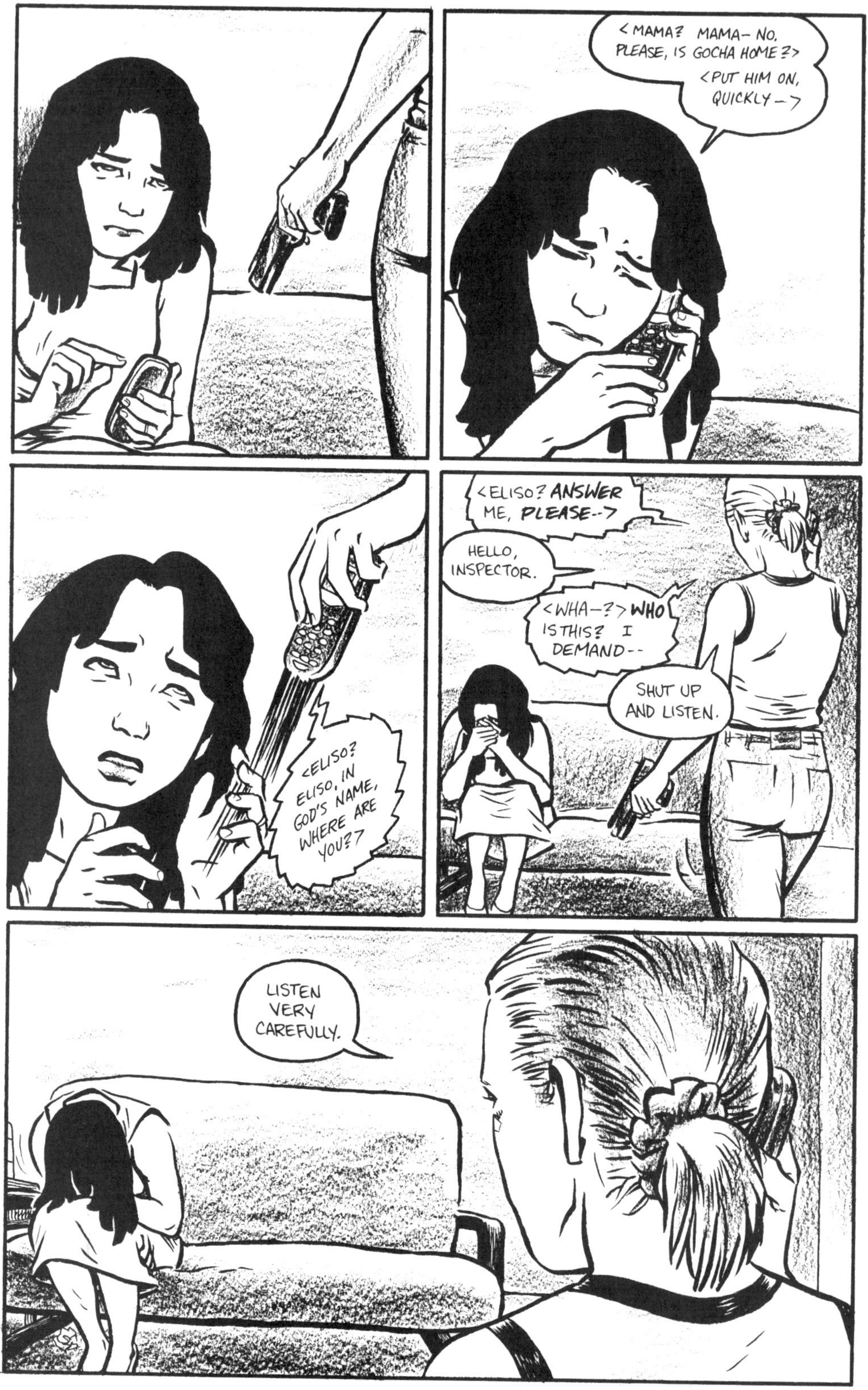
<MAMA? MAMA– NO. PLEASE, IS GOCHA HOME?>
<PUT HIM ON, QUICKLY–>
<ELISO? ELISO, IN GOD'S NAME, WHERE ARE YOU?>
<ELISO? ANSWER ME, PLEASE-->
HELLO, INSPECTOR.
<WHA–?> WHO IS THIS? I DEMAND--
SHUT UP AND LISTEN.
LISTEN VERY CAREFULLY.

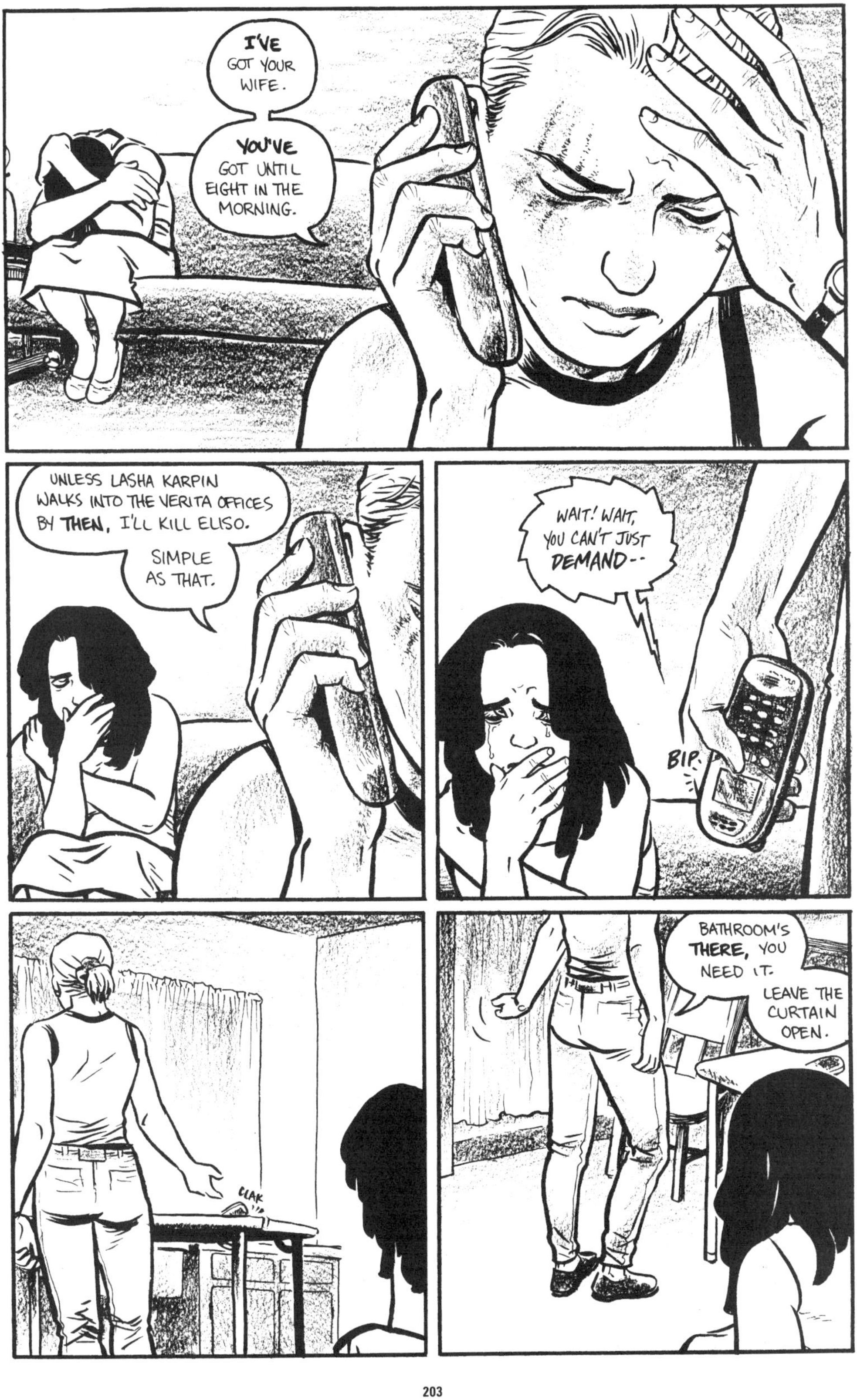
I'VE GOT YOUR WIFE.
YOU'VE GOT UNTIL EIGHT IN THE MORNING.
UNLESS LASHA KARPIN WALKS INTO THE VERITA OFFICES BY THEN, I'LL KILL ELISO.
SIMPLE AS THAT.
WAIT! WAIT, YOU CAN'T JUST DEMAND--
BIP.
CLAK
BATHROOM'S THERE, YOU NEED IT.
LEAVE THE CURTAIN OPEN.

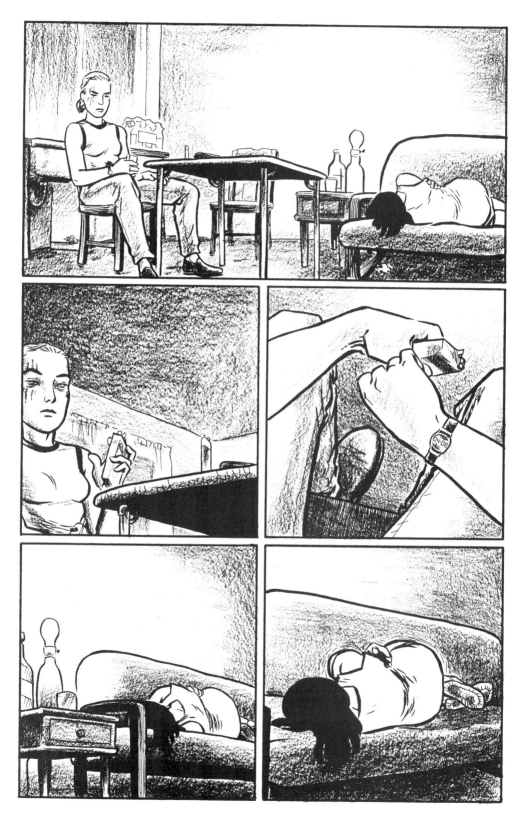

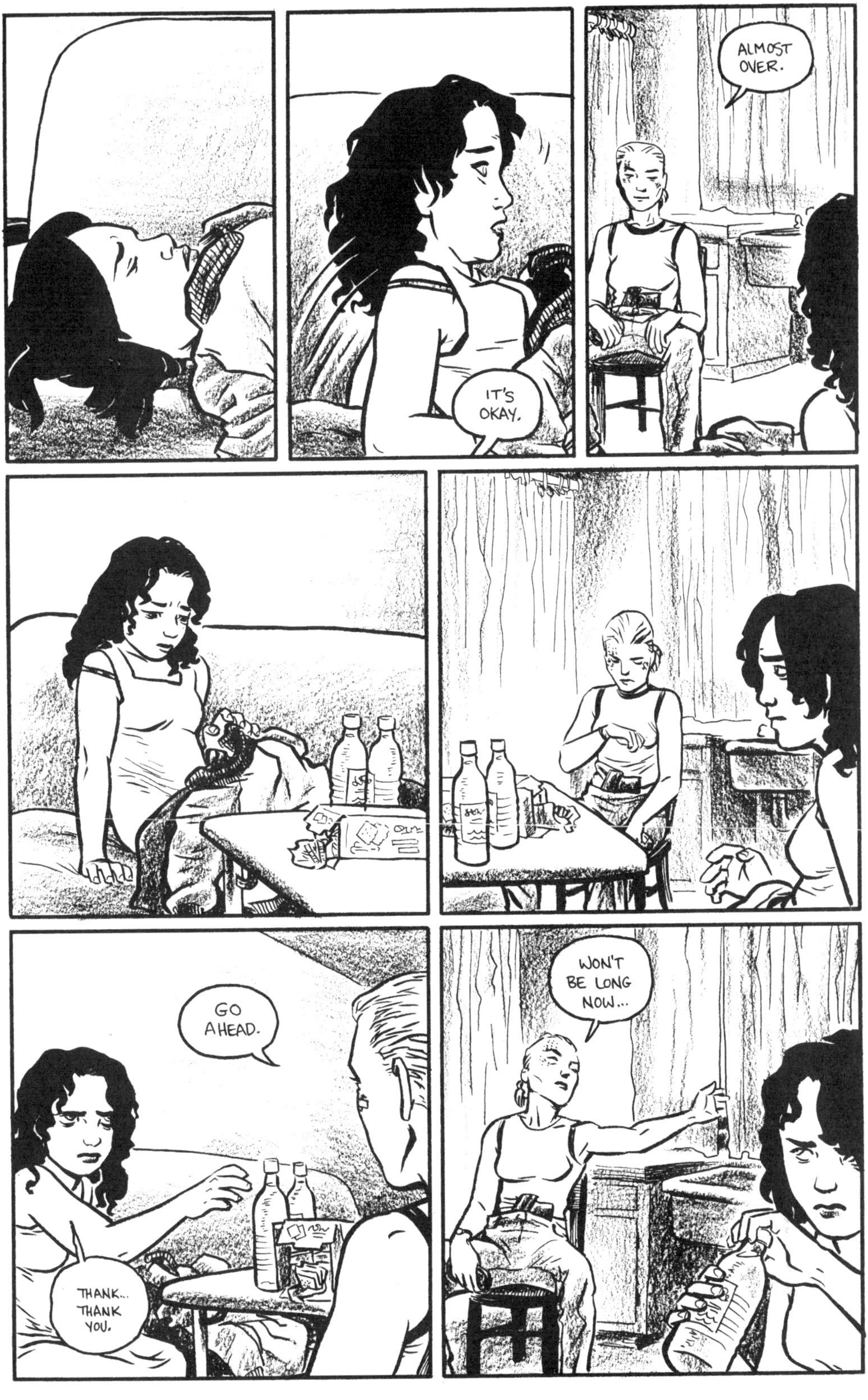
IT'S OKAY.
ALMOST OVER.
GO AHEAD.
THANK.. THANK YOU.
WON'T BE LONG NOW...

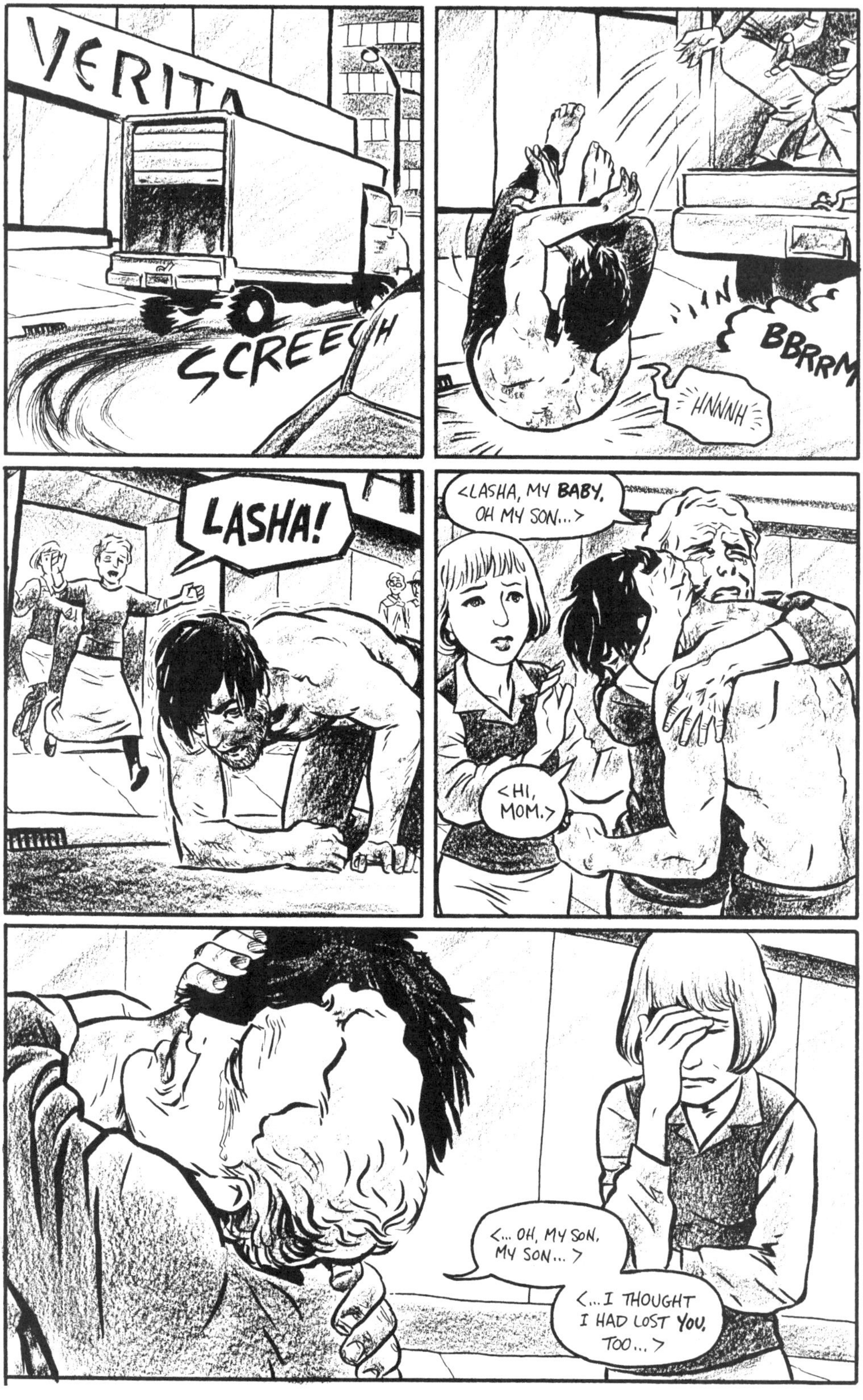
VERITA
SCREECH
N
BBRRRM
HNNNH
LASHA!
<LASHA, MY BABY, OH MY SON...>
<HI, MOM.>
<...OH, MY SON, MY SON...>
<...I THOUGHT I HAD LOST YOU, TOO...>

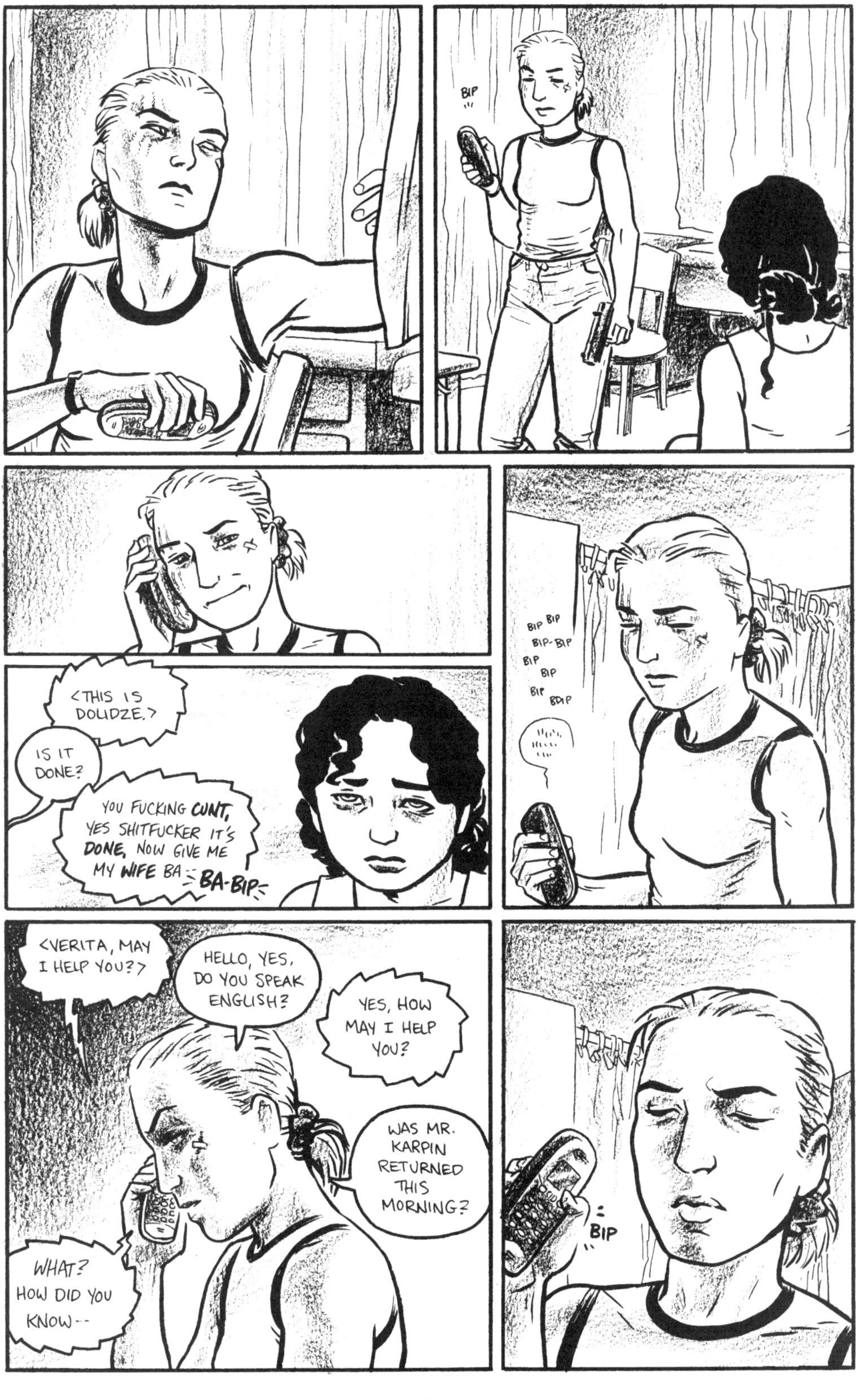

BIP
BIP BIP
BIP-BIP
BIP
BIP
BIP
BDIP
<THIS IS DOLIDZE.>
IS IT DONE?
YOU FUCKING CUNT, YES SHITFUCKER IT'S DONE, NOW GIVE ME MY WIFE BA
BA-BIP
<VERITA, MAY I HELP YOU?>
HELLO, YES, DO YOU SPEAK ENGLISH?
YES, HOW MAY I HELP YOU?
WAS MR. KARPIN RETURNED THIS MORNING?
WHAT? HOW DID YOU KNOW--
BIP

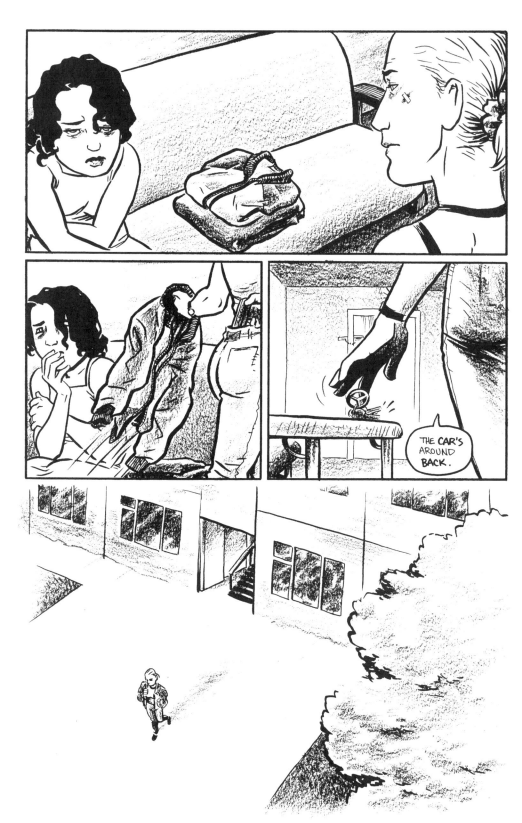

THE CAR'S AROUND BACK.

OPERATION: DANDELION

WRITTEN BY
GREG RUCKA

ILLUSTRATED BY
MIKE HAWTHORNE

LETTERED BY
JOHN DRANSKI

ORIGINAL SERIES EDITED BY
JAMIE S. RICH & JAMES LUCAS JONES

ROSTER

C—Ubiquitous code-name for the current head of SIS. Real name is Sir Wilson Stanton Davies.

DONALD WELDON—Deputy Chief of Service, has oversight of all aspects of Intelligence gathering and operations. Immediate superior to Crocker.

PAUL CROCKER—Director of Operations, encompassing all field work in all theaters of operations. In addition to commanding individual stations, has direct command of the Special Section– sometimes referred to as Minders–used for special operations.

TOM WALLACE—Head of the Special Section, a Special Operations Officer with the designation Minder One. Responsible for the training and continued well-being of his unit, both at home and in the field. Six year veteran of the Minders.

TARA CHACE—Special Operations Officer, designated Minder Two. Entering her third year as Minder.

FRANCES BARCLAY —Chief of Service, also known as 'C.' Distinguished service as CIA-Liaison, Chairman of the Joint Intelligence Committee, and as Head of Station Prague (85-88), Saigon (89-91), and Paris (91-94).

OPS ROOM STAFF   OTHERS

ALEXIS—Mission Control Officer (also called Main Communications Officer)– responsible for maintaining communications between the Operations Room and the agents in the field.

RON—Duty Operations Officer, responsible for monitoring the status and importance of all incoming intelligence, both from foreign stations and other sources.

KATE—Personal Assistant to Paul Crocker, termed PA to D.Ops. Possibly the hardest and most important job in the Service.

WALTER SECCOMBE —Permanent Under Secretary to the Foreign Office, a career civil servant with intimate knowledge of the inner workings of all levels of Government, and with the savvy to negotiate the corridors of power to achieve his own ends.

EDWARD KITTERING—Special Operations Officer, designated Minder Three. Has been with the Special Section for less than a year.

BRIAN BUTLER—A former sergeant in one of the British Army's oldest and most respected regiments. An unique individual who actually requested assignment with special section.

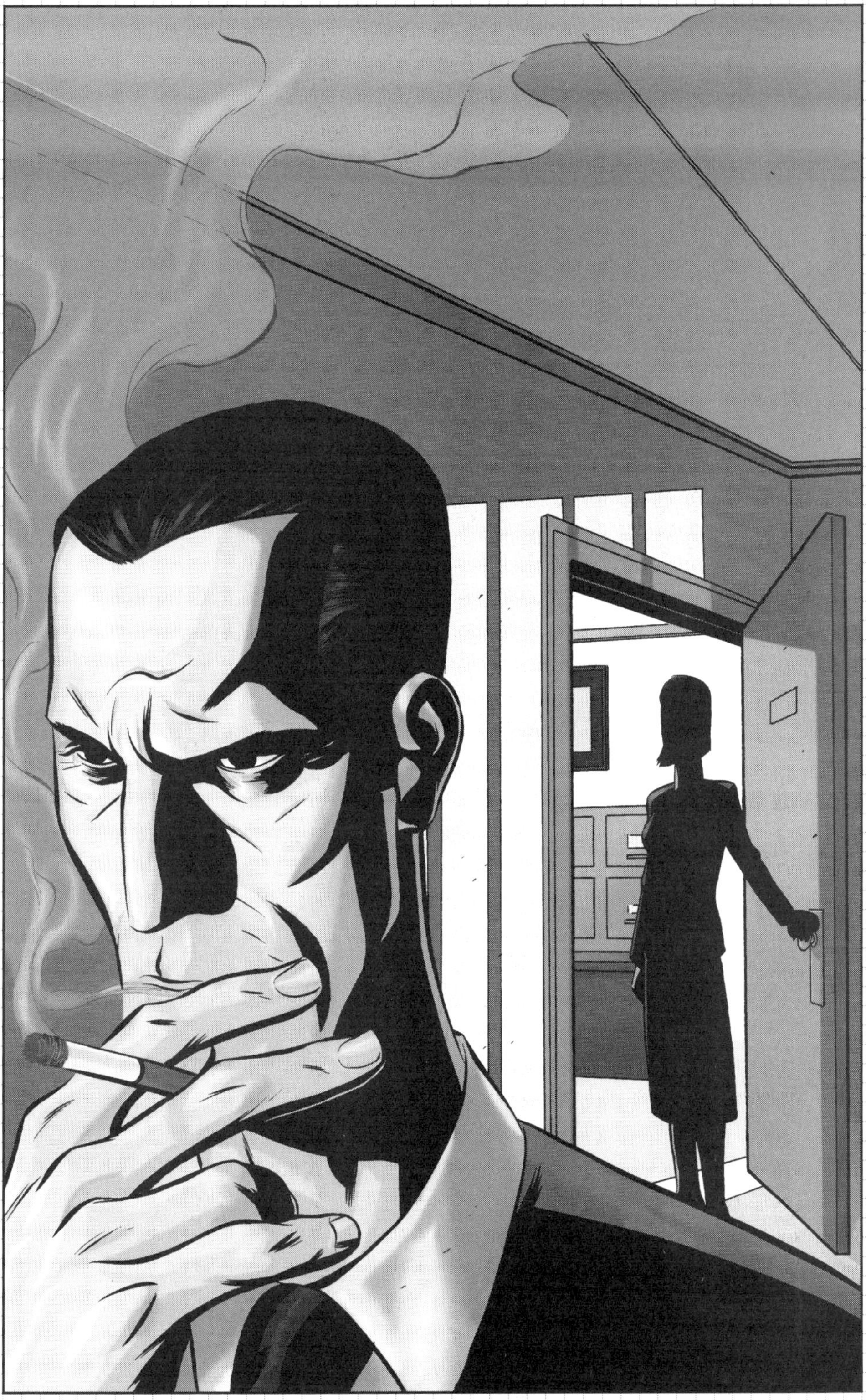

CHAPTER 1

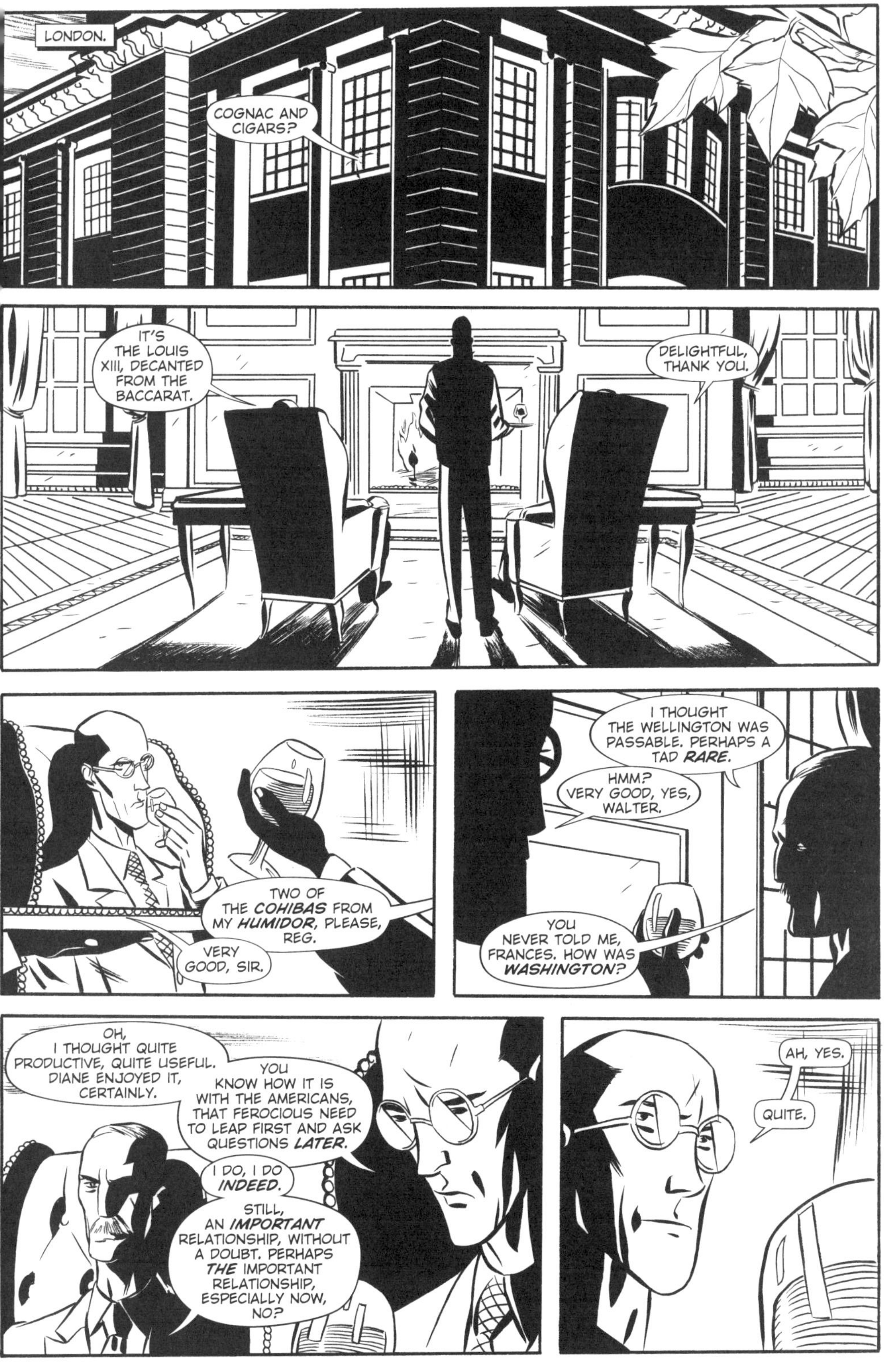
LONDON.
COGNAC AND CIGARS?
IT'S THE LOUIS XIII, DECANTED FROM THE BACCARAT.
DELIGHTFUL, THANK YOU.
TWO OF THE COHIBAS FROM MY HUMIDOR, PLEASE, REG.
VERY GOOD, SIR.
I THOUGHT THE WELLINGTON WAS PASSABLE. PERHAPS A TAD RARE.
HMM? VERY GOOD, YES, WALTER.
YOU NEVER TOLD ME, FRANCES. HOW WAS WASHINGTON?
OH, I THOUGHT QUITE PRODUCTIVE, QUITE USEFUL. DIANE ENJOYED IT, CERTAINLY.
YOU KNOW HOW IT IS WITH THE AMERICANS, THAT FEROCIOUS NEED TO LEAP FIRST AND ASK QUESTIONS LATER.
I DO, I DO INDEED.
STILL, AN IMPORTANT RELATIONSHIP, WITHOUT A DOUBT. PERHAPS THE IMPORTANT RELATIONSHIP, ESPECIALLY NOW, NO?
AH, YES.
QUITE.

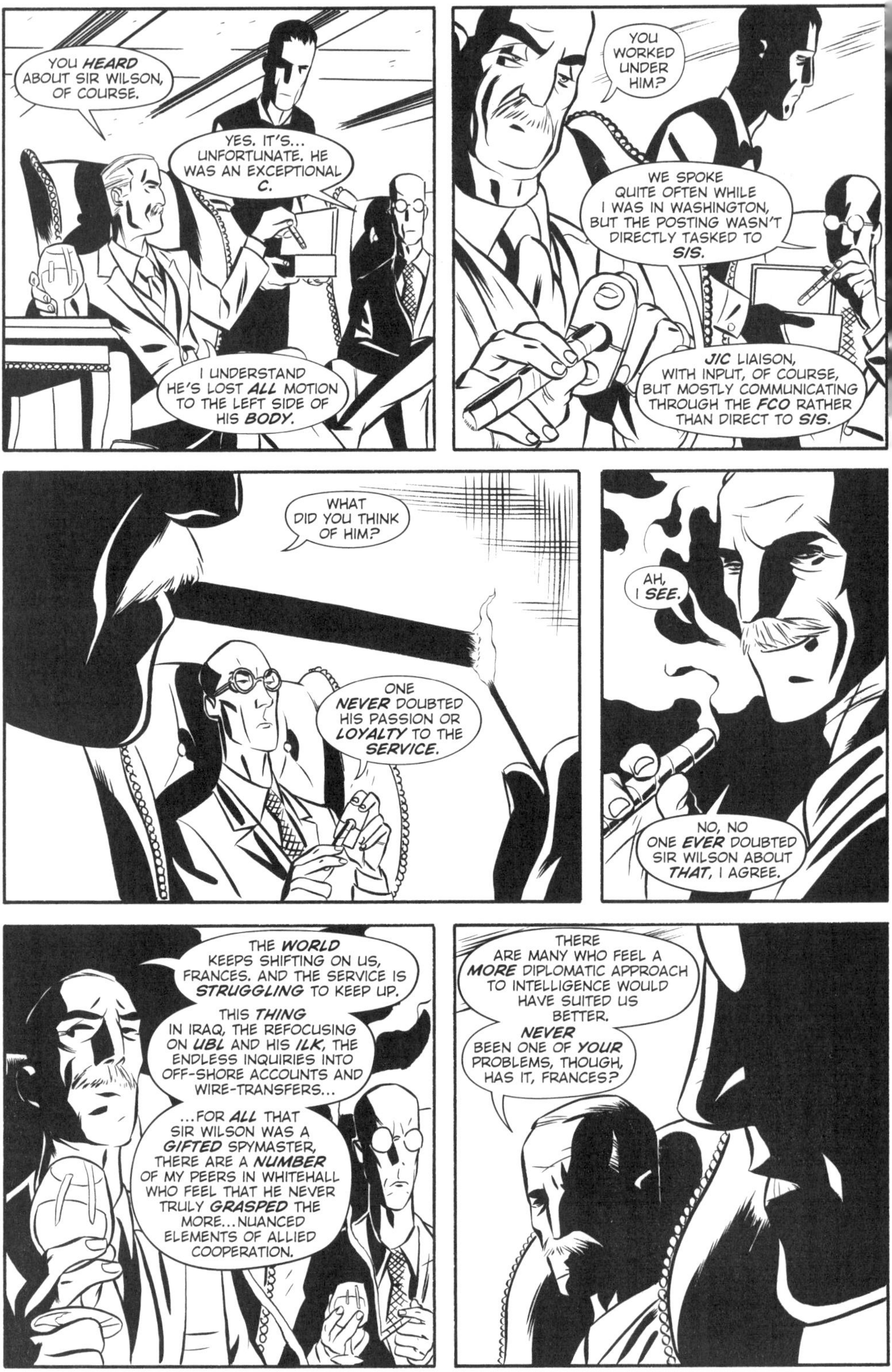
YOU HEARD ABOUT SIR WILSON, OF COURSE.
YES. IT'S... UNFORTUNATE. HE WAS AN EXCEPTIONAL C.
I UNDERSTAND HE'S LOST ALL MOTION TO THE LEFT SIDE OF HIS BODY.
YOU WORKED UNDER HIM?
WE SPOKE QUITE OFTEN WHILE I WAS IN WASHINGTON, BUT THE POSTING WASN'T DIRECTLY TASKED TO SIS.
JIC LIAISON, WITH INPUT, OF COURSE, BUT MOSTLY COMMUNICATING THROUGH THE FCO RATHER THAN DIRECT TO SIS.
WHAT DID YOU THINK OF HIM?
ONE NEVER DOUBTED HIS PASSION OR LOYALTY TO THE SERVICE.
AH, I SEE.
NO, NO ONE EVER DOUBTED SIR WILSON ABOUT THAT, I AGREE.
THE WORLD KEEPS SHIFTING ON US, FRANCES. AND THE SERVICE IS STRUGGLING TO KEEP UP.
THIS THING IN IRAQ, THE REFOCUSING ON UBL AND HIS ILK, THE ENDLESS INQUIRIES INTO OFF-SHORE ACCOUNTS AND WIRE-TRANSFERS...
...FOR ALL THAT SIR WILSON WAS A GIFTED SPYMASTER, THERE ARE A NUMBER OF MY PEERS IN WHITEHALL WHO FEEL THAT HE NEVER TRULY GRASPED THE MORE...NUANCED ELEMENTS OF ALLIED COOPERATION.
THERE ARE MANY WHO FEEL A MORE DIPLOMATIC APPROACH TO INTELLIGENCE WOULD HAVE SUITED US BETTER.
NEVER BEEN ONE OF YOUR PROBLEMS, THOUGH, HAS IT, FRANCES?

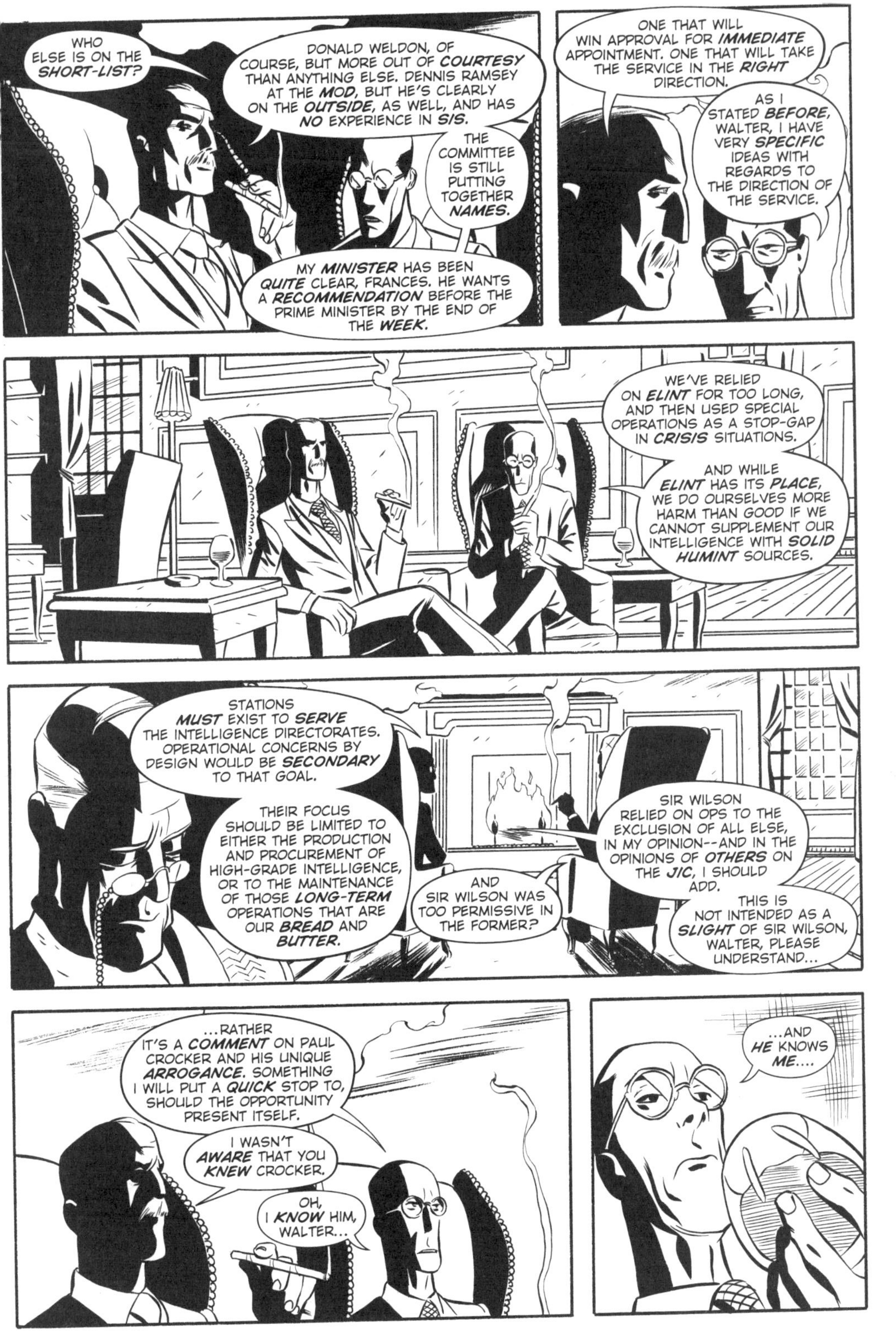
WHO ELSE IS ON THE SHORT-LIST?
DONALD WELDON, OF COURSE, BUT MORE OUT OF COURTESY THAN ANYTHING ELSE. DENNIS RAMSEY AT THE MOD, BUT HE'S CLEARLY ON THE OUTSIDE, AS WELL, AND HAS NO EXPERIENCE IN SIS.
THE COMMITTEE IS STILL PUTTING TOGETHER NAMES.
MY MINISTER HAS BEEN QUITE CLEAR, FRANCES. HE WANTS A RECOMMENDATION BEFORE THE PRIME MINISTER BY THE END OF THE WEEK.
ONE THAT WILL WIN APPROVAL FOR IMMEDIATE APPOINTMENT. ONE THAT WILL TAKE THE SERVICE IN THE RIGHT DIRECTION.
AS I STATED BEFORE, WALTER, I HAVE VERY SPECIFIC IDEAS WITH REGARDS TO THE DIRECTION OF THE SERVICE.
WE'VE RELIED ON ELINT FOR TOO LONG, AND THEN USED SPECIAL OPERATIONS AS A STOP-GAP IN CRISIS SITUATIONS.
AND WHILE ELINT HAS ITS PLACE, WE DO OURSELVES MORE HARM THAN GOOD IF WE CANNOT SUPPLEMENT OUR INTELLIGENCE WITH SOLID HUMINT SOURCES.
STATIONS MUST EXIST TO SERVE THE INTELLIGENCE DIRECTORATES. OPERATIONAL CONCERNS BY DESIGN WOULD BE SECONDARY TO THAT GOAL.
THEIR FOCUS SHOULD BE LIMITED TO EITHER THE PRODUCTION AND PROCUREMENT OF HIGH-GRADE INTELLIGENCE, OR TO THE MAINTENANCE OF THOSE LONG-TERM OPERATIONS THAT ARE OUR BREAD AND BUTTER.
AND SIR WILSON WAS TOO PERMISSIVE IN THE FORMER?
SIR WILSON RELIED ON OPS TO THE EXCLUSION OF ALL ELSE, IN MY OPINION--AND IN THE OPINIONS OF OTHERS ON THE JIC, I SHOULD ADD.
THIS IS NOT INTENDED AS A SLIGHT OF SIR WILSON, WALTER, PLEASE UNDERSTAND...
...RATHER IT'S A COMMENT ON PAUL CROCKER AND HIS UNIQUE ARROGANCE. SOMETHING I WILL PUT A QUICK STOP TO, SHOULD THE OPPORTUNITY PRESENT ITSELF.
I WASN'T AWARE THAT YOU KNEW CROCKER.
OH, I KNOW HIM, WALTER...
...AND HE KNOWS ME....

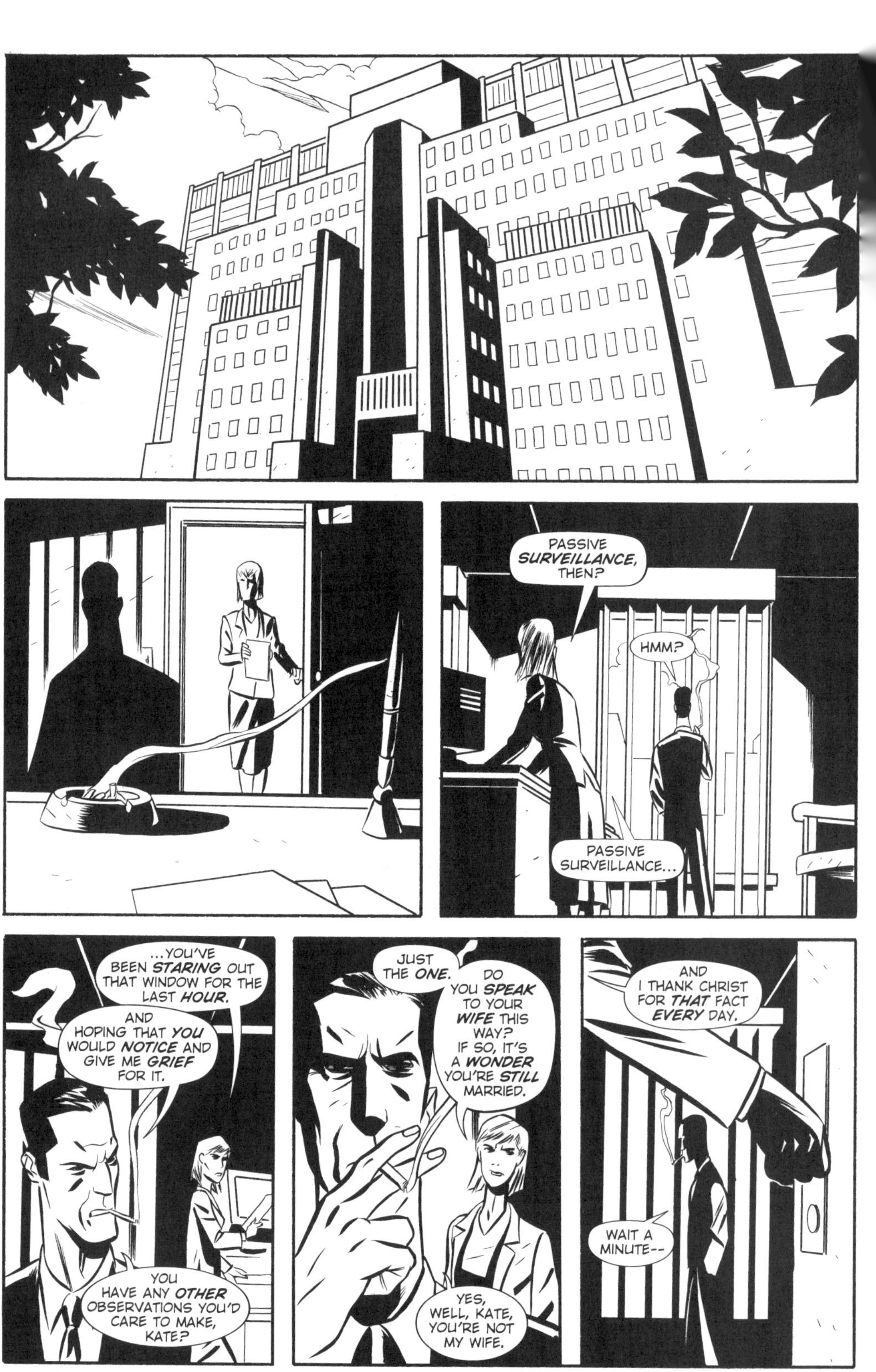
PASSIVE SURVEILLANCE, THEN?
HMM?
PASSIVE SURVEILLANCE...
...YOU'VE BEEN STARING OUT THAT WINDOW FOR THE LAST HOUR.
AND HOPING THAT YOU WOULD NOTICE AND GIVE ME GRIEF FOR IT.
YOU HAVE ANY OTHER OBSERVATIONS YOU'D CARE TO MAKE, KATE?
JUST THE ONE.
DO YOU SPEAK TO YOUR WIFE THIS WAY? IF SO, IT'S A WONDER YOU'RE STILL MARRIED.
YES, WELL, KATE, YOU'RE NOT MY WIFE.
AND I THANK CHRIST FOR THAT FACT EVERY DAY.
WAIT A MINUTE--

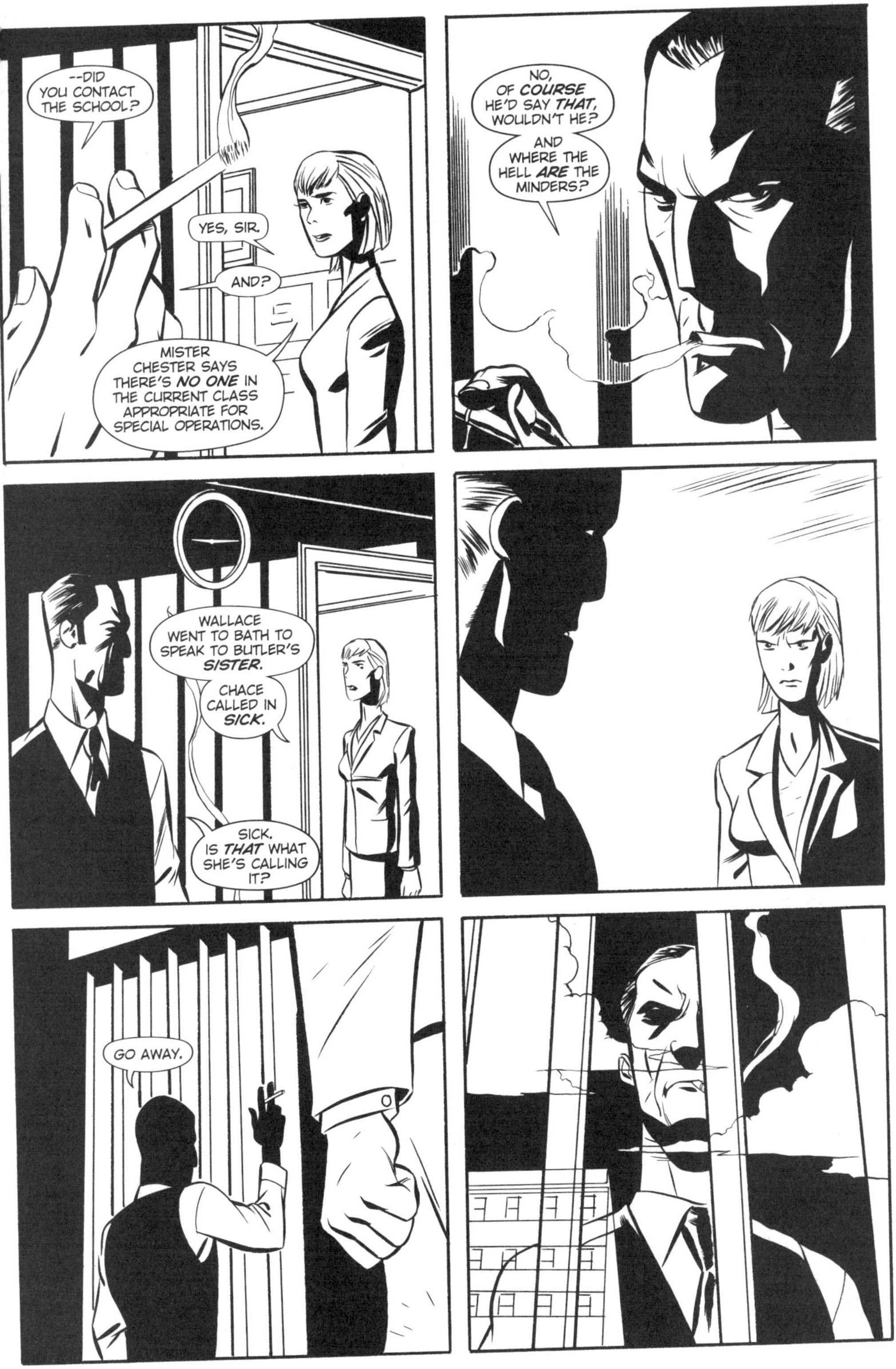
--DID YOU CONTACT THE SCHOOL?
YES, SIR.
AND?
MISTER CHESTER SAYS THERE'S NO ONE IN THE CURRENT CLASS APPROPRIATE FOR SPECIAL OPERATIONS.
NO, OF COURSE HE'D SAY THAT, WOULDN'T HE?
AND WHERE THE HELL ARE THE MINDERS?
WALLACE WENT TO BATH TO SPEAK TO BUTLER'S SISTER.
CHACE CALLED IN SICK.
SICK. IS THAT WHAT SHE'S CALLING IT?
GO AWAY.

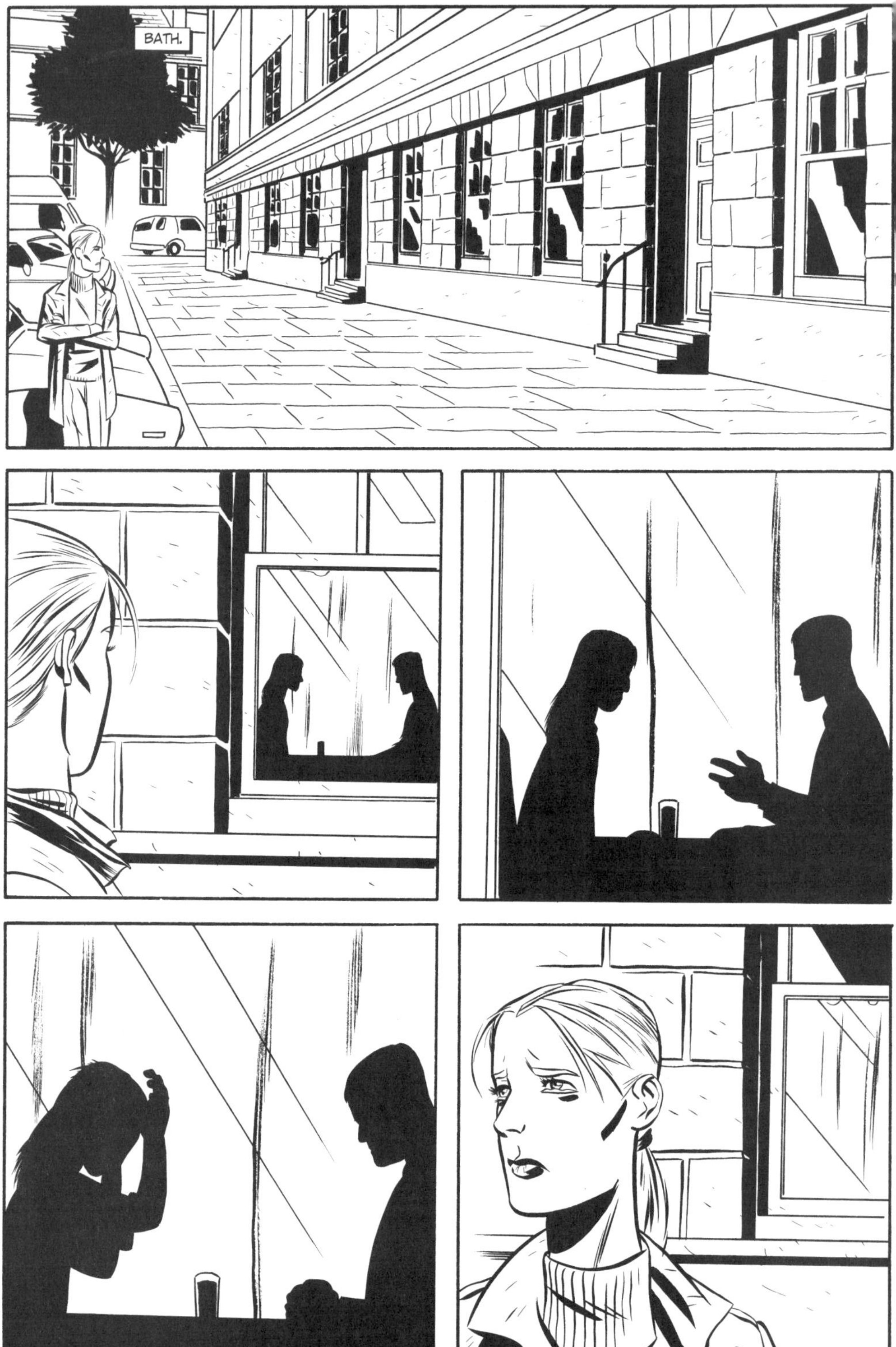
BATH.

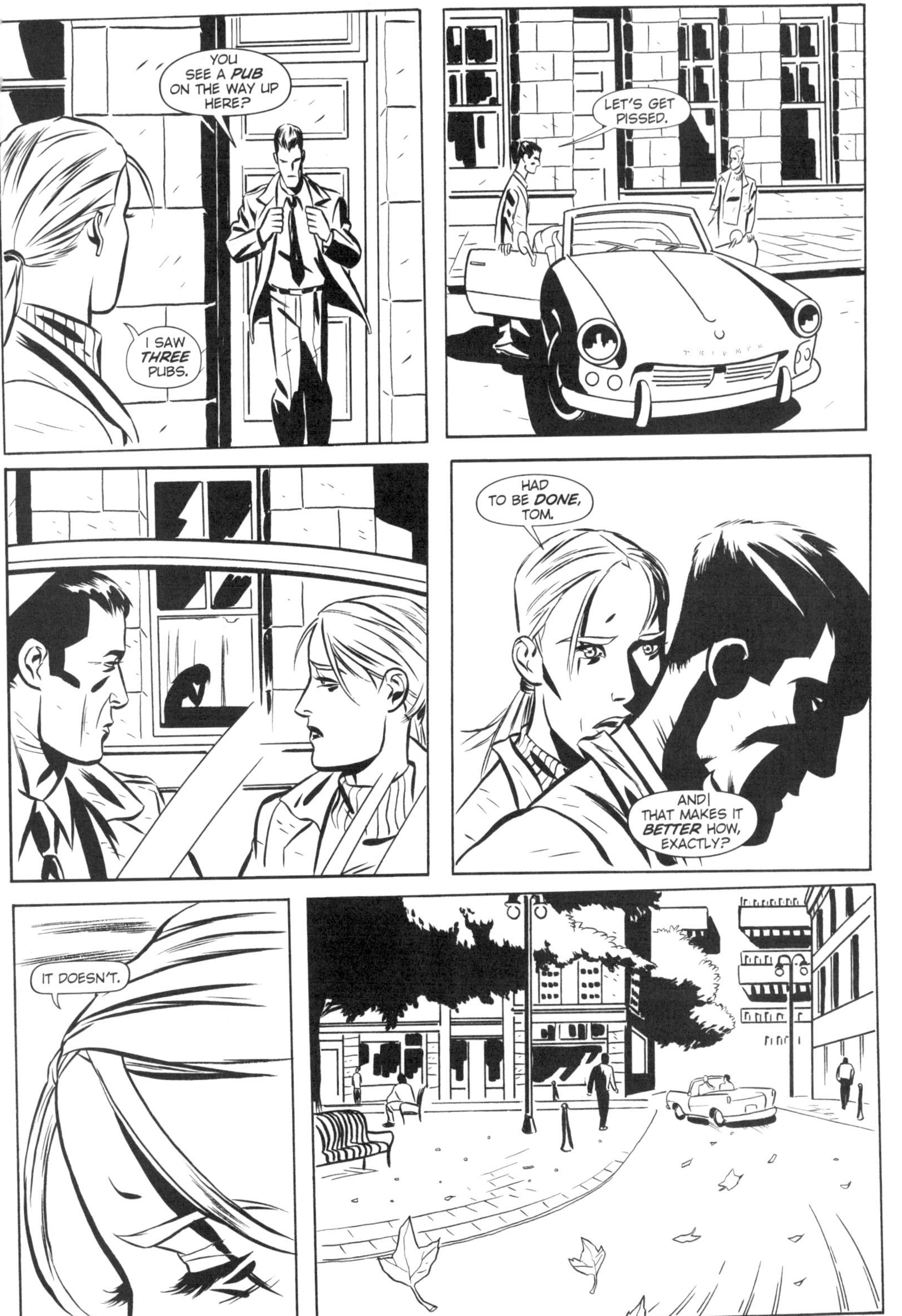
YOU SEE A PUB ON THE WAY UP HERE?
I SAW THREE PUBS.
LET'S GET PISSED.
HAD TO BE DONE, TOM.
AND THAT MAKES IT BETTER HOW, EXACTLY?
IT DOESN'T.

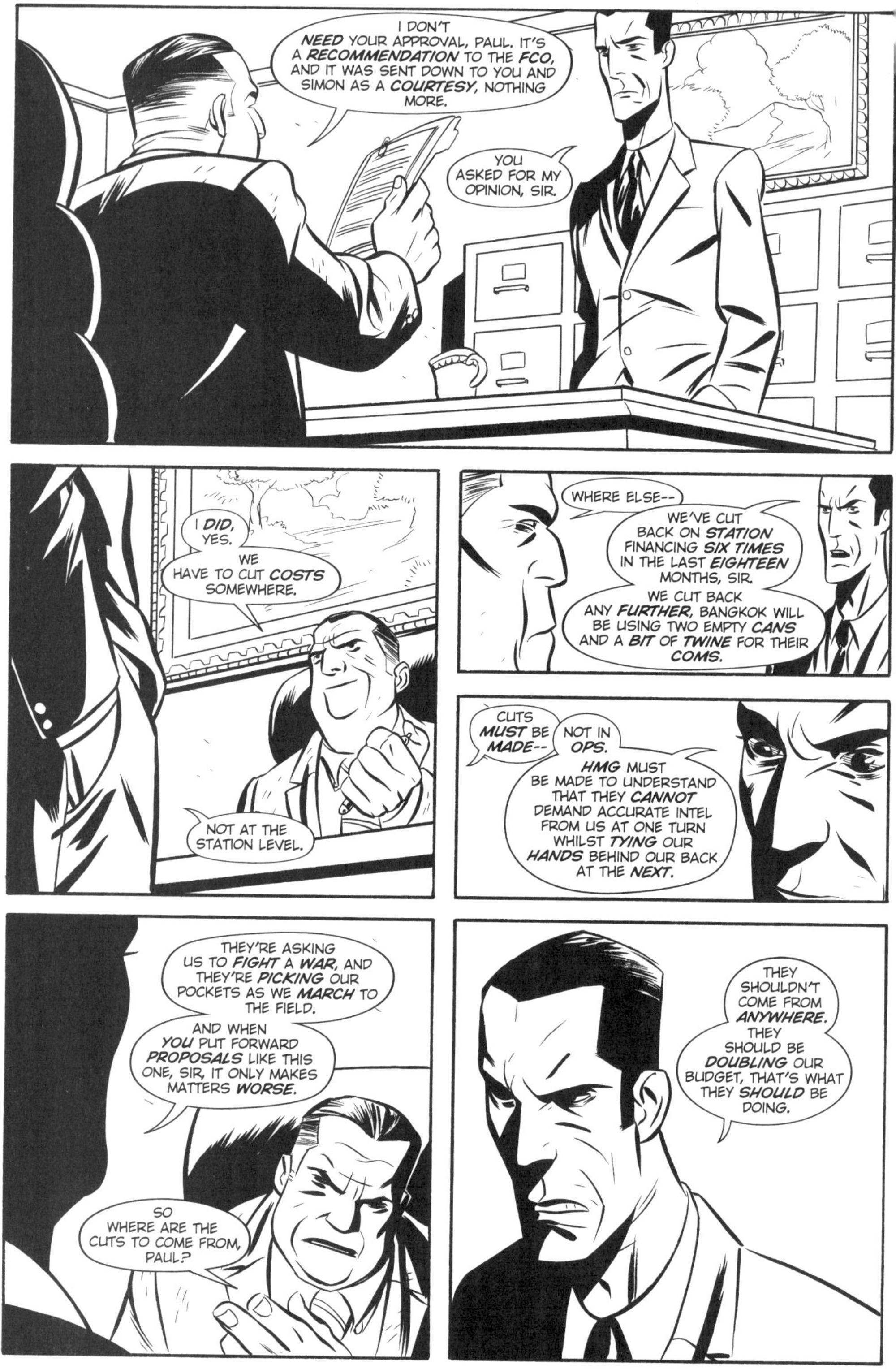
I DON'T NEED YOUR APPROVAL, PAUL. IT'S A RECOMMENDATION TO THE FCO, AND IT WAS SENT DOWN TO YOU AND SIMON AS A COURTESY, NOTHING MORE.
YOU ASKED FOR MY OPINION, SIR.
I DID, YES.
WE HAVE TO CUT COSTS SOMEWHERE.
NOT AT THE STATION LEVEL.
WHERE ELSE--
WE'VE CUT BACK ON STATION FINANCING SIX TIMES IN THE LAST EIGHTEEN MONTHS, SIR.
WE CUT BACK ANY FURTHER, BANGKOK WILL BE USING TWO EMPTY CANS AND A BIT OF TWINE FOR THEIR COMS.
CUTS MUST BE MADE--
NOT IN OPS.
HMG MUST BE MADE TO UNDERSTAND THAT THEY CANNOT DEMAND ACCURATE INTEL FROM US AT ONE TURN WHILST TYING OUR HANDS BEHIND OUR BACK AT THE NEXT.
THEY'RE ASKING US TO FIGHT A WAR, AND THEY'RE PICKING OUR POCKETS AS WE MARCH TO THE FIELD.
AND WHEN YOU PUT FORWARD PROPOSALS LIKE THIS ONE, SIR, IT ONLY MAKES MATTERS WORSE.
SO WHERE ARE THE CUTS TO COME FROM, PAUL?
THEY SHOULDN'T COME FROM ANYWHERE.
THEY SHOULD BE DOUBLING OUR BUDGET, THAT'S WHAT THEY SHOULD BE DOING.

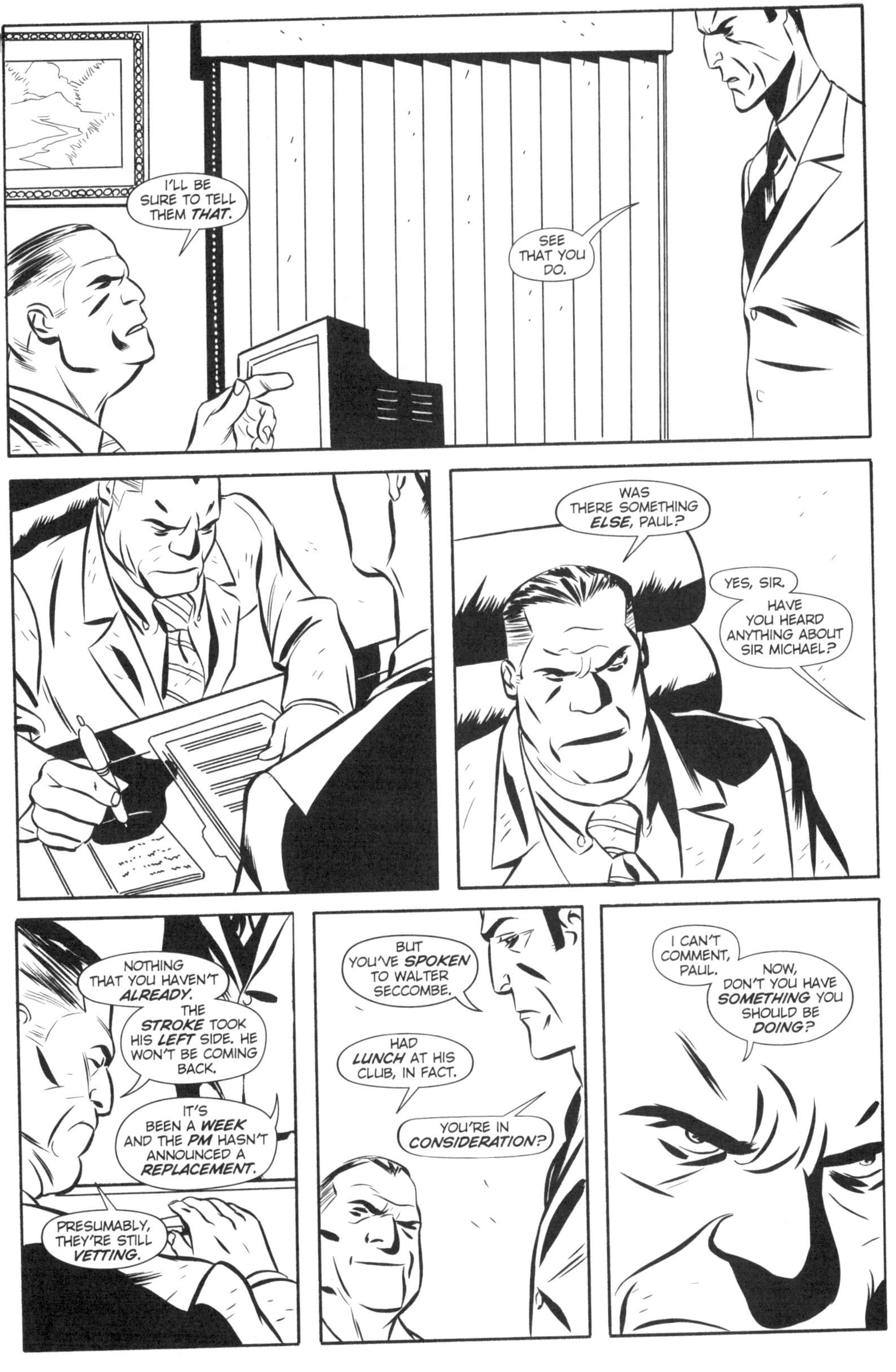
I'LL BE SURE TO TELL THEM THAT.
SEE THAT YOU DO.
WAS THERE SOMETHING ELSE, PAUL?
YES, SIR.
HAVE YOU HEARD ANYTHING ABOUT SIR MICHAEL?
NOTHING THAT YOU HAVEN'T ALREADY.
THE STROKE TOOK HIS LEFT SIDE. HE WON'T BE COMING BACK.
IT'S BEEN A WEEK AND THE PM HASN'T ANNOUNCED A REPLACEMENT.
PRESUMABLY, THEY'RE STILL VETTING.
BUT YOU'VE SPOKEN TO WALTER SECCOMBE.
HAD LUNCH AT HIS CLUB, IN FACT.
YOU'RE IN CONSIDERATION?
I CAN'T COMMENT, PAUL.
NOW, DON'T YOU HAVE SOMETHING YOU SHOULD BE DOING?

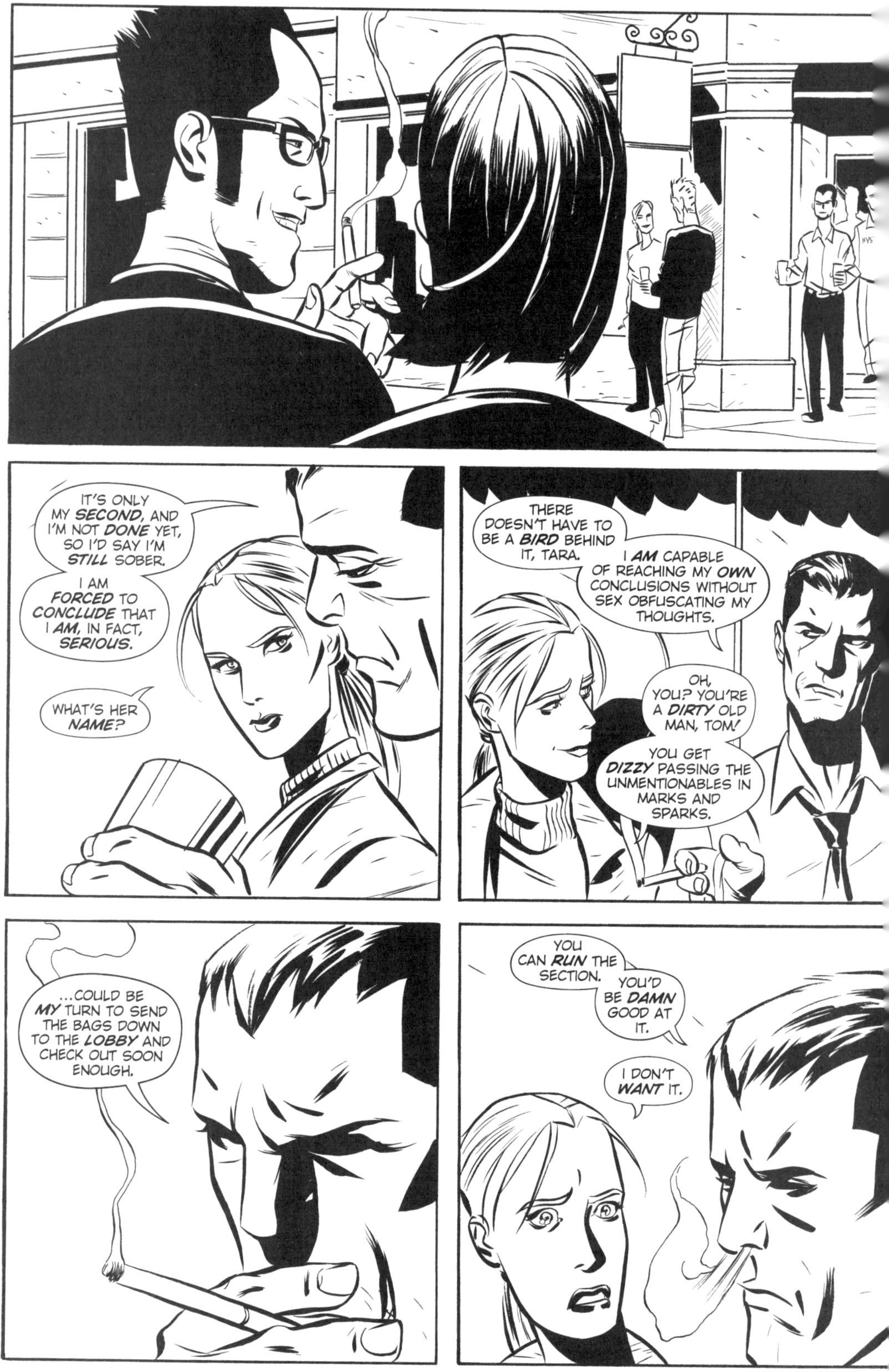
IT'S ONLY MY SECOND, AND I'M NOT DONE YET, SO I'D SAY I'M STILL SOBER.
I AM FORCED TO CONCLUDE THAT I AM, IN FACT, SERIOUS.
WHAT'S HER NAME?
THERE DOESN'T HAVE TO BE A BIRD BEHIND IT, TARA.
I AM CAPABLE OF REACHING MY OWN CONCLUSIONS WITHOUT SEX OBFUSCATING MY THOUGHTS.
OH, YOU? YOU'RE A DIRTY OLD MAN, TOM!
YOU GET DIZZY PASSING THE UNMENTIONABLES IN MARKS AND SPARKS.
...COULD BE MY TURN TO SEND THE BAGS DOWN TO THE LOBBY AND CHECK OUT SOON ENOUGH.
YOU CAN RUN THE SECTION.
YOU'D BE DAMN GOOD AT IT.
I DON'T WANT IT.

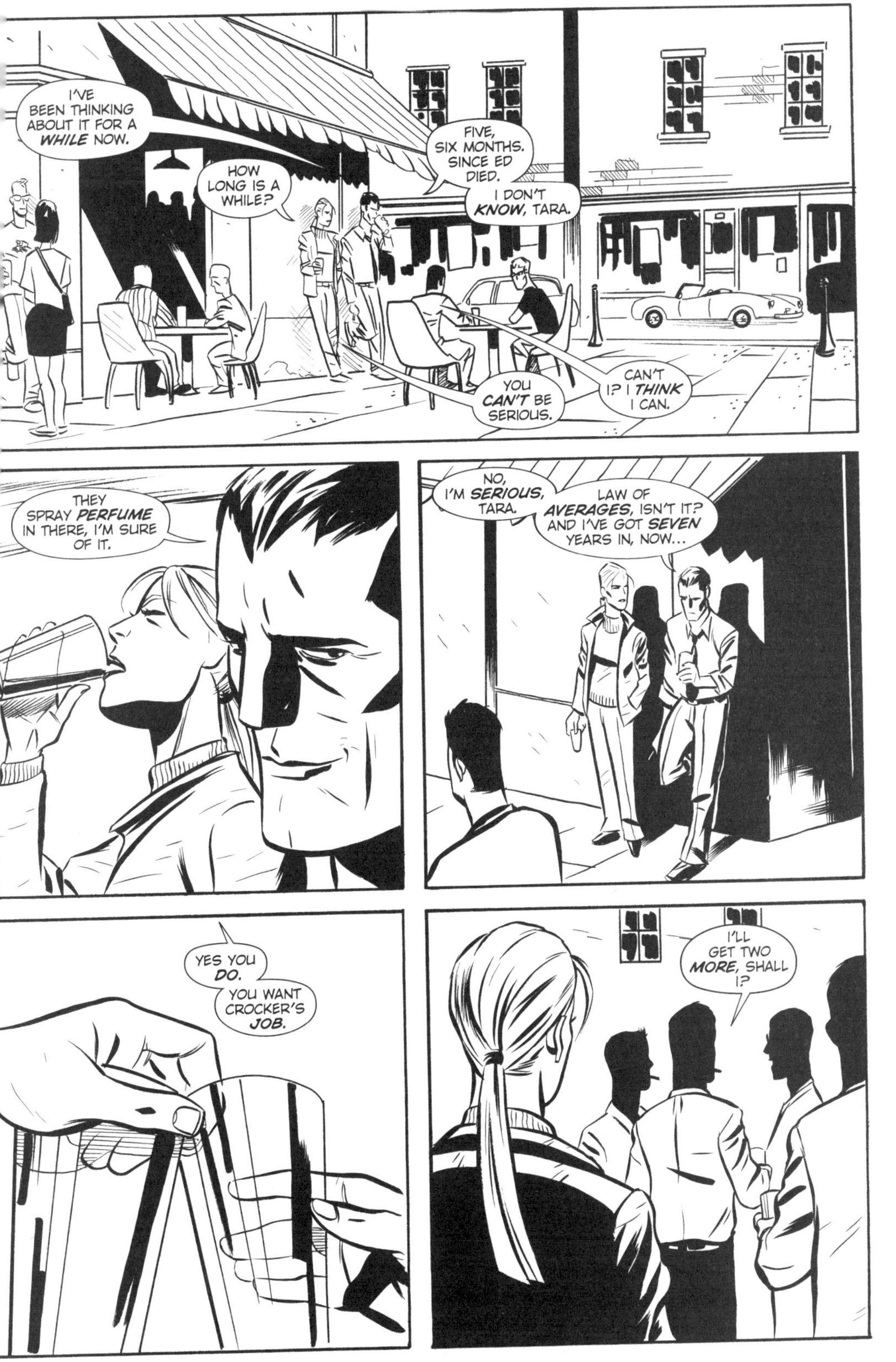
I'VE BEEN THINKING ABOUT IT FOR A WHILE NOW.
HOW LONG IS A WHILE?
FIVE, SIX MONTHS. SINCE ED DIED.
I DON'T KNOW, TARA.
YOU CAN'T BE SERIOUS.
CAN'T I? I THINK I CAN.
THEY SPRAY PERFUME IN THERE, I'M SURE OF IT.
NO, I'M SERIOUS, TARA.
LAW OF AVERAGES, ISN'T IT? AND I'VE GOT SEVEN YEARS IN, NOW...
YES YOU DO. YOU WANT CROCKER'S JOB.
I'LL GET TWO MORE, SHALL I?

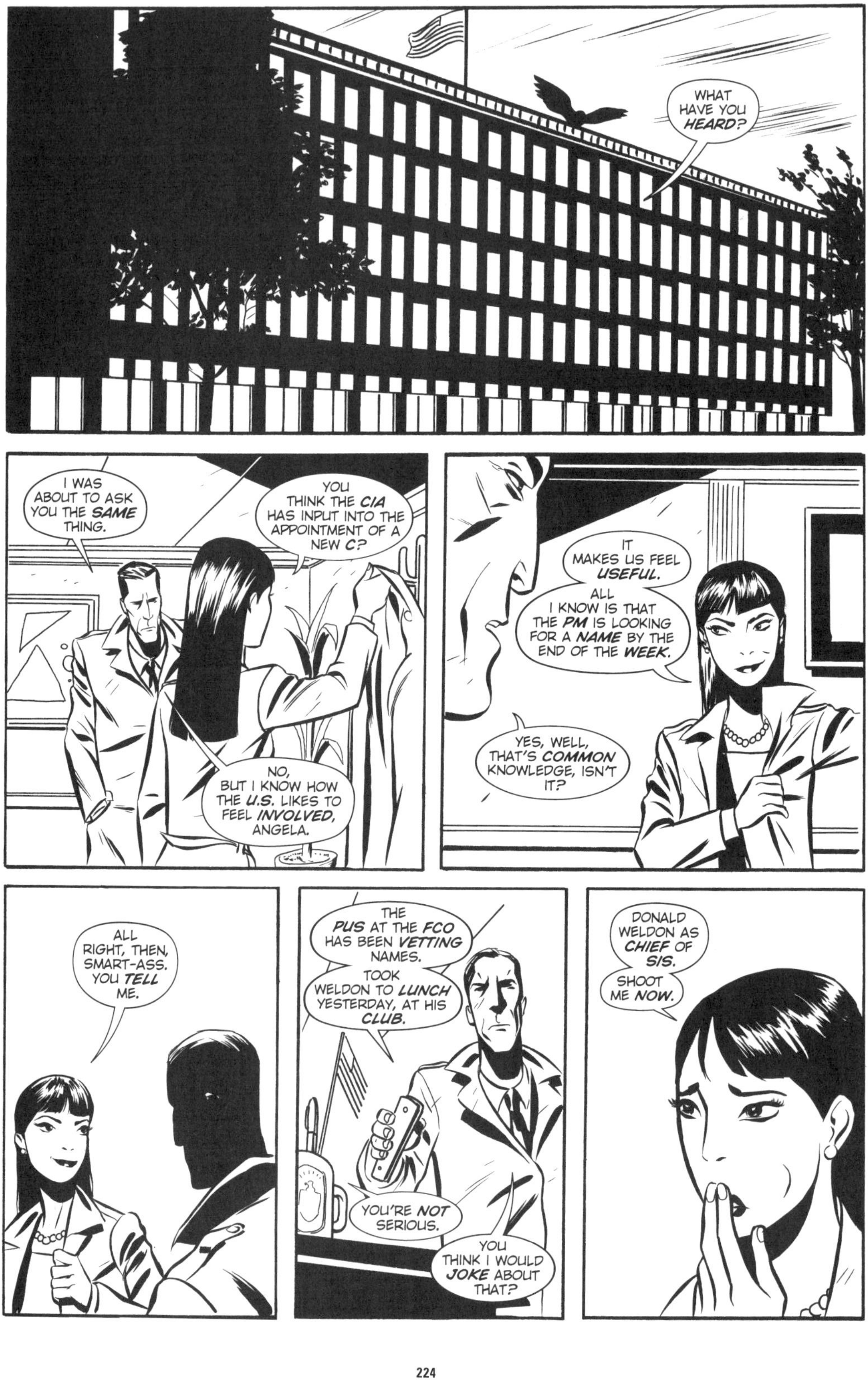
WHAT HAVE YOU HEARD?
I WAS ABOUT TO ASK YOU THE SAME THING.
YOU THINK THE CIA HAS INPUT INTO THE APPOINTMENT OF A NEW C?
NO, BUT I KNOW HOW THE U.S. LIKES TO FEEL INVOLVED, ANGELA.
IT MAKES US FEEL USEFUL.
ALL I KNOW IS THAT THE PM IS LOOKING FOR A NAME BY THE END OF THE WEEK.
YES, WELL, THAT'S COMMON KNOWLEDGE, ISN'T IT?
ALL RIGHT, THEN, SMART-ASS. YOU TELL ME.
THE PUS AT THE FCO HAS BEEN VETTING NAMES.
TOOK WELDON TO LUNCH YESTERDAY, AT HIS CLUB.
YOU'RE NOT SERIOUS.
YOU THINK I WOULD JOKE ABOUT THAT?
DONALD WELDON AS CHIEF OF SIS.
SHOOT ME NOW.

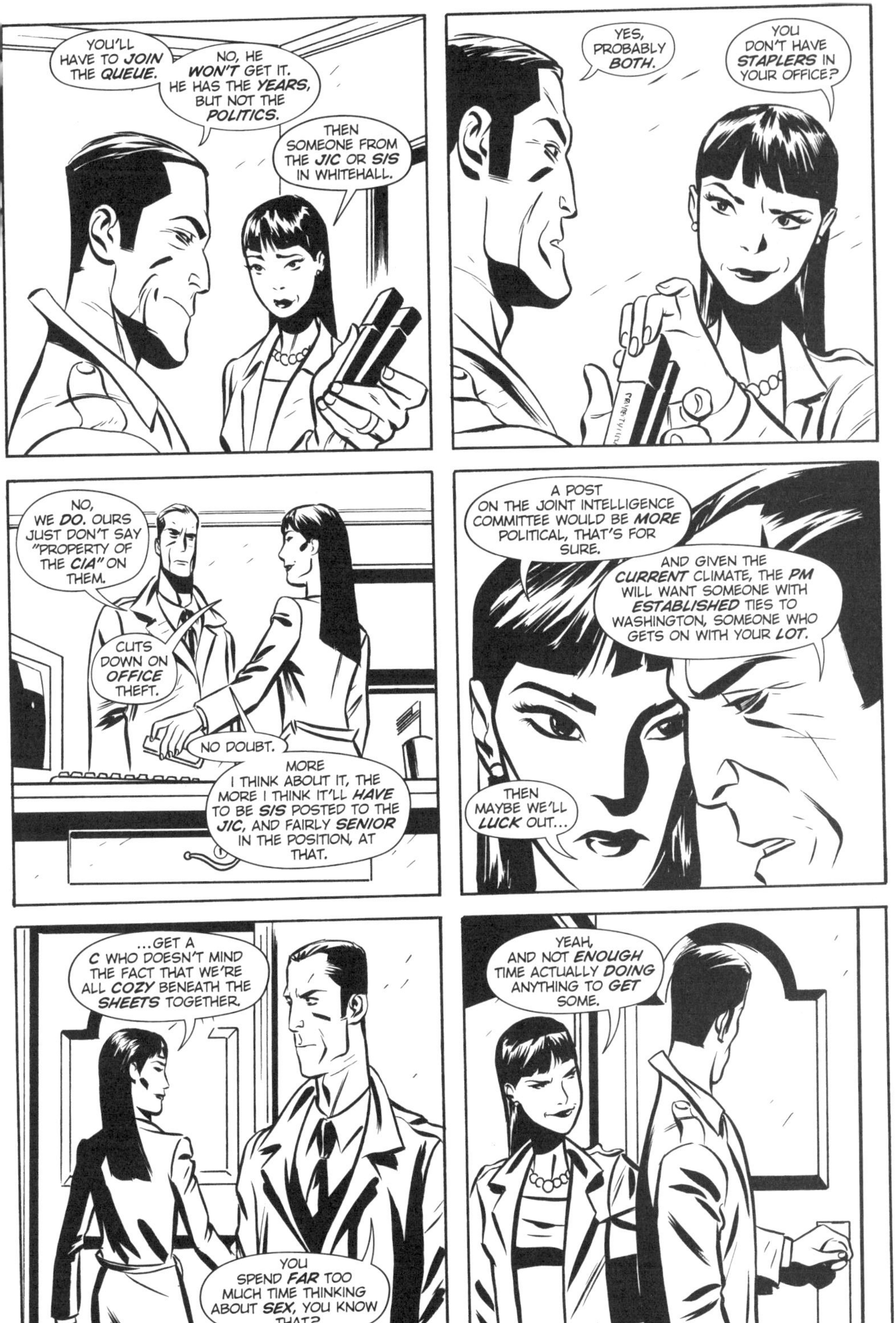
YOU'LL HAVE TO JOIN THE QUEUE.
NO, HE WON'T GET IT. HE HAS THE YEARS, BUT NOT THE POLITICS.
THEN SOMEONE FROM THE JIC OR SIS IN WHITEHALL.
YES, PROBABLY BOTH.
YOU DON'T HAVE STAPLERS IN YOUR OFFICE?
NO, WE DO. OURS JUST DON'T SAY "PROPERTY OF THE CIA" ON THEM.
CUTS DOWN ON OFFICE THEFT.
NO DOUBT.
MORE I THINK ABOUT IT, THE MORE I THINK IT'LL HAVE TO BE SIS POSTED TO THE JIC, AND FAIRLY SENIOR IN THE POSITION, AT THAT.
A POST ON THE JOINT INTELLIGENCE COMMITTEE WOULD BE MORE POLITICAL, THAT'S FOR SURE.
AND GIVEN THE CURRENT CLIMATE, THE PM WILL WANT SOMEONE WITH ESTABLISHED TIES TO WASHINGTON, SOMEONE WHO GETS ON WITH YOUR LOT.
THEN MAYBE WE'LL LUCK OUT...
...GET A C WHO DOESN'T MIND THE FACT THAT WE'RE ALL COZY BENEATH THE SHEETS TOGETHER.
YOU SPEND FAR TOO MUCH TIME THINKING ABOUT SEX, YOU KNOW THAT?
YEAH, AND NOT ENOUGH TIME ACTUALLY DOING ANYTHING TO GET SOME.

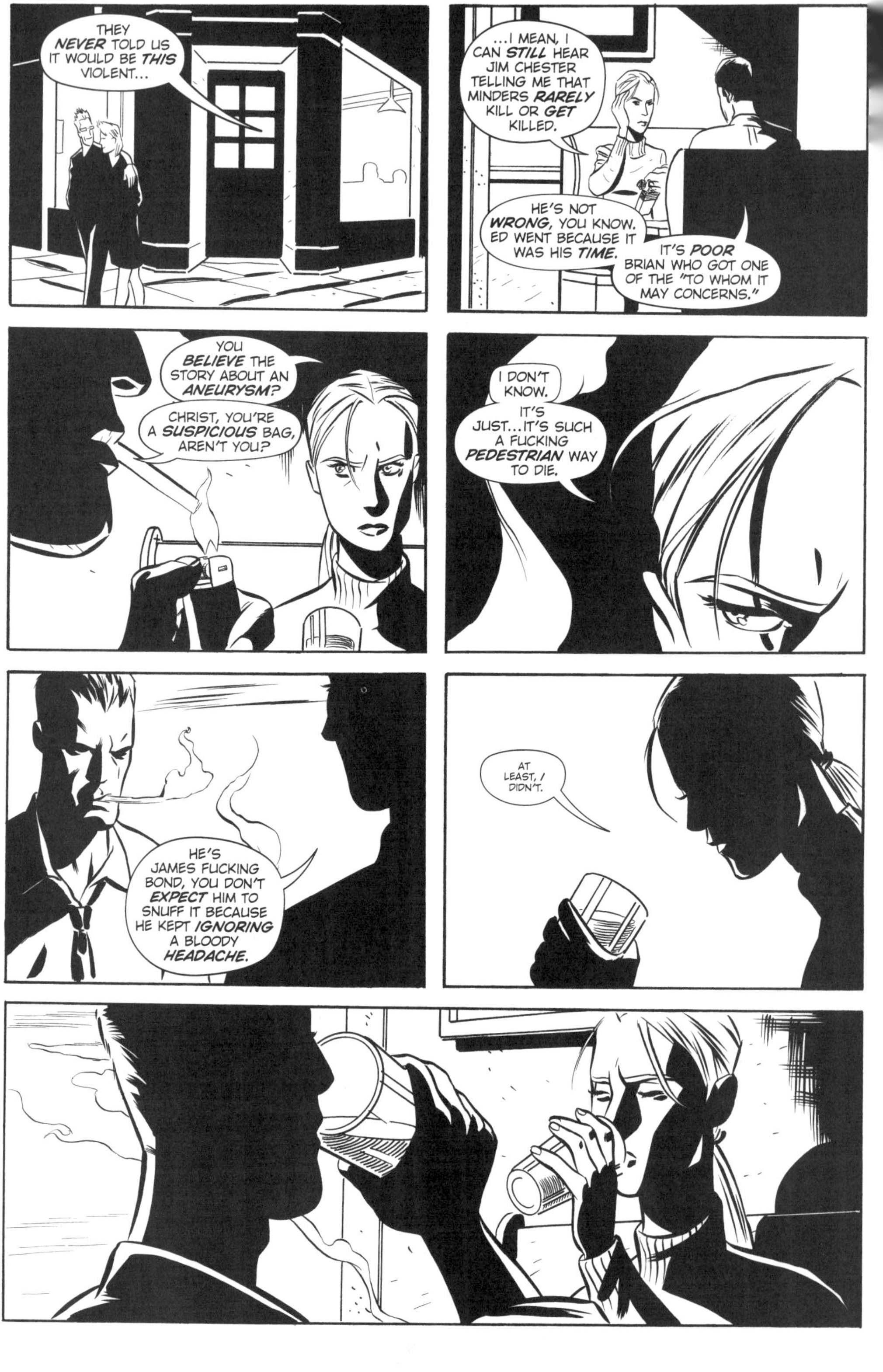
THEY NEVER TOLD US IT WOULD BE THIS VIOLENT...
...I MEAN, I CAN STILL HEAR JIM CHESTER TELLING ME THAT MINDERS RARELY KILL OR GET KILLED.
HE'S NOT WRONG, YOU KNOW. ED WENT BECAUSE IT WAS HIS TIME.
IT'S POOR BRIAN WHO GOT ONE OF THE "TO WHOM IT MAY CONCERNS."
YOU BELIEVE THE STORY ABOUT AN ANEURYSM?
CHRIST, YOU'RE A SUSPICIOUS BAG, AREN'T YOU?
I DON'T KNOW.
IT'S JUST...IT'S SUCH A FUCKING PEDESTRIAN WAY TO DIE.
HE'S JAMES FUCKING BOND, YOU DON'T EXPECT HIM TO SNUFF IT BECAUSE HE KEPT IGNORING A BLOODY HEADACHE.
AT LEAST, I DIDN'T.

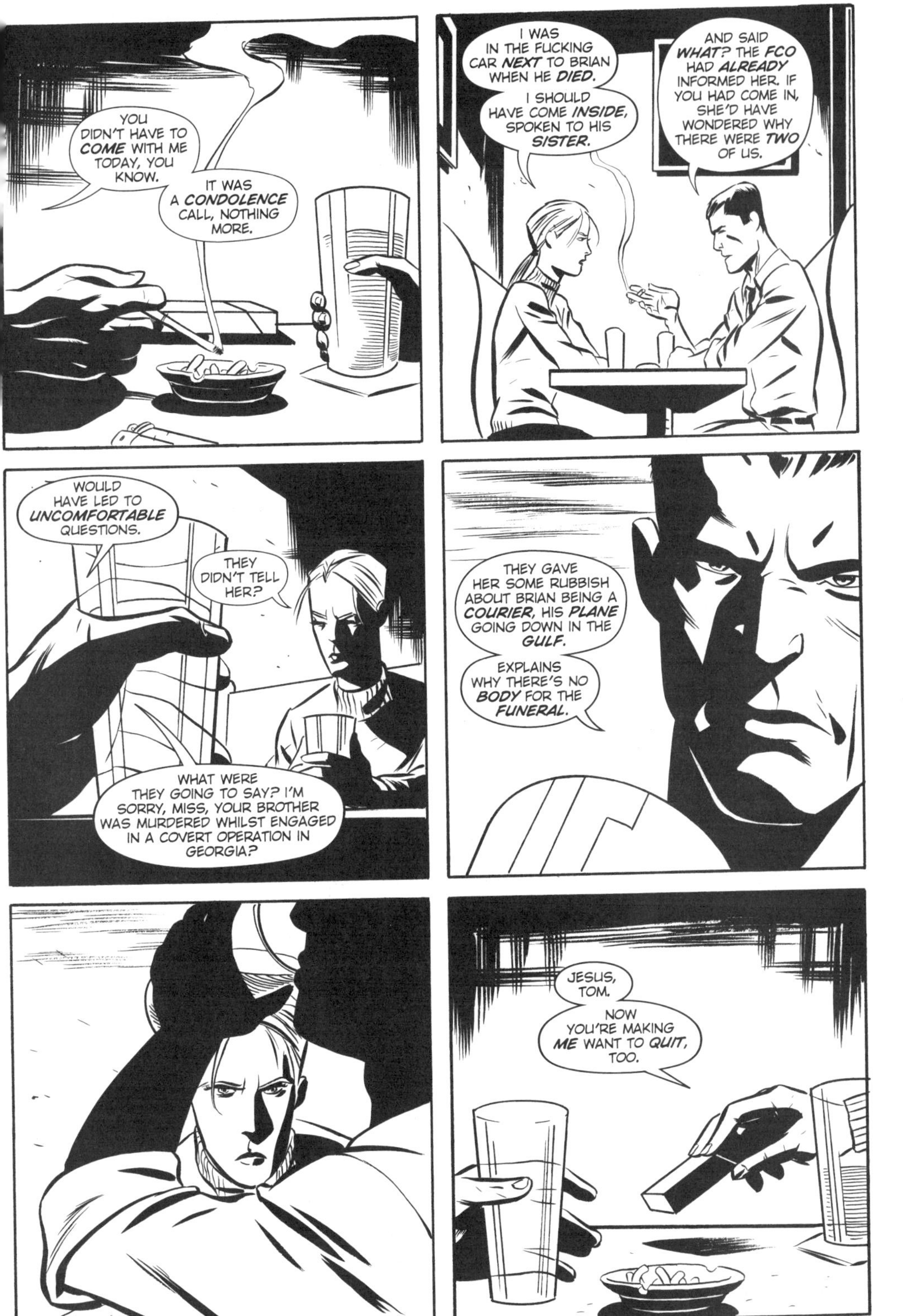
YOU DIDN'T HAVE TO COME WITH ME TODAY, YOU KNOW.
IT WAS A CONDOLENCE CALL, NOTHING MORE.
I WAS IN THE FUCKING CAR NEXT TO BRIAN WHEN HE DIED.
I SHOULD HAVE COME INSIDE, SPOKEN TO HIS SISTER.
AND SAID WHAT? THE FCO HAD ALREADY INFORMED HER. IF YOU HAD COME IN, SHE'D HAVE WONDERED WHY THERE WERE TWO OF US.
WOULD HAVE LED TO UNCOMFORTABLE QUESTIONS.
THEY DIDN'T TELL HER?
WHAT WERE THEY GOING TO SAY? I'M SORRY, MISS, YOUR BROTHER WAS MURDERED WHILST ENGAGED IN A COVERT OPERATION IN GEORGIA?
THEY GAVE HER SOME RUBBISH ABOUT BRIAN BEING A COURIER, HIS PLANE GOING DOWN IN THE GULF.
EXPLAINS WHY THERE'S NO BODY FOR THE FUNERAL.
JESUS, TOM.
NOW YOU'RE MAKING ME WANT TO QUIT, TOO.

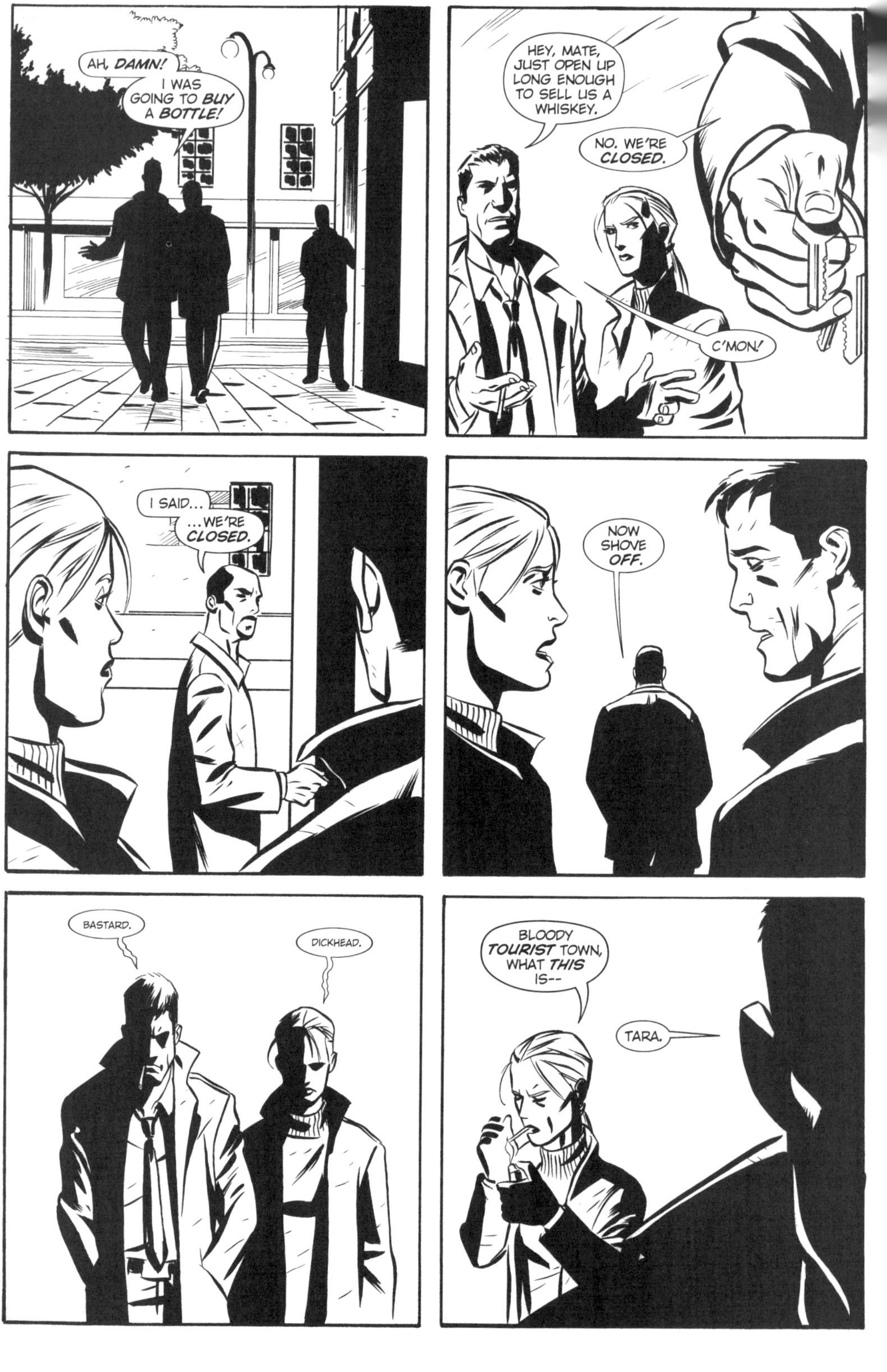
AH, DAMN!
I WAS GOING TO BUY A BOTTLE!
HEY, MATE, JUST OPEN UP LONG ENOUGH TO SELL US A WHISKEY.
NO. WE'RE CLOSED.
C'MON!
I SAID...
...WE'RE CLOSED.
NOW SHOVE OFF.
BASTARD.
DICKHEAD.
BLOODY TOURIST TOWN, WHAT THIS IS--
TARA.

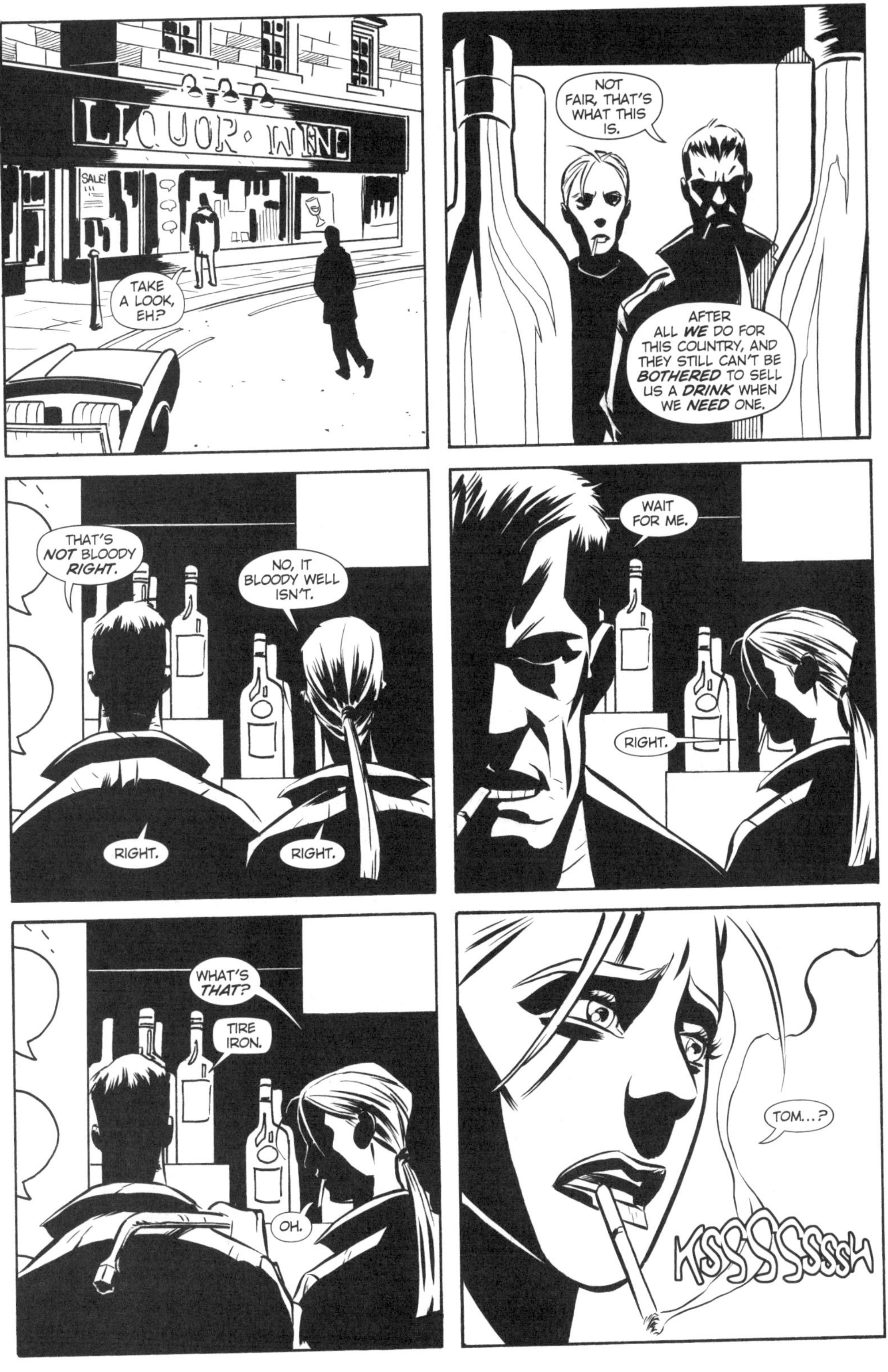
LIQUOR · WINE
SALE!
TAKE A LOOK, EH?
NOT FAIR, THAT'S WHAT THIS IS.
AFTER ALL *WE* DO FOR THIS COUNTRY, AND THEY STILL CAN'T BE *BOTHERED* TO SELL US A *DRINK* WHEN WE *NEED* ONE.
THAT'S *NOT* BLOODY *RIGHT*.
NO, IT BLOODY WELL ISN'T.
RIGHT.
RIGHT.
WAIT FOR ME.
RIGHT.
WHAT'S *THAT*?
TIRE IRON.
OH.
TOM...?
KSSSSSSSSH

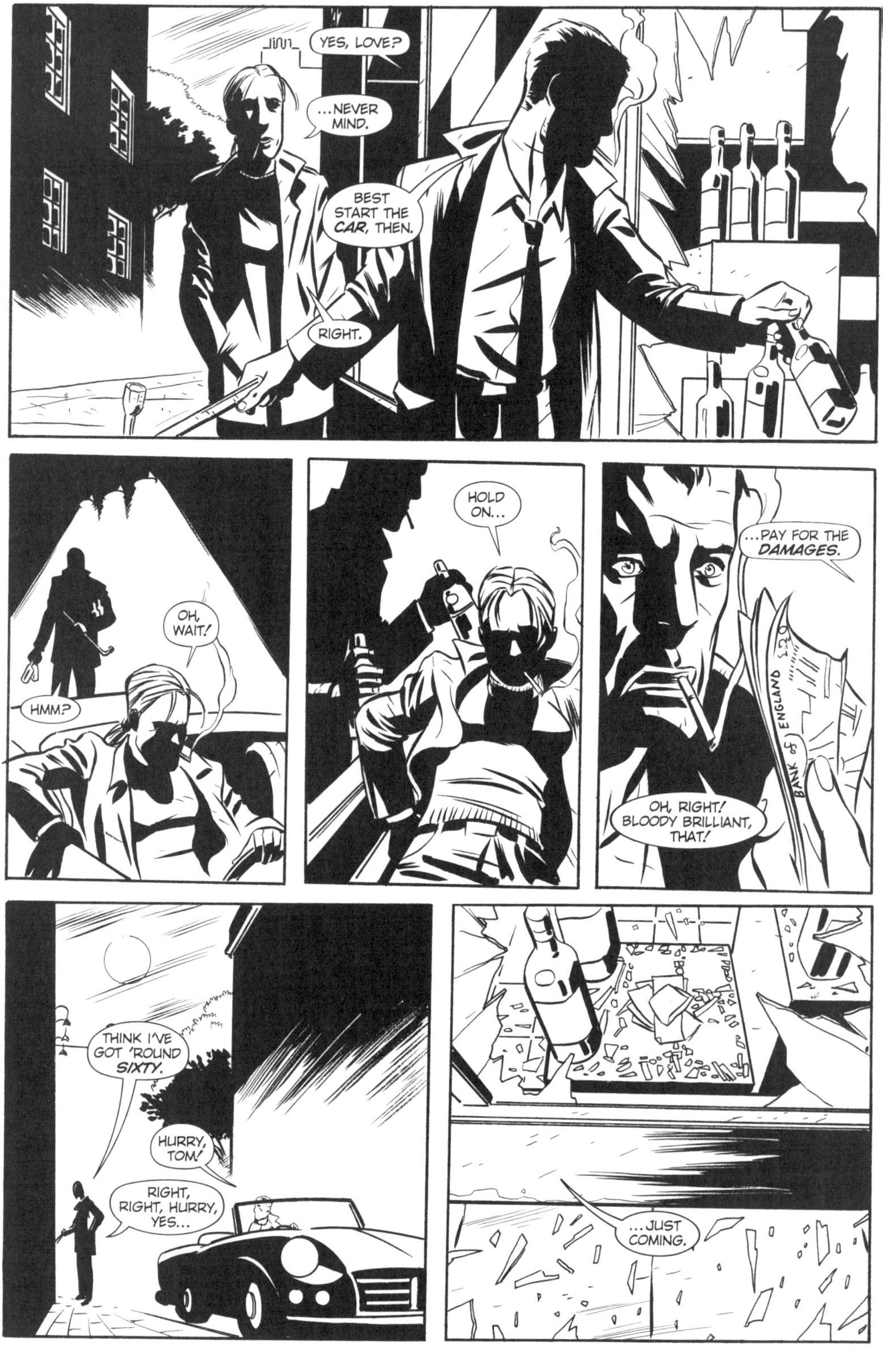

ʃʃʃʃ
YES, LOVE?
...NEVER MIND.
BEST START THE CAR, THEN.
RIGHT.
OH, WAIT!
HMM?
HOLD ON...
...PAY FOR THE DAMAGES.
BANK of ENGLAND
OH, RIGHT! BLOODY BRILLIANT, THAT!
THINK I'VE GOT 'ROUND SIXTY.
HURRY, TOM!
RIGHT, RIGHT, HURRY, YES...
...JUST COMING.

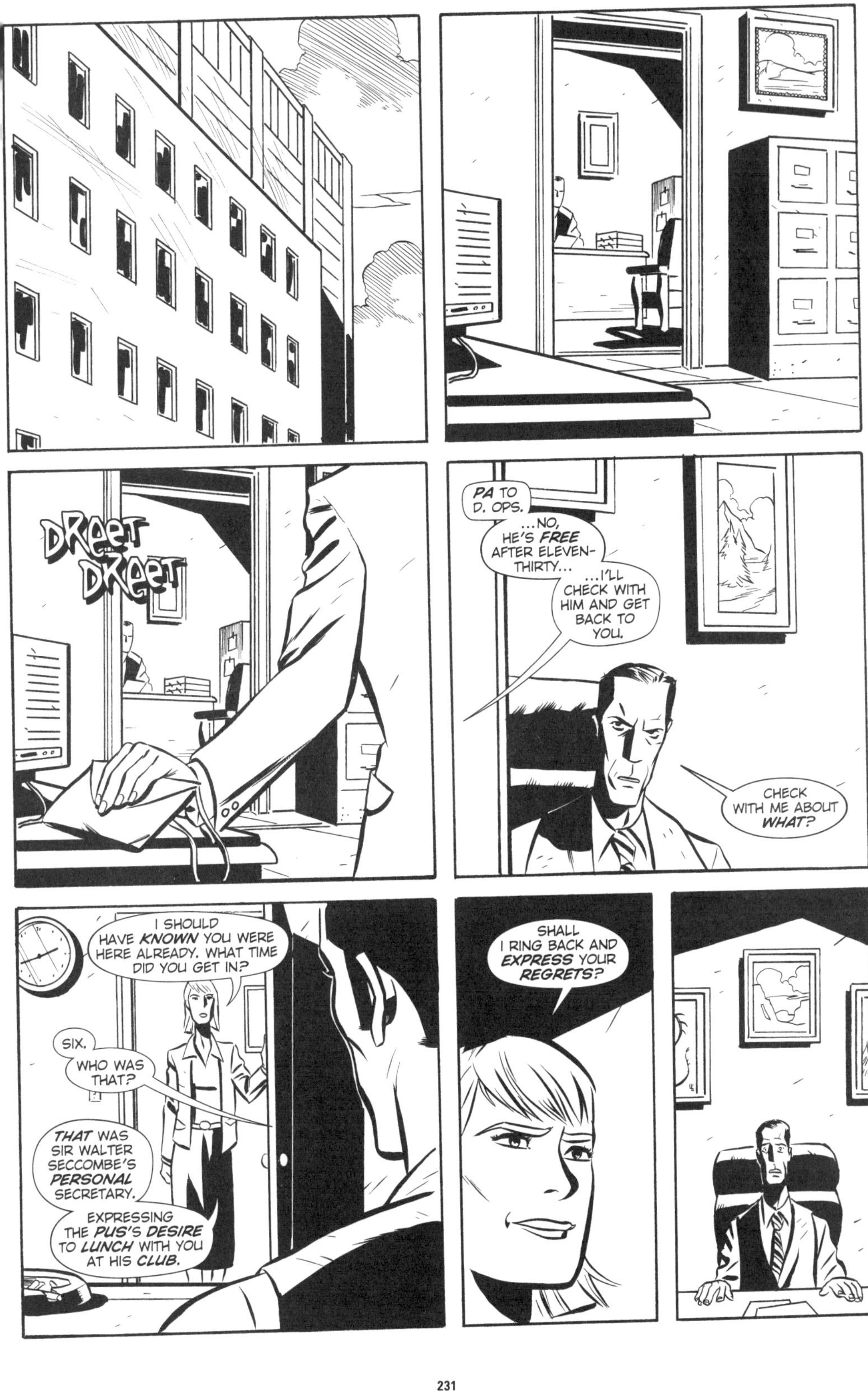
DREET DREET
PA TO D. OPS.
...NO, HE'S FREE AFTER ELEVEN-THIRTY...
...I'LL CHECK WITH HIM AND GET BACK TO YOU.
CHECK WITH ME ABOUT WHAT?
I SHOULD HAVE KNOWN YOU WERE HERE ALREADY. WHAT TIME DID YOU GET IN?
SIX.
WHO WAS THAT?
THAT WAS SIR WALTER SECCOMBE'S PERSONAL SECRETARY.
EXPRESSING THE PUS'S DESIRE TO LUNCH WITH YOU AT HIS CLUB.
SHALL I RING BACK AND EXPRESS YOUR REGRETS?

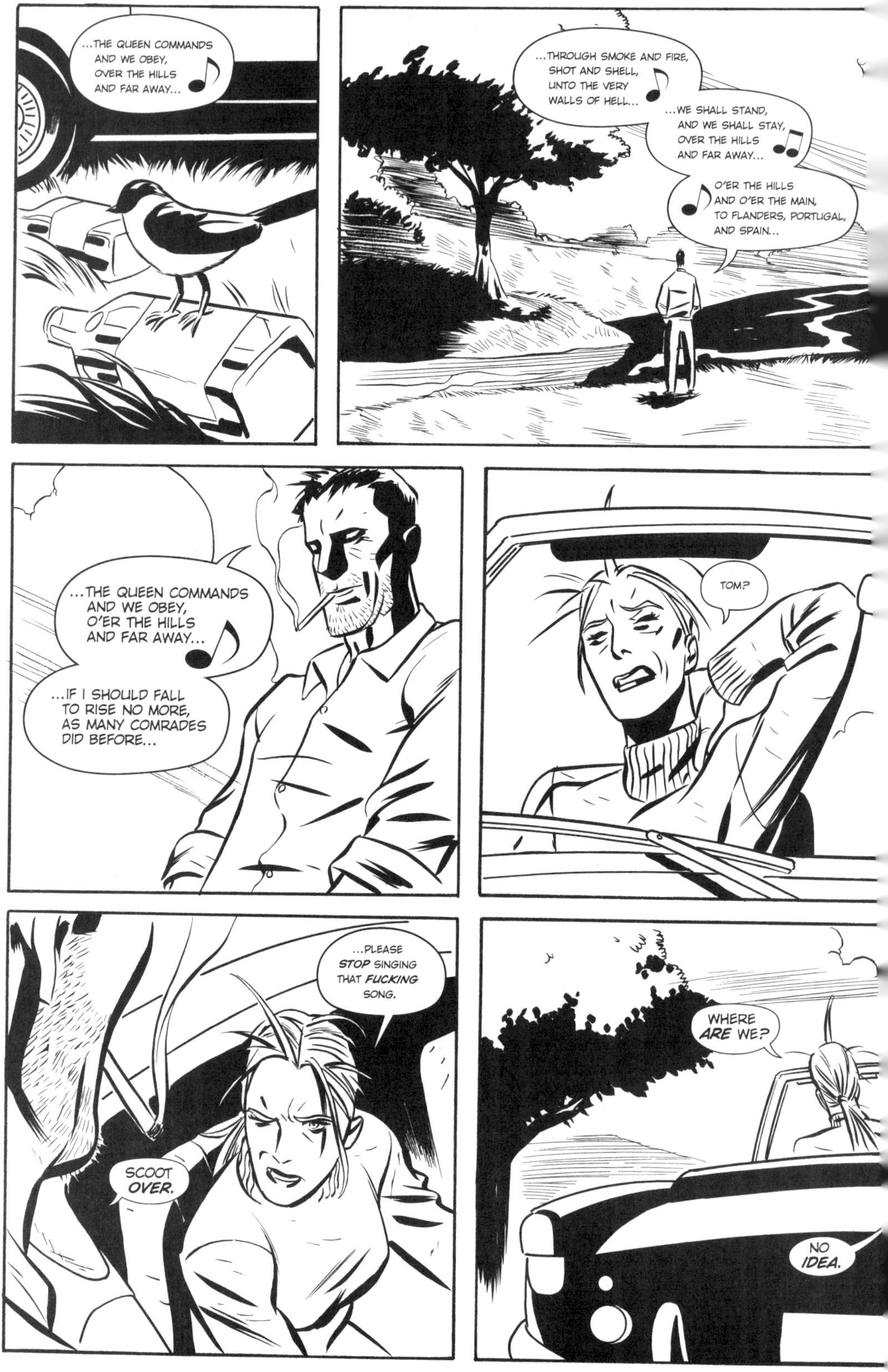
...THE QUEEN COMMANDS AND WE OBEY, OVER THE HILLS AND FAR AWAY...
...THROUGH SMOKE AND FIRE, SHOT AND SHELL, UNTO THE VERY WALLS OF HELL...
...WE SHALL STAND, AND WE SHALL STAY, OVER THE HILLS AND FAR AWAY...
O'ER THE HILLS AND O'ER THE MAIN, TO FLANDERS, PORTUGAL, AND SPAIN...
...THE QUEEN COMMANDS AND WE OBEY, O'ER THE HILLS AND FAR AWAY...
...IF I SHOULD FALL TO RISE NO MORE, AS MANY COMRADES DID BEFORE...
TOM?
...PLEASE **STOP** SINGING THAT **FUCKING** SONG.
SCOOT **OVER.**
WHERE **ARE** WE?
NO **IDEA.**

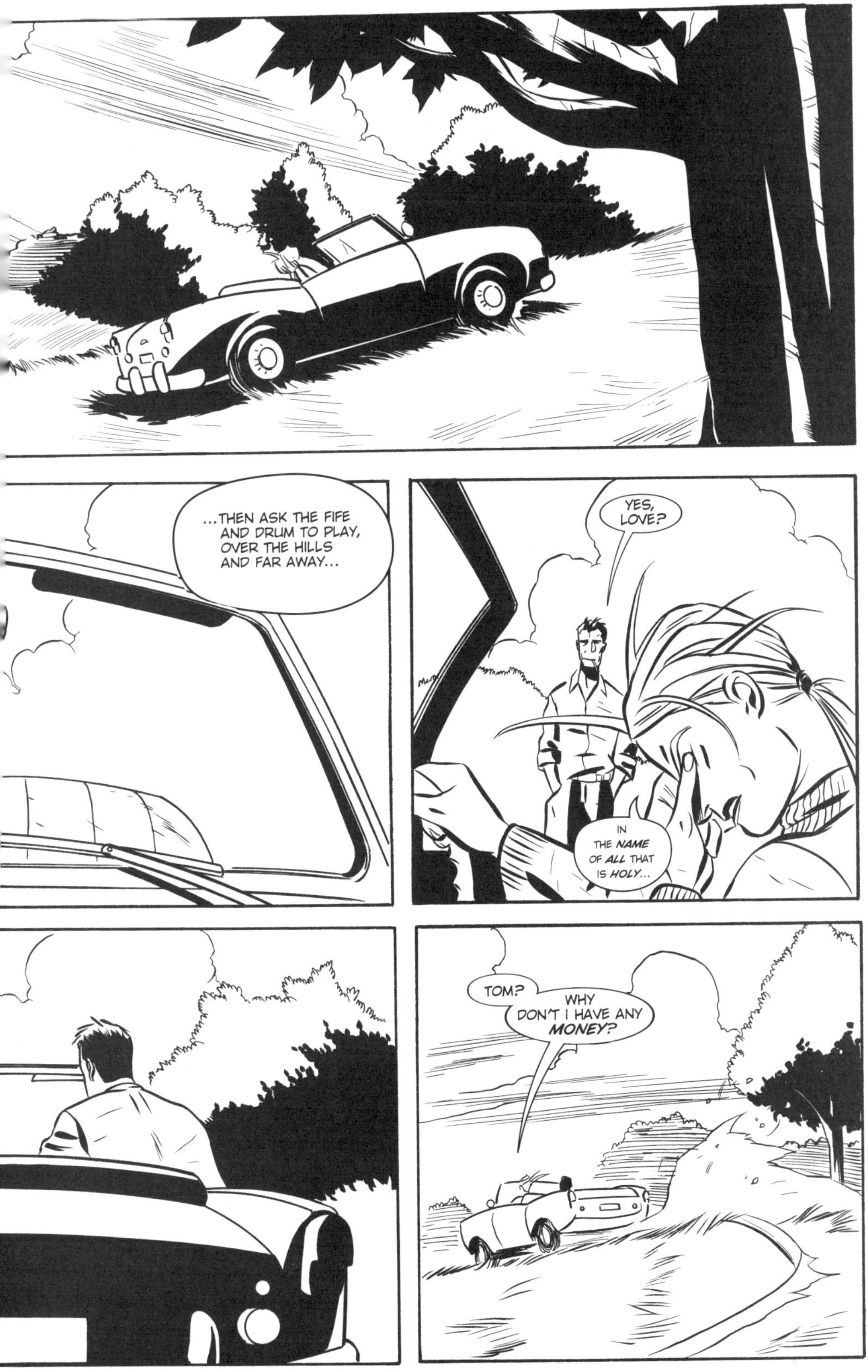
...THEN ASK THE FIFE AND DRUM TO PLAY, OVER THE HILLS AND FAR AWAY...
YES, LOVE?
IN THE NAME OF ALL THAT IS HOLY...
TOM?
WHY DON'T I HAVE ANY MONEY?

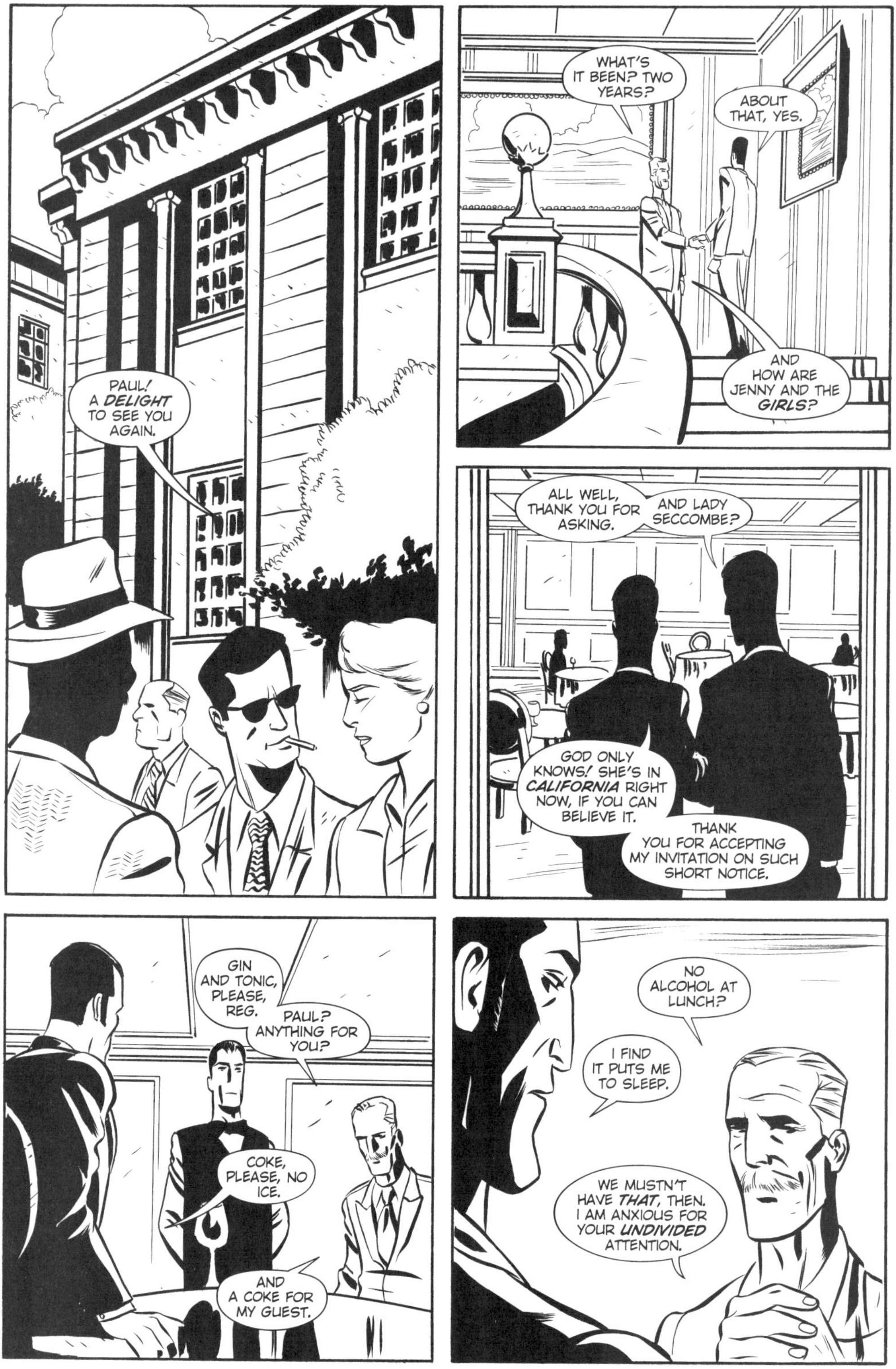
PAUL! A DELIGHT TO SEE YOU AGAIN.
WHAT'S IT BEEN? TWO YEARS?
ABOUT THAT, YES.
AND HOW ARE JENNY AND THE GIRLS?
ALL WELL, THANK YOU FOR ASKING.
AND LADY SECCOMBE?
GOD ONLY KNOWS! SHE'S IN CALIFORNIA RIGHT NOW, IF YOU CAN BELIEVE IT.
THANK YOU FOR ACCEPTING MY INVITATION ON SUCH SHORT NOTICE.
GIN AND TONIC, PLEASE, REG.
PAUL? ANYTHING FOR YOU?
COKE, PLEASE, NO ICE.
AND A COKE FOR MY GUEST.
NO ALCOHOL AT LUNCH?
I FIND IT PUTS ME TO SLEEP.
WE MUSTN'T HAVE THAT, THEN. I AM ANXIOUS FOR YOUR UNDIVIDED ATTENTION.

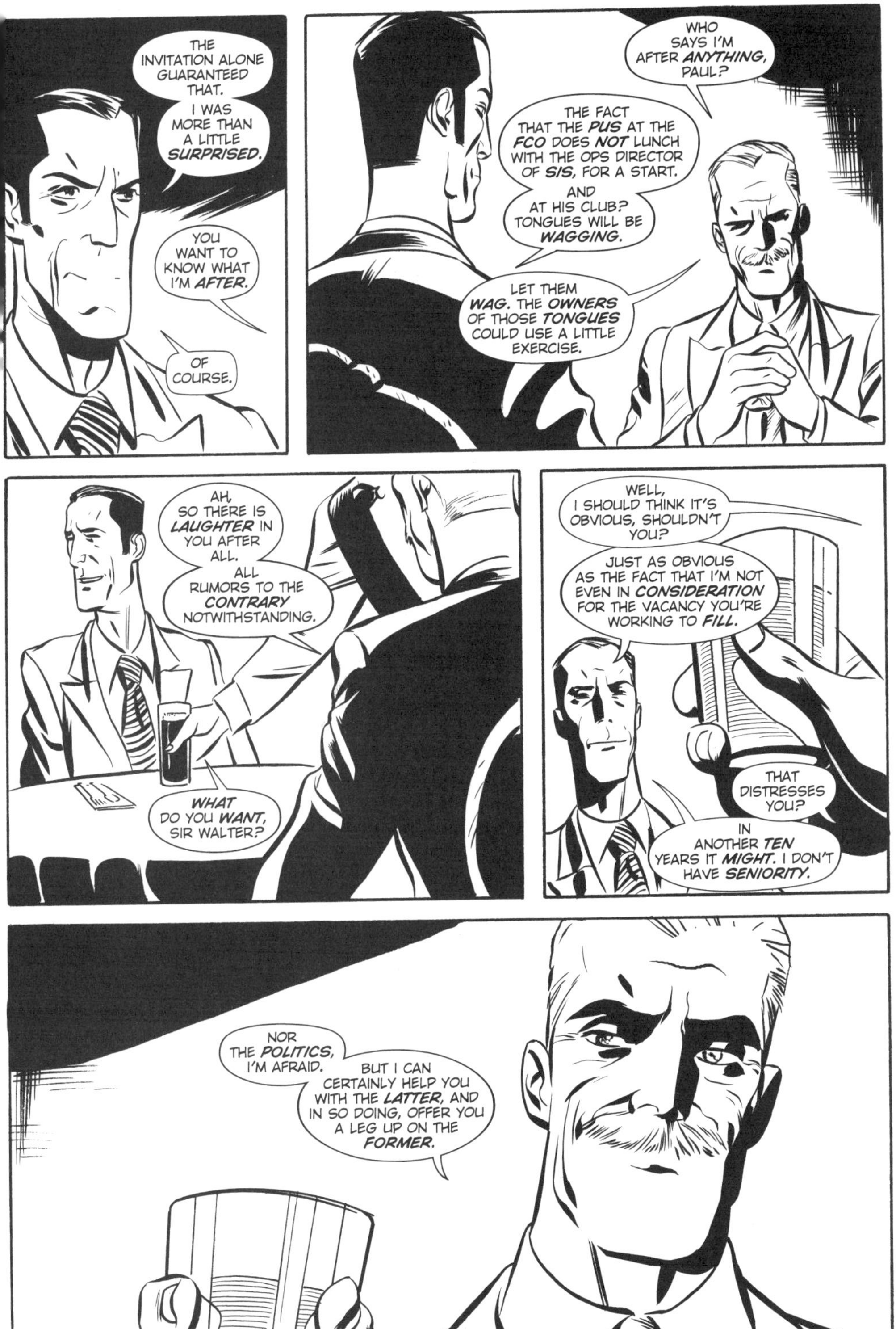

THE INVITATION ALONE GUARANTEED THAT.
I WAS MORE THAN A LITTLE SURPRISED.
YOU WANT TO KNOW WHAT I'M AFTER.
OF COURSE.
WHO SAYS I'M AFTER ANYTHING, PAUL?
THE FACT THAT THE PUS AT THE FCO DOES NOT LUNCH WITH THE OPS DIRECTOR OF SIS, FOR A START.
AND AT HIS CLUB? TONGUES WILL BE WAGGING.
LET THEM WAG. THE OWNERS OF THOSE TONGUES COULD USE A LITTLE EXERCISE.
AH, SO THERE IS LAUGHTER IN YOU AFTER ALL.
ALL RUMORS TO THE CONTRARY NOTWITHSTANDING.
WHAT DO YOU WANT, SIR WALTER?
WELL, I SHOULD THINK IT'S OBVIOUS, SHOULDN'T YOU?
JUST AS OBVIOUS AS THE FACT THAT I'M NOT EVEN IN CONSIDERATION FOR THE VACANCY YOU'RE WORKING TO FILL.
THAT DISTRESSES YOU?
IN ANOTHER TEN YEARS IT MIGHT. I DON'T HAVE SENIORITY.
NOR THE POLITICS, I'M AFRAID.
BUT I CAN CERTAINLY HELP YOU WITH THE LATTER, AND IN SO DOING, OFFER YOU A LEG UP ON THE FORMER.

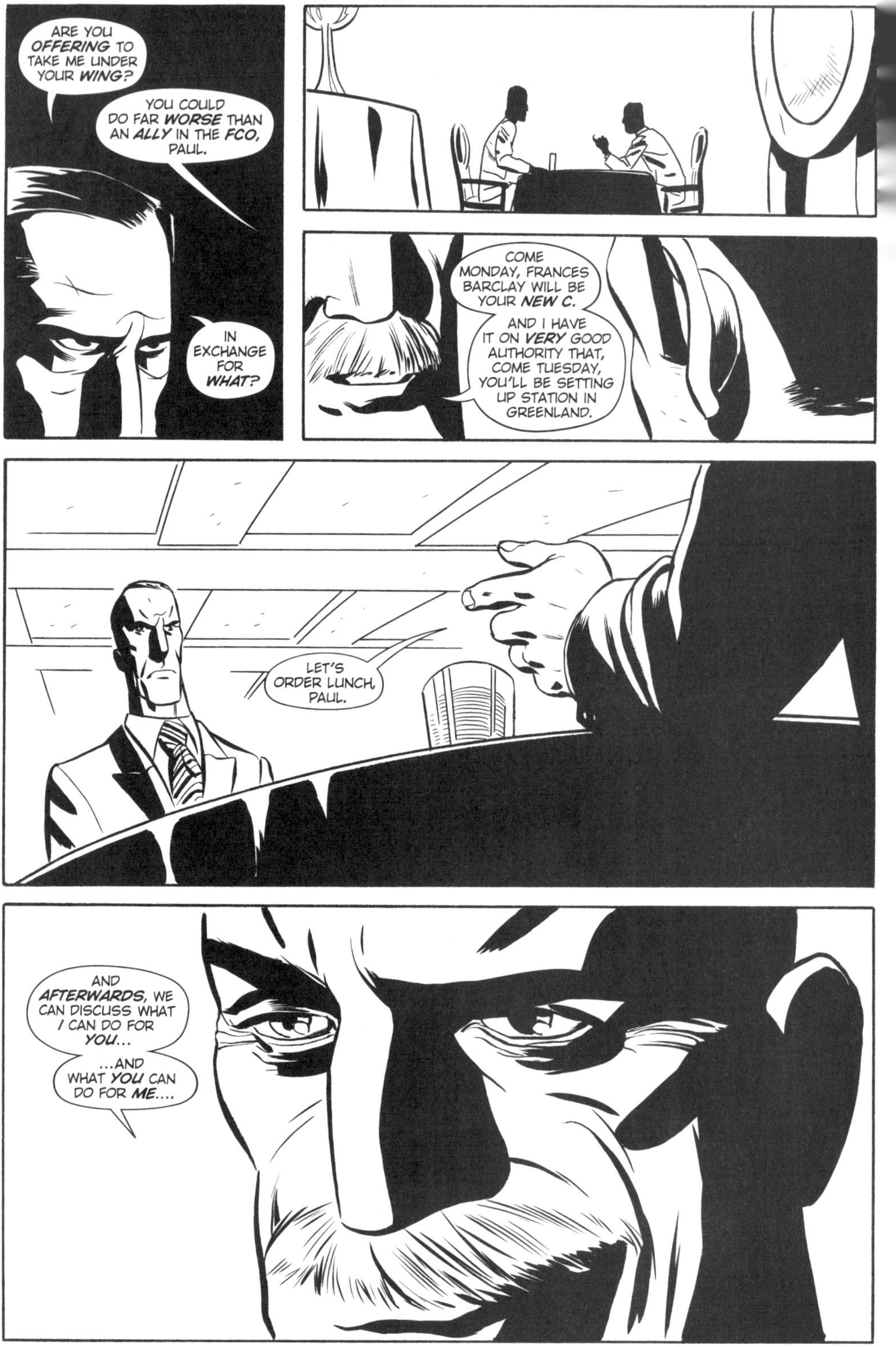
ARE YOU OFFERING TO TAKE ME UNDER YOUR WING?
YOU COULD DO FAR WORSE THAN AN ALLY IN THE FCO, PAUL.
IN EXCHANGE FOR WHAT?
COME MONDAY, FRANCES BARCLAY WILL BE YOUR NEW C.
AND I HAVE IT ON VERY GOOD AUTHORITY THAT, COME TUESDAY, YOU'LL BE SETTING UP STATION IN GREENLAND.
LET'S ORDER LUNCH, PAUL.
AND AFTERWARDS, WE CAN DISCUSS WHAT I CAN DO FOR YOU...
...AND WHAT YOU CAN DO FOR ME....

CHAPTER 2

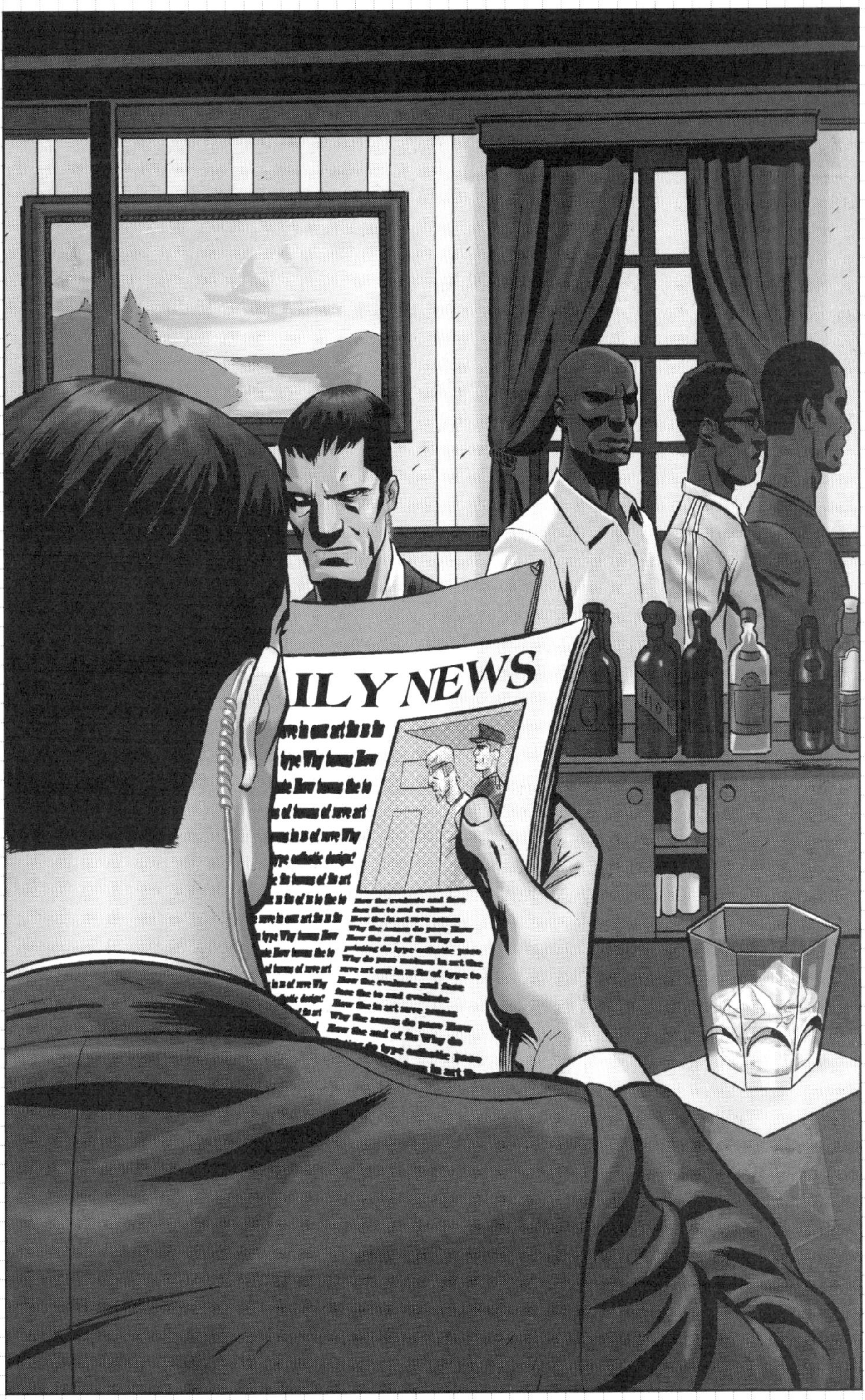
ILY NEWS

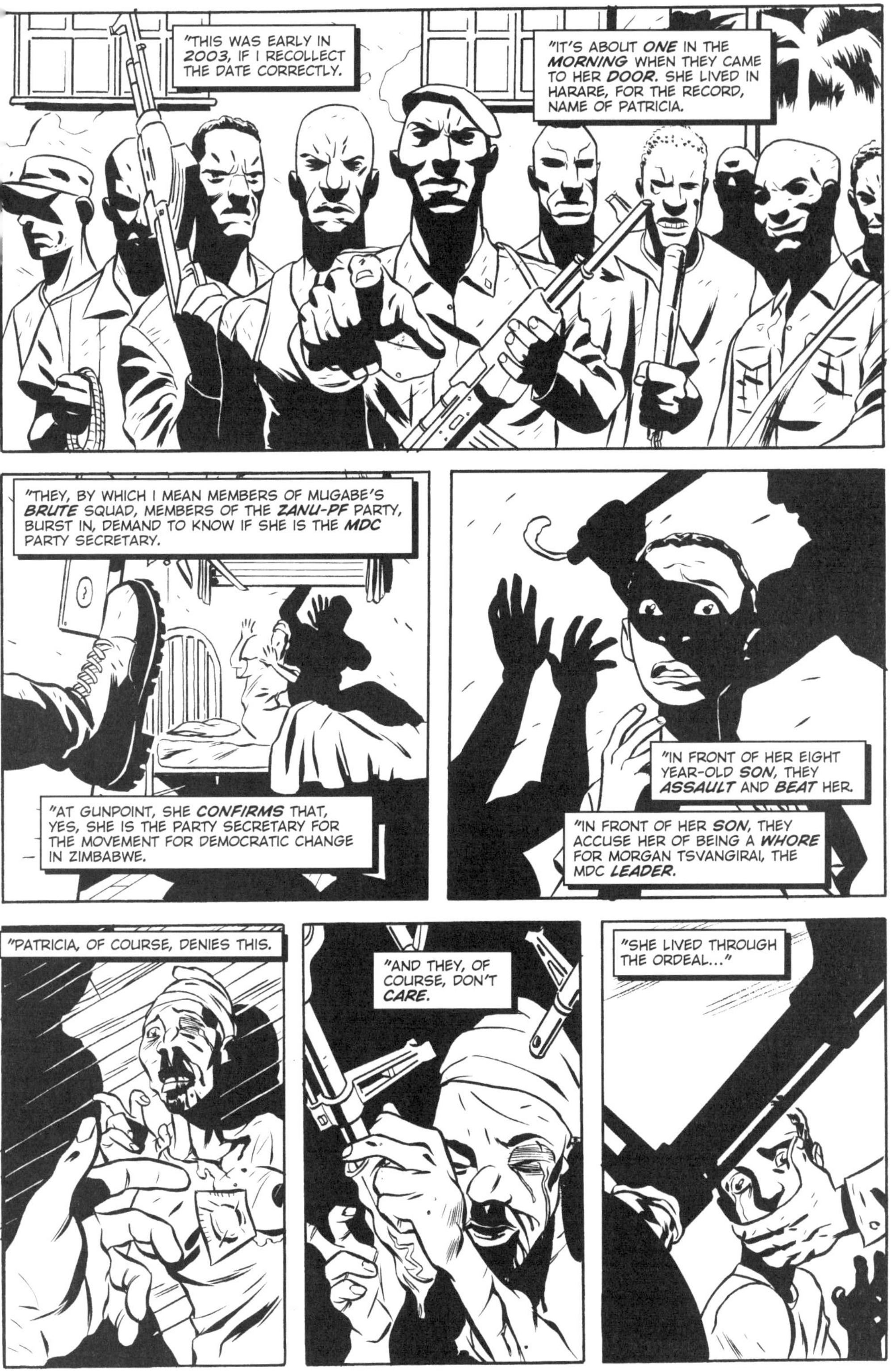
"THIS WAS EARLY IN 2003, IF I RECOLLECT THE DATE CORRECTLY.
"IT'S ABOUT ONE IN THE MORNING WHEN THEY CAME TO HER DOOR. SHE LIVED IN HARARE, FOR THE RECORD, NAME OF PATRICIA.
"THEY, BY WHICH I MEAN MEMBERS OF MUGABE'S BRUTE SQUAD, MEMBERS OF THE ZANU-PF PARTY, BURST IN, DEMAND TO KNOW IF SHE IS THE MDC PARTY SECRETARY.
"AT GUNPOINT, SHE CONFIRMS THAT, YES, SHE IS THE PARTY SECRETARY FOR THE MOVEMENT FOR DEMOCRATIC CHANGE IN ZIMBABWE.
"IN FRONT OF HER EIGHT YEAR-OLD SON, THEY ASSAULT AND BEAT HER.
"IN FRONT OF HER SON, THEY ACCUSE HER OF BEING A WHORE FOR MORGAN TSVANGIRAI, THE MDC LEADER.
"PATRICIA, OF COURSE, DENIES THIS.
"AND THEY, OF COURSE, DON'T CARE.
"SHE LIVED THROUGH THE ORDEAL..."

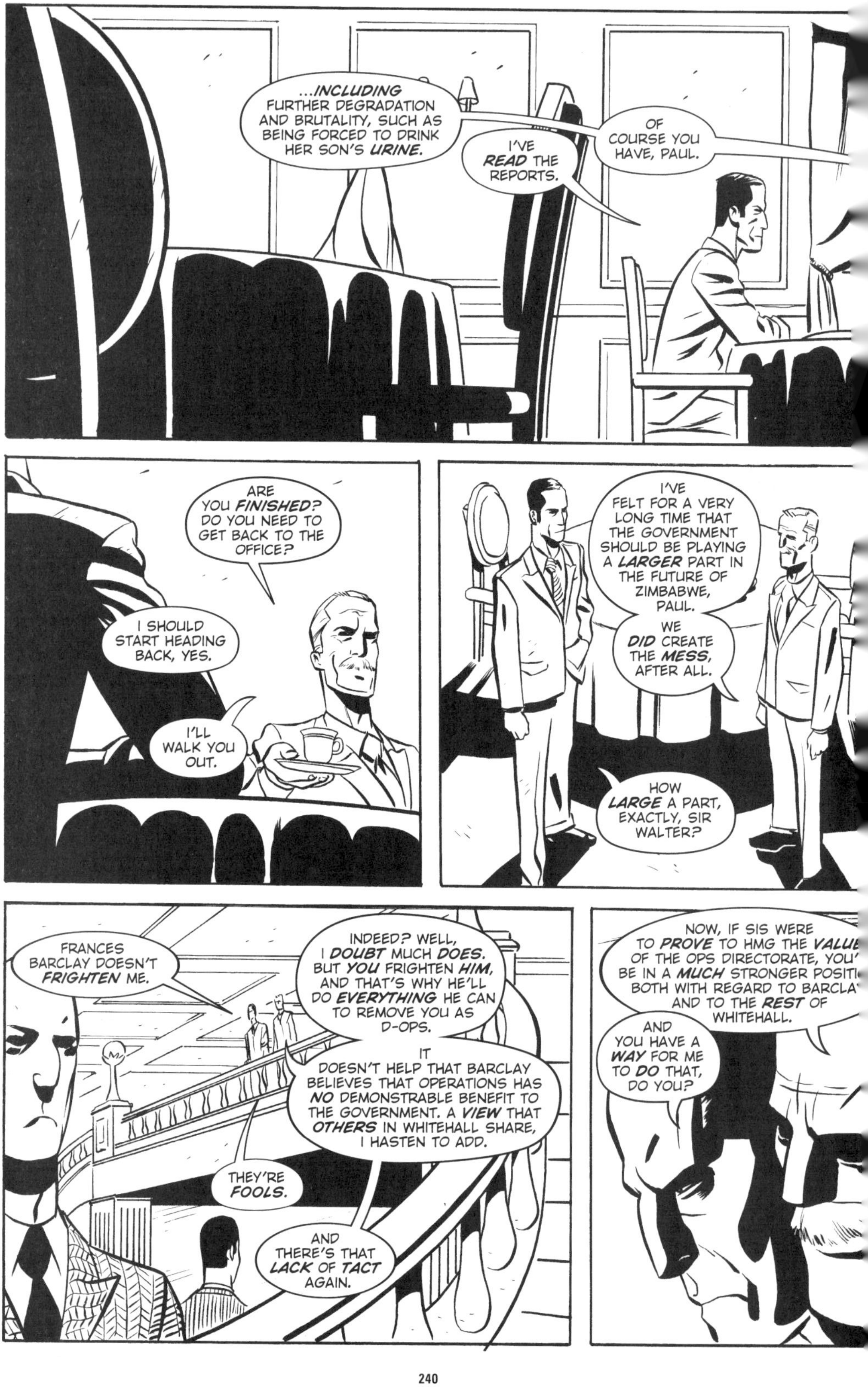
...INCLUDING FURTHER DEGRADATION AND BRUTALITY, SUCH AS BEING FORCED TO DRINK HER SON'S URINE.
I'VE READ THE REPORTS.
OF COURSE YOU HAVE, PAUL.
ARE YOU FINISHED? DO YOU NEED TO GET BACK TO THE OFFICE?
I SHOULD START HEADING BACK, YES.
I'LL WALK YOU OUT.
I'VE FELT FOR A VERY LONG TIME THAT THE GOVERNMENT SHOULD BE PLAYING A LARGER PART IN THE FUTURE OF ZIMBABWE, PAUL.
WE DID CREATE THE MESS, AFTER ALL.
HOW LARGE A PART, EXACTLY, SIR WALTER?
FRANCES BARCLAY DOESN'T FRIGHTEN ME.
INDEED? WELL, I DOUBT MUCH DOES. BUT YOU FRIGHTEN HIM, AND THAT'S WHY HE'LL DO EVERYTHING HE CAN TO REMOVE YOU AS D-OPS.
IT DOESN'T HELP THAT BARCLAY BELIEVES THAT OPERATIONS HAS NO DEMONSTRABLE BENEFIT TO THE GOVERNMENT. A VIEW THAT OTHERS IN WHITEHALL SHARE, I HASTEN TO ADD.
THEY'RE FOOLS.
AND THERE'S THAT LACK OF TACT AGAIN.
NOW, IF SIS WERE TO PROVE TO HMG THE VALU OF THE OPS DIRECTORATE, YOU' BE IN A MUCH STRONGER POSITI BOTH WITH REGARD TO BARCLA AND TO THE REST OF WHITEHALL.
AND YOU HAVE A WAY FOR ME TO DO THAT, DO YOU?

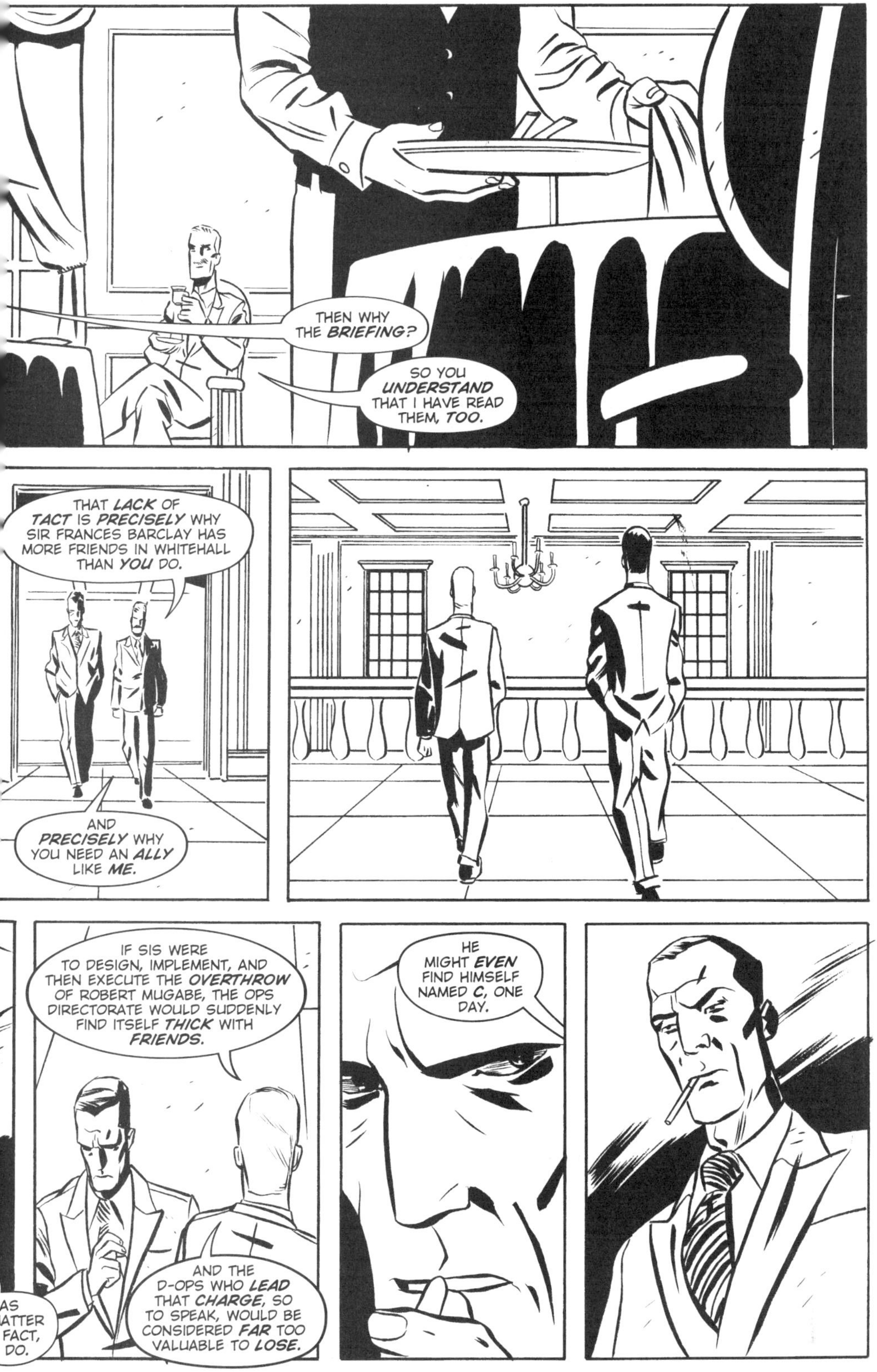
THEN WHY THE BRIEFING?
SO YOU UNDERSTAND THAT I HAVE READ THEM, TOO.
THAT LACK OF TACT IS PRECISELY WHY SIR FRANCES BARCLAY HAS MORE FRIENDS IN WHITEHALL THAN YOU DO.
AND PRECISELY WHY YOU NEED AN ALLY LIKE ME.
AS MATTER F FACT, I DO.
IF SIS WERE TO DESIGN, IMPLEMENT, AND THEN EXECUTE THE OVERTHROW OF ROBERT MUGABE, THE OPS DIRECTORATE WOULD SUDDENLY FIND ITSELF THICK WITH FRIENDS.
AND THE D-OPS WHO LEAD THAT CHARGE, SO TO SPEAK, WOULD BE CONSIDERED FAR TOO VALUABLE TO LOSE.
HE MIGHT EVEN FIND HIMSELF NAMED C, ONE DAY.

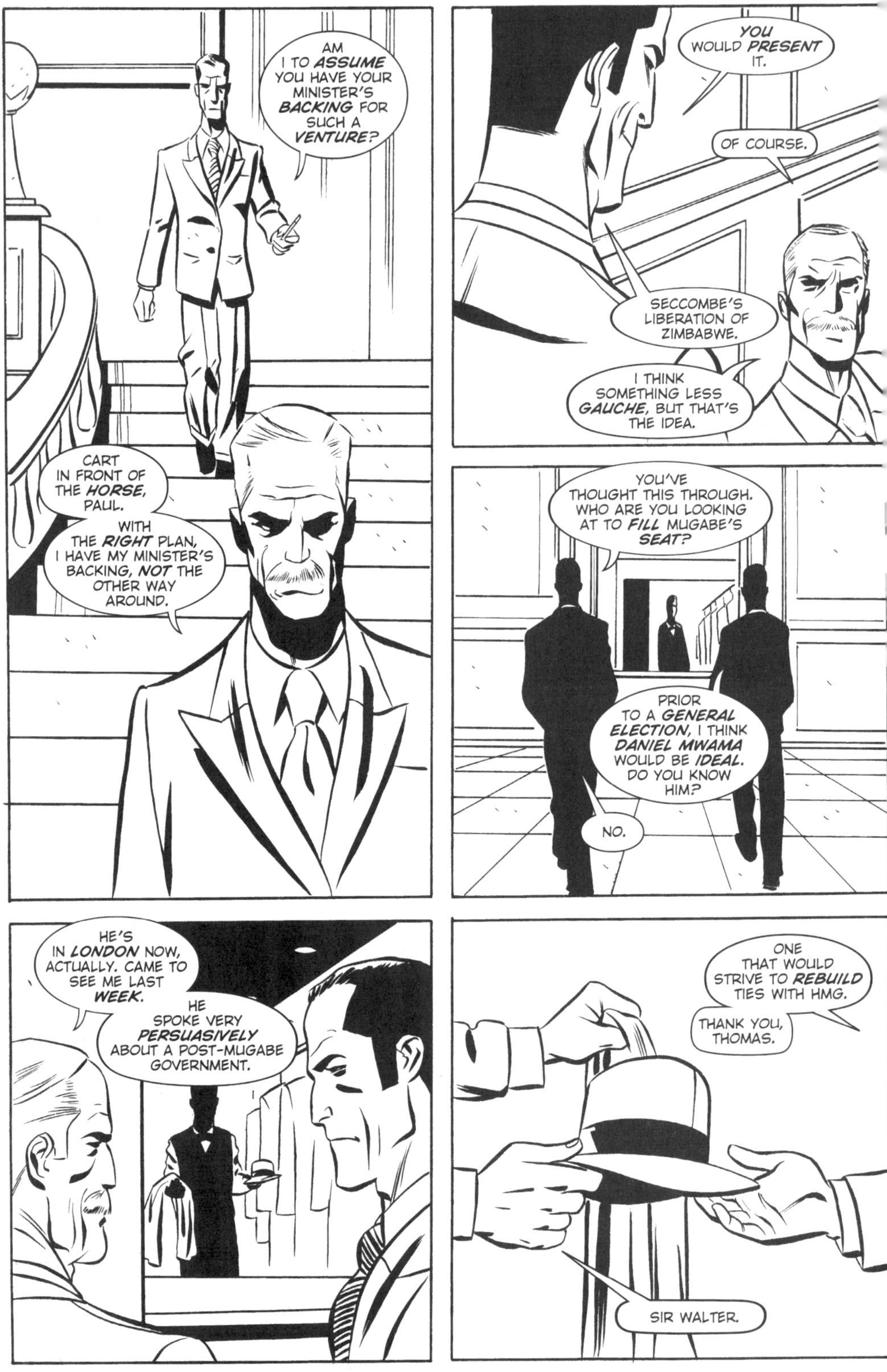
AM I TO ASSUME YOU HAVE YOUR MINISTER'S BACKING FOR SUCH A VENTURE?
CART IN FRONT OF THE HORSE, PAUL.
WITH THE RIGHT PLAN, I HAVE MY MINISTER'S BACKING, NOT THE OTHER WAY AROUND.
YOU WOULD PRESENT IT.
OF COURSE.
SECCOMBE'S LIBERATION OF ZIMBABWE.
I THINK SOMETHING LESS GAUCHE, BUT THAT'S THE IDEA.
YOU'VE THOUGHT THIS THROUGH. WHO ARE YOU LOOKING AT TO FILL MUGABE'S SEAT?
PRIOR TO A GENERAL ELECTION, I THINK DANIEL MWAMA WOULD BE IDEAL. DO YOU KNOW HIM?
NO.
HE'S IN LONDON NOW, ACTUALLY. CAME TO SEE ME LAST WEEK.
HE SPOKE VERY PERSUASIVELY ABOUT A POST-MUGABE GOVERNMENT.
ONE THAT WOULD STRIVE TO REBUILD TIES WITH HMG.
THANK YOU, THOMAS.
SIR WALTER.

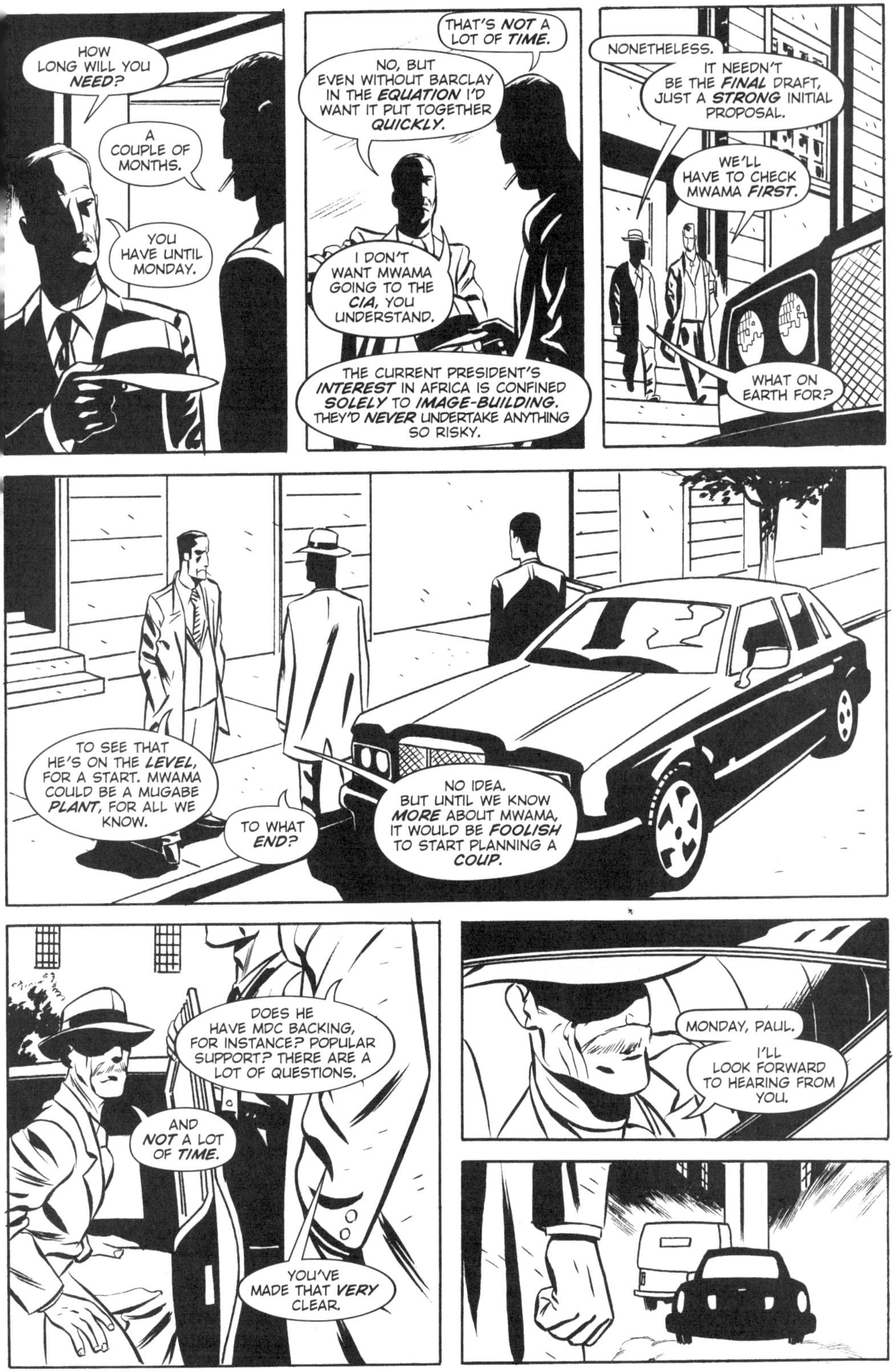
HOW LONG WILL YOU NEED?
A COUPLE OF MONTHS.
YOU HAVE UNTIL MONDAY.
THAT'S NOT A LOT OF TIME.
NO, BUT EVEN WITHOUT BARCLAY IN THE EQUATION I'D WANT IT PUT TOGETHER QUICKLY.
I DON'T WANT MWAMA GOING TO THE CIA, YOU UNDERSTAND.
THE CURRENT PRESIDENT'S INTEREST IN AFRICA IS CONFINED SOLELY TO IMAGE-BUILDING. THEY'D NEVER UNDERTAKE ANYTHING SO RISKY.
NONETHELESS.
IT NEEDN'T BE THE FINAL DRAFT, JUST A STRONG INITIAL PROPOSAL.
WE'LL HAVE TO CHECK MWAMA FIRST.
WHAT ON EARTH FOR?
TO SEE THAT HE'S ON THE LEVEL, FOR A START. MWAMA COULD BE A MUGABE PLANT, FOR ALL WE KNOW.
TO WHAT END?
NO IDEA. BUT UNTIL WE KNOW MORE ABOUT MWAMA, IT WOULD BE FOOLISH TO START PLANNING A COUP.
DOES HE HAVE MDC BACKING, FOR INSTANCE? POPULAR SUPPORT? THERE ARE A LOT OF QUESTIONS.
AND NOT A LOT OF TIME.
YOU'VE MADE THAT VERY CLEAR.
MONDAY, PAUL.
I'LL LOOK FORWARD TO HEARING FROM YOU.

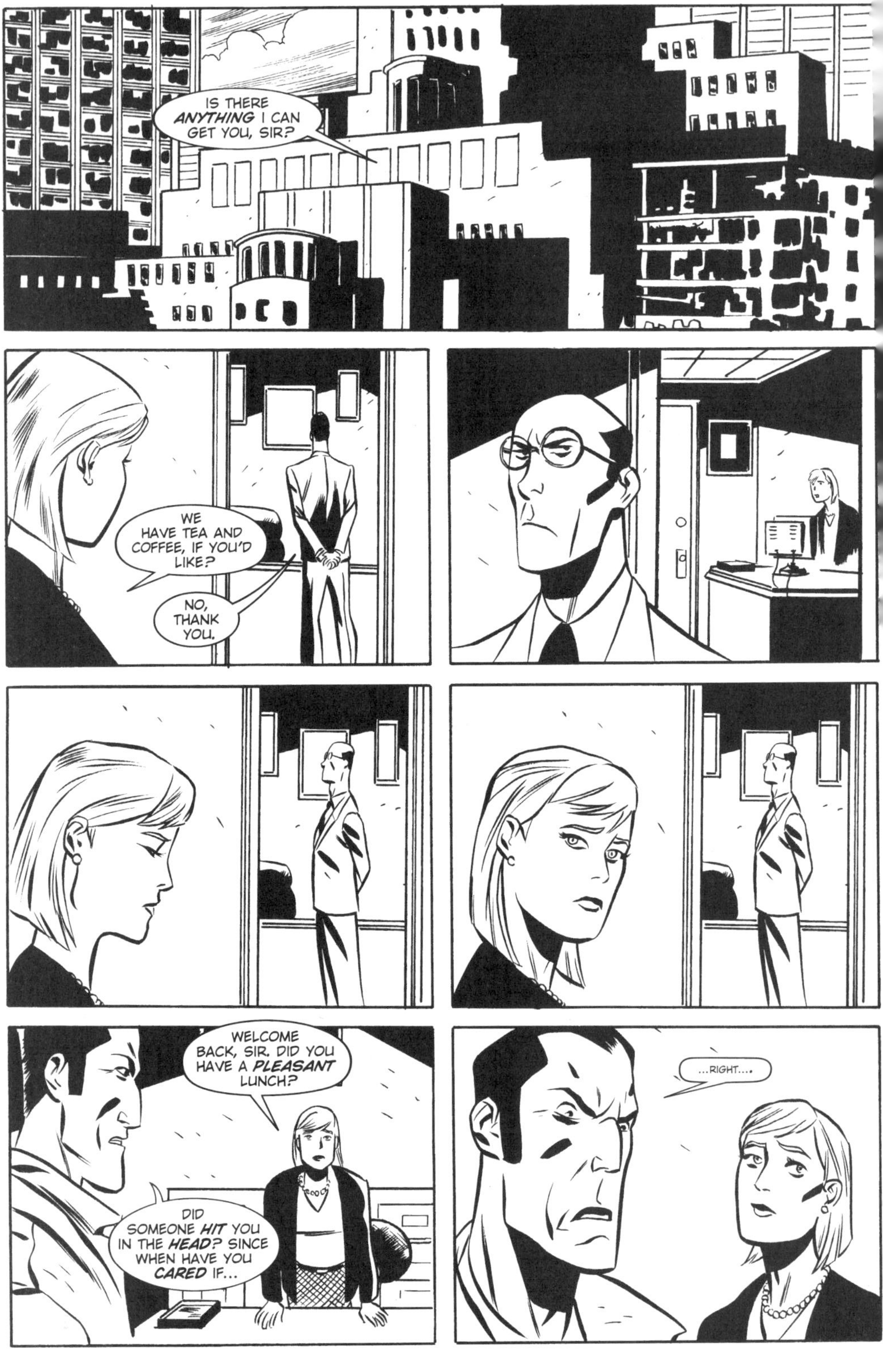
IS THERE ANYTHING I CAN GET YOU, SIR?
WE HAVE TEA AND COFFEE, IF YOU'D LIKE?
NO, THANK YOU.
WELCOME BACK, SIR. DID YOU HAVE A PLEASANT LUNCH?
DID SOMEONE HIT YOU IN THE HEAD? SINCE WHEN HAVE YOU CARED IF...
...RIGHT....

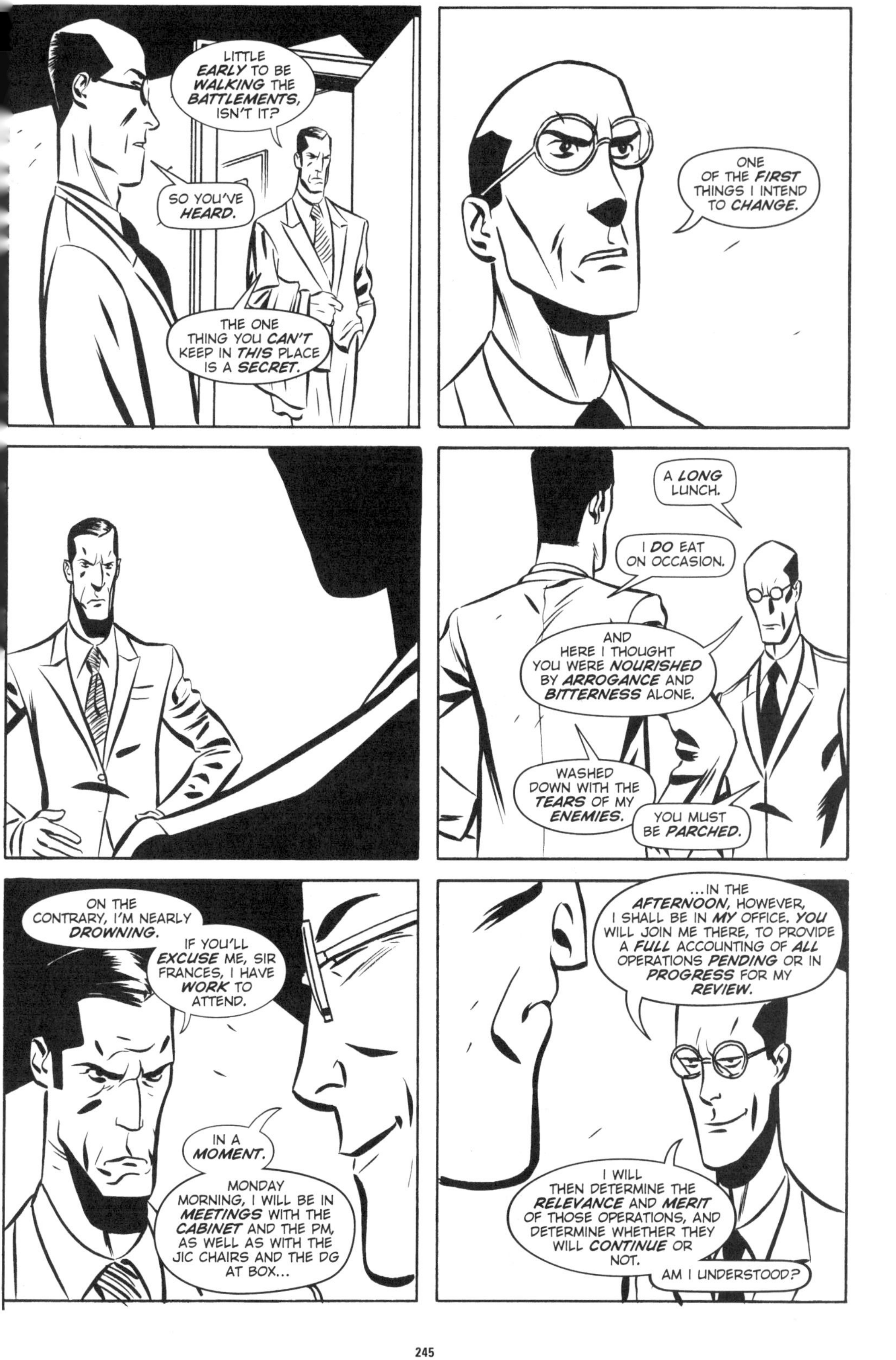
LITTLE EARLY TO BE WALKING THE BATTLEMENTS, ISN'T IT?
SO YOU'VE HEARD.
THE ONE THING YOU CAN'T KEEP IN THIS PLACE IS A SECRET.
ONE OF THE FIRST THINGS I INTEND TO CHANGE.
A LONG LUNCH.
I DO EAT ON OCCASION.
AND HERE I THOUGHT YOU WERE NOURISHED BY ARROGANCE AND BITTERNESS ALONE.
WASHED DOWN WITH THE TEARS OF MY ENEMIES.
YOU MUST BE PARCHED.
ON THE CONTRARY, I'M NEARLY DROWNING.
IF YOU'LL EXCUSE ME, SIR FRANCES, I HAVE WORK TO ATTEND.
IN A MOMENT.
MONDAY MORNING, I WILL BE IN MEETINGS WITH THE CABINET AND THE PM, AS WELL AS WITH THE JIC CHAIRS AND THE DG AT BOX...
...IN THE AFTERNOON, HOWEVER, I SHALL BE IN MY OFFICE. YOU WILL JOIN ME THERE, TO PROVIDE A FULL ACCOUNTING OF ALL OPERATIONS PENDING OR IN PROGRESS FOR MY REVIEW.
I WILL THEN DETERMINE THE RELEVANCE AND MERIT OF THOSE OPERATIONS, AND DETERMINE WHETHER THEY WILL CONTINUE OR NOT.
AM I UNDERSTOOD?

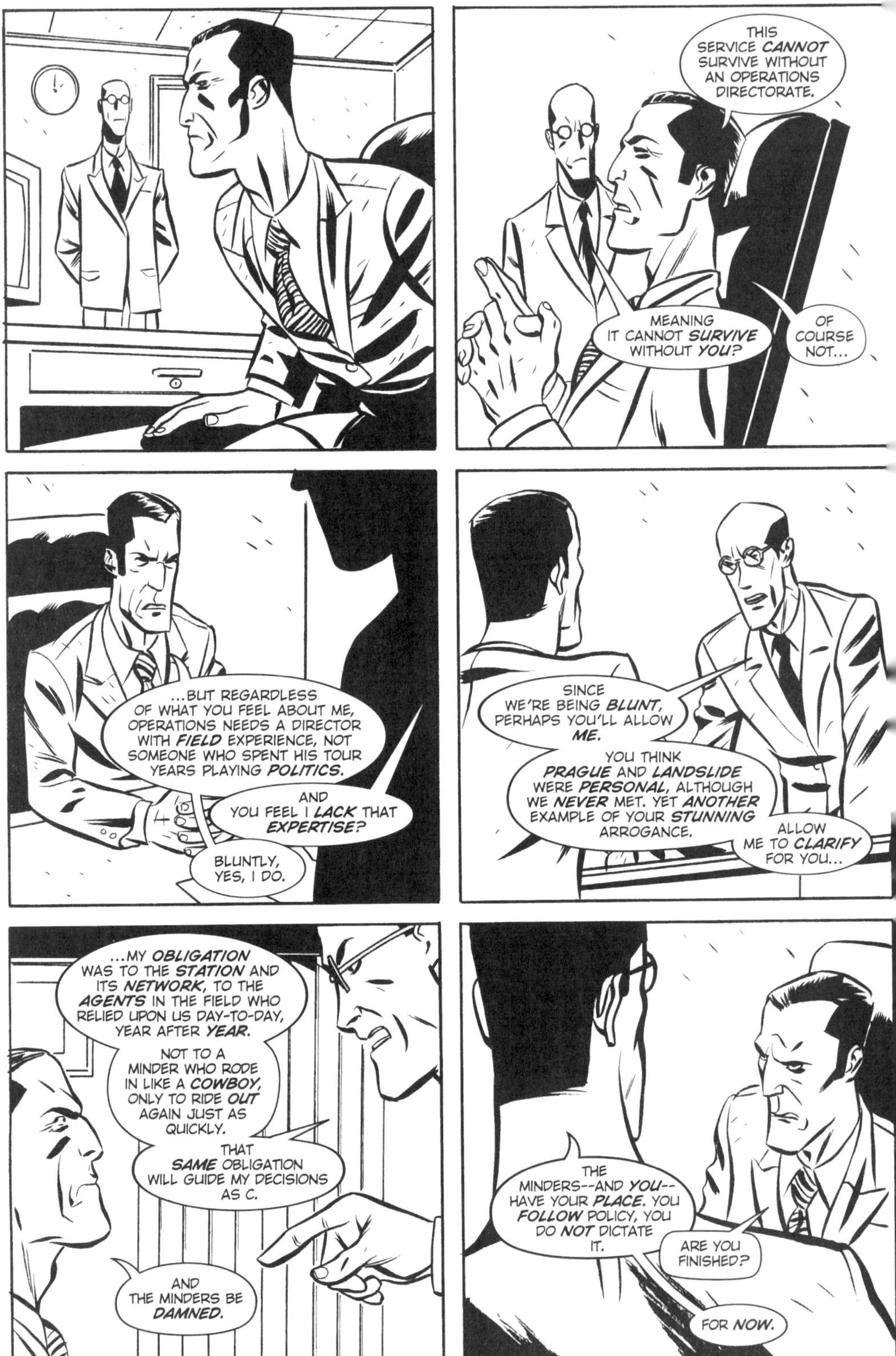
THIS SERVICE CANNOT SURVIVE WITHOUT AN OPERATIONS DIRECTORATE.
MEANING IT CANNOT SURVIVE WITHOUT YOU?
OF COURSE NOT...
...BUT REGARDLESS OF WHAT YOU FEEL ABOUT ME, OPERATIONS NEEDS A DIRECTOR WITH FIELD EXPERIENCE, NOT SOMEONE WHO SPENT HIS TOUR YEARS PLAYING POLITICS.
AND YOU FEEL I LACK THAT EXPERTISE?
BLUNTLY, YES, I DO.
SINCE WE'RE BEING BLUNT, PERHAPS YOU'LL ALLOW ME.
YOU THINK PRAGUE AND LANDSLIDE WERE PERSONAL, ALTHOUGH WE NEVER MET. YET ANOTHER EXAMPLE OF YOUR STUNNING ARROGANCE.
ALLOW ME TO CLARIFY FOR YOU...
...MY OBLIGATION WAS TO THE STATION AND ITS NETWORK, TO THE AGENTS IN THE FIELD WHO RELIED UPON US DAY-TO-DAY, YEAR AFTER YEAR.
NOT TO A MINDER WHO RODE IN LIKE A COWBOY, ONLY TO RIDE OUT AGAIN JUST AS QUICKLY.
THAT SAME OBLIGATION WILL GUIDE MY DECISIONS AS C.
AND THE MINDERS BE DAMNED.
THE MINDERS--AND YOU--HAVE YOUR PLACE. YOU FOLLOW POLICY, YOU DO NOT DICTATE IT.
ARE YOU FINISHED?
FOR NOW.

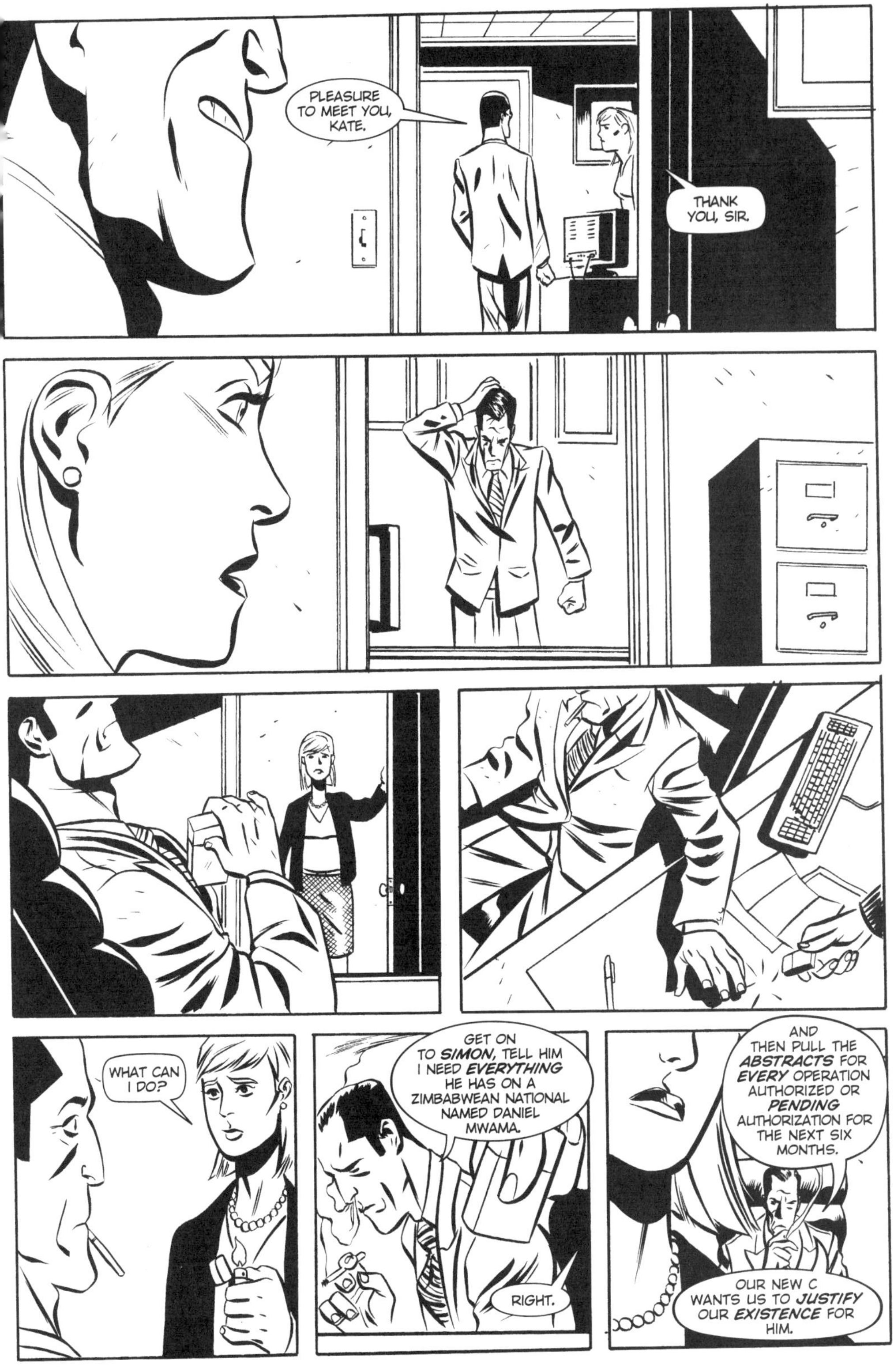
PLEASURE TO MEET YOU, KATE.
THANK YOU, SIR.
WHAT CAN I DO?
GET ON TO SIMON, TELL HIM I NEED EVERYTHING HE HAS ON A ZIMBABWEAN NATIONAL NAMED DANIEL MWAMA.
RIGHT.
AND THEN PULL THE ABSTRACTS FOR EVERY OPERATION AUTHORIZED OR PENDING AUTHORIZATION FOR THE NEXT SIX MONTHS.
OUR NEW C WANTS US TO JUSTIFY OUR EXISTENCE FOR HIM.

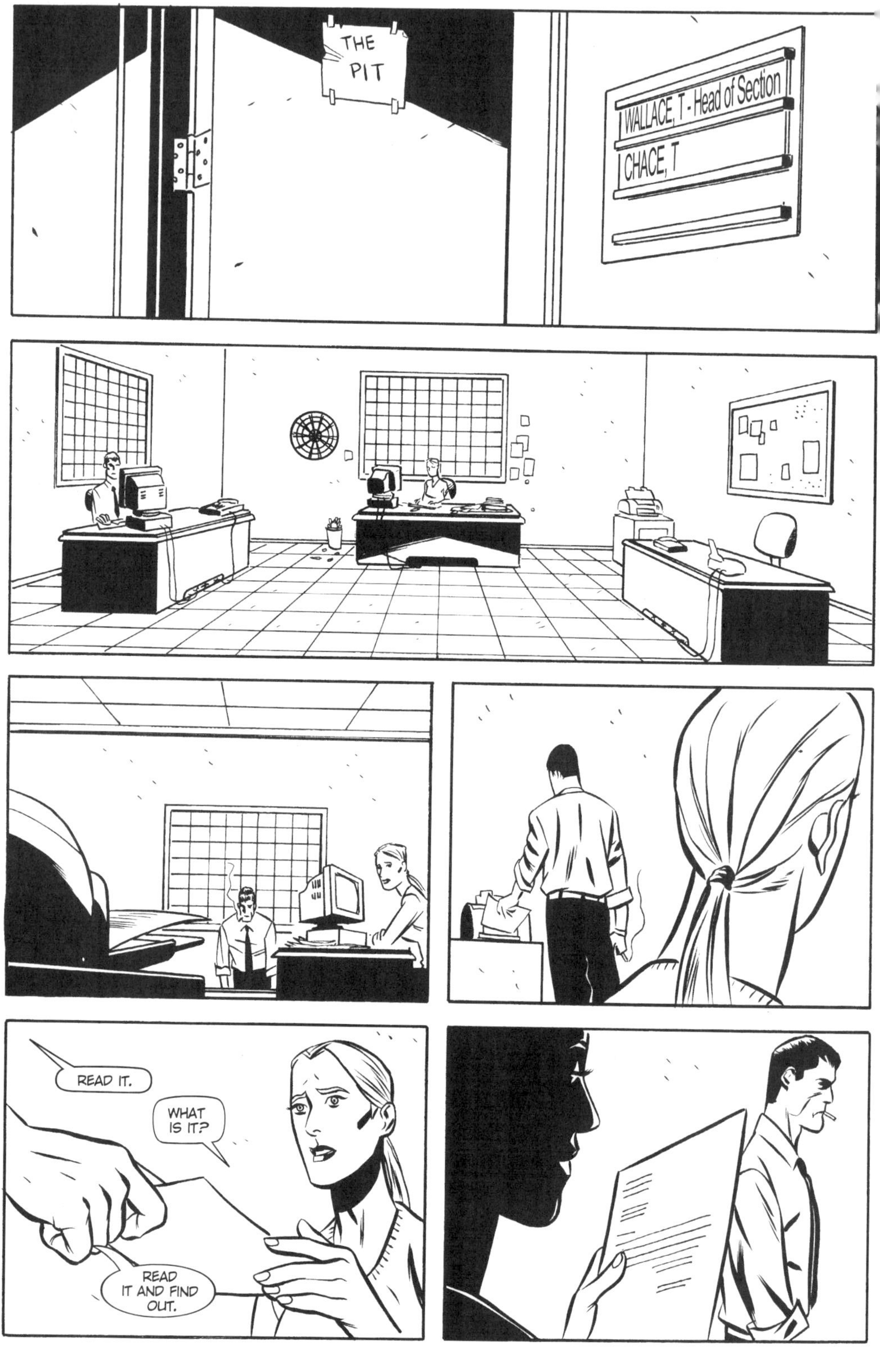
THE PIT
WALLACE, T - Head of Section
CHACE, T
READ IT.
WHAT IS IT?
READ IT AND FIND OUT.

YOU'RE OUT OF YOUR *SKULL*.

AM I? WHY'S THAT?

YOU'RE TRADING IN BEING A MINDER FOR *TEACHING* AT THE FIELD SCHOOL?

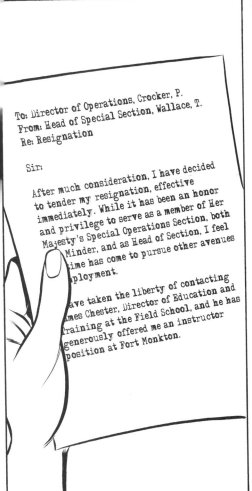

To: Director of Operations, Crocker, P.
From: Head of Special Section, Wallace, T.
Re: Resignation

Sir:

After much consideration, I have decided to tender my resignation, effective immediately. While it has been an honor and privilege to serve as a member of Her Majesty's Special Operations Section, both Minder, and as Head of Section, I feel time has come to pursue other avenues ployment.

ave taken the liberty of contacting mes Chester, Director of Education and raining at the Field School, and he has generously offered me an instructor position at Fort Monkton.

YOU'LL *DIE* OF *BOREDOM!*

BETTER TO GO *THAT* WAY THAN ANY *OTHER*, I THINK.

YOU *CAN'T* DO THIS, TOM!

REALLY, I *CAN*. REALLY, I AM.

I'M *DONE*, TARA. I'VE HAD *ENOUGH*. I'VE *DONE* MY BIT FOR QUEEN AND COUNTRY.

YOU'LL *KILL* THE SECTION, IF YOU GO.

YOU CAN HANDLE IT.

ONE MINDER TO COVER THE WORLD? I'M *GOOD*, I'M *NOT* THAT GOOD.

MAYBE *NOT* THAT GOOD AT *ALL*. I DIDN'T *DATE* THE LETTER. I'LL *WAIT* UNTIL CROCKER'S FOUND A *REPLACEMENT* FOR BUTLER BEFORE TURNING IT IN.

YOU'LL HAVE TO STAY *LONGER* THAN *THAT*. I'LL NEED YOUR HELP TO BREAK IN THE *NEW* GUY.

YOU'LL BREAK HIM IN JUST FINE.

THE WAY I *BROKE* THE LAST ONE? OH, BRILLIANT THAT.

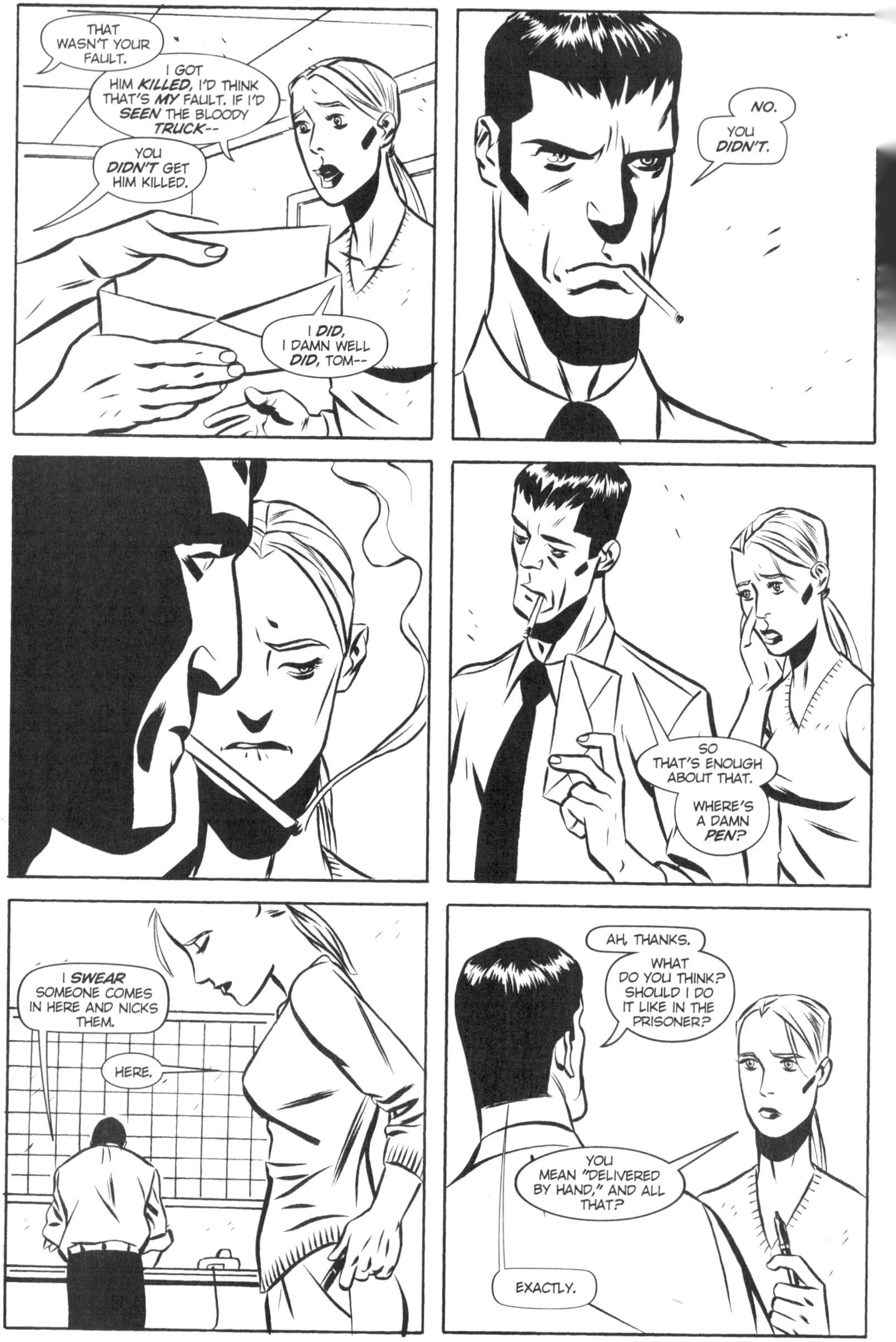

THAT WASN'T YOUR FAULT.
I GOT HIM KILLED, I'D THINK THAT'S MY FAULT. IF I'D SEEN THE BLOODY TRUCK--
YOU DIDN'T GET HIM KILLED.
I DID, I DAMN WELL DID, TOM--
NO.
YOU DIDN'T.
SO THAT'S ENOUGH ABOUT THAT.
WHERE'S A DAMN PEN?
I SWEAR SOMEONE COMES IN HERE AND NICKS THEM.
HERE.
AH, THANKS.
WHAT DO YOU THINK? SHOULD I DO IT LIKE IN THE PRISONER?
YOU MEAN "DELIVERED BY HAND," AND ALL THAT?
EXACTLY.

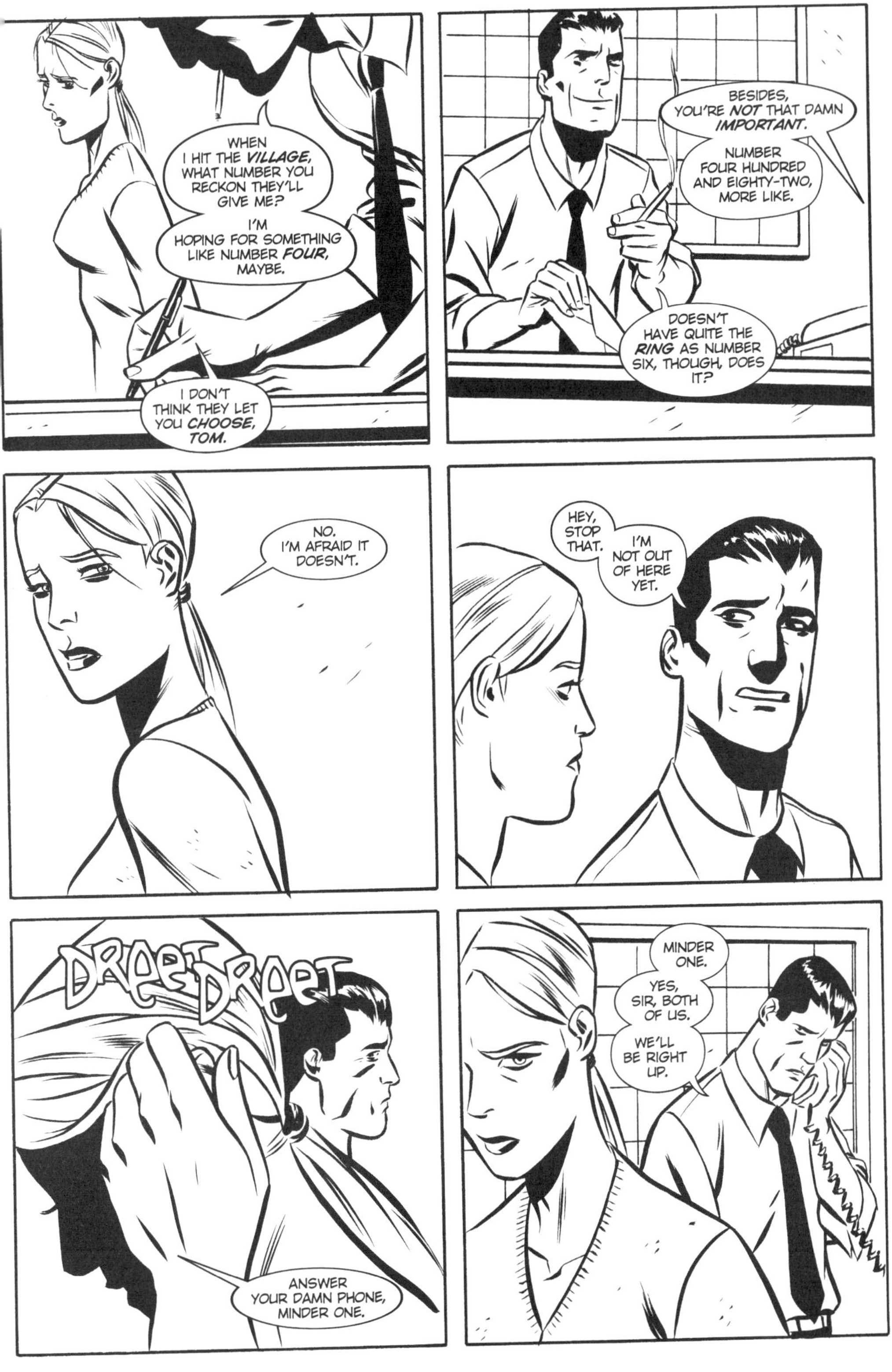
WHEN I HIT THE VILLAGE, WHAT NUMBER YOU RECKON THEY'LL GIVE ME?
I'M HOPING FOR SOMETHING LIKE NUMBER FOUR, MAYBE.
I DON'T THINK THEY LET YOU CHOOSE, TOM.
BESIDES, YOU'RE NOT THAT DAMN IMPORTANT.
NUMBER FOUR HUNDRED AND EIGHTY-TWO, MORE LIKE.
DOESN'T HAVE QUITE THE RING AS NUMBER SIX, THOUGH, DOES IT?
NO. I'M AFRAID IT DOESN'T.
HEY, STOP THAT.
I'M NOT OUT OF HERE YET.
DREET DREET
ANSWER YOUR DAMN PHONE, MINDER ONE.
MINDER ONE.
YES, SIR, BOTH OF US.
WE'LL BE RIGHT UP.

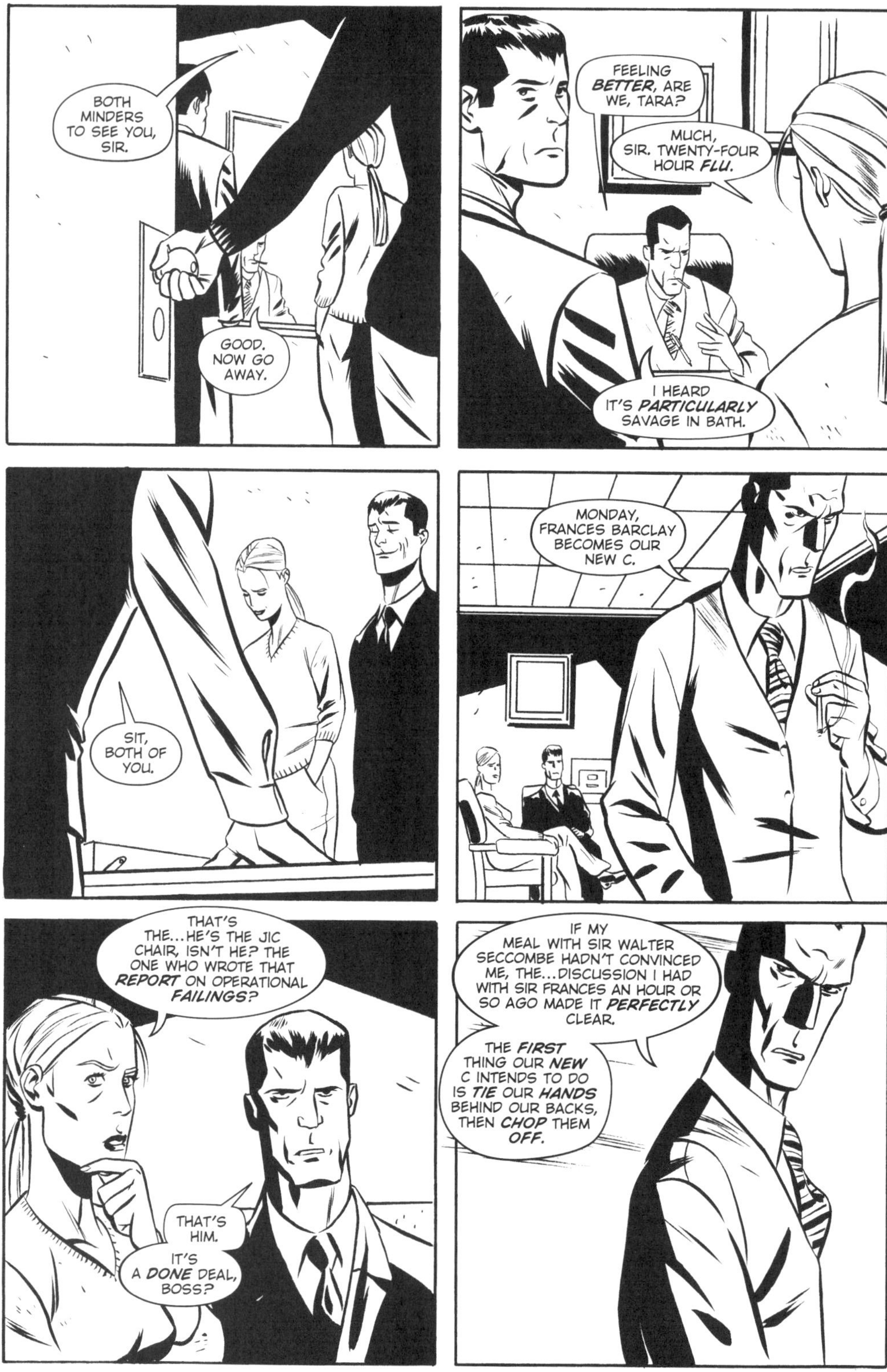
BOTH MINDERS TO SEE YOU, SIR.
GOOD. NOW GO AWAY.
FEELING **BETTER**, ARE WE, TARA?
MUCH, SIR. TWENTY-FOUR HOUR **FLU**.
I HEARD IT'S **PARTICULARLY** SAVAGE IN BATH.
SIT, BOTH OF YOU.
MONDAY, FRANCES BARCLAY BECOMES OUR NEW C.
THAT'S THE...HE'S THE JIC CHAIR, ISN'T HE? THE ONE WHO WROTE THAT **REPORT** ON OPERATIONAL **FAILINGS**?
THAT'S HIM.
IT'S A **DONE** DEAL, BOSS?
IF MY MEAL WITH SIR WALTER SECCOMBE HADN'T CONVINCED ME, THE...DISCUSSION I HAD WITH SIR FRANCES AN HOUR OR SO AGO MADE IT **PERFECTLY** CLEAR.
THE **FIRST** THING OUR **NEW** C INTENDS TO DO IS **TIE** OUR **HANDS** BEHIND OUR BACKS, THEN **CHOP** THEM **OFF**.

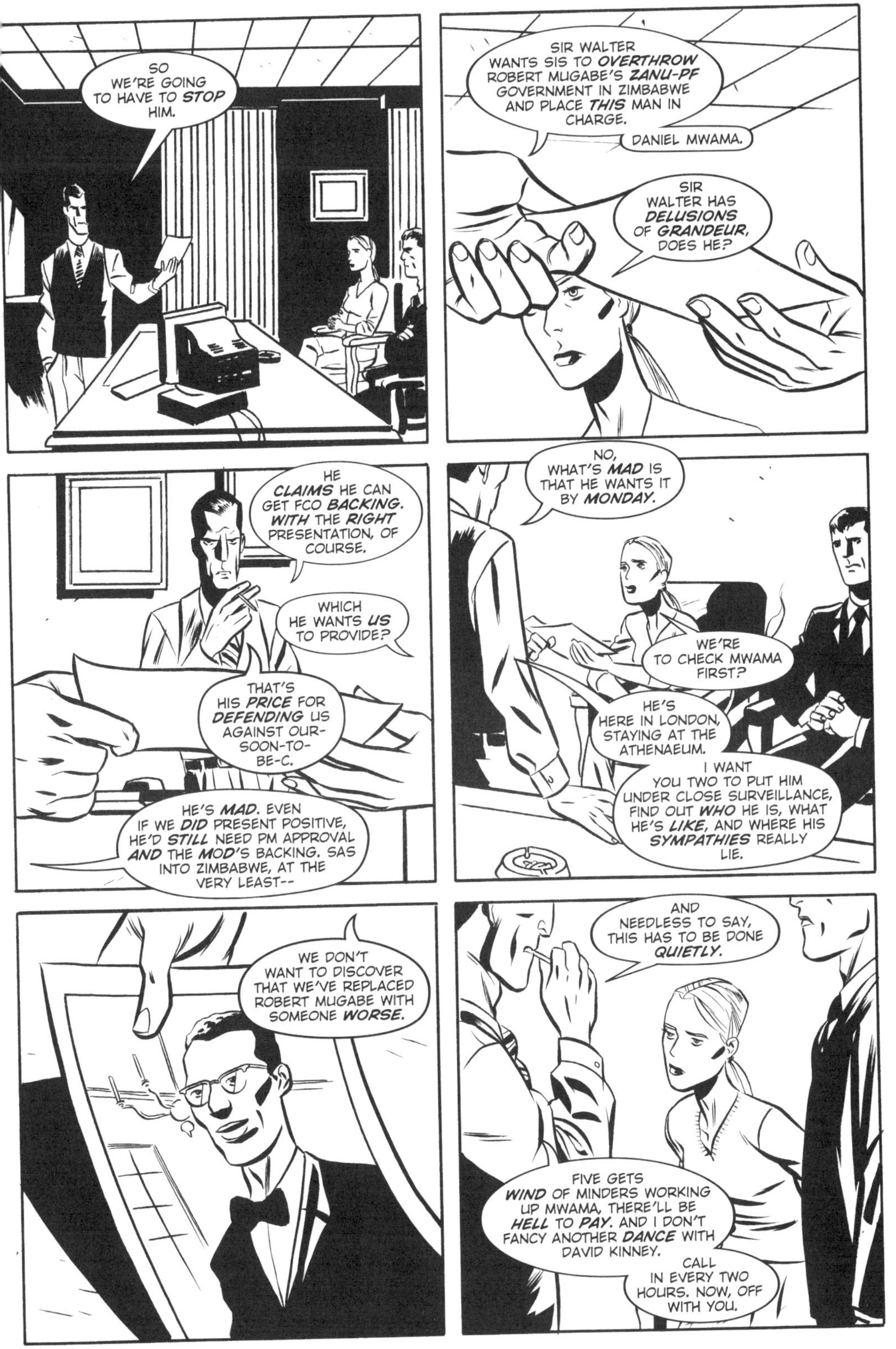
SO WE'RE GOING TO HAVE TO STOP HIM.
SIR WALTER WANTS SIS TO OVERTHROW ROBERT MUGABE'S ZANU-PF GOVERNMENT IN ZIMBABWE AND PLACE THIS MAN IN CHARGE.
DANIEL MWAMA.
SIR WALTER HAS DELUSIONS OF GRANDEUR, DOES HE?
HE CLAIMS HE CAN GET FCO BACKING. WITH THE RIGHT PRESENTATION, OF COURSE.
WHICH HE WANTS US TO PROVIDE?
THAT'S HIS PRICE FOR DEFENDING US AGAINST OUR-SOON-TO-BE-C.
HE'S MAD. EVEN IF WE DID PRESENT POSITIVE, HE'D STILL NEED PM APPROVAL AND THE MOD'S BACKING. SAS INTO ZIMBABWE, AT THE VERY LEAST--
NO, WHAT'S MAD IS THAT HE WANTS IT BY MONDAY.
WE'RE TO CHECK MWAMA FIRST?
HE'S HERE IN LONDON, STAYING AT THE ATHENAEUM.
I WANT YOU TWO TO PUT HIM UNDER CLOSE SURVEILLANCE, FIND OUT WHO HE IS, WHAT HE'S LIKE, AND WHERE HIS SYMPATHIES REALLY LIE.
WE DON'T WANT TO DISCOVER THAT WE'VE REPLACED ROBERT MUGABE WITH SOMEONE WORSE.
AND NEEDLESS TO SAY, THIS HAS TO BE DONE QUIETLY.
FIVE GETS WIND OF MINDERS WORKING UP MWAMA, THERE'LL BE HELL TO PAY. AND I DON'T FANCY ANOTHER DANCE WITH DAVID KINNEY.
CALL IN EVERY TWO HOURS. NOW, OFF WITH YOU.

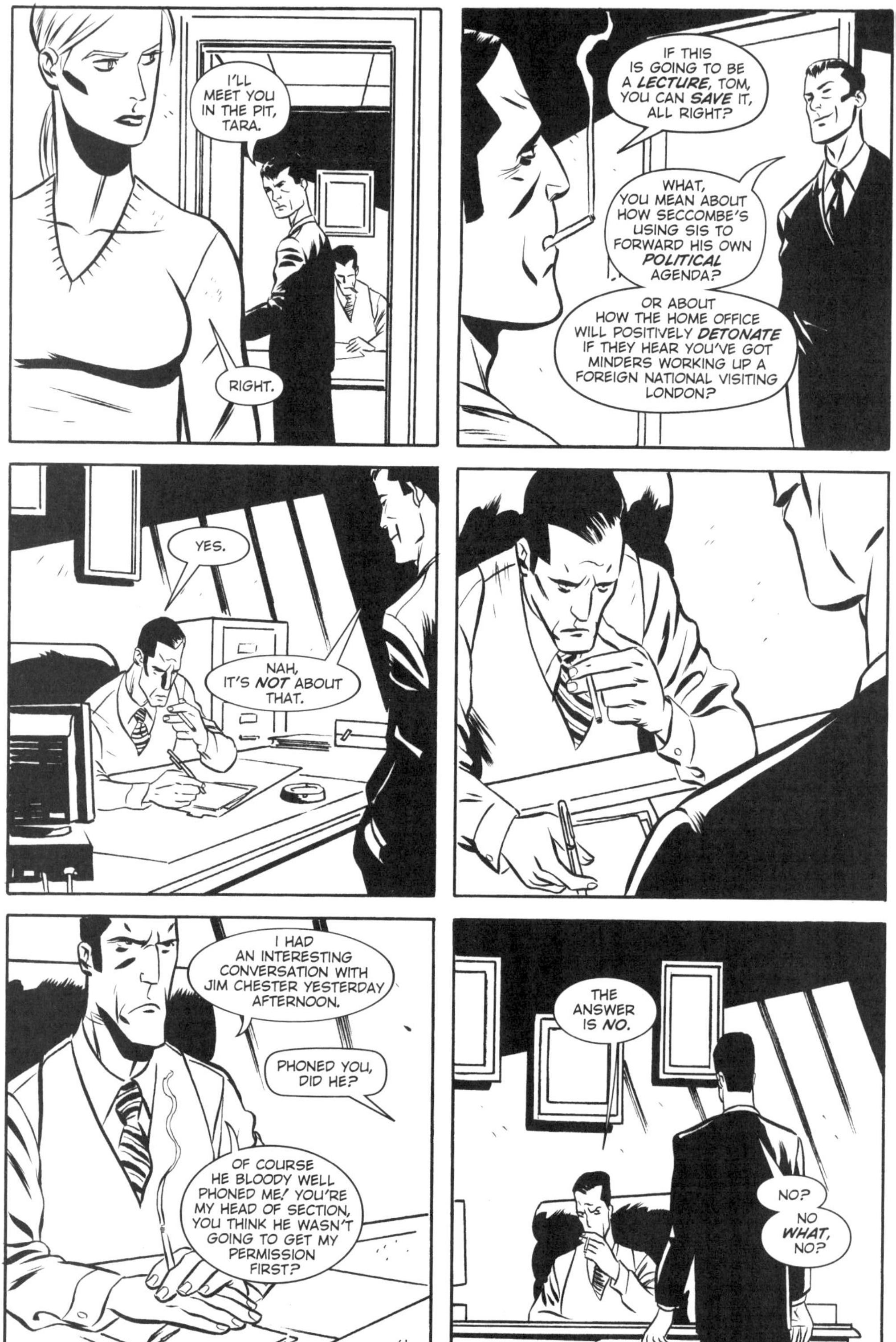
I'LL MEET YOU IN THE PIT, TARA.
RIGHT.
IF THIS IS GOING TO BE A LECTURE, TOM, YOU CAN SAVE IT, ALL RIGHT?
WHAT, YOU MEAN ABOUT HOW SECCOMBE'S USING SIS TO FORWARD HIS OWN POLITICAL AGENDA?
OR ABOUT HOW THE HOME OFFICE WILL POSITIVELY DETONATE IF THEY HEAR YOU'VE GOT MINDERS WORKING UP A FOREIGN NATIONAL VISITING LONDON?
YES.
NAH, IT'S NOT ABOUT THAT.
I HAD AN INTERESTING CONVERSATION WITH JIM CHESTER YESTERDAY AFTERNOON.
PHONED YOU, DID HE?
OF COURSE HE BLOODY WELL PHONED ME! YOU'RE MY HEAD OF SECTION, YOU THINK HE WASN'T GOING TO GET MY PERMISSION FIRST?
THE ANSWER IS NO.
NO?
NO WHAT, NO?

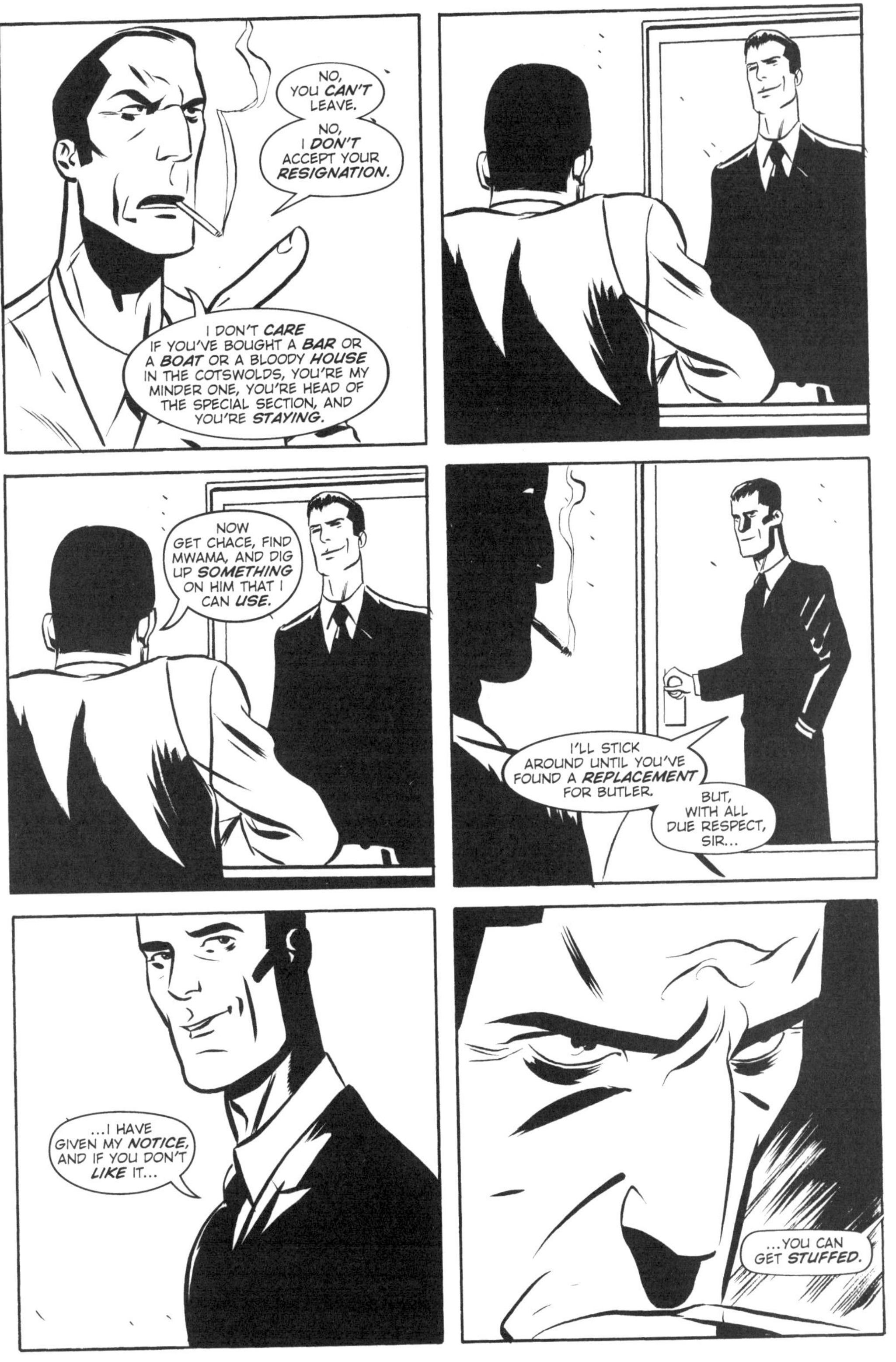
NO, YOU CAN'T LEAVE.
NO, I DON'T ACCEPT YOUR RESIGNATION.
I DON'T CARE IF YOU'VE BOUGHT A BAR OR A BOAT OR A BLOODY HOUSE IN THE COTSWOLDS, YOU'RE MY MINDER ONE, YOU'RE HEAD OF THE SPECIAL SECTION, AND YOU'RE STAYING.
NOW GET CHACE, FIND MWAMA, AND DIG UP SOMETHING ON HIM THAT I CAN USE.
I'LL STICK AROUND UNTIL YOU'VE FOUND A REPLACEMENT FOR BUTLER.
BUT, WITH ALL DUE RESPECT, SIR...
...I HAVE GIVEN MY NOTICE, AND IF YOU DON'T LIKE IT...
...YOU CAN GET STUFFED.

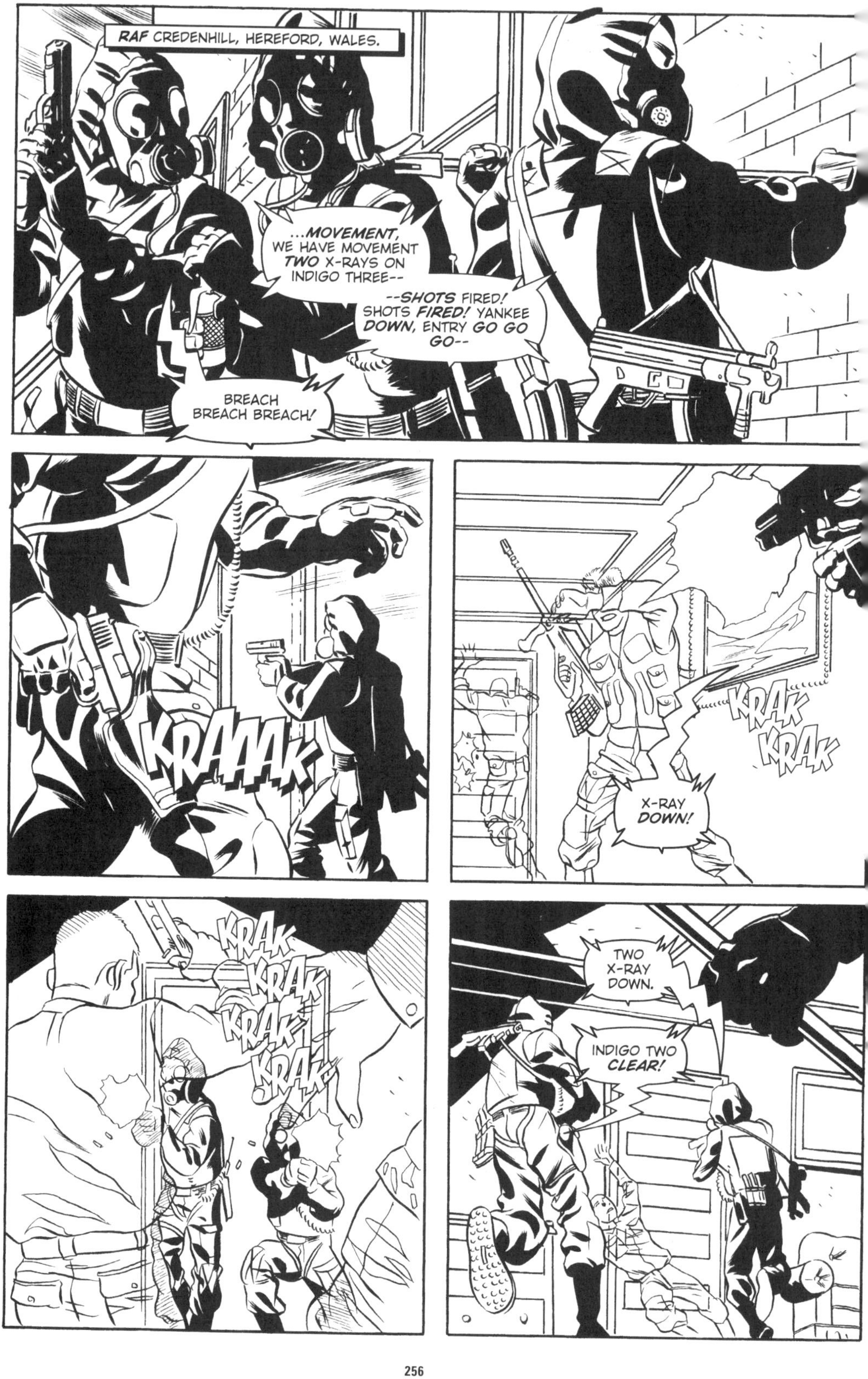
RAF CREDENHILL, HEREFORD, WALES.
...MOVEMENT, WE HAVE MOVEMENT TWO X-RAYS ON INDIGO THREE--
--SHOTS FIRED! SHOTS FIRED! YANKEE DOWN, ENTRY GO GO GO--
BREACH BREACH BREACH!
KRAAAK
KRAK KRAK
X-RAY DOWN!
KRAK KRAK KRAK KRAK
TWO X-RAY DOWN.
INDIGO TWO CLEAR!

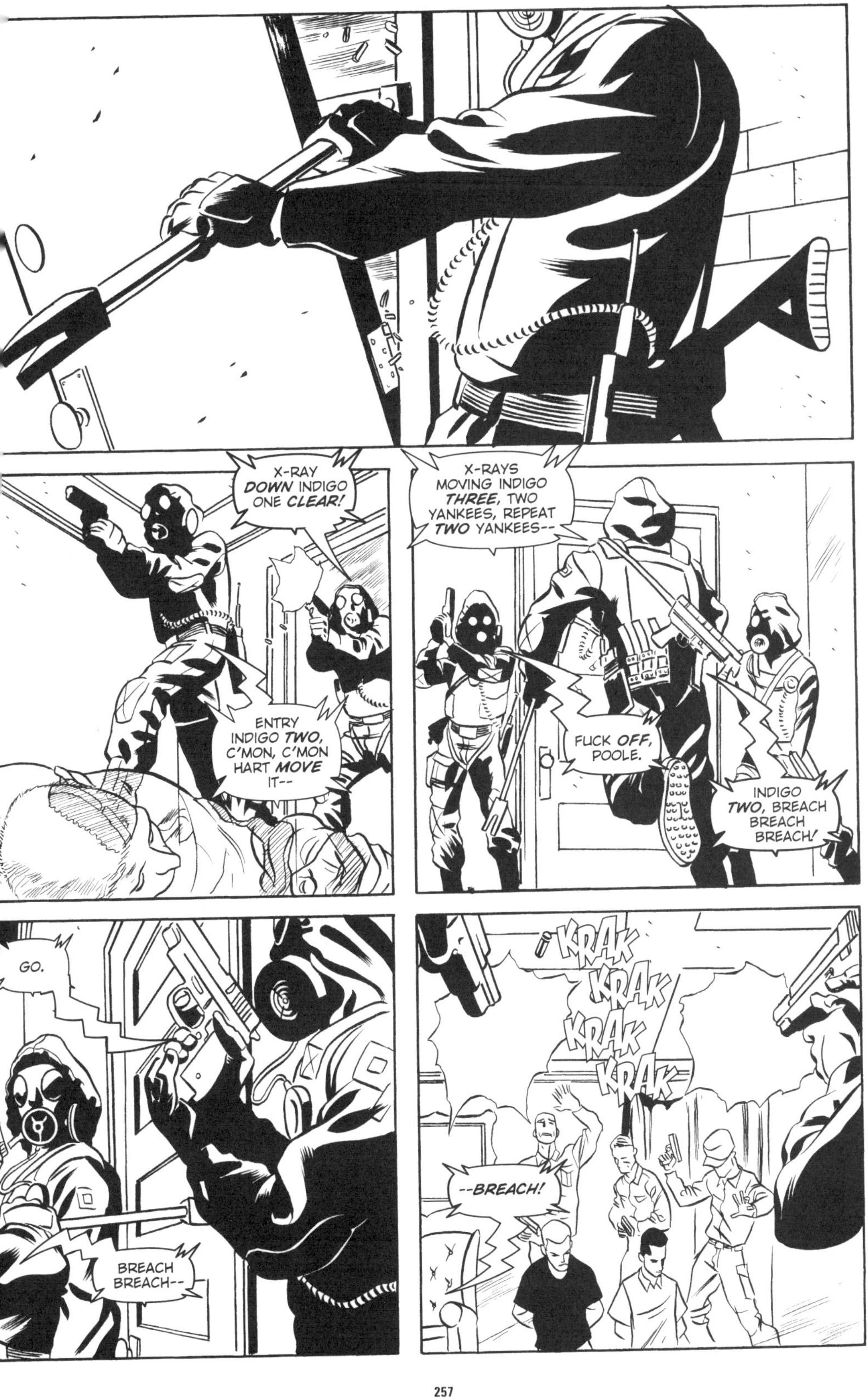
X-RAY DOWN INDIGO ONE CLEAR!
ENTRY INDIGO TWO, C'MON, C'MON HART MOVE IT--
X-RAYS MOVING INDIGO THREE, TWO YANKEES, REPEAT TWO YANKEES--
FUCK OFF, POOLE.
INDIGO TWO, BREACH BREACH BREACH!
GO.
BREACH BREACH--
KRAK KRAK KRAK KRAK
--BREACH!

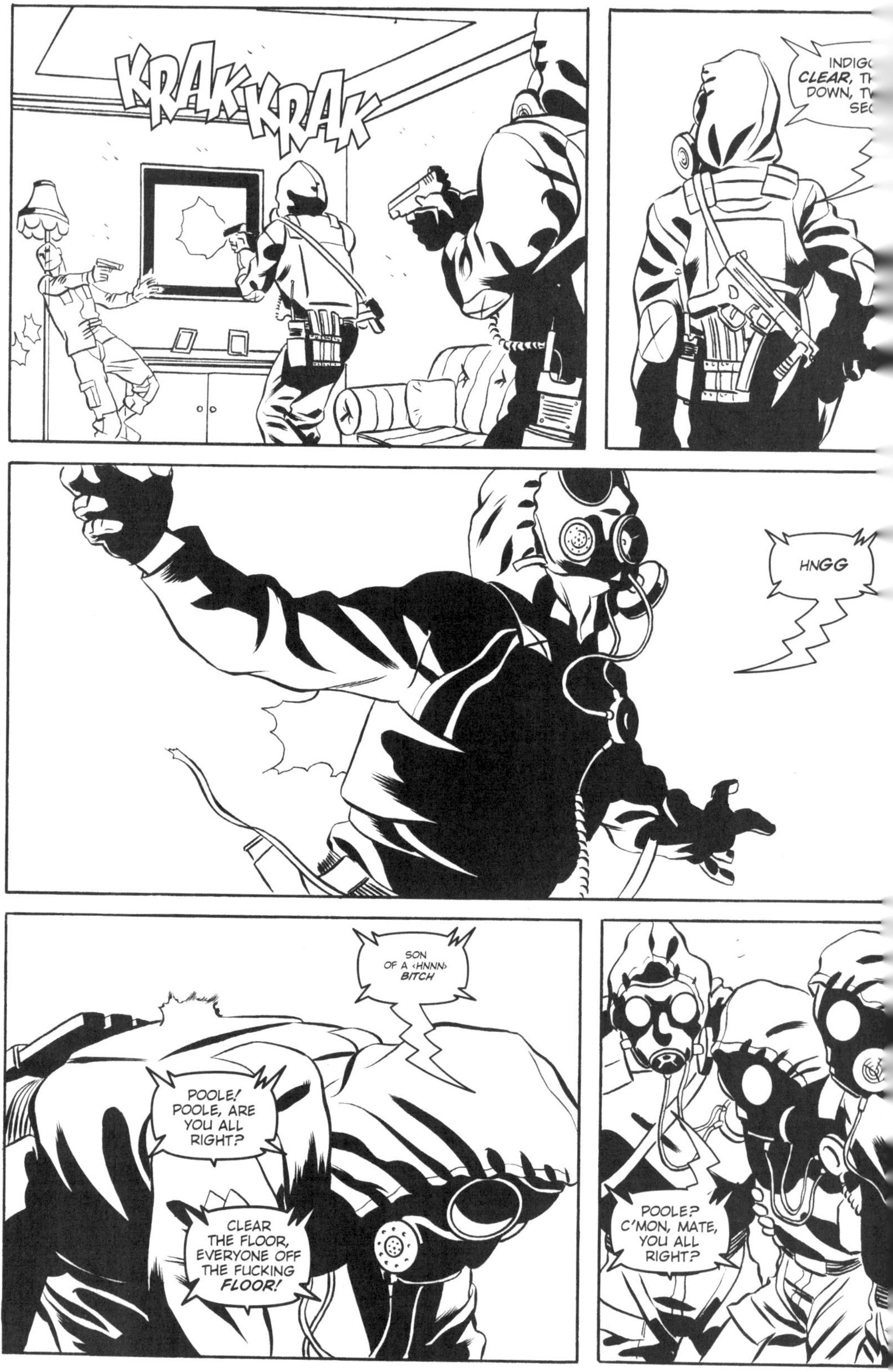
KRAK KRAK
HNGG
SON OF A <HNNN> BITCH
POOLE! POOLE, ARE YOU ALL RIGHT?
CLEAR THE FLOOR, EVERYONE OFF THE FUCKING FLOOR!
POOLE? C'MON, MATE, YOU ALL RIGHT?

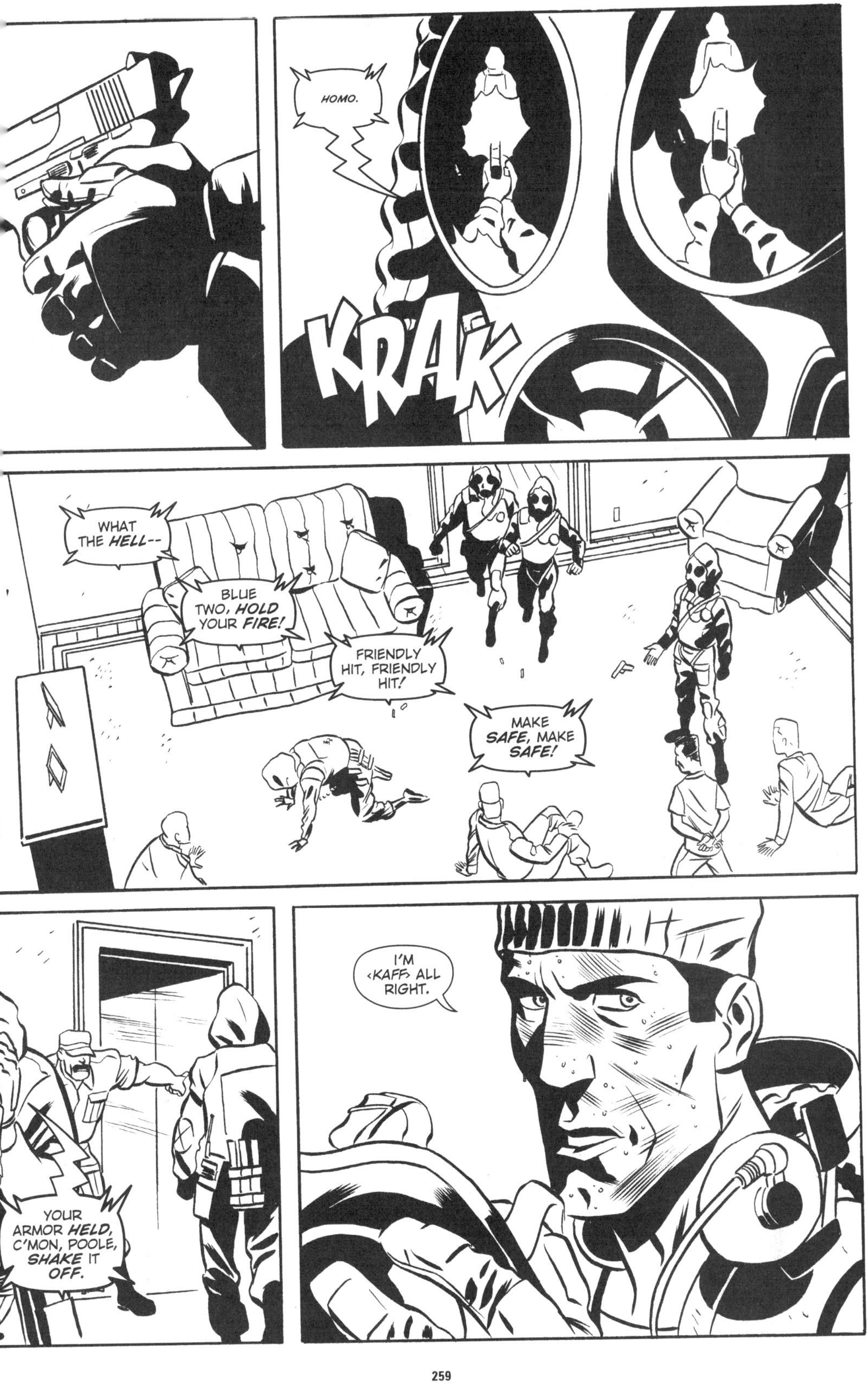
HOMO.
KRAK
WHAT THE HELL--
BLUE TWO, HOLD YOUR FIRE!
FRIENDLY HIT, FRIENDLY HIT!
MAKE SAFE, MAKE SAFE!
YOUR ARMOR HELD, C'MON, POOLE, SHAKE IT OFF.
I'M <KAFF> ALL RIGHT.

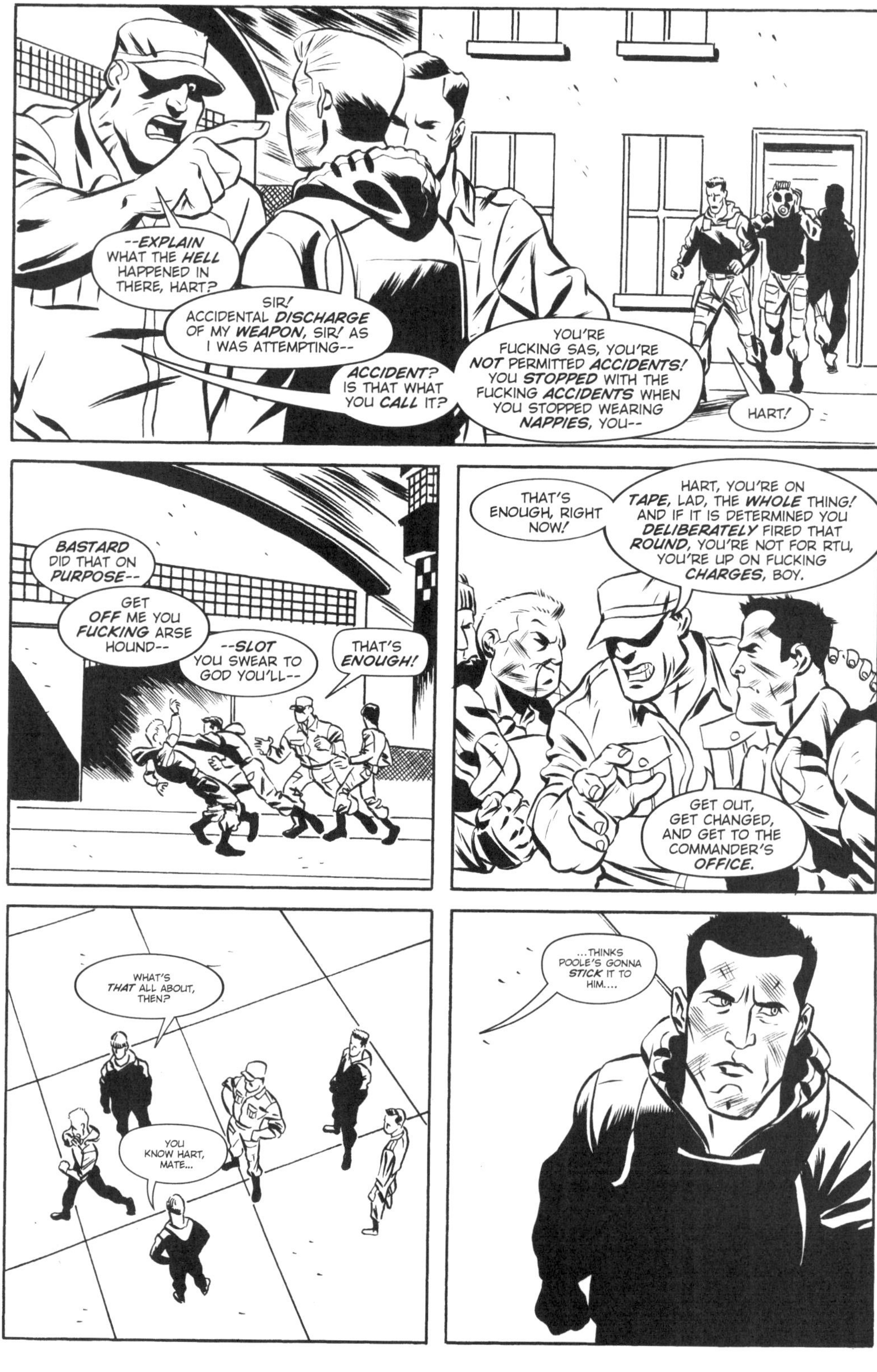
--EXPLAIN WHAT THE HELL HAPPENED IN THERE, HART?
SIR! ACCIDENTAL DISCHARGE OF MY WEAPON, SIR! AS I WAS ATTEMPTING--
ACCIDENT? IS THAT WHAT YOU CALL IT?
YOU'RE FUCKING SAS, YOU'RE NOT PERMITTED ACCIDENTS! YOU STOPPED WITH THE FUCKING ACCIDENTS WHEN YOU STOPPED WEARING NAPPIES, YOU--
HART!
BASTARD DID THAT ON PURPOSE--
GET OFF ME YOU FUCKING ARSE HOUND--
--SLOT YOU SWEAR TO GOD YOU'LL--
THAT'S ENOUGH!
THAT'S ENOUGH, RIGHT NOW!
HART, YOU'RE ON TAPE, LAD, THE WHOLE THING! AND IF IT IS DETERMINED YOU DELIBERATELY FIRED THAT ROUND, YOU'RE NOT FOR RTU, YOU'RE UP ON FUCKING CHARGES, BOY.
GET OUT, GET CHANGED, AND GET TO THE COMMANDER'S OFFICE.
WHAT'S THAT ALL ABOUT, THEN?
YOU KNOW HART, MATE...
...THINKS POOLE'S GONNA STICK IT TO HIM....

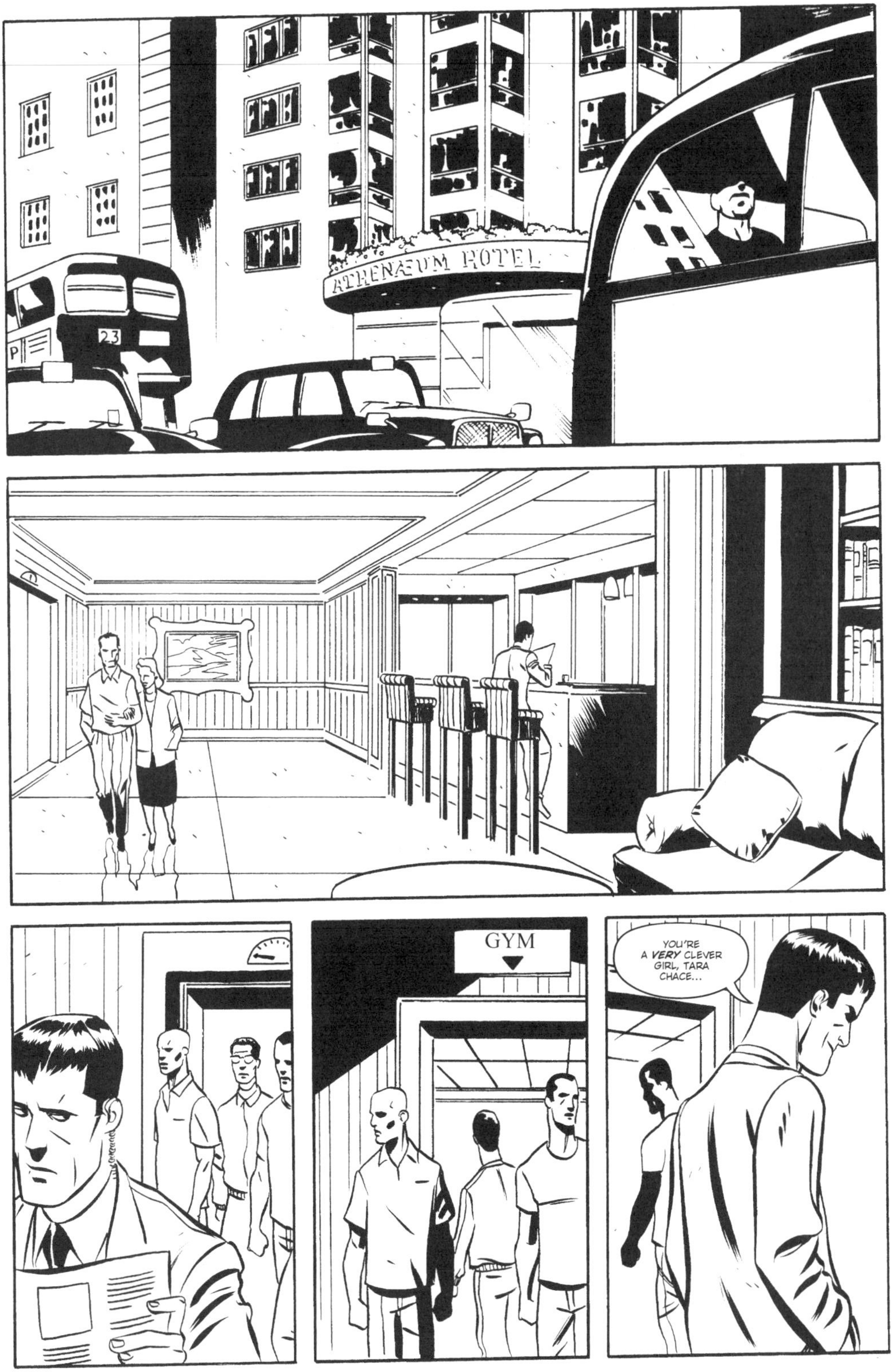
ATHENÆUM HOTEL
23
GYM
YOU'RE A *VERY* CLEVER GIRL, TARA CHACE...

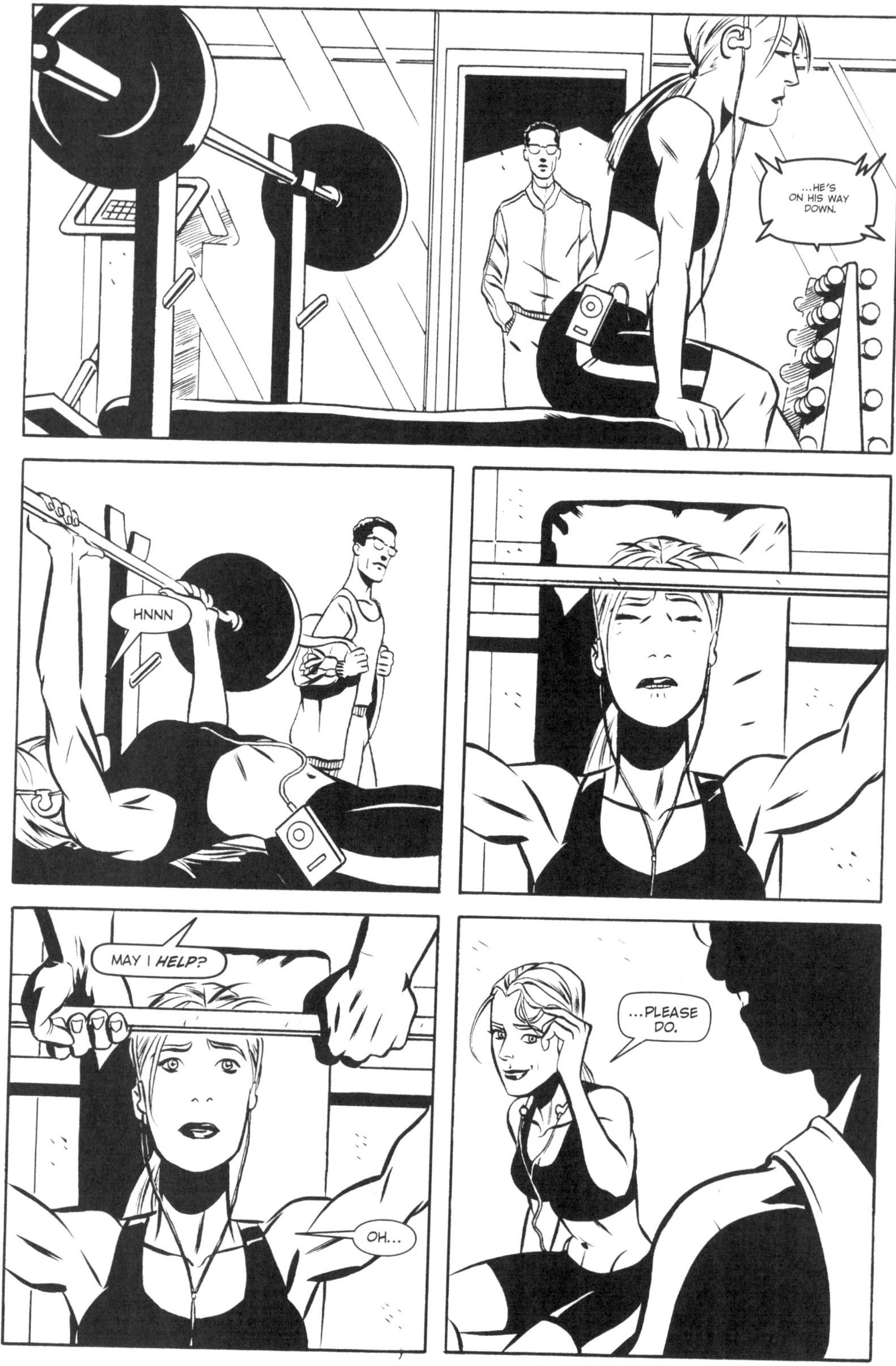
...HE'S ON HIS WAY DOWN.
HNNN
MAY I *HELP?*
OH...
...PLEASE DO.

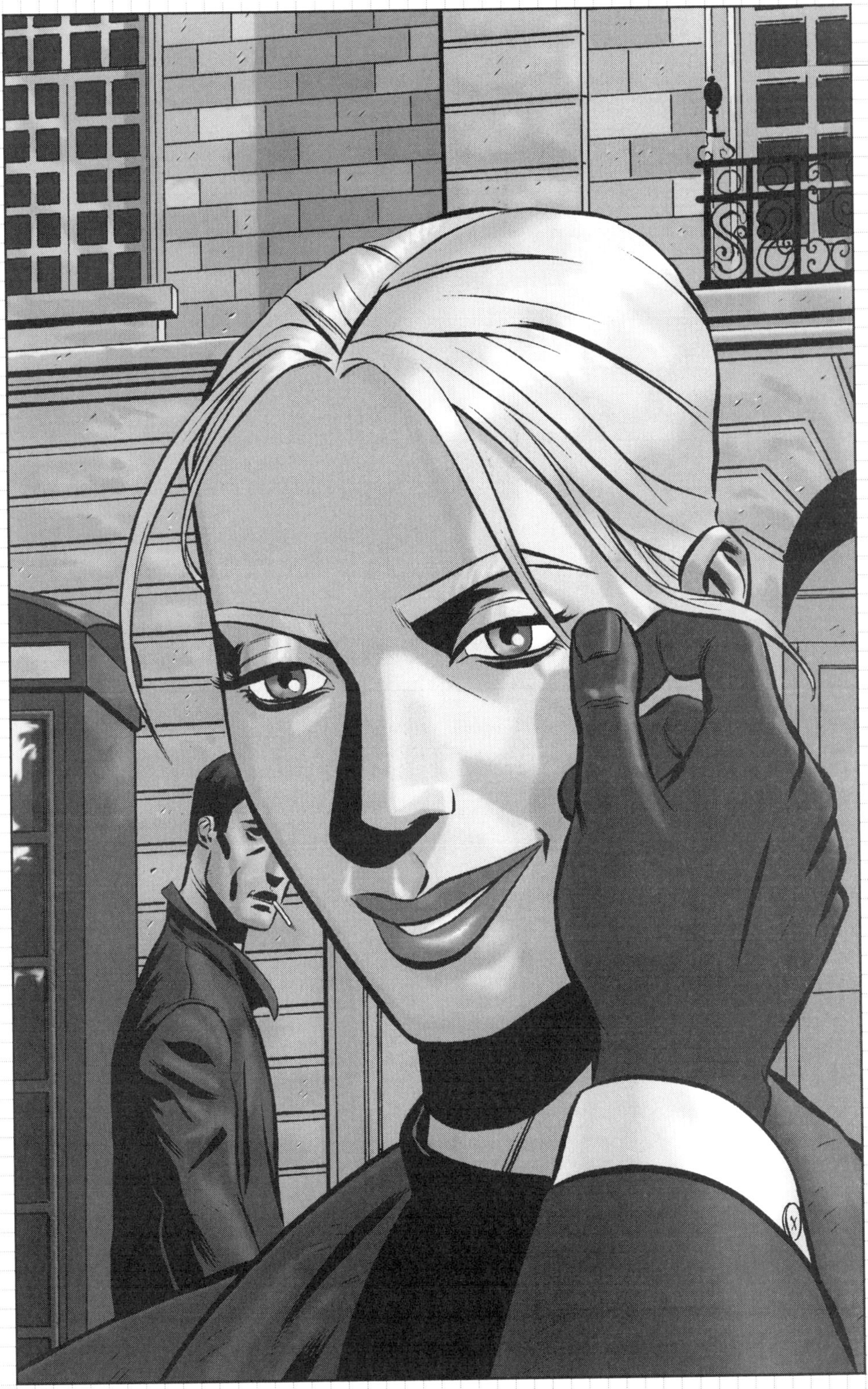

CHAPTER 3

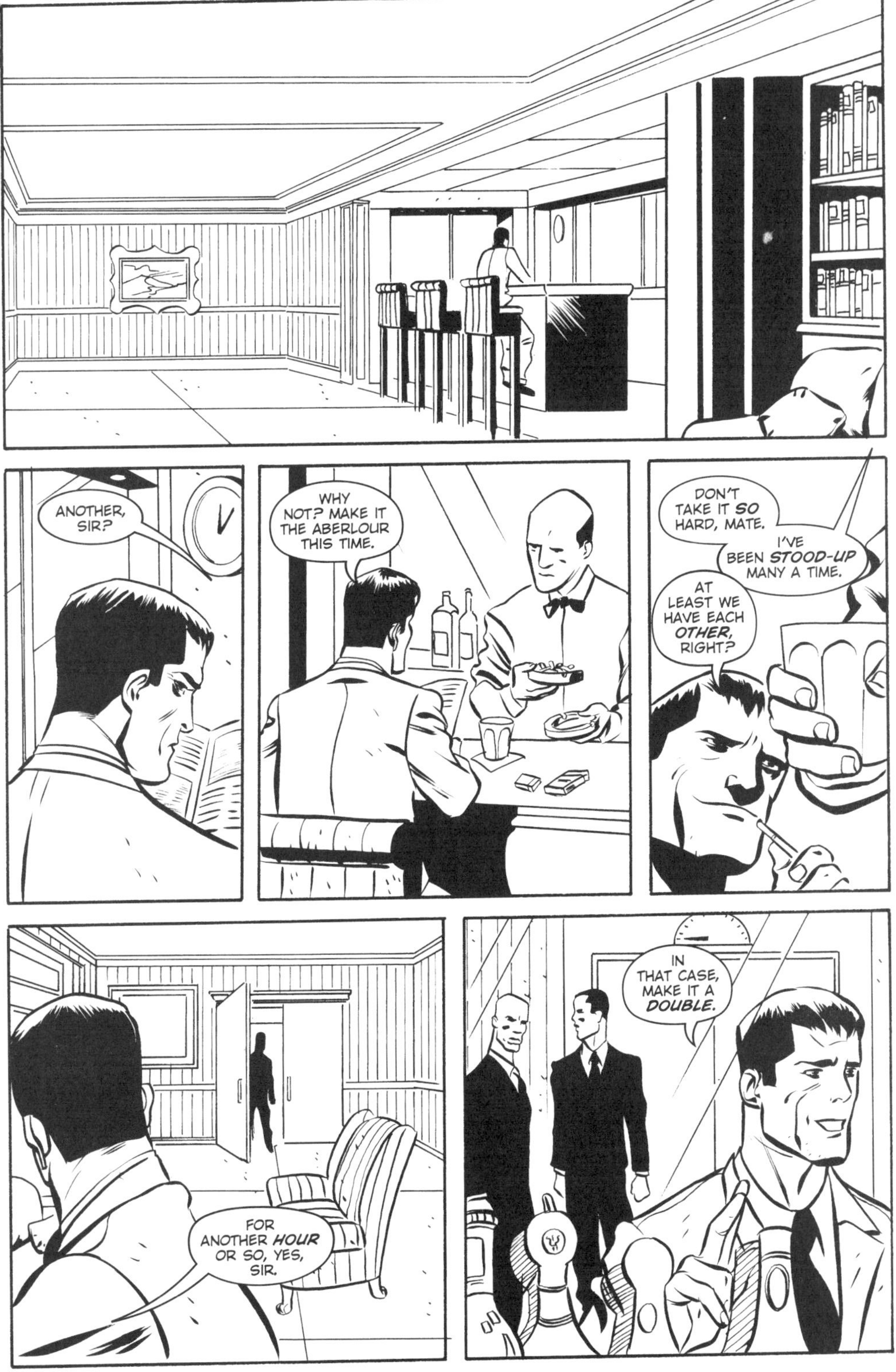
ANOTHER, SIR?
WHY NOT? MAKE IT THE ABERLOUR THIS TIME.
DON'T TAKE IT SO HARD, MATE.
I'VE BEEN STOOD-UP MANY A TIME.
AT LEAST WE HAVE EACH OTHER, RIGHT?
FOR ANOTHER HOUR OR SO, YES, SIR.
IN THAT CASE, MAKE IT A DOUBLE.

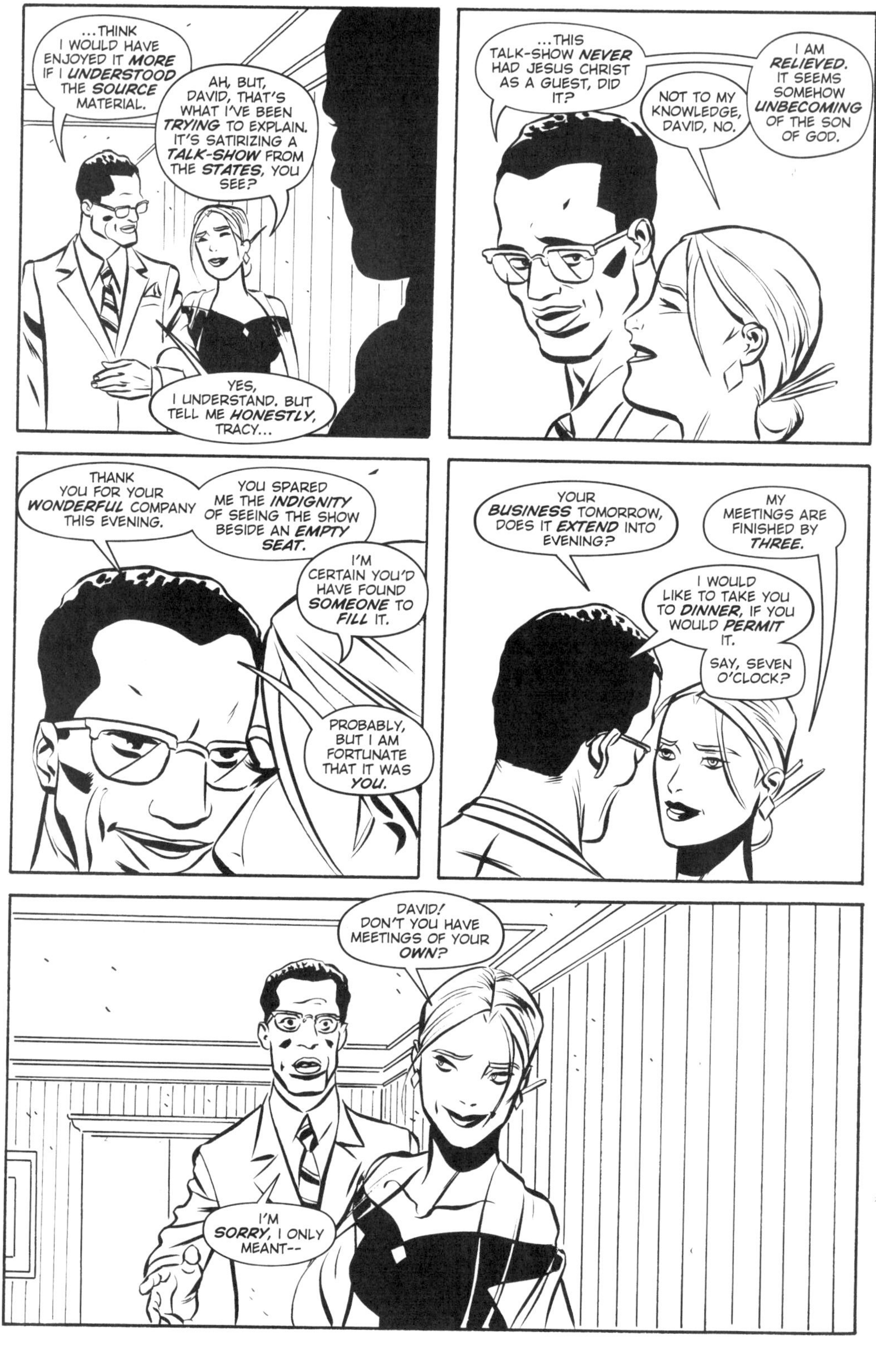
...THINK I WOULD HAVE ENJOYED IT MORE IF I UNDERSTOOD THE SOURCE MATERIAL.
AH, BUT, DAVID, THAT'S WHAT I'VE BEEN TRYING TO EXPLAIN. IT'S SATIRIZING A TALK-SHOW FROM THE STATES, YOU SEE?
YES, I UNDERSTAND. BUT TELL ME HONESTLY, TRACY...
...THIS TALK-SHOW NEVER HAD JESUS CHRIST AS A GUEST, DID IT?
NOT TO MY KNOWLEDGE, DAVID, NO.
I AM RELIEVED. IT SEEMS SOMEHOW UNBECOMING OF THE SON OF GOD.
THANK YOU FOR YOUR WONDERFUL COMPANY THIS EVENING.
YOU SPARED ME THE INDIGNITY OF SEEING THE SHOW BESIDE AN EMPTY SEAT.
I'M CERTAIN YOU'D HAVE FOUND SOMEONE TO FILL IT.
PROBABLY, BUT I AM FORTUNATE THAT IT WAS YOU.
YOUR BUSINESS TOMORROW, DOES IT EXTEND INTO EVENING?
MY MEETINGS ARE FINISHED BY THREE.
I WOULD LIKE TO TAKE YOU TO DINNER, IF YOU WOULD PERMIT IT.
SAY, SEVEN O'CLOCK?
DAVID! DON'T YOU HAVE MEETINGS OF YOUR OWN?
I'M SORRY, I ONLY MEANT--

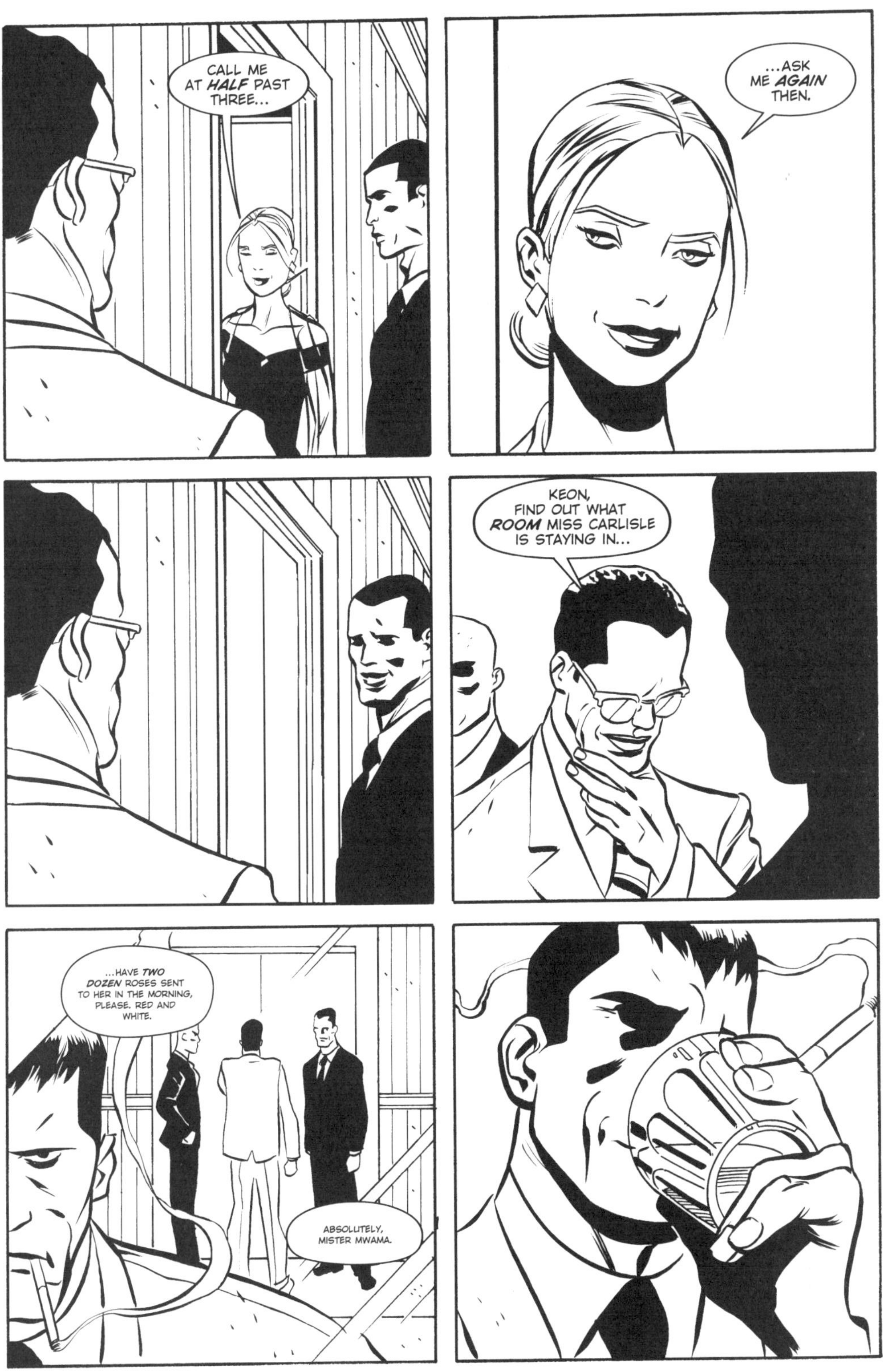
CALL ME AT HALF PAST THREE...
...ASK ME AGAIN THEN.
KEON, FIND OUT WHAT ROOM MISS CARLISLE IS STAYING IN...
...HAVE TWO DOZEN ROSES SENT TO HER IN THE MORNING, PLEASE. RED AND WHITE.
ABSOLUTELY, MISTER MWAMA.

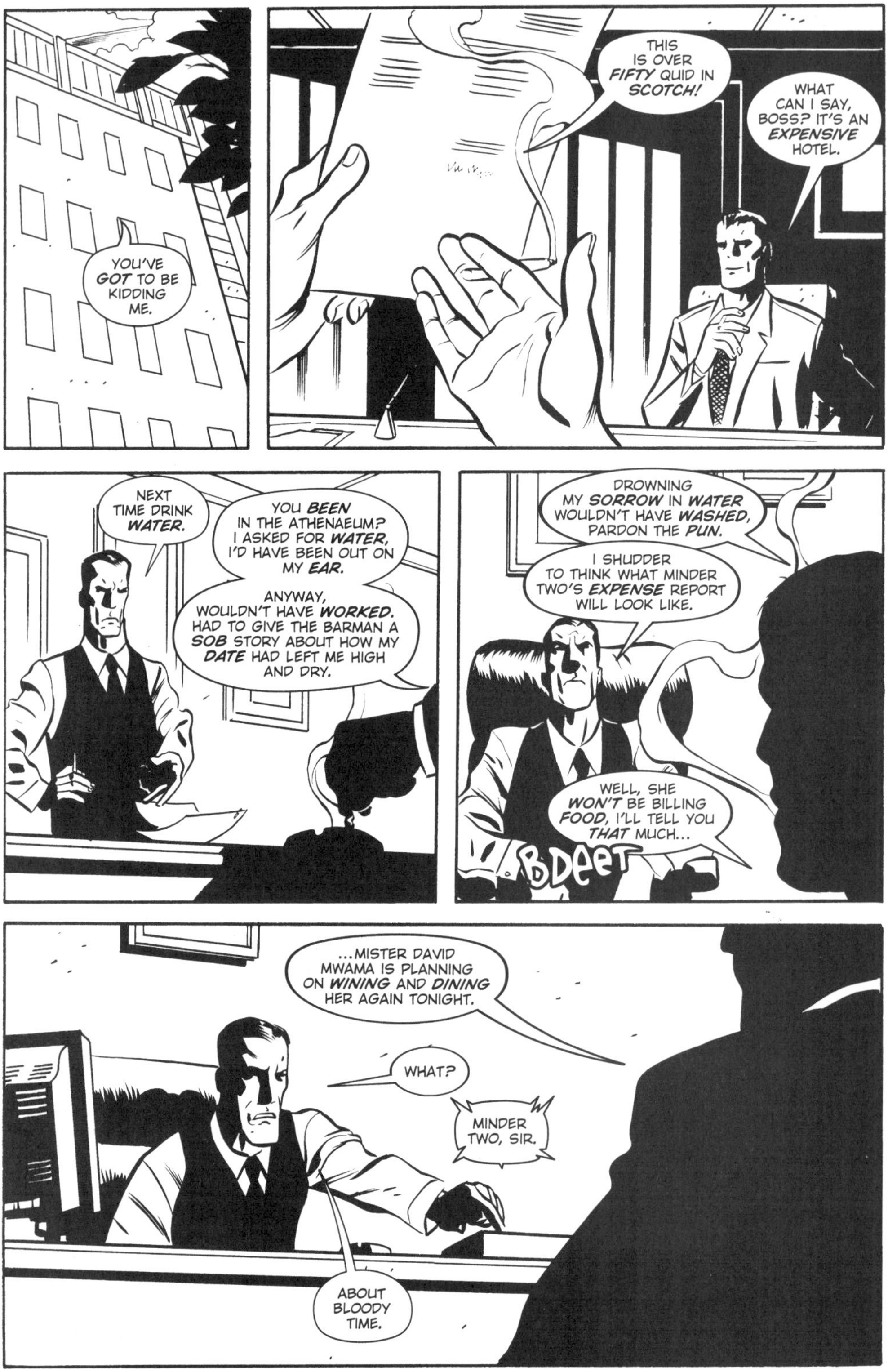
YOU'VE GOT TO BE KIDDING ME.
THIS IS OVER FIFTY QUID IN SCOTCH!
WHAT CAN I SAY, BOSS? IT'S AN EXPENSIVE HOTEL.
NEXT TIME DRINK WATER.
YOU BEEN IN THE ATHENAEUM? I ASKED FOR WATER, I'D HAVE BEEN OUT ON MY EAR.
ANYWAY, WOULDN'T HAVE WORKED. HAD TO GIVE THE BARMAN A SOB STORY ABOUT HOW MY DATE HAD LEFT ME HIGH AND DRY.
DROWNING MY SORROW IN WATER WOULDN'T HAVE WASHED, PARDON THE PUN.
I SHUDDER TO THINK WHAT MINDER TWO'S EXPENSE REPORT WILL LOOK LIKE.
WELL, SHE WON'T BE BILLING FOOD, I'LL TELL YOU THAT MUCH...
BDEET
...MISTER DAVID MWAMA IS PLANNING ON WINING AND DINING HER AGAIN TONIGHT.
WHAT?
MINDER TWO, SIR.
ABOUT BLOODY TIME.

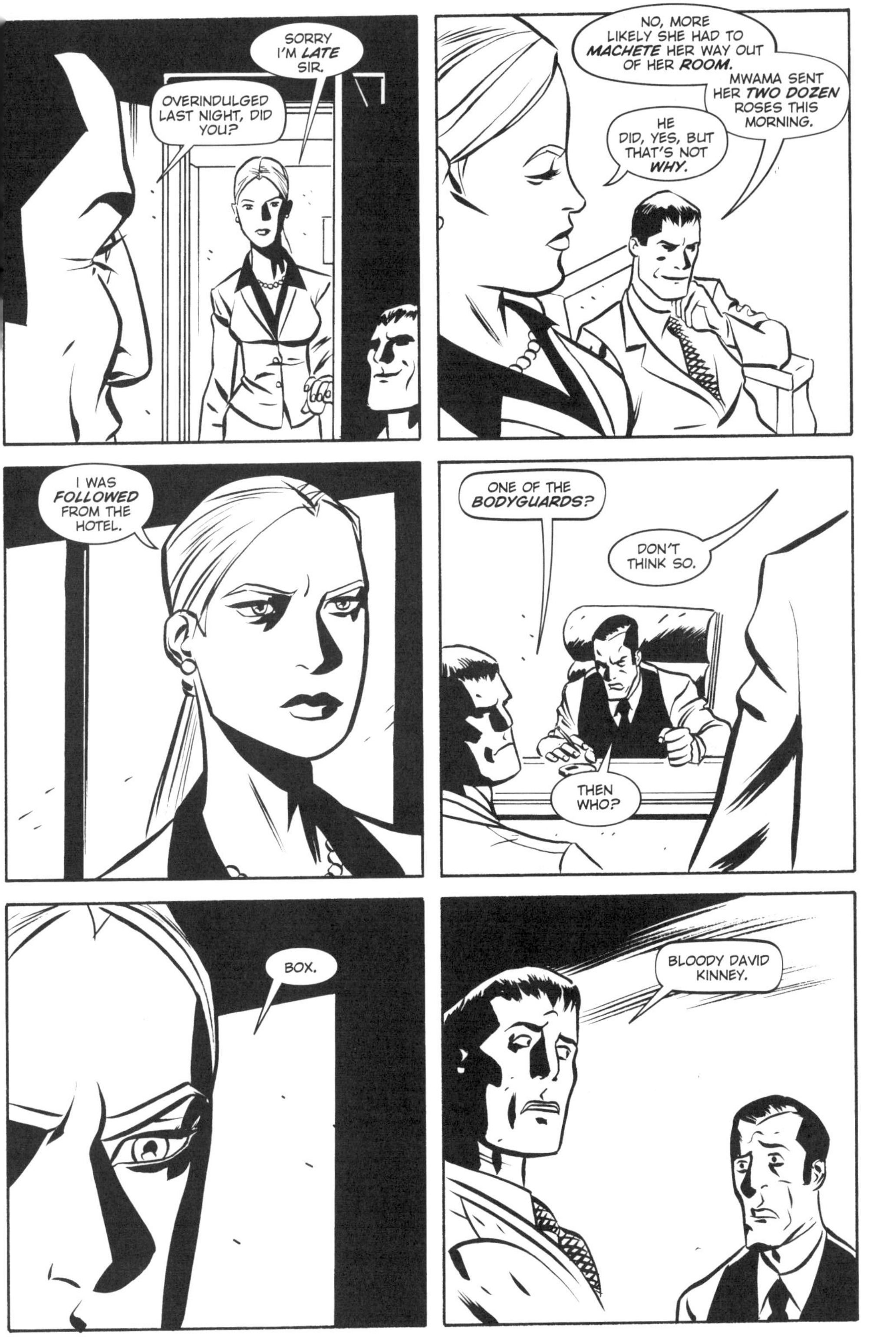
SORRY I'M *LATE* SIR.
OVERINDULGED LAST NIGHT, DID YOU?
NO, MORE LIKELY SHE HAD TO *MACHETE* HER WAY OUT OF HER *ROOM.*
MWAMA SENT HER *TWO DOZEN* ROSES THIS MORNING.
HE DID, YES, BUT THAT'S NOT *WHY.*
I WAS *FOLLOWED* FROM THE HOTEL.
ONE OF THE *BODYGUARDS?*
DON'T THINK SO.
THEN WHO?
BOX.
BLOODY DAVID KINNEY.

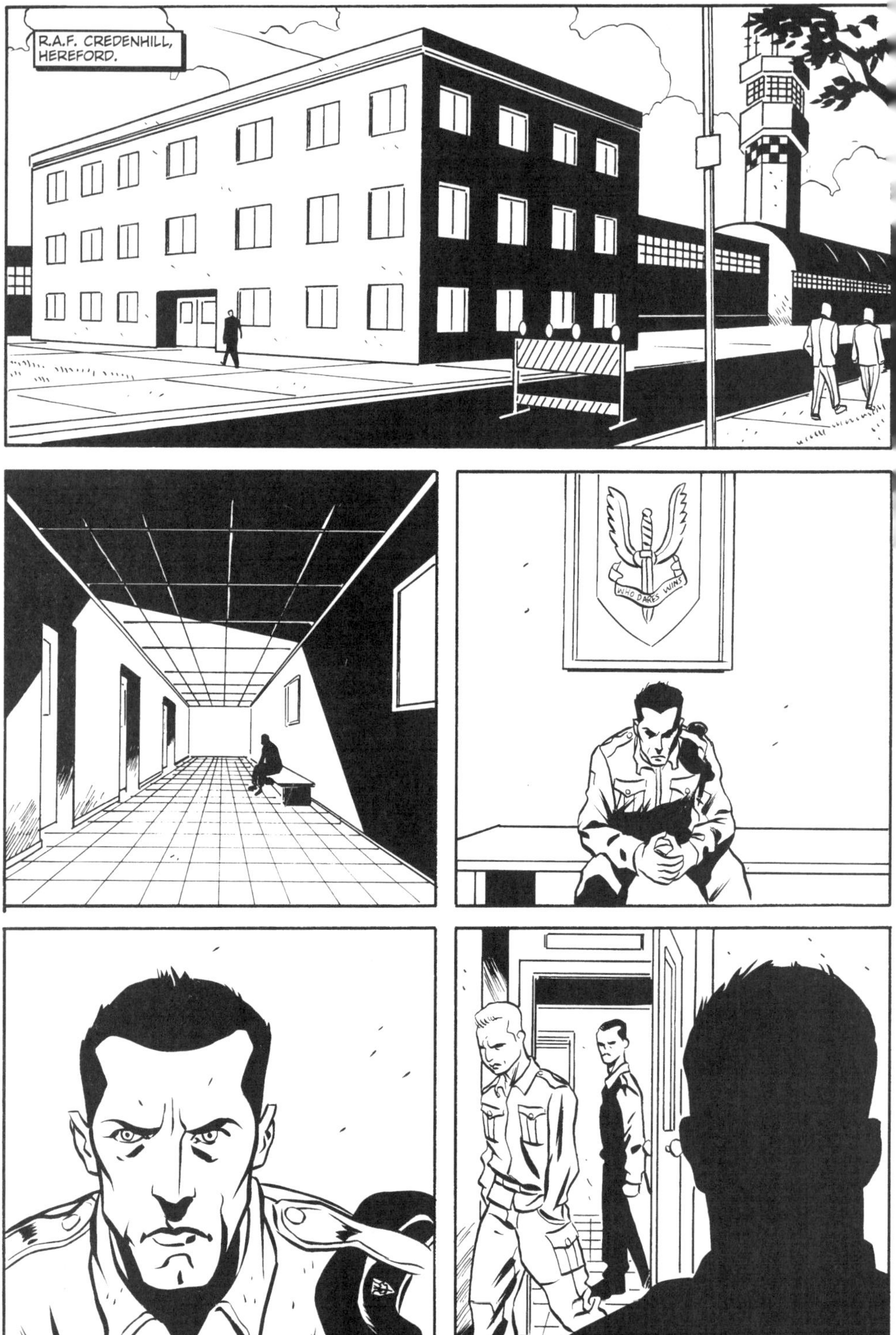
R.A.F. CREDENHILL, HEREFORD.
WHO DARES WINS

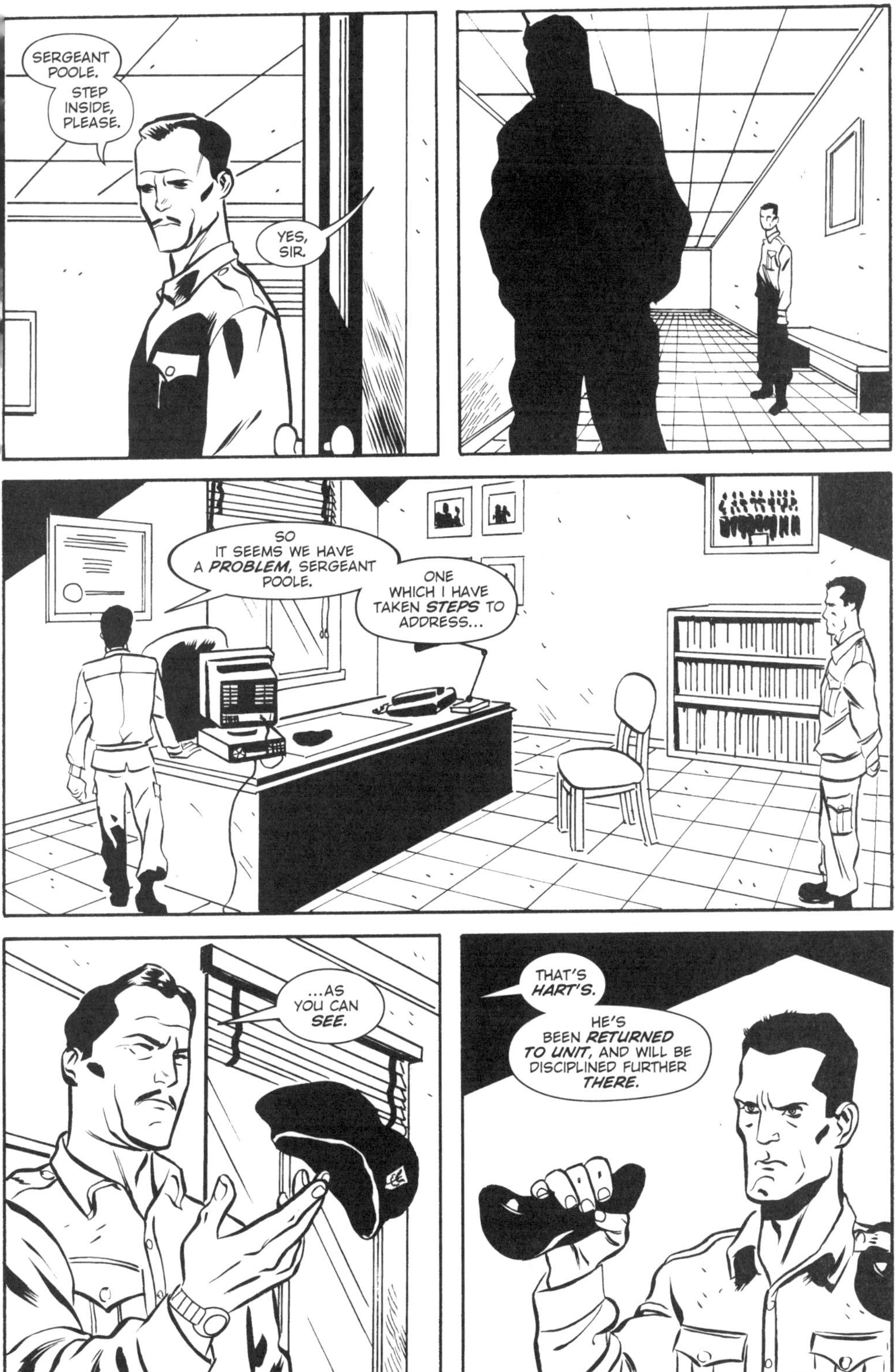
SERGEANT POOLE.
STEP INSIDE, PLEASE.
YES, SIR.
SO IT SEEMS WE HAVE A *PROBLEM*, SERGEANT POOLE.
ONE WHICH I HAVE TAKEN *STEPS* TO ADDRESS...
...AS YOU CAN *SEE*.
THAT'S *HART'S*.
HE'S BEEN *RETURNED TO UNIT*, AND WILL BE DISCIPLINED FURTHER *THERE*.

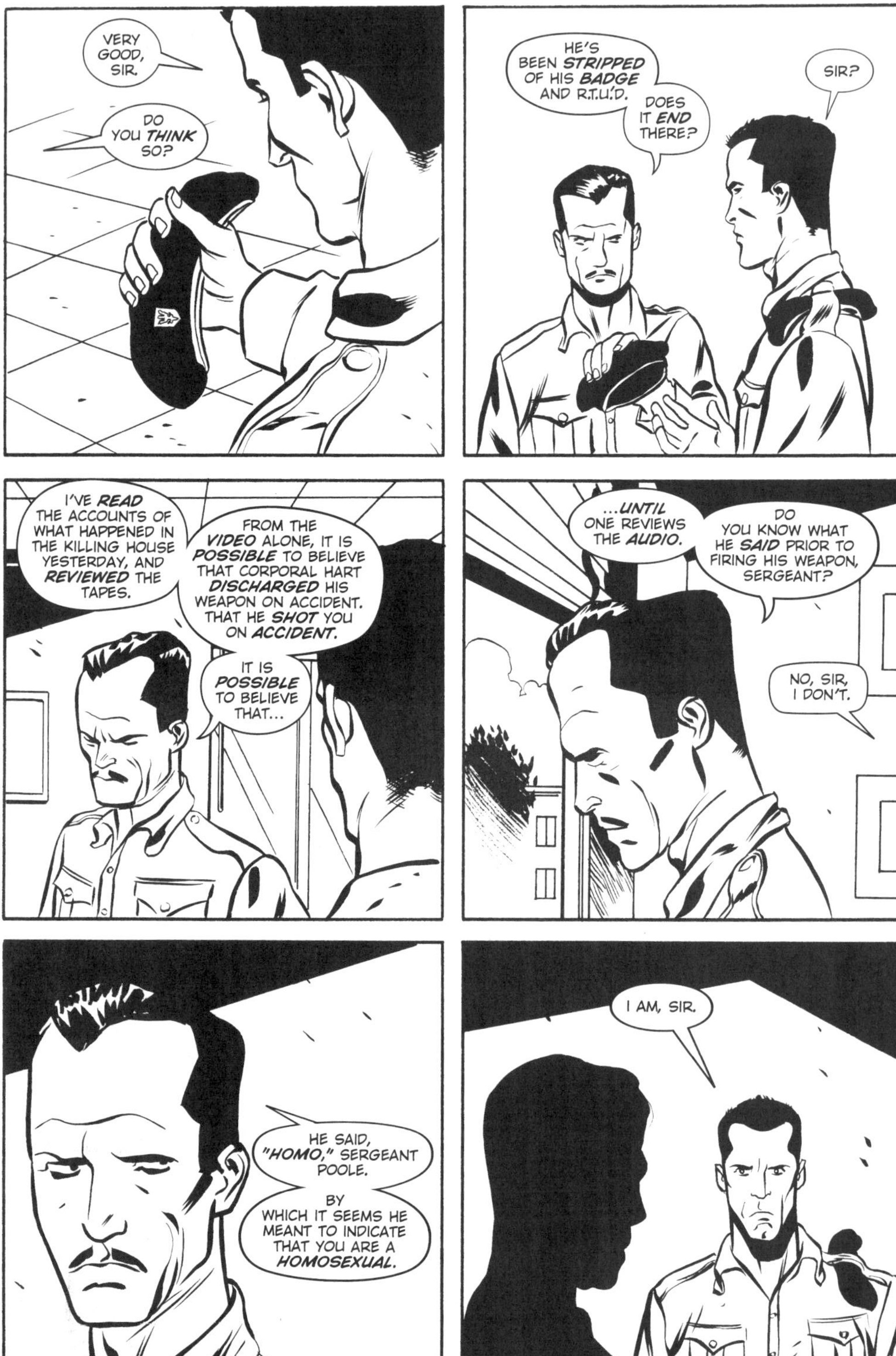
VERY GOOD, SIR.
DO YOU THINK SO?
HE'S BEEN STRIPPED OF HIS BADGE AND R.T.U.'D.
DOES IT END THERE?
SIR?
I'VE READ THE ACCOUNTS OF WHAT HAPPENED IN THE KILLING HOUSE YESTERDAY, AND REVIEWED THE TAPES.
FROM THE VIDEO ALONE, IT IS POSSIBLE TO BELIEVE THAT CORPORAL HART DISCHARGED HIS WEAPON ON ACCIDENT. THAT HE SHOT YOU ON ACCIDENT.
IT IS POSSIBLE TO BELIEVE THAT...
...UNTIL ONE REVIEWS THE AUDIO.
DO YOU KNOW WHAT HE SAID PRIOR TO FIRING HIS WEAPON, SERGEANT?
NO, SIR, I DON'T.
HE SAID, "HOMO," SERGEANT POOLE.
BY WHICH IT SEEMS HE MEANT TO INDICATE THAT YOU ARE A HOMOSEXUAL.
I AM, SIR.

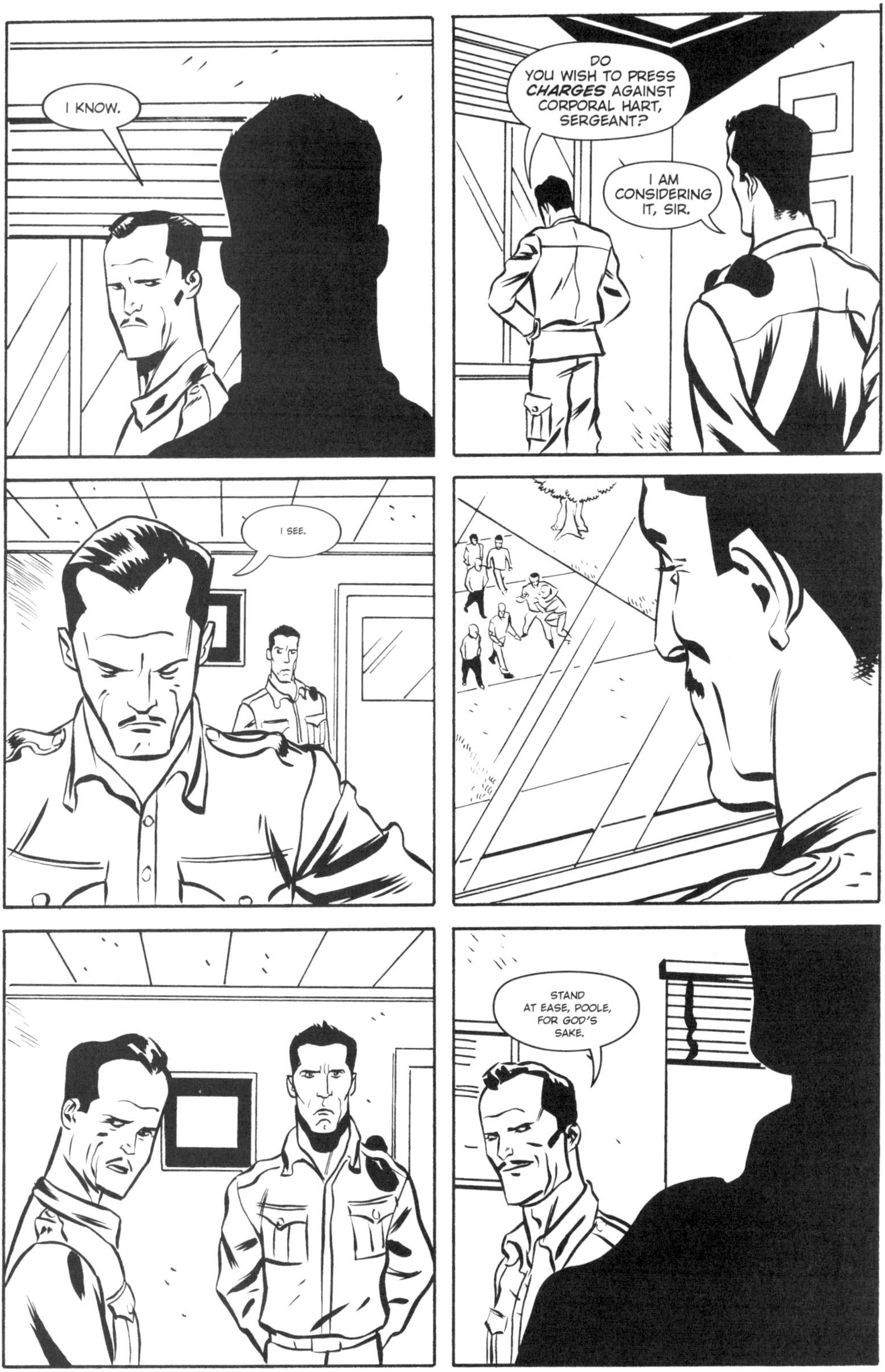
I KNOW.
DO YOU WISH TO PRESS CHARGES AGAINST CORPORAL HART, SERGEANT?
I AM CONSIDERING IT, SIR.
I SEE.
STAND AT EASE, POOLE, FOR GOD'S SAKE.

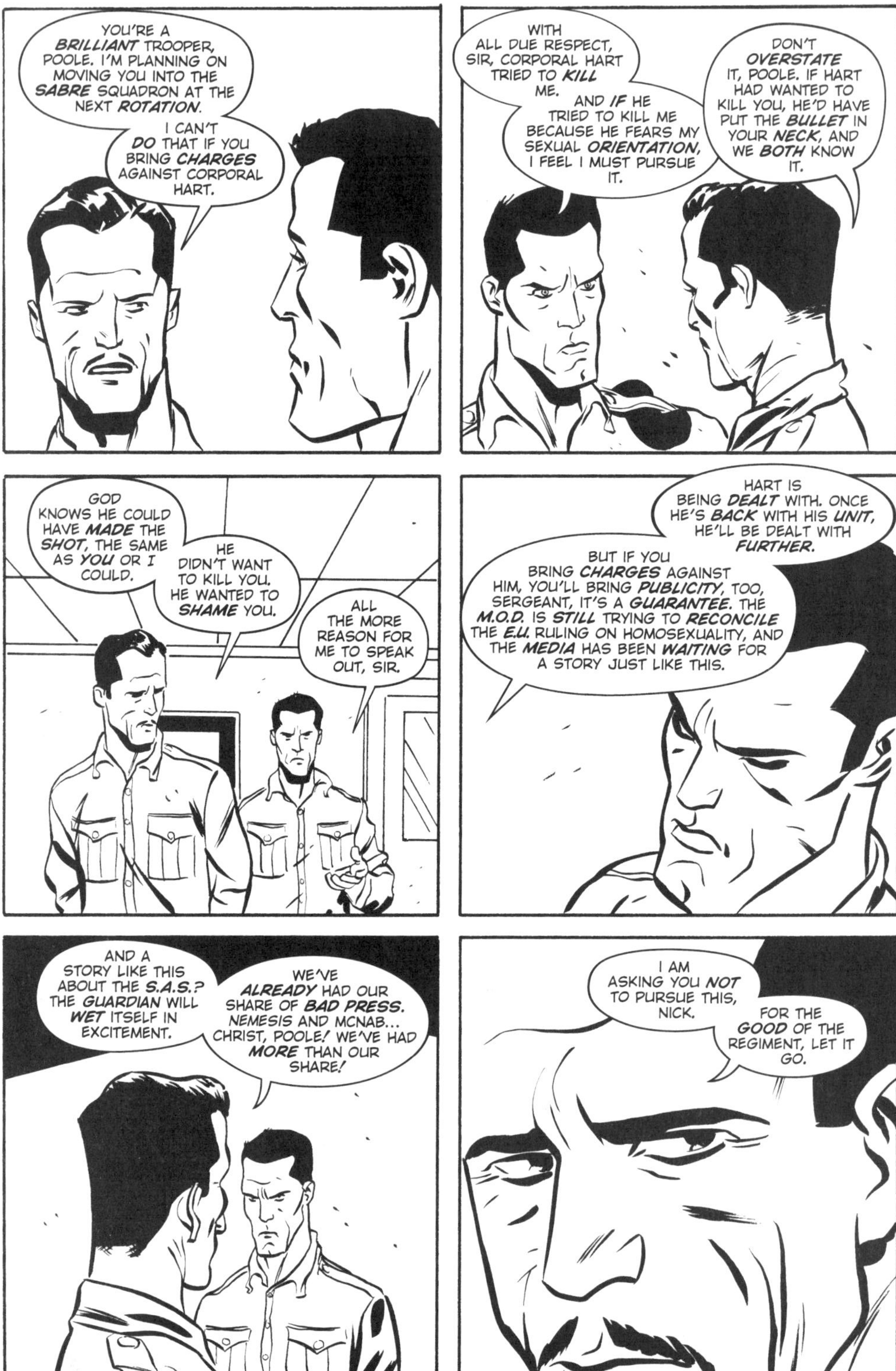
YOU'RE A BRILLIANT TROOPER, POOLE. I'M PLANNING ON MOVING YOU INTO THE SABRE SQUADRON AT THE NEXT ROTATION.
I CAN'T DO THAT IF YOU BRING CHARGES AGAINST CORPORAL HART.
WITH ALL DUE RESPECT, SIR, CORPORAL HART TRIED TO KILL ME.
AND IF HE TRIED TO KILL ME BECAUSE HE FEARS MY SEXUAL ORIENTATION, I FEEL I MUST PURSUE IT.
DON'T OVERSTATE IT, POOLE. IF HART HAD WANTED TO KILL YOU, HE'D HAVE PUT THE BULLET IN YOUR NECK, AND WE BOTH KNOW IT.
GOD KNOWS HE COULD HAVE MADE THE SHOT, THE SAME AS YOU OR I COULD.
HE DIDN'T WANT TO KILL YOU. HE WANTED TO SHAME YOU.
ALL THE MORE REASON FOR ME TO SPEAK OUT, SIR.
HART IS BEING DEALT WITH. ONCE HE'S BACK WITH HIS UNIT, HE'LL BE DEALT WITH FURTHER.
BUT IF YOU BRING CHARGES AGAINST HIM, YOU'LL BRING PUBLICITY, TOO, SERGEANT, IT'S A GUARANTEE. THE M.O.D. IS STILL TRYING TO RECONCILE THE E.U. RULING ON HOMOSEXUALITY, AND THE MEDIA HAS BEEN WAITING FOR A STORY JUST LIKE THIS.
AND A STORY LIKE THIS ABOUT THE S.A.S.? THE GUARDIAN WILL WET ITSELF IN EXCITEMENT.
WE'VE ALREADY HAD OUR SHARE OF BAD PRESS. NEMESIS AND MCNAB... CHRIST, POOLE! WE'VE HAD MORE THAN OUR SHARE!
I AM ASKING YOU NOT TO PURSUE THIS, NICK.
FOR THE GOOD OF THE REGIMENT, LET IT GO.

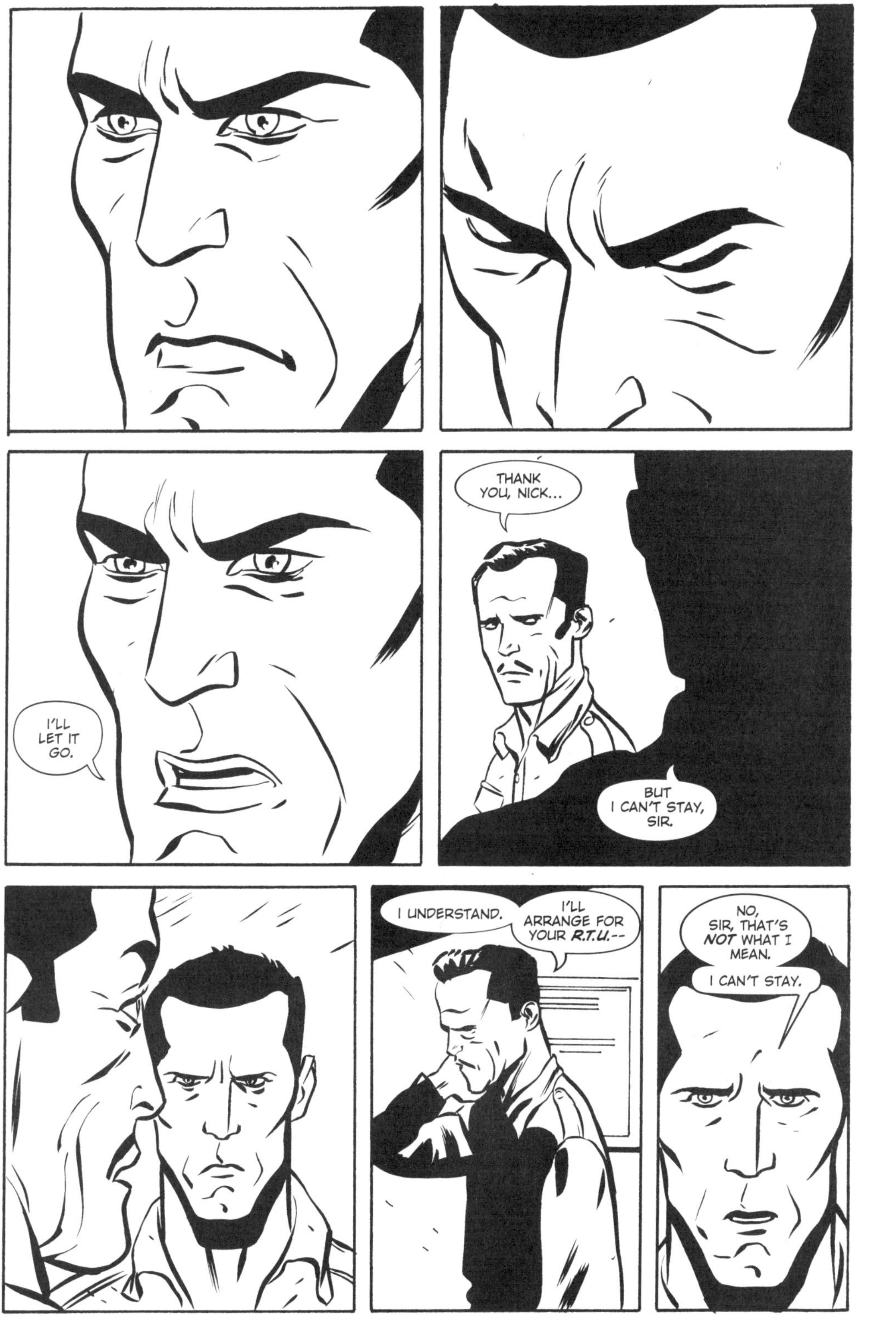
I'LL LET IT GO.
THANK YOU, NICK...
BUT I CAN'T STAY, SIR.
I UNDERSTAND.
I'LL ARRANGE FOR YOUR *R.T.U.*--
NO, SIR, THAT'S ***NOT*** WHAT I MEAN.
I CAN'T STAY.

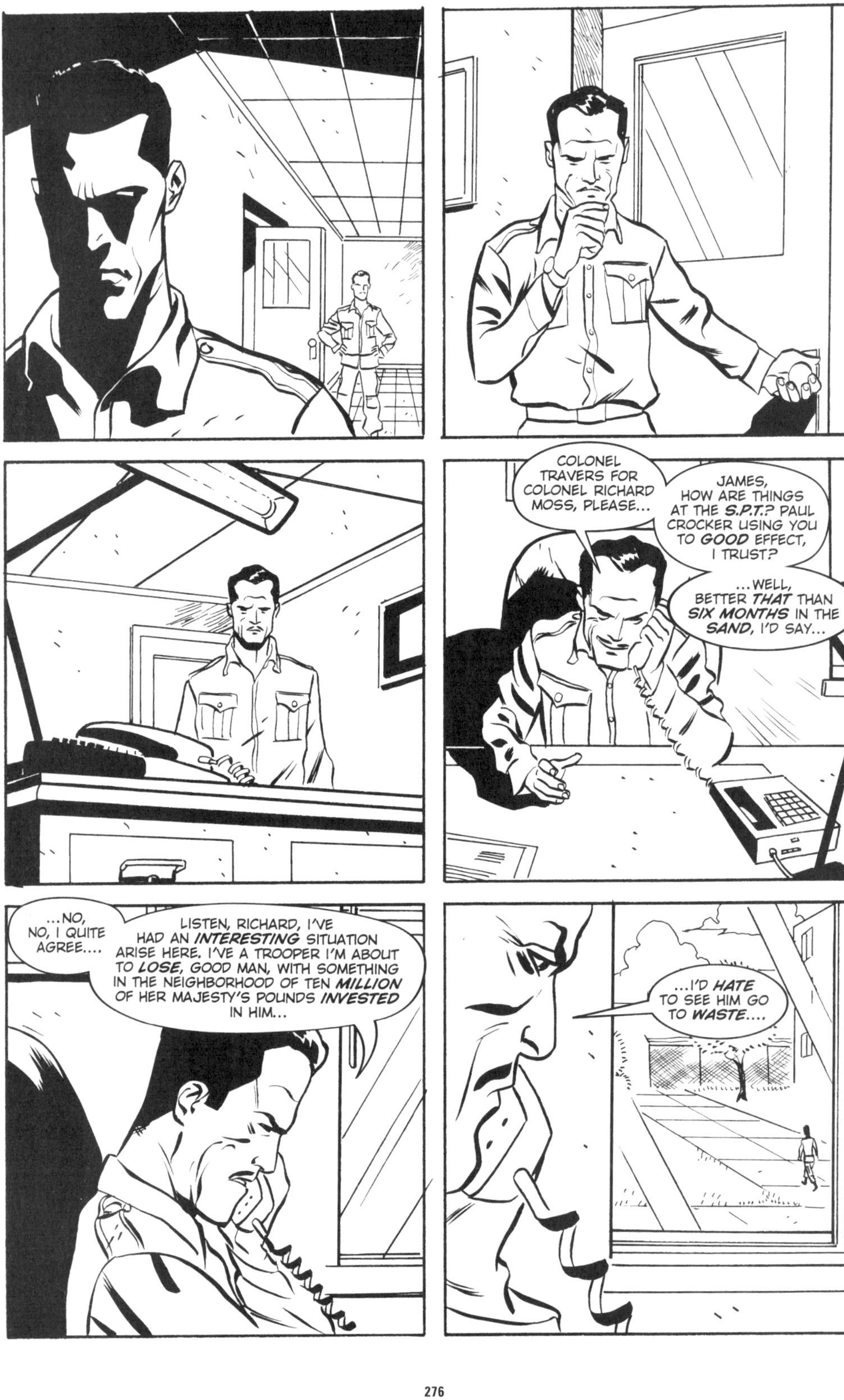
COLONEL TRAVERS FOR COLONEL RICHARD MOSS, PLEASE...
JAMES, HOW ARE THINGS AT THE S.P.T.? PAUL CROCKER USING YOU TO GOOD EFFECT, I TRUST?
...WELL, BETTER THAT THAN SIX MONTHS IN THE SAND, I'D SAY...
...NO, NO, I QUITE AGREE....
LISTEN, RICHARD, I'VE HAD AN INTERESTING SITUATION ARISE HERE. I'VE A TROOPER I'M ABOUT TO LOSE, GOOD MAN, WITH SOMETHING IN THE NEIGHBORHOOD OF TEN MILLION OF HER MAJESTY'S POUNDS INVESTED IN HIM...
...I'D HATE TO SEE HIM GO TO WASTE....

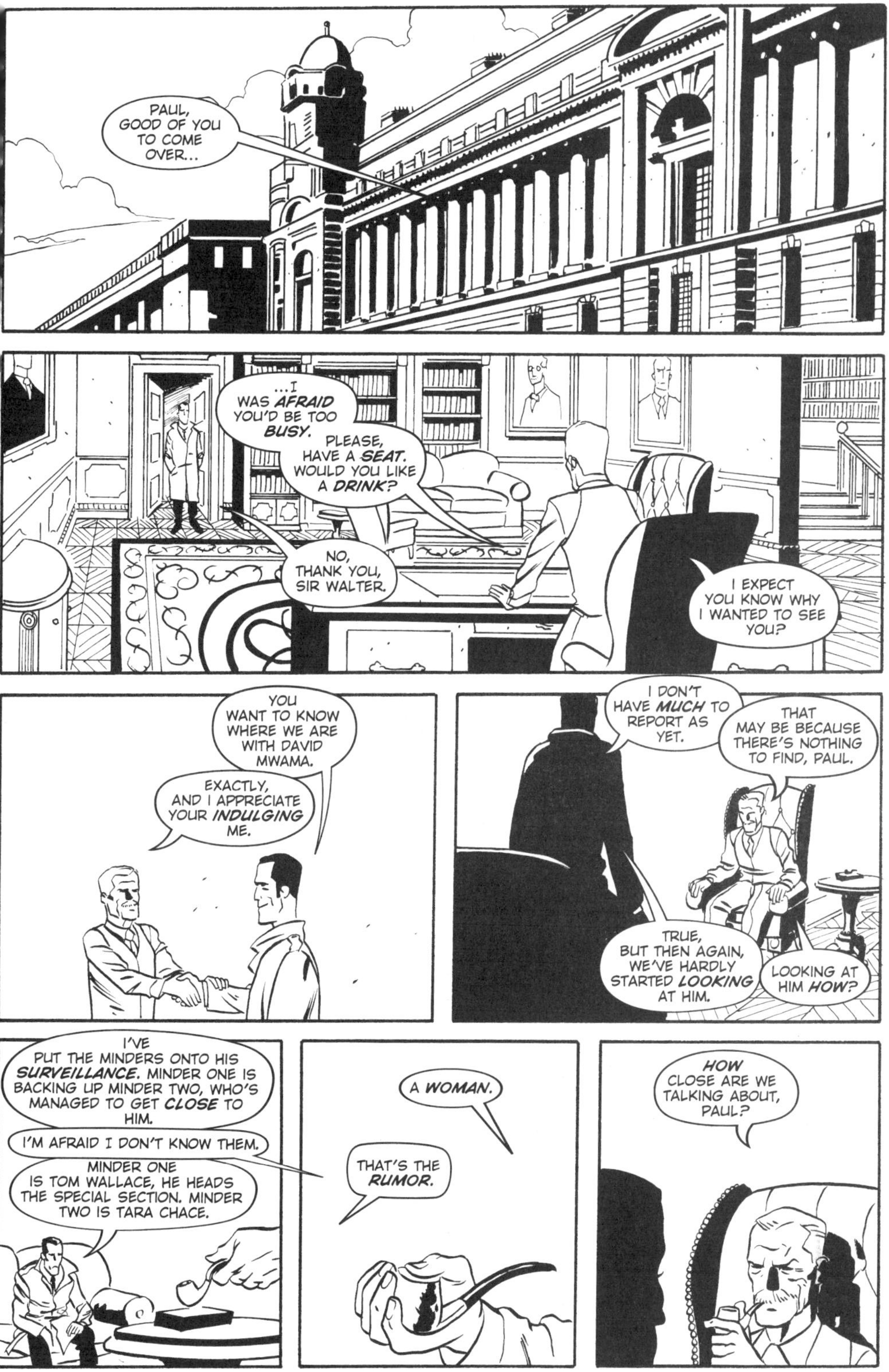

PAUL, GOOD OF YOU TO COME OVER...
...I WAS AFRAID YOU'D BE TOO BUSY.
PLEASE, HAVE A SEAT. WOULD YOU LIKE A DRINK?
NO, THANK YOU, SIR WALTER.
I EXPECT YOU KNOW WHY I WANTED TO SEE YOU?
YOU WANT TO KNOW WHERE WE ARE WITH DAVID MWAMA.
EXACTLY, AND I APPRECIATE YOUR INDULGING ME.
I DON'T HAVE MUCH TO REPORT AS YET.
THAT MAY BE BECAUSE THERE'S NOTHING TO FIND, PAUL.
TRUE, BUT THEN AGAIN, WE'VE HARDLY STARTED LOOKING AT HIM.
LOOKING AT HIM HOW?
I'VE PUT THE MINDERS ONTO HIS SURVEILLANCE. MINDER ONE IS BACKING UP MINDER TWO, WHO'S MANAGED TO GET CLOSE TO HIM.
I'M AFRAID I DON'T KNOW THEM.
MINDER ONE IS TOM WALLACE, HE HEADS THE SPECIAL SECTION. MINDER TWO IS TARA CHACE.
A WOMAN.
THAT'S THE RUMOR.
HOW CLOSE ARE WE TALKING ABOUT, PAUL?

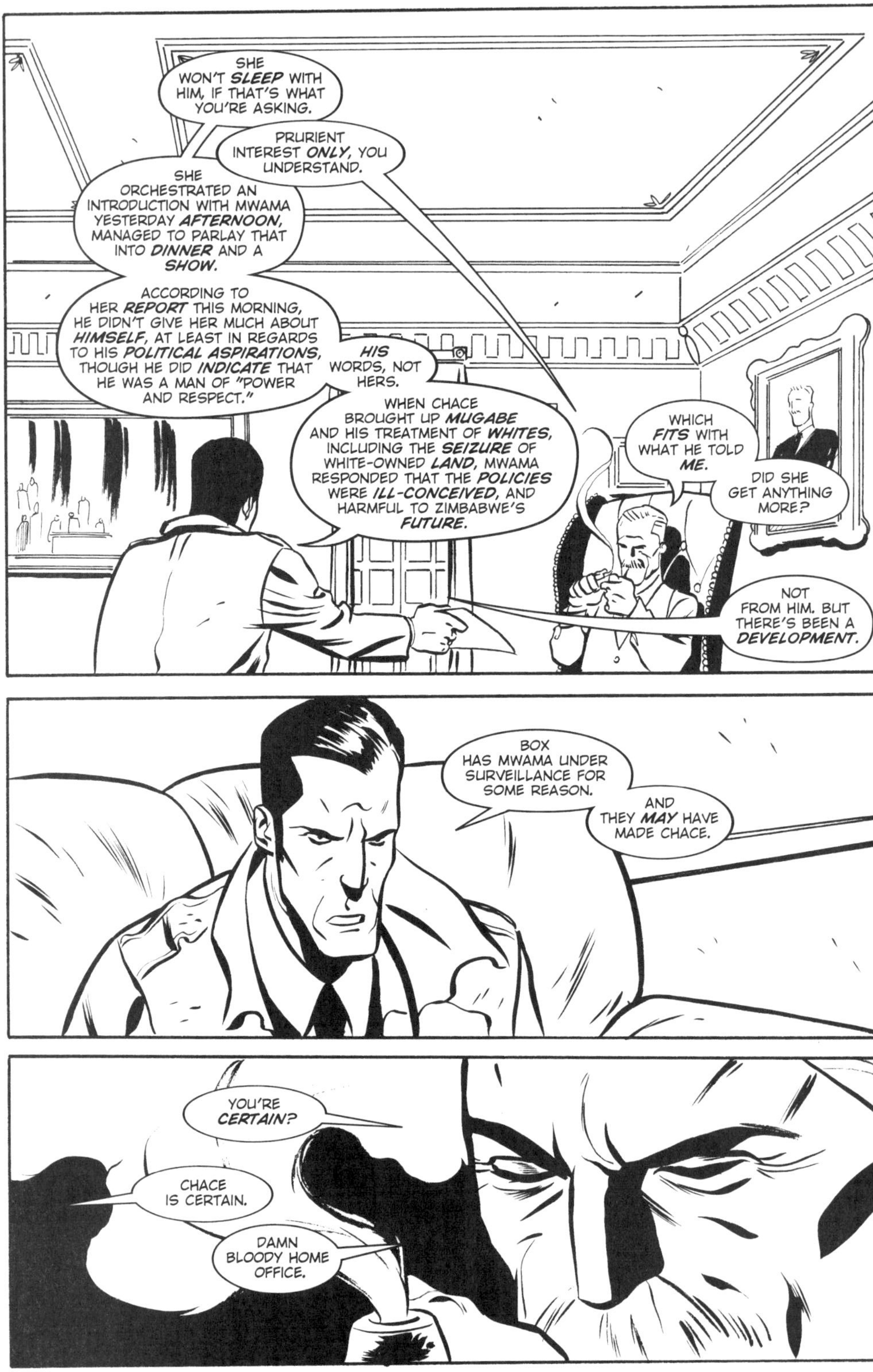
SHE WON'T SLEEP WITH HIM, IF THAT'S WHAT YOU'RE ASKING.
PRURIENT INTEREST ONLY, YOU UNDERSTAND.
SHE ORCHESTRATED AN INTRODUCTION WITH MWAMA YESTERDAY AFTERNOON, MANAGED TO PARLAY THAT INTO DINNER AND A SHOW.
ACCORDING TO HER REPORT THIS MORNING, HE DIDN'T GIVE HER MUCH ABOUT HIMSELF, AT LEAST IN REGARDS TO HIS POLITICAL ASPIRATIONS, THOUGH HE DID INDICATE THAT HE WAS A MAN OF "POWER AND RESPECT."
HIS WORDS, NOT HERS.
WHEN CHACE BROUGHT UP MUGABE AND HIS TREATMENT OF WHITES, INCLUDING THE SEIZURE OF WHITE-OWNED LAND, MWAMA RESPONDED THAT THE POLICIES WERE ILL-CONCEIVED, AND HARMFUL TO ZIMBABWE'S FUTURE.
WHICH FITS WITH WHAT HE TOLD ME.
DID SHE GET ANYTHING MORE?
NOT FROM HIM. BUT THERE'S BEEN A DEVELOPMENT.
BOX HAS MWAMA UNDER SURVEILLANCE FOR SOME REASON.
AND THEY MAY HAVE MADE CHACE.
YOU'RE CERTAIN?
CHACE IS CERTAIN.
DAMN BLOODY HOME OFFICE.

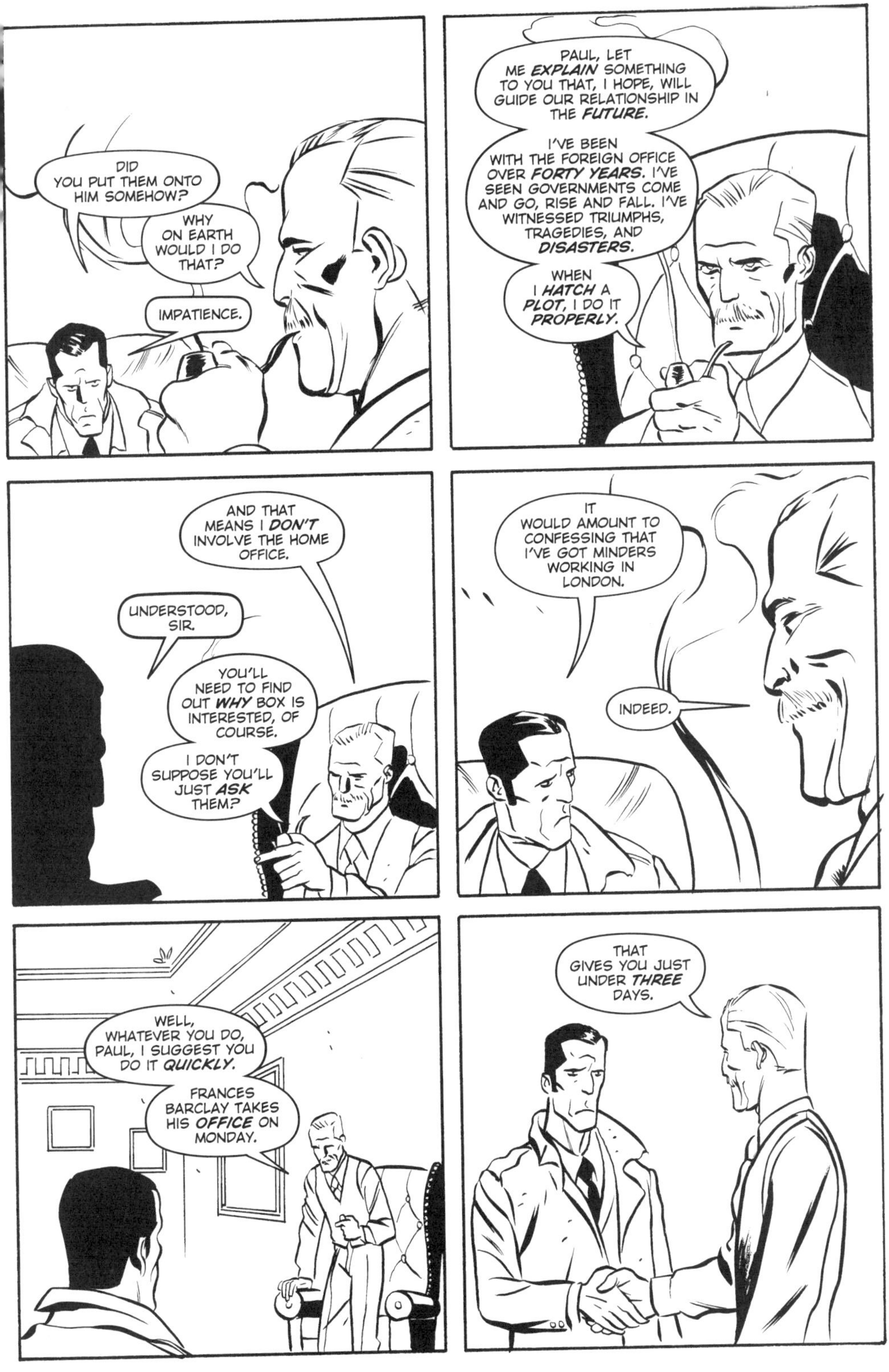
DID YOU PUT THEM ONTO HIM SOMEHOW?
WHY ON EARTH WOULD I DO THAT?
IMPATIENCE.
PAUL, LET ME EXPLAIN SOMETHING TO YOU THAT, I HOPE, WILL GUIDE OUR RELATIONSHIP IN THE FUTURE.
I'VE BEEN WITH THE FOREIGN OFFICE OVER FORTY YEARS. I'VE SEEN GOVERNMENTS COME AND GO, RISE AND FALL. I'VE WITNESSED TRIUMPHS, TRAGEDIES, AND DISASTERS.
WHEN I HATCH A PLOT, I DO IT PROPERLY.
AND THAT MEANS I DON'T INVOLVE THE HOME OFFICE.
UNDERSTOOD, SIR.
YOU'LL NEED TO FIND OUT WHY BOX IS INTERESTED, OF COURSE.
I DON'T SUPPOSE YOU'LL JUST ASK THEM?
IT WOULD AMOUNT TO CONFESSING THAT I'VE GOT MINDERS WORKING IN LONDON.
INDEED.
WELL, WHATEVER YOU DO, PAUL, I SUGGEST YOU DO IT QUICKLY.
FRANCES BARCLAY TAKES HIS OFFICE ON MONDAY.
THAT GIVES YOU JUST UNDER THREE DAYS.

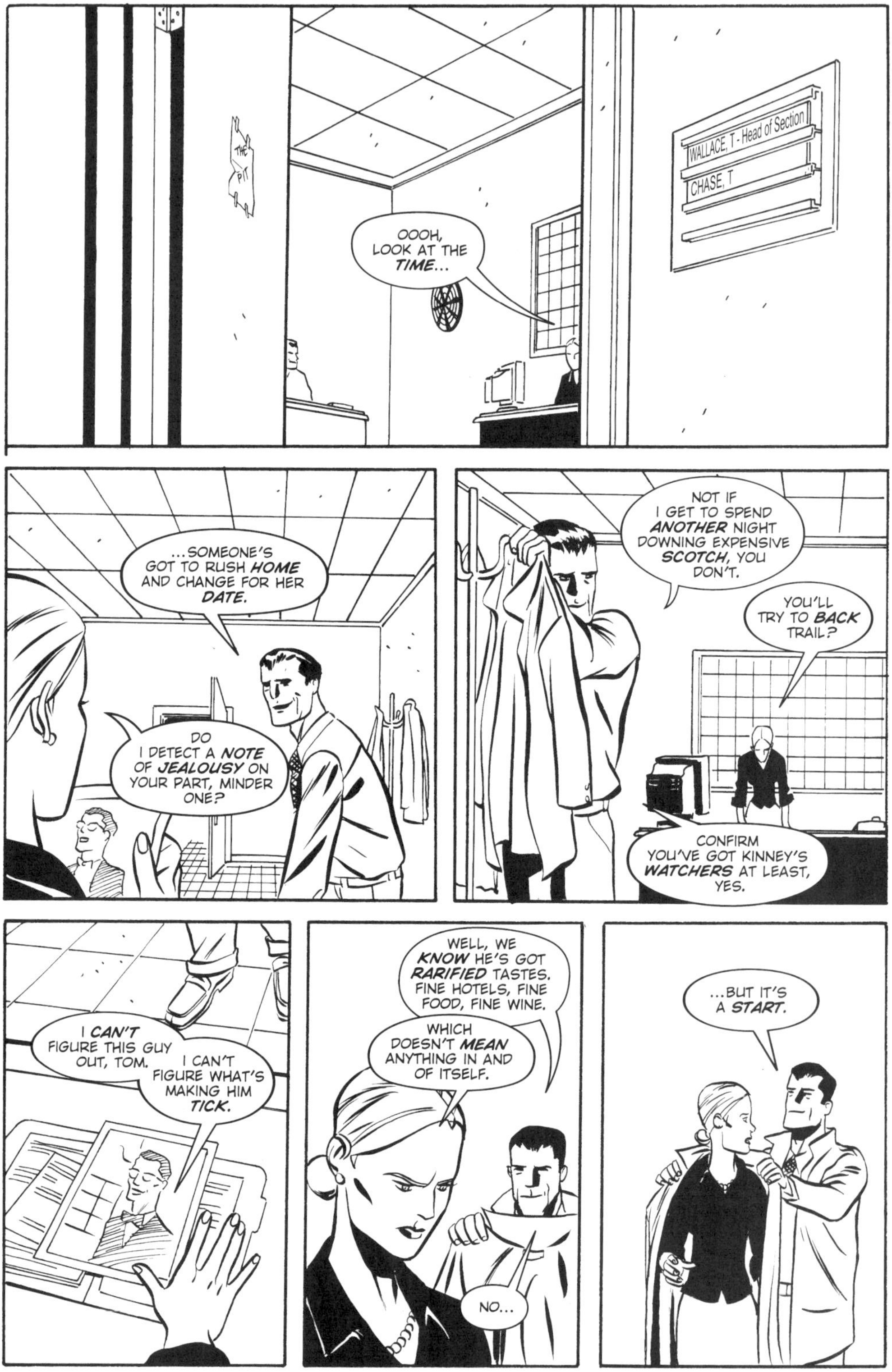
WALLACE, T - Head of Section
CHASE, T
OOOH, LOOK AT THE TIME...
...SOMEONE'S GOT TO RUSH HOME AND CHANGE FOR HER DATE.
DO I DETECT A NOTE OF JEALOUSY ON YOUR PART, MINDER ONE?
NOT IF I GET TO SPEND ANOTHER NIGHT DOWNING EXPENSIVE SCOTCH, YOU DON'T.
YOU'LL TRY TO BACK TRAIL?
CONFIRM YOU'VE GOT KINNEY'S WATCHERS AT LEAST, YES.
I CAN'T FIGURE THIS GUY OUT, TOM.
I CAN'T FIGURE WHAT'S MAKING HIM TICK.
WELL, WE KNOW HE'S GOT RARIFIED TASTES. FINE HOTELS, FINE FOOD, FINE WINE.
WHICH DOESN'T MEAN ANYTHING IN AND OF ITSELF.
NO...
...BUT IT'S A START.

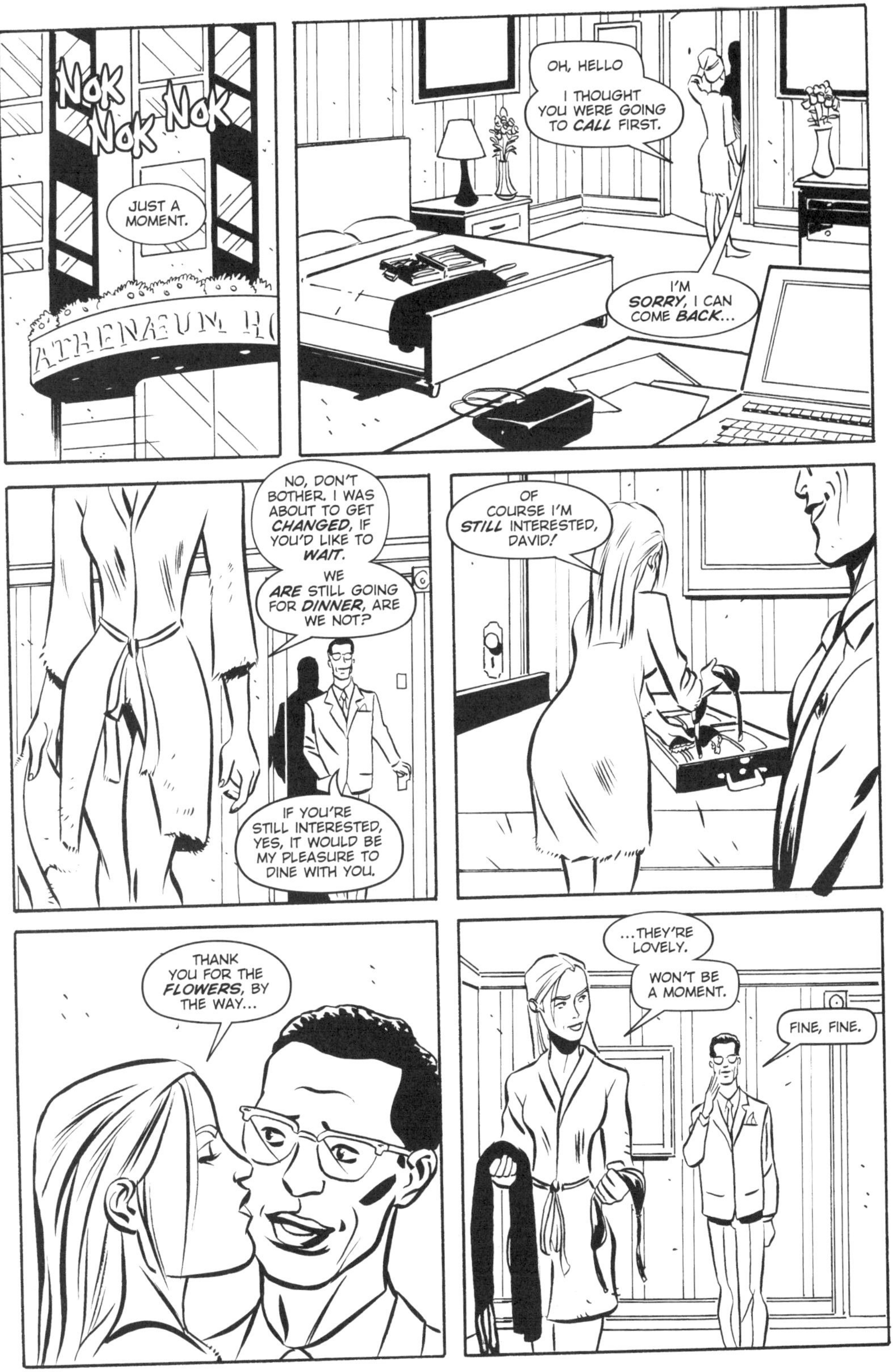
NOK NOK NOK
JUST A MOMENT.
ATHENAEUM H
OH, HELLO
I THOUGHT YOU WERE GOING TO CALL FIRST.
I'M SORRY, I CAN COME BACK...
NO, DON'T BOTHER. I WAS ABOUT TO GET CHANGED, IF YOU'D LIKE TO WAIT.
WE ARE STILL GOING FOR DINNER, ARE WE NOT?
IF YOU'RE STILL INTERESTED, YES, IT WOULD BE MY PLEASURE TO DINE WITH YOU.
OF COURSE I'M STILL INTERESTED, DAVID!
THANK YOU FOR THE FLOWERS, BY THE WAY...
...THEY'RE LOVELY.
WON'T BE A MOMENT.
FINE, FINE.

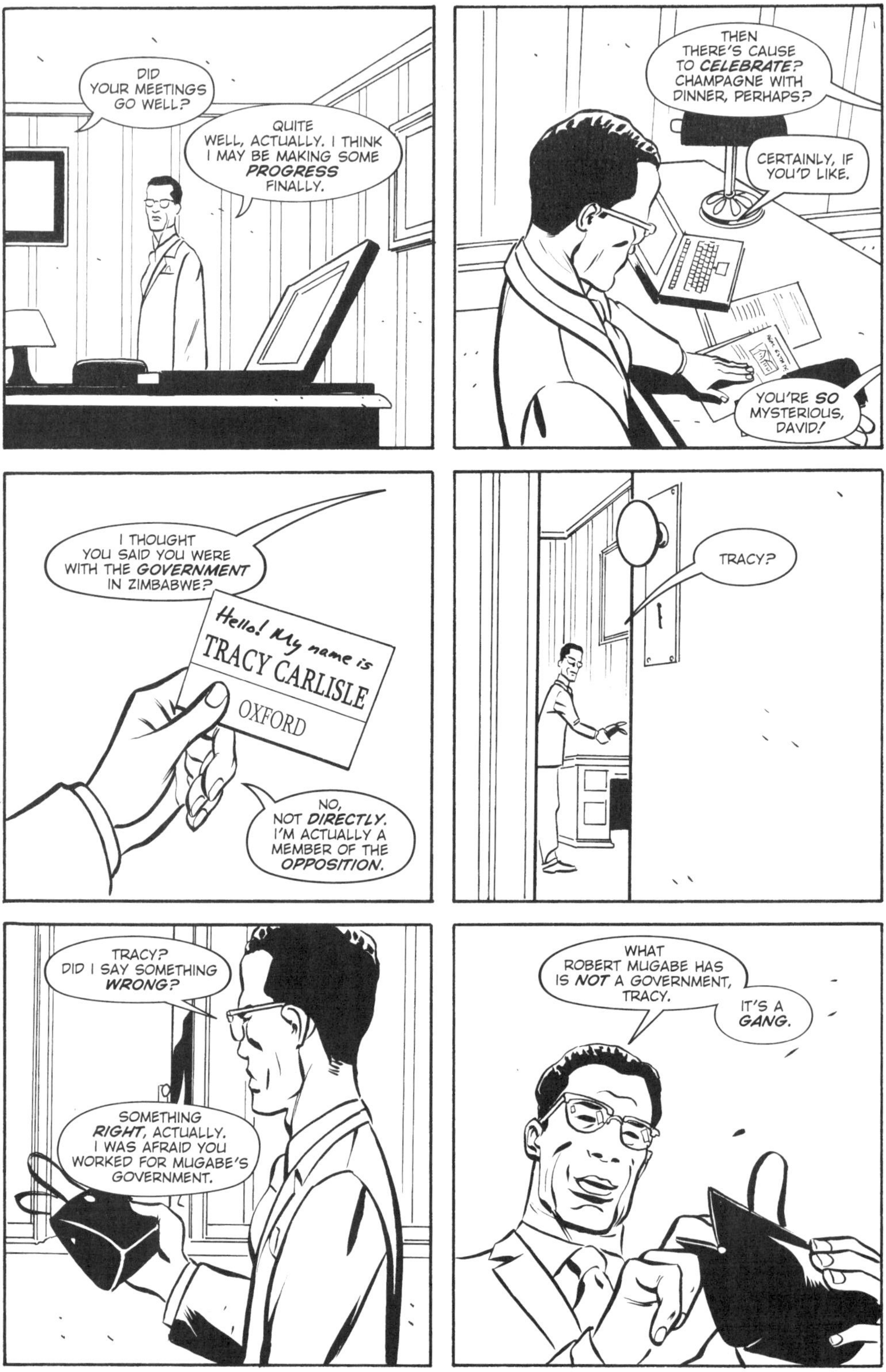
DID YOUR MEETINGS GO WELL?
QUITE WELL, ACTUALLY. I THINK I MAY BE MAKING SOME PROGRESS FINALLY.
THEN THERE'S CAUSE TO CELEBRATE? CHAMPAGNE WITH DINNER, PERHAPS?
CERTAINLY, IF YOU'D LIKE.
YOU'RE SO MYSTERIOUS, DAVID!
I THOUGHT YOU SAID YOU WERE WITH THE GOVERNMENT IN ZIMBABWE?
Hello! My name is
TRACY CARLISLE
OXFORD
NO, NOT DIRECTLY. I'M ACTUALLY A MEMBER OF THE OPPOSITION.
TRACY?
TRACY? DID I SAY SOMETHING WRONG?
SOMETHING RIGHT, ACTUALLY. I WAS AFRAID YOU WORKED FOR MUGABE'S GOVERNMENT.
WHAT ROBERT MUGABE HAS IS NOT A GOVERNMENT, TRACY.
IT'S A GANG.

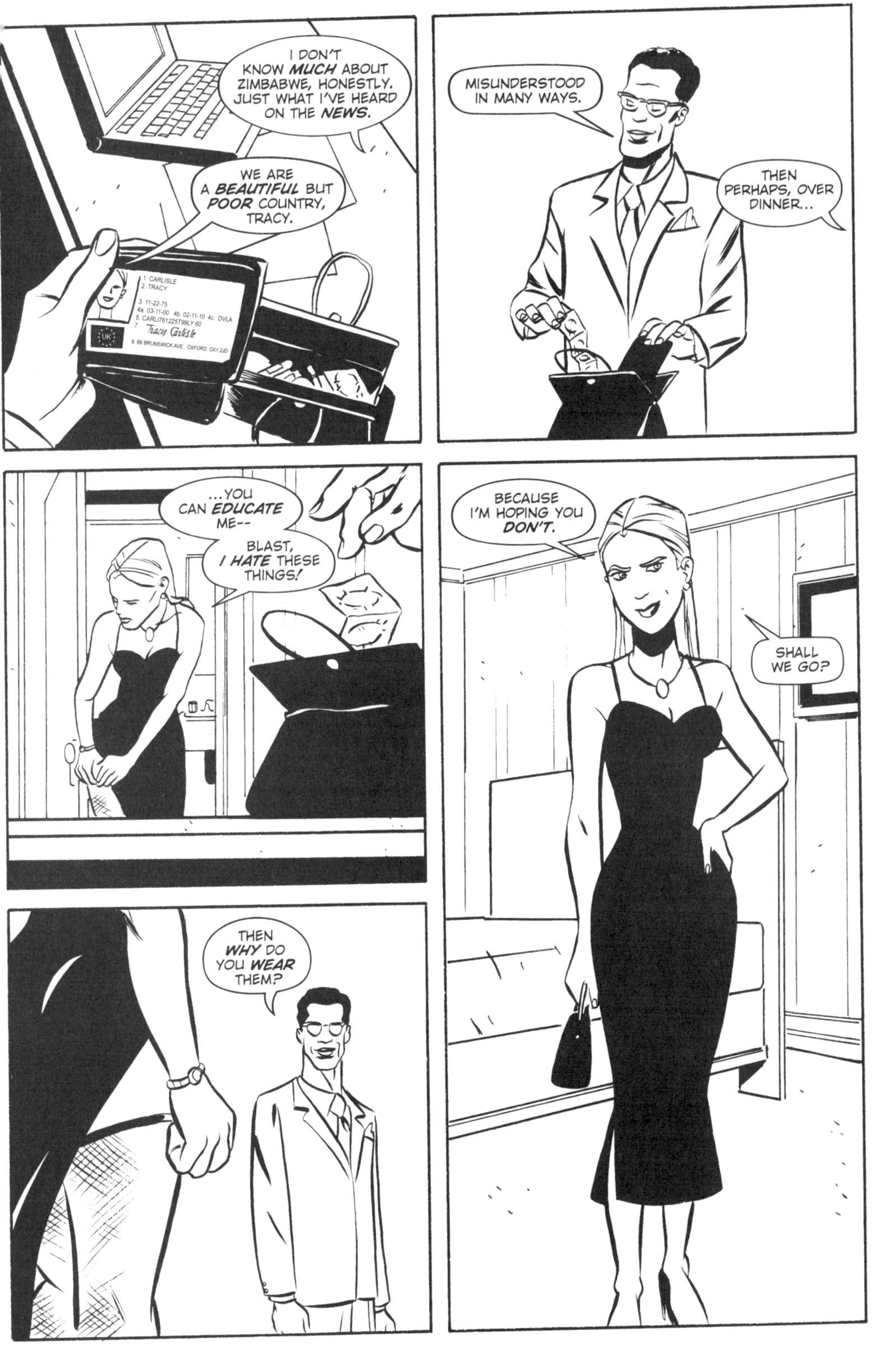
I DON'T KNOW *MUCH* ABOUT ZIMBABWE, HONESTLY. JUST WHAT I'VE HEARD ON THE *NEWS.*
WE ARE A *BEAUTIFUL* BUT *POOR* COUNTRY, TRACY.
1. CARLISLE
2. TRACY
3. 11-22-75
4a. 03-11-00 4b. 02-11-10 4c. DVLA
5. CARLI761225T99LY 60
7. Tracy Carlisle
UK
8. 66 BRUNSWICK AVE., OXFORD, OX1 2JD
MISUNDERSTOOD IN MANY WAYS.
THEN PERHAPS, OVER DINNER...
...YOU CAN *EDUCATE* ME--
BLAST, *I HATE* THESE THINGS!
THEN *WHY* DO YOU *WEAR* THEM?
BECAUSE I'M HOPING YOU *DON'T.*
SHALL WE GO?

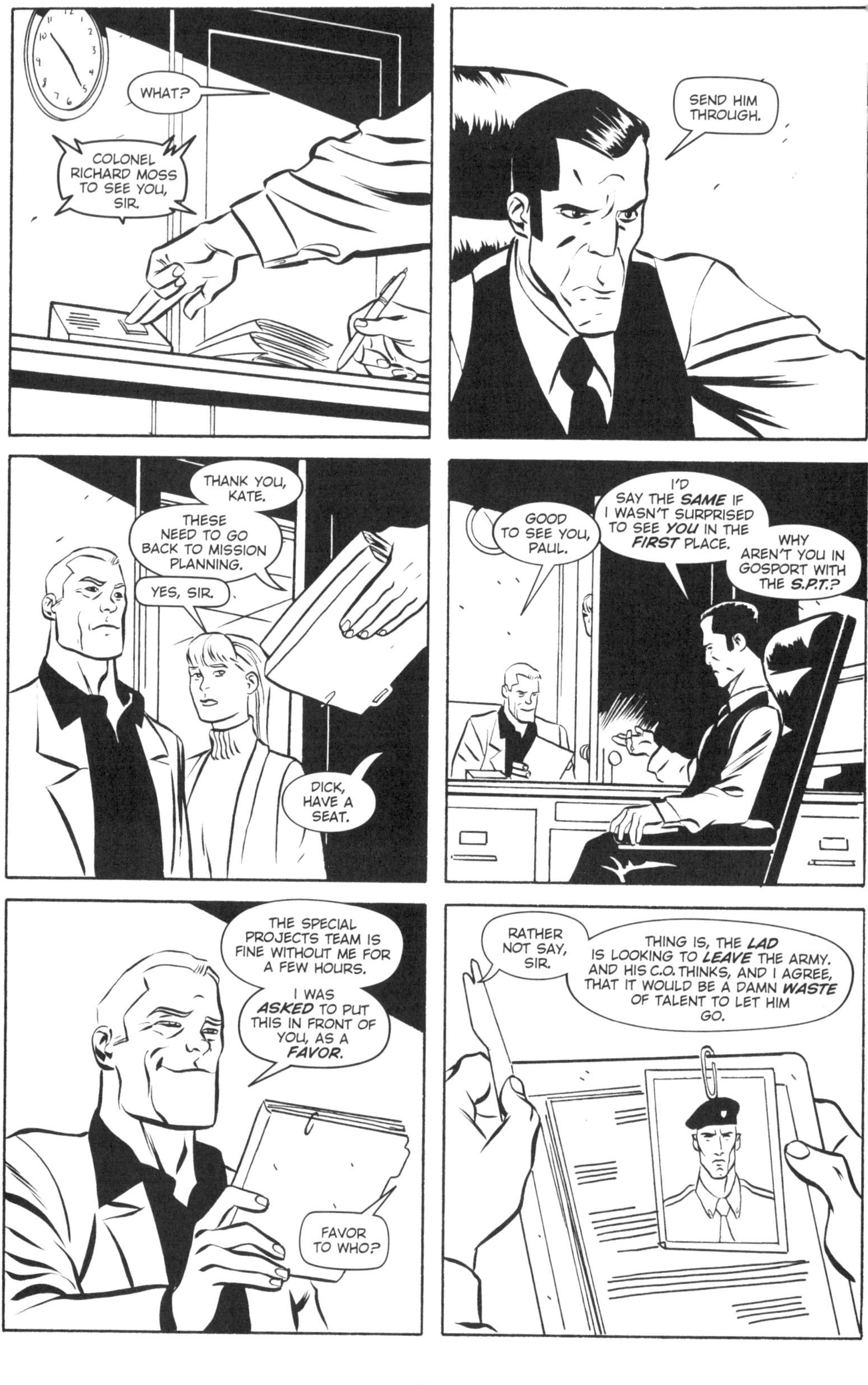
WHAT?
COLONEL RICHARD MOSS TO SEE YOU, SIR.
SEND HIM THROUGH.
THANK YOU, KATE.
THESE NEED TO GO BACK TO MISSION PLANNING.
YES, SIR.
DICK, HAVE A SEAT.
GOOD TO SEE YOU, PAUL.
I'D SAY THE **SAME** IF I WASN'T SURPRISED TO SEE **YOU** IN THE **FIRST** PLACE.
WHY AREN'T YOU IN GOSPORT WITH THE **S.P.T.**?
THE SPECIAL PROJECTS TEAM IS FINE WITHOUT ME FOR A FEW HOURS.
I WAS **ASKED** TO PUT THIS IN FRONT OF YOU, AS A **FAVOR.**
FAVOR TO WHO?
RATHER NOT SAY, SIR.
THING IS, THE **LAD** IS LOOKING TO **LEAVE** THE ARMY. AND HIS C.O. THINKS, AND I AGREE, THAT IT WOULD BE A DAMN **WASTE** OF TALENT TO LET HIM GO.

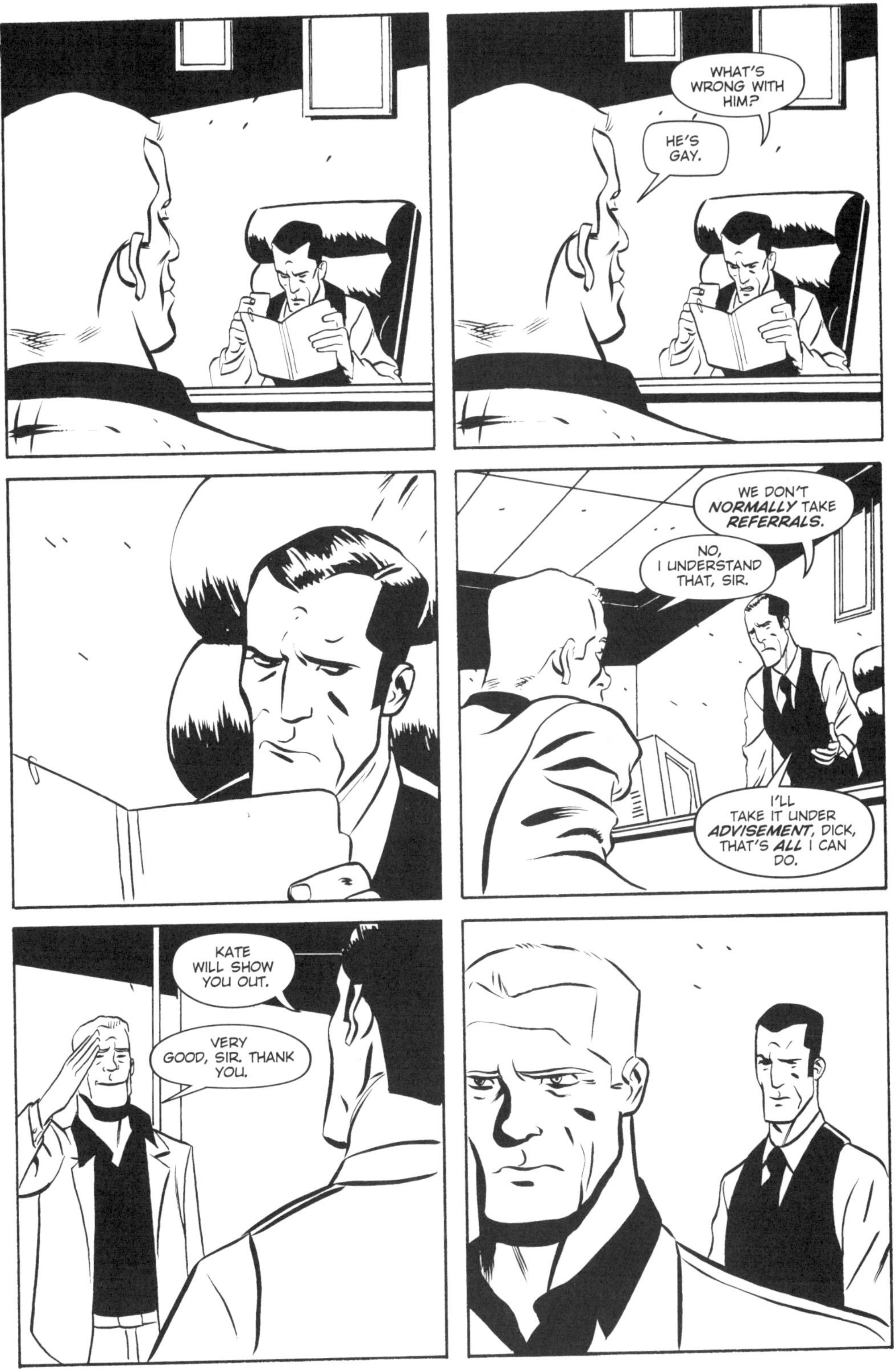
WHAT'S WRONG WITH HIM?
HE'S GAY.
WE DON'T **NORMALLY** TAKE **REFERRALS.**
NO, I UNDERSTAND THAT, SIR.
I'LL TAKE IT UNDER **ADVISEMENT,** DICK, THAT'S **ALL** I CAN DO.
KATE WILL SHOW YOU OUT.
VERY GOOD, SIR. THANK YOU.

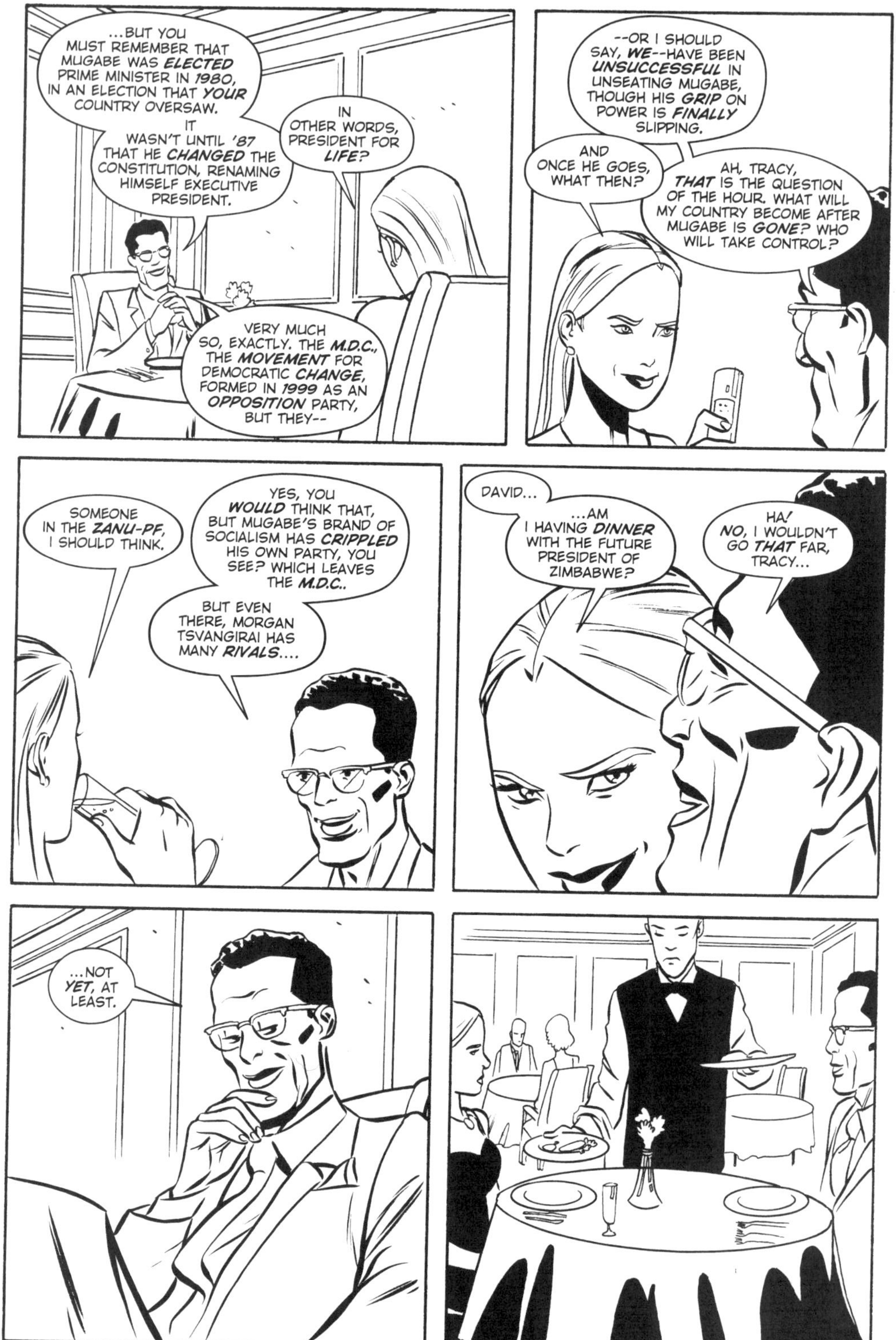
...BUT YOU MUST REMEMBER THAT MUGABE WAS ELECTED PRIME MINISTER IN 1980, IN AN ELECTION THAT YOUR COUNTRY OVERSAW.
IT WASN'T UNTIL '87 THAT HE CHANGED THE CONSTITUTION, RENAMING HIMSELF EXECUTIVE PRESIDENT.
IN OTHER WORDS, PRESIDENT FOR LIFE?
VERY MUCH SO, EXACTLY. THE M.D.C., THE MOVEMENT FOR DEMOCRATIC CHANGE, FORMED IN 1999 AS AN OPPOSITION PARTY, BUT THEY--
--OR I SHOULD SAY, WE--HAVE BEEN UNSUCCESSFUL IN UNSEATING MUGABE, THOUGH HIS GRIP ON POWER IS FINALLY SLIPPING.
AND ONCE HE GOES, WHAT THEN?
AH, TRACY, THAT IS THE QUESTION OF THE HOUR. WHAT WILL MY COUNTRY BECOME AFTER MUGABE IS GONE? WHO WILL TAKE CONTROL?
SOMEONE IN THE ZANU-PF, I SHOULD THINK.
YES, YOU WOULD THINK THAT, BUT MUGABE'S BRAND OF SOCIALISM HAS CRIPPLED HIS OWN PARTY, YOU SEE? WHICH LEAVES THE M.D.C..
BUT EVEN THERE, MORGAN TSVANGIRAI HAS MANY RIVALS....
DAVID...
...AM I HAVING DINNER WITH THE FUTURE PRESIDENT OF ZIMBABWE?
HA! NO, I WOULDN'T GO THAT FAR, TRACY...
...NOT YET, AT LEAST.

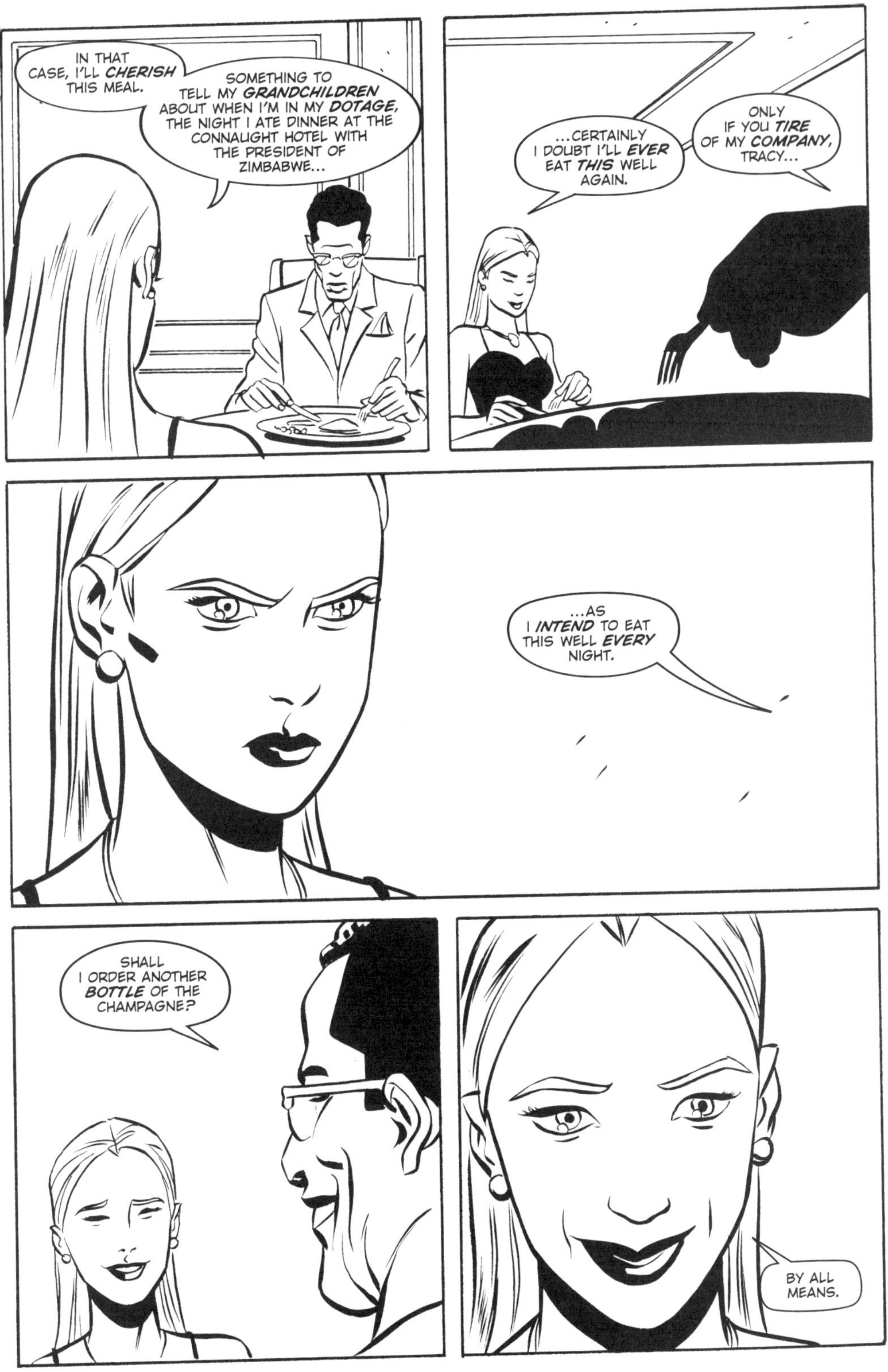
IN THAT CASE, I'LL CHERISH THIS MEAL.
SOMETHING TO TELL MY GRANDCHILDREN ABOUT WHEN I'M IN MY DOTAGE, THE NIGHT I ATE DINNER AT THE CONNAUGHT HOTEL WITH THE PRESIDENT OF ZIMBABWE...
...CERTAINLY I DOUBT I'LL EVER EAT THIS WELL AGAIN.
ONLY IF YOU TIRE OF MY COMPANY, TRACY...
...AS I INTEND TO EAT THIS WELL EVERY NIGHT.
SHALL I ORDER ANOTHER BOTTLE OF THE CHAMPAGNE?
BY ALL MEANS.

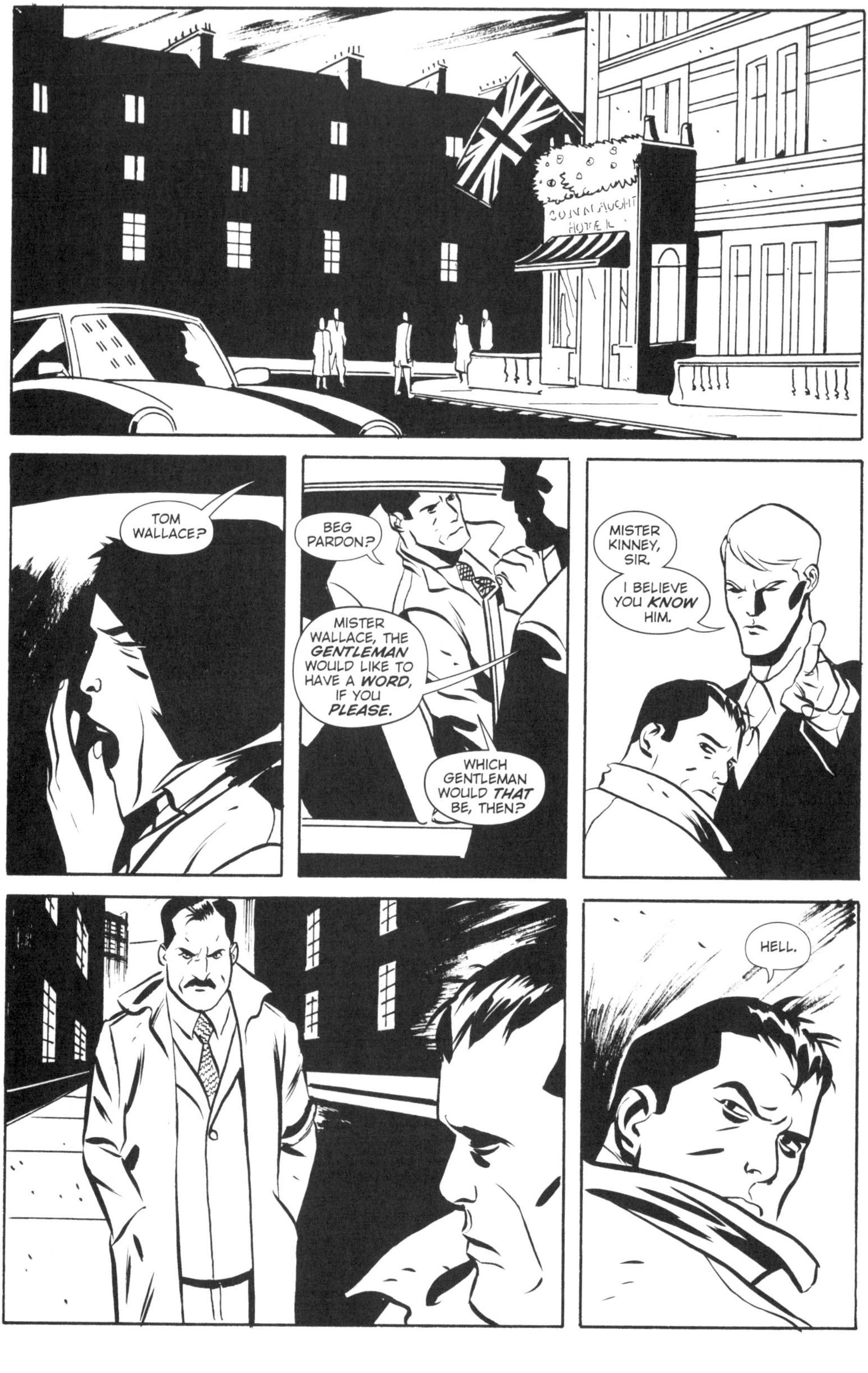
CONNAUGHT HOTEL
TOM WALLACE?
BEG PARDON?
MISTER WALLACE, THE GENTLEMAN WOULD LIKE TO HAVE A WORD, IF YOU PLEASE.
WHICH GENTLEMAN WOULD THAT BE, THEN?
MISTER KINNEY, SIR.
I BELIEVE YOU KNOW HIM.
HELL.

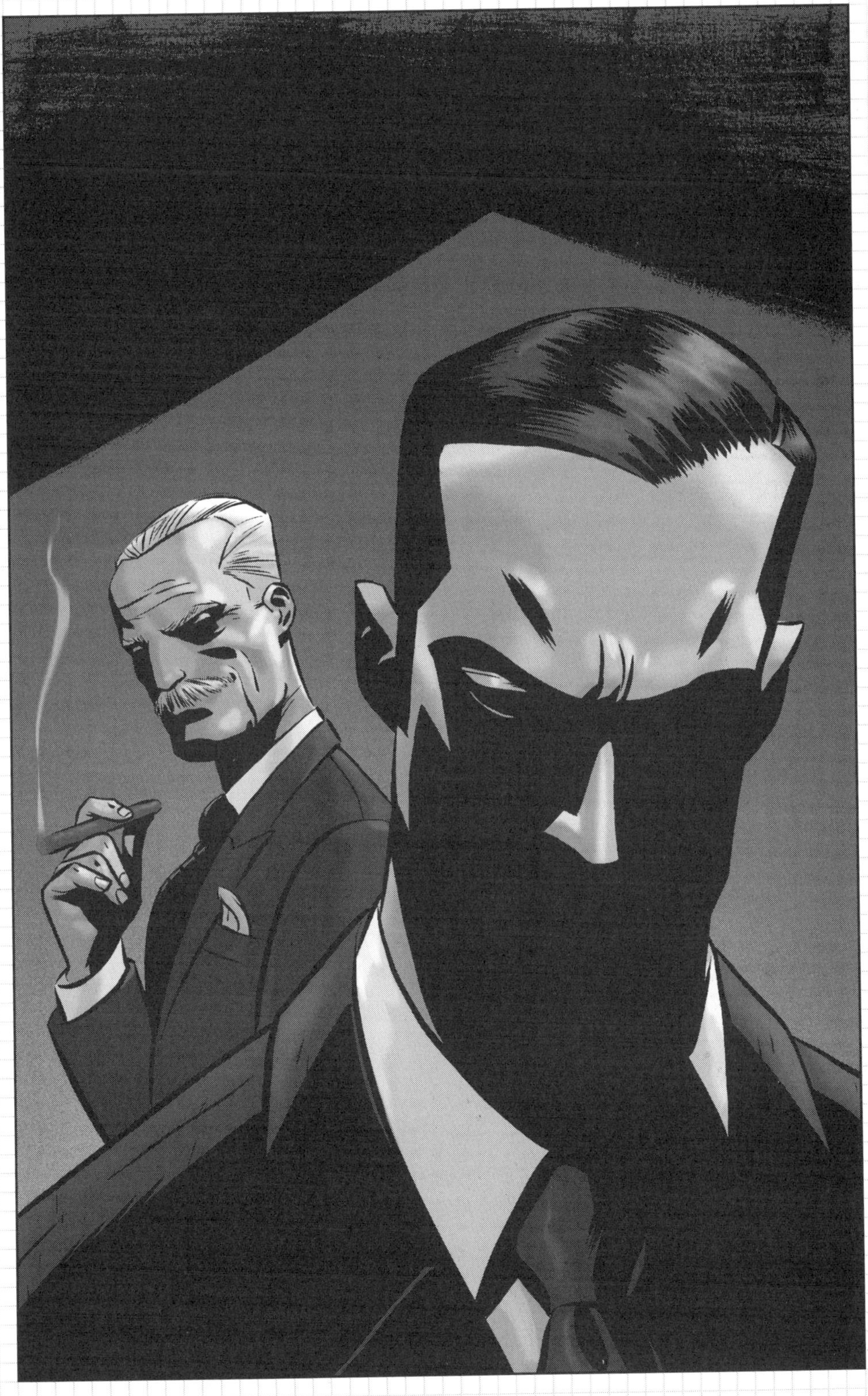

CHAPTER 4

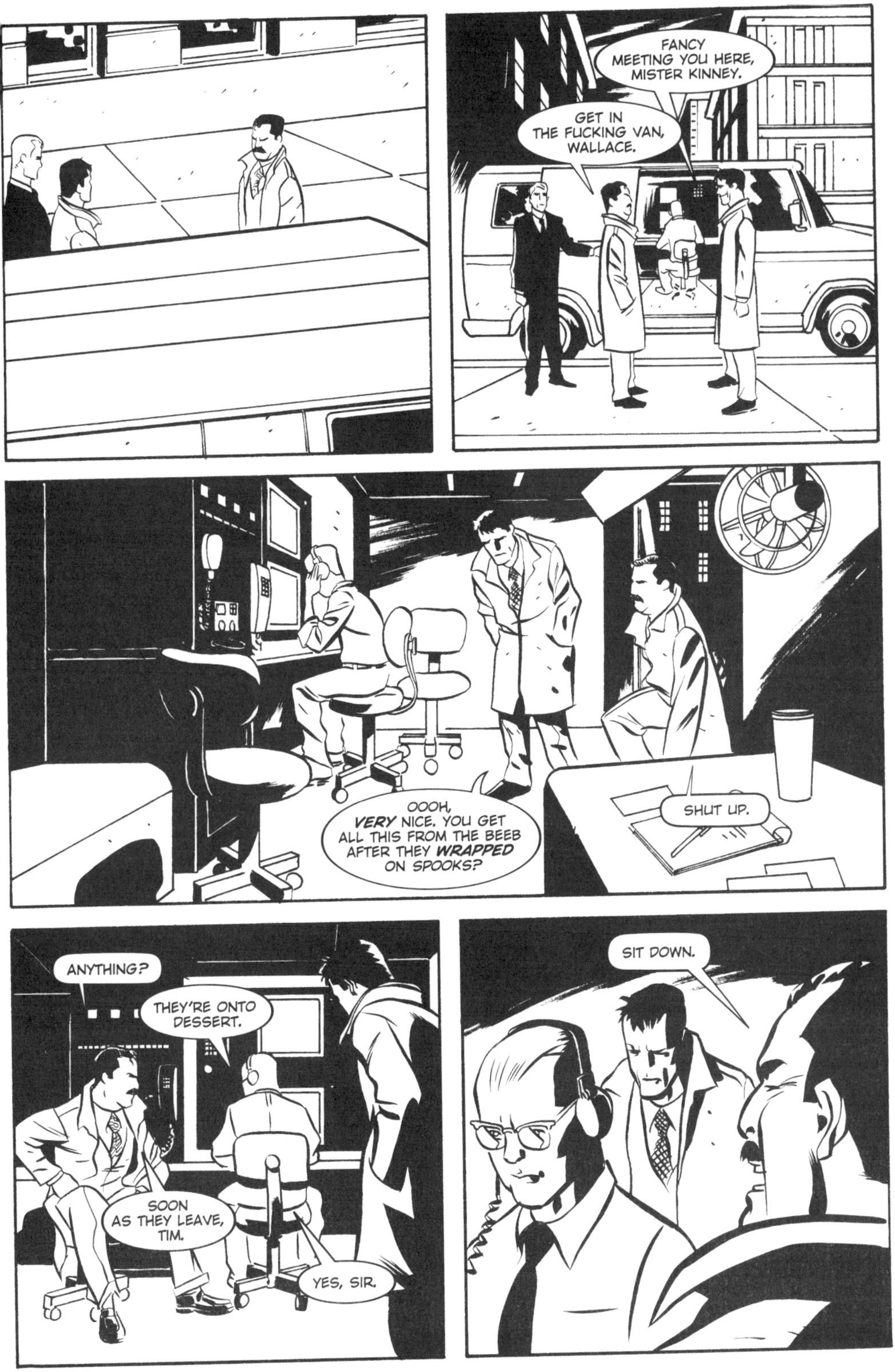
FANCY MEETING YOU HERE, MISTER KINNEY.
GET IN THE FUCKING VAN, WALLACE.
OOOH, VERY NICE. YOU GET ALL THIS FROM THE BEEB AFTER THEY WRAPPED ON SPOOKS?
SHUT UP.
ANYTHING?
THEY'RE ONTO DESSERT.
SOON AS THEY LEAVE, TIM.
YES, SIR.
SIT DOWN.

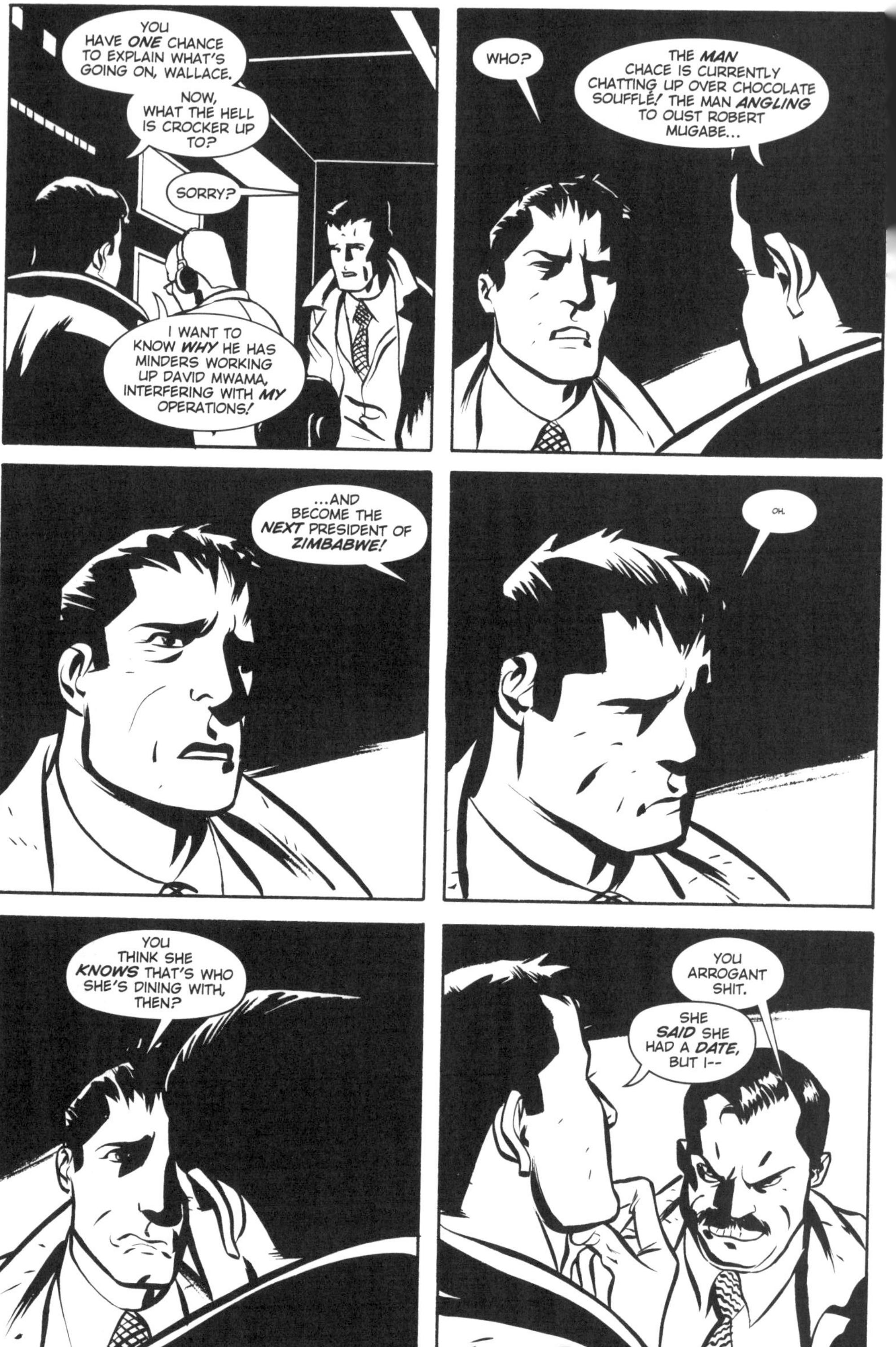
YOU HAVE ONE CHANCE TO EXPLAIN WHAT'S GOING ON, WALLACE.
NOW, WHAT THE HELL IS CROCKER UP TO?
SORRY?
I WANT TO KNOW WHY HE HAS MINDERS WORKING UP DAVID MWAMA, INTERFERING WITH MY OPERATIONS!
WHO?
THE MAN CHACE IS CURRENTLY CHATTING UP OVER CHOCOLATE SOUFFLÉ! THE MAN ANGLING TO OUST ROBERT MUGABE...
...AND BECOME THE NEXT PRESIDENT OF ZIMBABWE!
OH.
YOU THINK SHE KNOWS THAT'S WHO SHE'S DINING WITH, THEN?
YOU ARROGANT SHIT.
SHE SAID SHE HAD A DATE, BUT I--

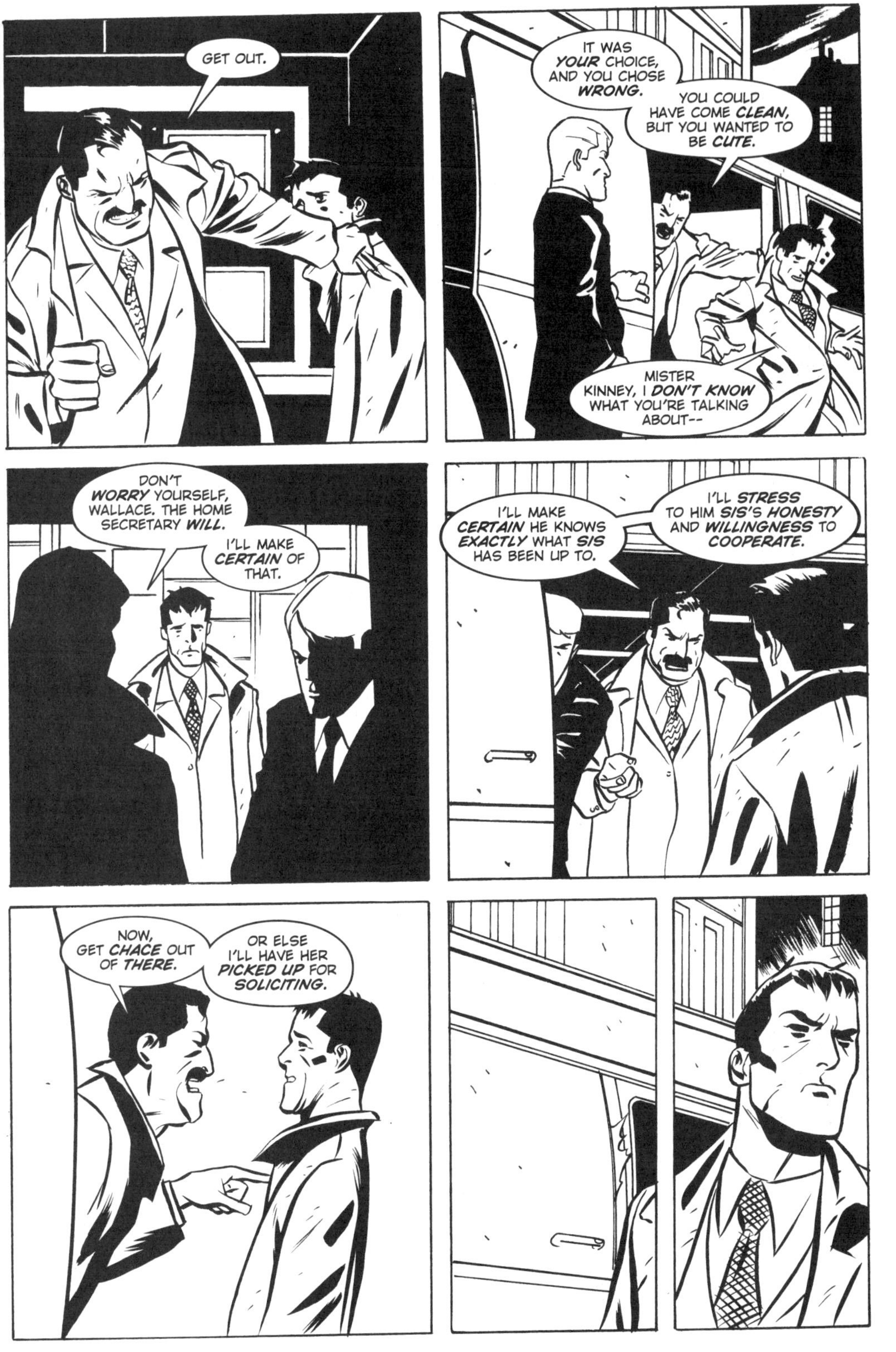
GET OUT.
IT WAS YOUR CHOICE, AND YOU CHOSE WRONG.
YOU COULD HAVE COME CLEAN, BUT YOU WANTED TO BE CUTE.
MISTER KINNEY, I DON'T KNOW WHAT YOU'RE TALKING ABOUT--
DON'T WORRY YOURSELF, WALLACE. THE HOME SECRETARY WILL.
I'LL MAKE CERTAIN OF THAT.
I'LL MAKE CERTAIN HE KNOWS EXACTLY WHAT SIS HAS BEEN UP TO.
I'LL STRESS TO HIM SIS'S HONESTY AND WILLINGNESS TO COOPERATE.
NOW, GET CHACE OUT OF THERE.
OR ELSE I'LL HAVE HER PICKED UP FOR SOLICITING.

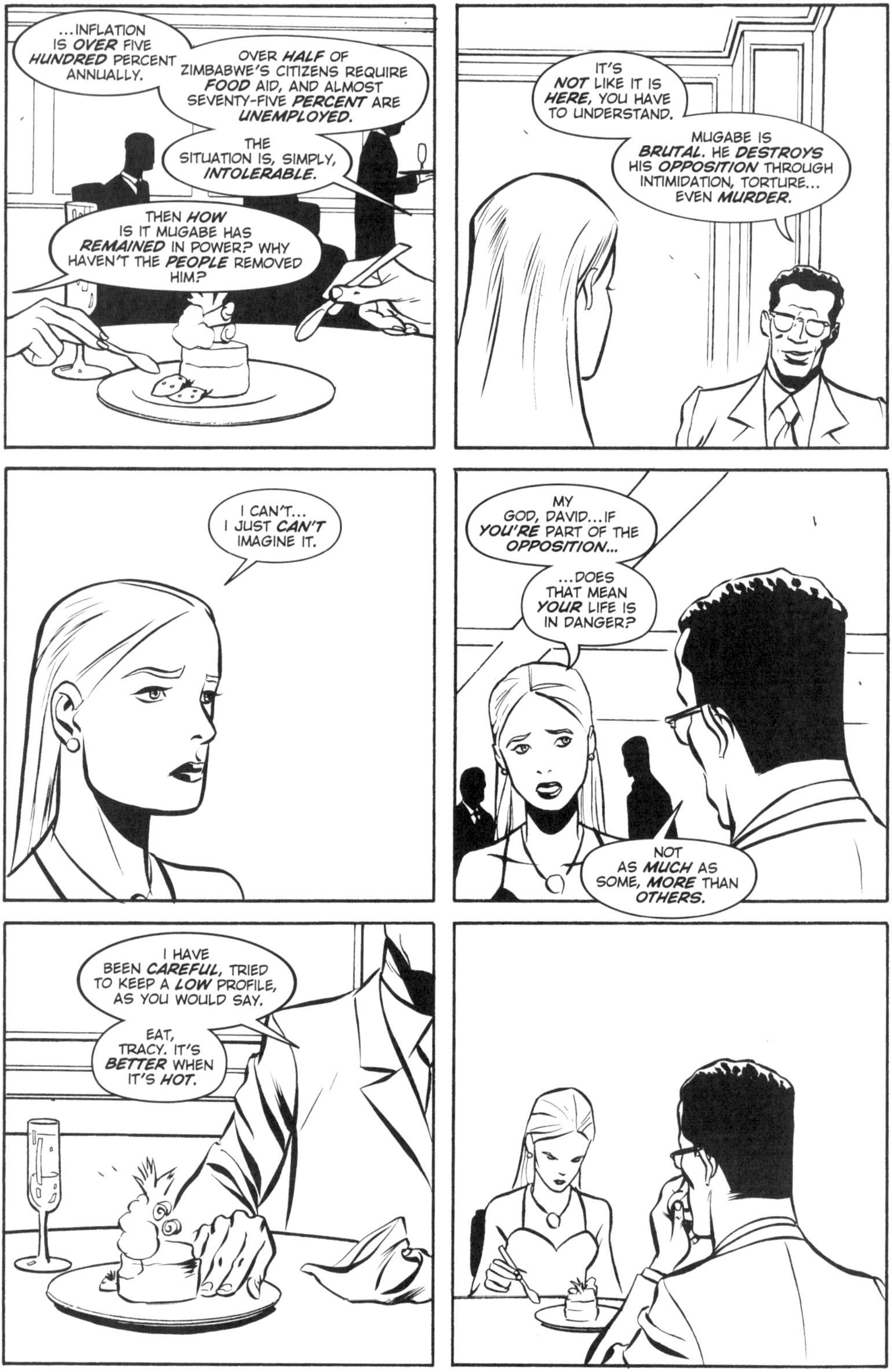
...INFLATION IS OVER FIVE HUNDRED PERCENT ANNUALLY.
OVER HALF OF ZIMBABWE'S CITIZENS REQUIRE FOOD AID, AND ALMOST SEVENTY-FIVE PERCENT ARE UNEMPLOYED.
THE SITUATION IS, SIMPLY, INTOLERABLE.
THEN HOW IS IT MUGABE HAS REMAINED IN POWER? WHY HAVEN'T THE PEOPLE REMOVED HIM?
IT'S NOT LIKE IT IS HERE, YOU HAVE TO UNDERSTAND.
MUGABE IS BRUTAL. HE DESTROYS HIS OPPOSITION THROUGH INTIMIDATION, TORTURE... EVEN MURDER.
I CAN'T... I JUST CAN'T IMAGINE IT.
MY GOD, DAVID...IF YOU'RE PART OF THE OPPOSITION...
...DOES THAT MEAN YOUR LIFE IS IN DANGER?
NOT AS MUCH AS SOME, MORE THAN OTHERS.
I HAVE BEEN CAREFUL, TRIED TO KEEP A LOW PROFILE, AS YOU WOULD SAY.
EAT, TRACY. IT'S BETTER WHEN IT'S HOT.

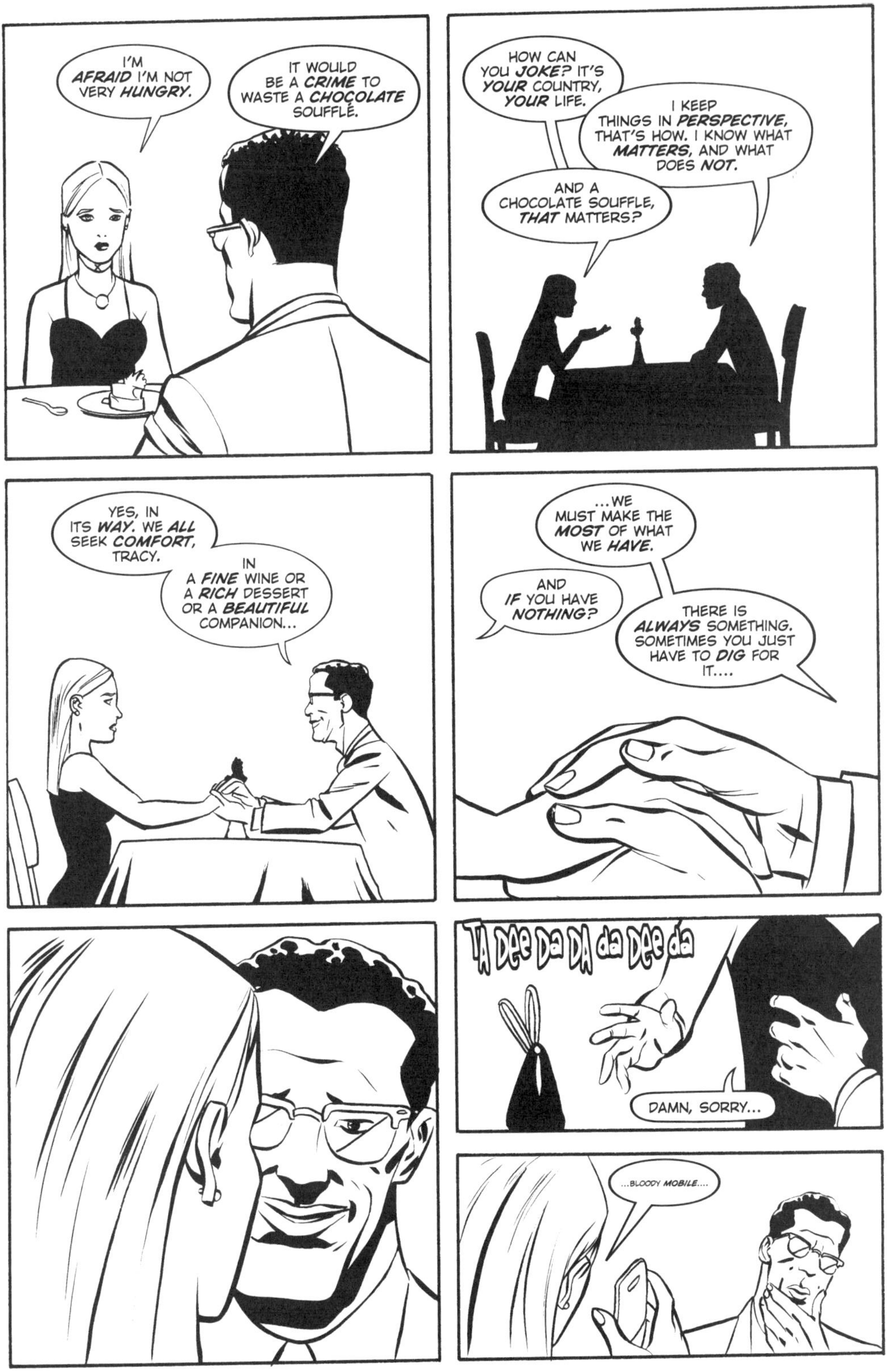
I'M AFRAID I'M NOT VERY HUNGRY.
IT WOULD BE A CRIME TO WASTE A CHOCOLATE SOUFFLÉ.
HOW CAN YOU JOKE? IT'S YOUR COUNTRY, YOUR LIFE.
I KEEP THINGS IN PERSPECTIVE, THAT'S HOW. I KNOW WHAT MATTERS, AND WHAT DOES NOT.
AND A CHOCOLATE SOUFFLE, THAT MATTERS?
YES, IN ITS WAY. WE ALL SEEK COMFORT, TRACY.
IN A FINE WINE OR A RICH DESSERT OR A BEAUTIFUL COMPANION...
...WE MUST MAKE THE MOST OF WHAT WE HAVE.
AND IF YOU HAVE NOTHING?
THERE IS ALWAYS SOMETHING. SOMETIMES YOU JUST HAVE TO DIG FOR IT....
TA DEE DA DA da DEE da
DAMN, SORRY...
...BLOODY MOBILE....

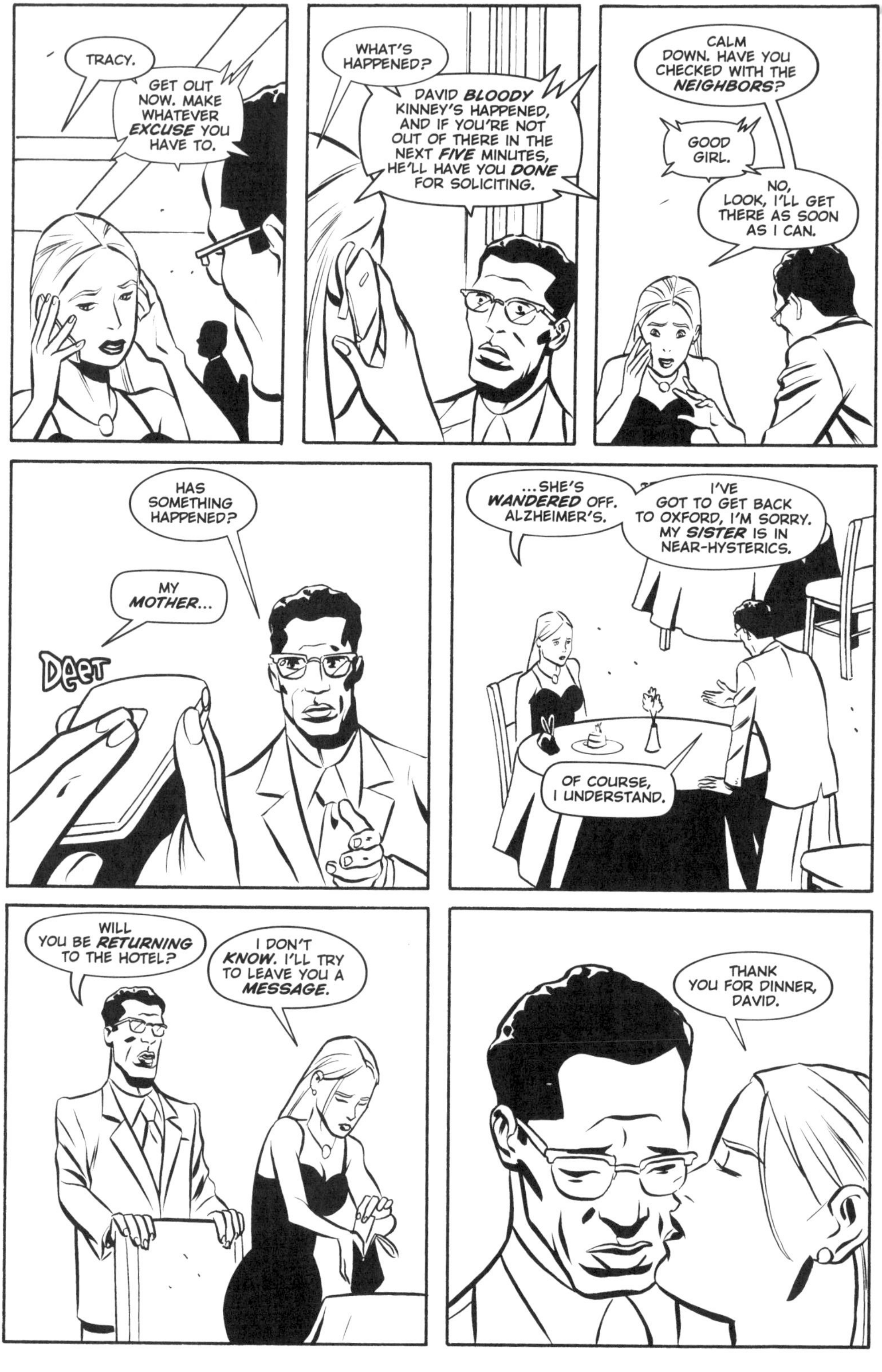
TRACY.
GET OUT NOW. MAKE WHATEVER EXCUSE YOU HAVE TO.
WHAT'S HAPPENED?
DAVID BLOODY KINNEY'S HAPPENED, AND IF YOU'RE NOT OUT OF THERE IN THE NEXT FIVE MINUTES, HE'LL HAVE YOU DONE FOR SOLICITING.
CALM DOWN. HAVE YOU CHECKED WITH THE NEIGHBORS?
GOOD GIRL.
NO, LOOK, I'LL GET THERE AS SOON AS I CAN.
HAS SOMETHING HAPPENED?
MY MOTHER...
DEET
...SHE'S WANDERED OFF. ALZHEIMER'S.
I'VE GOT TO GET BACK TO OXFORD, I'M SORRY. MY SISTER IS IN NEAR-HYSTERICS.
OF COURSE, I UNDERSTAND.
WILL YOU BE RETURNING TO THE HOTEL?
I DON'T KNOW. I'LL TRY TO LEAVE YOU A MESSAGE.
THANK YOU FOR DINNER, DAVID.

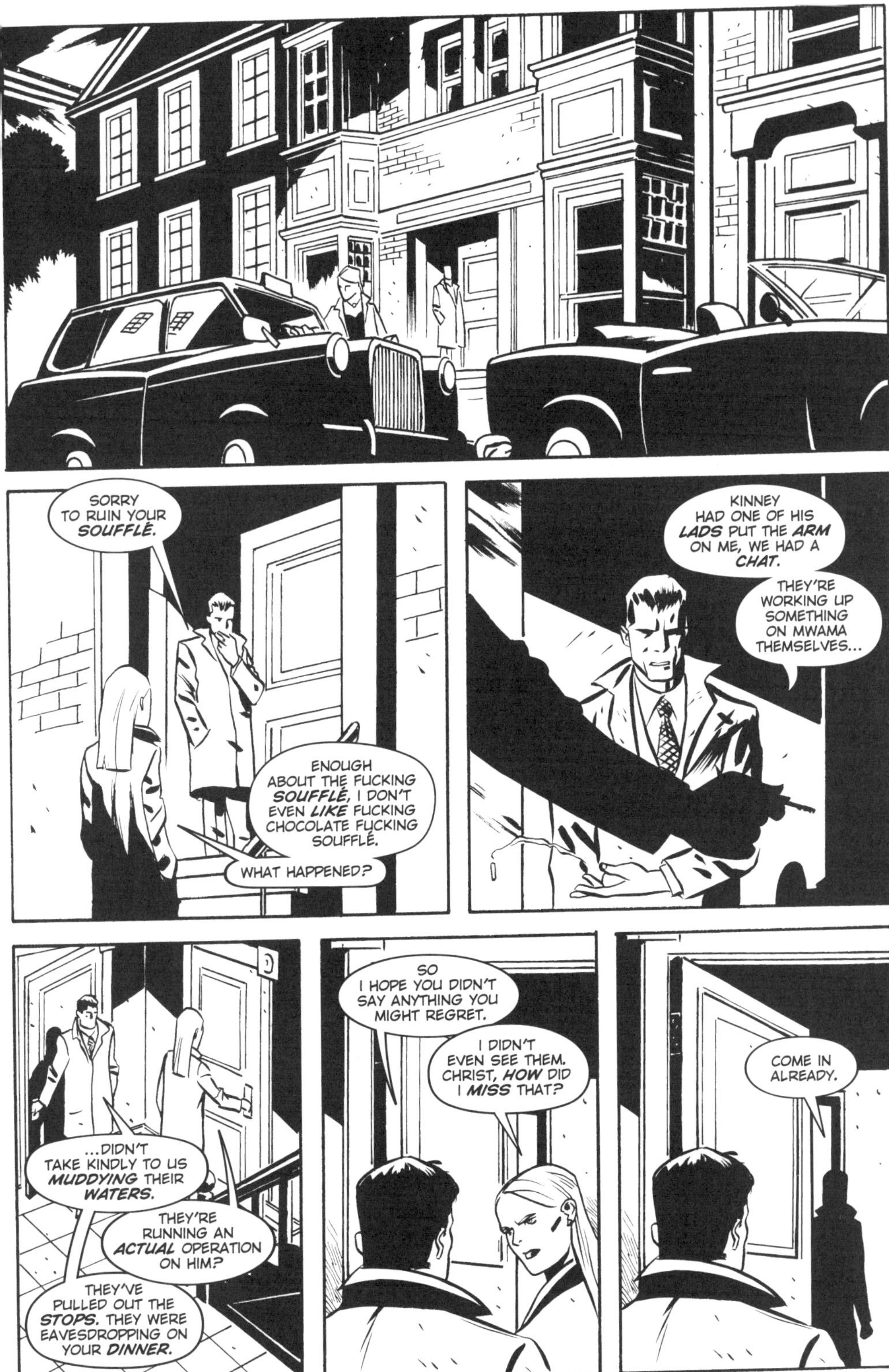
SORRY TO RUIN YOUR SOUFFLÉ.
ENOUGH ABOUT THE FUCKING SOUFFLÉ, I DON'T EVEN LIKE FUCKING CHOCOLATE FUCKING SOUFFLÉ.
WHAT HAPPENED?
KINNEY HAD ONE OF HIS LADS PUT THE ARM ON ME, WE HAD A CHAT.
THEY'RE WORKING UP SOMETHING ON MWAMA THEMSELVES...
...DIDN'T TAKE KINDLY TO US MUDDYING THEIR WATERS.
THEY'RE RUNNING AN ACTUAL OPERATION ON HIM?
THEY'VE PULLED OUT THE STOPS. THEY WERE EAVESDROPPING ON YOUR DINNER.
SO I HOPE YOU DIDN'T SAY ANYTHING YOU MIGHT REGRET.
I DIDN'T EVEN SEE THEM. CHRIST, HOW DID I MISS THAT?
COME IN ALREADY.

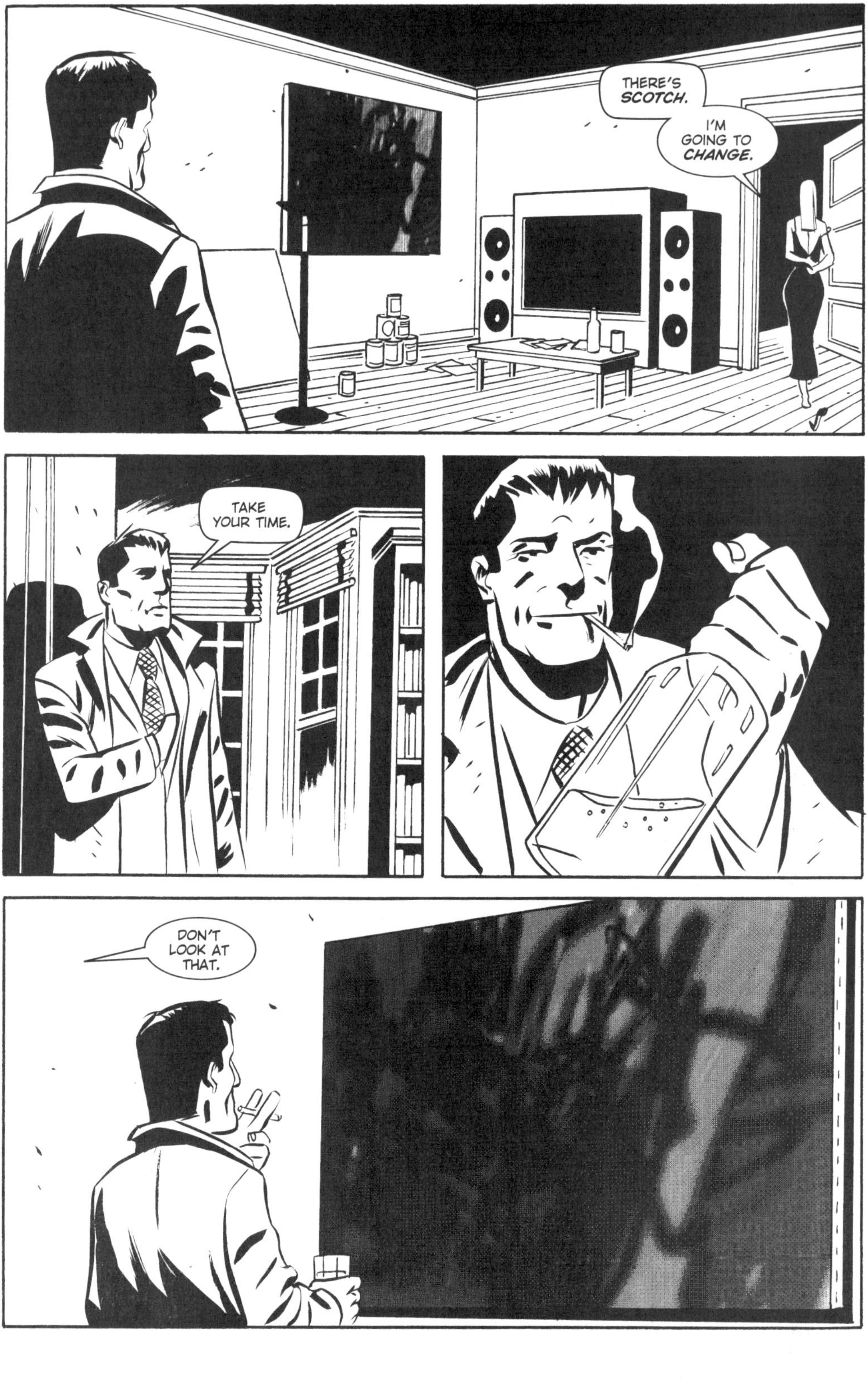
THERE'S SCOTCH.
I'M GOING TO CHANGE.
TAKE YOUR TIME.
DON'T LOOK AT THAT.

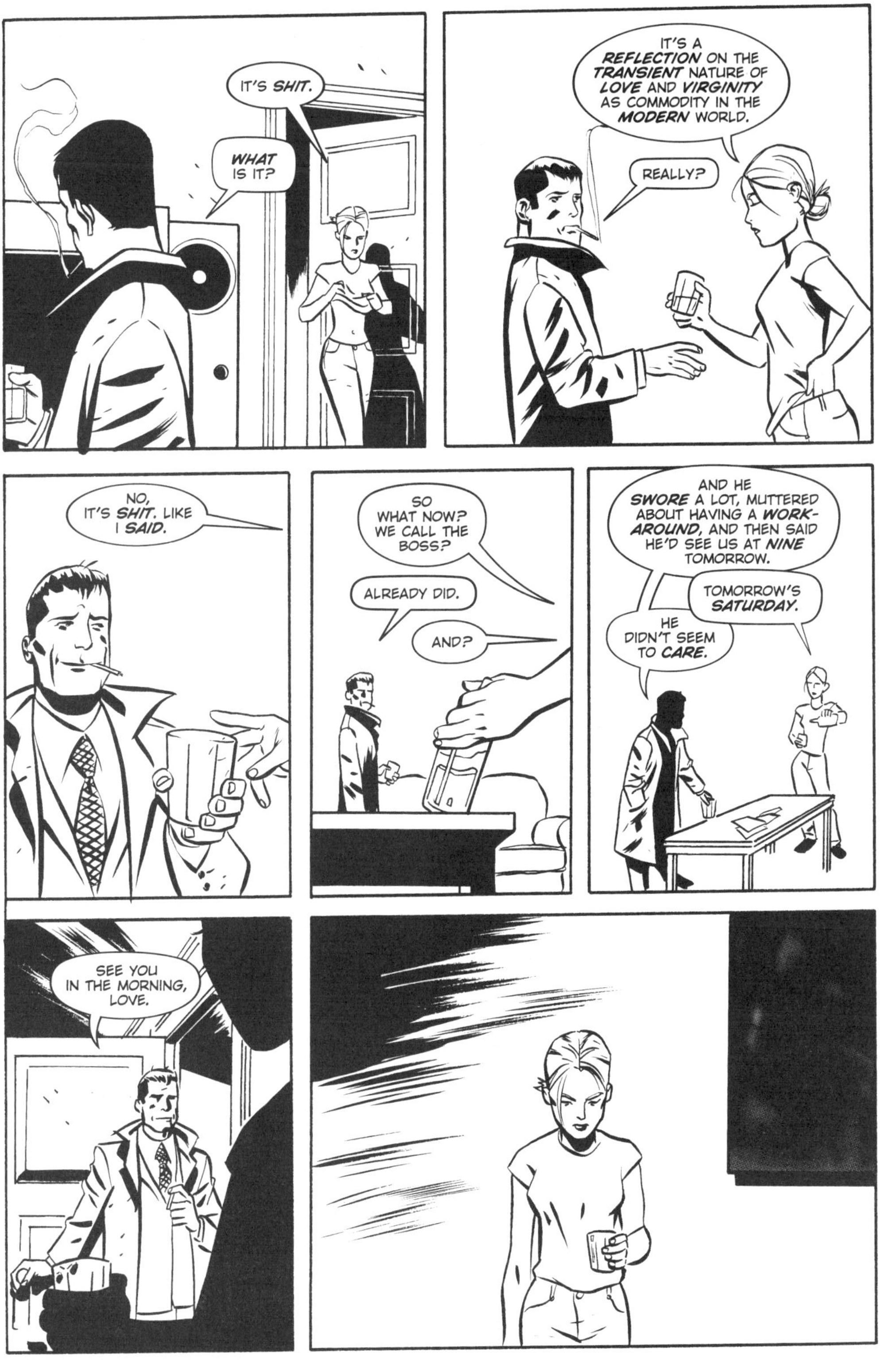

IT'S SHIT.
WHAT IS IT?
IT'S A REFLECTION ON THE TRANSIENT NATURE OF LOVE AND VIRGINITY AS COMMODITY IN THE MODERN WORLD.
REALLY?
NO, IT'S SHIT. LIKE I SAID.
SO WHAT NOW? WE CALL THE BOSS?
ALREADY DID.
AND?
AND HE SWORE A LOT, MUTTERED ABOUT HAVING A WORK-AROUND, AND THEN SAID HE'D SEE US AT NINE TOMORROW.
TOMORROW'S SATURDAY.
HE DIDN'T SEEM TO CARE.
SEE YOU IN THE MORNING, LOVE.

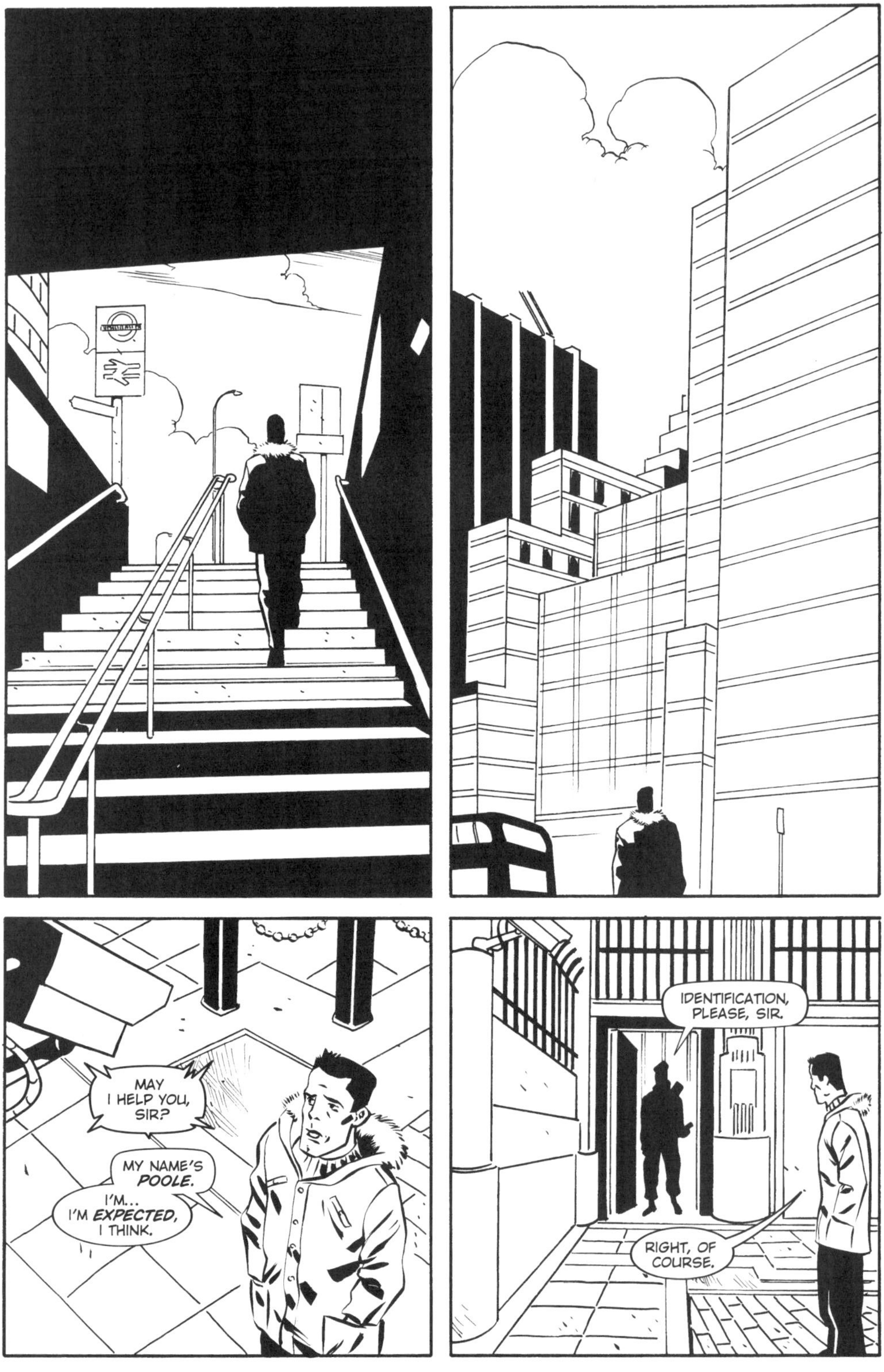
MAY I HELP YOU, SIR?
MY NAME'S POOLE.
I'M... I'M EXPECTED, I THINK.
IDENTIFICATION, PLEASE, SIR.
RIGHT, OF COURSE.

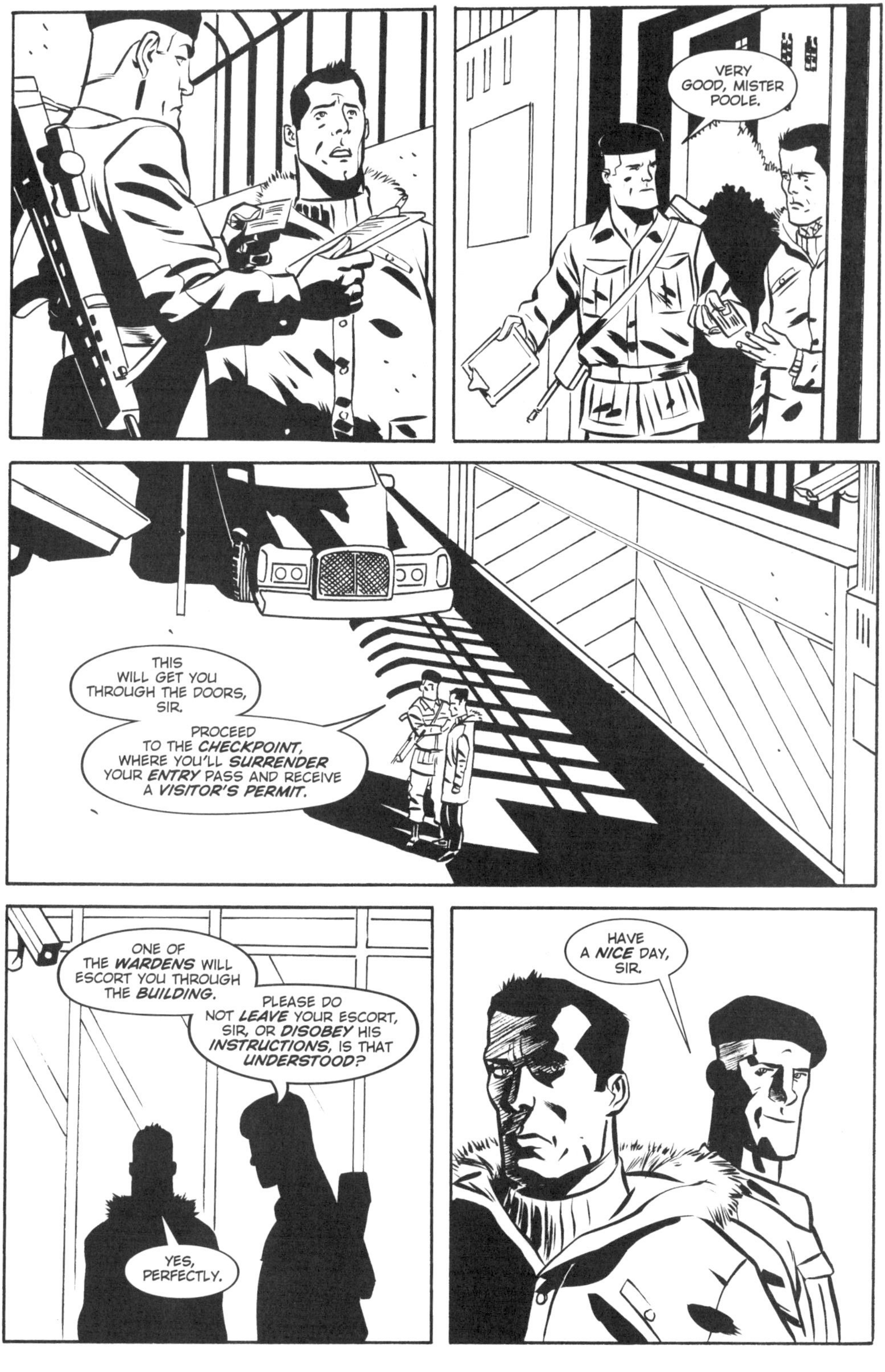
VERY GOOD, MISTER POOLE.
THIS WILL GET YOU THROUGH THE DOORS, SIR.
PROCEED TO THE CHECKPOINT, WHERE YOU'LL SURRENDER YOUR ENTRY PASS AND RECEIVE A VISITOR'S PERMIT.
ONE OF THE WARDENS WILL ESCORT YOU THROUGH THE BUILDING.
PLEASE DO NOT LEAVE YOUR ESCORT, SIR, OR DISOBEY HIS INSTRUCTIONS, IS THAT UNDERSTOOD?
YES, PERFECTLY.
HAVE A NICE DAY, SIR.

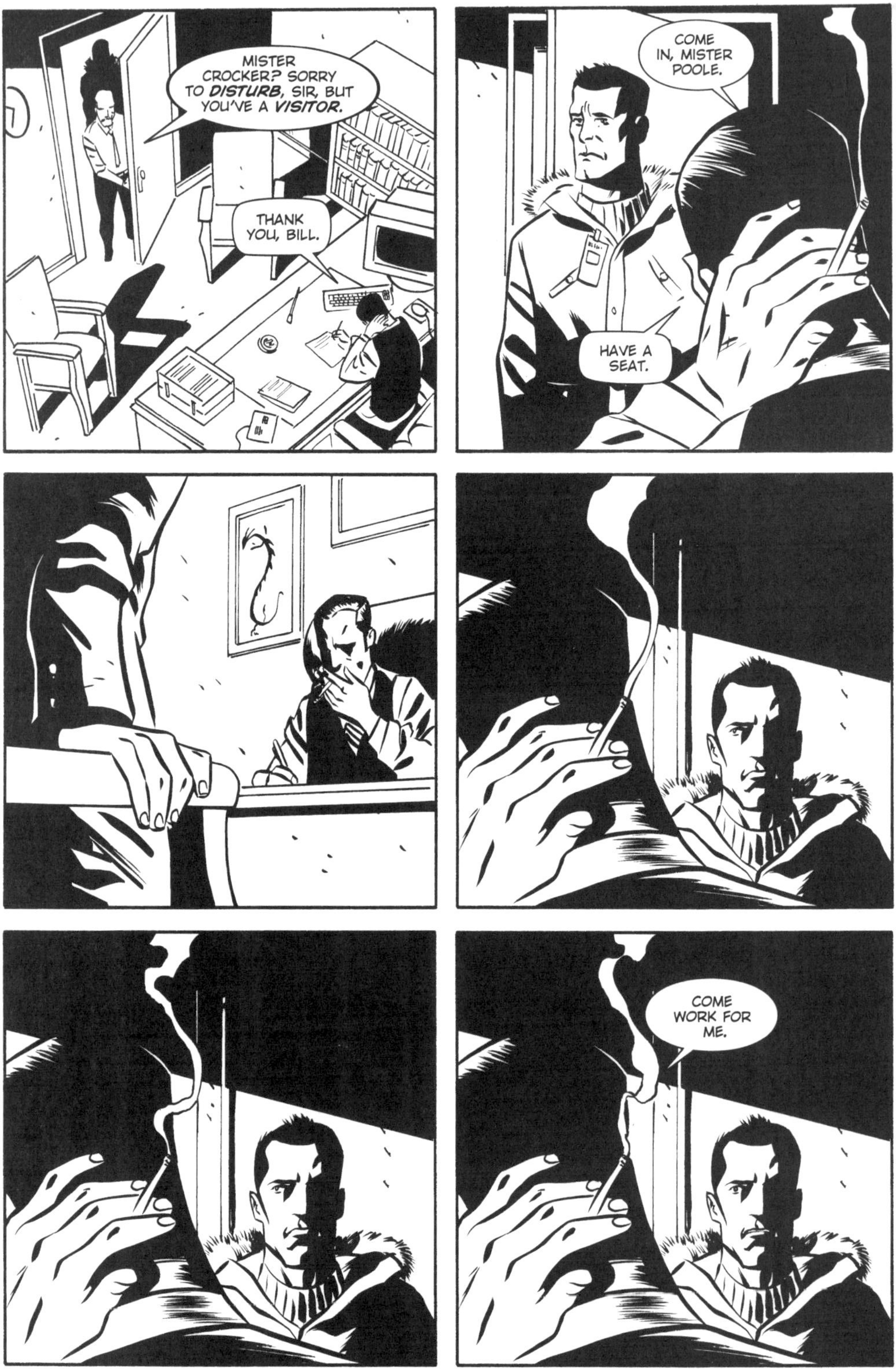
MISTER CROCKER? SORRY TO DISTURB, SIR, BUT YOU'VE A VISITOR.
THANK YOU, BILL.
COME IN, MISTER POOLE.
HAVE A SEAT.
COME WORK FOR ME.

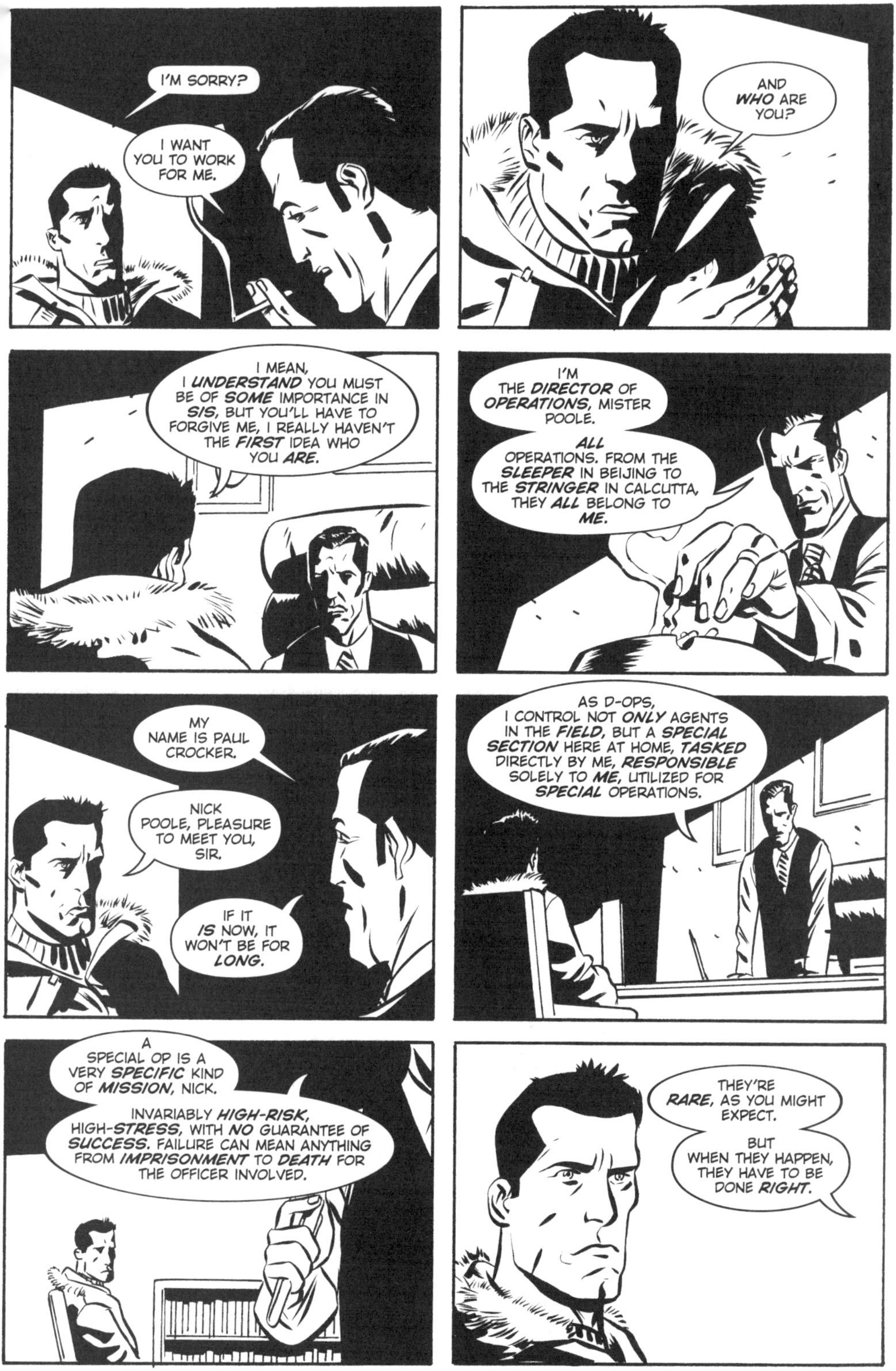
I'M SORRY?
I WANT YOU TO WORK FOR ME.
AND WHO ARE YOU?
I MEAN, I UNDERSTAND YOU MUST BE OF SOME IMPORTANCE IN SIS, BUT YOU'LL HAVE TO FORGIVE ME, I REALLY HAVEN'T THE FIRST IDEA WHO YOU ARE.
I'M THE DIRECTOR OF OPERATIONS, MISTER POOLE.
ALL OPERATIONS. FROM THE SLEEPER IN BEIJING TO THE STRINGER IN CALCUTTA, THEY ALL BELONG TO ME.
MY NAME IS PAUL CROCKER.
NICK POOLE, PLEASURE TO MEET YOU, SIR.
IF IT IS NOW, IT WON'T BE FOR LONG.
AS D-OPS, I CONTROL NOT ONLY AGENTS IN THE FIELD, BUT A SPECIAL SECTION HERE AT HOME, TASKED DIRECTLY BY ME, RESPONSIBLE SOLELY TO ME, UTILIZED FOR SPECIAL OPERATIONS.
A SPECIAL OP IS A VERY SPECIFIC KIND OF MISSION, NICK.
INVARIABLY HIGH-RISK, HIGH-STRESS, WITH NO GUARANTEE OF SUCCESS. FAILURE CAN MEAN ANYTHING FROM IMPRISONMENT TO DEATH FOR THE OFFICER INVOLVED.
THEY'RE RARE, AS YOU MIGHT EXPECT.
BUT WHEN THEY HAPPEN, THEY HAVE TO BE DONE RIGHT.

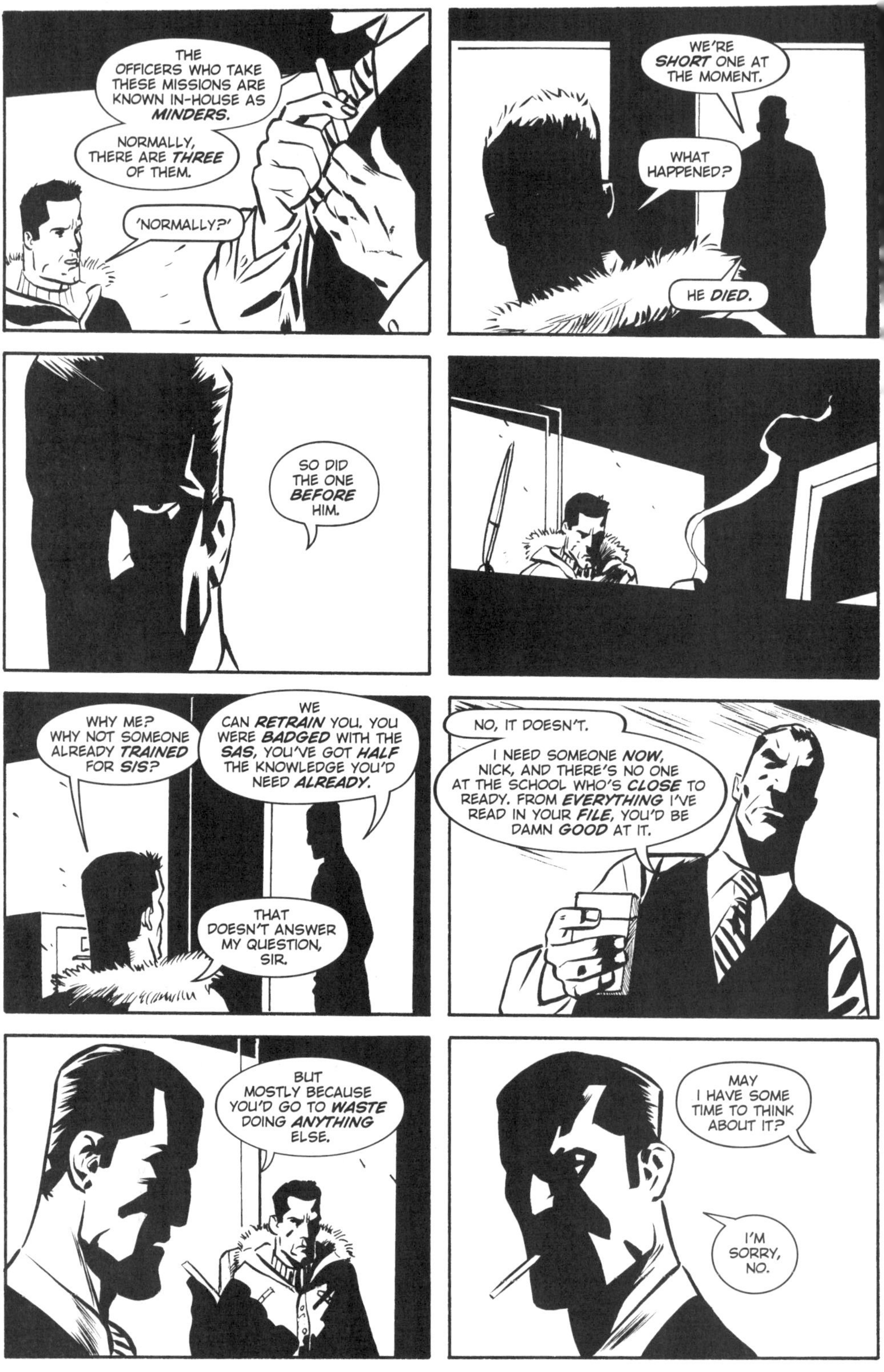

THE OFFICERS WHO TAKE THESE MISSIONS ARE KNOWN IN-HOUSE AS MINDERS.
NORMALLY, THERE ARE THREE OF THEM.
'NORMALLY?'
WE'RE SHORT ONE AT THE MOMENT.
WHAT HAPPENED?
HE DIED.
SO DID THE ONE BEFORE HIM.
WHY ME? WHY NOT SOMEONE ALREADY TRAINED FOR SIS?
WE CAN RETRAIN YOU. YOU WERE BADGED WITH THE SAS, YOU'VE GOT HALF THE KNOWLEDGE YOU'D NEED ALREADY.
THAT DOESN'T ANSWER MY QUESTION, SIR.
NO, IT DOESN'T.
I NEED SOMEONE NOW, NICK, AND THERE'S NO ONE AT THE SCHOOL WHO'S CLOSE TO READY. FROM EVERYTHING I'VE READ IN YOUR FILE, YOU'D BE DAMN GOOD AT IT.
BUT MOSTLY BECAUSE YOU'D GO TO WASTE DOING ANYTHING ELSE.
MAY I HAVE SOME TIME TO THINK ABOUT IT?
I'M SORRY, NO.

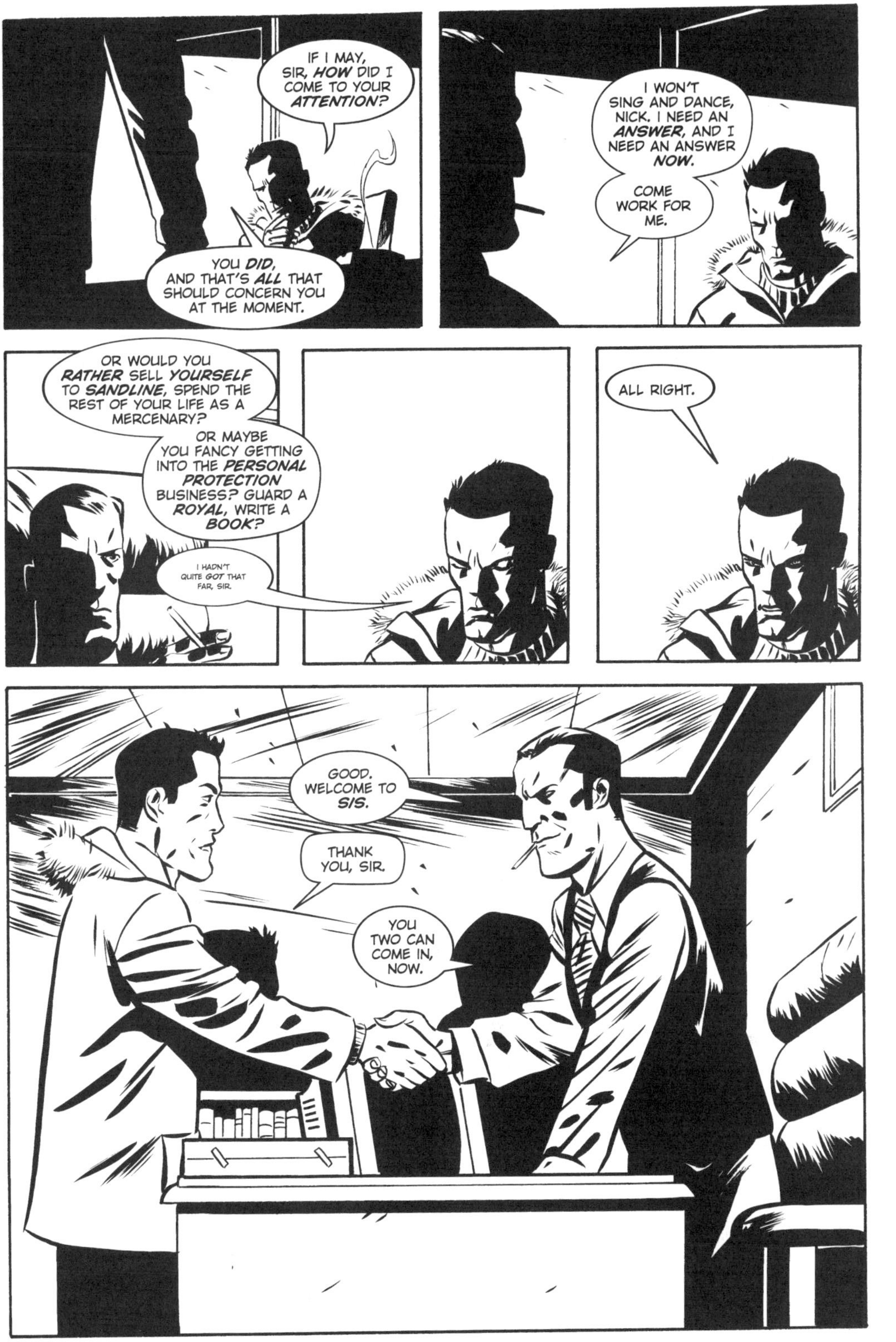
IF I MAY, SIR, HOW DID I COME TO YOUR ATTENTION?
YOU DID, AND THAT'S ALL THAT SHOULD CONCERN YOU AT THE MOMENT.
I WON'T SING AND DANCE, NICK. I NEED AN ANSWER, AND I NEED AN ANSWER NOW.
COME WORK FOR ME.
OR WOULD YOU RATHER SELL YOURSELF TO SANDLINE, SPEND THE REST OF YOUR LIFE AS A MERCENARY?
OR MAYBE YOU FANCY GETTING INTO THE PERSONAL PROTECTION BUSINESS? GUARD A ROYAL, WRITE A BOOK?
I HADN'T QUITE GOT THAT FAR, SIR.
ALL RIGHT.
GOOD. WELCOME TO SIS.
THANK YOU, SIR.
YOU TWO CAN COME IN, NOW.

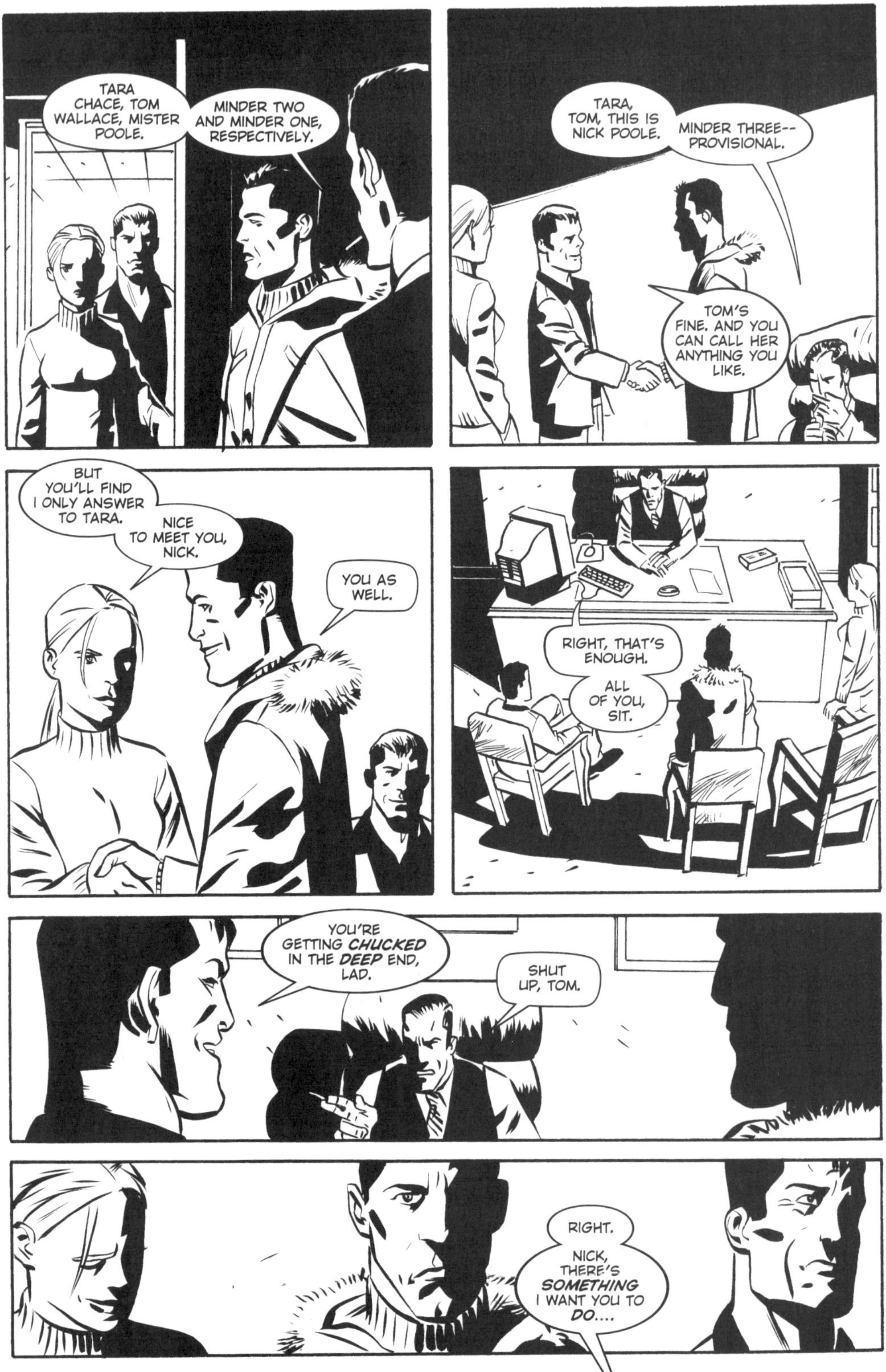
TARA CHACE, TOM WALLACE, MISTER POOLE.
MINDER TWO AND MINDER ONE, RESPECTIVELY.
TARA, TOM, THIS IS NICK POOLE.
MINDER THREE-- PROVISIONAL.
TOM'S FINE. AND YOU CAN CALL HER ANYTHING YOU LIKE.
BUT YOU'LL FIND I ONLY ANSWER TO TARA.
NICE TO MEET YOU, NICK.
YOU AS WELL.
RIGHT, THAT'S ENOUGH.
ALL OF YOU, SIT.
YOU'RE GETTING CHUCKED IN THE DEEP END, LAD.
SHUT UP, TOM.
RIGHT.
NICK, THERE'S SOMETHING I WANT YOU TO DO....

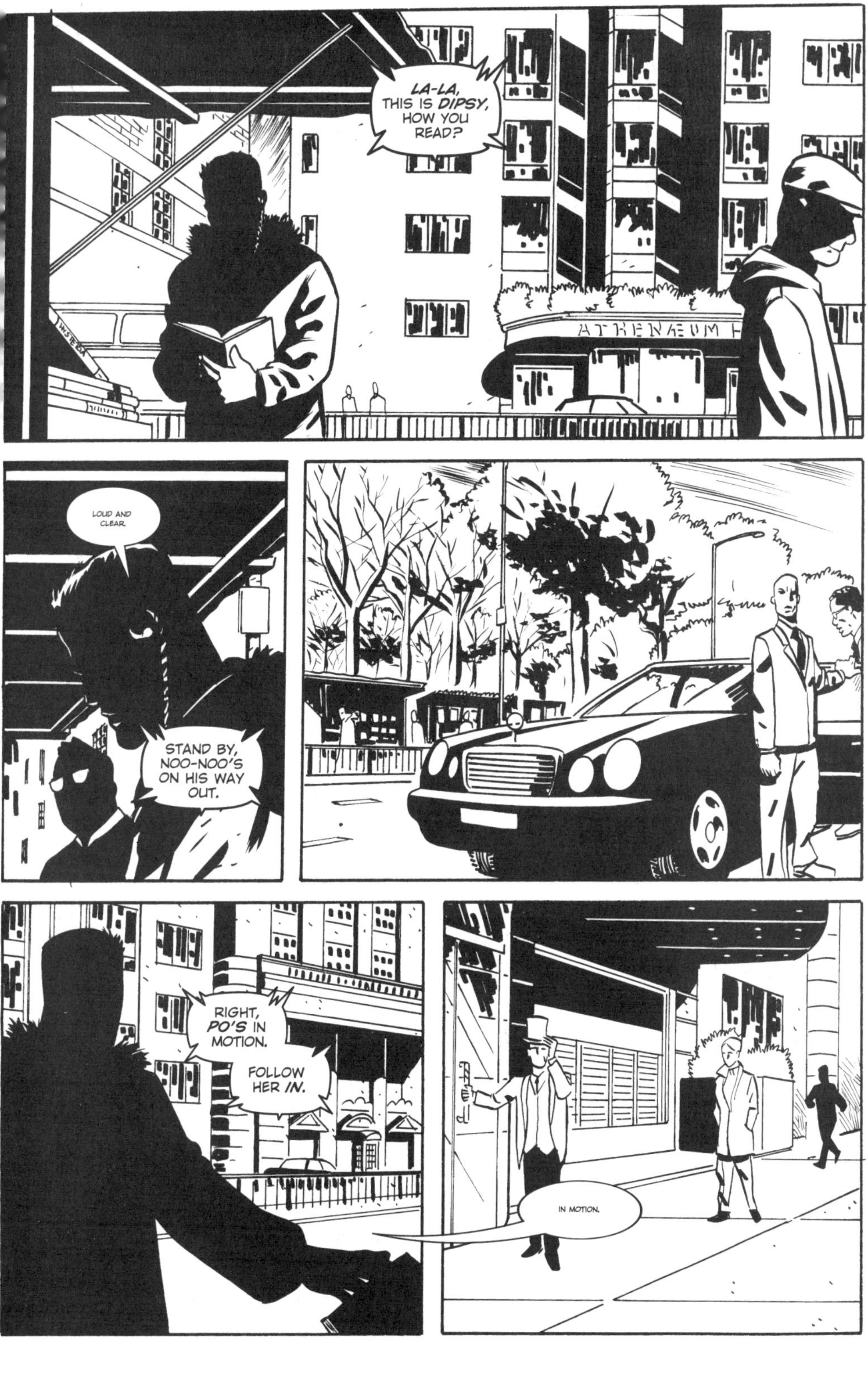
LA-LA, THIS IS DIPSY, HOW YOU READ?
ATHENAEUM
LOUD AND CLEAR
STAND BY, NOO-NOO'S ON HIS WAY OUT.
RIGHT, PO'S IN MOTION.
FOLLOW HER IN.
IN MOTION.

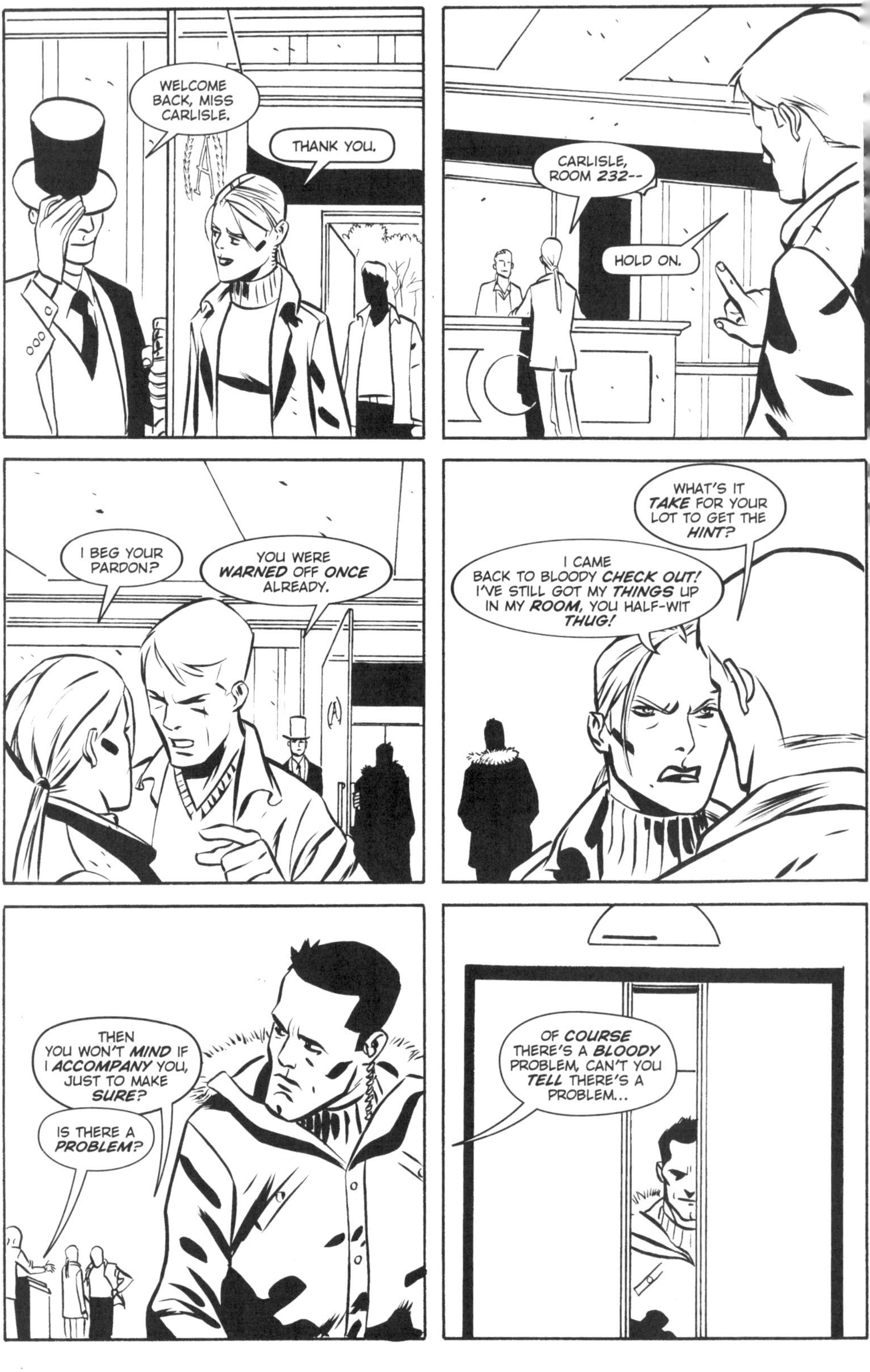
WELCOME BACK, MISS CARLISLE.
THANK YOU.
CARLISLE, ROOM 232--
HOLD ON.
I BEG YOUR PARDON?
YOU WERE WARNED OFF ONCE ALREADY.
WHAT'S IT TAKE FOR YOUR LOT TO GET THE HINT?
I CAME BACK TO BLOODY CHECK OUT! I'VE STILL GOT MY THINGS UP IN MY ROOM, YOU HALF-WIT THUG!
THEN YOU WON'T MIND IF I ACCOMPANY YOU, JUST TO MAKE SURE?
IS THERE A PROBLEM?
OF COURSE THERE'S A BLOODY PROBLEM, CAN'T YOU TELL THERE'S A PROBLEM...

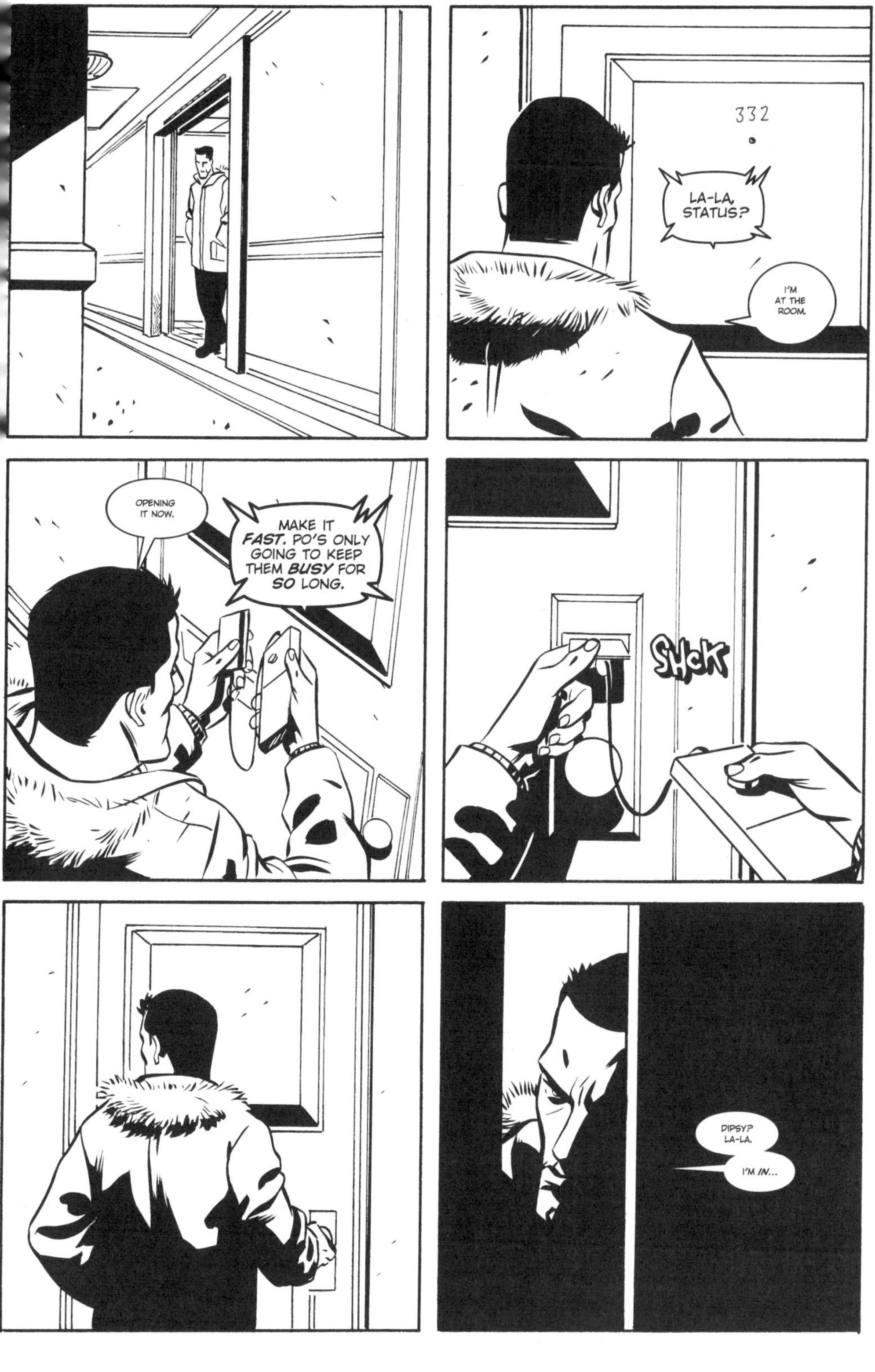
332
LA-LA, STATUS?
I'M AT THE ROOM.
OPENING IT NOW.
MAKE IT FAST. PO'S ONLY GOING TO KEEP THEM BUSY FOR SO LONG.
SHCK
DIPSY? LA-LA.
I'M IN...

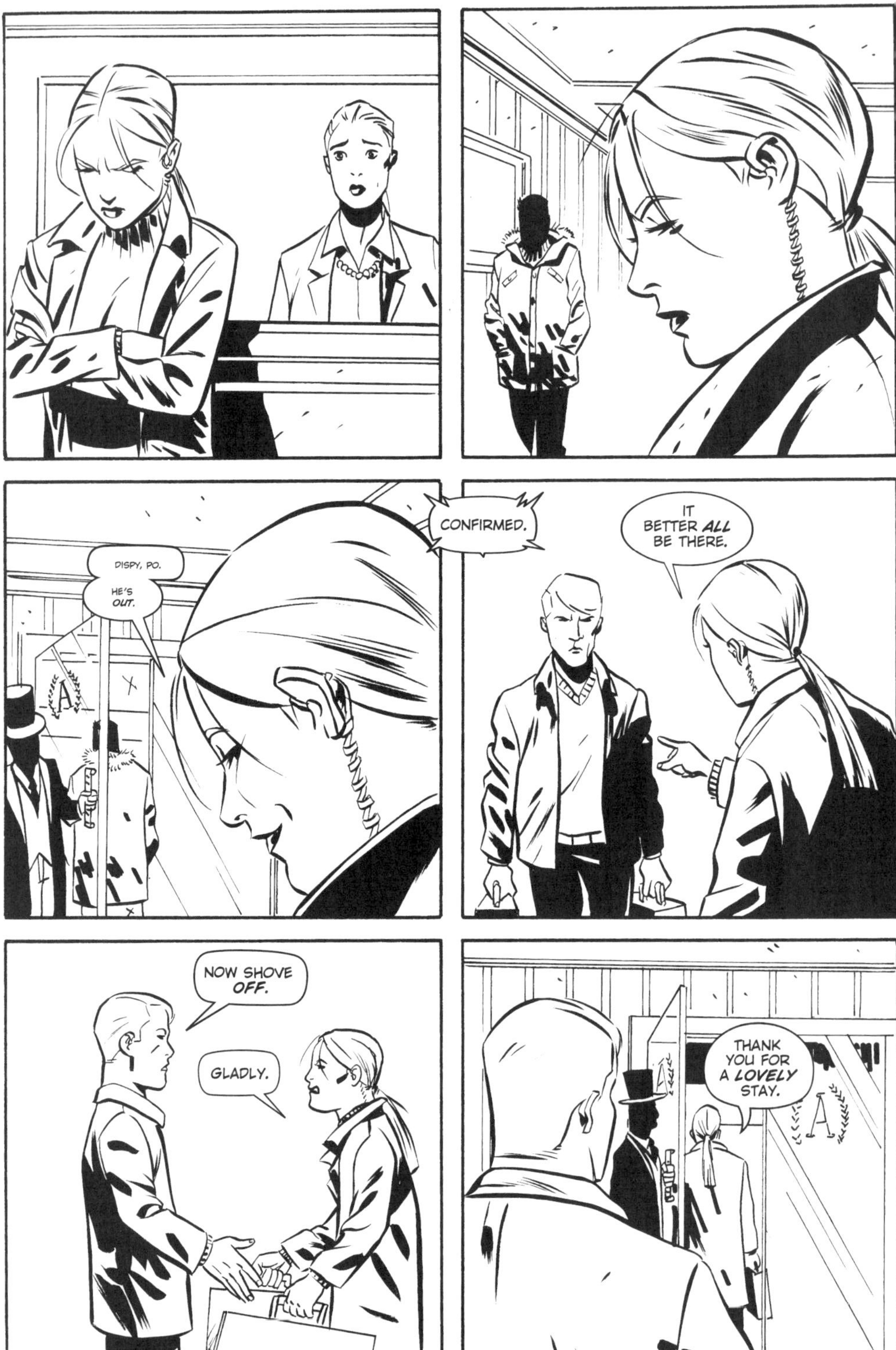
DISPY, PO.
HE'S OUT.
CONFIRMED.
IT BETTER ALL BE THERE.
NOW SHOVE OFF.
GLADLY.
THANK YOU FOR A LOVELY STAY.

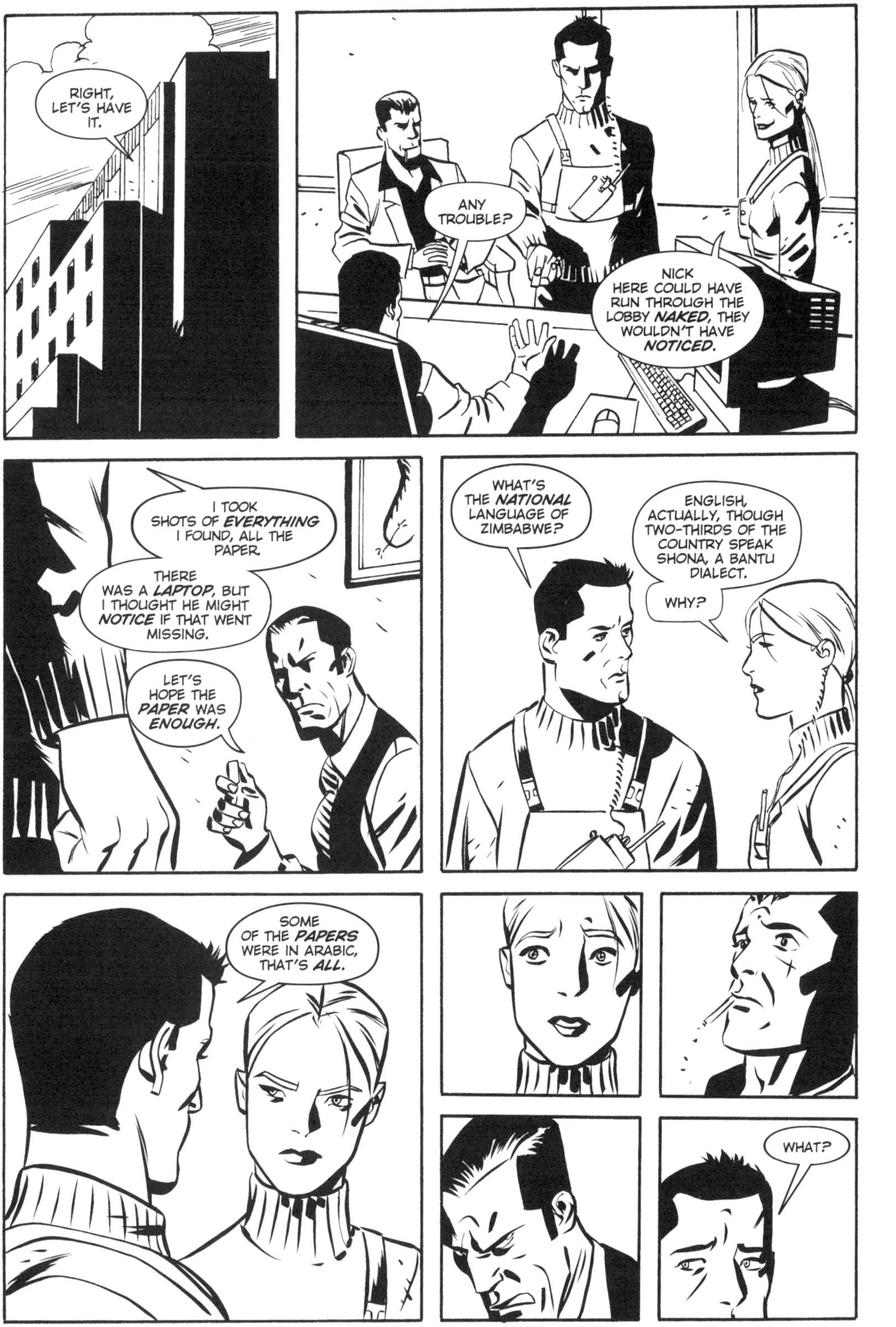
RIGHT, LET'S HAVE IT.
ANY TROUBLE?
NICK HERE COULD HAVE RUN THROUGH THE LOBBY *NAKED*, THEY WOULDN'T HAVE *NOTICED*.
I TOOK SHOTS OF *EVERYTHING* I FOUND, ALL THE PAPER.
THERE WAS A *LAPTOP*, BUT I THOUGHT HE MIGHT *NOTICE* IF THAT WENT MISSING.
LET'S HOPE THE *PAPER* WAS *ENOUGH*.
WHAT'S THE *NATIONAL* LANGUAGE OF ZIMBABWE?
ENGLISH, ACTUALLY, THOUGH TWO-THIRDS OF THE COUNTRY SPEAK SHONA, A BANTU DIALECT.
WHY?
SOME OF THE *PAPERS* WERE IN ARABIC, THAT'S *ALL*.
WHAT?

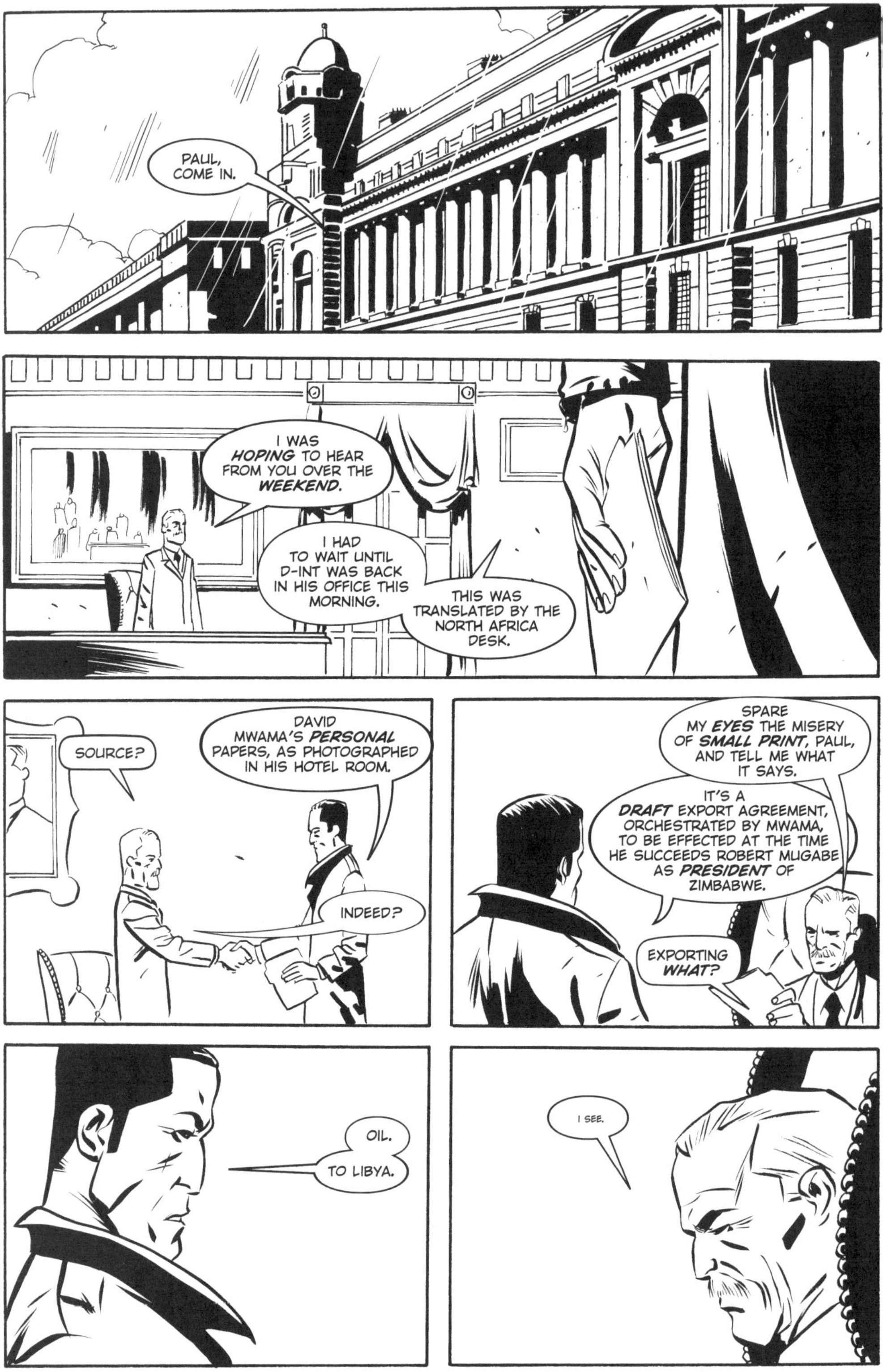
PAUL, COME IN.
I WAS HOPING TO HEAR FROM YOU OVER THE WEEKEND.
I HAD TO WAIT UNTIL D-INT WAS BACK IN HIS OFFICE THIS MORNING.
THIS WAS TRANSLATED BY THE NORTH AFRICA DESK.
SOURCE?
DAVID MWAMA'S PERSONAL PAPERS, AS PHOTOGRAPHED IN HIS HOTEL ROOM.
INDEED?
SPARE MY EYES THE MISERY OF SMALL PRINT, PAUL, AND TELL ME WHAT IT SAYS.
IT'S A DRAFT EXPORT AGREEMENT, ORCHESTRATED BY MWAMA, TO BE EFFECTED AT THE TIME HE SUCCEEDS ROBERT MUGABE AS PRESIDENT OF ZIMBABWE.
EXPORTING WHAT?
OIL.
TO LIBYA.
I SEE.

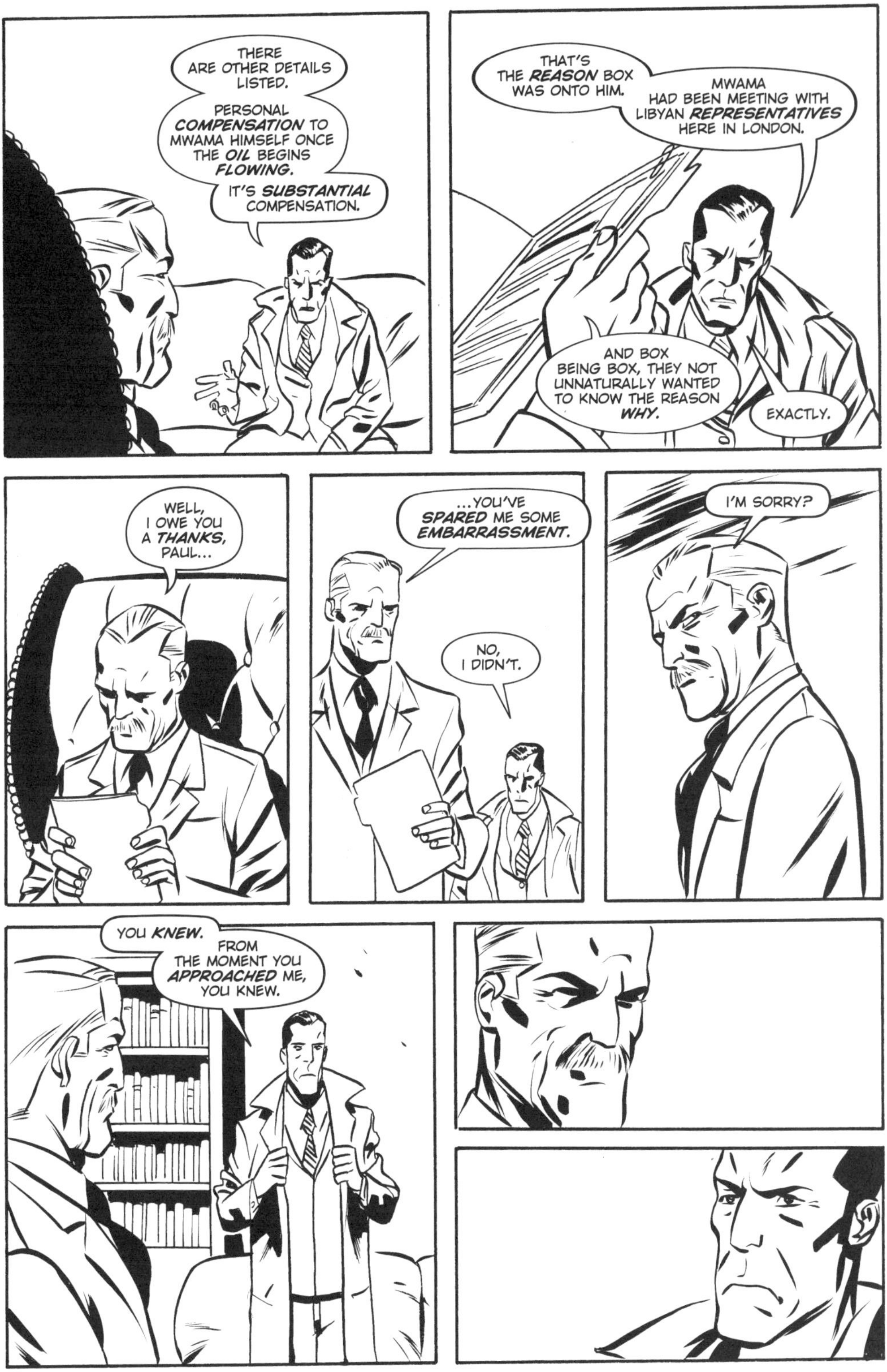
THERE ARE OTHER DETAILS LISTED.
PERSONAL COMPENSATION TO MWAMA HIMSELF ONCE THE OIL BEGINS FLOWING.
IT'S SUBSTANTIAL COMPENSATION.
THAT'S THE REASON BOX WAS ONTO HIM.
MWAMA HAD BEEN MEETING WITH LIBYAN REPRESENTATIVES HERE IN LONDON.
AND BOX BEING BOX, THEY NOT UNNATURALLY WANTED TO KNOW THE REASON WHY.
EXACTLY.
WELL, I OWE YOU A THANKS, PAUL...
...YOU'VE SPARED ME SOME EMBARRASSMENT.
NO, I DIDN'T.
I'M SORRY?
YOU KNEW.
FROM THE MOMENT YOU APPROACHED ME, YOU KNEW.

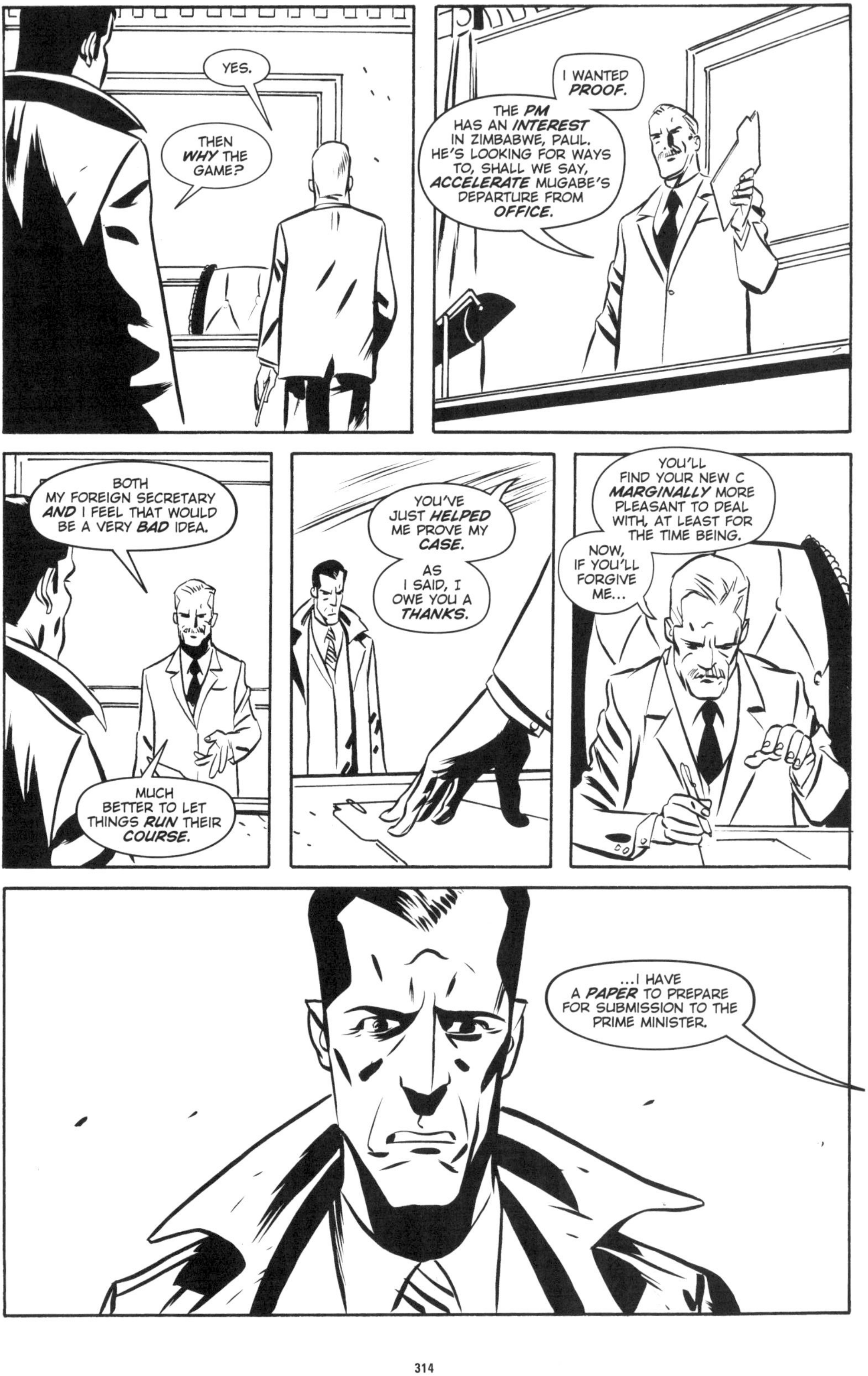
YES.
THEN WHY THE GAME?
I WANTED PROOF.
THE PM HAS AN INTEREST IN ZIMBABWE, PAUL. HE'S LOOKING FOR WAYS TO, SHALL WE SAY, ACCELERATE MUGABE'S DEPARTURE FROM OFFICE.
BOTH MY FOREIGN SECRETARY AND I FEEL THAT WOULD BE A VERY BAD IDEA.
MUCH BETTER TO LET THINGS RUN THEIR COURSE.
YOU'VE JUST HELPED ME PROVE MY CASE.
AS I SAID, I OWE YOU A THANKS.
YOU'LL FIND YOUR NEW C MARGINALLY MORE PLEASANT TO DEAL WITH, AT LEAST FOR THE TIME BEING.
NOW, IF YOU'LL FORGIVE ME...
...I HAVE A PAPER TO PREPARE FOR SUBMISSION TO THE PRIME MINISTER.

QUEEN & COUNTRY™

BEHIND THE SCENES

The following pages contain samples of some of Jason Shawn Alexander's development process, taking cover art from sketches to final designs. Above is the cover painting to *Queen & Country - Operation: Blackwall* in progress at Alexander's art studio.

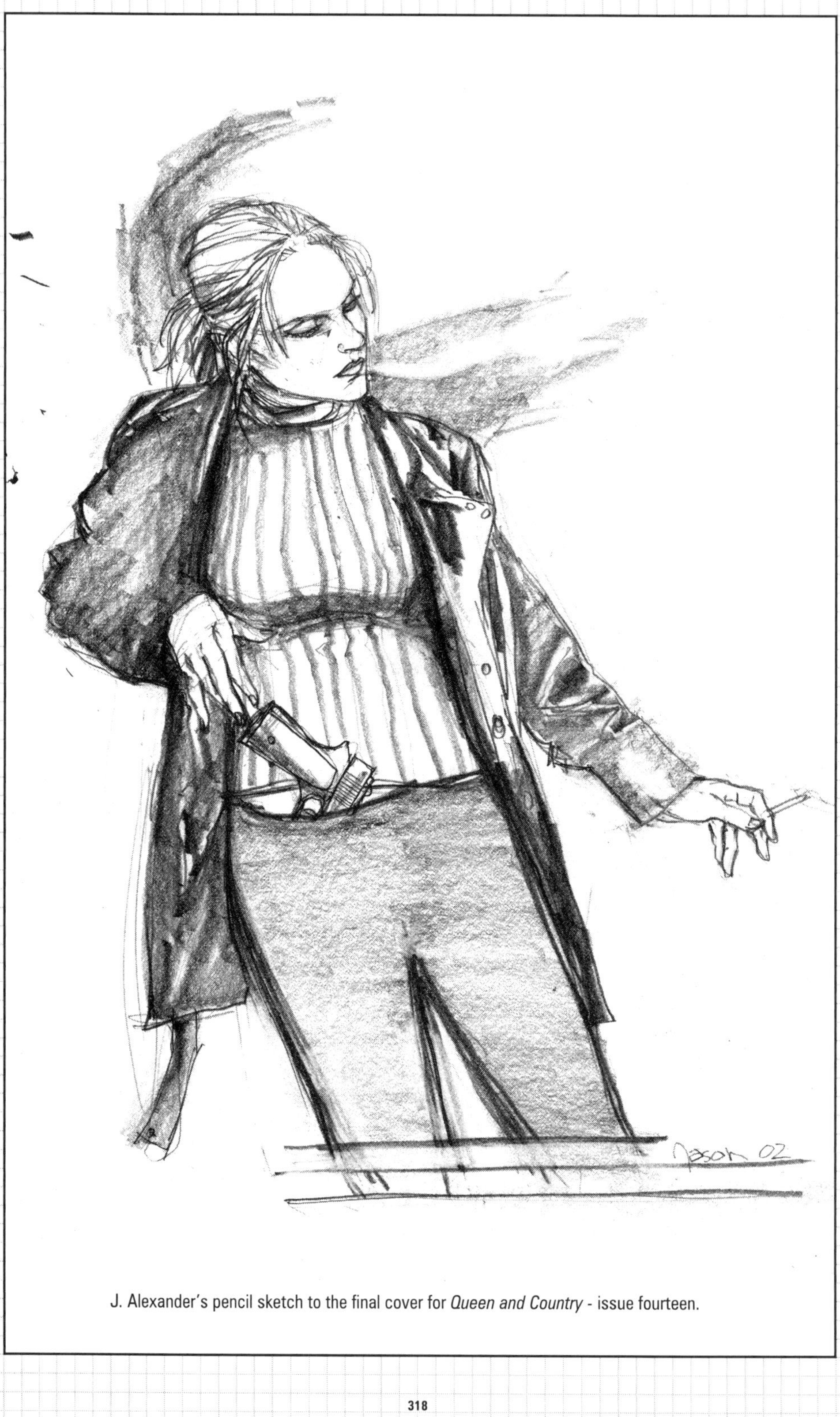
Jason 02

J. Alexander's pencil sketch to the final cover for *Queen and Country* - issue fourteen.

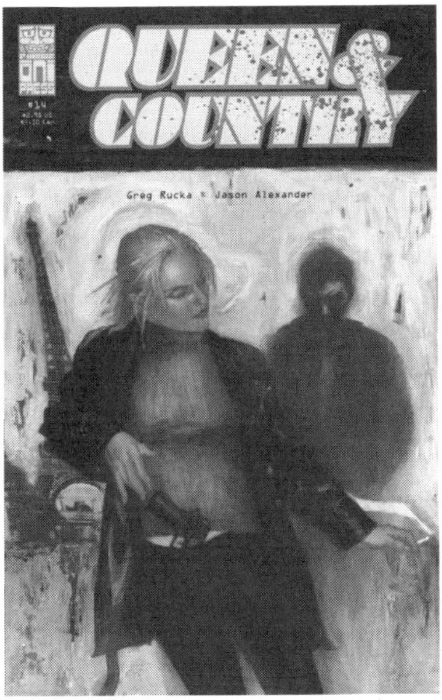
QUEEN & COUNTRY
#14
Greg Rucka * Jason Alexander

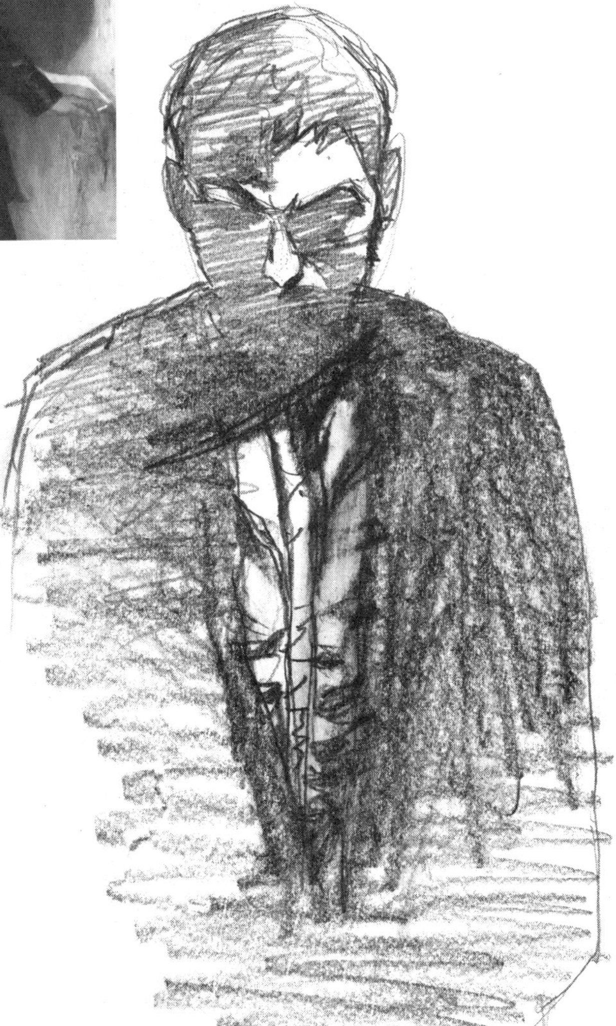

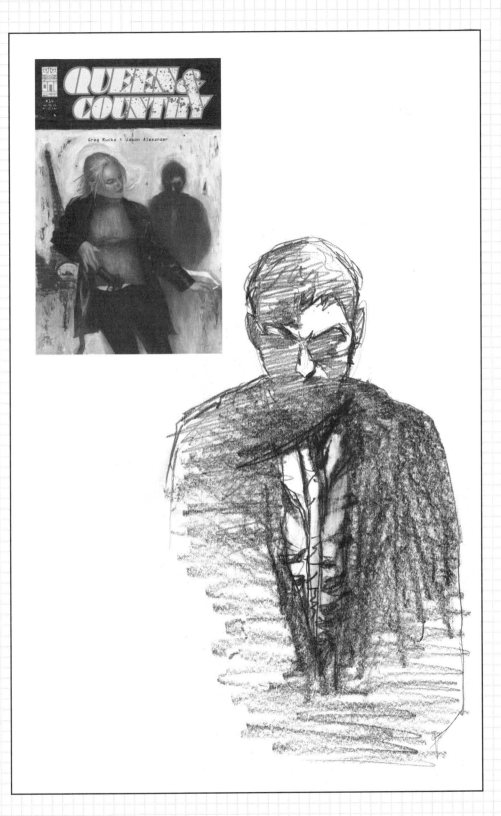

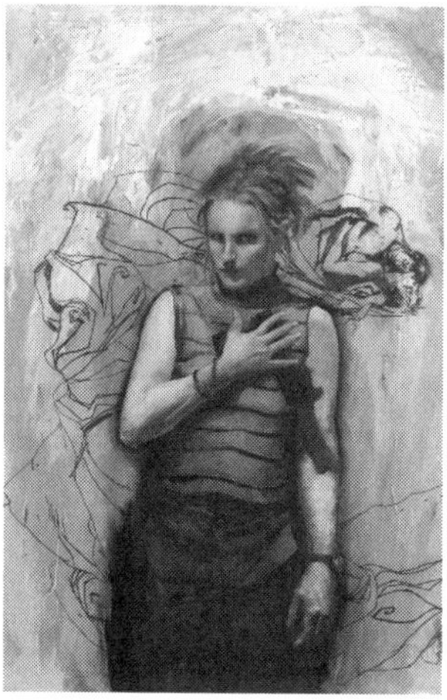

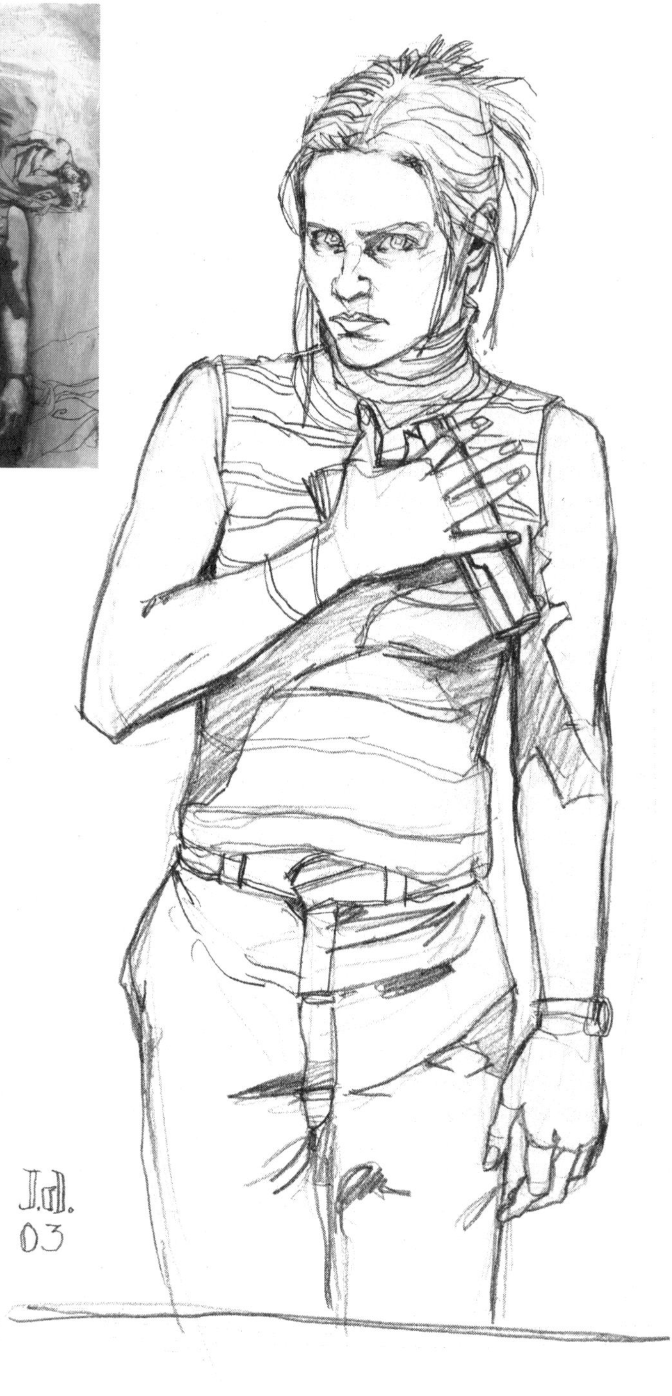

Alexander's pencil sketch to the final painting for *Queen & Country - Operation: Blackwell*.

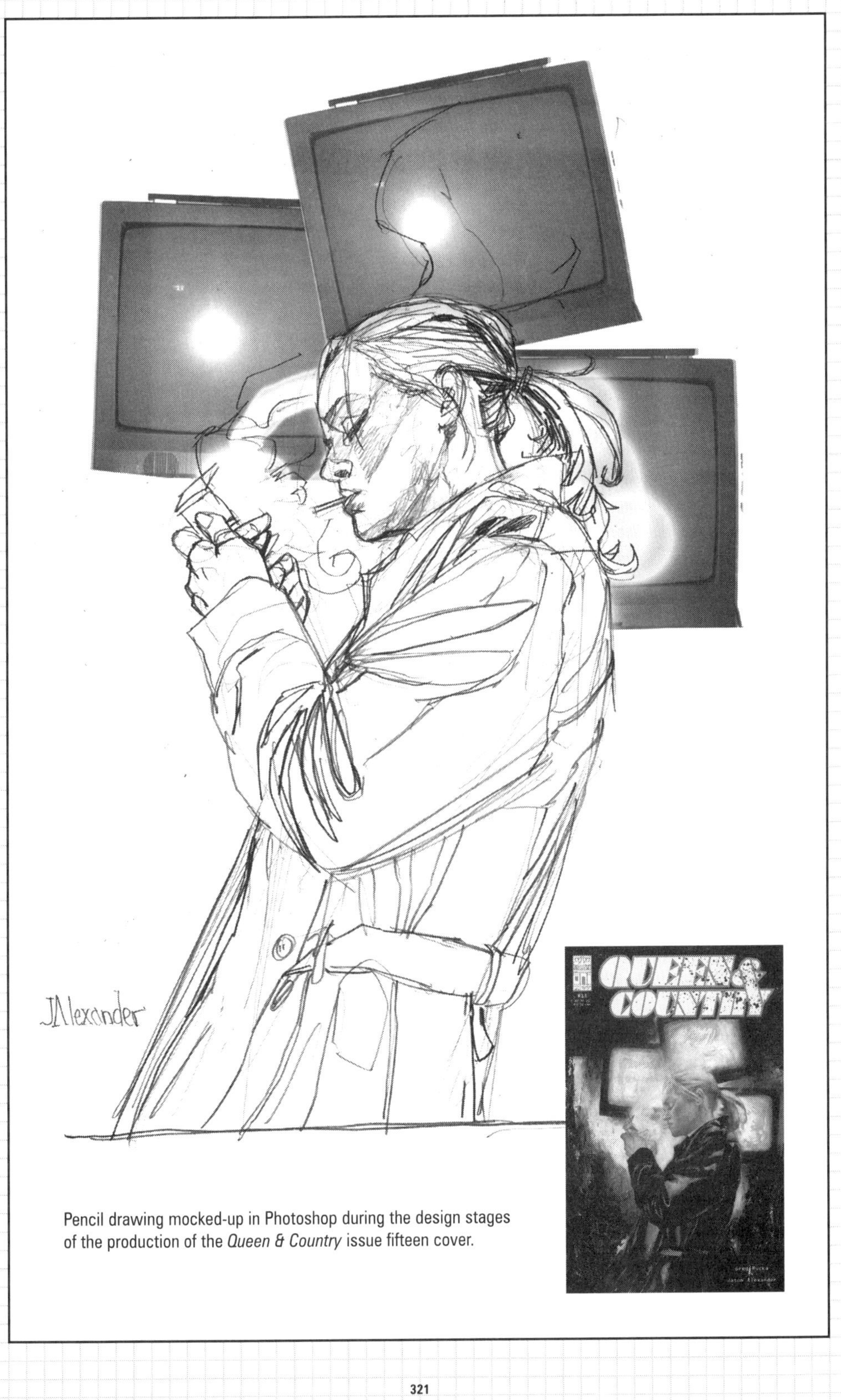
JAlexander
QUEEN & COUNTRY

Pencil drawing mocked-up in Photoshop during the design stages of the production of the *Queen & Country* issue fifteen cover.

QUEEN & COUNTRY
OPERATION: BLACKWALL
GREG RUCKA J. ALEXANDER

QUEEN & COUNTRY
OPERATION: STORM FRONT
GREG RUCKA ★ CARLA SPEED McNEIL

QUEEN & COUNTRY
OPERATION: DANDELION
GREG RUCKA
★
MIKE HAWTHORNE

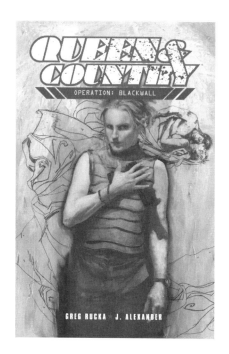

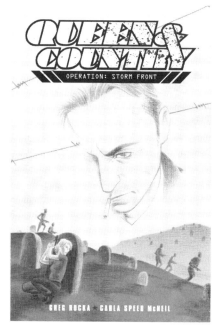

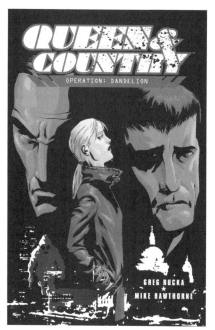

Original cover designs for *Queen & Country* trade paperback collections volumes four through six.

Operation: Blackwall by Jason Shawn Alexander.
Operation: Storm Front by Carla Speed McNeil.
Operation: Dandelion by Mike Hawthorne.

QUEEN & COUNTRY™

THE TRANSLATED SCENES

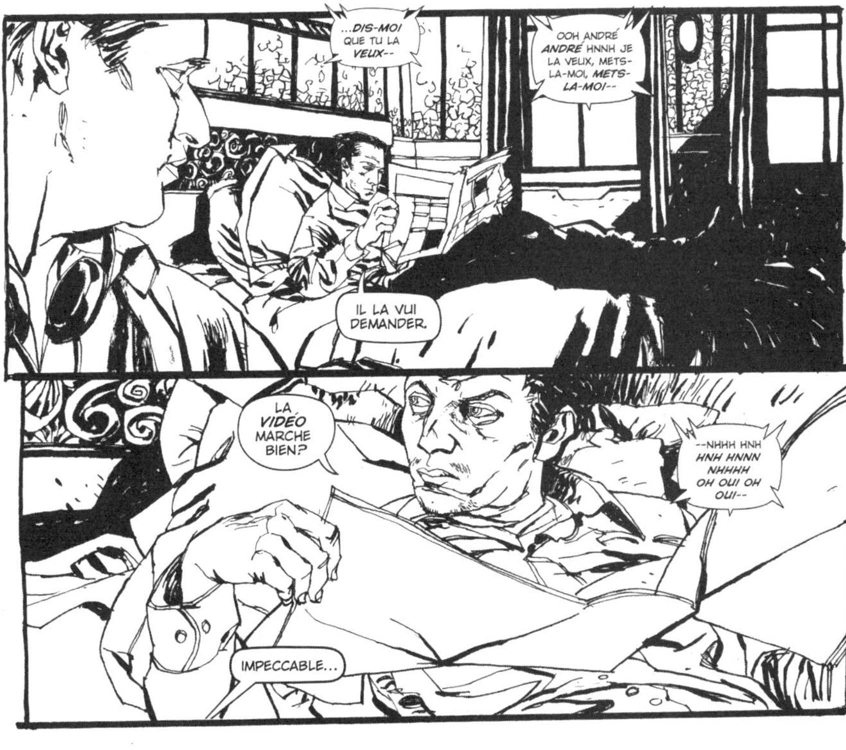
...DIS-MOI QUE TU LA VEUX--
OOH ANDRÉ ANDRÉ HNNH JE LA VEUX, METS-LA-MOI, METS-LA-MOI--
IL LA VUI DEMANDER.
LA VIDÉO MARCHE BIEN?
--NHHH HNH HNH HNNN NHHHH OH OUI OH OUI--
IMPECCABLE...

The following pages contain english translations of the first three pages of this book.

Page 1

MARION/inside:	*I hope you like the room.*
BECK:	*It's lovely.*
MARION:	*Do you want a drink? I could order champagne.*
BECK:	*If I have another drink, I don't think I'll be able to walk.*
MARION:	*Then it's a good thing walking wasn't what I had in mind. I want you so badly, Rachel. I've been wanting you for weeks.*
MARION/linked:	*Every time I see you I get turned on, I can't help myself.*
BECK:	*Andre…*
MARION:	*I've been dying to touch you…*
MARION/linked:	*…to pleasure you…*
MARION/off:	*…to make love to you.*

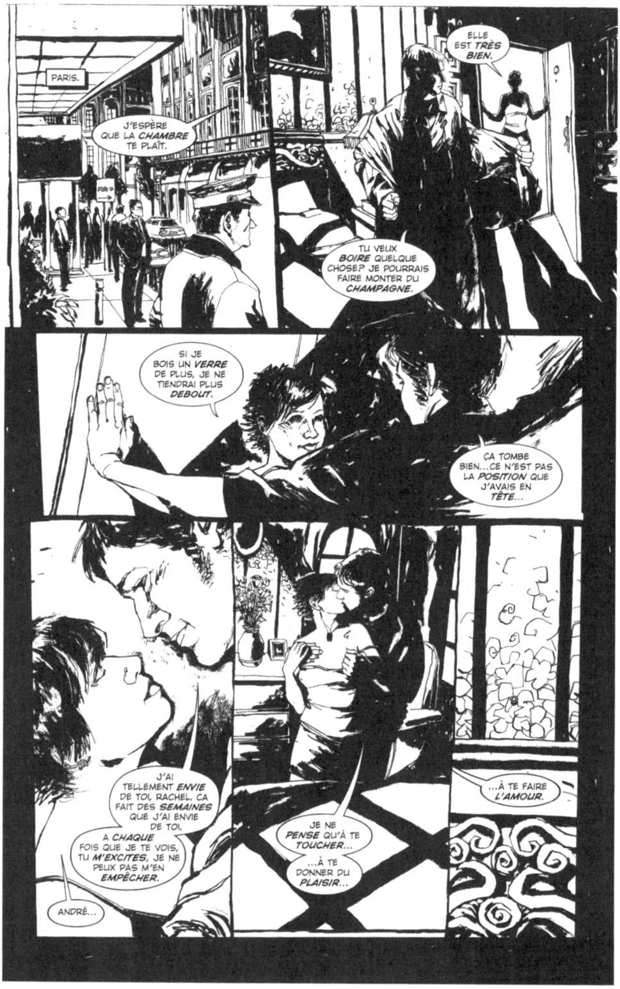

PARIS.
J'ESPÈRE QUE LA CHAMBRE TE PLAÎT.
ELLE EST TRÈS BIEN.
TU VEUX BOIRE QUELQUE CHOSE? JE POURRAIS FAIRE MONTER DU CHAMPAGNE.
SI JE BOIS UN VERRE DE PLUS, JE NE TIENDRAI PLUS DEBOUT.
ÇA TOMBE BIEN...CE N'EST PAS LA POSITION QUE J'AVAIS EN TÊTE...
J'AI TELLEMENT ENVIE DE TOI, RACHEL. CA FAIT DES SEMAINES QUE J'AI ENVIE DE TOI.
A CHAQUE FOIS QUE JE TE VOIS, TU M'EXCITES, JE NE PEUX PAS M'EN EMPÊCHER.
ANDRÉ...
JE NE PENSE QU'À TE TOUCHER...
...À TE DONNER DU PLAISIR...
...À TE FAIRE L'AMOUR.

...TU AS LES MAINS TELLEMENT CHAUDES...
...OOH C'EST BON OOHHH...
VAS-Y, BOUGE COMME ÇA, REMUE TON CUL COMME ÇA
TU AIMES ÇA, HEIN? TU AIMES ÇA QUAND JE TE METS LES DOIGTS DANS LE CUL...
...DIS-MOI QUE TU AIMES AVOIR MES DOIGTS DANS LE CUL.
NHHH OOOH OUI N'ARRÊTE PAS CE QUE TU FAIS OH OUI--
--OOOH MMMM N'ARRÊTE OOOHH PAS MMMM OOHHHH MA CHÉRIE NNGGGGG MON AMOUR...
NGHH OOHHH C'EST BON OUI COMME ÇA...
...TU LA SENS, DANS TA CHATTE, QUAND JE TE BAISE COMME ÇA?
NHH OH OUI OUI COMME ÇA COMME ÇA SUR MON CLITO GNNH HHN OOH OUI TU VAS ME FAIRE JOUIR--
--JE VAIS JOUIR TELLEMENT FORT SUR TA BITE
DIS-MOI, RACHEL...
JE CROYAIS QU'IL ALLAIT AU MOINS LUI DEMANDER DE LE SUCER D'ABORD.
...DIS-MOI QUE TU LA VEUX--
OOH ANDRÉ ANDRE HNNH JE LA VEUX, METS-LA-MOI, METS-LA-MOI--
IL LA VUI DEMANDER.
LA VIDÉO MARCHE BIEN?
--NHHH HNH HNH HNNN NHHHH OH OUI OH OUI--
IMPECCABLE...

Page 2

ELEC/tailless/small:	*...your hands, they're so hot...*
ELEC/tailless/small:	*...ooh that feels sooo good unhh...*
ELEC/tailless/small:	*Yeah, move like that, move your ass just like that.*
ELEC/tailless/small:	*You like that, don't you? You like my fingers in your ass, tell me how you like my fingers up your ass.*
ELEC/tailless/small:	*Jesus—nhhh oooh don't stop whatever you do God—*
ELEC/tailless/small:	*—ungh unh don't huh stop uhhh uh-huh oh honey ooh ngg love...*
ELEC/tailless/small:	*nghh uhh good yes like this...*
ELEC/tailless/small:	*...you feel this, me inside you, fucking you like this?*
ELEC/tailless/small:	*nnnh oh yeah, yeah like that like that on my clit gnnh hhn huh God I'm gonna come—*
ELEC/tailless/small:	*—gonna come so hard around your cock nhh...*
ELEC/tailless/small:	*Tell me, Rachel...*
CLAUDE:	*I thought he'd at least have her blow him first.*
ELEC/tailless/small:	*...tell me hnnn how much you want it—*
ELEC/tailless/small:	*God Andre Andre hnnh I want it, I want it so nhhh bad—*
PHILIPPE:	*He'll get to it.*
PHILIPPE:	*How's the video?*
CLAUDE/off:	*Perfect, really...*
ELEC/tailless/small:	*—nhhh hnh HNH HNNN NHHHH OH GOD OH GOD—*

Page 3

CLAUDE:	*. . . I can count the hairs on her cunt—*
ELEC/tailless/small:	*—OHMYGODANDRE GNHHhh. . .*
CLAUDE:	*HEY!*
ELEC/tailless/small:	*. . . hnn huh huh huh oh oh baby. . .*
PHILIPPE:	*No smoking.*
PHILIPPE/linked:	*She could smell it through the hole in the wall.*
ELEC/tailless/small:	*. . . oh baby oh lover. . .*
CLAUDE:	*I don't think we have to worry about that.*
ELEC/tailless/small:	*. . . I think it's my turn now. . .*
CLAUDE:	*Anton has her more than occupied for the time being.*
ELEC/tailless/small:	*Ooh, oh Rachel, baby, you don't have to. . .*
ELEC/tailless/small:	*Shhh I want to. . . .*

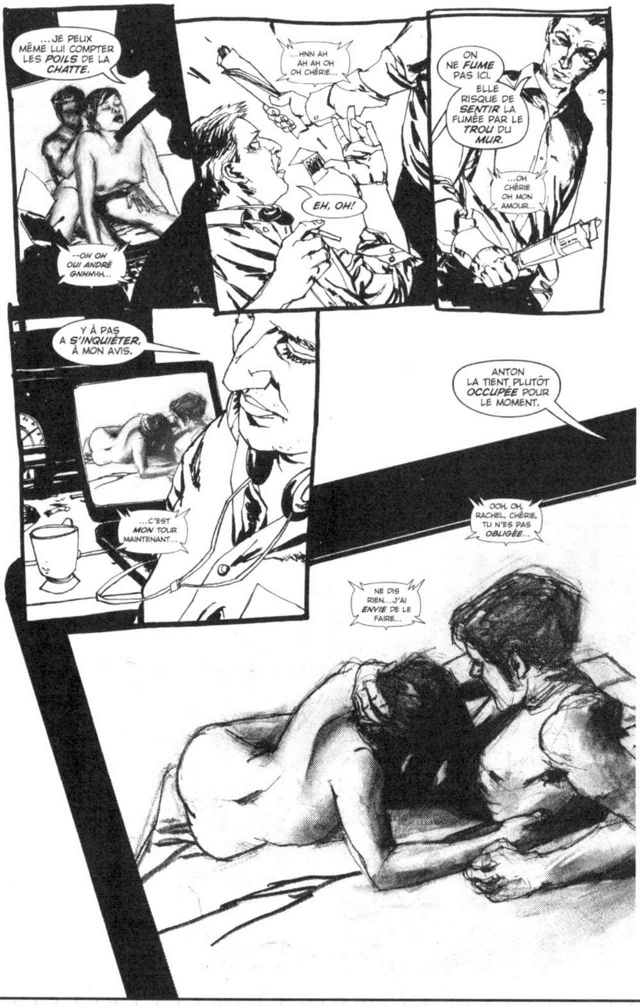

...JE PEUX MÊME LUI COMPTER LES POILS DE LA CHATTE.
--OH OH OUI ANDRÉ GNHHHH...
...HNN AH AH AH OH OH CHÉRIE...
EH, OH!
ON NE FUME PAS ICI.
ELLE RISQUE DE SENTIR LA FUMÉE PAR LE TROU DU MUR.
...OH CHÉRIE OH MON AMOUR...
Y À PAS A S'INQUIÉTER, À MON AVIS.
...C'EST MON TOUR MAINTENANT...
ANTON LA TIENT PLUTÔT OCCUPÉE POUR LE MOMENT.
OOH, OH, RACHEL, CHÉRIE, TU N'ES PAS OBLIGÉE...
NE DIS RIEN...J'AI ENVIE DE LE FAIRE...

QUEEN & COUNTRY™

ABOUT THE AUTHORS . . .

GREG RUCKA was born in San Francisco and raised on the Central Coast of California, in what is commonly referred to as "Steinbeck Country." He began his writing career in earnest at the age of 10 by winning a county-wide short-story contest, and hasn't let up since. He graduated from Vassar College with an AB in English, and from the University of Southern California's Master of Professional Writing program with an MFA.

He is the author of nearly a dozen novels, six featuring bodyguard Atticus Kodiak, and two featuring Tara Chace, the protagonist of his *Queen & Country* series. Additionally, he has penned several short-stories, countless comics, and the occasional non-fiction essay. In comics, he has had the opportunity to write stories featuring some of the world's best-known characters—Superman, Batman, and Wonder Woman—as well as penning several creator-owned properties himself, such as *Whiteout* and *Queen & Country*, both published by Oni Press. His work has been optioned several time over with *Whiteout*—starring Kate Beckinsale—being the first to actually be made. His services are also in high demand in a variety of creative fields as a story-doctor and creative consultant.

Greg resides in Portland, Oregon, with his wife, author Jennifer Van Meter, and his two children. He thinks the biggest problem with the world is that people aren't paying enough attention.

JASON SHAWN ALEXANDER Not unlike the music of the blues, Jason Shawn Alexander's work often explores the darker side of life. The subject is suspended in moments of pain or sorrow. The ultimate expression, however, is one of survival, if not hope.

Alexander, originally from Tennessee, now resides in Hollywood, California. He began painting seriously in 2002 and has had no formal training. Since then, his work has been exhibited in galleries in Los Angeles, Memphis, and Savannah.

He has participated in various teaching workshops, art forums, and has received a Silver Medal from the Society of Illustrators-West and two Eisner Award nominations for his sequential art. It has yet to be verified that he made a deal with the devil.

CARLA SPEED McNEIL is a science fiction writer, cartoonist, and illustrator. Her chief work is the ongoing science fiction comic series *Finder*. Since beginning publication in 1996, McNeil and her imprint, Lightspeed Press, has become a lasting and revered force in self-published comics. She has also written and illustrated comics for anthologies including *Dignifying Science* and *Smut Peddler*, worked as an illustrator on the *Queen & Country* story "Operation: Storm Front" and did a two-page guest-illustration spot for *Transmetropolitan: Filth of the City*. She is editor in chief and print manager of Saucy Goose Press, which produces *Smut Peddler* and other related projects. Her adaptation of D. J. MacHale's first Pendragon book, *The Merchant of Death* is scheduled for release in mid-2008

Her work has been nominated for Eisner Awards in several categories over the years. In 1997 she won a Kimberley Yale Award from the Friends of Lulu at Comic-Con International.

MIKE HAWTHORNE has worn many hats during his short lifetime—everything from "teacher" to "commercial illustrator" to "comic artist"—his favorites remain "dad" and "hubby." His pencil has graced the romantic comedy *Three Days in Europe*, his own one-man, high-octane adventure series *Hysteria*, and an insane array of titles for Marvel, DC, Beckett, and Image.

Working 20-some odd hours a day in his Pennsylvania bunker, Hawthorne hopes to one day have a day off.

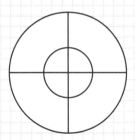

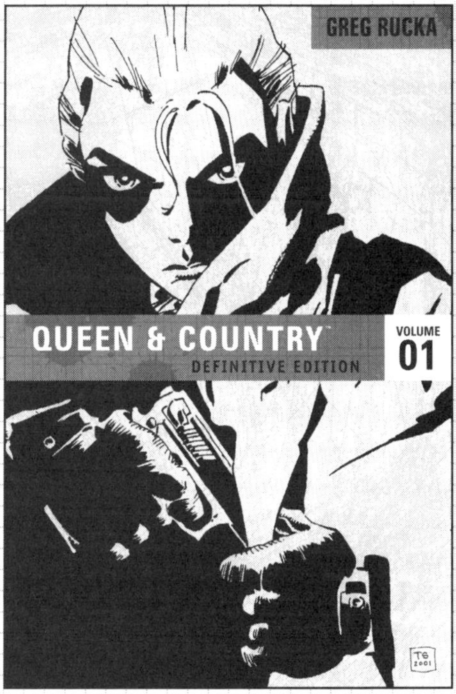
GREG RUCKA
QUEEN & COUNTRY
DEFINITIVE EDITION
VOLUME
01

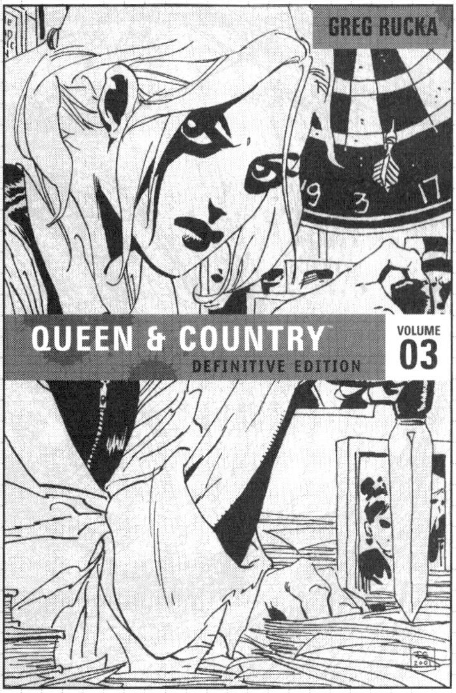
GREG RUCKA
QUEEN & COUNTRY
DEFINITIVE EDITION
VOLUME
03

COMING IN 2008 TO FINER COMICS SHOPS & BOOKSTORES.

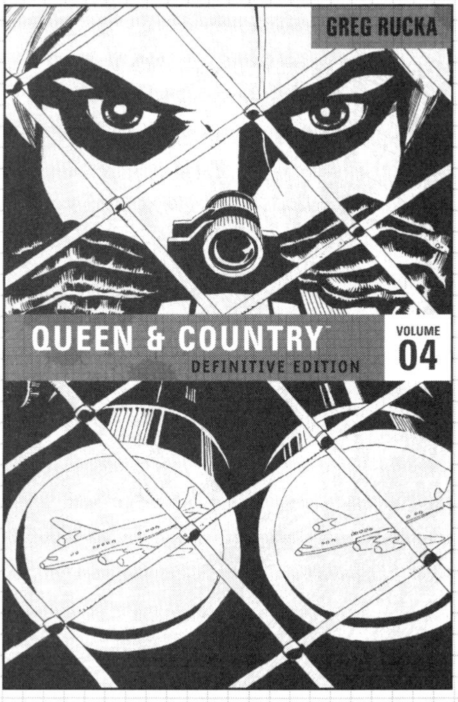
GREG RUCKA
QUEEN & COUNTRY
DEFINITIVE EDITION
VOLUME
04

QUEEN & COUNTRY, VOL. 1:
THE DEFINITIVE EDITION
written by Greg Rucka; illustrated by Steve Rolston,
Brian Hurtt, & Leandro Fernandez
376 pages, 6x9 trade paperback
ISBN-13 978-1-932664-87-4
$19.95 US
AVAILABLE NOW!

QUEEN & COUNTRY, VOL. 3:
THE DEFINITIVE EDITION
written by Greg Rucka; illustrated by Mike Norton,
Chris Samnee, & Steve Rolston
296 pages, 6x9 trade paperback
ISBN-13 978-1-932664-96-3
$19.95 US
COMING JULY 2008!

QUEEN & COUNTRY, VOL. 4:
THE DEFINITIVE EDITION
written by Greg Rucka & Antony Johnston;
illustrated by Brian Hurtt, Rick Burchett,
& Christopher Mitten
296 pages, 6x9 trade paperback
$19.95 US
COMING DECEMBER 2008!